C++
From the Beginning

INTERNATIONAL COMPUTER SCIENCE SERIES

Consulting Editor **A D McGettrick** University of Strathclyde

SELECTED TITLES IN THE SERIES

Concurrent Systems: An Integrated Approach to Operating Systems, Database, and Distributed Systems (2nd Edn) *J Bacon*
Programming Language Essentials *H E Bal and D Grune*
Programming in Ada 95 (2nd Edn) *J G P Barnes*
Java Gently: Programming Principles Explained (3rd Edn) *J Bishop*
Software Design *D Budgen*
Concurrent Programming *A Burns and G Davies*
Real-Time Systems and Programming Languages: Ada 95, Real-Time Java and Real-Time POSIX (3rd Edn) *A Burns and A Wellings*
Comparative Programming Languages (3rd Edn) *Wilson and Clark, updated by Clark*
Distributed Systems: Concepts and Design (3rd Edn) *G Coulouris, J Dollimore and T Kindberg*
Principles of Object-Oriented Software Development (2nd Edn) *A Eliëns*
Fortran 90 Programming *T M R Ellis, I R Philips and T M Lahey*
Program Verification *N Francez*
Introduction to Programming using SML *M Hansen and H Rischel*
Functional C *P Hartel and H Muller*
Ada 95 for C and C++ Programmers *S Johnston*
Algorithms and Data Structures: Design, Correctness, Analysis (2nd Edn) *J Kingston*
Introductory Logic and Sets for Computer Scientists *N Nissanke*
Human-Computer Interaction *J Preece et al.*
Algorithms: a Functional Programming Approach *F Rabhi and G Lapalme*
Foundations of Computing: System Development with Set Theory and Logic *T Scheurer*
Ada 95 From the Beginning (3rd Edn) *J Skansholm*
Java from the Beginning *J Skansholm*
Software Engineering (6th Edn) *I Sommerville*
Object-Oriented Programming in Eiffel (2nd Edn) *P Thomas and R Weedon*
Miranda: The Craft of Functional Programming *S Thompson*
Haskell: The Craft of Functional Programming (2nd Edn) *S Thompson*
Discrete Mathematics for Computer Scientists (2nd Edn) *J K Truss*
Compiler Design *R Wilhelm and D Maurer*
Discover Delphi: Programming Principles Explained *S Williams and S Walmsley*
Compiler Construction *N Wirth*
Software Engineering with B *J B Wordsworth*
Database Systems (3rd Edn) *T Connolly and C Begg*
Discover Pascal in Delphi *S Walmsley and S Williams*

C++ From the Beginning

Jan Skansholm

An imprint of Pearson Education

Harlow, England · London · New York · Reading, Massachusetts · San Francisco · Toronto · Don Mills, Ontario · Sydney
Tokyo · Singapore · Hong Kong · Seoul · Taipei · Cape Town · Madrid · Mexico City · Amsterdam · Munich · Paris · Milan

Pearson Education Limited
Edinburgh Gate
Harlow
Essex CM20 2JE

and Associated Companies throughout the World.

Visit us on the World Wide Web at:
www.pearsoneduc.com
First published in 1997
Second edition published in 2002

ISBN 0-201-72168-6

British Library Cataloguing in Publication Data
A catalogue record for this book is available from the British Library

Library of Congress Cataloging-in-Publication Data
Skansholm, Jan, 1949–
C++ from the beginning / Jan Skansholm.
p. cm. — (International computer science series)
Includes bibliographical references and index.
ISBN 0-201-72168-6 (alk. paper)
1. C++ (Computer program language) I. Title. II. Series.
QA76.73.C153 S548 2002
005.13′3—dc21 2002190375

10 9 8 7 6 5 4 3 2 1
05 04 03 02

Typeset by 35 in 10/13pt Times
Printed in Great Britain by Henry Ling Ltd, at the Dorset Press, Dorchester, Dorset

Preface

C++ is without doubt a programming language that has won great popularity during the past few years. It is used in many different applications. For anyone who wants to work professionally writing programs, it is almost a necessity to be familiar with C++. If you want to become a good C++ programmer, your road will be a long one; C++ is a very comprehensive language. This book attempts to make your journey as short as possible, and the recipe is simple: program directly in C++!

C++ is a development of the older, popular programming language C, which has been supplemented time and time again. Most of the C++ programmers working today are old C programmers who have taken a step further and learnt C++, so many believe that you should master C before you go on to C++. They argue that C++ is such a difficult language that a detour via C is recommended. This is why most of the books on C++ assume that you already know C and therefore deal with those sections of the language that are found in C++ and not in C. In addition, many comparisons can be made between C and C++.

This book has been planned in a completely different way. There is no onus on the reader to know C, or any other programming language for that matter. Everything is taken in a natural order, from the most simple things such as expressions and assignments to extremely advanced language constructs such as virtual functions, exceptions and generic classes. Since the goal is to learn C++ and not C, language constructs belonging to C++, and not to C, are used from the very beginning. We shall treat C++ as a completely independent language. As a result, there will be no reason to confuse the issue by comparing it with C and discussing the differences between the two languages.

This book is designed both for beginners in elementary programming and for those with some programming experience. The aim is to teach C++ as well as the basics of designing 'good' computer programs. For this reason such things as algorithms, objects, classes, modular program development and generic units are discussed. Special emphasis has been placed throughout on developing programs and sections of programs to make them general and reusable.

I have based the tutorial input on many years of teaching programming, both in C++ and in other languages. I have tried to understand which aspects students find difficult, and have gone into more detail in these. I have also been well served by my experience of writing other books. This is especially true of my book *Ada 95 from the Beginning*, which, I am pleased to say, has been well received by students. It has been a useful point of departure and has contributed a number of examples.

This second edition of the book is based on the international ISO standard from 1998 (ISO/IEC 14882). One novelty in this standard is a library with generic standard classes and functions that can be used to build data structures. This library is generally known as STL (Standard Template Library). Previously STL was not a part of the C++ language. It was considered to be a detached library that could be bought from various software producers. Since STL is now a part of the C++ standard, the generic classes and functions in STL are described fully in this second edition of the book. This is not only done in a separate chapter and a detailed appendix; the new classes have also been integrated into the rest of the book. The intention is that you should learn how to use them early so that you consider them to be a natural part of the C++ language. The generic class `vector` is introduced in Chapter 2 and the standard class `string` in Chapter 3, for instance.

Another novelty in this second edition of the book is that objects, classes and relations are shown graphically with the use of UML (Unified Modeling Language). UML has become a de facto standard for the graphic presentation of object-oriented concepts.

Chapter 1 provides a general background to programming. It gives an overview of the way a computer is constructed and how compiling, linking and execution are carried out. In addition, it contains a short account of the most common programming languages. Algorithms and 'software engineering' are also discussed.

The other chapters in the book (except Chapter 6) deal entirely with C++. Chapters 2 to 5 tell you what you need to know to come to grips with the more advanced language constructs. Chapter 2 gives you the basics: variables, expressions, the most common statements and arrays. Chapter 3 describes how you deal with texts. Chapter 4 looks at functions and the guidelines for dividing large programs into files. In Chapter 5, we go through the different types inherent in C++. We also look at pointers and type conversions.

Chapter 6 gives an introduction to object-oriented programming development. Object-oriented analysis, design and programming are discussed in this chapter, together with such important concepts as classes and objects. Various kinds of relations are also discussed.

Chapters 7 to 10 constitute an essential part of the book. Here an account is given of the parts of C++ that deal with classes. Chapters 7 and 8 give basic constructions

– member functions, constructors, and so on. Chapter 9 deals with inheritance, virtual functions and dynamic binding. Chapter 10 describes exceptions. I have used the new classes, found in the standard, in order to highlight the kinds of error that can be found in programs.

Chapter 11 gives an account of streams and files. Up to this point in the book the C++ standard library for reading and writing from the keyboard and screen has been used. This library can also be used to handle different kinds of files and streams, and this is demonstrated here. Text files, as well as binary files, are discussed. The way you store 'heterogeneous object collections' (collections in which the objects belong to different classes) in files is given particular attention.

Chapter 12 contains a detailed description of the generic classes that are now a part of the C++ standard. For instance, classes for construction of lists, queues, sets and maps are described. Iterators and function objects, two important tools that are used in conjunction with the standard classes, are also discussed.

Chapter 12 concentrates on the *use* of existing classes and functions. Chapters 13 and 14 go deeper. They discuss how complicated program components are *implemented*. Chapter 13 describes how dynamic data structures – lists, queues, stacks, and trees – are constructed with the use of classes. It also describes how iterators are implemented.

Chapter 14 demonstrates how you can use templates to build general – so-called generic – program components. In particular it discusses how the generic standard classes are constructed. It also discusses different ways to build heterogeneous collections of data.

Chapter 15 is a depository for all the material that did not fit into any of the other chapters, such as name spaces, unions and bit operators.

Appendix A contains a compilation of all reserved words and operators in C++.

In Appendix B there is a table showing the so called LATIN_1 code. This code is now standard, and is used to represent printable letters and other characters. LATIN_1 contains not only the letters a–z, but also various letters with diacritics such as é, ñ and ö.

Appendix C is the most important. It contains a compilation of all so-called *algorithms* in the generic standard library. These algorithms are generic functions that are used to handle collections of data. For each algorithm there is a description and also examples showing how the algorithm works.

The book contains lots of examples. I have tried, as far as possible, to present 'real-world' examples. The examples should either show fairly complete programs, or demonstrate classes and other parts of programs in a general way and be usable for different purposes. I have seriously tried to avoid fictitious examples of the type 'a class A which is a subclass of a class B which contains a member function M which happens to write the text: now we are in M'. Every chapter, except Chapter 6, concludes with a set of exercises that the reader can practise with.

Inserted in the text are a good many 'information windows' that contain summaries of rules, language constructs or concepts that have just been dealt with. The purpose of these windows is to give the reader a little revision, but they can also serve as a quick reference when a point of language has to be looked up.

Addresses

A web page with information about the book can be found at the address `www.cs.chalmers.se/~skanshol/cpp_eng/`. There you can find some examples from the text and solutions to all exercises. There is also a class named `alpha`, which can be used to sort text correctly in different languages: English, Spanish and German, for instance. There is also a class that can be used to read and write letters in a correct way in an MS-DOS window. (Without this class only the 'pure' letters a–z are shown as they should be.)

The ISO standard for C++ can be ordered from the web address `web.ansi.org/public/std_info.html`. Unfortunately it is not free of charge. On the other hand the documentation of STL is available at `www.dinkum.com/htm_cpl/index.html`. Another useful web address is `www.accu.org`. There you can find links to many interesting things concerning C++. If you are interested in finding a C++ compiler, free of charge, you can visit the web pages `sourceware.cygnus.com/cygwin` and `www.delorie.com/djgpp/` (for Windows) and `www.gnu.org/home.html` (for Unix and Linux).

Contents

Computers and programming

1

This book is about programming, or, more precisely, about how you write programs in C++. The different chapters will describe different program constructions in C++. This first chapter is an exception, as it is not about C++ but about programming in general and the prerequisites for programming. It gives a short introduction to the way a computer is constructed, its most important components and their functions. We look at a very simple program. Further on we deal with how programs are translated and how the computer is made to carry them out. After this, there is an overview of the most common and important programming languages and their historical development.

Program development is not simply about the act of programming. In a wider perspective, the programming itself is only a part of the total work. Therefore in this chapter there is also a short discussion about *software engineering* and the place of programming in the program development process. The important concepts of *algorithms* and *top-down design* are also introduced.

1.1 A computer's structure and operation

You could say that a computer is a 'machine' that can process and store information. (Computers were of course called *data processing machines* at first.) A very rough illustration of how it looks when you run a program in a computer is shown in Figure 1.1. We see that the computer can be regarded as a unit into which you put certain data, or *input data*. The computer processes this data and produces *output data*. Indata and outdata can really be anything: text, pictures, or sound. You may think that, in principle, a computer communicates with a person via a keyboard, screen and mouse, but computers are also used in a variety of different conditions where communication with people is not the main consideration. Computers can, for instance, control industrial manufacturing processes, or they may be components in technical systems (aeroplanes, cars, and so on). Here the indata is often in the form of signals from so-called *monitoring devices*, which give the computer information about the current situation in the system concerning, for example, temperatures and speeds. Output data from the computer may then be control signals to relays and motors.

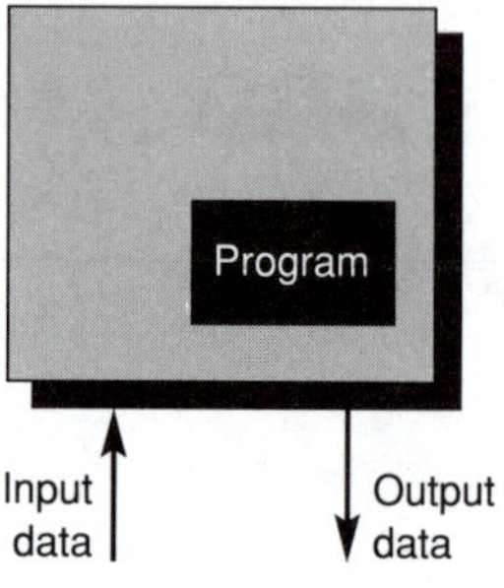

Figure 1.1

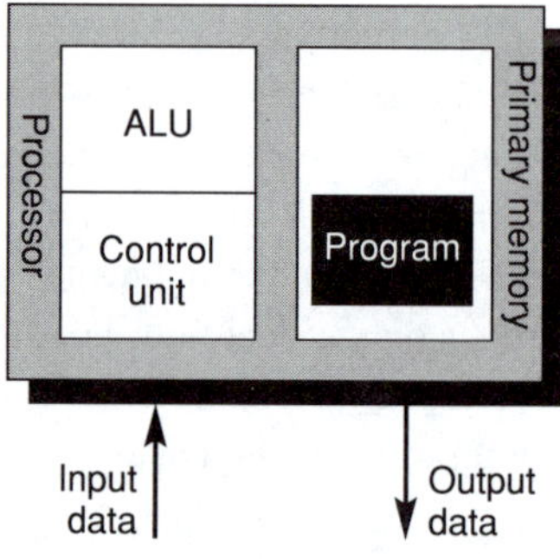

Figure 1.2

A very important principle, which is clear from the diagram, is that the computer's behaviour is controlled by a program stored inside it. By changing the program you can make the computer produce different things. It is this that makes the computer so different from an 'ordinary' machine, which, of course, is built to produce certain predetermined things.

Figure 1.2 shows the main components of a computer in a little more detail. The computer's 'brain' consists of the *processor* (the *central processing unit*, or *CPU*). Here you find the *control unit*, which controls and coordinates all the computer's activities. The control unit decides which operations the computer will perform and the order in which they will be carried out. It sends out control signals that regulate all the computer's other parts.

There is also an *arithmetic logic unit*, or *ALU*, in the processor, which contains electronic circuits to perform various operations on the data to be processed. These might be, for example, addition, subtraction, multiplication and division. Advanced processors may contain several ALUs, which means that several operations can be performed in parallel. Modern processors often contain, in addition, a special *mathematics processor*, whose job it is to perform special time-consuming mathematical operations.

Another very important unit in the computer is the *primary memory* (random access memory, or RAM). When a program is performed, or is run, by a computer we say that it is *executed*. For the program to be executed, it must first be placed in the primary memory. In the primary memory there is also various data and temporary storage space that the executing program needs in order to be able to function.

Execution
When a program is performed (run) in a computer, we say that it is *executed*.

So that the processor can get at the data from the primary memory more quickly, many fast processors often use an extra-fast *cache memory* for intermediate storage of data between the processor and the primary memory. The cache memory is often built into the processor.

The primary memory can be thought of as consisting of *memory cells*. (These memory cells are also sometimes called *words*, which do not have anything to do with ordinary words.) Each memory cell has a certain *address* (a number) that gives its position in the memory. The number of memory cells in the primary memory varies, depending on the computer type and model, but it is usually a matter of millions. Each memory cell consists of a certain number of bits (normally 8). Each bit is a *binary digit*: that is, a 'zero' or a 'one'. A group of 8 bits is called a *byte*. You normally express memory size in units of *kilobytes* (Kb), *megabytes* (Mb) and *gigabytes* (Gb), which correspond to 1024, one million and one billion respectively.

A program that is executed, and which therefore is to be found in the primary memory, consists of a number of continuous memory cells. A memory cell or a group of memory cells contains an *instruction* in the program. Different instructions can be represented by combining the bits in the memory cells in different ways. Thus a program consists of a sequence of instructions. An instruction tells the computer that it must do a certain particular thing: for instance, move a memory cell from the primary memory to the central processing unit, or add up two numbers in the arithmetic logic unit.

When a program is being executed, the control unit reads the instructions from the primary memory one by one and sees that the instructions are performed in the order in which they are read.

You could therefore say that an instruction in the program consists of a certain number of ones and zeros. The way these combinations look will depend on the computer. The program must be stored in this form in the primary memory for it to be performed in the computer. We usually say that the program exists in the form of *machine code*. This

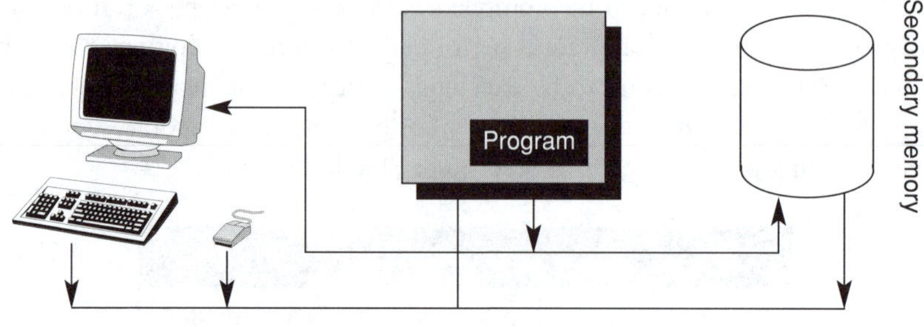

Figure 1.3

is a code that is very 'user *un*friendly': that is, it is difficult for us either to read or to write it. In the infancy of computers, you had to program them directly in machine code. Luckily, things have progressed and normally programmers today don't have to worry about the computer's machine code. As we shall see, programs are written in a 'high-level language' (for example, C++ or Java), which is much more user-friendly than the computer's machine code. Nowadays there are special translation programs that translate from high-level language to machine code, so that the programs that have been written can be run in the computer.

In Figure 1.3 our computer system has been extended by two very familiar units. In order to communicate with its surroundings, a computer must have one or more *input* and *output* units. The diagram shows the most common input and output units for communication with people: a *screen* (*monitor*), a *mouse* and a *keyboard*. Other common input and output units are printers and loudspeakers.

We saw that a computer's primary memory is used, among other things, to store the program currently being executed, but a computer also normally needs to be able to store programs that may not be running. There is also a need to store various pieces of information that will be used as input data for different programs. In order to store this type of data, which will be saved more permanently, *secondary memories* are used.

Common types of secondary memory are *disk memory* (hard disks) and *diskettes*. (A hard disk is shown in the diagram.) You can also have secondary memories that are only readable; they cannot be written to. The most common example of this is *CD-ROM* (compact disc read-only memory). These contain completed programs or data.

Disk memories are also used in certain systems to create *virtual memory*. This technique makes the primary memory appear much larger than it is in reality, which makes things easier for the programmer, who does not have to worry about the primary memory's physical limitations. When you use this virtual memory technique, you store only that data that is currently needed in the actual primary memory. Other data is stored in the disk memory and is retrieved automatically into the primary memory when needed.

Data in secondary memories is usually organized in the form of *files*. A file is a collection of data that belongs together. It may, for example, contain a program or indata for a particular program. You could think of a file as an 'envelope' in which you put data that belongs together. You can create new files, delete files, or make changes in files. Each file is given a special name for easy reference.

It is often important with modern computers to have equipment that makes it possible to communicate with other computers. If the computer is equipped with a *network card* it can be connected to a local data network, where several computers are connected together, so that they can, for example, access and share each other's disk memories and other input and output devices. If the computer has a *modem* it can communicate with distant computers. You can be connected to the Internet or send electronic mail, for example.

1.2 How you get the program into the computer

A computer program written in a programming language has the form of normal text. You could write the program on an ordinary piece of paper. In this section, we are going to see what happens when this original *program text*, or *source code* as it is sometimes called, is translated into the machine's special machine code and loaded in the computer. In order to do this, we shall study a very simple program that, when it is run, will only print out the text `C++ From the Beginning` on the screen:

```
#include <iostream>
using namespace std;
main()
{
  cout << "C++ From the Beginning" << endl;
  return 0;
}
```

Important components in a computer
• The *processor* (CPU) controls the computer and manipulates the data. • The *primary memory* is used to store the program to be executed and the data this program needs. • *Input and output devices* are used to read and print data. • *Secondary memories* are used to store data permanently. • *Network cards* make it possible to connect to a local data network. • With the help of a *modem*, the computer can communicate with distant computers.

Before we discuss how the program is translated, let's talk about how it looks. (More detailed descriptions of the various program constructions will, of course, come further on in the book.)

The language C++ itself contains no special constructions to read and write data, but there are a number of complete 'libraries' with resources for reading and writing. One of these is `iostream`, and the first line in the program indicates that the program will make use of this. Actually, `iostream` is the name of a *header file* that contains declarations of the resources to be found in the library.*

All declarations in the standard libraries are done in a *namespace* called `std`. The second line in the program makes the declarations in that namespace directly visible in the program. The line must be present. (It is not necessary to understand this now. It is enough to know that the second line in the program must be present in every program that includes any of the standard libraries.)

In a C++ program there can be one or more *functions* that indicate what the program will do. Only one function was shown in the example above. The name of the function is `main`, which is on the third line. A C++ program must contain exactly one function with the name `main`, and when the program is run, execution will begin in this function. The empty parentheses after the word `main` indicate that the function lacks parameters. On the fourth line there is a left brace, and on the last line a right brace. These symbols indicate where the 'guts', or the *body*, of the function begins and ends. (The symbols `{` and `}` correspond to the words 'begin' and 'end', which are normally used in many other programming languages.)

On the fifth and sixth lines we find a description of what the function will do. This is expressed in *statements*. A semicolon is normally written after every statement. In this example there are two statements, one on each line. The first statement indicates that the text `C++ From the Beginning` must be written out. The output operator `<<` from the '`iostream`' library is used here. Output takes place with '`cout`', which is a predefined *output stream*. Whatever is output in this stream will automatically be written in a text window on the screen. The word '`endl`' is a *manipulator* that says that the cursor on the screen will be moved forward to a new line (after output).

---

* In C, and previously also in C++, it has been a convention that all header files have a name that ends with `.h`. Therefore in an old C++ program the first line would look like this:

```
#include <iostream.h>
```

Furthermore, the second line in the program, the one starting with `using`, would not be there. You can let your programs look like that if you are using an old compiler that does not follow the standard. (It should also work for a new compiler since the standard says that a compiler should be able to compile old programs.)

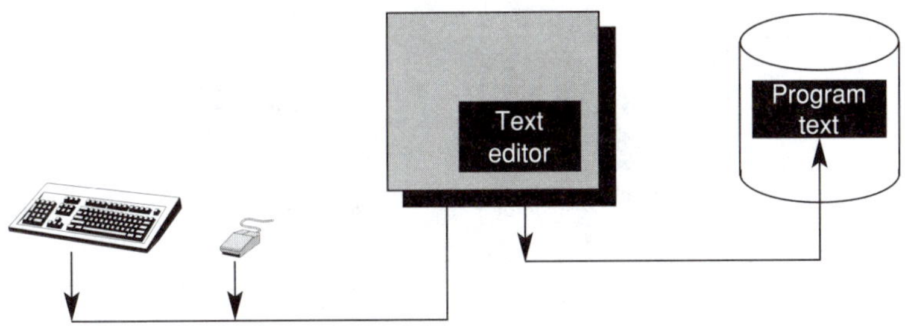

Figure 1.4

The sixth line in the program contains a `return` statement. This indicates that execution of the function will come to an end. (The value `0` indicates that execution has finished normally.)

Since the program consists of normal text, it can be entered at the keyboard. There are usually a great many support programs in all computer systems. One such support program that can always be found is a text-editing program, or *text editor*. Figure 1.4 gives an idea of how this program is run. Using the text editor you can input any text in the computer and store the text in the secondary memory. A file that contains text is usually called a *text file*. With the help of the text editor, you can also easily edit the text: that is, delete, change, move and add text. You can usually see a part of the text on the screen and so you are able, with the help of the keys or a mouse, to mark parts of the text to be edited. Exactly how the text editor functions, and which commands it understands, vary from system to system. A simple text editor does not worry about what the text itself contains, but you can also find text editors that 'understand' what kinds of text they are processing. A text editor that knows that it is editing a C++ program can help the programmer by marking various program constructions with different styles or colours.

Let us suppose that we have edited the program text above with the help of a text editor and stored it in a text file with the name `example1.cpp`. As you can see, the text file has the suffix `.cpp`. In most computer systems you use suffixes to keep your files in order. Files that contain texts from C++ programs often have the suffix `cpp`, but they may have other suffixes, such as `c` or `cc`.

In the next step the program texts are translated from normal text to machine code. This is done, as shown in Figure 1.5, with the help of a special translating program, a *compiler*. Every compiler is constructed to handle a particular programming language. To be able to translate a C++ program, therefore, you must have access to a C++ compiler. A compiler can either be a separate program, or it can be part of an integrated program development system. A system like this contains all the resources you need to develop and test run programs: for instance, text editors and compilers. Later we shall

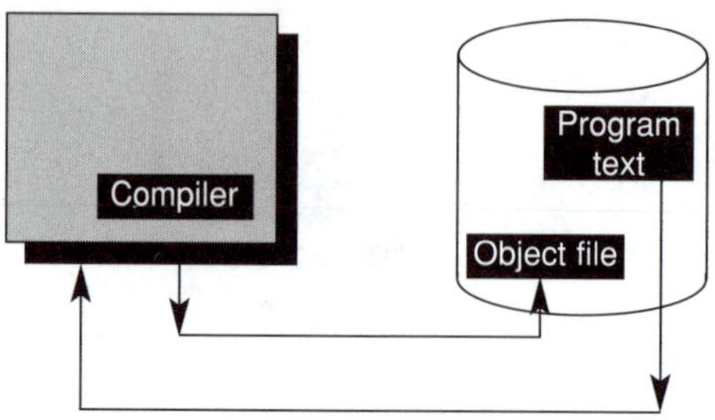

Figure 1.5

show an example of such an integrated system in a Windows environment, but first we demonstrate how to use a compiler as a separate program. In this case the compiler is normally started from a command line in a console window (the MS-DOS prompt in Windows). As an example we show how to write in an MS-DOS window when you use the free compiler from Gnu.[†]

```
gxx -c example1.cpp
```

If you run Unix or Linux you should write `g++` instead of `gxx`.

For every programming language there are special rules for how different programming constructions may look (compare this with the rules for sentence construction in normal languages). We say that every language has a certain *syntax*. The compiler reads the program from the text file created earlier and checks first that the program is following the rules of the language: that is, that the program is following the given syntax. If the compiler finds errors, error outputs will appear on the screen. There may also be warnings for things that may not be clear errors but which the compiler thinks look doubtful. Sometimes, the compiler will try to correct the errors if they are not too serious, but usually the compiling will break off when errors have been discovered. You then have to go back to the previous step and, with the help of the text editor, edit your program text and correct the errors. Once this has been done, you can attempt once more to compile the program. This process normally has to be repeated several times.

If the compiler does not discover any errors, it goes further and translates the program from text to machine code. The compiler usually creates a file with the suffix `o` or `obj`, in which it saves the machine code produced. This file is called an *object file*. In our example, the compiler will generate the file `example1.o`.

Notice that since the various types of computer have different machine codes, object files meant for one computer will not do for another. Different computers must have

[†] The latest Windows version of this compiler can be downloaded from `www.delorie.com/djgpp/` and the Unix and Linux versions from `www.gnu.org/home.html`.

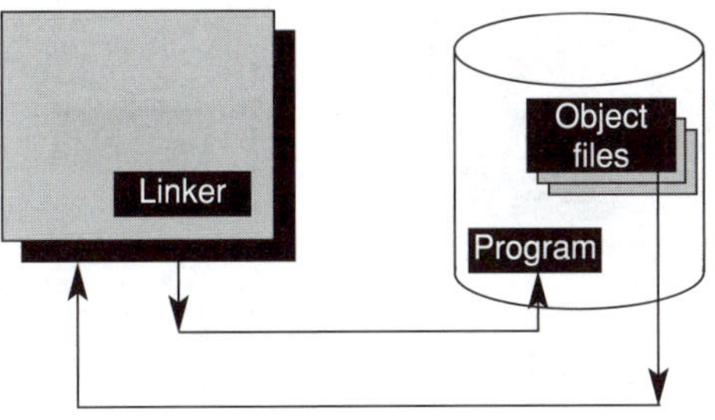

Figure 1.6

different compilers. This does not cause the programmer problems, since a C++ compiler always requires a C++ program as indata, whichever computer you are using. Program text developed on one computer system can thus be moved to another system and run there. For this to be done easily, you should not use too many system-dependent details in your program. A program that can be easily moved from one computer system to another is called a *portable* program.

Usually, a program consists of several program parts that have been compiled *separately*. You therefore have several object files. You will have created a number of the object files yourself by compiling your program texts, as with the file `example1.o`. There may also exist object files that were created before, and which will also be a part of the program. This is true, for instance, with standard functions. In our example the output operator `<<` exists in a prefabricated standard object file. In order to put the various object files together into a program that can be run, you run a special *linking program*, a *linker*. This is shown in Figure 1.6. The linker produces a complete unit, an *executable file*.

Sometimes a special suffix, for example '`exe`', may be used in the file name to indicate that the file contains an executable program. The linker can be a separate program or can be part of a program development system. In an MS-DOS window the program is linked with the command

```
gxx -o example1.exe example1.o
```

(As before you write `g++` instead of `gxx` in Unix and Linux.)

We give the names of the object files as arguments. We only have one here, `example1.o`. We can see that the linking program automatically finds the standard object files without their having to be indicated. The argument `-o` is used to indicate what the executable file is to be called. We want it to be called `example1.exe`.

Linking can take place either *statically* or *dynamically*. With static linking, all the parts of the program are put into the executable file, while with dynamic linking, references to the required object files are placed in the executable file. The object files themselves

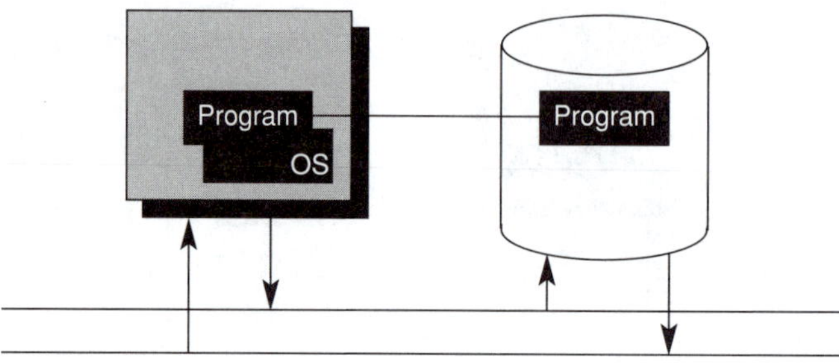

Figure 1.7

are not found in the executable file. When a dynamically linked program is run, the different object files will be automatically retrieved and stored in the primary memory when necessary. The advantage with dynamic linking is, of course, that you can save a lot of file space, since different programs often contain common parts, for instance input and output or window handling: these parts do not then need to be copied to all the executable files but can exist in only one copy, which all the executable files will refer to.

Now the last step remains: to get the executable program into the primary memory so that it can be run. This leads us to the question: how does the computer know which program it is to run? For the answer, let us look at Figure 1.7.

In earlier diagrams, we have shown only one program at a time in the primary memory, the program being executed. In fact there are always parts of yet another program permanently stored. This is termed the *operating system*, or OS. Examples of common operating systems are Windows XP, MS-DOS, Unix and Linux. The operating system is the program that is always run when no 'ordinary' program is being executed. It is automatically started when a normal program has finished being executed, or for some reason has been broken off. The operating system also begins automatically when the computer is started.

The user normally communicates with the operating system via the screen, keyboard and mouse. The user can write the command on the keyboard, or point and click with the mouse. A common command is for a particular program to be loaded and executed. The operating system then searches for the desired executable file in the secondary memory and copies it into the primary memory, as suggested in the diagram. Control is then transferred to the loaded program, which can execute until it has finished or until it is broken off. In order to start our program in an MS-DOS environment, we give the operating system the command

```
example1.exe
```

In a text window on the screen we then get the output

```
C++ From the Beginning
```

We have now seen how a program is written and how it is loaded and run. This process can often be simplified so that you, the programmer, do not need to see all the separate steps and a program can be found that both compiles and links in one step. For instance we would have been able to compile and link our program with the more simple command

```
gxx -o example1.exe example1.cpp
```

Modern program development systems usually offer the programmer an integrated environment where all the resources necessary to develop programs can be found. Examples of such systems are Borland's C++ and Microsoft's Visual C++. Both of these are for the development of programs under Windows.

The different steps

- The program text (the source code) is created with the help of a text editor.
- The compiler translates the program text to an object file.
- The linker puts together several object files to form an executable file.
- The operating system puts the executable file in the primary memory and the program is executed.

A modern program development system not only has the obvious resources of text editor, compiler and linker, it also has support to keep order in the different parts that go to make up a programming project. There is a *debugger* (a program that makes it possible to test run your programs step by step and search for possible errors in them) and there are help texts, documentation and examples. There may also be advanced resources to produce programs with a graphical user interface: that is, programs that communicate with the user via menus, windows, click-buttons, and so on.

As an example of a modern program development system we shall show how you write and run our program example in Visual C++. You start the program development system in the usual way, by clicking on its symbol. When the system has started, you get a window like the one in Figure 1.8.

Choose the alternative *New* in the *File* menu and click on the tab *Files*. The window in Figure 1.9 is then shown. In this window you should select the option *C++ Source File*. Then a text editor area is opened in which you can enter the program text. When you have typed the text you can save it in a file named `example1.cpp`. (Choose the option *Save As* in the *File* menu.)

For every program that will be developed there must be a *project* (Workspace in Visual C++). A project contains a mass of information about the current program. Among other things, it keeps a check on all the files needed to construct the program. The

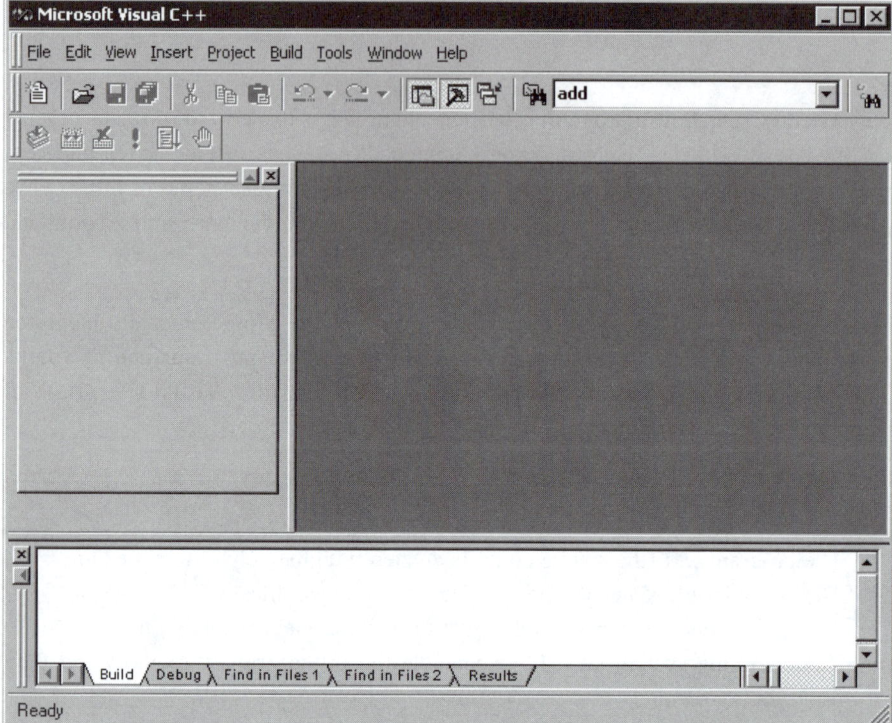

Figure 1.8

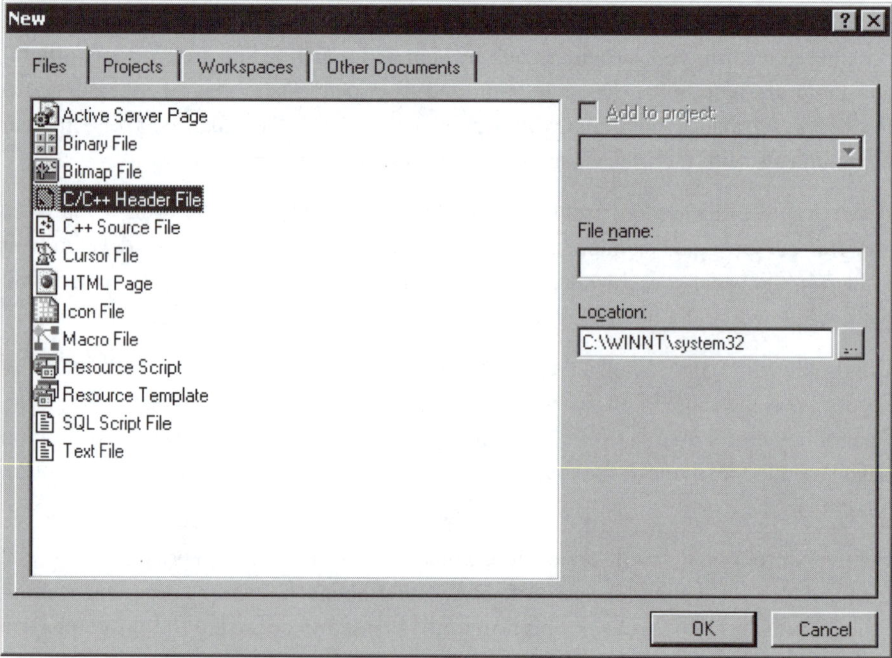

Figure 1.9

easiest way in the beginning is to let Visual C++ create the project for you. This will be done if you try to compile the program. Choose the alternative *Build* in the *Build* menu. Then Visual C++ will ask you if a default project workspace should be created. Answer 'yes' to this question.

You can also create a project yourself. Choose the option *New* in the *File* menu and click on the tab *Project*. In the dialog window that appears you should select the type of project to be *Win32 Console Application*. You should also type the name of the project, `example1`, and indicate the directory where the files of the project are to be placed. Then you have to indicate that the file `example1.cpp` should be a part of the project. Choose the option *Add To Projec*t in the *Project* menu and then choose the option *Files*. Select the file `example1.cpp` in the dialog window. After that you can compile the program by choosing the option *Build* in the *Build* menu. You could also click on the *Build* button (the one with two small arrows).

When the project has been created the window in Figure 1.10 can be obtained. At the left there is a graphics picture of the classes and files that constitute the project. In our example there is only one program text file, the file named `example1.cpp`. You can

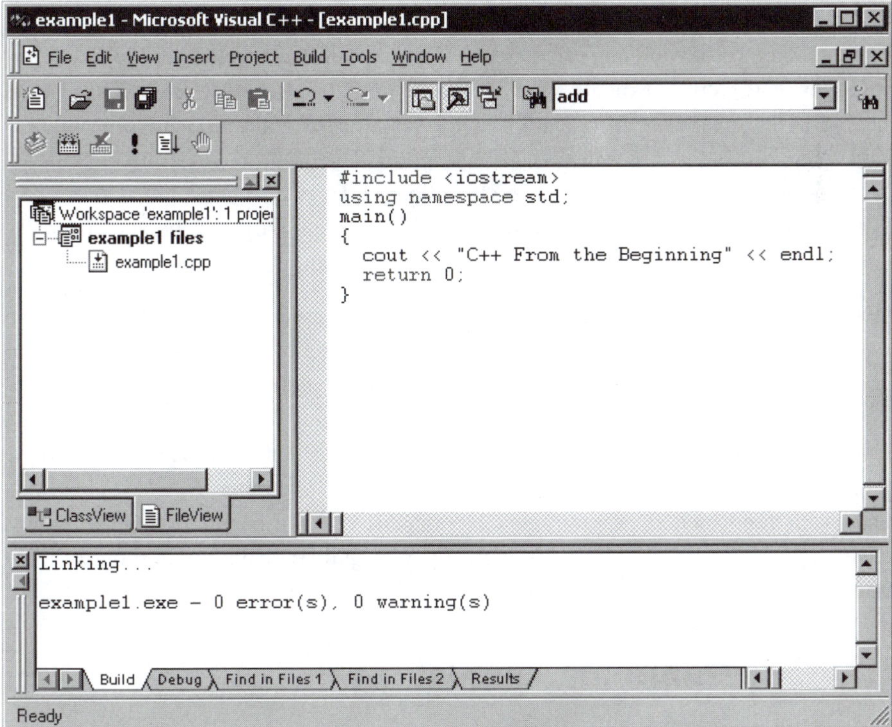

Figure 1.10

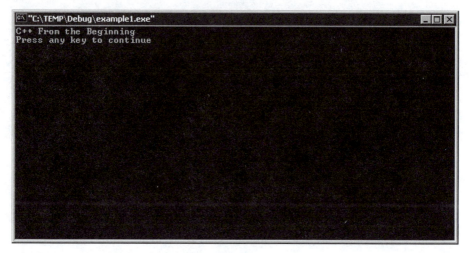

Figure 1.11

see this if you click on the tab *File View* and click on the little plus sign. (When you open the project at a later time you can get the file `example1.cpp` into the text editor area simply by clicking on the filename.)

If the compiler discovers any errors when the program is compiled you will get error messages at the bottom of the window in Figure 1.10. A faulty line could also be marked in the text editor area. (Simply click on the error message.) If the program is fault-free, it is linked into an executable program. The program is run by clicking on the 'run' button (the button with an exclamation mark), or by choosing the alternative *Execute* in the *Build* menu. The window in Figure 1.11 will then be shown on the screen. This is a text window in which the program's outputs are showns.

Modern applications programs make use of windows, menus, and so on to communicate with the person running the program, and program development systems such as Borland C++ or Visual C++ make it possible to write such programs. Unfortunately, it is not trivial to construct windows-oriented programs, even if there is adequate support in the program development system, for much depends on the system, and the help functions that must be used vary in the different computer systems. This book deals with fundamental programming techniques, so the construction of windows-oriented programs lies outside its framework. We shall be dealing with programs that read and write in simple text windows such as that in Figure 1.11.

1.3 Programming languages

The earliest computers had to be programmed, as mentioned earlier, in machine code. A part of a program might then have looked like this:

```
0111000100001111 1001110110110001 1110000100111110
```

Naturally, it was regarded as an enormous advance when *assembler languages* began to be used. The program section above might then be written:

```
LOAD A    ADD B    STORE C
```

In assembler language every line in the program corresponds to an instruction in the machine code. The program section above thus consists of three instructions. For a program written in assembler language to be run in the computer, a translation program is needed, an *assembler*, which translates into machine code. A translation program like this need not be terribly complicated since the assembler language, in its structure, is very close to machine code.

In spite of the fact that assembler languages were such an improvement, there are still considerable disadvantages to using them. One is that every kind of computer has its own unique assembler language. An assembler programmer could have to learn many different kinds of assembler languages, which could vary greatly. Another disadvantage is that assembler languages are extremely detailed. Every single instruction must be given to the computer. This means that it is time consuming to use assembler languages, and it is very easy to make mistakes.

Programming work was changed radically with the development of high-level languages in the mid-1950s. A program written in a high-level language is more compatible with the way we express ourselves than with the computer's arranging of instructions. Programs are expressed in a kind of pidgin English, and arithmetical calculations are written in a form reminiscent of mathematics.

The program sections above could possibly look like this:

```
C = A + B
```

The programmer can concentrate on the problem to be solved without worrying about the details of how the computer works. In principle it is also possible to write programs in one high-level language to run on different computers. There is no need to learn a new language for every computer to be used.

The first high level language was *FORTRAN* (FORmula TRANslator), which was introduced in 1954. It was originally intended to simplify writing programs using arithmetical expressions. The great weakness is its poor structure. In addition, the language has poor facilities for input and output. FORTRAN has had a facelift with the new versions FORTRAN 77 and FORTRAN 90.

In 1959 a new programming language, *COBOL*, was introduced, designed for programming in the areas of finance and administration. A few years later the language was standardized, and it has become, and remains, one of the most used languages.

COBOL programs are very readable in that they resemble ordinary English. The disadvantage of this is that programs in the language are sometimes considered wordy and awkward. What was new about COBOL, compared with FORTRAN, was that it had better ways of describing the data a program had to handle.

A language that came to be very significant for subsequent developments was *ALGOL*, which was presented in 1960. The big advantage of the language is that it has good structure. It is possible to write a program so that the way it works is reflected in its appearance.

Another significant language for later language developments was *SIMULA*, the first version of which appeared in 1967, a direct extension of ALGOL. The language is used primarily, as its names implies, to write simulation programs. SIMULA is significant for being the first programming language that enabled *object-oriented* programs to be written. For instance, *classes* and *inheritance*, two concepts of importance in object-oriented languages today, could already be found in SIMULA.

The *Pascal* language was introduced in 1971. It was to be a simple language, suitable for use in teaching, and it has achieved wide usage in this field. The reason is that it has good program structure, which makes it easy for the beginner to acquire good 'programming style'. Pascal is based directly on ALGOL and on ideas from SIMULA, although a good many constructs have been deliberately simplified. Even so, variants of Pascal have appeared, for example UCSD Pascal and TURBO Pascal. The greatest weakness of the language is that it lacks constructs for enabling larger programs to be built up in a modular way. Further, it is limited in its handling of text, and in its input and output facilities.

C is a language that has become very popular in spite of its age (it was developed at the start of the 1970s). It is a language that can be said to be a 'high-level language at a low level'. It gives the programmer great freedom to control the computer in detail, and has therefore come largely to replace the assembler in the development of system programs. From the beginning C was closely connected to the operating system Unix, but today it is used in most computer environments. Most of today's operating systems and other system programs, such as those handling windows and menus, are written in C. C is relatively small but demands a lot of the programmer, as it is so easy to make mistakes.

Remarkably fast developments in the field of electronics, with more and more powerful components being produced ever more cheaply, led many to believe that it would similarly be possible to construct ever larger and more complex programs. In the event, this assumption was quite wrong. All too many programs failed to be ready on time, greatly exceeded their budget, contained many errors, or did not fulfil the customers' specifications. This phenomenon became known as the *software crisis*. Among the reasons for this crisis were poor project management, and the fact that the programmer often considered the program to be his or her own property. Many individual and curious programming styles developed, and it proved difficult to create error-free programs. In order to remedy this, the concept of *structured programming* was introduced, with the aim that a program should be written in such a way that it is both easily understood and free from errors. Structured programming can be said to be a set of rules and recommendations for how 'good' programs should be written. Such programming needs the support of a suitable programming language, and it was this need for well-structured programs that was behind the development of what became known as structured languages, such as Pascal.

During the 1970s it became clear that even well-structured programs were not enough for mastering the complexity involved in developing a large program system. It was also recognized that it was necessary to support the division of the program into well-defined parts, or *modules*, that could be developed and tested independently of one another, so that several people could work together within one large programming project. One way to divide a program into modules is to use so-called *objects* as building blocks in the program. An object in the program can be thought of as a representation of a real or conceptual thing in the program's environment.

This idea originated from the language SIMULA but was further elaborated in a project at Xerox, where a brand new language, *Smalltalk*, was constructed. The first available version of Smalltalk was presented in 1980, and the concept of *object-oriented* program development was introduced in connection with this project. Many of the special words that are used in the object-oriented programming languages, *messages* and *methods* for instance, come from Smalltalk. In Smalltalk, the concept of object is particularly emphasized. There are no data types in the language, and all data in a program is just objects. The syntax of Smalltalk is also somewhat particular: that is, the language looks very different compared with other languages. A Smalltalk system is an integrated interactive environment with a window-oriented user interface. Drawbacks of Smalltalk that are often mentioned are that the interactive environment demands large computer resources, and that the programs produced usually execute slowly. The latter is due to that fact that the program is not compiled, but *interpreted*, at execution.

The US Department of Defense was hit hard by the software crisis. It was an important customer for independent companies producing programming systems. To put this right, the initiative was taken to develop a new programming language capable of meeting the specifications envisaged. Developments continued in the form of an international competition between different research groups and companies. The winning project was given the name *Ada* and was accepted in 1983 as a standard in the USA. Ada also became an international ISO standard. Apart from being a well-structured language,

Ada also supports the modular development of programs. The concept of the *package* has been introduced, and it is possible to build up libraries of packages that can be put together to make large programs. One thing that distinguishes Ada from most other programming languages is that it can be used to write *parallel programs*: that is, programs that contain several active parts that are to be executed simultaneously and interact with one another. Such programs, called *realtime programs*, are encountered in applications for computer control of technical systems.

After a few years of use the decision was made to revise the standard. The new standard is called *Ada 95*. One important innovation compared with the old standard (Ada 83) is that of object-oriented language constructs. Another important addition is that of child libraries, which further simplify the construction of large programs.

C++ is, however, without any doubt the most popular object-oriented programming language at the moment. One of the reasons for this is that it is an expansion of the popular language C. There are compilers or complete development systems in C++ for all common types of computer.

C++ was constructed by Bjarne Strostrup at AT&T Bell Laboratories. The first commercial version came out in 1985. There was no official standard until 1998.

C++ is a straight expansion of C. In the basics of the languages there are only marginal differences. You can compile a C program with a C++ compiler but not the other way around; meanwhile the additions made to C are quite comprehensive. It is mainly a question of language constructs for object-oriented programming. The concept of class, central to C++, does not exist at all in C. Again, C++ contains many improvements on C, especially, for instance, the mechanism for the transfer of parameters to functions, which is more reliable. In this book C++ will be treated as a separate language, and we shall learn it from the beginning: so we will not be discussing substantial differences between C and C++.

Another interesting language is *Java*, which was developed by Sun Microsystems. Java became generally available in 1995. At first, Java was probably best known as a programming language used on the Internet to create dazzling effects on web sites. A web site can contain applets, which are small programs written in Java. When a browser such as Internet Explorer or Netscape Navigator downloads and displays a web site containing a program in Java, the program will be run. Java can then generate sounds and moving pictures, or permit the user to communicate with the program by using the mouse and keyboard. But Java is really a fully fledged programming language. By using Java, much as with C++, complete application programs can be created that by no means need to be run through a browser.

One advantage with Java is that it contains classes to generate graphical user interfaces (GUIs). These classes can be used to construct *GUI programs*: that is, programs communicating with the user through windows, menus, buttons and so on. Another important characteristic of Java is that it is platform-independent. This means that Java programs can be run on different types of computer system without having to be changed. When a Java program is compiled the code generated is not machine code but a platform-independent code called *Java bytecode*. This code is interpreted by a special program, a *Java interpreter*. The disadvantage with interpreting is that it takes longer to interpret a program than it does to execute a program that is in the form of machine code. This means that a Java program is normally slower that a program written in, for instance, C++.

When Java was designed, C++ was used as a model, which means that the syntax of Java is very similar to that of C++. The most important difference is that the handling of pointers and memory has been much simplified in Java.

1.4 The process of developing programs

This book is all about programming or, in other words, how one builds or constructs a program. However, developing a program is not only a question of programming. It might be compared with what happens when a house is built – it is not just a case of going ahead and laying the bricks. A good deal of careful preparation is needed. First, you have to decide how the house will be used, then the plans can be drawn, and after that all the calculations have to be made before the actual building can commence. And even when the house is completely built it cannot be left to itself: it needs to be maintained. The work of building a house can thus be divided into a number of *phases* – from the decision about its future usage to its maintenance. This is quite similar to what has to happen if you are going to develop a computer program: the programming, corresponding to the actual carpentry and bricklaying, is only one phase of the whole process.

This is where a useful distinction can be made between *programming in the small* and *programming in the large*. Programming in the small means that you work alone and produce a little program of a temporary nature. Programming in the large means that you work with the development of a larger program and that the work is often the joint effort of a group of programmers. Most programming in education settings is on the small scale, but on occasion it can also be large scale, for example in project-based courses and the sort of applied project work incorporated in many education programmes. In the case of commercial and industrial program development, it is almost always a question of programming in the large.

When you want to develop a program, it is so easy to sit down and start to write it at once – one could call this the *direct programming* method. In the case of professional programming, in the large, this practice leads to greater costs, and it is questionable whether a functioning and usable program can ever be produced in this way. It is generally admitted that such direct programming brought about the software crisis that was discussed previously. It is less serious to use the direct programming approach for programming in the small, but even then it is worthwhile to decide in advance what the program should do and how it should do it.

The overall goal when developing a professional program is to produce a high-quality program within given constraints of time and cost. A program should match the demands of the user, and be reliable, well documented and easy to maintain. To achieve these ends the program has to be developed with a well-structured approach: just as with building a house, this calls for engineer-like work in accordance with a clear plan. The term *software engineering* is often used to refer to such a well-structured approach.

In order to draw up a work plan you need a model for the way in which program development proceeds, and there are several models to choose from. The most widely used is that known as the *waterfall model*, of which there are several variants. The program development process is here divided up into the following phases:

1. Requirements analysis and requirements specification.
2. Design.
3. Implementation.
4. Test and installation.
5. Operation and maintenance.

The reason why this is called the waterfall method is that each phase results in a set of documents that run down to the next phase.

During the first phase, *requirements analysis* and *specification*, the goal is to determine what has to be done. You have to try to understand the environment in which the desired program will have to function. You should specify what the program is required to do, what different functions it should be capable of, and the principles for its communication with the user. Such questions as the sort of computers it should be run on should also be addressed now. This work should result in a written *requirements specification* that states clearly all these demands. The specification is the document that defines the program that is to be constructed, and it has to be accepted both by the customer and by the program developer(s). The specification might include a *preliminary user manual*, and it can also prescribe *trial procedures*, which state how the final program will be tested.

In the second phase, that of *design*, the question being addressed is: *how* should the program meet the demands now specified? You could say that this is producing a blueprint for the program. You decide what different parts should go to make up the program, what each of these should do, how they should interface, and how they should communicate with one another. This is done first in outline and then in greater detail. The detailed design really means that you have decided how the program is to be implemented. For example, it is now that decisions are made about suitable algorithms (see the next section) and data structures. The details of the interface with the user are worked out: what it should look like, how commands will be given to the program, what the menus should include, and so on. The documents that are produced during the design phase are first a *detailed system description*, laying out the program's design, and second a *user manual*, which gives directions for how the program should be used.

It is only in the third phase, *implementation*, that any programming starts to be done, when there is already a detailed system specification and user manual to adhere to. This phase also sees the testing of the parts of the program, one by one, as they are completed. The result of the implementation phase is, naturally, the *program code*, but there might also be *test protocols* resulting from the tests carried out on parts of the program.

In the fourth phase of development, *test and installation*, all the parts of the program are put together for a check that everything works. If the program is to be installed at a particular site, that is also done now. Testing is carried out according to the prescribed test procedures that were defined earlier. This phase results in a *test protocol*, and it is only after this has been found acceptable that the program developer gets paid in full by the customer.

The final phase, *operation and maintenance*, is the longest phase in the life of the product. Now the program is in full use, but errors that were missed in earlier tests have to be put right, and the program might have to be adjusted to cope with new demands, for example to work in a more modern hardware environment.

There is a criticism of the waterfall model in that it is too static: if one should happen upon a mistake made in an earlier phase it cannot be corrected. Of course, the waterfall model is not in reality used too strictly: some degree of feedback is allowed. There is, after all, no point in implementing something known to be incorrect or unsuitable. For example, one might discover during the design phase that some of the demands made in the first phase are impossible, or very expensive, to implement, and then it is only natural to relax the demands.

The specifications that are drawn up during the program development process should be as clear as possible, so that there is no possibility of misunderstanding. There are no generally recognized formal methods for writing specifications. The most common method is to use *graphic notation*, *ordinary text*, or a *program description language*. When using normal text it is usual to make it as formal as possible, by filling in sets of prespecified forms, for example. Program description languages (PDLs) are simplified programming languages that contain certain simple language constructs and which enable one to include explanatory text.

1.5 Algorithms

When designing a program the problem has to be faced of deciding on suitable methods of solving the different partial problems of the whole program. A description of how a particular problem is solved – a computational method – is called an *algorithm*. An algorithm consists of a number of elementary operations and instructions about the order in which these operations should be carried out. Certain demands can be made of an algorithm:

- It should solve the given problem.
- It should be unambiguous (not 'fuzzy' in its formulation).
- If the problem has an end view, such as computing a certain value, then the algorithm should terminate after a finite number of steps.

Note: Not all algorithms have to terminate. For instance, the algorithm that describes the control program for a nuclear power plant should certainly not terminate.

We come across algorithms every day. One example is a recipe. The problem is to prepare a particular dish, and the algorithm gives us the solution. Another example is the assembly instructions we get when we buy furniture in kit form; and then there are all the different kinds of instruction manuals. Knitters will recognize that a knitting pattern is nothing other than an algorithm.

Algorithms can be expressed in many different ways. One common way is in natural language. Pictures and symbols can also be used; so can formal languages such as mathematical notation. Flow charts have also been popular. Here we are dealing with programming, so what is naturally of interest to us is that algorithms can be expressed in programming languages. The programming language ALGOL, which lies at the root of most of today's conventional programming languages, was designed specifically so that it could be made to express algorithms – hence the name.

Algorithm
Description of how a particular problem is to be solved (a calculation method).

Let us look at an example. We shall describe an algorithm that shows the sum 1 + 2 + 3 . . . + n can be evaluated, if n is a given whole number > 0. One way of describing the algorithm in natural language is:

1. Set `sum` equal to 0 and the counter `k` equal to `1`.
2. Repeat the following steps until `k` is greater than `n`:
   2.1. Calculate the sum of `sum` and `k` and save the result in `sum`.
   2.2. Increase the value of `k` by `1`.
3. The result required is now the number in `sum`.

Expressed as part of a C++ program, the algorithm looks like this:

```
cin >> n;
sum = 0;
for (int k=1; k<=n; k++)
  sum += k;
cout << sum;
```

These lines of program read in the number `n` from the keyboard and display the calculated sum on the screen.

To describe general algorithms the description method must be able to express the following three constructs:

- A *sequence* is a series of steps that are carried out sequentially in the order in which they are written. An example is the assembly instructions for bookshelves:

  1. Put the side pieces in position.
  2. Screw the back piece onto the sides.
  3. Put the shelves into the frame.

- *Selection*. Selection means that one of two or more alternatives should be chosen. Calculating the absolute value of a number t can be taken as an example:

  if $t > 0$ then the result is t, otherwise the result is $-t$.

- *Iteration*. Part of the algorithm should be capable of repetition, either for a defined number of times or until a certain condition has been met. We saw an example of repetition for a defined number of times in the algorithm above, when the sum $1 + 2 + 3 + \ldots + n$ was calculated. An example of the latter repetition could be:

  Whisk the egg whites vigorously, until they become fluffy.

The most important algorithmic constructs
• Sequence – series of steps
• Selection – choice between alternative paths
• Iteration – repetition

Another kind of construct that is commonly used in algorithms, and which can sometimes replace iteration, is *recursion*. This construct seldom occurs in 'everyday' algorithms and may therefore feel a little strange. The principle is to break down the original problem into smaller, but structurally similar, problems. The smaller problems can then be solved by reapplying the same algorithm. The previous example, calculating the sum of the first *n* positive integers, can be solved with recursion in the following manner:

1. If `n` = 0 set the result to 0,
2. otherwise:
   2.1. Compute the sum 1 + 2 + 3 + . . . (*n* – 1) using this algorithm.
   2.2. The required result is obtained by adding *n* to the result from step 2.1.

1.6 Top-down design

When a complicated problem has to be solved, it is helpful to split it into smaller subproblems, which are then solved separately. The subproblems can then be split into further subproblems, and so on. This is a very important technique in algorithm and program construction and is known as *top-down design*. Let us look at an 'everyday' algorithm that describes washing your car. A first, rough algorithm might be simply:

1. Wash car.

This can be quickly refined to:

1.1. If you are feeling lazy:
  1.1.1. Wash it at a car wash.
1.2. otherwise
  1.2.1. Wash it by hand.

Step 1.1.1 can be refined to:

1.1.1.1. Drive to the nearest car wash.
1.1.1.2. Buy a token.
1.1.1.3. Wait in a queue.
1.1.1.4. Have the car washed.

Step 1.1.1.4 can be refined further:

1.1.1.4.1. Check that the doors and windows are closed.
1.1.1.4.2. Wind down the driver's window.
1.1.1.4.3. Put the token into the machine.
1.1.1.4.4. Wind up the window.
1.1.1.4.5. Drive into the car wash.
1.1.1.4.6. Wait until the car wash is finished.
1.1.1.4.7. Drive away.

In this way, different parts of an algorithm can be refined until a level is reached where the solution becomes trivially simple.

Top-down design

- Divide into subproblems.
- Solve the subproblems one by one.
- Divide the subproblems into further subproblems.
- Continue in this way until all the subproblems are easily solvable.

Let us look at another example where iteration is also involved. Imagine the following situation. In your bookcase you have a compact disc holder for ordinary compact discs. You keep your CDs there, neatly arranged alphabetically according to the name of the composer. (For simplicity, assume that you only have classical music.) CD holders are made of small slots, each large enough for one CD so that they cannot be moved sideways. We assume that the CDs are kept in the left part of the holder, so that there are no gaps or empty slots on the left, but at least five empty ones on the right.

Now suppose you have bought five new CDs that need to be put in the holder in their correct positions, so that alphabetical order is maintained. Assume also that the bookshelves are so full that there is nowhere to put the CDs, so you have to hold them in your hands while you shift them around. To avoid the risk of dropping any, you cannot have more than one CD in your hand at a time. The five new CDs are on the floor and you pick them up one after the other and position them in the holder.

We can make up a rough algorithm:

```
1. Sort the new CDs into the CD holder.
```

The first refinement will be:

```
1.1. For each new CD:
     1.1.1. Lift the CD from the floor with your left hand.
     1.1.2. Sort it into its correct place.
```

The way we have written points 1.1.1 and 1.1.2 inset on the line shows that they have to be repeated several times (once per new CD). We have thus introduced iteration into the algorithm. Point 1.1.1 needs no further refinement so we can refine point 1.1.2:

```
1.1.2.1. Locate the slot in the CD holder where the new CD is to be placed.
1.1.2.2. Shift all the CDs to the right of (and including) the located slot one place to the right,
         so that the located one becomes empty.
1.1.2.3. Place the new CD in the located slot.
```

Refining point 1.1.2.1 gives:

```
1.1.2.1.1. Put your left index finger on the leftmost slot of the CD holder. (You can do this even
           though you have the new CD in that hand.)
```

1.1.2.1.2. Repeat the following point until the located slot is empty or until the composer's name on the CD in the located slot comes alphabetically after the composer's name on the new CD.

  1.1.2.1.2.1. Move your left index finger one slot to the right.

1.1.2.1.3. Your left index finger has now located the slot where the new CD is to be inserted.

Point 1.1.2.2 now becomes:

1.1.2.2.1. Put your right hand on the CD furthest to the right and repeat the following steps until the slot indicated by your left index finger is empty.

  1.1.2.2.1.1. Move the CD held by your right hand one slot to the right.
  1.1.2.2.1.2. Move your right hand to the nearest CD on the left.

If we now put all the refined steps together, we get the following complete algorithm. The numbering of the steps has been removed to make it look neater. Note that the inset lines are repeated a defined number of times.

For each of the newly bought CDs:

  Lift the CD from the floor with your left hand.

  Put your left index finger on the slot in the CD holder furthest to the left.

  Repeat the following steps until the slot pointed to is empty, or until the composer's name on the CD pointed to comes alphabetically after the composer's name on the new CD.

    Move your left index finger one slot to the right.

  Your left index finger now points to the slot where the new CD is to be inserted.

  Put your right hand on the CD that is furthest to the right and repeat the following steps until the slot pointed to by your left index finger is empty.

    Move the CD you are holding in your right hand, one slot to the right.

    Move your right hand to the nearest CD on the left.

  Insert the new CD in the located slot.

We have just seen an example of a *sort algorithm*. This is not the only algorithm that can be used to sort the CDs into position. You could think of several other ways of doing this. Sort algorithms often occur in programming.

There are usually several alternative algorithms for solving a particular problem. In general, it is sensible to design an algorithm that is simple and easy to understand because it will then have the best chance of working as intended.

Exercises

1.1 Try to find out the following about the computer system you intend to use:

(a) What operating system is being used?
(b) How large is the primary memory?
(c) How large is the hard disk memory?
(d) What possibilities are there for communicating with other computers?

(e) Which C++ compiler or C++ development environment is to be used?
(f) What other programming languages, apart from C++, are available?

1.2 Write a C++ program to display your name and address at the terminal. Compile, link and test run the program with the help of the compiler or program development environment you intend to use.

1.3 Give an algorithm for calculating the sum

$$\sum_{i=1}^{n} i^2$$

1.4 Find an algorithm for calculating

$$n! = 1 \cdot 2 \cdot 3 \cdot \ldots \cdot n, \langle n > 0 \rangle$$

1.5 A table contains *n* different numbers. Design an algorithm that searches the table to find the smallest number. At the end, the algorithm will give the lowest number's position number in the table (an index between 1 and *n*).

1.6 A table contains *n* different numbers. Design an algorithm that changes the table's contents so that the numbers appear in order of size, the smallest number first and largest last. Use a method that first places the smallest number in the table's first position, then the next smallest number in the table's second position, and so on. (*Tip*: The algorithm in the previous exercise may help.)

The basics

2

This chapter presents some of the basic concepts behind C++. We shall see how programs that read and write input data are constructed. In this context, we shall look at *variables*. A variable is like a container in computer programs; it is used to handle data. There are different kinds of variable, and they may contain different sorts of data, or *types*, as they are often called. In this chapter we shall be looking at the most common types so that we can handle different kinds of numbers, and we shall be going over various forms of arithmetical and logical expressions.

We shall also deal with `if` statements, `while` statements and `for` statements, the most common constructions for performing choice and repetition.

Finally, the various errors that can occur in the programming process are discussed.

2.1 Variables and reading/writing

On page 5 we saw a simple program to output text. Now we begin to study programs that are more useful: programs that can calculate more important things. We now design, as a first example, a program that calculates how much a car costs to hire. Suppose that you know the number of days you want to hire the car for and how much it costs per day. You give the program this information, and let it calculate the total cost and output it. When the program is running, the output might look like this:

```
Number of days? 3
Rate per day?   42
Total cost:     126
```

The numbers `3` and `42` are called *input data*. They are written by the person running the program. The rest of the output is produced by the program. The number `126` is the result calculated by the program – the *output data*. The program looks like this:

```
#include <iostream>
using namespace std;
main ()
{
   int day_number;
   int daily_rate;
   cout << "Number of days? ";
   cin  >> day_number;
   cout << "Rate per day?   ";
   cin  >> daily_rate;
   cout << "Total cost:     "
        << day_number * daily_rate << endl;
}
```

The first line says that we want to use the standard library `iostream`, which contains a facility for input and output. (If you have an old compiler that does not follow the standard, you can write `#include <iostream.h>` instead of `#include <iostream>` and delete the second line.) A variable, as mentioned above, is a kind of container into which data can be put: in this program the two variables are `day_number` and `daily_rate`. A particular variable can contain only information of a certain kind, or *type*. Before you can use a variable in a program, you have to say what you are going to call it and what kind of data it will contain. To do this is to *declare* the variable. In our program the declarations are made on the two lines that begin with the word **`int`**. These lines say that the variables will be called `day_number` and `daily_rate` and that both of them will contain values of the type **`int`**. (We usually say that the variables *are* of the type **`int`**, or that they *have* the type **`int`**.) The type **`int`** is a standard type in C++, and 'int' is an abbreviation of 'integer', which means 'whole number'. The two variables in the program will thus contain whole numbers: that is, numbers without decimal parts.

A function contains, as we have seen, a number of *statements*, which describe what is to be performed. The declarations are often written in front of the statements. In our program the statements begin on the sixth line.

As we saw in Chapter 1, output from a program can be generated with the help of the output operator `<<`. The first statement in the program writes out the text `Number of days?`. The next statement:

```
cin >> day_number;
```

uses the input operator `>>` to read input data from the input stream `cin` to the variable `day_number`. The stream `cin` is normally connected to the keyboard.

This means that, when this statement is carried out, the program will stop for a moment and wait until a number is typed in from the keyboard. When the number has been typed (normally finished by pressing the 'enter' key) the program will continue. The number typed in from the keyboard now lands in the variable `day_number`. If the user, as in our example, types the number `3`, then `day_number` will get the value `3`.

The input data is then read in a similar way for the variable `daily_rate`, which in our example has the value `42`. The output of the result takes the form of the statement

```
cout << "Total cost: "
     << day_number * daily_rate << endl;
```

First the text `Total cost:` is written, then the product of `day_number` and `daily_rate`. The sign `*` means multiplication. As we know, many things can be output one after the other in the same output statement. Last of all in the stream is the manipulator `endl`, which generates a new line in the output. There are many different kinds of manipulator, and they can be inserted in the outstream to edit the output. We shall shortly be looking at a few more common manipulators.

Output on the screen
cout << out1 << out2 << out3 . . . ;
where *outi* can be a constant, a variable, an expression or a manipulator.

In C++ there are a number of *reserved words*, words with particular meanings. There is one in our program called **`int`**. We often write these reserved words in bold so that they may be seen more clearly, and this will be the case in this book. When you write the program yourself, you don't have to mark reserved words in any particular way. (In modern program development systems reserved words are often marked automatically by special text editors when they are written.)

The observant reader will notice that we have not put a statement such as

```
return 0;
```

as we did in the example on page 5 of Chapter 1. There really ought to be a **`return`** statement like this at the end of every program, but according to the standard you can omit this statement. So we shall not include it in our examples from now on. Most of the C++ compilers today will give a warning about this, but you can go ahead and compile the program anyway.

Now we shall make some additions to our program so it becomes a little more usable. Suppose you are on holiday somewhere in Europe and want to hire a car there. This will mean that the rate per day is given in euros. Suppose that you also have to pay an extra, fixed payment of 10 euros in tax. To avoid the mental arithmetic, you want the program to output the total cost both in euros and in dollars. For this to be possible, you have to give the current rates of exchange as input data. Here is an example of how the program might look when you run it.

```
Indicate number of days and cost per day: 3 31
Exchange rate? 0.885
Total cost: 103 euro ($91.155)
```

The program will then look like this:

```
#include <iostream>
using namespace std;
main ()
{
  int         day_number, daily_rate, tot_cost;
  const int tax = 10;
  double      exchange_rate;
  cout << "Indicate number of days and cost per day: ";
  cin  >> day_number >> daily_rate;
  cout << "Exchange rate? ";
  cin  >> exchange_rate;
  tot_cost = tax + day_number * daily_rate;
  cout << "Total cost: " << tot_cost << " euro"
       << " ($" << tot_cost*exchange_rate << ")"<< endl;
}
```

The three variables `day_number`, `daily_rate` and `tot_cost` are declared on the fifth line. They are all of the type **`int`**. We can see that we don't have to declare a variable per line but are allowed to enumerate several variables one after another. They must all be of the same type, however.

The constant `tax` is declared on the next line. It has a constant value and may (can) not be changed in the program. The fact that `tax = 10` in the program means that the constant `tax` is *initialized* to the value `10`, and it will have this value during the execution of the entire program.

If a variable is not initialized, its starting value will be undefined. Constant variables must always be initialized, since they cannot be changed later in the program. It is also possible for variables that are not constant to be initialized upon declaration. We might have been able to put it in the following way, where the variables `day_number` and `tot_cost` are initialized to the value `0` and the variable `daily_rate` is left uninitialized:

```
int day_number=0, daily_rate, tot_cost=0;
```

The variable `exchange_rate`, which will contain the exchange rate, is declared on the seventh line of the program. Obviously, the exchange rate cannot be a whole number and so the type **`int`** will not work. Instead, we have to make use of another standard type, `double`. Variables of this type can contain real numbers, numbers with decimals. (Double actually stands for 'double precision'.)

> **Variable declarations**
>
> *type name1, name2 . . . ;*
> ⇒ changeable, uninitialized variables
>
> or
>
> *type name1=value1, name2=value2 . . . ;*
> ⇒ changeable, initialized variables
> (each variable is initialized separately)
>
> or
>
> ***constant*** *type name1=value1, name2=value2 . . . ;*
> ⇒ constant variables
> (each variable is initialized separately)

When you declare a variable, you can decide yourself what to call it. The name of the variable may be as long as you like, and can consist of letters, numbers and the underline character. It may not, however, begin with a number. Only the letters 'a' to 'z' may be used in C++. Note that upper-case and lower-case letters are treated as being *different*. The names `n1` and `N1` thus designate two different variables. Reserved words may not be used as names of variables, so variables such as `while` and `if` may not be declared.

Let us return to our program. In the line

```
cin >> day_number >> daily_rate;
```

the values of the variables `day_number` and `daily_rate` are entered. Several values can be input one after another in the same statement. The user can input freely formatted input data extending to more than one line in the program. Either the different numbers can be input one after the other on the same line, or you can press the Enter key after every number. Normally, the operator `>>` automatically skips over all the 'white' characters (spacings, tab stops and end-of-line breaks) in the input stream. Thus input could just as well look like this:

```
Indicate number of days and cost per day: 3
31
```

The variable `tot_cost` is used for storage of the total cost, expressed in euros. It gets its value through an *assignment statement*:

```
tot_cost = tax + day_number * daily_rate;
```

Input from the keyboard

cin >> variable1;
cin >> variable2;
cin >> variable3;

or

cin >> variable1 >> variable2 >> variable3 . . . ;

Input data is written in free format. Spacings, tab stops and end of lines are normally skipped over.

The expression on the right of the equation is calculated first. Then the calculated value is placed in the variable `tot_cost`. A value must have the same type as a variable if it is to be assigned to it. Thus the expression to the right of the equation in an assignment statement must either have the same type as the variable to the left, or the value must be able to be automatically converted into the type of this variable. There is no problem if the types in question are *arithmetic types*, types that contain mathematical numbers, since they can always be automatically converted into one another. When run, the last program statement reads:

```
Total cost: 103 euro ($91.155)
```

Assignment

variable names = expressions;

- The value of the expression to the right of the equation is calculated first.
- This value is then placed in the variable to the left.
- The variable's previous value is destroyed.
- The expression to the right must have the same type as the variable or must be able to be automatically transformed into this type.
- Arithmetic types, and possibly others, can be automatically transformed.

When a real number is output, the output operator automatically edits the output to facilitate reading the number as much as possible. This means, among other things, that the number of decimals shown will depend on the value of the number. This can be useful, although mostly you might like to control how the number will be output. In our example above, it could well be that you always want two decimals in the output of the sum in dollars. One way of editing the output is to use manipulators. To do this, you may have to include the file `iomanip` as well in your program. You do this by entering the line

```
#include <iomanip>
```

at the beginning of the program. The last statement in our program is then rewritten:

```
cout << "Total cost: " << tot_cost << " euro"
     << setiosflags(ios::fixed) << setprecision(2)
     << " ($" << tot_cost*exchange_rate << ")"<<endl;
```

Two manipulators have been put into the stream here. The first manipulator, `setiosflags`, is used to give certain characteristics to the current stream. One such characteristic is `fixed`, which indicates that real numbers will be output with a fixed decimal point. The other manipulator, `setprecision`, is used to indicate how many decimals we want to have in the output (in our case, two). The output will be *rounded off* to the number of decimals we indicate. The program will now produce the output

```
Total cost: 103 euro ($91.16)
```

Note that the output of the number of euros has not been affected. Manipulators affect only the output that comes after them in the stream. A manipulator normally applies not only to the next values that are output but also to the values following these. If, for instance, we were to insert a further series of real numbers into our program, these would also be output with two decimals and a fixed decimal point. There is a manipulator called `fixed`, which is easier to use than `setiosflags`. So an alternative would be:

```
cout << "Total cost: " << tot_cost << " euro"
     << fixed << setprecision(2)
     << " ($" << tot_cost*exchange_rate << ") " << endl;
```

A commentary should be provided for `precision`. The standard value for `precision` is 6. If the standard format in the output is used, `precision` will indicate the total number of figures in the output; but if you have indicated, as has been done here, that the output form should be `fixed`, `precision` will indicate the number of decimals.

If a return to the default output form is desired, the manipulators `setprecision` and `resetiosflags` can be used:

```
cout << setprecision(6) << resetiosflags(ios::fixed);
```

Let us now look at an example of a program that can be used with the sale of goods. Let us imagine that a customer has bought a certain number of goods of the same kind and that he now wants an invoice. The invoice should say how many articles the customer has bought, what the total cost is (including sales tax), and how much of the cost the sales tax accounts for. When the program is run, it can look like this:

```
Number of articles? 30
Cost per article? 42.50
```

```
INVOICE
=======
Number of articles:     30
Cost per article:       42.50
Total cost:           1593.75
Of which sales tax:    318.75
```

Particularly noticeable here is that all the figures in the output of the invoice have been adjusted so that there is a straight right-hand margin. We say that the figures have been *right-justified*. When a number is to be printed, a certain number of positions are used in the output. The number will usually be placed to the right in these positions; the space in front of the number will be filled in with blank characters. If you don't indicate the number of positions to be used, there will automatically be just enough of them for the number. As a result, the number will be left-justified directly after the previous output.

Some common manipulators in output

The following lines must be found at the beginning of the program:

```
#include <iomanip>
using namespace std;
```

- `endl`

  Line feed.
- `setprecision (n)`

  Output of numbers of the form `fixed` will occur with *n* decimals. *n*=0 means standard value.
- `fixed` or `setiosflags (ios::fixed)`

  Real numbers will be printed out with fixed decimal point and with decimals.
- `resetiosflags (ios::fixed)`

  Return to standard kind of output form.
- `setw(n)`

  Next printout will take place with *n* positions.
- `setfill('x')`

  In the next printout, fill-in will occur with the sign 'x' instead of with blanks.

To indicate the number of output positions, the manipulator `setw` is used. The expression `setw (9)` indicates that nine positions will be used in the next output. Note that the manipulator `setw`, unlike `setprecision` and `setiosflags`, applies only to the next output. Note, too, that `setw` can be used for all kinds of ouput, not only for outputting real numbers.

The sales tax and the cost with and without sales tax are calculated in three separate variables. The exact percentage for sales tax has been declared as a constant and, since it has been expressed as a percentage, we must divide it by 100. The program then looks like this:

```
#include <iostream>
#include <iomanip>
using namespace std;
main ()
{
  int number;
  double per_art, excl_sales_tax, incl_sales_tax, sales_tax;
  const double sales_tax_percent = 25.0;
  cout << "Number of articles? "; cin >> number;
  cout << "Cost per article? "; cin >> per_art;
  excl_sales_tax = per_art * number;
  sales_tax = excl_sales_tax * sales_tax_percent / 100;
  incl_sales_tax = excl_sales_tax + sales_tax;
  cout << endl <<
  "INVOICE" << endl << "=======" << endl <<
  "Number of articles:" << setw(9) << number << endl <<
  setprecision(2) << setiosflags(ios::fixed) <<
  "Cost per article:" << setw(11) << per_art << endl <<
  "Total cost:" << setw(17) << incl_sales_tax << endl <<
  "Of which sales tax:" << setw(9) << sales_tax << endl;
}
```

Sometimes you need to indicate the constant values in your programs. In this program, for instance, we have the values 25.0 and 100. Constant values of this kind are called *literals*. Literals need not designate numerical data. You can have literals of another kind, for example literals to designate constant texts, such as `"INVOICE"`. In calculating the sales tax, you could of course have written

```
sales_tax = excl_sales_tax * 0.25;
```

The constant `sales_tax_percent` would not then have been needed. However, it is a good rule to avoid having numerical literals inserted among statements in a program. If the percentage for sales tax is changed, it could be difficult to find all the places in the program where changes are needed. (The percentage might be used several times in a big program.) If a constant variable is used, as in this example, you need only make the change in one place.

2.2 Arithmetic expressions

Types used to describe ordinary numbers are called *arithmetic types*. The types **`int`** and **`double`** are examples of such types. Often, expressions occur in programs where ordinary numbers are calculated. These expressions are called *arithmetic expressions*.

The ordinary arithmetical operations of addition, subtraction, multiplication and division, designated by `+`, `-`, `*` and `/` respectively, can be used in these expressions. The most common form of arithmetic expression has two operands which can be variables or literals. Here are some examples of these expressions:

```
i1 + i2     weight + 12.6    1 - i     x - y
x * y       25 * n           i / 10    x / y
```

The two operands may be of different arithmetic types. The result type of the expression will be determined by the types of the operands entered. If both have the same type, the result will also be of this type. If one of the operators is an integer and the other a real number, the result will be a real number. If, for example, the types **`int`** and **`double`** are mixed, the result will be of the **`double`** type.

Division needs to be explained further. It is not unusual for one of the operands to be a real number. Then ordinary division takes place and the result will be a real number, the quotient of the two operands. If, on the other hand, the two operands are of integer type, for instance **`int`**, *integer division* will be performed. This means that you will see how many times the right-hand operand 'goes into' the left-hand one. If the variables `i` and `j` are of type **`int`** and have the values `14` and `5` respectively, then the expression `i/j` will give a result of `2`, since `5` goes into `14` twice. The result will *not* be `2.8`.

To obtain the remainder upon integer division, the *modulus operator* `%` is used. If, as before, the variables have the values `14` and `5` respectively, the expression `i%j` will produce a result of `4`. For this operator to give a well-defined result, both operands must be positive.

Unary variants of the operators `+` and `-` also occur. These variants have only one operand, which is written to the right of the operator. The unary minus operator is especially useful in the following kinds of construct:

```
k = -1;    k * (-3)    cout << -k;    k = -k;
```

More complicated expressions can be created by combining several operators. The result will be an expression containing several partial expressions. An example is the expression

```
tax + day_number * daily_rate
```

from the program in the last section. The result of a partial expression will be a value that, in its turn, constitutes the one operand for a new operation. The different priorities of operators in a complicated expression will decide the order in which the expression is to be calculated. Operators with a higher priority are calculated before operators with a lower one. Calculation takes place from left to right if two operators have the same priority. In the case of the arithmetic operators discussed, the unary operators `+` and `-`

have highest priority; then come the operators `*`, `/` and `%`, which have the same priority. The ordinary operators `+` and `-` have lowest priority. In the above expression, multiplication will therefore take place before addition. Another example is the expression `-2+4/2*3`, which will have a value of `4`. Parentheses can also be used to control the order of calculation. The expression `(-2+4)/2*3` will, for instance, have a value of `3`. In fact statements such as

```
i = i + 1;
k = k - 1;
```

are extremely common in programming.

There are two useful operators in C++, `++` and `--`, which can be used to increase or decrease a variable's value by `1`. With the help of these, the two statements above can be simplified to

```
i++;
k--;
```

These increment and decrement operators occur in two variants. You can put `++` or `--` either in front (*prefix* variants) or after (*postfix* variants) the variable's name. The two statements might then have been written

```
++i;  // prefix
--k;  // prefix
```

In the examples above it does not matter which of the two variants you choose, but there is an important difference between them. The expressions `i++` and `++i` both mean that the variable `i` is increased by `1`, but the *values* of the two expressions are different. The value of the expression `i++` is the value `i` had *before* the increase; the value of the expression `++i` is the value `i` has *after* the increase. The same holds for the decrement operator. This is best illustrated by a couple of examples:

```
int i, k, m, n;
i = 4; k = 7;
m = i++ * j--;  // postfix. m gets the value 4*7, i.e. 28
i = 4; k = 7;
n = i++ * --j;  // prefix. n gets the value 5*6, i.e. 30
```

Apart from increasing or decreasing by `1`, it often happens that you want to change a variable's value in other ways. You may for instance want to add a value to the variable, subtract a value from it, or multiply it by a certain number. Some examples are

```
i = i + 2;
j = j - k;
k = k * i;
n = n / 3;
```

In these situations it is useful to use the compound forms of the assignment operator.

With the help of these, the statements above can be written

```
i += 2;  // same as i = i + 2;
j -= k;  // same as j = j - k;
k *= i;  // same as k = k * i;
n /= 3;  // same as n = n / 3;
```

There are several compounded forms of the assignment operator.

Arithmetic operators	
`+ - *`	Addition, subtraction and multiplication.
`/`	Division (division of integers, if both operands are integral, otherwise ordinary division).
`%`	Gives the remainder with division of integers.
`++`	Increases the operand's value by `1`. The value `k++` is `k`'s old value. The value `++k` is `k`'s new value.
`--`	Decreases the operand's value by `1`. The value `k--` is `k`'s old value. The value `--k` is `k`'s new value.
`+= -= *= /= %=`	Compound assignment operators. The expression: `x ·= y;` is equivalent to: `x = x · y;`

There are often several mathematical functions in the common calculator, and you can usually work out logarithms and trigonometric functions. Are functions of this sort available in C++ and, if so, how do you use them? Standard mathematical functions are not built into the programming language itself but they can be found in the standard library. The two most interesting standard libraries are called `cmath` and `cstdlib`. The letter `c` at the beginning indicates that these are libraries taken from the programming language C. The library `cmath` contains trigonometric functions, logarithmic functions and square roots. (See the information window on page 41.) The library `cstdlib` contains a number of functions of a more general nature, but some of them can be used for performing arithmetical calculations.

You should have the following lines at the beginning of your program if you want to have access to the functions in the `cmath` and `cstdlib` libraries:

```
#include <cmath>
#include <cstdlib>
using namespace std;
```

Standard functions in the cmath library

All functions return a real number. The arguments `x` and `y` shall also be real numbers. (There are versions of these functions for the types **float**, **double** and **long double**.)

`exp(x)`	Gives e^x.
`log(x)`	Gives the natural logarithm (ln) of x.
`log10(x)`	Gives the common logarithm (base 10) of x.
`sqrt(x)`	Gives $\sqrt{x}$.
`ceil(x)`	Gives the smallest integer that is $\geq x$.
`floor(x)`	Gives the greatest integer which is $\leq x$.
`fabs(x)`	Gives the absolute value of x.
`pow(x,y)`	Gives x^y (If $x < 0$, y must be an integer).
`fmod(x,y)`	Gives the remainder upon division x/y.
`sin(x), cos(x), tan(x)`	x is given in radians.
`asin(x), acos(x), atan(x)`	Gives arcsines, etc.
`sinh(x), cosh(x), tanh(x)`	Hyperbolic functions.

Arithmetic functions in the cstdlib library

`abs(n)`	n has the type **int**. Gives the absolute value of n.
`labs(n)`	n has the type **long int**. Gives the absolute value of n.

The call of functions can be a part of arithmetic expressions such as

```
3.6*sqrt(z)   log(z)/log10(x+y)   fabs(sin(y))
```

As an example, let's look at a program that calculates compound interest. Suppose that your account at the bank is credited with \$$b$ and that the annual interest rate is r%. The capital you will have accumulated over n years if you haven't touched the money is calculated by the formula $b \cdot (1 + r/100)^n$:

```
#include <iostream>
#include <iomanip>
#include <cmath>
using namespace std;
main ()
{
  double b, r;
  int n;
```

```
    cout << "Amount? "; cin   >> b;
    cout << "Interest? "; cin >> r;
    cout << "Number of years? "; cin >> n;
    cout << setprecision(2) << setiosflags(ios::fixed)
         << "The capital becomes " << b*pow(1+r/100, n);
}
```

2.3 `if` statements

The three most important algorithm constructs, *sequence*, *selection* and *iteration*, were discussed in Chapter 1 on page 23. You can get a sequence in C++ by placing several statements in succession, one after the other. In this section we shall examine the `if` statement, which is one of the most simple and common constructs in C++ for obtaining selection – that is, choice. We begin by giving another variant of the program that calculates sales prices. This time, we shall omit the sales tax. When you run the program, you simply indicate the number of items bought and the cost per item. The program will then calculate the total cost. Let us now suppose that, if you spend more than $100, you will get 10% discount on the cost of the goods. If you spend less, you don't get a discount. When you run the program, it can look like this:

```
Number of items? 25
Cost per item? 4.50
The cost becomes: 101.25
```

The program will look as below. Constant variables have been used to indicate how much percentage discount is received and the bound where the discount begins.

```
#include <iostream>
#include <iomanip>
using namespace std;
main ()
{
  int number;
  double per_item, cost, discount;
  const double discount_percent = 10, bound = 100;
  cout << "Number of items? "; cin >> number;
  cout << "Cost per item? "; cin >> per_item;
  cost = per_item * number;
  if (cost > bound)
  {
    discount = cost * discount_percent / 100;
    cost     = cost - discount;
  }
  cout << "The cost becomes: " <<setprecision(2) <<
  setiosflags(ios::fixed) << cost << endl;
}
```

Indentation

- A program is made more readable when text on the lines is indented to reflect the program's structure.
- A well-structured program is always indented.
- When writing programs, indentation should always be used.

The interesting part of this program are the four lines preceded by the word **`if`**. An expression *in parentheses* should come after this word. Here, however, we have the expression `cost > bound`. If the expression is true, the statements inside the following braces `{}` will be executed. If the expression is false, these statements will not be executed. It is a good thing to write the left brace immediately above the right brace, so that they can be seen to belong together. We have indented the text so that the conditional statements can be seen more clearly. This indentation facilitates the reading and understanding of your programs.

In an **`if`** statement there can be as many statements as you like within the braces. If there is only a single statement, you do not need to put it within braces. For instance, we could write

```
if (cost > bound)
  cost -= cost * discount_percent / 100;
```

An **`if`** statement can also have an **`else`** part, a sequence of statements that are executed if the condition is false. You can write, for example,

```
if (cost > bound)
{
  discount = cost * discount_percent / 100;
  cost -= discount;
}
else
  cout << "No discount, sorry" << endl;
```

Now *either* the two statements within the braces, *or* the statement after **`else`**, will be executed.

You can also have several statements in the **`else`** part but then you must have braces:

```
if (cost > bound)
  cost -= cost * discount_percent / 100;
else
{
  cout << "No discount, sorry" << endl;
  cout << "Buy more next time" << endl;
}
```

Different forms of `if` statement	

`if` (*expression*)
  statement;
———
`if` (*expression*)
  statement;
`else`
  statement;
———
`if` (*expression*)
{
  one or more statements
}
`else`
{
  one or more statements
}
	`if` (*expression*)
	{
	  one or more statements
	}
	———
	`if` (*expression*)
	  statement;
	`else`
	{
	  one or more statements
	}
	———
	`if` (*expression*)
	{
	  one or more statements
	}
	`else`
	  statement;

Here we have rewritten the two statements after `if` to make one statement. Note particularly that there must not be a semicolon in front of `else` when braces include the statements after `if`. When the braces have been left out, however, there must be a semicolon.

The `if` statement can be used in multiple-choice situations even if it has only two alternatives. Let us suppose that we have two discount levels in our example. If you buy goods totalling more than $500 you get a 15% discount; if you buy goods totalling less than $500 but more than $100 you get a 10% discount. If anything less than $100 is spent there is no discount. Let us now then declare two 'boundaries' and two discount percentages:

```
const double discount_percent1 = 10, bound1 = 100,
             discount_percent2 = 15, bound2 = 500;
```

Then we rewrite the `if` statement like this:

```
if (cost > bound2)
  cost -= cost * discount_percent2/100;
else if (cost > bound1)
  cost -= cost * discount_percent1/100;
else
  cout << "No discount, sorry" << endl;
```

Two `if` statements have been put together here, with the result that the `else` part of the first `if` statement contains a new `if` statement.

There can be all kinds of statement in an `if` statement, or the `else` part of an `if` statement – even new `if` statements. When one `if` statement is contained within another we say that the `if` statements are *nested*. This structure will become clearer if the indentation is done slightly differently:

```
if (cost > bound2)
   cost -= cost * discount_percent2/100;
else
   if (cost > bound1)
      cost -= cost * discount_percent1/100;
else
   cout << "No discount, sorry" << endl;
```

When pure multiple-choice situations occur, as in this example, you usually indent in the way we did first; then the appearance of the program itself becomes a satisfying reflection of its logic.

2.4 Comparison operators and logical operators

The expression within the parentheses after `if`, which will be true or false, can appear in different forms. We usually use *comparison operators*, as in our example. The following comparison operators are used:

```
<    >    <=    >=    ==    !=
```

These mean 'less than', 'greater than', 'less than or equal to', 'greater than or equal to', 'equal to' and 'not equal to' respectively. Note in particular that the operator 'equal to' is written with two equal signs. (One equal sign of course means 'assignment'.) Some examples are given below.

Comparison operators		
`==` equal to	`<` less than	`>` greater than
`!=` not equal to	`<=` less than or equal to	`>=` greater than or equal to

```
if (number == 0)
   cout << "None left";
if (number != 0)
   cout << "Some exist";
if (cost <= 0)
   cout << "Noteworthy pricing" << endl;
```

More complicated *logical expressions* could be constructed using the operators `&&`, `||` and `!`, which execute the logical operations *and*, *or* and *not*. It is important to write two

`&` signs or two of the `|` signs when using these operators, since the two operators `&` and `|`, written singly, also exist. These operators are used when dealing with bits. The operators `&&` and `||` have two operands, and the operator `!` one operand. The expression `A && B` is true if *both* `A` and `B` are true but false otherwise. The expression `A || B` is true if *at least one* of `A` or `B` is true but false otherwise. The expression `! A` is true if `A` is false and false if `A` is true. Some examples:

```
if (temp>20 && temp<30)
   cout << "suitably warm" << endl;
if (i==1 || i==3 || i==5 || i==7 || i==9)
   cout << "Odd number";
if (!(temp>20 && temp<30))
   cout << "Not nice";
```

The operators `&&` and `||` have lower priority than the arithmetic operators `+`, `-`, `*` and `/` and the comparison operators `<`, `>`, etc. This means that expressions such as

```
i + j > k * l && m == n
```

are interpreted as

```
(i + j) > (k * l) && (m == n)
```

which is quite natural. In the last **if** statement above, the extra parentheses are necessary because the operator `!` has a higher priority than `&&` and `||`. Had we not written parentheses, the expression `! temp>20 && temp<30` would have been interpreted in the same way as the expression `(! temp>20) && temp<30`.

The operators **and**, **or** and **not** have been introduced in the standard of C++ as an alternative to the operators `&&`, `||` and `!`. Using these operators, the last **if** statement above would have been written

```
if (not(temp>20 and temp<30))
   cout << "Not nice";
```

Logical operators		
A `&&` *B* *A* **and** *B* true if *both* *A* and *B* are true	*A* `||` *B* *A* **or** *B* true if *at least one of* *A* or *B* is true	`!` *A* **not** *A* true if *A* is false

- `&&` and `||` have *lower* priority than comparison operators.
- `!` has *higher* priority than arithmetic operators and comparison operators.

Every expression in C++ has a certain type. You need to ask yourself which type the result of an expression with comparison operators, or logical operators, will have. In the C++ standard a standard type `bool` has been introduced. The comparison and logical operators give a result that has a value of this type. There are only two values for the type `bool`, `true` and `false`. The `if` statement is constructed in such a way that it expects a value of the type `bool` within the parentheses.

A special type to designate logical values was not found in C++ in the past. Instead, such values were described using the type `int`. As a result the compiler expected the expression within the parentheses in an `if` statement to have the type `int`. When an `if` statement was executed, the value `0` was treated as being 'false' and all other values as 'true'. Comparison and logical operators were also constructed in such a way as to leave integers as a result. If an expression was true the result was equal to `1`, and if an expression was false the result was equal to `0`. Here now are two strange examples. On the first line `i` is assigned the value `1`:

```
i = 5 > 2;
if (i)
  cout << "i is not equal to 0";
```

An automatic type conversion, from the type `int` to the type `bool`, has been introduced to ensure that old C++ programs can function as they used to when they are compiled with a compiler that follows the standard. The value `0` is automatically converted into `false` and all other values into `true`. Thus the choice can be made either to use the old style with the type `int` describing logical values, or to use the type `bool`.*

An `if` statement can be used to see whether the input has gone as planned. As an example, let us look at the statement

```
cin >> number;
```

where we assume that the variable `number` has the type `int`. This statement inputs a number from the keyboard and places the input value into the variable `number`. This will work well, provided the person running the program actually types in an integer from the keyboard. If incorrect input data is entered (perhaps a letter instead of a number is typed), the input will miscarry and the variable `number` will remain

---

* If the compiler you use does not as yet support the type `bool`, you can proceed in the following way. Put the program lines below into a text file with the name `bool.h`.

```
typedef int bool;
#define false 0
#define true 1
```

Then let every program start with the extra line

```
#include "bool.h"
```

unchanged, keeping its previous value. The input stream will also get into an error state, which will have to be cleared before more data can be entered.

We shall now use the fact that the expression `cin >> number` gives a result value. This value can be automatically converted into the type **`bool`**. If input has proceeded satisfactorily, the result of the conversion will be **`true`**; if not, it will be **`false`**.

```
if (cin >> number)
  cout << "The number was" << number;
else
{
  cout << "Incorrect input";
  cin.clear();
}
```

The statement `cin.clear();` clears the error that has arisen in the input stream. This statement must be included if more input data from the stream is to be entered later in the program.

2.5 `while` statements

Besides sequence and selection, the third important construct is *repetition*. The easiest way of producing repetition in C++ is by using a **`while`** statement. Let us begin with a simple example. Suppose that the variable `j` has the type **`int`**. The program section

```
j = 0;
while (j < 6)
{
  cout << setw(3) << j;
  j += 2;
}
```

gives the output

```
0 2 4
```

Execution of the **`while`** statement takes place in the following way. The expression in parentheses after **`while`** is calculated first. (The same rules hold as for the **`if`** statement.) If the expression is false, nothing more is done. If, however, the expression is true, the statements within the braces are executed once. When these statements have been executed, the expression in parentheses is calculated once more. If it is false, the **`while`** statement is terminated; if it is true, the statements within the braces are executed once more, and so on. The **`while`** statement will be executed three times in the example above. The variable `j` has the value `0` from the beginning, and is increased by `2` at the end of every 'round'. This means that `j` will have a value of `6` at the end of the third round. The expression `j<6` will then be false, and the **`while`** statement will be terminated.

In a **while** statement, the braces may be left off (exactly as with **if** statements) if only one statement is to be executed at each round.

Different forms of while statement	

while (*expression*)
    statement
	while (*expression*)
	{
	    one or more statements
	}

Our next example will be taken from a somewhat unreal situation. You have been offered a very dangerous job. There is a risk of being seriously injured, or even killed, if you take the job. The settling of wages is also rather unusual. For the first day of work, you are offered 1c, for the second day 2c, for the third 4c, for the fourth day 8c, and so on: in other words, the wages are doubled every day. Since you are careful about your health but don't mind taking certain risks to reach your goal and become rich, you want to check out the offer. You ask yourself this question: How many days must I work to become a millionaire? To get an answer to this, we shall write the following program:

```
#include <iostream>
#include <iomanip>
using namespace std;
main ()
{
   int number_days = 1 ;
   double daily_wage = 0.01, total_sum = 0.01;
   const double desired = 1000000.0;
   while (total_sum < desired)
   {
      number_days++;
      daily_wage *= 2;
      total_sum += daily_wage;
   }
   cout << "You will be a millionaire after "
        << number_days << " days" << endl;
}
```

The three variables `number_days`, `daily_wage` and `total_sum` are used in the program. They are initialized to start values that enable the program to give the situation after one day of work. The constant variable `desired` has been given a value of 1 million.

The three statements in the **while** statement will be repeated once per day worked, from and including day 2. We see that the day counter is increased by `1` for each day; the new daily wage (which is equal to double that of the old) is calculated and added to the total sum. After two days `number_days` will have a value of `2`, `daily_wage` a value of `0.02`, and `total_sum` a value of `0.03`.

We don't know for how many rounds the **`while`** statement will be executed. Each round corresponds to a day worked. Remember it was simply the number of days worked that the program was to calculate. Since the value in the variable `total_sum` increases all the time, the condition after **`while`** must sooner or later be false. If you run the program you will get the output

```
You will be a millionaire after 27 days
```

We shall now look at a more complicated example. We shall write a program to calculate the sum of the mathematical series

$$\frac{1}{1\times1}-\frac{1}{2\times2}+\frac{1}{3\times3}-\frac{1}{4\times4}+\frac{1}{5\times5}-\ldots$$

The series has an infinite number of terms, so it is impossible to take account of all of them in the program. The signs of the terms alternate between plus and minus, and the absolute value[†] of the terms decreases with each new term. The sum of the series therefore approaches a certain limit. (We say that the series is *convergent*.) We shall decide to ignore terms that are so small that they won't have any effect on the final result. If the result is to be written to five decimal places, terms with an absolute value of less than 0.000001 can be ignored without any effect on the end result.

To find the solution, we shall make use of the technique of top-down design discussed in section 1.6. First, we produce an algorithm:

1. Initialize the sum to 0 and the first term to 1.
2. If the absolute value of the next term ≥ 0.000001, carry out the following two steps:
   - 2.1. Put the next term to the sum.
   - 2.2. Calculate a new next term.
3. Write out the sum.

We can refine step 1:

```
double the_sum = 0, next_term = 1;
```

We have introduced two variables here, `the_sum` and `next_term`. They will both be of real type, since the sum and its terms are real numbers. The second variable is called `next_term`, even if it gives the value of the first term at this stage, because it can then be used in the rest of the program when calculating the values of the remaining terms.

[†] The absolute value of a number is calculated in the following way: If $x \geq 0$, the absolute value is x; if not, it is $-x$.

(Before beginning, the next term is of course the same as the first term.) We initialize the variables at the same time as we declare them.

In the continuing program construction we shall be using *comments* in the program code. Comments serve to help you to construct and clarify your programs. The compiler will not attempt to translate whatever is contained in a comment. In C++ there are two ways of writing comments:

```
// This is a comment
/* This is a comment
   that will continue on several lines */
```

The combination of characters `//` introduces a comment, and everything written after these characters on the *same* line will be interpreted as a comment. If instead the combination of characters `/*` is used to introduce a comment, the whole text, including the end mark `*/` will be interpreted as a comment. In the latter case, a comment can extend over several lines.

Step 2 in our algorithm will be a **`while`** statement. For the time being, we can let the substeps 2.1 and 2.2 be comments. The standard function `fabs` from the `math` library is used to calculate the absolute value of `next_term`:

```
while (fabs(next_term) >= epsilon)
{
   // 2.1 Put next term to the sum
   // 2.2 Calculate a new next term
}
```

We have introduced the constant `epsilon` to avoid having literals in the program. You declare `epsilon` in the following way (`1e-6` means 1×10^{-6}):

```
const double epsilon = 1e-6;
```

Step 2.1 in the algorithm is simply

```
the_sum += next_term;
```

Step 2.2, 'Calculate a new next term', requires a little extra thought. Any particular term in the sum (let us call this term number k) will have the form $1/(k \times k)$. To be able to calculate it, we need a counter k for the number of terms. It is just as well that this counter is an integer that is initialized to 1 and then increased by 1 every time we want to calculate a new term. Thus we get the declaration

```
int k = 1;
```

and the statement

```
k++;
```

which will be executed first in step 2.2.

Having alternate terms that are positive and negative presents a complication. It can be resolved by introducing a variable `sign`, which alternately takes the value `+1` and `-1`. If the calculated terms are multiplied by `sign`, they will become alternately positive and negative. For simplicity, we let `sign` be a real variable.

Since term number 1 should be positive, we initialize `sign` to `+1`. We then get the declaration

```
double sign = 1;
```

By putting the statement

```
sign = -sign;
```

in step 2.2, we make `sign` alternate between `+1` and `-1` each time a new term is to be calculated. The actual calculation of the next term is then

```
next_term = sign/(k*k);
```

If we had declared `sign` to be an integer, both the operands of the division operator would have been integers and we would have got integer division, the result of this being an integer. The variable `next_term` should not contain an integer, however, so we let one of the operands of the division operator be a real number and we get an 'ordinary' division. If we put the three statements in 2.2 together, we get

```
k++;
sign = -sign
next_term = sign/(k*k);
```

In step 3, 'Write out the sum', we use a constant variable, `num_dec`, to control the number of decimal places in the output:

```
cout << "The sum is: " << setprecision(num_dec)
     << the_sum << endl;
```

The constant `num_dec` is declared in the following way:

```
const num_dec = 5;
```

This is useful. If on another occasion we want to alter the number of decimal places in the output, all we have to do is change the two constants `num_dec` and `epsilon`.

Now we can assemble all the steps into a complete program:

```
#include <iostream>
#include <iomanip>
#include <cmath>
using namespace std;
main ()
{
```

```
    double the_sum = 0, next_term = 1, sign = 1;
    int    k = 1;
    const  num_dec = 5;
    const double epsilon = 1e-6;
    while  (fabs(next_term) >= epsilon)
    {
      // Add next term to the sum
      the_sum += next_term;
      // Calculate a new next term
      k++;
      sign      = -sign;
      next_term = sign/(k*k);
    }
    cout << "The sum is: " << setprecision(num_dec)
         << the_sum <<endl;
}
```

When the program is run, you get the output

```
The sum is: 0.82247
```

It is of course possible to have `if` statements inside `else` statements and vice versa. This is shown in the next example. We shall look at a program that inputs an arbitrary number of real numbers (≥0) from the keyboard. The program is tailored to write out the largest number and the mean value of all the numbers. The four variables `num`, `max_num`, `sum` and `n` are used in the program. One number at a time is input to the variable `num`. The sum of the numbers is calculated in `sum`, and `n` contains the number of numbers entered. The variable `max_num` is used to calculate the largest number.

```
#include <iostream>
using namespace std;
main ()
{
    double num, max_num = -1, sum = 0;
    int    n = 0;
    while  (cin >> num)
    {
      sum += num;
      n++;
      if (num > max_num)
        max_num = num;
    }
    cout << "Largest num: " << max_num << endl
         << "Mean value: " << sum / n << endl;
}
```

For every number input, a round of the `while` statement is executed. The expression `cin>>num` in parentheses after `while` may look a little strange. The program tries to read a number from the keyboard using this expression. If input is successful, the expression will be true and the `while` statement will be executed one more time; otherwise, the expression will be false and the `while` statement will be terminated. (Compare with the example on page 48.) This means that the program will be terminated as soon as anything but a number has been input. You can write a letter, for instance, but it is more natural to use a special combination of characters denoting *end of file*. If you are using MS-DOS or Windows, you normally make use of Ctrl-Z to indicate 'end of file'. If you use Unix, the keys will be Ctrl-D.

When a number has just been entered, it is added to the sum and `n` is increased by `1`. The `if` statement is also executed for every new number, since you want to test whether the new number is larger than the largest number (previously found in the variable `max_num`). If this is the case, the new number will now become the current largest number. Since we have a precondition that all input numbers should be greater than, or equal to, zero, `max_num` will have been initialized to a negative number.

Sometimes it may be necessary to stop a `while` statement in the middle of a repetition. In this case, a `break` statement can be used. A `break` statement can be placed among the statements to be executed in each round. It has the simple form

```
break;
```

A `break` statement normally lies in an `if` statement and is executed only conditionally.

When a `break` statement is executed, the `while` statement is immediately stopped, and there is a jump in the program to the first statement immediately after the `while` statement. Note that `break` statements can also be used with the two other repetition statements in C++, namely `for` statements, covered in the next section, and `do` statements, described later in the book.

`break` statements

- May be placed among statements executed in every round of a repetition statement.
- They immediately stop the repetition statement.
- There is a jump to the first statement after the repetition statement.
- They are often placed in an `if` statement:

```
if (condition_to_quit)
  break;
```

A good opportunity for using `break` statements often presents itself with the use of *interactive* programs. Here, the user is invited to indicate the input. The program then determines the output and presents it to the user at the terminal. Interactive programs are very common. All our examples so far have been examples of interactive programs. We have seen how important it is, in interactive programs, that before each input of data there should be a communication with the user indicating what input should be written. A program stops when it reaches an input statement, and does not proceed until the user has entered input data. If there is no message before the input statement, the user will not notice that the program is waiting for input.

A computation of any sort has the following general form:

- Read input data.
- Perform computations.
- Write out the result.

You will often require a program to perform several computations in a row without having to restart it between each computation. The program is thus required to follow this pattern:

- Repeat the following three steps again and again:
  - Read input data.
  - Perform computations.
  - Write out the result.

Repetition should not stop until the person running the program enters special input data to indicate that it is time to stop.

As examples, we will show a couple of variants of a program which calculates the length of the hypotenuse in a right-angled triangle. The input data for the program are the lengths of the two shorter sides. If we designate these to be a and b and the length of the hypotenuse to be c, then c can be easily calculated using the well-known formula: $c = \sqrt{}(a^2 + b^2)$. In our first example, we let the user of the program indicate that it is time to quit by giving a negative value of a or b.

```
#include <iostream>
#include <cmath>
using namespace std;
main ()
{
  double a, b, c;
  while (true)
  {
    cout << "Give lengths of shorter sides. " <<
            "Close with a negative number." <<endl;
    cin >> a;
    if (a <= 0)
      break;
    cin >> b;
    if (b <= 0)
      break;
```

```
      c = sqrt(a*a+b*b);
      cout << "Hypotenuse has length " << c <<endl;
    }
}
```

The statements occur in the right order inside the **while** statement thanks to the **break** statement. The input comes first in every round, and it is preceded by a request to the user to enter input data. When this is read, a check is done to see whether the user has entered the special data indicating that the program should finish. If this is so, the **while** statement is stopped with a **break** statement. Otherwise, the result is computed and output at the end of the round.

Special input data is not always available to indicate that it is time to quit. A little earlier we constructed a program that input an arbitrary number of real numbers and calculated both the largest number and the mean value of all the numbers. In that program, all the real numbers are normal input data and cannot be used as end indicators. Instead we let the user indicate the end of the input by writing the special combination for *end of file*. We can use this technique here too:

```
#include <iostream>
#include <cmath>
using namespace std;
main ()
{
  double a, b, c;
  while (true)
  {
    cout << "Give lengths of shorter sides. " <<
            "Close with Ctrl-Z. " << endl;
    if (not (cin >> a))
      break;
    if (not (cin >> b))
      break;
    c = sqrt(a*a+b*b);
    cout << "Hypotenuse has length " << c <<endl;
  }
}
```

2.6 `for` statements

We have seen how a **while** statement can be used to produce repetition. In this section we shall be looking at **for** statements, which are an alternative to **while** statements. Often, **for** statements are used for repetition where there is a counter to be incremented or decremented for each round in the program. The **for** statement in C++ differs slightly from corresponding statements in other programming languages. After the reserved word **for** come parentheses that contain three separate parts: an initialization, a condition, and a change part. A semicolon must be placed between the different parts. The **for** statement has the form

```
for (init; condition; change)
  statement;
```

The statement on the second line can consist of several statements in braces exactly as with **if** statements and **while** statements. Execution is done in the following way. First `init` is computed and then `condition`. If `condition` is true, `statement` is executed. When this has been done, `change` is computed; then `condition` is computed again. If this is still true, another round is executed, which means that first `statement`, then `change` are computed again; whereupon `condition` is computed and tested again. The whole process is repeated until `condition` is shown to be false.

Note that `init` is performed only once, before the first round, while the other expressions are computed once per round, `condition` before each round and `change` after each round.

Here are some examples of **for** statements. The following statement writes out the multiplication table for 12: 1 times 12, 2 times 12, and so on up to 12 times 12:

```
int i;
for (i=1; i<=12; i++)
  cout << i*12 << endl;
```

If there is a counter, as there is here, it need not be incremented by 1. The counter may be changed at will at the end of each round. For instance, we could easily write

```
int i;
for (i=12; i<=144; i+=12)
  cout << i << endl;
```

The counter can also be declared in the initialization expression; then it will only be recognized inside the **for** statement.

```
for (int i=12; i<=144; i+=12)
  cout << i << endl;
```

The three different parts `init`, `condition` and `change` in the parentheses of the **for** statement can each contain several expressions. Sometimes you may want to initialize several variables at the beginning of repetition, or change more than one counter after each round. Here is an example where x^n is computed. We want `x` to have the type **double** and `n` the type **int**. The result will be calculated in a variable `r` of the type **double**. Both the variable `r` and a counter `i` must be initialized before the first round. When one of the parts `init`, `condition` and `change` contains several expressions, then a *comma* should be placed between those expressions. A semicolon of course serves to demarcate the three parts.

```
for (r=1.0, i=1; i <=; i++)
  r *= x;
```

Sometimes it happens that the statement to be repeated at every round is an empty statement, when nothing is to be done. In this case you write only a lone semicolon. The **for** statement above may, for example, be rewritten

```
for (r=1.0, i=1; i <=n; i++, r*=x)
  ;
```

In this case you should, as in this example, write the semicolon on a separate line so that it will be quite clear that it is an empty statement. Because a semicolon is counted as an empty statement and will be the statement repeated at every round, you should *never write a semicolon directly after the end of parentheses*. This also applies to **while** statements.

> **for statements**
>
> **for** (*init; condition; change*)
>   *statement*;
>
> is equivalent to the statements
>
> *init*;
> **while** (*condition*)
>   {
>   *statement*;
>   *change*;
>   }
>
> - The parts *init*, *condition* and *change* may be omitted but the semicolon should remain.
> - Each part can consist of several expressions divided by a comma.

In a **for** statement, one of the three parts `init`, `condition` and `change` may be left out. If there is no initializing to be done, the initializing part may be omitted. If a part is omitted, this must be indicated by a semicolon. There should always be two semicolons in the parentheses of a **for** statement. You can even omit all the parts. If the `condition` part is omitted, the statement will be regarded as 'true'. An infinite repetition can be produced, for instance, with

```
for (;;)
  cout << "Help, I cannot stop" << endl;
```

2.7 Arrays

A variable of the type **int** or **double** can contain only one value at a time, but you will often want to handle aggregates containing many values of the same type. Then you

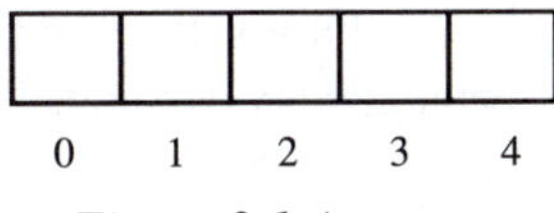

Figure 2.1 An array

can make use of *arrays*. An array is a kind of table that contains several components, all numbered, of the same kind. Let us begin by declaring an array with five components of the type **double**:

```
double f[5];
```

This is a declaration of a variable with the name `f`. We recognize `f` as an array and not an ordinary variable from the `[5]` after the name of the variable. The contents of the square brackets must have a *constant* value indicating the number of elements in the array. The word **double** indicates that the components of the array will be of the same type. Figure 2.1 shows how the variable `f` looks.

Every component in an array has a unique number, or *index*. Numbering of the components begins with `0`, so that the first component has an index of `0`. This is *always* the case with arrays. (In C++ it is not possible to indicate, as it is in a number of other programming languages, how the components are to be numbered. The first component always has the index `0`.) It follows, therefore, that the last component in an array is always a number that is 1 less than the number of components in the array. If you want to access a particular component of an array, you make use of the component's index through *indexing*. For example, to give the last component (the one numbered `4`) in the array `f` the value `2.75`, we shall write the statement

```
f[4] = 2.75
```

Note the use of square brackets here. The index in square brackets need not be a constant number; it can be an arbitrary integer expression. If the variables `i` and `j` are of type **int**, it is possible to write

```
f[i + j] = 2.75;
```

The index expression has to have a value lying inside the bounds of the array. In this example, therefore, the value `i+j` will lie in the interval from `0` to `4`. It is natural to ask what would happen if the index expression's value lay outside the bounds of the array. Would the compiler produce error output? No! In C++, responsibility is handed over completely to the programmer. There is no index check. Even if indexing is incorrect, the program will run; but it will not run as it should, and there won't be any warnings or error messages. Suppose, for example, that the value `i+j` in our example happens to be `5`. When the statement above is performed, the value `2.75` is placed in the primary memory in the position where the component number `5` *would* have been *if* such a component had existed. This could of course be disastrous for the program. Any information could be put there – variables that have nothing to do with `f`, for instance.

Components in an array can be of arbitrary type. We could, for example, declare another array with the name `a` containing six components of type **`int`**:

```
int a[6];
```

If nothing particular is indicated upon declaration of an array, all its components will be *uninitialized*. An array can be initialized in connection with declaration. We would be able to write

```
int a[6] = {2, 2, 2, 5, 5, 0};
```

The first three components here are initialized to the value `2`, the following two to the value `5` and the last to the value `0`. The number of components inside the square brackets should conform to the size of the array (but this is not checked by the compiler). When you initialize an array, the compiler itself can compute its size. You can omit the number of components and simply write

```
int b[]= {0, 0, 0, 0, 0, 0};
```

Here the array `b` consists of six components, all set at zero upon declaration. The initialization expressions inside the braces need not be constants; they can be arbitrary expressions. If the variables `i` and `j` have type **`int`**, we could write

```
int b[]= {i, i-1, i+j};
```

Note that it is only in initializations that you may assign values to all the components all at once. The following statement would not be allowed

```
b = {0, 0, 0, 0, 0, 0}; // Not allowed!
```

If, for example, you want to assign the value `0` to all the components in `b`, you have to do this for each component one at a time:

```
for (int k=0; k<6; k++)
   b[k] = 0;
```

The following statement is also not allowed:

```
a = b; // Not allowed!
```

If you want to assign the whole array `b` to `a`, you must instead do it in this way:

```
for (int k=0; k<6; k++)
   a[k] = b[k];
```

Neither can you compare two complete arrays with each other. If we write

```
if (a == b) // Allowed but not what is intended
   ...
```

it will certainly be allowed, but this comparison does not mean that the contents of the two arrays will be compared, only that a check will be made on whether `a` and `b` are referring to the same array.

We will now look at a simple program that uses arrays. Ten real numbers, constituting a measurement series, are entered from the keyboard. The program then computes the mean value of the measurements and outputs this data. Finally, the program will output all the measurements which are greater than the computed mean value.

```
#include <iostream>
using namespace std;
main ()
{
  const int number = 10;
  double meanv, sum = 0;
  double series[number];
  int i;
  cout << "Give measurement values" << endl;
  for (i = 0; i<number; i++)
  {
    cin >> series[i];
    sum += series[i];
  }
  meanv = sum / number;
  cout << "Mean value is " << meanv << endl;
  cout << "Measurements greater than mean value:"<<endl;
  for (i = 0; i<number; i++)
    if (series[i] > meanv)
    cout << "Measurement no. " << (i+1) << " is "
    << series[i] << endl;
}
```

Note in particular that, in the program, a constant with the name `number` has been declared. Instead of writing the literal `10`, we have used the constant `number` in the declaration of the array `series`. The constant `number` is also used in other parts of the program itself. By using a constant in this way, the program has become easy to change. If we wanted a measurement series containing 20 numbers, then we would simply have to change the declaration of the constant `number`. Nothing else in the program would have to be changed. It is good practice to use constants in this way.

We shall now demonstrate a slightly larger example of the use of arrays. Suppose that a company has a number of sales representatives working on commission. The total number of reps is at most 100, and each rep has a unique identity number (an integer in the interval 1 to 100). Every time a rep has sold something, he or she leaves a record of the sale with the company. A sales record consists of the rep's number and the amount the goods have been sold for. We shall now design a program that inputs a lot of sales records and outputs a compilation of how much the different reps have sold. The program will also show what commission the reps are to receive. This is 10% of total sales if less than, or equal to, $5000. If total sales is greater than $5000, the rep's commission will include 15% of the amount over $5000. If the following data is input into the program

```
78 1000
32 50
2 1200
100 2500
78 6000
2 100
5 6000
```

the program will give the output

```
Number      Amount      Commission
======      ======      ==========
     2        1300         130
     5        6000         650
    32          50           5
    78        7000         800
   100        2500         250
```

No sales records are entered for those reps who have not sold anything. The various sales records can be input in arbitrary order into the program, and if a rep has left more than one sales record with the company, this will be accepted by the program (here, for instance, reps no. 2 and no. 78 each made two sales).

The program looks like this:

```
#include <iostream>
#include <iomanip>
using namespace std;
main ()
{
  const int max_number=100;
  const float bound=5000., pro1=0.1, pro2=0.15;
  float tab[max_number], amount, commission;
  int i, no;
  // reset table
  for (i=0; i<max_number; i++)
    tab[i] = 0;
  // Input sales records
  while (cin >> no && cin >> amount)
  {
    if (no < 1 || no > max_number || amount < 0)
      cout << "Incorrect input data" << endl;
    else
      tab[no-1] += amount;
  }
```

```
    // Write compilation
    cout << endl
         << "Number    Amount    Commission" << endl
         << "======    ======    ==========" << endl;
    for (i=0; i<max_number; i++)
    {
      if (tab[i] > 0)
      {
        if (tab[i] <= bound)
          commission = pro1 * tab[i];
        else
          commission = pro1*bound + pro2*(tab[i]-bound);
        cout << setw(4) << (i + 1)
        << setprecision(0) << setiosflags(ios::fixed)
        << setw(12) << tab[i]
        << setw(13) << commission << endl;
      }
    }
}
```

Note that we have used constants to indicate the maximum number of sales reps, the bound for getting a higher commission, and the two commission percentages. This makes it easy to change the program if these figures should change – for example, if the number of sales reps should increase.

The expression in parentheses in the line

```
while(cin >> no && cin >> amount)
```

will be true if both inputs are successful (compare with the program example on page 53). When the program is run, therefore, you can indicate the end of the input by using Ctrl-Z or Ctrl-D (depending on the operating system).

You will often want to construct computer programs that will search for certain information in tables or lists: then it is natural to use arrays in the programs. There are two operations in particular that you will often perform in arrays: *search* and *sort*. We shall first demonstrate a simple way of searching in an array. Suppose that we have an integer array `f` with `n` elements and that we want to see whether a certain number is in the array. This is the simplest kind of search, a *linear search*. The array `f` is searched from the beginning until the element containing the searched number is found, or until the whole array has been searched without producing the number looked for:

```
cout << "What number are you looking for? "; cin >> number;
for (int k = 0; k < n && f[k]!= number; k++)
  ;
if (k < n)
  cout << "The number is in place no. " << k << endl;
else
  cout << "The number was not found" <<endl;
```

The first condition in the **if** statement, `k<n`, tests whether the index `k` still lies in the array. If so, it will check whether `k` is the number looked for. If it is not, another round is executed, which means that `k` is increased by 1. The value of `k` can be examined after the end of the **for** statement. If `k` has a value inside the bounds of the array, the **for** statement must have been stopped because the partial condition `f[k]!=number` will have been false. The number looked for will then have been found in position `k`.

You may often want to have sorted arrays, because they speed up search. There are many ordinary algorithms that describe how an array can be sorted, one of them being the sort algorithm on page 25, when we put compact discs into a CD holder. We shall be looking at another sort algorithm here. We shall write a program that inputs a maximum of 100 integers, where the input is finished by the user indicating an end to the input by typing Ctrl-Z or Ctrl-D at the terminal. The program puts the integers entered into an array, sorts the array, and prints out the numbers in order of size. We use an algorithm called *search for the least and swap* to carry out the sorting itself. The idea is that the smallest number in the array is found and placed in the array's first position, the second smallest is found and placed in the array's second position, and so on. The algorithm can be described as follows:

1. Set k as the index for the first element of the array.
2. While k is smaller than, or equal to, the index for the array's last element:
   - 2.1. Search for the smallest element in that part of the array that begins with element k and ends with the last element in the array.
   - 2.2. Let the smallest element (from step 2.1) and element k swap places.
   - 2.3. Increase k by 1.

Step 2.1 can be refined to

- 2.1.1. Set m to k.
- 2.1.2. Let i run from k+1 to the number of the last element in the array:
  - 2.1.2.1. If element i is less than element m, set m to i.
- 2.1.3. The smallest element is now in the mth position.

Step 2.2 can be refined to

- 2.2.1. Move the kth element to a temporary position.
- 2.2.2. Move element m to position k.
- 2.2.3. Move the element in the temporary position to the mth position.

Using this, we can now put the program together:

```
#include <iostream>
using namespace std;
main ()
{
  const int max_number = 100;
```

```
  int f[max_number], n = 0; // n is the number of input numbers
  cout << "Write in at most 100 integers" << endl;
  while (n < max_number && cin >> f[n])
    n++;
  // Sort the array
  for (int k = 0; k < n; k++)
  {
    // Search for the smallest among the numbers no. k to n-1
    int m = k;
    for (int i = k+1; i < n; i++)
      if (f[i] < f[m])
        m =i;
    // Let the numbers no.k and m swap places
    int temp = f[k];
    f[k] = f[m];
    f[m] = temp;
  }
  // print out the sorted array
  for (int j=0; j<n; j++)
    cout << f[j] << ' ';
}
```

2.8 Sequences: `vector` and `deque`

In the previous section we saw how you can make use of arrays to construct data sets with several values of the same type. Arrays are basic constructions that were part of the very first versions of C and C++. For this reason, a C++ programmer must know how arrays work. However, we saw that there are some missing aspects of arrays that make them a bit difficult to work with. For instance, you cannot assign and compare complete arrays. There is no control of indexing, and you cannot change the size of an array if you wish to add or delete elements. Therefore a more advanced type is needed. As you will learn in a later chapter, in C++ you can use something called *classes* to construct new types that can be more powerful than the built-in standard types and arrays. The individual programmer can construct such types, but C++ now also has a number of standard classes that accompany the C++ compiler. An important group of such standard classes[‡] is used to describe different kinds of data sets, for instance lists, sets and maps. Such classes are called *container classes*. Using standard classes can very much facilitate programming. Instead of needing to write all the program code, the programmer can make use of tried and tested program components.

‡ These classes are not actually ordinary classes, but templates that can be adapted to different conditions by the programmer. Later in this book we describe how such templates are constructed and how you can develop your own templates.

In this part of the chapter, we study how you make use of standard classes that describe *sequences*. These are sets where the elements are lined up logically. The container classes you can use to construct sequences are `list`, `vector` and `deque`. (The word 'deque' is an abbreviation of 'double-ended queue'.) These classes have many common characteristics. In this chapter we go through the classes `vector` and `deque`. The class `list` and other container classes are described in Chapter 12.

2.8.1 General characteristics of sequences

In order to have access to a container class, you must first include the header file that contains the declarations of the class. The header files have the same names as the container classes. For instance, if you want access to the class `vector` you must have the following lines at the beginning of your program (to use the class `list` or `deque` you write `list` and `deque` respectively instead of `vector`):

```
#include <vector>
using namespace std;
```

Sequences are declared as variables, in the same way as arrays. When we declared arrays we had to indicate which type the individual elements should have. We also had to indicate how many elements should be in the array. When you declare sequences you must also indicate which type the elements will have, but you do not need to indicate the number of elements. The sequence size can, in contrast, be changed dynamically. The syntax for declaring a sequence is a little different from what we saw earlier. You first write the word `list`, `vector` or `deque` (depending on which kind of sequence you want), and then within the characters `<>` you indicate which type the elements will have. For instance, to declare a vector `v` where the elements are of type `double` and another vector `u` where the elements are of type `int`, we write

```
vector<double> v; // a vector with elements of type double
vector<int> u;    // a vector with elements of type int
```

Both these sequences are empty, with a length of 0. If you like, you can indicate how many elements you want in the sequence. For instance, you can declare

```
vector<double> v2(3); // v2 contains {0, 0, 0}
```

If you do not indicate anything special, as here, all the elements in the sequence will take the value 0. If you like, you can explicitly indicate a start value for the elements. For instance, we can write

```
vector<double> v3(4, 1.5); // v3 contains {1.5, 1.5, 1.5, 1.5}
```

There is another way to state an initialization value for a sequence as well. You can state another sequence as argument. Then the new sequence will be a copy:

```
vector<double> v4(v3); // v4 becomes a copy of v3
```

If you want to know the number of elements in a sequence, you can use the function `size` that returns a whole number. If you just want to determine whether a sequence is empty you can alternatively use the function `empty`, which returns a value of the type **`bool`**.

```
int i = v3.size(); // i gets the value 4
if (v.empty())
   cout << "The vector is empty";
```

It is easy to assign a whole sequence to another sequence of the same kind. For instance, we can write

```
v = v2; // v becomes a copy of v2, it contains {0, 0, 0}
```

(This was not allowed for arrays.) If you want to assign a certain value to all the elements in a sequence, you can use the function `assign`:

```
v.assign(4, 1.0); // v gets the values {1.0, 1.0, 1.0, 1.0}
```

All the three sequence classes are constructed so that it will be easy to add new elements at the end. You use the function `push_back` as illustrated in the following example. It is also easy to delete the last elements in a sequence. Then you use the function `pop_back`. There are also two functions, `front` and `back`, that you can use to read or change the first and last elements respectively in a vector. For the classes `list` and `deque` there are also two functions, `push_front` and `pop_front`, which are used to add and delete, respectively, elements at the beginning of a sequence. Note that these two functions are not in the class vector.[§] Here are some examples:

```
v.clear();          // remove all elements from v
v.push_back(0.0);   // v contains {0.0}
v.push_back(6.2);   // v contains {0.0, 6.2}
v.push_back(7.3);   // v contains {0.0, 6.2, 7.3}
v.front() = 5.1;    // v contains {5.1, 6.2, 7.3}
v.pop_back();       // v contains {5.1, 6.2}
deque<int> d;
d.push_front(5);    // d contains{5}
d.push_front(4);    // d contains {4, 5}
d.pop_front();      // d contains {5}
```

Another useful function is `resize`. For example, we can write

```
v.resize(5); // v contains {5.1, 6.2, 0.0, 0.0, 0.0}
```

The argument indicates how long the sequence will be. In this case, when the sequence previously was shorter, the new elements are added at the end. The new elements will then get zero value. (Furthermore, it is also possible to state a further argument that

---

[§] You can also add and delete elements at the beginning of a vector with the help of iterators. However, this is ineffective because it demands rearrangement of the elements.

indicates the value of the new elements). If the new length is shorter than the old, elements are cut off at the end:

```
v.resize(3); // v contains {5.1, 6.2, 0.0}
```

The function `swap` swaps the contents in two sequences of the same kind:

```
swap(v,v2); // swap the contents of v and v2
```

Sequences can be compared in a simple way with all the usual operators =, !, =, <, >, <= and >=. Suppose that we have declared two vectors

```
vector<int> a, b;
```

For instance, we can write

```
if (a < b)
  cout << "a is less than b" << endl;
else if (a == b)
  cout << "a and b are equal" << endl;
```

Two sequences are regarded as being equal if they contain the same number of elements and all the corresponding elements are equal. If they are different, the comparison occurs according to the same principle as for the alphabetical ordering of texts. Let us take the comparison `a<b` as an example. If the first element in `a` is less than the first element in `b`, then the whole of `a` is regarded as being less than `b` and the expression `a<b` is true. However, if the first element in `a` is bigger than the first element in `b`, then `a` is regarded as being bigger than `b` and the expression `a<b` is false.

If the first elements in both sequences are equal, the comparison goes on to the second elements, which are examined in the same way. If the second elements are equal, the third is examined, and so on. If the sequences have the same number of elements and all of them are equal, the sequences are regarded as being equal and the expression `a<b` is false. If the sequences have a different number of components and all the elements in the shorter sequence are equal to the corresponding elements in the longer sequence, the shorter sequence is regarded as being the least.

In the facts table the operations for the classes `list`, `vector` and `deque` are shown. Besides these operators there are a number of operations that have *iterators* as parameters. (This is described in section 12.1). There are also a number of standard functions, called *algorithms*, that you can use to handle sequences.

2.8.2 Special characteristics of the classes `vector` and `deque`

What makes the classes `vector` and `deque` special is that you can use indexing in the same way as with arrays. Both classes work in the same way. The only difference is that the functions `push_front` and `pop_front` appear in the class `deque` but not in the class `vector`. These two classes are internally built with the help of arrays. The class vector can be implemented by a simple array. (See Figure 2.1 on page 59.) To make it possible for a variable of the type deque to effectively add or delete elements at the beginning of a sequence without the elements being moved, the class deque must be internally more complicated than the class vector. For instance, it can be implemented with the help of several arrays linked together. If you want to be able to index, but do not need to add or delete elements at the beginning of a sequence, you should therefore use the class vector instead of the class deque.

Operations for the standard classes list, vector and deque

In the following compilation, seq either means list, vector or deque. s and t represent sequences of type list, vector or deque.

Operation	Description
seq<type> s;	Creates a sequence of zero length.
seq<type> s(n);	Creates a sequence of length n. Initializes with zeros.
seq<type> s(n, e);	Creates a sequence of length n. Initializes with e.
seq<type> s(t);	Creates a sequence that is a copy of the sequence t.
s = t	Assignment. s becomes a copy of the sequence t.
s.assign(n, e)	Assignment. s gets the length n. All the elements get the value e.
s.clear()	Deletes all the elements in the sequence s. The length becomes 0.
s.size()	Returns the number of elements in the sequence s.
s.empty()	Returns **true** if the number of elements in s is 0, otherwise **false**.
s.push_back(e)	Adds the element e at the end of the sequence s.
s.pop_back()	Deletes the last element in sequence s.
s.push_front(e)	Adds the element e at the beginning of s. Not available for vector.
s.pop_front()	Deletes the first element in s. Not available for vector.
s.front()	Returns the first element in the sequence s.
s.back()	Returns the last element in the sequence s.
s.resize(n)	Changes s length to n. Fills with zeros if n is bigger than the old length, otherwise cuts off elements at the end.
s.resize(n, e)	As above, but fills up with e instead of zeros.
s==t s!=t s<t etc.	Comparisons. Operates according to alphabetical principles.
v[i]	Indexing without index control. Not available for list.
v.at(i)	Indexing with index control. Not available for list.
v.capacity(n)	Returns the size of the internal array. Available only for vector.
v.reserve(n)	Indicates that you will need space for n elements. Available only for vector.

As an example of indexing, we illustrate how you can print all the elements in the vector v:

```
for (int i=0; i<v.size(); i++)
   cout << v[i] << ' ';
```

Here we have used the function size, which shows how many elements the vectors contain. Indexing occurs as usual from zero. When you index in this way, with square brackets, it is not checked that the index value lies within the allowed boundaries. There is therefore an alternative way to index. You can use the function at, which automatically makes an index control. (If the index value is outside the allowed boundaries, the program generates an exception of the type out_of_range.) Here we show two alternative ways to assign the value 5 to elements number j in vector v.

```
v[j] = 5;     // indexing without index check
v.at(j) = 5; // indexing with index check
```

When you are using the class vector, you do not normally need to worry about how the class is internally constructed. However, one thing can be good to know. In the class vector an array is used internally to store the vector's elements. For the elements to have enough space, this array must always be at least as long as the number of elements in the vector. When you add new elements to a vector, it might be that the internal array isn't big enough. In this case a new, bigger internal array is automatically allocated and the elements in the vector are copied to the new array. You can find out the size of the internal array by calling the function capacity:

```
cout << v.capacity();
```

It can be a little time-consuming to allocate a new internal array and copy all the elements in the vector. If you know beforehand that the vector will have a certain maximum size, you can avoid copying by telling the vector how many spaces will be needed from the start. An internal array of the appropriate size is then allocated directly. You can achieve this by calling the function reserve:

```
v.reserve(200); // use an internal array with 200 elements
```

One good thing about the classes vector and deque is that you can easily and quickly access individual elements inside a sequence with the help of indexing. However, neither of these classes is particularly efficient if you need to add or delete elements *within* a sequence when it is necessary to rearrange the elements in the internal array being used. To perform such operations then it is better to use the class list.

2.9 Errors in programs

Writing a computer program is not a trivial task, and it is normal to make a number of mistakes. Even an experienced programmer falls into traps of various kinds. It is therefore important when learning to program that we also learn how to find and correct errors in the program. This can be done by designing and writing programs, running tests and correcting any errors found. Three types of error can occur when writing programs:

- *Compiling errors.* These occur when the rules of the language have not been followed. This type of error is discovered during compilation of the program. Usually a listing of different errors is provided. This may include a misspelt variable, a forgotten brace, a lost semicolon, or the wrong key pressed when typing the program.
- *Execution errors.* Such errors do not occur until the program is run. The program may be syntactically correct – the language rules have been obeyed – but it still contains mistakes that prevent it from continuing normally when executed. An example of this is using a pointer to try to change memory space which either does not exist or is input protected. In C++ there is a very poor 'protective net' to catch execution errors. For instance, indexing outside an array does not register as an error. On the other hand, a number of errors can be found through 'exception handling'.
- *Logic errors.* These mistakes are caused by faulty reasoning when designing the program. An incorrect algorithm has been used. This type of error is the hardest to find, since the program can be compiled and run without getting any error messages. A logic error will show when the program is being run, and an incorrect result is obtained. If there is no verified data available for testing the program, it can be hard to be quite certain that the program is free from logic errors. Even if the program works correctly for a particular set of input data, it can be faulty for another set.

We shall demonstrate the different types of error by studying an example. We would like a program to calculate $n!$: that is, the product of $1 \times 2 \times 3 \times \ldots \times n$. We begin by writing in the program:

```
#include <iostream>
using namespace std;
main ()
{
  int prod = 0, n, i=1;
  cout << "n? ";
  cin >> n;
  while (i<=n)
  {
    pro *= i;
    i++;
  }
  cout << "Result: " << prod << endl;
}
```

We then compile the program. We then get an error message, which might be something like

```
Error line 9: Undefined symbol 'pro' in function main
```

We are dealing with a compiling error because we happened to write `pro` instead of `prod`. We correct the faulty line:

```
prod *= i;
```

Now the program can be compiled. No error messages appear. We want to test run the program and start it. We try to compute `4!`, which we know should be `24`:

```
n? 4
Result: 0
```

To our astonishment, the program returns a result of `0`. We test run the program again and this time we input another value for *n*. Whatever the value of *n*, we keep getting the result `0`. Something is wrong. There is a logic error in the program. We look at the program to see what the error might be. In the program, we let the counter `i` run from `1` to `n`, and with every round we multiply `prod` by `i`: that is, in the first round we multiply by `1`, in the second by `2`, and so on. This seems to be true, but what value does `prod` have from the beginning? The declaration tells us that `prod` has a value of `0` from the beginning. Here is our mistake! If you multiply a number that is `0` by another number, the result will of course always be `0`. The variable `prod` should naturally be initialized to `1`. We correct this:

```
int prod=1, n, i=1;
```

When the program is run again, the result is `24` when we input the number `4`. The program seems to be correct. We can try other values of `n` to get larger results. If the number `7` is entered, for instance, the program gives a result of `5040`. When we try `8`, we get a result of `-25216`. This is impossible! There has been an error at the execution stage, but the program had continued as though nothing had happened. What happened is that the result is so large, it is greater than the largest integer that can be stored in our system by a variable of type **`int`**. The result is therefore incorrect. If the program is to be able to compute `n!` for values of `n` larger than `7`, it must be changed. The best solution is to change `prod` to a variable of type **`double`**. A variable like this is capable of containing much larger numbers than an integer variable. Now the necessary changes are made and the corrected program can be test run after another compilation, as shown:

```
#include <iostream>
using namespace std;
main ()
{
```

```
  double prod=1;
  int n, i=1;
  cout << "n? ";
  cin >> n;
  while (i<=n)
  {
    prod *= i;
    i++;
  }
  cout << "Result: " << prod << endl;
}
```

Now if we try to compute `8!` we shall get the correct result, `40320`.

Looking for errors in a program and correcting them has come to be known, lightheartedly, as *debugging* the program. In some systems there are excellent aids for debugging. For example, it may be possible to test run a program step by step, or stop at particular points in the program, study the values of the various variables and change them. Such debugging aids are very valuable when errors have to be found in more complicated programs. If there is no access to such debugging aids, the values of the variables can still be studied at given points in the program by inserting temporary test printouts, and using them to find possible errors.

Exercises

2.1 Write a program to compute and print out how many kilometres a car has travelled during the last year. When the program is run, it should ask for the daily number of kilometres and for the number of kilometres one year ago. The number of kilometres should be given as whole numbers.

2.2 Modify the program in the previous exercise so that it can compute average litre consumption per kilometre. In addition to the two readings mentioned earlier, the program should input how many litres of petrol (given as a real number) are used for the year. The printout could look like this:

```
Total no. of kilometres:    14870
Total petrol consumption:   1234.5
Consumption per km:         0.083
```

2.3 When insuring a car, it is common for people to take out comprehensive insurance if the car is new, or not older than five years old. If the car is an older one, then a 'third party' insurance might be sufficient.

(a) Write a program that gives the type of insurance desired. The program should read the current year, and the year of the car's registration from the keyboard. One of the texts *Choose comprehensive insurance* or *Choose third party insurance* should be written out, depending on whether the car is less than, or more than, five years old.

(b) Some insurance companies have special policies for cars that are at least 25 years old. Modify your program so that it will write out *Choose a vintage car insurance* if the car is at least 25 years old.

2.4 In the USA litre consumption is usually given in *miles/gallon*. Write a program that inputs litre consumption given in this way and which translates these figures into the *litres/kilometre* format that is more common in Europe. Use the following conversion factors: *1 mile = 1.609 km* and *1 gallon = 3.785 litres.*

2.5 A running competition consists of two races. The winner is the one with the fastest time for both races together. Write a program to calculate the total time for a runner. The input should be the times for the two races, given in hours, minutes and seconds in the form *hh mm ss*. The results of the program should also be written in this format.

2.6 Write a program to calculate how much change should be received after making a purchase, and in which notes and coins the change should be given. Input to the program should be the price to be paid and the amount given in payment. For the sake of simplicity, assume that all prices are a whole number of dollars. For example, if a person bought goods for $51 and paid with one $100 bill, the program should print out that the change should be two $20 bills, one $5 bill, and four $1 bills (or coins).

2.7 The distance between two points in a coordinate system is given by the formula

$$s = \sqrt{((x_1 - x_2)^2 + (y_1 - y_2)^2)}$$

Write a program to read in the coordinates of the two points and write out the distance between them.

2.8 For radioactive decomposition, the amount of radioactive material, n, remaining after a certain time t, can be calculated using the formula

$$n = n_0 e^{-\lambda t}$$

where n_0 is the amount of radioactive material at time $t = 0$ and λ is a constant for the material. This is usually given as a half-life (the time taken for half the radioactive material to decompose). If the half-life is denoted by T, it is easy to calculate that

$$\lambda = \frac{\ln 2}{T}$$

The half-life for the isotope ^{14}C is 5730 years. Write a program to print out what percentage of this isotope is left after S years. S is the input to the program.

2.9 Suppose that a bank gives interest of $p\%$ on invested capital. Suppose further that you want to invest a sum of $\$k$. Write a program that shows how the capital yields interest at compound interest for the first 10 years. The printout should show your capital, including interest, after each of the 10 years. The input for the program should be the interest rate and the invested capital.

2.10 The same as for the previous exercise, but this time the program should instead calculate how long your capital should remain in the bank before you have $100 000 at your disposal.

2.11 A local authority has come up with the following forecast for population growth in the next few years. At the beginning of 1997, the borough had 26 000 inhabitants. The numbers of births and deaths for a year are estimated to be 0.7% and 0.6%, respectively, of the population at the beginning of the year. The numbers of new residents and people moving out are estimated each year to be 300 and 325 respectively. Write a program to calculate the borough's estimated population at the beginning of a particular year. The year in question should be read in as input data for the program.

2.12 If you don't have access to a library of arithmetical functions, you can use a Maclaurin series to calculate the value of certain common functions. The *sine* function can, for instance, be calculated using the following series:

$$\sin(x) = x - \frac{x^3}{3!} + \frac{x^5}{5!} - \frac{x^7}{7!} + \frac{x^9}{9!} - \ldots$$

Write a program that inputs a value of x and which calculates $\sin(x)$ using this series. The result should be printed out to four decimal places. Do not therefore include terms in the sum that are smaller than 10^{-5}.

2.13 Write a program that will produce a table for all the integers n in the interval n_1 to n_2. For every integer n, n and n^3 should be printed out. The two integers n_1 and n_2 should be input from the keyboard. Use a `for` statement.

2.14 Design a program to print out a neat table with values for the function $f(x) = 3x^3 - 5x^2 + 2x - 20$.

(a) Let the program print out the value of $f(x)$ for all integer values x in the interval from -10 to $+10$.

(b) Let the program print out the value of $f(x)$ for all values of x in the interval from -2 to $+2$, each time making the step 0.1, i.e. for the values –2.0, –1.9, –1.8, . . . , 1.9, 2.0.

2.15 A *prime number* is a positive integer greater than 1 that cannot be exactly divided by any other integer except itself and 1. A number will be a prime number if it cannot be divided exactly by a smaller prime number. Use this fact to design a program to compute the first 50 prime numbers and put them in a table. A vector should be used. (If you want to decide whether a certain number k is a prime number or not, check to see whether k can be divided exactly by any of the numbers listed in the table so far.) The program should stop when the table with your 50 prime numbers has been produced.

2.16 On page 63 we demonstrated how a linear search could be performed in an array. If the array is sorted, the search can be carried out more effectively when the number searched for is not inside the array. The search is simply stopped before the last element of the array is reached. Adjust the statements on page 63 using this method.

2.17 Write a program to read in a maximum of 100 integers and place them in an array, sorted into ascending numerical order. Your program should be designed so that one number at a time can be read in and put in the array. The numbers read in up to this point should be sorted before each new number is entered.

2.18 There is a very simple but not particularly effective sort algorithm called *bubble sort*. With this method, you run through the array to be sorted, again and again. As soon as you find two elements in the array lying side by side that are not in the right order, you let them change places. You stop this process when you haven't changed the places of any of the elements. The 'lighter' elements, those having small values, will, during execution, successively 'bubble up' to the front of the array: hence the name of this sorting method. Write a program to read in a number of integers and sort them with this algorithm. The program should stop when the input numbers have been printed out in ascending numerical order.

2.19 Write a program that first reads in an integer k from the terminal. The program should then read in a maximum of 500 integers from the terminal and place them in an array. The numbers in the array should then be rearranged to form two groups in the array. The left-hand group should contain all the numbers $\leq k$ and the right-hand group all the numbers $>k$. (The number in each group and the boundary between the two groups will depend on the numbers read into the array and the value of k.)

Example: If k is 20 and the array consists of the numbers

23 16 27 3 11 34 25 20 8

then one permissible rearrangement of the array will be

8 16 20 3 11 34 25 27 23

Other arrangements would be permissible. Note that it is not necessary to sort the array (even if it is a way of solving the problem).

2.20 Statistics of the rainfall for a certain location have been collected over the past 20 years. Write a program to read in the information for the 20 years and present the results in the form of a histogram. Assume that the annual rainfall lies in the interval from 0 to 3000 mm. Organize the output as a horizontal histogram, in the format

```
Year   0         1         2         3        × 1000 mm
  1    ****************
  2    ***********************
  3    *************
       etc.
```

Characters and texts

3

Most of the data handled by computers is probably not numerical at all, but text, characters and symbols. We shall now begin by describing the standard type `char`, which is used to handle individual characters. A character can be a letter, a digit, a special character (such as a question mark, full stop or colon) or a 'non-printing control character'. Non-printing control characters can be used for communication tasks when the computer needs to make a terminal do certain things – for example begin a new line, or give a 'chirping' sound.

3.1 Character codes and character literals

To store a character in a computer, a group of eight bits – a *byte* – is most often used. In C, only seven of these bits are used from the beginning. The eighth bit, or *parity bit*, is reserved for purposes of checking. The parity bit is usually the first bit of a byte. The other seven bits can be combined in 128 different ways, which means that there are 128 different character codes. There is a generally accepted standard, called the *ASCII standard*, which determines which characters can be coded with the seven available bits, and for each pattern of seven bits there is one character designated in the standard. For example, '`%`', '`9`' and '`A`' are represented by, respectively,

```
00100101  00111001  01000001
```

These patterns of bits can be interpreted as binary integers, called *character codes*. The codes start with 0, which means that the character codes lie between 0 and 127; the characters '`%`', '`9`' and '`A`' thus have character codes 37, 57 and 65 respectively. Even though a C++ compiler does not necessarily have to use the ASCII code, it is nevertheless the norm. This means that a variable of type `char` can contain (at least) the 128 characters in the ASCII standard. It also means that the different characters are represented in the computer in precisely the bit patterns specified by the standard.

The ASCII standard contains the letters a–z (both upper and lower case), the digits 0–9, various special characters ('`+`', '`!`' and '`.`') and a collection of non-printing control characters.

The ASCII standard is an American standard that was developed on the assumption that the language in use is English. The English alphabet has the 26 letters a–z, derived from the Latin alphabet. Almost all other living languages use either the Latin alphabet plus other characters, or a non-Latin alphabet or syllabaries. The ASCII standard on the other hand is spread throughout the world. The fact that the ASCII standard only contains the letters a–z has thus been a problem and a constant source of irritation for all those who work in the sphere of programming in countries with languages other than English. The solution to this problem is naturally to allow for more characters in the standard. If we dropped the use of the first bit in each byte as a parity bit, we could have eight bits instead of seven, and 256 different characters could be represented instead of 128. We could then use the characters from 128 to 255 to represent new letters and other characters. There is an international standard (ISO 8859) specifying which characters will be designated by the different codes. When you use Windows or a Unix system (but not MS-DOS) you follow this standard. ISO 8859 corresponds to the ASCII standard for the character codes 0 to 127. Character codes 128 to 255 are used partly for non-printing control characters and partly for a set of printable characters. The set of printable characters contained in the ISO 8859 standard is called *LATIN_1*. Among the characters of LATIN_1 are to be found the letters with diacritics that are used in the Romance and Germanic languages, for example á, å, è, æ, ö, ü, ñ and ç in both upper- and lower-case variants. (The only exceptions are the German character ß, indicating a double s, and the character ÿ, which are defined as lower-case letters only.) Apart from the letters with diacritical marks, LATIN_1 also contains graphical characters such as §, £ and ¶.

Character literals – that is, the constant character values – are written in single apostrophe marks. For instance, if we want to put a plus sign into the variable `chtr` of type **`char`**, we can write

```
chtr = '+';
```

In a C++ program you can normally use eight-bit codes in texts and comments but not in the names of variables and so on. The following assignments are allowed, however:

```
chtr = 'ê'; chtr = '¿';
```

An inner order is defined among the different values of type **`char`**. First come 32 non-printing control characters. Then come the 95 printable characters in the ASCII code and finally the characters with codes from 128 to 255 (for example, as in LATIN_1). Upper- and lower-case letters are not treated as the same, and the normal alphabetical order applies only to the letters a–z. The program lines below list two characters and write them out in ascending order. The two variables `chtr1` and `chtr2` both have type **`char`**, and we see that they can easily be compared in an **`if`** statement.

```
if (chtr1 < chtr2)
  cout << "chtr1 is smallest" << endl;
else
  cout << "chtr2 is smallest" << endl;
```

Character literals for the printable characters can easily be given as shown above. Exceptions are the characters ' (single quote), " (double quote) and \ (backslash). When choosing these, *escape sequences* must be used. To assign an apostrophe to the variable chtr1, for instance, and a backslash to the variable chtr2, you can write

```
chtr1 = '\''; chtr2 = '\\';
```

Escape sequences are also used to indicate non-printing control characters. Some of the most common control characters have been given special escape sequences. The sequence \n means, for example, the character for a new line, and \t means tabulator. If you want to indicate a character that you can't write and which does not have a special escape sequence, you can use an escape sequence where the character's code is given directly. After the character \, an *octal* number, consisting of at most three digits, can be written. Some examples are:

```
'\0'    '\33'    '\177'    '\266'    '\377'
```

Alternatively, the character code can be given in hexadecimal form. An 'x' is then written after the character \. The same examples as the ones above can then be written

```
'\x0'    '\x1b' '\7f'    '\xb6'    '\xff'
```

Although LATIN_l is used to code characters in Windows, for historical reasons it is not used in the MS_DOS window. (There are several MS-DOS codes. One multi-language code used in many countries is 850.) This may create problems when you run a PC (even if you use Windows 95/98 or Windows NT/XP). For instance, suppose we have the program line

```
cout << "Would you like some pâté?" << endl;
```

In that case, the print out in MS-DOS might look as awful as this:

```
Would you like some pótú?
```

The coding used in MS-DOS corresponds to LATIN_l only for the first 128 characters. For the other 128 characters (including letters with accents) a different code is used. Therefore the printout looks correct only if you limit yourself to using the 'pure' letters a–z, which of course gives rise to a problem in most non-English-speaking countries. The corresponding problem arises when reading into a program. When you write text in an MS_DOS window that contains letters with accents or other diacritical marks, the program will consider them to be other, erroneous characters. One solution to this problem is to translate all characters from LATIN_l to MS_DOS code at printout and vice versa at read-in. Of course this is a bit difficult. Therefore, on this book's website, there is a header file, `iodos.h`, that contains the help you need. How this is used is clear from the following little example:

```
#include <iostream>
#include "iodos.h"    // included in main
using namespace std;
main() {
   dos_console();      // place this line first in main
   cout << "Would you like some pâté?" << endl; // correct output
}
```

You should include the file `iodos.h` in the program file that contains the function `main` and then call the function `dos_console` at the beginning of the program. After that all the printouts and read-ins in the MS-DOS window will be correct.

3.2 Single characters: reading and writing

The values of type **`char`** can be read and written using the common input and output operators `<<` and `>>`. Let us write a small program to read in and write out a character:

```
#include <iostream>
using namespace std;
main ()
{
   char chtr;
   cout << "Write a character" << endl;
   cin  >> chtr;
   cout << "The character was " << chtr << endl;
}
```

Escape sequences		
`\n`	*new line*	Moves the printout position to the start of the next line.
`\a`	*alert*	Gives a sound signal (e.g. a 'chirp').
`\b`	*backspace*	Moves the printout position one step to the left.
`\r`	*return*	Moves the printout position to the start of the line.
`\f`	*form feed*	Moves the printout position to the start of the next page.
`\t`	*tab*	Moves the printout position to the next tab stop.
`\v`	*vertical tab*	Gives vertical tabulating.
nnn		The character with octal character code *nnn*.
\x*nn*		The character with hexadecimal character code *nn*.

In the program we have declared a variable `chtr` of type **`char`**. The expression `cin >> chtr` means that the character the user has written at the terminal will land in the variable `chtr`. Note that `chtr` can only contain a single character. If the user were to write several characters at the terminal, only the first one would land in `chtr`.

The input operator `>>` skips over any white characters. The program will only read and write out the first non-white characters typed in from the keyboard. But there are occasions when you will not want to skip over white characters. An example is when you want to write a program that copies a text exactly as it is written, including all the white characters: then the function `cin.get` can be used. As an example, here is a small program that reads the input from the keyboard and writes it out at the terminal:

```
#include <iostream>
using namespace std;
main ()
{
  char c;
  while (cin.get(c))
    cout << c;
}
```

The expression `cin.get(c)` reads the next character and puts it in the variable `c`. Like the input operator `>>`, `cin.get` gives an output value that can be taken to be 'true' if reading in went well and 'false' otherwise. This means that the **`while`** statement is executed a round for every character the user types in at the keyboard. When the user wants to stop input, 'end of input data' can be indicated by typing Ctrl-Z or Ctrl-D, depending on the operating system being used; then the input of the next character will miscarry, the result of `cin.get` will be interpreted as being 'false' and the program will be terminated.

It may seem pointless to write a program that reads what is typed at the keyboard and then writes it out at the terminal. Whatever is typed is normally seen on the screen anyway, without needing to run a program like this; but the program can be put to better uses. Certain operating systems, such as MS-DOS and Unix, will allow you to redirect the streams `cin` and `cout`. Suppose that we have compiled and linked the program above and given the executable program the name `my_copy`. When we start the program as usual with the command

```
my_copy
```

the program will function as described above: that is, whatever is typed in will be copied at the terminal. But if instead we start the program with the command

```
my_copy <f1.txt
```

it will display the contents of the text file `f1.txt` at the terminal. What we have done here is redirect the stream `cin` so that it will be connected not to the keyboard but to the file `f1.txt`. We can also redirect `cout`. We can give the command

```
my_copy >f2.txt
```

in which case the program's output will not appear at the terminal but will instead be stored in the file `f2.txt`. Since both `cin` and `cout` can be redirected, the program can be used to copy the contents of one file to another:

```
my_copy <f1.txt >f2.txt
```

There is another variant of the standard function `cin.get` that also reads the next character, whatever it might be, from `cin`. The difference, compared with the first version, is that you get the input character as a result of the function instead of giving the name of a variable as an argument. A call of the other version of `cin.get` can look like this:

```
c = cin.get();
```

There is a standard function called `cin.peek` that functions similarly to the other version of `cin.get`. It 'peeks' at the next character to be read but does not read it. As an example of this we shall show a **`while`** statement that skips the white characters of the input stream. At the beginning of every round the next character is checked to see whether it is a white character: that is, a blank space, tabulator or an end-of-line character. The **`while`** statement is stopped as soon as a non-white character is encountered.

```
while (cin.peek()==' ' or cin.peek()=='\t' or
       cin.peek()=='\n')
cin.ignore();
```

Input and output of simple characters	
`cout << c;`	Outputs the character `c`.
`cout.put(c);`	Outputs the character `c`.
`cin >> c;`	Inputs the next non-white character to `c`.
`cin.get(c)`	Inputs the next character to `c`.
`cin.get()`	Inputs and gives the next character as a result.
`cin.peek()`	Peeks at and gives the next character as a result. The next character remains unread.
`cin.ignore();`	Reads and skips the next character.
`cin.ignore(n,c);`	Reads and skips a maximum of `n` characters. Ends when the character `c` is encountered.
`cin >> ws;`	Skips the white characters.

We have used yet another standard function in this example, `cin.ignore`. When it is called without arguments, as here, it inputs but then skips over the next character. The function `cin.ignore` can also be called with arguments, in which case the first argument will be the maximum number of characters to be skipped and the second argument the character at which you want to stop. We show, as an example, how you can skip all the characters until you come to the character `'X'`. A maximum of 100 characters can be skipped.

```
cin.ignore (100, 'X');
```

Actually there is a much easier way of skipping white characters in the input stream. This may be done with the manipulator `ws` (short for 'white space'):

```
cin >> ws; // Skip white characters
```

We have seen that the first variant of the function `cin.get` gives a result value that can be interpreted as 'false' when *end of file* is entered. The second version of `cin.get` and the function `cin.peek` both give quite a special value when *end of file* is encountered. This value is called `EOF` and is defined in the file `iostream`. If you want to test whether there is input data to be read, you can write

```
if (cin.peek()!=EOF)
```

3.3 The standard class `string`

In our earlier program examples we saw several ways of printing out texts – sets of several characters. Such sets are called *text strings*. A constant text, a *text string literal*, is indicated by putting it between double quotes, as

```
"This is a text"
```

Note that simple characters of type **`char`** are put between single quotes, whereas texts consisting of several characters are put between double quotes. If you want to include non-printable characters in a text, you can use escape sequences. The statement

```
cout << "Line 1\nLine 2\tI \"chirp\" now\a\n";
```

gives the output

```
Line 1
Line 2    I "chirp" now
```

on the screen and some 'chirp' or other sound. After output, the cursor will move to the beginning of the next line.

If you want to enter texts or handle texts in any other way, you will need variables that contain these texts. Variables of the type `char` contain only a single character and thus cannot be used to store whole texts. The traditional way is to use a character array – that is, an array where the components are of the type `char` (we discuss character arrays in section 3.4 below) – but it is easier to use a standard class, called `string`. Therefore we begin this section by describing how you can handle variables of the class `string`, called *`string` variables*. To have access to the class `string` you must write `#include <string>` at the beginning of the program. In the first example we show a program that asks for the name of the user and then writes it:

```
#include <iostream>
#include <string>
using namespace std;
main ()
{
  string name;
  cout << "What is your name?" << endl;
  cin >> name;
  cout << "Hello " << name << endl;
}
```

When the program is run, it gives the following printout:

```
What is your name?
Sara
Hello Sara
```

In the program, in the line

```
string name;
```

a `string` variable is declared. We have chosen to call the variable `name`.

A `string` variable can contain an arbitrarily long text. As you can see, it is extremely simple to read a text into a `string` variable. You just need to use the operator `>>`. It is just as simple to print out a `string` variable. Then you use `<<`.

The input operator `>>` is easy to use, but there is a small problem. Suppose the user writes in both the first and last names when the program is run:

```
What is your name?
Peter Pan
Hello Peter
```

Here we see how the input is broken when it encounters a blank character. (The same is true for the tabulator and new line characters.) Therefore only the first name is accepted as the variable `name`. One way of solving this problem is to read a whole line. This can be done with the input function `getline`, as demonstrated in the following program:

```
#include <iostream>
#include <string>
using namespace std;
```

```
main ()
{
  string name;
  cout << "What is your name?" << endl;
  getline(cin, name);
  cout << "Hello " << name << endl;
}
```

The function `getline` has two arguments. The first indicates which input stream you wish to read from, and the second which `string` variable you wish to write to. Now both first and last names are accepted:

```
What is your name?
Peter Pan
Hello Peter Pan
```

Unlike the input operator `>>`, the function `getline` always reads a whole line. There is a further difference that should be pointed out. When you use the input operator `>>` to read, all the leading so-called white characters (space, tabulator and return) will be skipped, but the function `getline` also reads the leading white characters. Like the operator `>>`, the function `getline` returns the value `true` if the input is successful, otherwise it returns `false`. This means that we can use `getline` in a **`while`** statement in the same way as when we read with `>>`. The user can denote the end of the input by writing Ctrl-Z (or Ctrl-D). (See page 53.)*

If you do not write anything special when you declare a `string` variable it will start with an empty text at the beginning (a text of zero length), but a `string` variable can, like other variables, be initialized at declaration. You can initialize it either with a text string or with another `string`. For instance, we can write

```
string s1 = "Peter Pan";
string s2 = s1;
```

Both variables will contain the text `"Peter Pan"`. Alternatively, you can use

```
string s1("Peter Pan");
string s2(s1);
```

The result will be the same. If you want to initialize a `string` variable with part of a text from another `string` variable you can use another variant of the last line. For instance, you can write

```
string s2(s1, 6, 3); // s2 contains "Pan"
```

The two extra arguments indicate that you choose the text that begins in position 6 of `s1` and that the chosen text will be three characters long. (Numbering is from 0. The

---

* Unfortunately the function `getline` does not function properly in version 6.0 of Visual C++.

first character in `s1` thus has the number 0.) At times, you may want to have a text that contains a certain number of similar characters. In the following line the variable `s3` will be initialized so that this length is 5 and all the characters contain the value `'x'`:

```
string s3(5, 'x'); // s3 contains "xxxxx"
```

You can also initialize using the first part of a text string. As the second argument, you indicate the number of characters there should be. For instance,

```
string s1("Peter Pan", 5); // s1 contains "Peter"
```

Assignment is easily done with the help of the common assignment operator `=`. You can assign a text string, an individual character or a second `string` variable to a `string` variable:

```
s1 = "Peter Pan"; // s1 contains "Peter Pan"
s2 = 'z';         // s2 contains "z"
s3 = s1;          // s3 contains "Peter Pan"
```

Using the operator `+` it is easy to build a new `string`-value. One of the operators should be of type `string`. The second can either be a `string`, a text string or a simple `char`. Here are some examples:

```
s3 = "an";
s3 = 'P' + s3;
s2 = "Pe";
s1 = s2 + "ter " + s3; // s1 contains "Peter Pan"
```

Alternately, assignments can be done using the function `assign`. Here you can use the same variants as when initializing. For instance, you can write

```
s2.assign(s1, 6, 3); // s2 contains "Pan"
s3.assign(5, 'x');   // s3 contains "xxxxx"
```

You can easily add a text to the end of a `string` variable. You then simply use the compound allocation operator `+=`. Here are a couple of examples:

```
s2 += "cake"; // s2 contains "Pancake"
s2 += s3;     // s2 får värdet "Pancakexxxxx"
```

Alternatively, you can use the function `append`. This exists in the same variant as at initializing. A couple of examples are

```
s3.append(s1, 6, 3); // s3 contains "xxxxxPan"
s3.append(3, '!');   // s3 contains "xxxxxPan!!!"
```

You can determine the length of a `string` variable by calling the function `size` (this function is alternatively called `length`).

```
cout << s3.size() << endl; // prints out 11
```

It is easy to put an empty text (a text of zero length) into a `string` variable:

```
s3=""; // s3 gets length 0
```

To delete part of a text you can use the function `erase`, which has two arguments: the first indicates the start position and the second the number of characters to be deleted. For instance, we can write (assuming that the variable `s2` as above contains the text `"Pancakexxxx"`)

```
s2.erase(2, 9); // s2 becomes "Pax"
```

To access individual characters in a `string` variable you use indexing. Just as in the class `vector`, there two alternatives: you can either use square brackets `[]` and have no index control, or you can use the function `at` and have index control. For instance, regarding the variable `s1` that previously contained the text `"Peter Pan"`, we can write

```
s1[7] = 'o';     // s1 becomes "Peter Pon"
s1.at(8) = 'p'; // s1 becomes "Peter Pop"
```

`insert` and `replace` are two useful functions. The function `insert` is used when you want to add text to a `string` variable. This function has several variants. The first argument always indicates the position where you want to put the new text:

```
s1.insert(5, "man");        // s1 becomes "Peterman Pop"
s1.insert(9, s2);           // s1 becomes "Peterman PaxPop"
s1.insert(13, s2, 1, 2); // s1 becomes "Peterman PaxPaxop"
s1.insert(12, 3, '.');     // s1 becomes "Peterman Pax...Paxop"
```

On the next to last line the two final arguments specify which part of `s2` will be put into `s1`. The number 1 indicates that you will start in position number 1 and the number 2 that two characters will be included. On the last line the number 3 indicates how many times the last argument is to be added.

The function `replace` appears in the same variants as `insert`: the only difference is that you always have two arguments first indicating which part of the current `string` variable will be replaced. The first argument gives the starting position and the second the number of characters to be replaced. Here are some examples:

```
s1.replace(9,11, "Pop");        // s1 becomes "Peterman Pop"
s1.replace(5, 3, s2);           // s1 becomes "PeterPax Pop"
s1.replace(10, 2, s2, 1, 2); // s1 becomes "PeterPax Pax"
s1.replace(5, 4, 2, '*');      // s1 becomes "Peter**Pax"
```

In the following program example the use of indexing and the function `replace` is illustrated. The American style of indicating the date differs from the British style and can sometimes be a little misleading. For example, in the United States 15 October 2001 is written as 10/15/01, while in Britain the form 15/10/01 is used. The program below can translate a date in the American format. When the program is run it may look like this:

```
Indicate date in the format mm/dd/yy 10/15/01
The British form of the date is 15/10/01
```

The program looks like this:

```
#include <iostream>
#include <string>
using namespace std;
main ()
{
   string a, s=" / / ";
   cout << "Indicate date in the format mm/dd/yy ";
   cin >> a;
   if (a.size() == 8 && a[2] == '/' && a[5] == '/') {
      s.replace(0,2,a,3,2); // day
      s.replace(3,2,a,0,2); // month
      s.replace(6,2,a,6,2); // year
      cout << "The British form of the date is "
            << s << endl;
   }
   else
      cout << "Illegal date" << endl;
}
```

Another valuable function is `substr`, which chooses a substring (a part of the text) from a `string` variable. It has two arguments. The first indicates the position in which you should begin and the second the number of characters that should be chosen. Using the function `substr` further simplifies the date program shown above. The variable `s` is then not necessary, and we can replace the **if** statement as follows:

```
if (a.size() == 8 && a[2] == '/' && a[5] == '/')
   cout << "The British form of the date is "
        << a.substr(3,2) + '/' + a.substr(0,2) +
        '/' + a.substr(6,2) << endl;
```

There are several functions you can use to search for substrings or single characters in a `string` variable. All these functions return an integer number as the result. If the searched-for substring is in the `string` variable, the start position for the substring is returned, and if the searched-for substring is missing, the value `string:-:npos` is returned (a constant defined in the class `string`). The first function we shall demonstrate is `find`. In its simplest form it has only one parameter, indicating the substring you want to look for. This parameter can be either another `string` variable or a text string. Suppose that we have made the following assignments:

```
s1 = "subclasses and superclasses";
s2 = "class";
```

We can then make the following call:

```
s1.find(s2)     // gives the value 3
s1.find("ses") // gives the value 7
s1.find('a')    // gives the value 5
s1.find("but") // gives the value string::npos
```

If you want to examine whether a certain text is in a `string` variable you can use an **`if`** statement, as in the following example:

```
int i=s1.find("ses");
if (i == string::npos)
  cout << "Not found" <<endl;
else
  cout << "Found in position " << i << endl;
```

The search is performed from left to right and stops at the first hit. Alternatively, you can insert an extra parameter that indicates the position where you want the search to begin. For instance, we can write

```
s1.find("su",5) // gives the value 15
s1.find('a',14) // gives the value 22
```

If, instead, you want to search from behind, you can use the function `rfind`. It is in the same variants as the function `find`. Here are a few examples:

```
s1.rfind(s2)     // gives the value 20
s1.rfind("ses") // gives the value 24
```

In order for the functions `find` or `rfind` to make hits, all the substring must be present in the `string` variable. If you want to determine whether only some of several characters are found in a `string` variable, you can use the functions `find_first_of` or `find_last_of`. Both work in the same way, except that `find_first_of` searches from the front and `find_last_of` from behind. For instance, suppose we have made the assignment

```
s1 = "Java 2 Version 1.4.1";
```

We can then make the following call in order to examine whether `s1` contains numbers:

```
s1.find_first_of("0123456789") // gives the value 5
s1.find_last_of("0123456789")  // gives the value 19
```

The functions `find_first_not_of` and `find_last_not_of` work correspondingly, but they search for the first occurrence of a character that is *not* in the parameter. For instance, the following statements search for the first or last character in `s1`, respectively, that is not a number:

```
s1.find_first_not_of("0123456789") // gives the value 0
s1.find_last_not_of("0123456789")  // gives the value 18
```

When we discussed the class `vector` in section 2.8 we saw that in this class an internal array was used to store the elements in the vector. The same technique is used for the standard class `string`. An internal array with elements of the type `char` is used to store the text. Just as for the class `vector`, we can use the function `capacity` to determine the size of the array and the function `reserve` to indicate that we want the internal array to have a certain length. There is also a function called `c_str` that returns the text in the actual `string` variable converted to text stored in the usual C++ manner. The function returns a pointer to a text string that ends with a null character (see page 99). Never go right in and try to change the text returned by the function `c_str`. That might cause problems.

It is easy to compare one `string` variable with another `string` variable or with a text string. All the customary operators `==`, `!`, `=`, `<=`, `>` and `>=` are there. For instance, we can write

```
cin >> s1 >> s2;
if (s1 == "Sara")
  cout << "Hello Sara!" << endl;
if ("Hanna" == s2)
  cout << "Hello Hanna!" << endl;
if (s1==s2)
  cout << "equal";
else if (s1 < s2)
  cout << s1 << " comes before " << s2 << endl;
else
  cout << s2 << " comes before " << s1 << endl;
```

There is also a basic function called `compare`. It exists in several variants, and can compare a `string` variable with another `string` variable, with a text string or with a simple `char`. For instance, you can write

```
if (s1.compare(s2) < 0)
  cout << s1 << " comes before " << s2 << endl;
```

The function `compare` returns the value –1, 0 or +1. If the first `string` variable (`s1` in the example) is less than the text given as a parameter (`s2` in the example) the value –1 is returned; if the texts are equal the value 0 is returned; and if the first `string` variable is the biggest the value +1 is returned. The function `compare` can also be used to compare substrings. However, it is much simpler to use the usual comparison operators, as illustrated below.

Operations for the standard class `string`

Here `s` and `s2` are `string` variables; `x` is a text string or a character array; `c` is of type `char`; `t` is a `string` variable, a text string or a character array.

`string s;`	Declaration, `s` contains an empty text (with zero length)
`string s=t;`	Declaration initializing `s` as a copy of `t`
`string s(t);`	Declaration initializing, `s` is a copy of `t`
`string s (s2, p, n);`	Declaration that initializes `s` with `n` characters from position `p` in `s2`
`string s(x, n);`	Declaration that initializes `s` with the first `n` characters from `x`
`string s(n, c);`	Declaration with initializing, `s` is assigned a text consisting of `n` `c`s
`s=t s=c`	Assignment
`s.assign-(t)`	Assigns `t` to `s`
`s.assign-(s2, p, n)`	Assigns to `s` `n` characters from position `p` in `s2`
`s.assign-(x, n)`	Assigns to `s` the first `n` characters from `x`
`s.assign-(n, c)`	Assigns a text consisting of `n` `c`s to `s`
`s-[k]`	Indexing without index control
`s.at(k)`	Indexing with index control (returns `s-[k]`)
`s.substr-(k, n)`	Returns part of `s`, starting in position `k` and with length `n`
`cout<<s`	Prints `s`
`cin>>s`	Reads to `s`, ends at a white character
`getline-(cin, s)`	Reads a whole line to `s`; returns `true` if the input was OK
`s.erase-(k, n)`	deletes `n` characters from `s`, starting at position `k`
`s.-clear-()`	Deletes all characters from `s`
`s.size-()`	Returns the length of `s`
`s.resize-(n)`	Changes the length of `ss` to `n`. Fills with zeros if `n` is bigger than the old length, otherwise cuts off at the end
`s.resize-(n, c)`	As above, but fills with `c` instead of zeros
`s.capacity-(n)`	Returns the size of the internal array
`s.reserve-(n)`	Indicates that you will need space for `n` characters
`s.c_str()`	Returns a pointer to a text string with the text of the variables
`s<t s==t s>t` etc.	Comparisons, *not* alphabetically correct
`s+t s+c`	Returns a new `string` with concatenations of the texts
`s+=t s+=c`	Adds `t`, `x` or `c` at the end of `s`

Operations for the standard class `string`	
Here `s` and `s2` are `string` variables; `x` is a text string or a character array; `c` is of type `char`; `t` is a `string` variable, a text string or a character array.	
`s.append-(t)`	Adds `t` at the end of `s`
`s.append-(s2, p, n)`	Adds `n` characters from position `p` in `s2` to `s`
`s.append-(x, n)`	Adds the first `n` characters from `x` to `s`
`s.append-(n, c)`	Adds text consisting of `n` `c`s to `s`
`s.insert-(k, t)`	Inserts `t` in the position `k` in `s`
`s.insert-(k, s2, p, n)`	Inserts `n` characters from position `p` in `t` to position `k` in `s`
`s.insert-(k, x, n)`	Inserts the `n` first characters from `x` in position `k` in `s`
`s.insert-(k, n, c)`	Inserts text consisting of `n` `c`s in position `k` in `s`
`s.replace-(k, m, t)`	Replaces characters `k` to `k+m-1` in `s` with `t`
`s.replace-(k, m,s2,p,n)`	Replaces characters `k` to `k+m-1` in `s` with the characters `p` to `p+n-1` in `t`
`s.replace-(k, m, x, n)`	Replaces characters `k` to `k+m-1` in `s` with the first `n` characters from `x`
`s.replace-(k, m, n, c)`	Replaces characters `k` to `k+m-1` in `s` with text consisting of `n` `c`s
`s.find(t)`	Searches in `s` for the text `t`; returns the position in `s` if `t` is in `s`, otherwise returns the value `string: :npos`
`s.find(t, k)`	As above, but starts the search in position `k`
`s.find(c, n)`	Searches in `s` for text consisting of `n` `c`s. Result is as above
`s.rfind`	As `find`, but searches from behind
`s.find_first_of(t)`	Searches in `s` for the first occurrence of *any* of the characters that appear in text `t`. Returns the same result value as `find`.
`s.find_first_of(t, k)`	As above, but starts searching in position `k`
`s.find_last_of(t)`	As `find_first_of`, but searches from behind
`s.find_first_not_of(t)`	Searches in `s` for the first occurrence of any character that does *not* appear in text `t`. Returns the same result value as `find`
`s.find_first_not_of(t,k)`	As above, but begins searching in position `k`
`s.find_last_not_of(t,k)`	As `find_first_not_of`, but searches from behind

When using comparison operators or the standard function `compare` to examine whether one text is larger or smaller than another, the usual alphabetical comparison is performed. However, note that lower-case and upper-case letters are considered different (upper-case letters are actually considered smaller than lower-case letters), and that letters with diacritics, such as á, ê and ñ, are not treated as being alphabetically correct. This makes it difficult to perform a normal alphabetical comparison of texts, for instance to sort a number of names in alphabetical order. On this book's website there is a help class called `alpha` that you can download to your own computer. The class `alpha` contains functions for making alphabetical comparisons. (Note that `alpha` is not a standard class but a class we have constructed ourselves.)

To be able to use the class `alpha`, you must compile and link the file `alpha.cpp` into your program. You must also have the following line first in the program:

```
#include "alpha.h"
```

After that you should declare a *comparator* of the class `alpha`. If you want comparisons to occur according to the English alphabet you can, for instance, declare a comparator in the following way:

```
alpha a;
```

You can also indicate that the comparisons should occur in another alphabet, for instance in the Spanish alphabet:

```
alpha a("es");
```

It is also possible to interchange between different languages by calling the function `set_lang`. For instance, we change to German by writing

```
a.set_lang("de");
```

At present, the class `alpha` handles all those languages in which the alphabets are similar to the Latin alphabet (for instance English and French). It can also handle Spanish, German and Swedish, which have special letters or letter combinations. It is easy to increase the class `alpha`, if desired, to handle more languages.

A comparator of the class `alpha` has the functions `eq`, `ne`, `lt`, `gt`, `le` and `ge` (which are read as 'equal', 'not equal', 'less than', 'greater than', 'less than or equal' and 'greater than or equal' respectively). These functions can be used to compare texts or single characters. Each function has two parameters. A parameter can be either of type `string` or of type `char`, or can be a text string. The functions return a value of the type `bool`. For instance, we can write

```
if (a.eq(s1,s2))
  cout << s1 << " and " << s2 << " are equal";
if (a.lt(s1,'M'))
  cout << s1 << " comes before 'M'";
if (a.gt(s1,"hello"))
  cout << s1 << " comes before \"hello\"";
```

Note that in every function call you begin by indicating the name of the comparator you want to use (in these examples it is `a`). When you use a comparator of the class `alpha` it does not distinguish between upper- and lower-case letters, and letters with diacritics etc. are sorted alphabetically.

A comparator of class `alpha` also has a function called `compare`. It has two parameters that indicate the texts or the single characters that are to be compared. As for the standard function `compare` mentioned above, it returns one of the values –1, 0 or +1. If the first parameter is less it results in the value –1, the value 0 if the texts are similar, and the value +1 if the second parameter is less.

Note that if you run DOS and want to compare texts with the help of a comparator of the `alpha`, you must also use `iodos` so that all the letters will be read and written correctly from the DOS window (see page 82).

In addition to the functions for making comparisons, the class `alpha` also contains functions that you can use to test whether or not a certain character is a letter, and to change between lower-case and upper-case letters (see the information window). There are certainly standard functions in C++ (defined in the file `<cctype>`) that do this for individual characters, but they usually do not work satisfactorily for letters other than a–z.

Comparators of the class `alpha`

Include the file `alpha.h` and link the file `alpha.cpp` to the program.

Then declare a comparator:

`alpha cmp` ("*language*") ; // *language* is a language code, for instance `en`, `fr` or `pt`.

The comparator can be used to compare the texts `s1` and `s2`, as below. `s1` and `s2` can be `string` variables, character strings or values of type `char`. All comparisons are performed according to proper alphabetical rules. `c` is of type `char`.

Function	Description
`cmp.eq(s1, s2)`	Returns `true` when `s1` and `s2` are equal
`cmp.ne(s1, s2)`	Returns `true` when `s1` and `s2` are not equal
`cmp.lt(s1, s2)`	Returns `true` when `s1` comes before `s2`
`cmp.gt(s1, s2)`	Returns `true` when `s1` comes after `s2`
`cmp.le(s1, s2)`	Returns `true` when `s1` comes before or is equal to `s2`
`cmp.ge(s1, s2)`	Returns `true` when `s1` comes after or is equal to `s2`
`cmp.compare(s1, s2)`	Returns `-1` if `s1<s2`, `0` if `s1==s2`, and `+1` if `s1>s2`
`cmp.is_letter(c)`	Returns `true` if `c` is a letter
`cmp.is_upper_case(c)`	Returns `true` if `c` is an upper-case letter
`cmp.is_lower_case(c)`	Returns `true` if `c` is a lower-case letter
`cmp.to_upper_case(c)`	If `c` is a lower-case letter the corresponding upper-case letter is returned, otherwise `c` is returned
`cmp.to_lower_case(c)`	If `c` is an upper-case letter the corresponding lower-case letter is returned, otherwise `c` is returned
`cmp.to_upper_case(s1)`	Replaces all lower-case letters in `s1` with the corresponding upper-case letters
`cmp.to_lower_case(s1)`	Replaces all upper-case letters in `s1` with the corresponding lower-case letters

We conclude this section on the standard class `string` by illustrating a new version of the sales representatives program from section 2.7 (see page 62). This time we shall not number the sales representatives. Information about each person contains their sales figures and their name. For instance, input to the program looks like this:

```
1000 Taylor Helen
50 Cooper Charles
1200 Stevens Eric
2500 Harding Jenny
6000 Taylor Helen
100 Stevens Eric
6000 Wolf Elisabeth
```

In the printout from the program the names of the sales representatives are now included:

```
Amount        Commission        Name
======        ==========        ====
 7000            800            Taylor Helen
   50              5            Cooper Charles
 1300            130            Stevens Eric
 2500            250            Harding Jenny
 6000            650            Wolf Elisabeth
```

In the program we use two vectors, one with elements of type `string`, in which we save the names of the sales representatives, and the other with elements of type `float`, in which we keep track of how much every sales representative has sold. The program might look like this:

```
#include <iostream>
#include <iomanip>
#include <vector>
#include <string>
using namespace std;
main()
{
  const float bound=5000., pro1=0.1, pro2=0.15;
  vector<string> name; // contains the names
  vector<float> tab; // contains the total amounts
  string nn;
  float amount, commission;
  while (cin >> amount >> ws)
  {
    getline(cin ,nn); // input next name
    // search for the name nn
    int i;
    for (i=0; i<name.size() && nn != name[i]; i++)
      ;
    if (i==name.size())
    { // not found, insert the new name
      name.push_back(nn);
```

```
        tab.push_back(amount);
      }
      else
        tab[i] += amount; // found, add new amount
    }
    // write compilation
    cout << endl
         << "     Amount     Commission     Name" << endl
         << "     ======     ==========     ====" << endl;
    for (int j=0; j<name.size(); j++)
    {
      if (tab[j] <= bound)
        commission = pro1*tab[j];
      else
        commission = pro1*bound + pro2*(tab[j]-bound);
      cout << setiosflags(ios::fixed) << setprecision(0)
           << setw(9) << amount << setw(12) << commission
           << "        " << j->first << endl;
    }
}
```

3.4 Character arrays

The class `string` we studied in the previous section did not appear in the first version of C++. The usual way to manage texts in C++ has thus been to use character arrays – arrays in which the components are of type `char`. This is described in the section below. We begin with an example that asks for the name of the user and then prints it out:

```
#include <iostream>
using namespace std;
main ()
{
  char name[10];
  cout << "What is your name?" << endl;
  cin >> name; // Dangerous input
  cout << "Hello " << name << endl;
}
```

When the program is run, it gives the following printout:

```
What is your name?
Sara
Hello Sara
```

The interesting thing here is the declaration

```
char name[10];
```

which says that the variable `name` is a character array consisting of 10 characters. As we saw earlier, the numbering of the separate elements in an array always begins with 0, so that the elements in the array `name` are numbered from 0 to 9. The statement

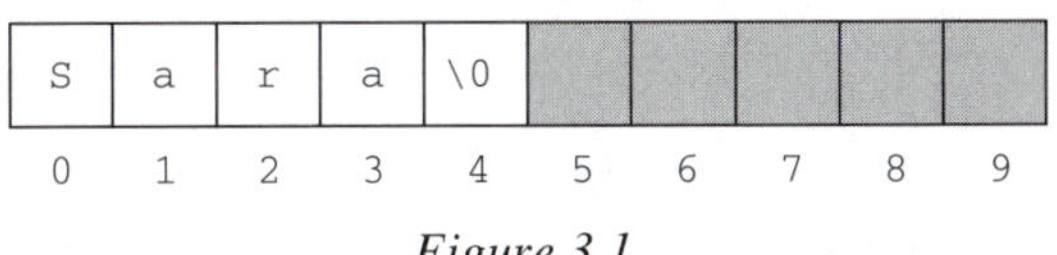

Figure 3.1

```
cin >> name;
```

inputs the text typed at the keyboard to the variable `name`. How this variable looks after input is shown in Figure 3.1. The characters written by the user have landed in the variable `name` beginning with element 0. Input finishes with the arrival of a white character (space, tabulator or end-of-line). The input operator `>>` then automatically puts a special *null character* into the variable `name` after the input characters. A null character is a byte that contains zeros in all of the eight bits. The null character is usually written with the escape sequence `\0` as in Figure 3.1. The elements 5–9 in `name` will not be influenced by the input in our example. Their contents are therefore undefined.

It is a convention in C and C++ to use null characters to indicate the end of a text. (This is not needed when you use the class `string` because the class itself keeps track of the length of the text.) A sequence of characters terminated by a null character, is usually called a *text string*. We thus differentiate between the concepts of character array and text string. A character array is like a container into which text strings are put. Since each text string terminates with an extra null character, a character array with *n* elements can contain text strings that are at most $n - 1$ characters long. When you work with texts in C++, you should always make sure that the texts terminate with a null character, because there are a number of standard functions for handling text strings, and they all require the use of null characters. The output operator `<<` in our examples uses, for instance, the null character in the variable `name` to decide where the text being written out is to finish.

Character arrays and text strings

`char` `a[n];`	The variable `a` is a *character array* with room for `n` characters. Numbered from `0` to `n-1`.

- A *text string* is an arbitrarily long sequence of characters.
- Terminates with a null character, indicated by `\0`.
- Can be put into a character array. There must then also be room for the null character.

The input statement `cin >> name;` seems to be easy to use, but there are two problems here. The first is that input is broken off when a white character is encountered. This means that if the user writes in both the first and last names of a person, it is only the first name that is read:

```
What is your name?
Peter Pan
Hello Peter
```

Of course you can easily solve this problem by introducing two variables in the program, and by writing in the first and last names independently.

The second problem is much more serious. Suppose that the user happens to have a long name:

```
What is your name?
Christopher
```

A pervading characteristic of C++ is that security with the handling of arrays is extremely poor. There are no checks to make sure that texts do not land outside the array. In this example the text `Christopher` is 11 characters long, but since a null character has also been inserted, 12 characters will be inserted in the variable name, in which there is room for only 10. The last two characters will therefore land outside the variable, and the program will be faulty. Anything can happen, and the program can behave in various ways, depending on which compiler you have used. Sometimes the program seems to work as intended, but at other times vital data in the vicinity of the variable `name` in the primary memory is destroyed and the program does not work as it should. The worst aspect of this type of error is that it may not be discovered while the program is tested, only later when it is in operation.

We saw in Chapter 2 how the manipulator `setw` could be used to indicate the number of positions in the output of data; but this manipulator can also be used when data is input. It will indicate how many bytes there are in the array you want to write to. We can change the input line in our program:

```
cin >> setw(10) >> name;
```

Then a maximum of nine characters will be entered. In this case the input operator will also put a null character last, and a position is needed for it. Notice that the manipulator `setw` will handle only *one* piece of input data; it must be repeated for all new data entered.

The use of `setw` solves the problem of long names as in our example. The first problem, namely that input stops after the first name, remains. Another alternative is to use the input function `getline` instead of the operator `>>`:

```
#include <iostream.>
using namespace std;
main ()
{
   char name[10];
   cout << "What is your name?" << endl;
```

```
    cin.getline(name, 10); // safe input
    cout << "Hello " << name << endl;
}
```

The function `getline` has two arguments. You first indicate which character array you want to write text to, and you then indicate how long this array is. Normally, `getline` writes a whole line from the keyboard, but if the input is too long, the function's second argument will determine the number of input characters allowed. If this argument has the value *n*, the function will read at most *n* – 1 characters. In both cases a null character is inserted after the input text. The end-of-line character terminating the input of a whole line is not normally put into the variable. On the other hand, it has been written in (and taken), which means that if you call the function several times in succession, every call will result in the input of a new line. An input line can contain both spaces and tabulators, and these will also land in the variable you are writing data to. We show here two examples of the latter version of the program as it is run:

```
What is your name?
Peter Pan
Hello Peter Pan
What is your name?
Christopher
Hello Christoph
```

Character arrays, like other arrays, can be initialized at declaration. For instance, we can write

```
char name[10] = "Sara";
```

In this case the variable name will look as it does in Figure 3.1: that is, the elements 0 to 3 will contain the letters `"Sara"`, element 4 a null character, and the other elements will not be initialized. Note that the null character is also put in automatically here, which means that the character array must be one character longer than the initialized text; otherwise there will be an error, even though the computer will not necessarily

Input and output of texts	
`cout << a;`	Types out the text string in character array `a`.
`cin >> a;`	Reads a text and puts it in `a`. Puts the null character last in `a`. Reading stops at the first white character. Dangerous; can put text outside `a`.
`cin >> setw(n);`	At most *n* – 1 characters may be read in the next input.
`cin.getline(a,n);`	Reads a text and puts it in `a`. `n` is the length of `a`. Puts in the null character itself. Normally reads a whole line, but at most *n* – 1 characters.

produce an error message from the compiler. When a character array is initialized, its length does not have to be indicated. The array will be exactly as long as is necessary. The variable `s` in the following declaration will have a length of `4`:

```
char s[] = "C++";
```

The syntax for declarations in C++ is somewhat special. Let us look at the following line as an example of this:

```
char a[4], b[4]="xyz", c, d[]="nn";
```

The variables `a` and `b` will be character arrays with a length of 4, `c` will be a simple variable of type **`char`** (not an array), and `d` will be a character array of length 3. The variables `a` and `c` will not be initialized.

Since character arrays can be *initialized* with text string literals, you would think that it would also be permissible to *assign* them to character arrays. You might want to write, for instance

```
name = "Sara"; // Not allowed !!
```

but this is in fact not allowed in C++. If you want to make assignments to arrays you must use special help functions. We shall soon show how this is done.

The next question is whether it is permissible to compare character arrays with each other. If we suppose that the variables `a` and `b` have been declared as above and we want to check whether they contain the same text string, we can write

```
if (a == b) // Allowed but not what is intended
```

As with other arrays, this can be compiled, but it doesn't mean, as you might think, that the contents of the variables `a` and `b` are being compared. Instead, the expression `a==b` will determine in this case whether `a` and `b` refer to the same variable, and of course they do not. The expression will therefore always be false. To compare character arrays, special help functions must be used.

Before we deal with help functions in the context of handling text strings, note that individual elements in a character array can be accessed by the use of *indexing*. To access element number 2 in the array `name`, for example, you write `name[2]`. The element you choose to select in a character array will have type **`char`** and can be handled in the same way as an ordinary, simple variable of this type. Here are some examples of indexing. We suppose that the variable `name` from the beginning contains the text `"Sara"`, as shown in Figure 3.1.

```
cout << name[2];   // Print an r
if (name[0]=='A') // See if the first character is an A
name[0] = 'b';     // Change element no.0 to a b
name[3] = '\0';    // Shorten the text to 3 characters
```

It can be seen from this that an individual element can be both read and changed by the use of indexing. After the two assignments in the example, the variable name will contain the text string `"bar"`. The index does not need to be a constant, and an arbitrary integer expression may be written inside the square brackets:

```
cout << name[i];
name[i+j] = 'X';
name[i-1] = name[i];
```

When the index is not a constant but an expression, it is easy to make mistakes when programming so that the index value lands outside the bounds of the array. We have already seen that there are no indexing checks in C++. If you want checks, you have to put them in yourself. Later in the book we shall see how classes can be constructed in which those checks are made.

As an example we give a new variant of the program that translates the American style date into the British format (see page 90). When the program is run it may look like this:

```
Indicate date in the format mm/dd/yy 10/15/01
The British form of the date is 15/10/01
```

The program appears as

```
#include <iostream>
using namespace std;
main ()
{
   char a[9], s[9]="  /  /  ";
   cout << "Indicate date in the format mm/dd/yy ";
   cin.getline(a, 9);
   s[0]=a[3]; s[1]=a[4]; // day
   s[3]=a[0]; s[4]=a[1]; // month
   s[6]=a[6]; s[7]=a[7]; // year
   cout << "The British form of the date is " << s << endl;
}
```

The variable `s` is initialized in the declaration. Blank characters have been inserted where the numbers for the year, month and day should be. These blank characters are then filled in with numbers for the year, month and day further down in the program.

In C and C++ there is a standard library with various useful help functions for handling text strings in character arrays. (When you use `string` variables these help functions are not needed because, as we have seen, the class `string` contains everything that is necessary to handle the `string` variables.) In order to have access to the library with the help functions you must include the file `cstring` at the beginning of your program.[†]

[†] If the compiler does not follow the standard you can include `string.h` instead.

Assignment and comparison of character arrays

The assignment and comparison of character arrays cannot be done using ordinary operators. Use the help functions in the standard string library.

```
#include <string>
```

The most common help functions:

`strcpy(s1, s2);`	Copies a string from `s2` to `s1`. No check that there is room.
`strncpy(s1, s2, n);`	Copies a string from `s2` to `s1`. Max. `n` characters (including the null character). The null character will be missing in `s1` if the length of `s2>n`.
`strcat(s1, s2);`	Puts a copy of `s2` last into `s1`. No check that there is room.
`strncat(s1, s2, n);`	Puts a copy of `s2` last into `s1`. Max. `n` characters added. `s1` always concluded with a null character.
`strcmp(s1, s2)` `strncmp(s1, s2, n)`	Compares two text strings. `strncmp` compares at most `n` characters. Result: <0 if `s1<s2`, 0 if `s1=s2` and >0 if `s1>s2`.
`strlen(s)`	Gives the length of the text string in `s` (excluding the null character).

We shall now give a few examples of the most useful help functions. The function `strlen` computes the length of a text string. If the variable `name` contains the text `"Sara"`, the following statement will give an output of `4`:

```
cout << strlen(name) << endl;
```

Note that it is the length of the *text string* in the variable `name` that is computed, not the length of the variable. The concluding null character is not counted.

The assigning of text strings can be done with `strcpy`. If we have the declarations

```
char a[4], b[4]="xyz", name[10];
```

we can assign the value of `b` – that is, the text string `"xyz"` – to `a`:

```
strcpy(a,b);         // Does the assignment a=b
cout << a << endl;  // Gives the output xyz
```

The whole text string in `b`, including the null character, is copied to the beginning of array `a`. A constant text string can also be assigned:

```
strcpy(name, "David"); // name="David"
```

A null character has also been put in at the end of the text here. No check is made to see whether the character array being copied into is big enough to hold the text string:

```
strcpy(a, name); // Dangerous!
```

If you want to make safer assignments, you can instead use the help function `strncpy`. This has an extra argument that indicates the maximum number of characters that may be copied. If we have two character arrays `s1` and `s2`, we can assign from `s2` to `s1`:

```
strncpy(s1, s2, n);
```

Here a maximum of *n* characters (possibly including the null character) are copied from `s2` to `s1`. This means that if the text string in `s2` (including the terminating null character) is longer than *n* characters, no null character will be copied to `s1`. The text string in `s1` will not then be completed. If we want to make a safe assignment from the variable `name` to the variable `a`, we have to ensure that there is a null character in `a` after the assignment:

```
strncpy(a, name, 3);
a[3]='\0';
cout << a << endl; // Gives the printout Dav
```

The first statement copies the characters '`D`', '`a`' and '`v`' to elements 0, 1 and 2 in variable `a`. The second statement puts an end-of-line character last in variable `a`. You need to have this statement for safety's sake.

When you copy to or from an array, you don't need to start copying at the first element in the array. The statement

```
strcpy(a+2, name+5);
```

copies a string that begins in element number 5 in the variable `name` to an array `a` that begins at element number 2. (As usual, numbering begins at zero, so that it will be the same thing to write `a+0` as to write `a`.) Using this, we can now write a new version of the date program:

```
#include <iostream>
#include <string>
using namespace std;
main ()
{
  char am_date[9], br_date[9] = "  /  /  ";
  cout << "Indicate date in the format mm/dd/yy "
  cin.getline(am_date, 9);
  strncpy(br_date+0, am_date+3, 2); // day
  strncpy(br_date+3, am_date+0, 2); // month
```

```
    strncpy(br_date+6, am_date+6, 2); // year
    cout << "The British form of the date is "
         << br_date << endl;
}
```

Above we saw the simplifications achieved by using `string` variables instead of character arrays. It is very simple to assign a `string` variable from a character array. Suppose that the variable `name` mentioned above is a character array. If we declare a `string` variable

```
string sname;
```

then it is easy to assign the character array `name` to it:

```
sname = name;
```

However, it is somewhat more complicated to assign in the reverse direction, from a `string` variable to a character array. You must then use `strcpy` or `strncpy`. In order to have a pointer to the text string inside the `string` variable, you use the function `c_str`. For instance, we can write

```
strcpy(name, sname.c_str());
```

There are two other help functions, `strcat` and `strncat`, that function roughly as `strcpy` and `strncpy` respectively. The statement

```
strcat(s1, s2);
```

copies the text string in `s2` to the *end* of the text string in `s1`. The earlier null character is thus overwritten. No check is made to see that the result will fit into `s1`. The statement

```
strncat(s1, s2, n);
```

copies the text string in `s2` to the end of the text string in `s1`. A maximum of *n* characters are copied and *then* a null character is put last into `s1`. This always happens (in contrast to `strncpy`). A maximum of *n* characters will thus be put into `s1`, since the old null character is taken away and a new one is added. Both `strcat` and `strncat` require `s1` to contain a correct text string from the beginning, otherwise there could be an error, and the assignment could land outside `s1`.

Suppose that we have two variables `name1` and `name2`, which contain a first name and a last name respectively. In addition, we have the variable `name`, which, as before, is 10 characters long. We can now combine the first name and the last name:

```
name[0]='\0';           // put an empty string in name
strncat(name, name1, 9-strlen(name));
strncat(name, " ",   9-strlen(name));
strncat(name, name2, 9-strlen(name));
```

The first statement sees that the variable name contains a correct text string (of zero length) from the beginning. Then we add the first name, a blank character and the last name. Note that the blank character should be between double quotes, not single quotes. We don't add a simple character but a *text string* that contains one null character. The total number of 'proper' characters in the variable name should not exceed nine. (There must always be room for the null character.) The text already in `name` when additions are made consists of a number of 'proper characters' dictated by `strlen(name)`. Thus a maximum number of `9-strlen(name)` new characters can be added each time.

To compare character strings, either of the functions `strcmp` or `strncmp` can be used. Both have two text strings as arguments, and these will be compared. The function `strncmp` also has an argument that indicates the maximum number of characters to be compared. If you want to compare the text strings in `s1` and `s2`, you can write the expressions

```
strcmp(s1, s2)    strncmp(s1, s2, n)
```

It is possible to check whether two texts are the same, or whether one is 'bigger' than the other. Ordinary alphabetical order is used. Note, however, that upper- and lower-case letters are regarded as being different (in the ASCII code, upper-case letters are treated as being smaller than lower-case letters) while only the letters a–z come in the correct order. If the texts `s1` and `s2` are the same and they are compared, the functions will give a result of `0`. If `s1<s2` the functions will give a result less than `0`, and if `s1>s2` they will give a result greater than `0`. As an example, here is a program that inputs and compares two names:

```
#include <iostream>
#include <string>
using namespace std;
main ()
{
  char name1[10], name2[10];
  cout << "Write two names" << endl;
  cin.getline(name1, 10);
  cin.getline(name2, 10);
  if (strcmp(name1, name2)<0)
    cout << name1 << " comes first" << endl;
  else if (strcmp(name1, name2)>0)
    cout << name2 << " comes first" << endl;
  else
    cout << "The names are the same" << endl;
}
```

A test run gives the following result:

```
Write two names
Hanna
David
David comes first
```

Note that the class `alpha` we described on page 94 can also be used to compare text strings in character arrays in a correct alphabetical way.

Exercises

3.1 Write a program to read in words from the keyboard to a character array, `s1`. The program should then copy the text string in `s1` to another character array, `s2`. (In this exercise you are not allowed to use the help function `strcpy`.)

3.2 Do the same as in the previous exercise, putting the characters in `s2` into the opposite order to that in `s1`.

3.3 A text that can be read forwards or backwards giving the same result is an example of a palindrome (e.g. madam, ada, radar). Write a program that reads in a word and then decides whether the word is a palindrome or not.

3.4 Write a program to enter a text file consisting of several lines and to compute the average number of characters per line in the file. Redirect the stream `cin`.

3.5 Write a program to enter a text file and print out the number of letters, digits and other characters in the file. Redirect `cin`.

3.6 Adjust the program on page 97 that prints out the sales information so that the names of the sales representatives are stored and printed out in alphabetical order. Use the help functions in the class `alpha` to perform correct alphabetical comparisons. If you run DOS you must also use `iodos` so that all the letters will be read and written correctly from the DOS window (see page 82).

3.7 Roman numerals are indicated with the letters I, V, X, L, C, D and M, which represent 1, 5, 10, 50, 100, 500 and 1000 respectively. First, declare a `string` variable containing the Roman numerals and then a table (an array) that can be used to translate a Roman numeral to an ordinary whole number (for instance, L to 50). Then write a program that reads a Roman number to a `string` variable, which translates the Roman number to an ordinary whole number. For instance, if the user writes MCMXLIX, the program will print 1949. However, the program should give an error message if the Roman number is written incorrectly.

In Roman numbers, if P appears immediately to the left of another Roman numeral Q, and if P represents a lower number than Q, the value of P will be subtracted from the total amount (for instance, LIX is 59), otherwise P is added to the total number (LXI is 61).

Functions

4

When designing programs that are somewhat bigger and more complicated than the ones we have dealt with so far, they have to be divided into several parts, or 'building blocks', that are of a size that can be handled. Essentially, there are only two kinds of building block in C++: functions and classes. In this chapter we shall begin to look at functions. Earlier, we saw how 'ready-made', standard functions could be used. Here we shall be constructing and calling our own functions.

In constructing an algorithm it is often useful to express certain steps on a 'higher level' than is possible with the fundamental statements in C++. Steps at such a higher level include, for example, 'calculate the logarithm of *x*', 'sort the table *t*' or 'calculate the mean of the measurements'. In C++ functions can be used to join fundamental statements at a higher level. As we have seen, higher-level steps in an algorithm occur naturally when the technique of top-down design is applied to a programming problem.

As we saw in Chapter 1, the program texts of a C++ program can be divided into several program text files, or *source code files*. Every such file can contain one or more functions, and the files can be compiled separately. In this chapter we shall be demonstrating the principles for dividing programs in this way.

In several other common programming languages, for example Ada and Pascal, we speak of *subprograms*. There are two types of subprogram: *functions* and *procedures*. The term 'function' is normally used for subprograms that compute a certain value, but the term 'procedure' is used for subprograms that 'do something', without this necessarily resulting in a value. In C++ only the concept of *function* is used; this will therefore correspond to both functions and procedures in other languages. There are thus two kinds of function in C++: those that compute and return a value and those that do not.

4.1 Functions that return a value

We begin by discussing functions that calculate a value. Such a function is like a black box into which one or more values can be placed. A result dependent on these initial

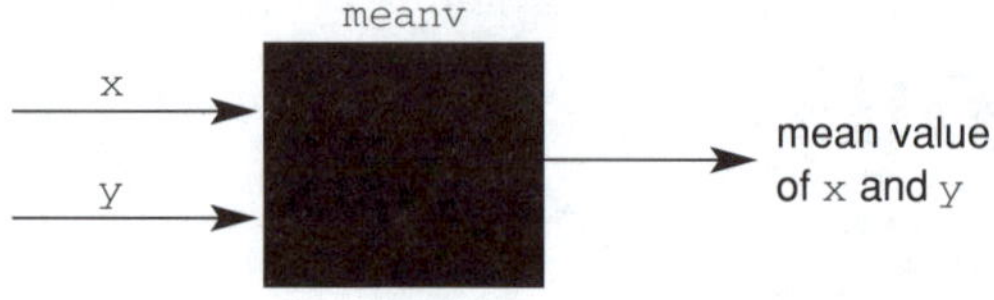

Figure 4.1

values then emerges from the box. As our first example, let us look at the function `meanv`, which computes the mean value of two real numbers. From the user program's point of view, the function will be like the black box in Figure 4.1.

In C++, the function looks like this:

```
double meanv (double x1, double x2)
{
   return (x1+x2)/2;
}
```

This is called a *function definition*. It consists of two parts: a *function head* and a *function body*. In this example the function head is on the first line. It will tell the user of the function how the function is to be used. First, the type of the result coming out of the function is indicated. In this example the mean value of two real numbers is to be calculated. The result type is therefore **double**. Then the name of the function is indicated; here it is `meanv`. After the function's name, whatever will be put into the function is indicated by giving a list of the function's *parameters* (also called *formal parameters* or *formal arguments*). The type and name is given for every parameter. We have indicated here that the function has two parameters, `x1` and `x2`, both of which are of type **double**. You may think that this looks much like a declaration of two variables `x1` and `x2`. In fact, `x1` and `x2` will come to be regarded as variables inside the function `meanv`. When the function is called, `x1` and `x2` will contain the values put into the function.

Function definition

result_type name (*type1 param1*, *type2 param2*, etc.)
{
   local declarations
   and statements
}

The contents of the 'black box' are described by the function body inside the braces, but the user of the function need not normally worry about this. A function body looks just like the contents of the function `main`. First, you normally write declarations (if there are any) and then a number of statements to be executed. There are no declarations in the function `meanv`, and there is only one statement:

```
return (x1+x2)/2;
```

A **`return`** statement does two things: it indicates which value is to be given as the function result, and it terminates the function. (If another statement were to follow the **`return`** statement, this statement would not be executed.) There should be an expression after the word **`return`**. The type of this expression should be the same as the type first indicated in the function head. If this is not the case, there will be an automatic type conversion into this type (if this is possible). A function may contain several **`return`** statements but often there is only one, which comes last in the function body.

`return` **statements**
`return` *expression*;
• Ends the function and gives the value *expression* as result. • The expression's type should be the same as the function's result type.

A function definition is only a description of how a particular computation is done. To actually have a computation done, we have to *call* the function. In other words, we must put something into the 'black box'. In the following example we have put our function into a complete program that reads in two numbers from the keyboard, computes their mean value, and writes it out at the end.

```
#include <iostream>
using namespace std;
double meanv (double x1, double x2)
{
   return (x1+x2)/2;
}
main ()
{
   double number1, number2, mv;
   cout << "Give two real numbers: ";
   cin >> number1 >> number2;
   mv = meanv(number1, number2);
   cout << "The mean value is " << mv << endl;
}
```

The program consists of two functions, `meanv` and `main`. Execution always begins in `main`. Let us suppose that the user enters the two numbers `2.0` and `2.5`. The call of the function `meanv` takes place in the expression

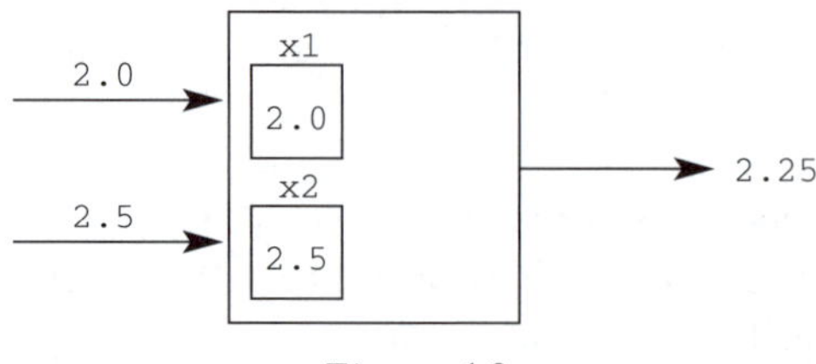

Figure 4.2

```
meanv(number1, number2)
```

First there is the name of the function being called and then, in parentheses, there is a list of the *arguments* of the function. (Sometimes the terms *actual parameters* or *actual arguments* are used.) When the call is executed, the values of the arguments are calculated first. (No calculations are necessary in this example, since the values are already in the variables `number1` and `number2`.) The values of the arguments are then put into the function. The arguments' values are *copied* to corresponding parameters. Figure 4.2 illustrates this. When the function is called, the value of the first argument is put into the parameter `x1` and the value of the second argument is put into the parameter `x2`. Note that neither `number1` nor `number2` is in any way influenced by this or by what will later take place inside the function. This method of transferring the arguments' values to a function is usually termed *call by value* and means that the arguments' values are copied to local copies inside the function. Another way of expressing this is to say that `x1` and `x2` are *value parameters*. Unless otherwise stated, all parameters in C++ are value parameters.

When the arguments' values are copied to `number1` and `number2` by a call to `meanv`, the expression in the **`return`** statement will be computed. The function call `meanv(number1, number2)` will thus have the value `2.25`. When the function call is finished, execution will continue as usual in `main` and the value `2.25` will be assigned to the variable `mv`. Note that when the function call has been ended, the two parameters `x1` and `x2` will cease to exist. They are only there while the function is being called. Inside the function they are regarded as ordinary variables, initialized at the start of the function.

The call of a function is regarded as an *expression* and is therefore allowed to be anywhere in the program where expressions may be put. It can, for instance, be a part of a bigger expression:

```
meanv(number1,number2)/number1*100
```

or be the operand for the output operator. We could have written

```
cout << "The mean value is " << meanv(number1,number2) << endl;
```

The arguments of a function can also be expressions. They need not be simple variables. You could, for instance, write the expression

```
meanv(number1*number2, number1+10)
```

In this example the parameter `x1` gets the value `5.0` and the parameter `x2` the value `12.0`. (We suppose that `number1` and `number2` have the same values as before.) The arguments in a function call should have the same type as the corresponding parameters. (Otherwise, automatic type conversion will occur, if this is possible.)

A common misunderstanding where functions are concerned is that what is put into a function and what comes out of a function should be typed at the keyboard and displayed on the screen respectively; but a function need not have anything whatever to do with input and output. The values going into a function come from the call program and are put in via the arguments (the values will not then be read from the keyboard). Similarly, the function's result value is given to the call program using the **`return`** statement and will not be displayed on the screen.

In our next example on functions we shall look at a function with several **`return`** statements. The function will compute the larger of two integers.

Function calls

function name(a1, a2, . . . an)

- *a1, a2, . . . an* are *arguments*. They may be expressions. Their types should agree with those of corresponding parameters.
- A function call is considered to be an *expression*.
- The following occur:
  1. The values of *a1, a2, . . . an* are computed.
  2. If nothing particular is indicated, the arguments *a1, a2, . . . an* are *copied* to the corresponding parameters. This is called *call by value*.
  3. The statements inside the function are executed.
  4. The function is ended by a **`return`** statement.
  5. The value of the function call is the value in the **`return`** statement.
  6. Execution continues after the function call.

```
int max (int x, int y)
{
  if (x > y)
    return x;
  else
    return y;
}
```

The following example shows a program with a max call:

```
main ()
{
   int a, b, c, m;
   cin >> a >> b >> c;
   m = max(a,b);
   m = max(m,c);
   cout << m << " is largest" << endl;
}
```

Three integers are entered in, and the largest one of them is computed and output. The function max is called in two places but with different arguments. We can get by without the variable m if we write instead

```
cout << max(max(a,b),c) << " is the largest" << endl;
```

The expression max(max(a,b),c) means that the function max should be called. The first argument is the expression max(a,b). This expression, which in its turn is a function call, must be computed before the outermost call of max can take place. The first thing to happen is therefore that max is called with the arguments a and b. The result will be the larger of the values in a and b. This value is then given as the first argument for max and the value in the variable c is given as its second argument. The outer call of max then takes place, and the result will be the largest of the three values in a, b and c.

A function can have parameters of different types. There can also be an arbitrary number of parameters, and their types can be different. Arrays can be parameters. One way of indicating that a parameter is an array is to write empty square brackets after the name of the parameter, as demonstrated below. Here the function computes the length of a text string. (Compare with the standard function strlen.)

```
int length(char s[]) // gives the length of the text string in s
{
   int n = 0;
   while (s[n] != '\0')
      n++;
   return n;
}
```

In the function there is a *local variable*, n, which gets the value 0 from the beginning. You then run through the array from the beginning, increasing n by 1 for every character until you find a null character. The function can be called with character arrays of different lengths. If we have the declarations

```
char a[100]="Hanna", b[10]="X";
```

then the statements give

```
cout << length(a);
cout << length(b);
```

the outputs 5 and 1 respectively. Note that it is the lengths of the text strings that are computed and not the lengths of the character arrays.

Here is another example of a function that has an array as a parameter. This function will have an array in which the elements have type **int**. The function should calculate the sum of all the elements in the array and give this sum as the result. The function will appear as

```
int sum(int a[], int n) // sums up the elements in a
{
  int s = 0;
  for (int i=0; i<n; i++)
    s += a[i];
  return s;
}
```

That the parameter a is an array can be seen by the empty square brackets. An extra parameter n, indicating the length of the array, is needed to establish the number of elements in the array within the function. Here is an example of a program section that uses the function sum to calculate the sum of a number of integers entered. The counter k indicates the number of the elements in the array used. The value of k will be given as the second argument of the function sum.

```
int tab[1000], k=0;
while (cin >> tab[k])
  k++;
cout << sum(tab, k);
```

A function can of course have parameters of *class type*: that is, of types that are defined with the use of classes. A parameter can be of a standard class, vector or string for instance, or of a class you have defined yourself. (This will be discussed in Chapter 7.) As an example we construct a new version of the function sum. We let the parameter be a vector instead of an array.

```
int sum(vector<int> a) // sums up the elements in the vector a
{
  int s = 0;
  for (int i=0; i<a.size(); i++)
    s += a[i];
  return s;
}
```

We do not need the second parameter that indicates the length because a vector keeps track of its length. (As you know you can call the member function `size` to find out the length of a vector.) The following program lines demonstrate how to read a number of whole numbers and calculate their sum with the use of the new version of the function `sum`:

```
vector<int> tab;
int tal;
while (cin >> tal)
  tab.push_back(tal);
cout << sum(tab);
```

We shall give yet another example of functions that have arrays as parameters. Here a method of making a more effective search than the linear one discussed on page 63 will be demonstrated. We shall write a function that searches for a given number in an integer array, a prerequisite being that the array to be searched will have been *sorted*. We shall use the following idea.

Look first at the element lying in the middle of the array. Suppose that this element contains the value *m*. If the number searched for is less than *m* we shall know that it must lie (assuming that it exists) in the array's left-hand side, since the array has been sorted. If the number searched for is bigger than *m* it must lie in the right-hand side of the array (again, assuming that it exists). A third possibility is that the number is equal to *m*, in which case the solution is trivial, since we happen to have found the number straight away. Thus, having looked at the number in the middle of the array, we shall either have found the desired number, or we shall know which half of the array we should continue to search.

If we continue our search we can consider the half to be searched as a new array, smaller than the original one. We can then use the same idea again: that is, looking at the element lying in the middle of the new, smaller array. If the desired number is not the one having the value of this element, we can decide whether we want to search in the array's left- or right-hand side. We now apply the same method yet again to the new, still smaller, partial array to be searched. The whole procedure is repeated again and again with ever-decreasing partial arrays until either we have isolated the number we are looking for, or the partial array we are left with is so small that it cannot contain any elements. In the latter case the desired number will not be in the array.

The method just given is a search method usually called a *binary search* (so called because it halves, at every step, the array to be searched).

We now show what the function looks like. It has three parameters, the first being the number we are searching for. The second parameter is the array, and the third is an integer that gives the number of elements in the array. The function gives as result an index for the position in the array occupied by the desired number. If the number does not happen to be in the array, a value of `-1` is returned. We use the variables `first` and `last` so that we shall know the first and last index in the partial array we are searching in. These variables are initialized so that they will describe the whole array from the beginning.

```
// Binary search
int bin_sch(int searched, int f[], int n)
{
  int first = 0, last = n-1;
  while (first <= last)
  {
    int middle = (first + last)/2;
    if (searched < f[middle])
      last = middle-1;
    else if (searched > f[middle])
      first = middle+1;
    else // equal
      return middle;
  }
  return -1; // not found
}
```

This search method is much more effective than a simple linear search. For instance, if you have an array with 100 elements, the binary search algorithm will need to investigate seven elements in the array, if it should come to that, to see whether a particular number is there or not. With a linear search, this 'worst case' would have meant investigating 100 elements. The bigger the array, the greater the efficiency of the method. In an array of 1000 elements, a binary search would have needed to investigate a maximum of only 13 elements at any one time, but with a linear search this figure would have been 1000. Note that there is a standard function `binary_search` that can be used to search for a certain element in a sequence – in a vector for instance.

Functions can be constructed that do not have parameters. As an example, let us write a function `get` that enters an integer from the keyboard. The function should give as result the number entered. To make the function usable, we shall design it so that it will ensure input from the programmer. In other words, if the person running the program happens to make an inputting mistake resulting in a number not being an integer, the function will give an error message warning the user to make a fresh attempt at typing an integer. The function will continue in this way until the user has typed a correct integer, and only then will it return the number entered. We shall use the result value from the input operator `<<` to decide whether a correct integer was entered or not. (Compare with the discussion on page 47.)

```
int get()
{
  int i;
  while (!(cin>>i) || cin.peek()!='\n')
  {
    cout << "Incorrect integer. Try again: ";
    cin.clear(); // clear error state
    cin.ignore(1000, '\n'); // jump to next line
  }
  return i;
}
```

Note that there must be empty parentheses after the function name on the first line. It would also have been permissible to have used the reserved word **void** and then to have written

```
int get(void)
```

The expression `cin>>i` on the fourth line in the function gives the value 'true' if input to the variable `number` has gone well and the value 'false' otherwise. The expression `!(cin>>i)` will then be 'true' if input to `number` has miscarried. The expression `cin.peek()!='\n'` is computed if input to the variable `number` has gone well. The function `peek` peeks at the next character waiting to be input. This character should be an end-of-line character, since the user is expected to press the Enter key after the integer has been typed. If the next character is not an end-of-line character, incorrect data has been input after the integer.

A round of the **while** statement is executed every time the user inputs incorrect data. First an error message is given; then `clear` is called to discontinue the error condition in the input stream. The standard function `cin.ignore` is used to skip the whole of the incorrect line the user has written. Of course the user would welcome the opportunity of writing a new number from the beginning. The argument `1000` of `ignore` means that at most 1000 characters may be skipped in the input stream, and the argument `'\n'` denotes that characters should be skipped until an end-of-line character has been encountered. The end-of-line character will then be the last one to be skipped. The statements

```
cout << "Write an integer: ";
n = get();
cout << n;
```

can give the following output at the terminal when the program is run:

```
Write an integer: xy23
Incorrect integer. Try again: 12.6
Incorrect integer. Try again: 45
45
```

When you call a function that does not have parameters, you still need the parentheses in the call. Thus we wrote `get()`. If the parentheses are forgotten, an error message will appear saying that the types are incorrect. Sometimes the outcome can be even worse: the program may be compiled but the function will not be called. Instead you will get a pointer to the function as a result. (Pointers will be dealt with later in the book.)

4.2 Functions that do not return a value

Up to now we have shown functions of a particular category – those that compute and return a value. Now we shall give some examples of functions of another category – functions that do not return a value but only perform something. As our first example we shall show a simple function that ensures that printout begins on a new line at the terminal. We call this function `new_line`.

```
void new_line() //Gives new printout line
{
   cout << endl;
}
```

The reserved word **void** that comes first indicates that the function will not return a value. A function that does not give a result does not need a **return** statement. Execution in the function stops when you come to the last right-hand brace. You can have **return** statements in functions that do not return a value, but then there should not be an expression after the word **return**. When you call a function which does not leave a value, there will not of course be a value to deal with. The function call becomes a statement as, for example,

```
new_line();
```

In the function `get`, on page 118, we called the standard function `cin.ignore` to skip all the input characters up to the beginning of the next line. We made the call `cin.ignore(1000,'\n');`. This does not look very nice; besides, an upper bound must be given for the number of characters to be skipped. We shall therefore write our own function `skip_line`, which will accomplish the same thing but which does not have any parameters. It also does not have an upper bound for the number of skipped characters. The function is called by writing

```
skip_line();
```

After the call, the first character comes on the next input line waiting to be read. The function is very simple. It reads one character at a time until either an end-of-file mark is encountered, or until an end-of-line character has been read in.

```
void skip_line() // Jumps to the next line to be read
{
  while (cin.peek() != EOF && cin.get() != '\n')
    ;
}
```

The functions `new_line` and `skip_line` did not have parameters. In the next example we shall look at the function `change_to`, which will not return a value but which has parameters. The purpose of the function is to change text strings. It changes a character to another character every time it occurs in a text string. How it is intended to function is best shown by the example below. The lines of the program

```
char a[100] = "C\tfor\tyourself";
cout << a << endl;
change_to(a, '\t', ' ');
cout << a << endl;
```

change all the tabulator characters in the text string in `a` to spaces. The output will be

```
C       for     yourself
C for yourself
```

Here is the function:

```
void change_to(char s[], char c, char cnew)
{
  int n = 0;
  while (s[n] != '\0')
  {
    if (s[n] == c)
      s[n] = cnew;
    n++;
  }
}
```

It is remarkable, if you think about it, that the argument `a` in the call should be changed. We stated earlier that values of arguments were *copied* to a function's parameters and that the function then worked with these copies; in which case it should not be possible for `a` to be changed. That this in fact happens, stems from the fact that `a` is an array. The rules for arrays are rather special. When a function is called, the values in an array are not copied to a corresponding parameter. The parameter will instead contain a pointer to the array. The parameter `s` in our example thus points to the array `a`, and this is why `a` is changed. We shall be studying the linkage between pointers and arrays in much more detail later in the book.

We saw in the previous chapter that, when you read in text strings, you had to combine the input operator `>>` with the manipulator `setw` so as not to run the risk of data landing outside the character array being read to. An alternative was to use the standard function `cin.getline`, but this always reads an *entire* line. We shall now write our own function that accomplishes the same thing as the operator `>>` in combination with `setw`: that is, it skips white characters and then reads up to the next white character. This function is called `get`:

```
void get(char s[], int n)
{
  int i = 0;
  cin >> ws; // skip over white characters
  while (i < n-1 &&
         cin.peek() != ' ' && cin.peek() != '\t' &&
         cin.peek() != '\n' && cin.peek() != EOF)
  {
    cin >> s[i]; // read a non-white character
    i++;
  }
  s[i] = '\0';
}
```

The function has two parameters: the first, `s`, is the character array we want to read into and the other, `n`, is an integer that indicates the size of the array. The function reads at most `n-1` characters from `cin`. Before it ends, it always puts a null character last in the text string in `s`. We first use the manipulator `ws` within the function to skip all initial white characters. Then comes a **`while`** statement that reads all the non-white characters. The **`while`** statement is ended when a new white character is encountered, or when the input data has finished.

The variable `i` is a counter that notes where the next character is to be inserted in the character array `s`. If we call the function `get` when there is no longer any input data to be read, no rounds of the **`while`** statement will be executed. This means that the variable `i` has the value `0` in the function's last statement and that the null character is placed first in `s`. The character array `s` will thus contain a text string of length `0`.

As we saw in Chapter 2, it can be rather difficult to edit outputs in C++. This is especially true of real numbers when the correction to a certain number of decimal places and right-hand justifying is required. Then the manipulators `setprecision`, `setiosflags` and `setw` must be used. We shall now construct a function that we shall call `put` and which is much easier to use. We let the function have three parameters. The first is the number that will be written out, the second gives how many positions the function will write out in front of the decimal point, and the third gives how many decimals are to be written out. Let us suppose, for example, that we want to write out the values in the variables `y` and `z` with three positions in front of the decimal point and to two decimal places. We can then call our new function `put`:

```
put(y,3,2);
new_line();
put(z,3,2);
```

(Here we have also called the new function `new_line`, which we defined on page 119.) If `y` contains the value `23.907` and `z` the value `318.2`, the function will write out

```
 23.91
318.20
```

The function looks as given below. The different manipulators for writing out and editing the parameter `x` are used on the first two lines inside the function. The last line restores the output stream to its standard values, so that any output coming after will not be affected by this output.

```
void put(double x, int before, int aft)
{
  cout << setprecision(aft)   << setiosflags(ios::fixed)
       << setw(before+aft+1)  << x
       << setprecision(6)     << resetiosflags(ios::fixed);
}
```

Let us now discuss for a moment the function `main`. Why does it look so different? We normally write

```
main()
{...
}
```

Shouldn't **void** be written in front of the function name to indicate that `main` will not leave a result? No; it would certainly be possible to do this but it would not be quite correct, since `main` actually leaves a value of type **int** as a result to the operating system. For historical reasons (an inheritance from C), it is assumed that the function will return a value of type **int** if a return type from a function has not been indicated. It would therefore be more correct to write

```
int main()
{...
  return 0;
}
```

The first way of writing this is more pleasing, and the standard permits you to omit having a **return** statement at this point in the function `main`.

4.3 Declaration scope and visibility

In programs you use entities, variables or functions for example, that you yourself have declared. Entities can be declared at many different places in a C++ program. Common functions are always defined at the outermost level in a program. It is in fact permitted to define variables there. Variables may also be declared in *blocks*. A block is an area of the program included in braces. All the variables seen so far have been declared within blocks. A third place where declarations may be made is in the function head, where function parameters are declared. Apart from these, declarations may also be made in classes and name spaces, but these will be discussed later in the book. Here are some examples of declarations:

```
int x;
int f1(char c)
{
  double y;
  while (y>0)
  {
    char x;
    ...
  }
  int w;
  ...
}
void f2()
{
  int y, z;
  ...
}
```

The integer variable `x` and the functions `f1` and `f2` are declared at the outermost level. The variables `y`, `w` and `z`, together with the **`char`** variable `x`, are declared in blocks. The variable `w` is an example to show that in C++ declarations can be put anywhere in a block. Thus they do not have to come before the statements.

An important concept is the *declaration scope* of an entity. The declaration scope of a program is that area of the program for which the declaration is valid. For all entities (except members of classes) the declaration scope begins at that point of the program where the entity is declared. How far the declaration scope extends will then depend on the position of the declaration. If the declaration occurs at the outermost level in a program, the declaration scope will extend right to the end of the program text file. If a declaration occurs in a block, the declaration scope will extend to the end of the block (to the right-hand brace), and if the declaration concerns a function parameter, the declaration scope will extend to the end of the function body (to the last right-hand brace).

Special rules apply to **`if`** statements, **`while`** statements, **`for`** statements and **`switch`** statements. (We shall discuss **`switch`** statements later.) If an entity is declared inside the parentheses following **`if`**, **`while`**, **`for`** or **`switch`**, the declaration scope will include both the area inside the parentheses and one or more statements controlled by the statement. Here are some examples:

```
if (int k = n)
{ // declaration scope for k
   ...
}
else
{ // k is also declared here
   ...
}
// Here k is NOT declared

for (int j=1; j<=n; j++)
{ // declaration scope for j
   ...
}
// Here j is NOT declared
```

For an entity to be used in a program it must be *visible* (for example, the use of a variable or the call of a function). An entity is visible in the whole of its declaration scope as long as it is not *hidden* (see below) by another entity of the same name. In the example on page 123 the parameter `c` and the **`double`** variable `y` are visible only in the function body of `f1` (also inside the inner block after **`while`**); the variable `x` of type **`char`** is visible only in the inner block of `f1`; the variable `w` is visible only in the last part of `f1`; and the variable `z` is visible only inside `f2`.

Normally, you may not declare several entities with the same name in a particular declaration scope. On the other hand, it is permissible to have the same name in different declaration scopes. In the previous example, for instance, we were allowed to have two variables called `x` and two called `y` since they did not lie in the same block. If an entity *e1* is declared in an inner block and if in the surrounding block there is another entity *e2* with the same name, the *e1* entity will hide the *e2* entity in the innermost block. (In the outer block, *e1* is not visible and *e2* is not hidden there.) In our example, the integer variable `x` is hidden in the inner block of `f1`. If `x` is written there, it would denote the **`char`** variable `x`.

If you want to access a hidden entity, the operator `::` can be used. For instance, we can write, in the innermost block of `f1`,

```
cout << x;   // the char variable is written out
cout << ::x; // the integer variable is written out
```

Where functions are concerned, there is in C++ an important exception to the rule that several entities may not have the same name in a declaration scope. It is permissible to have several different functions with the same name. In the previous section, on page 122, we constructed a function with the name `put`, which wrote out and edited real numbers. We can produce two other functions with the name `put`. One will write out and edit integers and the other one will write out text strings:

```
void put(int i, int width)
{
  cout << setw(width) << i;
}
void put(char s[])
{
  cout << s;
}
```

Now suppose that we have the following program lines:

```
double y = 43.138;
int k = 8;
put(y, 3, 2);
put(" and\n");
put(k, 3);
```

We then get written out

```
43.14 and
8
```

When two or more functions have the same name, we say that the functions are *overloaded*. It is permissible to have overloaded functions on condition that they have different parameters. The number of parameters and/or parameter types must be different. This is a condition because the compiler has to be able to compare the actual arguments with the parameters and 'understand' which function is to be called. Only one of the overloaded functions may pass; if this were not so, the program would be ambiguous.

Overloaded functions

Several functions may have the same name, or be overloaded, if they have a different number of parameters or parameter types.

4.4 Function declarations

The first complete program example in this chapter had the structure

```
#include <iostream>
using namespace std;
double meanv (double x1, double x2)
```

```
{
   return (x1+x2)/2;
}
main ()
{
   ...
   mv = meanv(number1, number2);
   ...
}
```

We see that the definition of the function `meanv` has been put before the definition of the function `main`. This is because a function in C++ must be visible before it can be called. If `main` had been put before `meanv`, `meanv` would have been unknown to the compiler when the call came up in `main`. The option still exists of putting `main` before the definition of `meanv`, however. In this case, a separate *function declaration* (also called a *prototype*) of the function `meanv` must be inserted before `main`.

In C++ the difference between the concepts *`declaration`* and *`definition`* is pointedly emphasized. When an entity is *declared*, it is given a name and its characteristics are listed. A *definition* gives an entity a name as well, but a definition also sees to it that memory space is reserved for the thing defined. A definition can be said to be that place in a program where the thing defined really 'exists', while a declaration is only an indication of something that exists somewhere else. You may often have only a definition, for example, when you declare a variable in a function. Then this also serves as a declaration.

A function *declaration* contains only the function head itself. When you have a separate function declaration, the complete *definition* of the function must exist in some other place: for instance, later in the program text. Our program could have the following structure:

```
#include <iostream>
using namespace std;
double meanv (double x1, double x2); // declaration
main ()
{
   mv = meanv(number1, number2);
   ...
}
double meanv (double x1, double x2) // definition
{
   return (x1+x2)/2;
}
```

In a function declaration, it is permissible to omit the names of the parameters; only the types have to be indicated. Thus the declaration of the function `meanv` could have looked like this:

```
double meanv (double, double);
```

For someone who wants only to call a function, it may of course be of little interest what the names of the parameters are inside the function. The important thing is to know what types they have, but sometimes it can be be useful to remember the parameter names, since they shed light on the order in which they are to come; this can be hard to remember if you have several parameters of the same type.

Function declarations

Before a function can be called, it must be *declared.*

This can be done either in a function *definition* or in a function *declaration.* A function declaration contains only the function head (it is also called a *prototype*):

result_type names (*type1 param1*, *type2 param2*, etc.);

The parameter names may be omitted.

4.5 Division of programs

We shall now discuss how you can divide a program into several program text files, or source text files, so that the different files can be compiled separately. As an example we shall write a program that reads in a text, word for word, and computes the number of words in the text, as well as the average length of a word. We can use several of the functions we constructed earlier in this chapter. We shall construct the following program and put it into a text file with the name `main.cpp`:

```
main()
{
char a[30];
double  sum = 0;
int n = 0;
get(a,30);
while(strlen(a) > 0)
{
  n++;
  sum += strlen(a);
  get(a,30);
}
put("Number of words:");
put(n, 13);
new_line();
put("Average length:");
put(sum/n, 3, 1); new_line();
}
```

If we try to compile this file as it is here, the compiler will complain that it does not recognize the functions `get`, `strlen`, `put` and `new_line`. We begin by discussing the function `strlen`.

This is a standard function. We know from experience that the following line must first be inserted in the program:

```
#include <cstring>
```

But why is it in order to call `strlen` when this line is included? The file `cstring` is a quite normal text file that contains program text. It is an example of a *header file*. Other header files we have met before are `iostream` and `iomanip`. There is a header file for each library of standard functions. It is an old tradition (an inheritance from C) that header files have names that end with `.h` , where the 'h' stands for 'header', but this does not apply to the standard libraries in the C++ standard. Suppose now that you have a program text file with the name `file1`, and that you insert a line with the directive `#include <file2>` at a certain position in this file: then the compiler, when it is about to compile `file1`, will read and compile all the text that is in `file2`, exactly as if this text had been in the position indicated in `file1`. So what kind of text is there in a header file? Most header files contain a number of function *declarations* – that is, declarations of function heads. Header files do *not*, however, contain function definitions, the complete functions. There is in the file `cstring`, for example, a line that looks roughly like this:

```
int strlen (char s[]);
```

After the file `cstring`, has been included in our program, the function `strlen` will have been declared and can be called.

We have written the other functions that are called in the program – that is, `get`, `put` and `new_line` – ourselves. They are useful in reading and writing, and could be useful in other programs too. We therefore choose to put their *definitions* into a separate file with the name `simpleio.cpp`. The functions must be *declared* in `main` so that they can be called there. One way is to put the following function declarations in the file `main.cpp` before the definition of `main`:

```
void get(char s[], int n);
void put(double x, int before, int aft);
void put(int i, int width);
void put(char s[]);
void new_line();
```

This is not a good solution, however. The first problem is that all the function heads in the file `main.cpp` must be written again. This is troublesome, and there is a great risk of making mistakes when typing: as a result the contents of the function definitions may not be exactly the same as in the file `simpleio.cpp`. The other problem is that lines at the beginning of every new program have to be entered to call the functions in `simpleio.cpp`.

A much better solution is to use a header file, just as you do for standard functions, since header files can also be created for functions you write yourself. If you include the file `myfile.h` that you yourself have created, you should give the directive

```
#include "myfile.h"
```

The file name is put between double quotes instead of the signs `< >`, which are used only for standard files. When double quotes are used, the compiler will know that it is a personally created file and it should search for this file in the programmer's current directory in the file system. When you include standard files, the compiler will look in another section of the file system.

We shall now make a text file with the name `simpleio.h` and in it put declarations of the functions `get`, `put` and `new_line`. We shall also include the function `skip_line` in the file, although it will not be called in this example. The file `simpleio.h` will afterwards be included in the main program. Our program will now consist of three files – `main.cpp`, `simpleio.h` and `simpleio.cpp`:

```
// The file main.cpp
#include <cstring>
#include "simpleio.h"
using namespace std;
main()
{
  ... // as before
}
```

```
// The file simpleio.h
void get(char s[], int n);
void skip_line(); // Jumps to the next input line
void put(double x, int before, int aft);
void put(int i, int width);
void put(char s[]);
void new_line(); // Gives new output line
```

```
// The file simpleio.cpp
#include <iostream>
#include <iomanip>
#include "simpleio.h"
using namespace std;
void get(char s[], int n)
{
  int i = 0;
  cin >> ws;  // Skip white characters
  while (i < n-1 &&
         cin.peek() != ' '  && cin.peek() != '\t' &&
```

```
          cin.peek() != '\n' && cin.peek() != EOF)
  {
    cin >> s[i]; // Read a non-white character
    i++;
  }
  s[i] = '\0';
}
void skip_line() // Jumps forward to next input line
{
  while (cin.peek() != EOF && cin.get() != '\n')
    ;
}
void put(double x, int before, int aft)
{
  cout << setprecision(aft)    << setiosflags(ios::fixed)
       << setw(before+aft+1)   << x
       << setprecision(6)      << resetiosflags(ios::fixed);
}
void put(int i, int width)
{
  cout << setw(width) << i;
}
void put(char s[])
{
  cout << s;
}
void new_line() // Gives new output line
{
  cout << endl;
}
```

Division of programs into several files

- A program can consist of several separate parts. Each part contains a pair consisting of a *definition file* and a *header file*.
- A definition file contains function definitions.
- A header file contains function declarations.
- The header file is included in its corresponding definition file and in other files where the functions in use will be called.

This is a general model that illustrates the division of programs. Files are always constructed *in pairs*. For every file that contains function definitions or *definition file*, a corresponding header file is written.

All the functions in the definition file capable of being called from other parts of the program should be declared in the header file. Note particularly that the header file is to be included in the definition file. In our example the file `simpleio.h` has been included in the file `simpleio.cpp` (on the fourth line). This may seem strange. Do you need to declare the functions again in the definition file? No, this is not actually necessary, although it's a very good habit to cultivate, for then the compiler, when the definition file is compiled, will check that the declarations in the header file really accord with the definitions in the definition file. You can then be sure that the header file is correct.

In order to run our example program, it must of course be compiled. Two separate compilings are needed, one for the file `main.cpp` and another for the file `simpleio.cpp`. Then the whole program will be linked together. In an MS-DOS Window, for instance, the following commands may be needed:

```
gxx -c main.cpp
gxx -c simpleio.cpp
gxx -o wordprog.exe main.o simpleio.o
```

The first two lines compile the files `main.cpp` and `simpleio.cpp`. The result of these compilings will be two object files, `main.o` and `simpleio.o` respectively. The last command links together the two object files into a program that can be run. The argument `-o wordprog` indicates that the program to be run will be called `wordprog`. Note that the header file `simpleio.h` does not need to be compiled separately. It will be compiled as soon as it is included in the other files.

This model can be generalized to programs that are made up of any number of separately compiled files. All the files (except the file with the main program) will be in pairs, every pair consisting of a definition file and a header file.

4.6 Reference parameters

On page 118 we wrote a function, `get`, that reads in an integer from the keyboard. If incorrect input data is entered, the function will output an error message asking the person running the program to enter the number again. The function can be called by writing

```
n = get();
```

This is a useful function, so we shall want to put it into our `simpleio` package from the previous section. We should also like to have a corresponding function there with the name `get`, which reads in a real number instead of an integer. This could be called in the following way (`y` has type **`double`**):

```
y = get();
```

We should then have two functions with the declarations

```
int get();
double get(); // Incorrect overload
```

But it does not work. The overload mechanism in C++ is valid only for parameters and not for result types. For two functions to have the same name they must have different parameters. If we redesign our `get` functions so that they do not give the number entered as a result but instead have a parameter, then overloading will work. They can then be called in the following way:

```
get(n);
get(y);
```

We begin by trying to rewrite the function get, which reads integers:

```
void get(int i) // Incorrect function
{
  while (!(cin >> i) || cin.peek() != '\n')
  {
    cout << "Incorrect integer. Try again: ";
    cin.clear();
    skip_line();
  }
}
```

(Here, the function `skip_line` from page 119 has been used.) Now we call the function `get` with the following lines:

```
int n=0;
cout << "Write an integer: ";
get(n);
cout << "The number is: " << n;
```

A test run will give the output

```
Write an integer: 45
The number is: 0
```

Now something is wrong here! In section 4.1 we discussed how function calls were implemented, and we saw that when a function was called, *value calls* were normally used: this meant that the values of the arguments were *copied* to corresponding parameters where the parameters could be considered as *local* variables inside the function. What happens here when `get` is called, therefore, is that a value of `0` is copied to the parameter `i`. The parameter `i` is a local variable inside the function, and in the expression `cin>>i` an integer is read to this local variable. The variable `n` is not at all affected by this. It will still have a value of `0`. But it is of course the variable `n` we want to read an integer to. How is `get` to be formulated so that this happens? To write `cin>>n` inside `get` is, of course, a silly idea because we cannot always be sure that the name of the argument will be `n` and the variable `n` is not visible in `get`. The solution is to use a *reference parameter*:

```
void get(int& i)
{
  while (!(cin >> i) || cin.peek() != '\n')
  {
    cout << "Incorrect integer. Try again: ";
    cin.clear();
    skip_line();
  }
}
```

The only change made is that the parameter type `i` has been changed from `int` to `int&`. The character `&` is the important thing here. It indicates that `i` is not an ordinary value parameter but a *reference parameter*. The parameter `i` is a *reference* to a variable of type `int`, and it will refer to the variable given as an argument when the function is called. This means that `i` can no longer be considered to be a local variable inside the function `get`. Instead, it can be thought of as an alternative name for the argument given in the call. If, as before, the call

```
get(n);
```

is made, then `i` is a reference to `n` and can be considered as an alternative name to `n`. This means that if the variable `i` in `get` is changed, the variable `n` will in fact be changed. An integer will thus be read into `n`. This is of course exactly what we wanted. Figure 4.3 shows how it looks. When reference parameters are used, we say that we use *call by reference* instead of 'value call', which is the usual mechanism in C++.

We can now write the second `get` function, the one that reads a real number:

```
void get(double& x)
{
  while (!(cin >> x) || cin.peek() != '\n')
  {
    cout << "Incorrect real number. Try again: ";
    cin.clear();
    skip_line();
  }
}
```

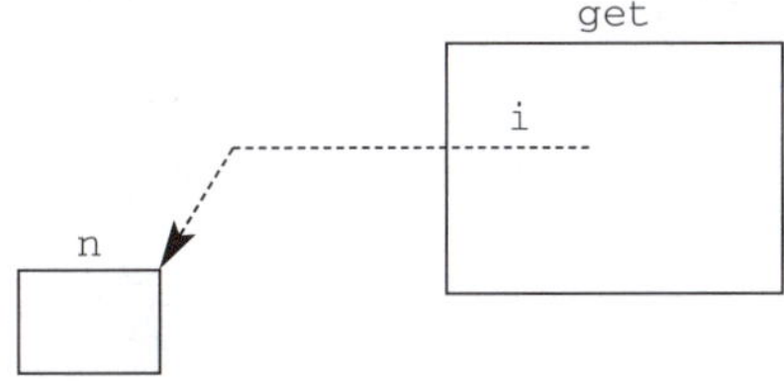

Figure 4.3

The overload mechanism will now work. If the variable `n` has type **`int`** and the variable `y` type **`double`**, we can carry out the following call, and the compiler will be able to decide which `get` is to be called:

```
get(n);
get(y);
```

We can now supplement our `simpleio` package with the two `get` functions. The definitions are put into the file `simpleio.cpp` and the declarations into the file `simpleio.h`, which will look like this:

```
// The file simpleio.h
void get(char s[], int n);
void skip_line();
void get(int& i);
void get(double& x);
void put(double x, int before, int aft);
void put(int i, int width);
void put(char s[]);
void new_line();
```

Thus there are now three overloaded functions with the name `get` here. We discussed the first of these on page 121. It reads a text into a character array. Note that you never have reference parameters when the parameter is an array because the name of an array is already a kind of reference to the array. You could say that arrays are always called by reference. This is not the case for parameters of class type, `vector` and `string` for instance. As an example let us study a new version of the function `change_to` from page 120. In the new version the parameter is a `string` instead of a character array:

```
void change_to(string s, char c, char cnew) // Incorrect
{
   for (int n=0; n<s.size(); n++)
      if (s[n] == c)
         s[n] = cnew;
}
```

Now let us test the function with the following lines. We try to change all tabulator characters to spaces.

```
string a = "C\tfor\tyourself";
cout << a << endl;
change_to(a, '\t', ' ');
cout << a << endl;
```

The printout will be

```
C     for     yourself
C     for     yourself
```

As you can see, the text in the `string` variable `a` is not changed by the call. This is because the parameter `s` is a *copy* of `a`. To be able to change the variable that is given as argument a reference parameter must be used. The first line in the function then becomes

```
void change_to(string& s, char c, char cnew) // Correct
```

When a function with reference parameters is called, the current argument must be able to be changed. Normally, a variable name is given to it. For example, the following call of `get` is not allowed:

```
get(n+k); // Incorrect reference call
```

A reference parameter must be used if an argument is to be changed in a function call. This may be necessary if you construct a function that gives more than one result. (Of course, only *one* result can be given with a **return** statement.) As an example of this we shall construct a function `roots` to calculate the two real roots of a second-order equation of the form $x^2 + px + q = 0$, the roots of which are given by the formula

$$x = \frac{-p}{2} \pm \sqrt{\left(\frac{p^2}{4} - q\right)}$$

We let the function we want to write have two reference parameters, `root1` and `root2`, in which the calculated roots are given as a result. The expression within the square root sign, the discriminant, must be greater or equal to zero if the equation has real roots. The function can therefore calculate the roots only if that is the case. For the function to be able to tell the caller whether or not the roots were calculated, it is given a third reference parameter `ok`, which we set to 'true' if the real roots were calculated, and to 'false' otherwise. The parameter `ok` may have type **bool**.

Here is a program in which the function `roots` is called. We shall make use of the input and output functions in `simpleio` in this example, to demonstrate how you can use your own packages with help functions.

```
#include <cmath>
#include <iostream>
using namespace std;
#include "simpleio.h"
void roots(double p, double q,
           double& root1, double& root2, bool& ok)
{
  double d = p*p/4-q;
  if (d < 0)
```

```
      ok = false;
    else
    {
      ok = true;
      root1 = -p/2+sqrt(d);
      root2 = -p/2-sqrt(d);
    }
  }
```

```
main ()
{
  double a, b, r1, r2;
  bool went_well;
  put("p? "); get(a);
  put("q? "); get(b);
  roots(a, b, r1, r2, went_well);
  if (went_well)
  {
    put("The roots are "); put(r1,1,2);
    put(" and "); put(r2,1,2);
  }
  else put("No real roots");
}
```

We have now discussed the two kinds of parameter you can have in functions – value parameters and reference parameters. When you want to write a function you must choose the parameters you need. A particular function can have parameters of both kinds. 'Value parameter' and 'reference parameter' are terms that reflect the technical aspect of how to transfer parameter values. Another way of looking at it is not to worry about the technical aspect at all but, instead, to think of which values will go *in* and which values will come *out* of a function; then the terms *inparameter* and *outparameter* are often used. Inparameters are used to carry data into a function from the calling program, and outparameters are used to carry data in the opposite direction. In the function `rooter` above, for example, `p` and `q` are inparameters, while `root1`, `root2` and `ok` are outparameters. Sometimes there is also a third category of parameter, *in/outparameters*. These are used to carry data both into and out of a function. If we write a function with a parameter `p` that is a character array and the function's task is to change all the lower-case letters to upper-case in the text string in `p`, then `p` can be considered to be an in/outparameter. The text string's old values must, of course, be carried into the function for it to know which characters are to be transformed, and the altered text string must be carried out of the function.

What then is the relationship between in- and outparameters and between value and reference parameters? You could say that if a choice must be made between an in- and an outparameter (or possibly an in/outparameter), then it is a question of choosing the one that gives the correct technical solution; you can choose either value parameters or

> **Reference parameters**
>
> *Function name*`(`*type*`& p);` // declaration
> *Function name*`(a);` // call
>
> - The parameter `p` is a reference to argument `a`.
> - Can be thought of as another name for `a`.
> - The argument `a` must be changeable, e.g. to a variable.
> - Are not used for arrays. An array is already a kind of reference.

reference parameters. For arrays, there is no choice: you must always have some kind of reference parameter, since a parameter that is an array is in fact a reference to the array given as argument when the function is called. If it is not a question of an array, you have to choose. Outparameters and in/outparameters are the simplest to use. Here you must always have reference parameters.

In terms of inparameters, we have used value parameters in all our examples so far. Since an inparameter should be used only to carry data into a function, corresponding arguments in the call should remain constant, and technically speaking this is the case with value parameters. Now you might not see why you should not use reference parameters as inparameters, since the function could get at the argument's value directly. The problem here is that it would be possible to change the argument's value inside the function, but this is not meant to be possible for inparameters. There are occasions when it is more effective to use reference parameters as inparameters. This is when you have large parameters that need a great many bytes of memory space. It is impractical here to use value parameters, since the entire argument value must be copied when a call is made. A reference, on the other hand, always consists of a small number of bytes and is therefore always easy to transfer. To eliminate the risk of an argument's value somehow changing inside the function, you can declare the parameter as a reference to a *constant* value.

Before we give an example, let us simply discuss which parameters can be considered to be large. The built-in types, such as, for example, **`int`** and **`double`**, are not large. They can be transferred as quickly as a reference. When you have inparameters of one of the built-in types, it is therefore easiest to use ordinary value parameters. It is parameters of class type that can be large. Classes will be described in more detail later in the book, but we have in fact already come upon types which are defined with the help of classes: they are the standard types `vector`, `deque` and `string`. A variable of some of this type can be very large. (Note that a variable of type `vector`, `deque` or `string` is not an array; it contains an array, but also more information.)

As an example we shall now construct a function with the name `word`, which will check whether a variable of type `string` contains a word. As result, the function will leave the value **true** or **false**. When we speak of a 'word', we mean a text that consists only of letters. The variable to be checked is given as argument for the function. It is clear that here we should use an inparameter. The variable's value must of course be carried into the function in order to be checked, but it may not be changed. It would be inappropriate to let the parameter be a value parameter in this example, since it could be large, and then copying would be unproductive. Instead, we shall let the parameter be a reference to a constant `string`. In this example there is also a main program that reads the groups of characters typed in at the keyboard and indicates whether they can be considered to be words.

```
#include <iostream>
#include <string>
using namespace std;
bool word (const string& s)
{
  int i = 0;
  while (i<s.length())
  {
    char c = s[i];
    if ((c >= 'a' & c <= 'z') &
        (c >= 'A' & c <= 'Z'))
      i++;
    else
      return false;
  }
  return true;
}
main ()
{
  string w;
  while (cin >> w)
    if (word(w))
      cout << "A word"  << endl;
    else
      cout << "No word" << endl;
}
```

It is common in C++ to use references to constants when the parameters have class type.

4.7 Parameters with default values

If a function has a certain number of parameters, then normally the same number of arguments must be indicated when the function is called. In C++, however, it is possible to leave out certain arguments when making the call. A condition for this is that the corresponding parameters should have default values. An example will best show how this works. We shall construct a function, `write_several`, which has two parameters. The first one indicates a character to be written and the second indicates how many times the character should be written.

```
void write_several (char c, int num=1)
{
  for (int i=1; i<= num; i++)
    cout << c;
}
```

We have given the parameter `num` a default value of `1` here. This value will automatically be used if the corresponding argument is omitted in a call. If the argument is not omitted, then its value will be used as usual. Examples of calls that are allowed are:

```
write_several('x', 4); // Four 'x's are written out
write_several('y');    // One 'y' is written out
```

A default value may not be redefined, not even to the same value. This means that if you have a separate function declaration (prototype), you ought to indicate the default value in it and not in the complete function definition. This is shown here for the function `write_several`:

```
void write_several (char c, int sum=1); // declaration
void write_several (char c, int sum)    // definition
{
  ...
}
```

If a parameter has a default value, all the parameters *following* it must have default values. For instance, we could extend our function with yet another parameter that indicates whether or not each character should be written on its own line:

```
void write_several (char c, int num=1, bool separate_lines=false)
{
  for (int i=1; i <= num; i++)
  {
    cout << c;
    if (separate_lines)
      cout << endl;
  }
}
```

Here are a few examples of calls:

```
write_several('+');           // One + is written
write_several('?', 7);        // Seven ?s on the same line
write_several('%', 5, true); // Five %s on separate lines
```

4.8 Recursive functions

We have seen that a function can call another function. Furthermore, a function can call itself, and such a function is called a *recursive function*. Recursive functions are used to solve certain types of problem. The problems for which recursion is most useful are those that are defined from the start in a recursive way: this occurs often in mathematical calculations. The most common example of a recursive function – an example that occurs in almost all books about programming – is a function to calculate the factorial of a number n. We studied this problem earlier (in section 2.9, page 71). We then used iteration to solve the problem, but now we shall see how recursion can be used instead.

The factorial of a number n, written $n!$, can be defined by

$$n! = \begin{cases} 1 & \text{if } n = 0 \\ 1 \times 2 \times 3 \times \ldots \times n & \text{if } n > 0 \end{cases}$$

Another way of writing the definition is

$$n! = \begin{cases} 1 & \text{if } n = 0 \\ n(n-1)! & \text{if } n > 0 \end{cases}$$

There is one case where the value is given (that is $0! = 1$) and one case where induction is used to express the solution in terms of values already defined. This second definition leads naturally to the following C++ function:

```
int nfac(int n) // calculate n!
{
  if (n <= 0)
    return 1;
  else
    return n * nfac(n-1);
}
```

It is the last line but one that is the most interesting. There the function `nfac` calls itself. (The parameter `n` should never be less than zero, but we have written the condition `n<=0` in the `if` statement to avoid problems if the function should be incorrectly called with a negative value in the parameter.)

Those who have not worked with recursion before usually think that it is a little strange. But remember a fundamental rule: recursive function calls work in *exactly the same way* as other function calls. There are no special rules for recursion. This means that when a function is called (itself, or another one), the current parameters are calculated first. Memory space is then generated for the called function's formal parameters, and the current parameters are copied into this space. More memory space is generated for the formal parameters at *every* new call. If a particular function is called several times, this will mean that *each* instance of the function will have its *own instance* of the formal parameters. The statements are then executed in the function called. When these statements are completed, you return to the point where the function was called. Thus if a function calls itself, you return to a point inside the function in question.

Let us take a concrete case and discuss exactly what happens. We shall suppose that in a program there is the following statement:

```
m = nfac(3);
```

The function `nfac` is called. Space is generated for the formal parameter `n`, which will have a value of `3`. Since `n` is greater than `0`, the statement after **`else`** will be performed. Now there is a new call of the function `nfac`. The value of the current parameter `n-1` will be `2`. New space is generated for the formal parameter `n`, and this space has the value `2`. At this moment, then, there will be two different formal parameters, both with the name `n`. The first one, with a value of `3`, belongs to the first instance of `nfac` and the second one, with a value of `2`, belongs to the second instance of `nfac`.

In the second instance of `nfac`, `n` is greater than zero as well, so the statement after **`else`** is performed. Now `nfac` is called for the third time, and another formal parameter `n`, which has a value of `1`, is generated. The statement after **`else`** in the third instance of `nfac` will also be executed, since 1 is greater than 0. The function `nfac` is called for the fourth time, and this time another formal parameter with the name `n` is created. This will have a value of `0`. No less than four different formal parameters with the name `n` will be existing at the same time.

In the fourth instance of `nfac` the condition after **`if`** will be true. The statement

```
return 1;
```

will therefore be executed. As usual, this means that the function is interrupted, a result value of `1` is returned, and there is a jump to the point where the call took place. Since the fourth call of `nfac` took place from the statement

```
return n * nfac(n-1);
```

the function will jump back to this point. That the result value is `1` means that the expression `n*1` should be calculated. But what value does `n` have? In the fourth instance of `nfac`, `n` had a value of `0`, but the fourth instance has now been terminated. We have returned to the third instance, and there `n` had a value of `1`. Thus the expression `1*1` is calculated. Now execution of the **`return`** statement can be completed, which means that the third instance of `nfac` will now be terminated. A result value of `1` is returned, and the function jumps back to the point where the call took place. We return again to the statement

```
return n * nfac(n-1);
```

Since we now return to the second instance of `nfac`, `n` will this time have a value of `2`. Therefore the expression `2*1` is calculated. Instance number 2 is now terminated with a result value of `2`, and the function jumps back again to the point of the call: that is, to the statement

```
return n * nfac(n-1);
```

We have now returned to instance number 1 of `nfac`, where `n` had a value of `3`. Since the result value of the expression `nfac(n-1)` was `2`, the expression `3*2` will now be calculated. Thus the result of instance number 1 of `nfac` will be a value of `6`. Now instance number 1 will be terminated, and there will be a return to the point of call. The first call of `nfac` took place from the statement

```
m = nfac(3);
```

so the return will be to this point, and the variable `m` will be assigned a value of `6`.

Recursive function

- A function that directly or indirectly calls itself.
- During execution there are as many instances of the function as the number of non-terminated calls made.
- Each instance of the function has its own values for formal parameters and local variables.

Recursive solutions always follow the same pattern. Given a problem, first identify one (or more) special case(s) where the solution is trivial (`n=0` in `nfac`). Then try to reformulate the problem so that it somehow becomes simpler ($(n-1)!$ is simpler than $n!$). You may then have the idea that the function you are trying to write already exists, and this will solve the simpler problem.

As an example of this, we shall construct a recursive function that reads text from the terminal and writes it out backwards. To solve this problem, we use the following recursive idea:

1. Try to read the first character in the text and store it.
   If it could be read, do the following:
   1.1. Read in the rest of the text and write it out backwards.
   1.2. Write out the first character of the text.

The trivial special case is that the text has no characters, in which case we do not do anything. In step 1.1 we assume that there already exists a function that can read the text and write it out backwards. We make use of this function to solve the simpler problem that arises when the text is one character shorter than it was at the beginning. If we now translate this algorithm to a C++ function, we shall get:

```
void backwards() // reads a text and writes it out backwards
{
  char c;
  if (cin.get(c))
  {
    backwards();
    cout << c;
  }
}
```

We suppose that the user will terminate the text by marking the end of the file (with Ctrl-Z or Ctrl-D). The function will occur in as many instances (plus one) as the number of characters in the text. The first instance will read the first character. This instance will not be terminated until all of the others have been terminated. The last thing to happen will therefore be that the first character will be written out. Note that each instance of the function has its own unique instance of the local variable `c`. Thus there are in principle as many variables `c` as there are characters in the text.

In the examples we have looked at, recursion has always occurred because a function called itself. This is called *direct recursion*. It is also possible to have *indirect recursion*. A function `f` can call another function `g`, which in turn calls `f`. Then `f` and `g` are said to be *mutually recursive*. It is even possible for recursion to occur through several stages (`f` calls `g`, which calls `h`, which calls `f`).

We shall see several examples of recursion later in the book. We shall find recursion especially useful when we deal with such dynamic data structures as lists and trees.

Exercises

4.1 Write a function to evaluate the sign of an integer in the following way. The function should return as its result the value 1 if the integer is greater than 0, the value 0 if the integer is equal to 0, and the value –1 if the integer is less than 0.

4.2 A number can be shown to be a prime number if it is exactly divisible only by itself and by 1. Write a function that checks whether or not a given number is a prime number.

4.3 A 'perfect number' is a number for which the sum of its factors, including 1 but not the number itself, is equal to the number. A couple of examples are the numbers 6 and 28. Write a function that decides whether or not a given positive number is perfect.

4.4 The binomial coefficients can be defined for non-negative integers n and k in the following way:

$$\binom{n}{k} = \frac{n!}{k! \cdot (n-k)!}$$

Write a function, with the help of the function `nfac` on page 140, that evaluates the binomial coefficients for two numbers.

4.5 Write a function that uses the following Maclaurin series to calculate the value of e^x. Exclude terms that are less than 10^{-7} from the sum.

$$e^x = 1 + \frac{x}{1!} + \frac{x^2}{2!} + \frac{x^3}{3!} + \frac{x^4}{4!} + \ldots$$

4.6 Construct a function `raise`, which evaluates x^y where both x and y are real numbers. Using common mathematical formulas for the calculation of logarithms, we find that

$$x^y = e^{y \cdot \ln(x)}$$

4.7 *Euclid's algorithm* for evaluating the greatest common divisor of two positive integers m and n can be described as follows:

(a) Divide m by n and denote the remainder by r.

(b) If $r = 0$, the evaluation is finished and the result is in n.

(c) Otherwise, set the value of m to that of n and the value of n to that of r, and return to step 1.

Use this algorithm to write a function `gcd`, which evaluates the greatest common divisor of two positive integers. Then write a program that reads in an arbitrary number of pairs of positive integers and writes out the greatest common divisor for each pair.

4.8 To calculate the square root of a number x we can use Newton's method as follows:

Start by guessing a number $g \geq 0$. When we guess g, we know that there must be a number h such that $g \cdot h = x$. (The number h can thus be written as $h = x/g$.) If we are very lucky and have made a good guess, g and h are approximately equal and we have found the solution. In general, however, guesses are not that good. A new better guess is the mean of g and h:

$$g_{new} = \frac{g + \frac{x}{g}}{2}$$

Now we can replace *g* by the new guess and calculate a new value of *h*. By taking the mean of the new values of *g* and *h* we can get a still better guess, and so on. Use this method to write a function that evaluates $\sqrt{x}$. Use $x/2$ for the first guess and let the guesses continue until the difference between two consecutive guesses is less than 10^{-6}.

4.9 All the previous exercises 4.1 to 4.8 require the construction of functions of a mathematical character. These functions can be useful in a number of different contexts. Show how, with the help of a header file and a definition file, a 'package' with these functions can be created. Then in a separate file write a main program that uses at least two of the functions.

4.10 Write a function that determines whether a given text string contains a variable name allowed in the C++ sense (see Chapter 2 page 33). The function will return as result the value `true` or the value `false`. Use this function to write a program that reads in a line with a number of words from the terminal and which writes out how many of the words are permissible variable names. The different words on the line are separated by one or more blank characters.

4.11 Write a function that determines how many lower- and upper-case letters (in the interval a–z) there are in a given text string. The result should be given in two outparameters.

4.12 Write a function that takes two text strings, `t1` and `t2`, as parameters. The function should determine whether `t1` is a substring of `t2`. If this is true, the function should return as a result the index of the start of the substring in `t2`. (An index is normally calculated from 0.) If `t1` is not a substring of `t2`, the function should return as result a value of `-1`. If, for example, `t1` has the value `"declaration"` and `t2` the value `"General declaration office"`, the function should give as the result a value of `8`.

4.13 Do the same thing as in the previous example but use the standard type `string` instead of ordinary text strings. Use reference parameters that refer to constants.

4.14 In the Romany language all the consonants are doubled, and an 'o' is placed between the doubled consonants. Vowels and other characters remain unchanged. Write a function `put_romany` that has a text string written in the Romany language as parameter. The function should write out the text in plain English. If, for example, the parameter contains the text `"hoheyoy alololol yoyou roromomanoniesos"`, the function should write out `"hey all you romanies"`. Use the function to write a program that reads a text file containing a secret message in Romany. The program should write out the secret message in plain English at the terminal. Redirect `cin`.

4.15 Write a function that decides whether two integer arrays are equal. (Two arrays are equal if they contain the same number of components and the corresponding components are equal.) The function should have as parameters the two arrays and two integers that indicate the length of the arrays. The function should give a result of type `bool`.

4.16 In an array of integers, 'rotation to the right' can be defined as an operation that moves each element one place to the right and the last element into the first position. Write a function that rotates an array an arbitrary number of places to the right. The function should have three parameters: the array to be rotated, the length of the array, and an integer that gives the number of places to be rotated.

4.17 In this chapter we constructed the 'package' `simpleio`, which contains two output functions with the name `put`. These write out integers and real numbers and edit them. Both functions have parameters that indicate how editing is to proceed. Complete the declarations of the functions so that their edit parameters take on appropriate default values. In which file should the changes be made – the header file or the definition file?

4.18 A trade union makes the following offer for a long-term wage agreement:

- The first year (year number 1) each employee will receive a monthly wage of $1790.
- In the following years (years number 2, 3, 4, and so on) there will be an increase of 4% over the previous year's wage and an additional general rise of $60 per year.

Write a recursive function that will calculate the monthly wage for a particular year according to the scheme presented here. The only input parameter is to be the year number.

4.19 Write a recursive function `gcd` that evaluates the greatest common divisor of two positive integers m and n based on the following definition.

$$gcd(m, n) = \begin{cases} m & \text{if } m = n \\ gcd(m - n, n) & \text{if } m > n \\ gcd(m, n - m) & \text{otherwise} \end{cases}$$

4.20 By making use of the output operator `<<`, integers can be written out in decimal, octal or hexadecimal form, but the operator will not write out in binary form. Write a recursive function that will produce a positive integer in binary form.

4.21 Write a new version of the program in Exercise 3.7 on page 108. In the new version the translation from Roman number to an ordinary whole number should be done in a separate function called `rom_value`. The function should get a string as parameter and return a value of type `int`. If the roman number is incorrect the function should return the value `-1`.

Types

5

When we talk about phenomena in the real world, we nearly always use a technique known as *abstraction*. Abstraction means creating a concept of something so that it can be talked about and described. The word 'truck', for example, is an abstraction for a vehicle that can be used for transporting things. We can talk about a truck and say that it has certain properties, such as capacity, length and running cost.

The abstraction can be made at different levels. For a maintenance mechanic it is natural to think of a truck as consisting of many components, such as a gearbox and brake system. To go down another level, it can be said that the gearbox is made up of many parts: axles, gearwheels, and so on. This level is appropriate for the design or repair of a gearbox. The level of abstraction chosen therefore depends on the context in which the phenomenon is to be studied. The advantage of deliberately choosing an abstraction is that it allows non-essential details to be ignored in favour of those properties important for the study in hand. The driver of a truck is not interested in how the different gearwheels inside the gearbox are moving. He or she needs only know how to use the gearlever.

The concept of a *type* is used in a computer program to indicate characteristics for data objects. When a variable is said to have a certain type, this explains *both* which values the variable can have *and* which operations are allowed to be performed on the variable. In earlier chapters use has been made of the predefined data types `int` and `double`. These are examples of *arithmetic types* (or *numeric types*), useful when numbers in mathematics are dealt with. The type `int` is an *integer type* and can be used to describe things that can have only integer values, such as counters and numbers of different kinds. The type `double`, which is a *real type* (or *floating-point type*), can be used to deal with other kinds of numeric values – physical characteristics such as temperature and length, for instance.

A question could be raised on the need for two number types: surely the standard type `double` would be sufficient to handle all numeric figures? In principle the answer is a guarded 'yes'. We still keep the type `int` as well because most computers handle integers more quickly than real numbers. Again, integers can be stored in a very exact way in the computer, whereas real numbers are stored more approximately.

We shall go through all the arithmetic types in C++ in this chapter and give a short account of how they are represented in the computer. We shall also be looking at *enumeration types*, which in C++ are treated as a kind of integer type. When programming in C++, so-called *pointers* often have to be used. Ordinary texts, such as those discussed in Chapter 3, are in fact represented with the help of pointers. In this chapter we shall be describing how pointers work.

In order to make models of more complicated objects than mere numbers we must be able to declare our *own* types, where we can say how an object of the type is to be constructed (and which values it is to have) and which operations it will be possible to perform on the object. The important language construct *class* is used in C++ to declare our own types. We shall be looking at classes in more detail later in the book.

We also discuss *type conversions* in this chapter. When working with different types it is sometimes necessary to convert data from one type to another. We shall be discussing when this can happen, and what then takes place.

5.1 Integer types

5.1.1 Storing integers in a computer

In order to understand the characteristics of integer types, we give here a brief description of the principles for the storage of integers in a computer. The details here are not essential for the programmer to know, and may be skipped on a first reading.

As we stated in Chapter 1, the memory of a computer consists of a number of memory cells. Each memory cell is made up of a certain number of bits, and every bit can hold a binary digit (a zero or a one). This means that numbers are naturally stored in binary form in a computer's memory. Let us therefore begin by considering the *binary number system*.

In our culture the decimal system dominates (presumably because we have ten fingers). So if we write a number, such as 158.32, we assume automatically that it is expressed in the decimal system, in which the base is 10. We interpret 158.32 as

$$1 \times 10^2 + 5 \times 10^1 + 8 \times 10^0 + 3 \times 10^{-1} + 2 \times 10^{-2}$$

Expressing this more generally, we can say that a decimal number

$$a_n a_{n-1} \ldots a_1 a_0 \cdot d_1 d_2 \ldots d_m$$

(where the *a*s denote the integral part and the *d*s the decimal part) really means

$$a_n \times 10^n + a_{n-1} \times 10^{n-1} + \ldots + a_1 \times 10^1 + a_0 \times 10^0 + d_1 \times 10^{-1} + d_2 \times 10^{-2} + \ldots + d_m \times 10^{-m}$$

Using base 2 instead of base 10, the binary number

$$b_n b_{n-1} \ldots b_1 b_0 \cdot c_1 c_2 \ldots c_m$$

is interpreted as

$$b_n \times 2^n + b_{n-1} \times 2^{n-1} + \ldots + b_1 \times 2^1 + b_0 \times 2^0 + c_1 \times 2^{-1} + c_2 \times 2^{-2} + \ldots + c_m \times 2^{-m}$$

Here the *b*s denote the integral part and the *c*s denote what is sometimes called the *bicimal* part. For example, the binary number 10111.101 can be interpreted as

$$1 \times 2^4 + 0 \times 2^3 + 1 \times 2^2 + 1 \times 2^1 + 1 \times 2^0 + 1 \times 2^{-1} + 0 \times 2^{-2} + 1 \times 2^{-3}$$

or

$$16 + 0 + 4 + 2 + 1 + 0.5 + 0 + 0.125 = 23.625$$

When an integer is stored in a computer, a certain number of the bits are used. The actual number of bits used varies from computer to computer, but it is commonly either 16 or 32. If, for example, the integer 23 has to be stored in 16 bits, we get the binary pattern

```
0000000000010111
```

If every bit is allowed to represent a binary digit, an *unsigned* storing form is obtained. The greatest number that can be stored in unsigned form with *N* bits is then $2^N - 1$. If there are 16 bits, the greatest number that can be stored then becomes $2^{16} - 1 = 65\,535$. The unsigned form for storing integers cannot be used to store negative numbers. So the smallest number that can be stored using an unsigned form is always 0.

Generally, it is desirable to be able to use both positive and negative integers. To make this possible, a form of storing numbers called *two's complement* is used. With this form, the bit on the extreme left gives the number's sign, zero and one indicating a positive and negative number respectively. The greatest positive number that can be stored in 16 bits is therefore

```
0111111111111111
```

This is actually $2^{15} - 1 = 32\,767$. Using the two's complement form, the number –1 is stored in 16 bits as

```
1111111111111111
```

The number –2 is obtained by subtracting 1 from this, thus yielding

```
1111111111111110
```

The number –3 is

```
1111111111111101
```

By continuing to subtract 1 at a time we see that the least number (that is, the most negative number) that can be stored in 16 bits is

```
1000000000000000
```

This has the value $-2^{15} = -32\,768$. In general it can be stated that, if integers are stored in N bits, the least number that can be stored is -2^{N-1}, and the greatest is $2^{N-1} - 1$.

Values of the standard type `int` are normally stored in this form, and can therefore be both positive and negative. As we shall see, there are also standard types where integers are stored in unsigned form. The programmer does not need to know exactly how the storage works because the compiler takes care of it.

There is a certain risk attached to using a standard type such as `int`. Because the size of the numbers that can be stored depends on the design of the particular computer being used, the type `int` will not have the same properties in all implementations of C++. Suppose we develop a program in a computer that uses 32 bits for storing integers of the type `int`. Now suppose that a variable of type `int` at some point in the program takes the value 100 000. This is fine, because there is room in 32 bits to store 100 000. But if we wanted to transfer our program to another computer that uses 16 bits to store integers we would have a problem. The program would not run as it should.

5.1.2 Predefined integer types

There are eight different predefined integer types in C++. These are divided into two groups: signed types – that is, types that allow both positive and negative numbers – and unsigned types, which will allow only storage of positive numbers. The signed integer types are **`signed char`**, **`short int`**, `int` and **`long int`**. For every one of these four, there is a corresponding unsigned type. The unsigned integer types are **`unsigned char`**, **`unsigned short int`**, **`unsigned int`** and **`unsigned long int`**. Signed integer types and the corresponding unsigned types (for example `int` and **`unsigned int`**) are always stored in the same number of bits in the computer. When variables of different integer types are declared it is sometimes permissible to omit key words. For example, the word **int** is understood if it is omitted. So if we write

```
unsigned m;
```

it will mean the same as

```
unsigned int m;
```

Furthermore, the word **signed** is understood except for type **char**. The line

```
long n;
```

is equivalent to

```
signed long int n;
```

For the type **char**, unfortunately, the notation can be ambiguous (for historical reasons). If you write

```
char c;
```

it will not be clear whether the variable `c` is **signed** or **unsigned**. How it is interpreted depends on which version of C++ is implemented. If the variable `c` is to be used to store 8-bit character codes, it can be useful to declare `c` as an **unsigned char**. (The character codes, of course, have values from `0` to `255`.)

The standard does not state exactly how many bits are used to store the different types. This obviously depends on implementation. It can be stated, however, that the type **char** is usually stored in 8 bits, the type **short int** in 16 bits, the type **int** in 16 or 32 bits and the type **long int** in 32 bits.

With unsigned types, arithmetic overflow can never occur. We say that computations are carried out 'modulo 2^N', where N is the number of bits for the type in question. Suppose, for example, that the type **int** is stored in 16 bits and that we have declared a variable `u` of type **unsigned int**. The greatest number that can be contained in `u` is then 65 535, and we can make the following assignment:

```
u = 65535;
```

The statement

```
u = u + 1;
```

now does not result in overflow, and the result is `0`. If instead we had made the statement

```
u = u + 2;
```

the result would have been `1`, and so on.

Integer types	
Signed types Can have both positive and negative values	*Unsigned types* Can only have positive values

`signed char`
`short int`
`int`
`long int`
	`unsigned char`
	`unsigned short int`
	`unsigned int`
	`unsigned long int`

Which integer type should be chosen when a variable is declared? If the variable is to be used for counting, the normal choice would be type `int`. When dealing with large integers, which cannot be stored in `int`, the type `long int` must be used. If there are many small integers to be stored, possibly in large arrays, then a great deal of memory space can be saved by using the types `short int` or `signed char`. Unsigned types are used to calculate modulo 2^N, and may also be used to store bit patterns. Naturally, the type `char` is used primarily to store texts.

The arithmetic operation symbols `+`, `-`, `*` and so on are defined for all the integer types, and may therefore be used for these operations in variables of type `char`. If `c` has type `char`, we can write

```
c = c * 3 - 5;
```

This may seem surprising at first. The type `char` is used mainly to store printable (or non-printable) characters, so we would not expect arithmetic operations of this kind to be performed with `char`. Upon reflection, however, we can see that what is stored in a variable of type `char` is the *code* for the character we want to store, and the code is of course an integer. In certain situations it might be natural to use arithmetic operations to handle character codes. If, for example, we want to write out all the lower-case letters from ‘a’ to ‘z’, we might have the statement

```
for (char c = 'a'; c <= 'z'; c++)
  cout << c;
```

The expression `c++` increases the character code in `c` by 1, which means that `c` will store the next letter.

That the type `char` should be counted as one of the integer types indicates something even more surprising: that character literals are in fact a kind of integer literal. If we write

```
c = 'a';
```

this will mean that the variable `c` should be assigned the character code for the letter `a`. Since this character code has the number `97`, we could just as well have written

```
c = 97;
```

This is quite correct, but may not be easy to recognize. The use of character literals is therefore an alternative way of writing integers. A character literal has type **char** and so is an integer. The character literals '+', '5', 'ñ', '\33' and '\\', for example, are equivalent to the integer literals 43, 53, 241, 27 and 92 respectively.

To demonstrate that the type **char** is an integer type, we shall first look at a function in which the values of this type are used for indexing. The function determines whether two texts are each other's anagram. (Anagrams are created by jumbling the letters in a word or phrase so that another word or phrase is formed.) The function will have as parameters, called s1 and s2, the two texts to be examined, and the function will return a result value of type **bool**. Two integer arrays, f1 and f2, used internally in the function, serve to count the number of different letters in the two texts. The character codes for the different characters in the texts are used as an index in f1 and f2. Because there are 256 different character codes, the arrays f1 and f2 must each have 256 components. As an example, let us take the letters 'a' and 'é'. The character code for 'a' is 97 and for 'é' it is 233. The components f1[97] and f1[233] will then contain the number of lower-case as and lower-case és, respectively, in the text s1. When the two arrays f1 and f2 have been filled, we can decide whether s1 and s2 are each other's anagram simply by comparing f1 and f2. If they are the same, s1 and s2 are each other's anagram. The function looks like this:

```
bool anagram(char s1[], char s2[])
{
  int f1[256], f2[256], i;
  // Put f1 and f2 to zero
  for (i=0; i<256; i++)
    f1[i] = f2[i] = 0;
  // Count the number of different characters in s1
  for (i=0; s1[i]; i++)
    f1[(unsigned char)s1[i]]++;
  // Count the number of different characters in s2
  for (i=0; s2[i]; i++)
    f2[(unsigned char)s2[i]]++;
  // Compare f1 and f2
  for (i=0; i<256; i++)
    if (f1[i] != f2[i])
    return false;
  return true;
}
```

Let us comment on some of the details in this function. The statement f1[i]=f2[i]=0; means that both f1[i] and f2[i] are set to 0. (Assignment of values goes from right to left.) The statement

```
f1[(unsigned char)s1[i]]++;
```

also needs explaining. The expression `s1[i]` has type **`char`** and is component number `i` in the text `s1`. This component is, as we now know, a character code – an integer. Because it is not clear whether type **`char`** is unsigned or not, we do not know whether the value of `s1[i]` lies in the interval from `-128` to `127` or the interval from `0` to `255`. If we want to use the value of `s1[i]` as index in the array `f1`, we must ensure that `s1[i]` is understood to be a number in the interval from `0` to `255`. This we can do by writing `(unsigned char)` in front of `s1[i]`. (We are actually making a *type conversion* from type **`char`** to **`unsigned char`**. We shall be discussing type conversions in greater detail later.) The expression `(unsigned char)s1[i]` is therefore a number in the interval from `0` to `255`, and we use this number as index in the array `f1`. The component we then get is increased by 1.

There is a standardized header file `climits` that contains information about the different standard types for integers, including type **`int`**. The two constants `INT_MIN` and `INT_MAX` indicate the least and greatest number, respectively, that can be stored by the type **`int`**. (There are corresponding constants for the other integer types.) A test program to determine which numbers can be stored in a computer can look like this:

```
# include <limits>
# include <iostream>
using namespace std;
main()
{
  cout << "The smallest int is: " << INT_MIN << endl;
  cout << "The largest int is: " << INT_MAX << endl;
}
```

5.2 Floating-point types

5.2.1 Storing real numbers in a computer

In science and engineering, to avoid using too many zeros in a number, standard notation is often used for writing very large and very small numbers. In standard notation the numbers 350 000 000 and 0.000 000 73, for example, are written respectively as

$$0.35 \times 10^{9} \qquad 0.73 \times 10^{-6}$$

The same technique is employed for storing real numbers in a computer, but the base 2 is used instead of 10. The decimal number 10.5 can be translated into binary form, giving the binary number 1010.1, and this can be written as

$$0.10101 \times 2^{100}$$

The first part, 0.10101, is usually called the *mantissa* and the second part, 100, the *exponent*. Both the mantissa and exponent are written as binary numbers (the exponent 100 meaning 4 in base 10).

When a real number is stored in a computer, its mantissa and exponent can each use a certain number of bits, the numbers varying from computer to computer. In addition, one bit is used to store the sign of the number.

The principle of storing real numbers is demonstrated in the following example, where we assume that the decimal number 10.5 is stored in a computer that uses 32 bits to store real numbers; the first of the 32 bits holds the sign (0 for plus, 1 for minus), the next eight bits are used for the exponent, and the remaining 23 bits are used to store the mantissa. The integral part of the mantissa does not need to be stored because it is always zero. (Sometimes, the first digit in the mantissa is not stored either, because it is always possible to adjust the number so that this digit is 1.)

```
t exponent    mantissa
0 00000100    10101000000000000000000
```

Note that the details of storing real numbers vary considerably from one computer to another. This example merely shows the general principles.

Note that the exponent can also be negative when a small number is stored. For example, the number 0.0625 (= 1/16) would be stored as follows, using the same format as the previous example:

```
0 11111101 10000000000000000000000
```

Here, the value of the exponent (–3) is expressed in two's complement form.

This method of storing real numbers means that some numbers, such as the example of 10.5 above, can be stored exactly, whereas others, such as 0.6, cannot. If the number –0.6 is to be stored in a computer using the form outlined above, the pattern of bits would look like this:

```
1 00000000 10011001100110011001100
```

The bit pattern in the mantissa should be repeated infinitely many times, but only 23 bits are available.

The number of significant decimal figures obtained depends on the number of bits used to store the mantissa. (It takes, on average, 3.32 bits per decimal figure.) The number of bits used for the exponent determines the largest and smallest numbers (excluding zero) that can be stored. The number zero is usually handled specially and stored exactly, using a particular pattern of bits.

The type `double` uses the above technique to store real numbers. This means that the number of significant figures is the same over the whole range of possible numbers, and that the position of the decimal point 'floats'. It is said the numbers are stored as floating-point numbers and that `double` is a floating-point type.

Storing real numbers is therefore complicated, but it is reassuring to know that the programmer need not worry about the details of what is happening. However, he or she should be aware of the accuracy that the decimal numbers retain. Furthermore, the programmer should remember that real numbers are not always stored in their exact form: that is, care must be taken when determining whether two real numbers are equal. Even if they are equal in principle, they can still differ by one bit in their mantissas, and the computer will then see them as unequal.

5.2.2 Predefined floating-point types

There are three floating-point types in C++: `float`, `double` and `long double`. They are all stored according to the principles described in the previous section. Exactly how many bits are required is not specified in the standard, and will depend on the installation used. The type `float` is often stored in 32 bits and the type `double` in 64 bits. The floating-point type most often used is that of `double`, because in many compilers `float` offers accuracy to only six or seven significant figures.

Floating-point types

- `float`
- `double`
- `long double`

The header file `cfloat` contains miscellaneous information about the different standard types for real numbers. If we want to find out the number of significant figures and the largest and least number that can be stored for type `double`, the constants `DBL_DIG`, `DBL_MAX` and `DBL_MIN`, respectively, can be used. (For the type `float`, the corresponding constants are `FLT_DIG`, `FLT_MAX` and `FLT_MIN`; for the type `long double` the constants are `LDBL_DIG`, `LDBL_MAX` and `LDBL_MIN`.) This is demonstrated in the following test program.

```
# include <cfloat>
# include <iostream>
using namespace std;
main()
{
  cout << "Characteristics for type double" << endl;
  cout << "Sig.Figs: " << DBL_DIG << endl;
  cout << "Largest number: " << DBL_MAX << endl;
  cout << "Least number: " << DBL_MIN << endl;
}
```

5.3 The `sizeof` operator

If we want to find out how many bytes an expression or type consists of, we can use the operator `sizeof`. We write either

```
sizeof expression
```

or

```
sizeof (typename)
```

If we suppose that type `int` consists of four bytes and type `double` of eight bytes, then the following expressions will give the values `1`, `4` and `8`, respectively

```
sizeof (char)
sizeof (unsigned int)
sizeof (double)
```

The `sizeof` operator can also be appplied to expressions. We can write

```
cout<<"The variable k is " << sizeof k <<" bytes";
cout<<"The expression a+b is " << sizeof (a+b) <<" bytes";
```

If the `sizeof` operator is used in an array, it will give the number of bytes for the whole array. If, for example, an array `f` has 10 elements of type `double` and type `double` is stored in eight bytes, the following expression will give a result of 80:

```
sizeof f
```

A common trick to find out the number of elements in an array is to write

```
sizeof f / sizeof f[0]
```

where the length of the whole array is quite simply divided by the length of one element.

5.4 Pointers

5.4.1 Primary memory addresses

When a program is run, the program variables will be in the computer's primary memory. We saw from Chapter 1 that the primary memory consists of a number of memory cells, each cell being made up of eight bits or one byte. These memory cells are numbered, with each cell having a unique number called a *primary memory address* or, quite simply, an *address*. A variable can consist of one or more memory cells (bytes). The number of bytes a variable may have will depend on the type of the variable. The type `char`, for instance, normally takes up one byte and the type `int` two or four bytes. As a variable lies in the primary memory it can be said to have a primary memory address. This address is the same as the address of that variable memory cell that has the lowest address.

As we know, the size of the primary memory depends on the computer. Its physical construction may also be different. But from the programmer's point of view the primary memory consists logically of a memory, which in principle is infinitely large and where each byte has a unique address.

Numbering of the cells begins at zero and continues upwards. The operating system and the computer's hardware take care of the generating process, from the logical memory the programmer sees to the computer's physical primary memory. The size of memory addresses that can be indicated depends on the computer's construction and the characteristics of the operating system. Modern operating systems (Windows and Unix, for example) permit 32-bit addressing, which means that the largest memory address that can be indicated is equal to $2^{32} - 1 = 4\,294\,967\,295$. Older computers and operating systems may be more limited. MS-DOS, for example, uses 20-bit addresses, which are put together by combining two 16-bit words. Primary memory addresses are usually indicated as octal or hexadecimal numbers. For example, the largest memory address that can be indicated with 32 bits can be written in hexadecimal form as `ffffffff`, or in octal form as `37777777777`.

In a C++ program we can work with a special kind of variable that contains primary memory addresses. These are called *pointers*. Suppose, for example, that we have a variable `k` of type **`int`**, and that this variable happens to have the primary address `00000561234` (octal form). If we now have another variable with the name `p`, and this variable contains the number `00000561234`, then we say that `p` *points to* `k`.

Modern programs are normally designed to be loaded anywhere in the memory when they are to be executed. Programs do not have to be found at a special, predetermined place in the memory in order to function. We say that programs like this are *relocatable*, and we also use this term for the variables in the program. A variable can therefore land in different places in the primary memory and have different addresses every time the program is run. Only in special cases is it meaningful to give an absolute primary memory address of `00000561234` in a program. (The only occasion when this might be necessary is in the writing of system software, such as drive routines.) When values are to be given to pointer variables, therefore, only what the pointer variables point to should be indicated and not exact addresses. We say that we work with *relative addresses*. As a program is loaded to be run, the loader will automatically convert the relative addresses to absolute addresses valid for that particular run.

5.4.2 Pointer variables

Let us now look at our first example of the use of pointers. The syntax used for declaring pointer variables is rather unusual. To declare a pointer variable `pi`, which is allowed to point to an **`int`**, we write

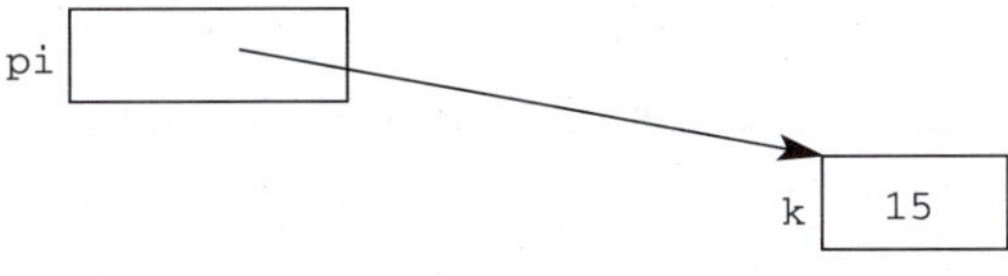

Figure 5.1

```
int *pi;
```

The asterisk shows that the operation involves a pointer. C++ distinguishes between pointers for different types. A pointer variable declared as a pointer for the type `int` may not, for example, point to a value of type `double` or `char`. Two further pointer variables, one for type `double` and another for type `char`, are declared here:

```
double  *pd;
char    *pc;
```

The `&` operator is used to find the address for a particular variable. For example, we can declare a variable `k` of type `int` and let the pointer `pi` point to `k`:

```
int k = 15;
pi = &k;
```

The operator `&` can be read as 'address for'. Figure 5.1 illustrates this.

Several pointers may point to the same variable. We can write

```
int *pi2;
pi2 = pi;
```

The value in the variable `pi` is a pointer for `k` – that is, the primary memory address for `k`. This value has here been assigned to the variable `pi2`. We then have the situation shown in Figure 5.2 (we would naturally have arrived at the same situation if we had instead written `pi2=&k;`).

The `*` operator should be used to get at whatever a pointer points to. For example, the following statement can be given to write out the variable that `pi` points to:

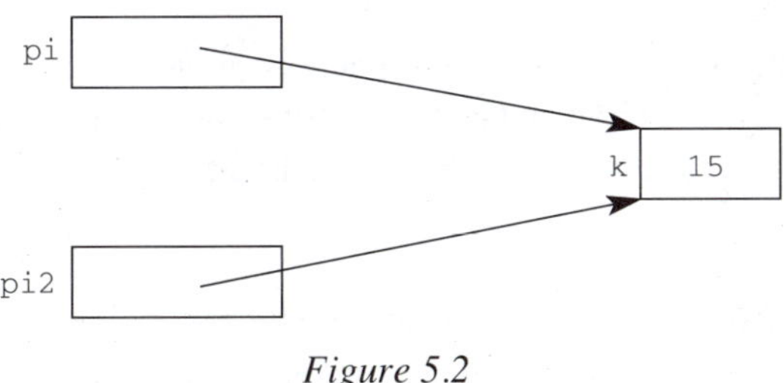

Figure 5.2

```
cout << *pi; // writes out 15
```

The `*` operator can also be used to the left of the equality sign when making an assignment. We can write the following statement, which assigns a value of `20` to the variable `k`:

```
*pi = 20;
```

Note the difference between changing a pointer and changing what the pointer points to. If we have the following lines, where `pi` points to `k` and `pi2` to `n`:

```
int k = 15, n;
int *pi, *pi2;
pi   = &k;
pi2  = &n;
*pi2 = *pi;
```

the last line will assign a value of `15` to the variable `n`. If the last line had instead been

```
pi2 = pi;
```

the pointer `pi2` itself would have been changed, and the situation in Figure 5.2 would have been the result.

Several pointer variables can be declared on the same line. We wrote

```
int *pi, *pi2;
```

Note that the asterisk must be repeated. If an asterisk had not been written in front of `pi2`, the variable name, `pi2`, would have been understood as a common **`int`**. Declarations of common variables and pointer variables can also be combined on the same line. Of course, the different variables can also be initialized in a declaration. The first four lines of the above example could have been written in a single declaration with initializations:

```
int k=15, n, *pi=&k, *pi2=&n;
```

Note also that an asterisk can be used in two different ways; these should not be confused! When a pointer variable is declared, the asterisk is used to indicate that the variable should be a pointer, but an asterisk can also be used as an operator to get at the value a pointer points to.

Sometimes a pointer variable may not be pointing at anything for the time being, in which case a value of zero is put inside the pointer. (Integers may not really be assigned to pointers without a type conversion, but the constant 0 is an exception.)

```
pi = 0;
```

A pointer that contains a value of zero is called a *null* pointer. When variables are declared in C++ they are uninitialized as long as an explicit initialization is not made at the same time; this also applies to pointer variables. Thus pointer variables are not automatically null when they are declared.

It is of course also possible to have a pointer to variables of class types, for instance to variables of the type `vector` or `string`. For instance, we can write

```
vector<double> v;
vector<double> *pv;
pv = &v;
```

Here the variable `pv` will point to the vector `v`. For instance, in order to call the operation `push_back` for the vector that `pv` is pointing at, we can write

```
(*pv).push_back(4.5);
```

First we take out what `pv` points to with help of the operator `*`, and then we call the operator `push_back` for this object. (The parentheses are essential here, since the dot operator has higher priority than the `*` operator.) This is a bit complicated to write. Fortunately, there is an easier way to write it. You can use the operator `->` in the following way:

```
pv->push_back(5.8);
```

This means exactly the same thing as what we wrote in the previous line. The rule to remember is this: if you want to call an operation for a variable of class type you should use a dot if you have stated the name of the variable itself, and the operator `->` if, instead, you have a pointer to the variable. We can illustrate this with a further example. The following lines print all the elements in the vector that `pv` points to:

```
for (int i=0; i<pv->size(); i++)
  cout << pv->at(i) << endl;
```

Finally, we also illustrate how you can have a pointer that points to constants. Suppose we make the following declarations:

```
int k;            // changeable int
const int c=100;  // constant int
const int *pc;    // pointer for constant int
int *pi;          // pointer for changeable int
```

Then the following is allowed:

```
pc = &c;
pc = &k;
```

but this is not allowed:

```
pi = &c; // Error! pi may not point to a constant
*pc = 0; // Error! pc points to a constant
```

Finally, note the difference in the declaration below, where a constant pointer, `cp`, is declared:

```
int *const cp = &k;
```

The pointer `cp` may not itself be changed, as it always points to the variable `k`, but `k` may be changed via the pointer.

Pointers	
type `*p;`	`p` has the type 'pointer to *type*'
`p = &v;`	`p` is assigned the address for `v`
`*p`	Means 'what `p` points to'
`p1 = p2`	`p1` will point to the same thing as `p2`
`*p1 = *p2`	What `p1` points to will be changed

5.4.3 Pointers and arrays

We discussed arrays in section 2.7. Arrays and pointers are closely connected to each other in C++. Every time we work with arrays we make use of pointers. In this section we shall attempt to describe how they are connected. We begin by declaring an array where the elements are of type **`float`**:

```
float f[4];
```

The variable `f` has the type 'array with 4 elements of type **`float`**'. Suppose now that we wish to declare a pointer that can point to the array `f`; the problem is then to indicate the right type for the pointer. A pointer for an array can be considered to be a pointer for the first element of the array, so the pointer's type can be given as a pointer for the element's type. A pointer with the type 'pointer to **`float`**' can therefore point to the array `f`. We shall now declare this pointer:

```
float *pd;
```

Then `pd` can be made to point to the first element in `f` (element number 0):

```
pd = &f[0];
```

We first choose element number `0`, using indexing, and then we apply the address operator `&`. There is, however, a much easier way of obtaining the address of the array's first element. We simply write

```
pd = f;
```

At first glance, this may seem strange. What is on the left of the equality sign is a pointer, and what is to the right of it is an array. Surely you can't assign a whole array

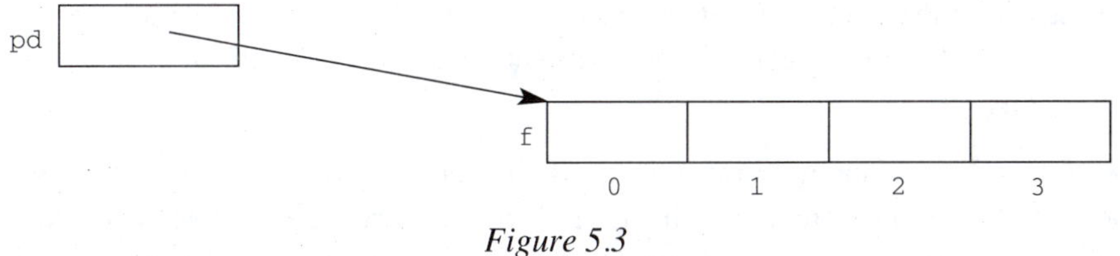

Figure 5.3

to a pointer? The secret lies in the fact that array names are treated rather specially in C++. As soon as an array name occurs in an expression, there is an automatic type conversion to a pointer, and the pointer will point to the first element in the array. If the array has the type 'array with an *n* number of T', the automatic conversion will result in the type 'pointer to T'. In the assignment above there is therefore an automatic type conversion to the type 'pointer to **float**', the same type as that of the variable pd. The assignment above is then correct, since the type is the same on both sides of the equality sign. In Figure 5.3 we see how this looks after the assignment has occurred.

We can now get at the first element in the array via the pointer pd. We can write out, for example,

```
cout << *pd; // Write out element number 0 in f
```

If we want to get at another element in the array via the pointer pd, we must take care to point to the desired element. We may write, for example,

```
cout << *(pd+3); // Write out element number 3 in f
```

It may seem strange that the expression pd+3 points to element number 3 in the array. The variable pd, of course, contains the primary memory address of the array f. If we suppose that the type **float** is stored with four bytes in the computer, then pd+3 should point somewhere to the middle of the first element of f. That this is not the case is due to the fact that C++ makes use of what is normally called *pointer arithmetic*. If there is an expression of the form p+n, n+p or p-n, where p is a pointer and n an integer, then n is interpreted as the number of *steps*, and n is automatically multiplied by the length of the step. The length of a step depends on what the pointer p is pointing to. If the pointer points to a **char**, the step is equal to 1; if the pointer points to something that is two bytes long, the step will be equal to 2; and so on. If we suppose that type **float** is stored with four bytes, the expression pd+3 will mean 'the address that is in pd plus 12'. If pd points to the array's first element, therefore, pd+3 will be the address of the element number 3 (the fourth element) in the array. The expression *(pd+3) also means 'that which is where the address pd+3 points': that is, element number 3 in the array.

The difference between two pointers can also be calculated. Suppose that there are two pointers p1 and p2, which both point to the same type. Then we can calculate the expression p1-p2, the result of which is an integer that indicates the number of steps between what the pointers point to. When working with pointer arithmetic we never need to know how many bytes a step represents. The compiler will automatically take care of this.

Let us now look at another strange thing. If an expression is written in the form `x[n]`, the compiler will interpret this as if `*(x+1)` had been written. Therefore we could also have written out element number `3` in the array `f` by giving the statement

```
cout << pd[3];    // Write out element number 3 in f
```

When an expression of the form `x[n]` is written, where `x` is an array, an automatic type conversion to a pointer is performed. If `x` has the type 'an array with an *n* number of T', then a conversion to the type 'pointer to T' will occur, as before. This means that the four expressions `f[3]`, `*(f+3)`, `3[f]` and `*(3+f)` are identical. All of them will give element number `3` in the array `f`.

When programming in C++, we often use pointers for indexing when we want to run through an array. If, for example, we want to set all the elements in the array `f` to zero, we can of course do this with the statements

```
for (int i=0; i<4; i++)
  f[1] = 0;
```

But this can be done just as easily with pointers:

```
for (float *p=f; p < f+4; p++)
  *p = 0;
```

The pointer `p` is initialized to point to the first element in `f`. Figure 5.4 shows how this looks just after `p` has been initialized and before the first round has been run through. At the end of each round, `p` is increased by one step (pointer arithmetic comes in here). Thus in the first round `p` will point to `f[0]`, in the second round to `f[1]`, and so on. The condition for continuing another round is that `p` is *less* than `f+4`. But since the array consists of only four elements, the last one will have the number `3`, and there will not be an element number `4`. As a result the last round to be run through is the one where `p` points to `f[3]`.

We have seen that when the name of an array occurs in an expression there is an automatic type conversion to a pointer, and this also applies to function calls. We

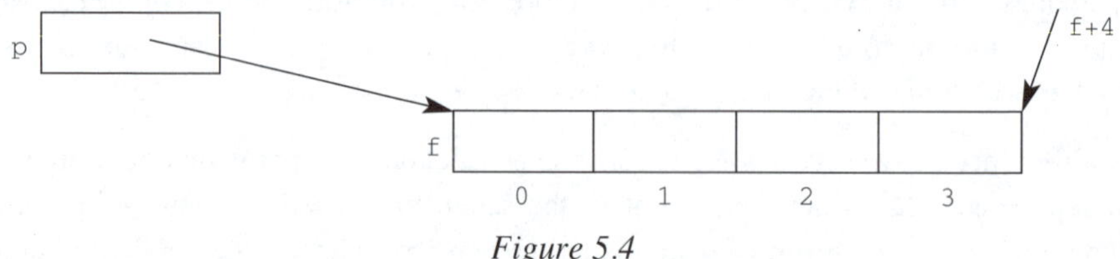

Figure 5.4

demonstrated in Chapter 4, page 115, how a function with the name `sum` calculated the sum of elements in an array of integers. The function `sum` has two parameters: an array, and an integer that indicates the number of elements. If we have an array with the declaration

```
int b[] = {1,2,3,4,1,2,3,4,1,2};
```

we can calculate and write out the sum of the elements with the statement

```
cout << "The sum is " << sum(b,10) << endl;
```

When the function is called, the first argument, `b`, will be automatically converted to a pointer for type **int**, and this pointer will point to the first element in the array `b`. The function `sum` will therefore get as first parameter not a copy of the whole array `b` but a *pointer* to it. This accords with what was discussed in Chapter 4: arrays are always transferred as a kind of reference parameter. Here is an alternative version of the function `sum`:

```
int sum(int *a, int n)  // Sums the elements in a
{
  int s = 0;
  for (int *ip=a; ip < a+n; ip++)
    s += *ip;
  return s;
}
```

In the list of parameters, **int** `a[]` could have been written (as was done earlier in the book) instead of **int** `*a`. Both ways of writing mean exactly the same where function parameters are concerned: the parameter is a pointer to an element of type **int**.

The constant `10` in the call of `sum` indicates that the array has 10 elements. When writing programs it is often desirable to make them easy to change. To insert constants in this way can therefore be dangerous. It would be easy to forget to change the constant `10` if later the array `b` had to be changed to a different length. The operator **sizeof** (see section 5.3) is therefore used instead to calculate the number of elements in `b`. We then write

```
cout << "The sum is "
     << sum(b,sizeof b/sizeof b[0]) << endl;
```

The observant reader will realize that no conversion of `b` to pointers occurs in the expression **sizeof** `b`; instead, the number of bytes in the whole array is calculated.

In certain cases it can be practical to have recursive functions, which in turn have pointers to arrays as parameters. To demonstrate this, we shall write an alternative version of the function `sum`. As before, the first parameter, `a`, is a pointer to the array in question, and the other parameter, `n`, indicates how many elements there are in the array:

Pointers and arrays

type a[...];

- The array name a is automatically converted to the type *type* * in expressions, and the value becomes a pointer to the array's first element.
- Applicable to assignments and function calls, for example.
- Arrays as parameters can be declared either as *type* a[] or as *type* *a
- *Pointer arithmetic*: p+n means the pointer value p plus n *steps*
- *(p+n) is the same thing as p[n]
- *(a+n) is the same thing as a[n]

```
int sum(int *a, int n) // sums the elements in a
{
  if (n <= 0)
    return 0;
  else
    return *a + sum(a+1, n-1);
}
```

The recursive idea is simple. The trivial case is that the array has no elements, in which case the sum will be equal to zero. If there are elements in the array, the sum of these can be calculated by adding the value of the first element, that which a points to, to the sum of all the other elements in the array. The expression a+1 is a pointer to the second element in the array. The function sum thus calls itself recursively in order to calculate the sum of the elements in an array that is one element shorter than the original one.

We shall demonstrate another example in which recursion is used in connection with arrays. A function that carried out a binary search in a sorted array was shown on page 117. A new, recursive variant of this function will now be constructed. The new version will have three parameters: the number desired, a pointer to the array's first element, and a pointer to the array's last element. As a result, we allow the function to give a pointer to that element in the array where the desired number is. If this is not in the array we shall let the function return a value of 0. If, for example, we have an array b with 100 elements, we can get a pointer to the element that contains the value 317 by making the call

```
int *p = bin_search (317, b, b+99);
```

The function will look like this:

```
int *bin_search (int searched, int *first, int *last)
{
  if (first > last) // The array has no elements
    return 0;
```

```
    int *middle = first + (last-first)/2;
    if (searched < *middle)
      return bin_search (searched, first, middle-1);
    else if (searched > *middle)
      return bin_search (searched, middle+1, last);
    else // Equal, the desired number lies in the middle
      return middle;
}
```

If the pointer to the array's first element points to the right of the pointer to the array's last element, the array will not have elements and the desired number cannot therefore be found. If the array contains elements, we let the pointer `middle` point to the element lying in the middle of the array. We then decide whether the desired number lies in the array's left-hand half or in its right-hand half, or whether it is the same as the middle element. If the last case is true, we have found the number we were looking for and can return a pointer to it. In the recursive calls of `bin_search`, `middle-1` means a pointer to the element lying to the left of the middle element and `middle+1` a pointer to the element lying to the right of the middle element.

5.4.4 Pointers and text strings

Text strings were discussed in section 3.3. We stated there that text strings were stored in character arrays with the type 'arrays with *n* number of **`char`**'. We can, for example, make the declarations

```
char txt[5];
char name[] = "Sara";
```

The variable `name` will automatically get a length of `5` and be initialized with the text `"Sara"`, which is terminated with a null character. An automatic type conversion to a pointer is performed when the name of a character array occurs in an expression, exactly as for other arrays. For character arrays this pointer gets the type 'pointer to **`char`**', that is **`char*`**. We can therefore write

```
char *p;
p = name;
cout << p << endl;       // Sara is written out
cout << p+2 << endl;     // ra is written out
cout << *(p+2) << endl;  // r is written out
```

Figure 5.5 illustrates this. Note that when the output operator `<<` has an operand of the type 'pointer to **`char`**' as on lines 3 and 4 above, it writes out all of the text string that the operand points to. If separate characters are to be written out, the `*` operator may be used, as on the last line.

There can also be pointers to constant text strings:

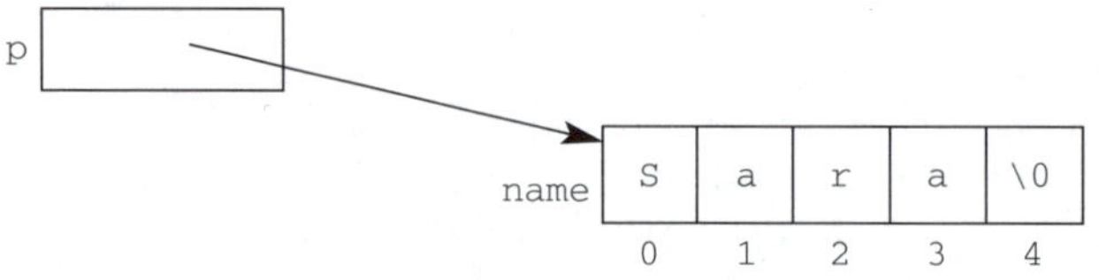

Figure 5.5

```
const char *q = "Hanna";
```

A text string literal, such as `"Hanna"`, has the type 'array with *n* number of **char**' but when it occurs in an expression, as it does here, it is automatically converted into the type 'pointer to **char**'. This means that the pointer `q` will point to the text string `"Hanna"`. The pointer `q` is one of several variables in our program, but the text `"Hanna"` is itself at another position in the primary memory.

Since the pointer `q` has the type 'pointer to a *constant* **char**', what `q` points to cannot be changed. But what would happen if we used the pointer `p` instead, which has the type 'pointer to **char**'?

```
char *p = "Hanna";
*(p+1) = 'i';        // Doubtful!!
```

It is not clear what happens here. In the standard it is stated that the result of an attempt to change the contents of a text literal remains undefined. Different C++ compilers may function differently. The operation may work, but it may also result in an execution fault.

Pointers are often used instead of indexing when working with text strings. As the first example of this we shall write our own version of the function `strlen`, which calculates the length of a text string. If the variable `p`, as above, points to the text string `"Sara"`, the call `strlen(p)`, for example, should give a value of `4` as result, and the call `strlen("C++")` a value of `3`. The function looks like this:

```
int strlen (const char *s) // Gives the length of s
{
  const char *p=s;
  while (*p++)
    ;
  return p-1-s;
}
```

The parameter `s` has the type 'pointer to a constant **char**'. This means that the function cannot change the text, the length of which is to be calculated. But the function can be called with pointers to constant and non-constant texts. In the **for** statement a help pointer, `p`, initialized to `s`, is used: that is, it points from the beginning to the same text string as the parameter `s`. If, for example, we suppose that the function is called with a pointer to the text "Sara" as argument, p will point to this text. This was illustrated in Figure 5.5.

In the **for** statement, the third part inside the parentheses is empty and so is the statement performed at every round. This means that the only step to be performed in the **for** statement occurs in conjunction with the calculation of the test expression *p++. Expressions in this form are very common in connection with the handling of text. In the case of unary operators (operators with only one operand), those *after* the operand have a higher priority than those *before* the operand. In the expression *p++, therefore, ++ has a higher priority than *. So the partial expression p++ is calculated first. This expression increases the pointer p by 1 so that p will point to the next character in the text string: that is, to the character 'a'. Note, however, that the resulting value of the partial expression p++ is the old value for p: that is, a pointer to the character 'S'. The operator * is then applied to this old value, and the result is the character 'S'. Since the character code for 'S' is not equal to zero, the result of the test expression *p++ is understood as 'true', and the **for** statement will be performed for another round.

This process is repeated time after time. At the beginning of every round the pointer p is increased by 1, so that it points to the next character. The character that p pointed to in the previous round is then tested. If it is 'false' – that is, equal to zero – the **for** statement is terminated. Since the text string is terminated by a null character, the **for** statement will stop in the position where p has just been changed so that it points to the character after the null character. Then p-1 must point to the null character. The length of the text string can then be calculated by calculating the difference between p-1 and the pointer s, which will still point to the beginning of the text string.

Here is another example of a function for the handling of text strings where pointers are used instead of indexing. We shall write our own version of the function strcpy, which copies one text string to another. This function has two parameters. The first, s1, is a pointer to the character array to which the text string will be copied, and the second, s2, is a pointer to the text string which is to be copied. Since it should not be possible for the function strcpy to change the text to be copied, s2 can be declared as a pointer to a *constant* **char**. The function looks like this:

```
void strcpy (char *s1, const char *s2)
{
  while (*s1++ = *s2++)
    ;
}
```

An empty statement is also performed with this function at every round of the repetition statement. Let us suppose that strcpy(txt, "ab") has been called. The copying of all characters occurs in conjunction with the calculation of the test expression in parentheses. This test expression is an assignment. First, the expression to the left of the equality sign is calculated. This expression first increases the pointer `s1` by `1`, but the result of the expression is the character that `s1` was pointing to before the increase – that is, `txt[0]`. The expression to the right of the equality sign is similarly calculated. The pointer `s2` is increased by `1`, but the result of the expression is the character that `s2` was pointing to – that is, the character '`a`'. As a result, at the beginning of the first round, the character '`a`' will be copied to `txt[0]`. The resulting value of the assignment is the assigned value, the character '`a`', which is understood as 'true'. One round of the **`while`** statement is therefore performed. Similarly, the character '`b`' will be assigned to `txt[1]` at the beginning of the second round. When the function tests whether a third round should be performed, the third character in the text string `"ab"` – that is, the null character – will be copied to `txt[2]`. The **`while`** statement will now be terminated since this character is understood as 'false'. As a result, a third round will not be performed.

Here are examples of calls to the function `strcpy`:

```
strcpy(txt, q);          // "Hanna" is copied to txt
strcpy(txt, name);       // "Sara" is copied to txt
strcpy(txt+4, " Maria");
cout << txt << endl;     // "Sara Maria" is written out
```

The elements of an array may have any type whatever. It is permissible to have arrays where the separate elements are pointers. This is useful when constructing tables with different texts, as in the following example:

```
const char *mess[4] =
          {"Put on your safety belt", "Start the motor",
           "Release the handbrake", "Close the door"};
```

The variable `mess` is an array consisting of four elements, where each element has the type 'pointer to constant **`char`**'. Figure 5.6 illustrates this. We note, for example, that

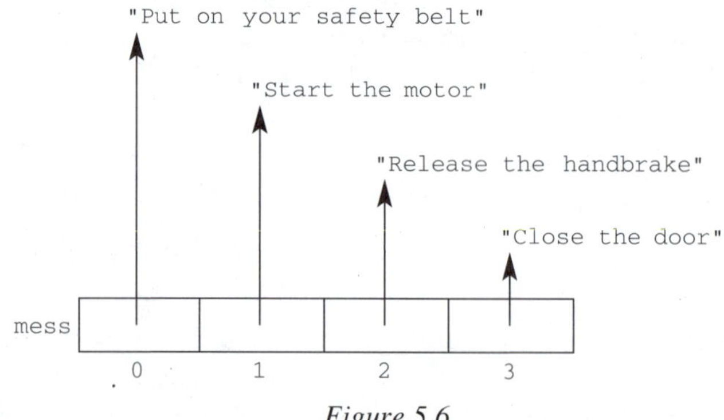

Figure 5.6

the element `mess[0]` contains a pointer to the text string `"Put on your safety belt"` and that `mess[1]` contains a pointer to the text string `"Start the motor"`. Note that the four text strings pointed out automatically have a null character last, as usual. If we want to write out a particular message, we can simply index in the array `mess`:

```
cout << mess[i] << endl;
```

If necessary, this can be written out with the help of a function:

```
void write(const char *pp[], int i)
{
  cout << pp[i] << endl;
}
```

Message number 2 can, for example, be written out with the call `write(mess,2);`. The type of the parameter has been indicated here as '**const char** `*pp[]`', but we know that a type conversion occurs automatically when the name of an array is indicated in the call of a function, sending a pointer to the array as a parameter for the function. A pointer of this kind has, as we have seen, the type 'pointer to the array's element type'. Because the element type in the array `mess` is '**const char** `*`', the function `write` will get a pointer of the type 'pointer to **const char** `*`' as parameter. The parameter `pp` is therefore *a pointer to a pointer* and can be declared, alternatively, as:

```
void write(const char **pp, int i)
  as earlier
```

These two ways of indicating the type of the parameter `pp` are equivalent.

5.4.5 Memory allocation

In order to work with a variable there must be a space reserved for it in the computer's primary memory. When we reserve memory space for a variable, we usually say that we *allocate* memory space; when memory space is no longer needed for a variable, we say that we *deallocate* this memory space. We normally speak of a variable's *life*, this being the time for which memory space is allocated for the variable. When a variable has been declared in the usual way, memory space will be allocated and deallocated *automatically*. But the programmer need not worry about this. For variables declared within a function (or local variables) and function parameters, memory space is allocated automatically each time the function is called, and deallocated automatically each time a return from the function occurs. A function parameter or a local variable will therefore have a life only for the duration of a particular call. Each time a function is called, memory space is once again allocated for the parameters and local variables. On the other hand, a variable declared at the outermost level in a program, outside all functions, will have a life as long as the program is being executed.

For the great majority of cases the programmer will know how many variables are needed. The variables can then be declared in the usual way and the problem of memory allocation can be ignored, since it will happen automatically. For some applications, however, it will not be known in advance how many variables will be necessary, nor of what size they need to be. One example is when we need an array but do not know the exact size when writing the program. Another example is when we work with *dynamic data structures* that increase or decrease during execution. Examples of such dynamic data structures are lists, stacks and trees. (Dynamic data structures will be dealt with in Chapter 13).

In our examples up to now we have seen that pointers point to other variables. The variables pointed to have been variables that we declared in the usual way. Pointers are very useful to us, but not simply because they can point to ordinary variables. Why make a detour with a pointer when it is much simpler to use the variable's name? Pointers prove particularly useful when memory space is allocated dynamically, for they are used to point to the memory space that has been allocated.

To allocate memory space a **new** expression is used. This consists of the reserved word **new** followed by a type name. To allocate memory for a variable of type **double**, for example, **new double** is written. The result of a **new** expression is a pointer to the allocated memory space. The type of pointer will correspond to the type of the memory space. If memory is allocated for a variable of type **double**, the **new** expression will return a result of the type 'pointer to **double**'. This result can be placed into a suitable pointer variable. We can write, for example,

```
double *pd;
pd = new double;
```

The variable for which memory space is allocated does not have a name. The only way of getting to the memory space, therefore, is via a pointer. To assign a value to the allocated memory space, we can write

```
*pd = 2.5; // Initialize the allocated space
```

If memory space is to be allocated for an array, the number of elements desired can be indicated in the **new** expression. In the following lines an array consisting of `n` integers is allocated. The number `n` is read as input data.

```
int n;
cin >> n;
int *pi = new int[n];
```

The allocated memory space will be uninitialized (as long as objects with constructors are not allocated; a discussion of this occurs later in the book). If we wish to set all the `n` elements in the array to zero, we can write

```
for (int i=0; i<n; i++)
  pi[i] = 0;
```

If you try to allocate more memory than is available, the expression **new** reacts by generating an *exception* of the type `bad_alloc`. In Chapter 10 we discuss how you can capture and handle exceptions in your program. Here, we simply mention that a **new** expression can have an alternative form, where you add the parameter `nothrow`. For instance, we can write

```
pd = new (nothrow) double;
pi = new (nothrow) int[n];
```

When using this alternative form you will get no exception if there is not enough memory available. Instead, the **new** expression returns an empty pointer as result. For instance, to see if the last allocation above worked, we can write

```
if (pi == 0)
  cout << "Allocation failed" << endl;
else
  // Allocation succeeded. Continue normally.
```

If you want to use the alternative form of the expression **new** you should include the standard file `new` at the beginning of your program:

```
#include <new>
```

Variables that have been allocated dynamically will have a life until their memory space has been expressly deallocated, and this can be done with a **delete** expression. To deallocate the memory the pointer `pd` points to, we can write

```
delete pd;
```

If we wish to deallocate a memory space that has been allocated for an array, we should use the alternative form

```
delete[] pi;
```

(Note that the square brackets may be left out, but generally speaking it is important for them to be used when the allocated array contains objects with their own destructors; otherwise the destructors will not be called for all the objects that are deallocated. Destructors will be dealt with later in the book.) In this case, all of the array pointed to by `pi` and consisting of `n` **int** is deallocated. The pointer in a **delete** expression will have got its value earlier from a **new** expression. The number of bytes deallocated automatically will be exactly the same as the number allocated earlier. (This is possible since the system automatically registers the number of bytes of memory space allocated and the pointer value that points to the allocated memory space.) It is also permissible to have a pointer with a value of `0` in a **delete** expression: in this case nothing happens.

Memory allocation	
`p = new type;`	Allocates space for a variable of the type *type*. `p` points to the allocated space.
`p = new type[n];`	Allocates space for an array with `n` elements of the type *type*. `p` points to the array.
`delete p;`	Frees that which `p` points to (not arrays).
`delete[] p;`	Frees the array that `p` points to.

The above forms of **new** generate an exception of the type `bad_alloc` if the allocation is unsuccessful. The forms below return an empty pointer. In order to use them you must include the file `new`.

```
#include <new>
p = new (nothrow) type;
p = new (nothrow) type[n];
```

As an example of the allocation of arrays, we shall look at a function `read_line`, which can be used to read one line at a time from the keyboard. We saw earlier that input could be effected either with the input operator `>>` or with the help of the standard function `cin.getline`. We could, for example, write `cin >> a`, where `a` must be an array sufficiently large to accommodate the text read in. The new function `read_line`, which we shall now write, does not require an array to have been declared in advance. Instead, the function reads a line and then itself allocates a memory space exactly large enough to accommodate the line read in. The characters that are read in are put in the allocated memory space, and as a result the function `read_line` gives a pointer to the allocated memory space. Here is an example of a call of this function:

```
char *s;
cout << "What is your name? ";
s = read_line();
cout << "Hello " << s << endl;
```

The function `read_line` looks like this:

```
char *read_line() // Reads a line
{
  char temp[1000];
  cin.getline(temp, 1000);
  char *res = new char[strlen(temp)+1];
  strcpy(res, temp);
  return res;
}
```

The standard function `cin.getline` is called first to read in a whole line from the keyboard. The input line is then placed in the local variable `temp`, an array big enough to hold lines of up to 1000 characters. An array as big as the text to be read is now allocated. The length of the text is calculated with the function `strlen`. This length must be increased by `1` in order to accommodate the null character, which comes last. Finally, the text that has been read is copied from the local array `temp` to the allocated memory space.

5.4.6 Common errors

Programming using pointers is not always a simple matter. It places big demands on the programmer, and mistakes are easily made. Such mistakes may be discovered during compiling: it is possible, for example, to confuse a pointer value with the value the pointer points to, resulting in a type error. However, a number of mistakes may not be discovered during compiling, and may then cause problems later when the program is being executed. The following are common errors:

- using a pointer that is uninitialized or contains a value of `0`;
- using a *lingering pointer*, which points to a memory space allocated earlier but now deallocated;
- allocating new memory space repeatedly, without deallocating memory space no longer needed.

Here is an example of the first kind of error, often made by inexperienced programmers. Since the name of an array is automatically converted to a pointer in an expression it may be assumed that it doesn't matter whether a variable is declared as an array or as a pointer. Look at the following program lines:

```
char a[10];
char *p;
*a = 'X'; // OK! a[0] = 'X'
*p = 'X'; // Execution error!
```

Since initializing of the pointer `p` does not occur when it is declared, it will contain an undefined, worthless value. When an attempt is made on the last line to copy the character `'X'` to the place where `p` points, there is of course an error, since `p` may be pointing anywhere.

As an example of the problem with lingering pointers we shall look at the following, incorrect version of the function `read_line` from the previous section:

```
char *read_line() // Incorrect function!!!
{
  char temp[1000];
  cin.getline(temp, 1000);
  return temp;    // Return of lingering pointer
}
```

Here, too, a line is read in with the use of the standard function `cin.getline`, and the characters read in are placed in the array `temp`. The function `read_line` should as a result give a pointer to the characters read in. Since these are now in the array `temp`, we try to get a result by quite simply giving a pointer to this array. This can be compiled and, possibly, also test run. But the problem is that the array `temp` has a life that stops as soon as the function call is terminated. This means that the pointer given as a result points to a memory space no longer reserved for the array `temp` but which later in the program can be used to store other variables and input data. If we were to try to change something in the line read in using the pointer obtained as a result from `read_line`, we could really make a mess of things, and the program might well behave in the most unexpected ways.

The third kind of common error can be illustrated by the following program lines, where the function `read_line` (the correct version) is called again and again:

```
while(true)
{
  cout << "Write input data";
  s = read_line();
  // Make calculations
  ...
}
```

A program containing these lines may certainly function excellently. However, problems may arise if it is designed to be in continuous operation. With every new round memory is allocated for the line read in, but the allocated memory is not returned anywhere. If the program is in operation for a long time, the accessible memory space must end sooner or later. The result will be an execution fault.

5.4.7 Pointers and references: a comparison

In C++ there is a language construct called a *reference*. References are closely related to pointers, and the inexperienced programmer may easily confuse them. So let us try to clarify the two terms.

A reference can be declared either as an ordinary variable or as a function parameter; this was discussed in section 4.6, page 131. Let us look at the following declarations:

```
int n;
int &ri = n;
```

A reference with the name `ri` is declared on the second line. The character `&` indicates that we are dealing with a reference. Do not confuse the character `&` used here with the address operator used in connection with pointers. A reference can be understood as a *constant* pointer to a particular variable. A reference is said to be a constant because it always refers to the same variable and cannot itself be changed. Since references are not changeable, they must always be initialized, which is what happens on the second line above. The reference `ri` is initialized so that it refers to the variable `n`. A reference could also be understood as an alternative name for another variable. We could write, for example,

```
ri = 15;     // same as n = 15
cout << ri; // same as cout << n;
```

Note that although `ri` is a reference, a `*` operator should not be included – as it is with pointers – to get to what `ri` refers to; because `ri` is constant, we mean 'what `ri` refers to' when we write `ri`.

There are two exceptions to the rule that references must always be initialized. One of these has to do with reference parameters. As we saw in section 4.6, a reference parameter is automatically initialized with every function call so that it refers to a corresponding actual parameter. The other exception applies when a reference is a data member of a class, in which case it must be initialized through a special initialization function called a constructor. This will be discussed in Chapter 7.

To shed some light on the difference between references and pointers, we show here two versions of a function that changes the values of two variables of type **`int`**. The first version of the function uses references:

```
void change1 (int& a, int& b)
{
  int c = a;
  a = b; b = c;
}
```

To change the values of two variables `i` and `j`, the following may be written:

```
int i = 5, j = 10;
change1(i, j);          // i gets a value of 10 and j a value of 5
```

Since the parameter `a`, for the whole of the call, refers to the variable `i` and the reference `b` to the variable `j`, the variables `i` and `j` will change values after the call of `change1`.

Alternatively, the same result can be achieved with pointers, instead of references. Let us look at the second version of the function:

```
void change2 (int *pa, int *pb)
{
  int c = *pa;
  *pa = *pb; *pb = c;
}
```

Here the parameters are of the type 'pointers to **int**', so we must change the * operator within the function to get at what they point to. When the function change2 is called, the *addresses* to the variables that are to change values must be given as actual parameters. This can look as follows:

```
int i =5, j =10;
change2(&i, &j);    // i gets a value of 10 and j a value of 5
```

Note that the use of references makes everything a little simpler for the programmer, both within the function and when the function is to be called. When we need to use changeable function parameters in this book, therefore, we shall use reference parameters instead of pointers. This does not apply to arrays, of course, since array parameters, as we have seen, are always transferred via pointers.

5.4.8 Pointers to functions

A pointer may point to a function, and functions may be called via pointers. We begin by declaring a pointer pf, which may point to functions. The syntax is not particularly easy to read. (The rules for interpreting complicated declarations are discussed in section 5.5.)

```
float (*pf)(int);
```

This should be understood as 'pf is a pointer to a function that has an **int** as parameter and which returns a **float**'. We can see that this is a function because the word **int** is in parentheses after the variable name. The first parentheses, around *pf, are necessary. If they had not been put there, the declaration would have indicated instead that pf was a function with an **int** as parameter, which returned a pointer to a **float**.

Now suppose that we have the function g with the declaration

```
float g(int);
```

Then the pointer pf can be made to point to this function by making the assignment

```
pf = g;
```

An automatic type conversion occurs here so that the part on the right is converted to a pointer to a function. (Compare this with automatic type conversions, where names of arrays are indicated.) Now the function that pf points to can be called:

```
x = pf(n);
```

Here the function g is called, but if pf had pointed to some other function, this one would have been called instead.

Note that the pointer pf may only point to functions that have an **int** as parameter and which return a **float**. If a pointer to another kind of function is required, another pointer must be used. The following line, for example, declares a pointer `pf2`, which may point to functions with three parameters – a **double**, a pointer to a **char** and an **int** – and which does not give a result (returns **void**):

```
void (*pf2)(double, char *, int);
```

Pointers to functions can be handled like other pointers. Arrays can be formed, for example, by pointers such as these:

```
float (*apf[10])(int);
```

Here `apf` is an array in which the elements are pointers to functions with an **int** as parameter, which return the type **float**. We can, for example, calculate the function number `i` with the parameter `n`:

```
x = apf[i](n);
```

Pointers to functions are very useful. They are often used in connection with numeric calculations. Many numeric functions are formed so that they have a pointer to a mathematical function as one of their parameters. A function that performs mathematical integration has, for example, a parameter that indicates the mathematical function to be integrated. As an example, we shall construct a function `zeropos`, which calculates a zero position for mathematical functions. The function `zeropos` will have the declaration

```
double zeropos(double (*f)(double),
               double a, double b, double eps=1e-10);
```

The first parameter, `f`, is a pointer to the mathematical function for which a zero position is to be sought. The two parameters `a` and `b` indicate the interval in which the search for the zero position is to occur. We are thus looking for a value `x` in the interval (`a, b`) such that `f(x)=0`. We suppose that the function that `f` points to is monotonous, and that it has exactly one zero position in the given interval. The parameter `eps` indicates the greatest error that may be found in the result. We have given this parameter a default value of 10^{-10}. We shall use the notion of 'surrounding' the zero position by moving the end points `a` and `b` ever nearer to each other. The definition of the function will be

```
double zeropos(double (*f)(double),
               double a, double b, double eps=1e-10)
{
  if (f(a) > 0 && f(b) < 0)
  { // Change a and b
    double temp = a;
    a=b; b=temp;
  }
  if (! (f(a) < 0 && f(b) > 0))
```

```
    {
      cout << " No zero position " << endl;
      abort();
    }
    // Now holds f(a) < 0 < f(b)
    while (fabs(a-b) > eps)
    {
      double xm=(a+b)/2, fm=f(xm);
      if (fm < 0)
        a=xm;
      else if (fm > 0)
        b=xm;
      else
        return xm; // We happened to find the zero position
    }
    return (a+b)/2;
  }
```

In the first part of the function we ensure that the condition `f(a)<0<f(b)` is true. If it turns out that `f(b)<0<f(a)`, we quite simply exchange `a` with `b`. If `f(a)` and `f(b)` are both greater than zero or less than zero, a zero position can be absent from the interval. In that case an error printout is given, and the program is terminated. This is done with the standard function `abort`, which is declared in the header file `cstdlib`.

We then calculate the mid-point `xm` in the interval (`a, b`) and the function's value at this point. This is done in the call `f(xm)`. Here the function that `f` points to is called. If the function value is less than zero, the zero position must lie to the right of `xm`. Then we make a change inside the interval so that `a` is set to `xm`. If the function value is greater than zero, the zero position must similarly lie to the left of `xm`, and `b` is changed to `xm`. This process is repeated until the interval (`a, b`) is shorter than `eps` or until we happen to find the zero position.

The function `zeropos` can now be used to calculate the zero position for different functions. For example, if we have the two functions

```
double f1(double x)
{
  return x-1;
}
double f2(double x)
{
  return 2*x*x*x - 3*x*x - 18*x - 8;
}
```

their zero positions can be calculated and written out with the statement

```
cout << zeropos(f1, -10, 10) << endl
     << zeropos(f2, -1, 1)   << endl;
```

Another very important area of use for pointers to functions should be mentioned here. Most modern programs today use a graphic user interface; in other words different windows and menus are shown on the screen, and the user communicates with the program through the medium of a mouse. To work in this way a program has to have a special structure. The program is started by calling prepared help functions in the windows system and specifying which windows, menus etc. are to be found. Then a special wait function in the windows system, which allows the user to wait until an event occurs, is called. An event can be the moving of the mouse, or the pressing of a key or a mouse button.

Before the wait function is called, it is necessary to indicate what should be done when different events occur. This is effected by calling the help functions that should have as parameters pointers to *callback functions*. These are functions that we write ourselves and which are to be called for various events. For example, a callback function can be written specifically to be called when the user clicks with the mouse on a certain button on the screen. Thus we need to know how to make pointers to functions.

5.5 Complicated declarations: `typedef`

Declarations in C++ are not always very easy to read, particularly when we begin to handle more complicated types such as arrays of pointers. First of all here are some fundamental examples:

```
float f(int); // f is a function
float a[10];  // a is an array
float *p;     // p is a pointer
```

Variable names, type names, ordinary parentheses, braces and the character `*` are some examples of what might occur in declarations. (References can also be declared, but these are not often complicated.) Ordinary parentheses coming after a name that is declared signify a function; square brackets coming after the name signify an array; and when the character `*` precedes a name, it is a question of a pointer. This is relatively simple as long as not too many of these characters – `()`, `[]` and `*` – appear in the same declaration.

Here are some more complicated examples:

```
float *fp(int);  // fp is a function which returns
                 // a pointer to float
float *ap[10];   // ap is an array where the elements are
                 // of the type pointer to float
float **pp;      // pp is a pointer to a pointer
                 // to a float
```

The following rules may be used to interpret these declarations correctly:

1. Begin by finding the name of what is to be declared (example: 'fp is').
2. If there is a (..) or a [..] directly after what is being declared, this will have highest priority. In this case, read 'a function', 'an array', respectively. Repeat this point until there are no more (..) or [..] following to the right.
3. If there is a * in front of what is to be declared, read 'pointer to'. Repeat this point until no more * are left.
4. Last of all, read the type name that comes first.

Simplifying matters we can say that (..) and [..] have higher priority than * in a declaration, but if this order of priority is not satisfactory it can be changed by including extra parentheses. We could, for example, write

```
float (*pf) (int);       // pf is a pointer to a function
                         // which returns a float
float (*pa) [10];        // pa is a pointer to an array
                         // where the elements are of type float
float (*apf[10])(int); // apf is an array where the elements
                         // are pointers to functions
```

Unfortunately, declarations can be even more complicated than those illustrated in these examples. In order to simplify the treatment of declarations, and to understand them more easily, a language construct called **typedef** can be used. If we have a complicated type, we can use **typedef** to give it a name and subsequently use this name instead of the complicated type formulation. Suppose, for example, that we wish to work with variables of the type **unsigned long int**. This may be awkward to write in some places, so we can make the following declaration:

```
typedef unsigned long int ulong;
```

A **typedef** declaration has exactly the same form as an ordinary variable declaration. The only difference is that the word **typedef** comes first. In a **typedef** declaration we declare a type name, not a variable name. Thus we declared the name `ulong` here. This name can then be used as a simple type name wherever a type can be indicated. We can, for example, declare a variable with the name `u1`:

```
ulong u1;
```

The variable `u1` will get the type **unsigned long int** just as if we had written it in the declaration. The use of **typedef** therefore does not lead to the creation of a new type; we have simply found an easier way of indicating the type **unsigned long int**. Let us show a few examples:

```
typedef char *text;
typedef float array[10];
typedef float (*funct_point)(int);
typedef vector<int> intvector;
```

The type names `text`, `array`, `funct_point` and `intvector` have been entered here. Now pointers to text strings can be declared more simply:

```
text t = "Hello";
```

The type names can be used to give simplified declarations of the variables `a`, `pf` and `apf` that were used above and a vector `v` with elements of type **int**:

```
array a;
funct_point pf;
funct_point apf[10];
intvector v;
```

5.6 The type void

There is a standard type called **void**. This is no common type. There are, for instance, no values of type **void**, and variables of this type may not be declared. The most important use of the type **void** is at the declaration of functions, when it is used to indicate that a function will not return a result:

```
void f(int);
```

We can also write **void** to show that a function has no parameters. The following two lines have the same meaning:

```
int g();
int g(void);
```

Variables of type **void** may not be declared; neither is it permissible to have references to type **void**, but it is permissible to declare variables and parameters with the type 'pointer to **void**':

```
void *p;
int f(void *q);
```

Because there are no values of type **void**, it is not permissible to try to find out what a pointer of this kind is pointing to; neither is it allowed to perform pointer arithmetic on the **void** pointer:

```
cout << *p; // Not allowed!!
p++;        // Not allowed!!
```

Pointers to **void** can be used as intermediate results when we wish to make conversions between different pointer types (see section 5.7 below).

5.7 Type conversions

Every expression computed in a C++ program has a certain type, and the compiler will keep a careful account of the types that different expressions have. However, the value of an expression can be converted in certain cases from one type to another. This either happens *automatically*, without anything particular being written by the programmer, or *explicitly*, when the programmer writes a *type conversion expression*.

5.7.1 Automatic type conversions

Let us begin by listing the occasions when the compiler tries to produce an automatic type conversion.

- When an expression of the form `x · y` is written, where · is an operator, the compiler tries to convert the operands `x` and `y` so that the operation can be carried out. If, for example, we have the expression `a + k`, where `a` has type **`double`** and `k` type **`int`**, then the value of `k` is automatically converted to type **`double`**. (Naturally, the variable `k` itself is not changed by this. What is converted is a copy of the value of `k`.)
- With assignments and initializing, for example, `x = y`, an attempt is made to convert the part on the right so that it gets the same type as the value in the left-hand part. (Assignment is actually a special case of the point above.)
- When a function is called, the compiler tries to convert the arguments' values (the actual parameters) so that they correspond to the types of the formal parameters. The same applies to a **`return`** statement. Then the value after the word **`return`** is refashioned to the type the function should return.
- In an **`if`** statement, the value in parentheses should be of type **`bool`**. If it is not, the compiler will try to carry out an automatic type conversion.
- In a **`switch`** statement (which we have not yet dealt with), the expression after **`switch`** should be of integer type. An automatic type conversion can also occur here.

What kind of type conversions are possible with automatic type conversion? For example, can a pointer be automatically converted to an **`int`**? We list here some of the possible kinds of automatic type conversion:

- *Arithmetic type conversions*. A value of arithmetic type can be converted to a value of another arithmetic type. A value of an enumeration type (see section 5.8) can also be converted to an integer. In many cases the value is not changed as a result of this conversion, but sometimes it is. An example of this occurs when a conversion is made from a long integer type to a short integer type. Then the bits furthest to the left that will not fit in are cut off. Another example is a conversion from a floating-point type to an integer type, when the decimals will disappear.

- *Conversion to and from the type* `bool`. An arithmetic value, an enumeration value (see section 5.8) or a pointer value can be automatically converted to the type `bool`. A value of `0` is then interpreted as `false` and all other values as `true`. A value of the type `bool` can alternatively be automatically converted to the type `int`. A value of `false` will then be converted to `0`, and a value of `true` to `1`.
- *Arrays and functions.* The name of an array or a function can be automatically converted to a pointer to the array's first element or, in the case of a function, to a pointer to the function.
- *Null pointers.* The integer literal `0` can be automatically converted to a pointer type and will then mean 'null pointer'.
- *Pointers to* `void`. A pointer of the type 'pointer to T' can be automatically converted to the type 'pointer to `void`'. Note that type conversions in the other direction cannot take place automatically.
- *Classes.* A number of automatic type conversions can also occur when we work with classes. We shall be describing these later in the book. For the sake of completeness we shall simply name here those automatic type conversions that can occur:
  - If there are user-defined type conversions (type conversion constructors or type conversion operators) to be carried out, these can be carried out automatically.
  - If `D` is a class with a base class `B`, a value of type `D` can be converted to type `B`. In the same way, a pointer of the type 'pointer to `D`' will automatically be converted to the type 'pointer to `B`'. Special rules also apply to pointers to class members.

5.7.2 Explicit type conversions

If, in a particular situation, a type conversion has to be made and this does not occur automatically as described above, an *explicit type conversion* can be effected. It is permissible to carry out several different types of type conversion. For example, conversions may be made between pointers and integers and between different kinds of pointer types. Note that the normal safety mechanisms in the compiler will no longer function when explicit type conversions are made. A program that contains explicit type conversions can therefore behave strangely if no extra care is taken. In C++ there are two alternatives for indicating an explicit type conversion. Either a type conversion expression of the form

```
(typename) expression
```

can be used, or the form

```
typename (expression)
```

C++ has inherited the first form, called a *cast*, from C. We write in parentheses the type that we want the expression to be converted to. Here are some examples:

```
char *p = (char *) 07650;    // integer → pointer
long int i = (long int) p;   // pointer → integer
double *q = (double *) p;    // pointer → another pointer
void *v;
q = (double *) v;            // void pointer → another pointer
```

The other, newer form of explicit type conversion is reminiscent of a function call. A couple of examples are:

```
cout << int(p);      // pointer → integer
typedef char *text;
cout << text (v);    // void pointer → another pointer
```

To be able to use the second form we have to be able to express the type we want to make the conversion to, with a simple type name. In order to achieve this, we can, as in the second example, give the type a simpler name using **typedef**.

The four type conversion operators **dynamic_cast**, **static_cast**, **reinterpret_cast** and **const_cast** have been introduced in the standard, the intention being that these should be used instead of the ones shown above. Using an explicit type conversion is always risky. If errors arise in a program when it is test run the explicit type conversions should always be checked to make sure they are correct. But it can be difficult to find all the places where explicit type conversions have been made. If the four operators suggested in the draft standard are used, the problem disappears, since it would be an easy matter to search for the word 'cast' in the program text.

5.8 Enumeration types

We have seen that much use is made of integer types when designing programs, but there are many phenomena in the real world that are described in words rather than numbers – the days of the week, for example. The second day of the week is usually called Tuesday rather than day number 2. In the same way, the suits in a pack of cards are not numbered but have names: clubs, diamonds, hearts and spades. To describe the state of something we commonly use different terms rather than numbers, such as the state of an elevator being 'going up', 'going down', or 'stationary'. If phenomena like these are to be represented in a program, numeric types will not suffice. Instead, there is the opportunity to use *enumeration types*. When an enumeration type is declared, the possible values are simply enumerated or listed.

Let us look at the three examples already mentioned: the days of the week, the suits in a pack of cards and the states of an elevator. We can make the following declarations:

```
enum day_of_the_week {Monday, Tuesday, Wednesday, Thursday,
                      Friday, Saturday, Sunday};
enum suit {clubs, diamonds, hearts, spades};
enum elevator_status {going_up, going_down, stationary};
```

The words day_of_the_week, suit and elevator_status will now designate three new types. These types can be used in the same way as the built-in types. We can, for example, declare the variables:

```
day_of_the_week today, tomorrow;
suit current_trump, suit_played;
elevator_status condition_1 = stationary;
```

The variables today and tomorrow will be of the type day_of_the_week, current_trump and suit_played of the type suit, and condition_1 of the type elevator_status. A variable of enumeration type may accept only one of the enumerated values for the type. The variable suit_played may, for example, accept only one of the four values clubs, diamonds, hearts and spades. Although we are perhaps accustomed to values being numeric, we must also become accustomed to the notion that diamonds is a value of type suit just as 257 is a value of type **int**.

Here are some examples of statements that are allowed:

```
suit_played = diamonds;
current_trump = suit_played;
if (condition_1 == stationary)
  cout << "The elevator is stationary" << endl;
```

It is not permissible to mix types. The following are incorrect:

```
int i = 4;
today = i;          // Error!
today = diamonds; // Error!
```

In fact, enumeration values are stored as integers but it is not permissible to assign an integer to an enumeration value. On the other hand, we may assign an enumeration value to an integer, so it would have been correct to write

```
int i = today;     // OK!
```

If nothing else has been indicated, the first enumeration value will be represented by the integer 0, the second by the integer 1, and so on. The value Friday is represented, for example, by the integer 4. The programmer may choose which integer is to be used to represent the different enumeration values. Look at the following declaration, for example:

```
enum etype {a, b = 100, c = -10, d};
```

Here a will be represented by the value 0, b by the value 100, c by the value -10 and d by the value -9 (the previous value +1). Enumerations can be used as an alternative way to give integer constants. We shall find this useful when we work with classes later. We could define two constants, k and number, for example:

```
enum {k = 100, number = 200};
```

Note that it is not necessary to indicate a name for the enumeration type. The enumeration values can then be used as constant integers. An example is:

```
double array[number];
```

We must have a way of reading and writing enumeration values simply for it to feel natural to use enumeration types. Unfortunately, there are no input and output operators for enumeration types in C++. If we were to carry out the following statements:

```
today = Saturday;
cout << "Today it is " << today << endl;
```

we would get written out

```
Today it is 5
```

The enumeration value is thus converted automatically to an `int` and is written out as an integer. One way to get the printout in fully written-out text is to declare a table:

```
const char *day_tab[] =
           {"Monday", "Tuesday", "Wednesday", "Thursday",
            "Friday", "Saturday", "Sunday", 0};
```

The variable `day_tab` is an array in which each element is of the type `const char *`: that is, a pointer to a constant text. The table contains an entry for each enumeration value, and we have added an extra null pointer in an extra element at the end of the array. This null pointer will be useful later when we come to use the table for input. It is quite complicated to write the type of the table. Therefore it will be convenient to introduce a name for it, using `typedef`:

```
typedef const char *enum_txt[];
```

The type `enum_txt` is called, and the table `day_tab` can now be declared more easily:

```
enum_txt day_tab =
          {"Monday", "Tuesday", "Wednesday", "Thursday",
           "Friday", "Saturday", "Sunday", 0};
```

The value of an enumeration variable can then be written out by indexing in the table:

```
cout << "Today it is " << day_tab[today] << endl;
```

If the variable `today` has the value `Saturday`, as before, the sixth element in the table (the one with number `5`) will be written out. We then get the printout

```
Today it is Saturday
```

We also want it to be possible for the user of the program to write input data in fully written-out text. The following lines might be wanted in a program:

```
cout << "What day of the week is it today?";
cin >> today; // ERROR!!
```

and it might be desirable to have the user be able to reply, for example,

```
Sunday
```

This is simply not possible, unfortunately. For the input we must therefore construct a help function with the declaration

```
int get_enum(enum_txt tab);
```

The function will get as argument a table containing a text for each enumeration value. As result, the function will return an integer that is equal to the number in the integer value. If the call of the function looks as follows, for example,

```
cout << "What day is it today? ";
today = day_of_the_week(get_enum(day_tab));
```

and the user writes the value `Sunday`, the function will return a value of `6`. (Numbering takes place, as usual, from `0`.) Since the return value is of type **`int`**, we must make an explicit type conversion to the correct enumeration type (here the type `day_of_the_week`) before we can assign the next read value to an enumeration variable. Here is the definition of the function `get_enum`:

```
int get_enum(enum_txt tab) {
  char s[100];
  if (cin>>s) {
    for (int k=0; tab[k]; k++)
      if (strcmp(s, tab[k])==0)
      return k;
    cout << "Error in input data" << endl;
  }
  return -1;
}
```

The function begins by reading the next word from the keyboard. The expression `cin>>s` will be true if reading went successfully. The text will then be in the text array `s`. The function then compares the text with each one of the texts described by the parameter `tab`. These comparisons occur with the standard function `strcmp`, which returns a value of zero if the two texts compared are the same. If the text read is the same as a particular text in `tab`, the number `k`, equal to the text's number in the table, is returned. The expression `tab[k]` is used in the **`for`** statement as the condition to continue for one more round. The elements in `tab` are pointers to texts. All the pointers, except for the last one, which was intentionally set to `0`, contain non-null pointers and can therefore be understood as true. If the text in `s` is not the same as one of the texts described by `tab`, the **`for`** statement will be interrupted when we reach the last (false) element in `tab`. An incorrect word must then have been written by the user, with the result that the function gives an error printout. A result of `-1` is then returned. This value is returned even if the input `cin>>s` has miscarried, for example if the user typed Ctrl-Z (or Ctrl-D).

Note that output and input of enumeration values using a text table will not function if we indicate our own integers for the enumeration values.

We shall conclude this section on enumeration types by illustrating a program that mixes colours. The colours are described by enumeration types. The program asks the user to indicate two of the colours red, yellow and blue. The program then writes out which colour is obtained by mixing them. Here is an example of how this can look when the program is run:

```
Indicate two of the colours red, yellow, blue.
yellow blue
The colour mixing will be green
Indicate two of the colours red, yellow, blue
yellow yellow
The colour mixing will be yellow
Indicate two of the colours red, yellow, blue.
The user writes here Ctrl-Z (or Ctrl-D)
```

The program looks like this:

```
# include <iostream>
# include <cstring>
using namespace std;
typedef char *enum_txt[];
int get_enum(enum_txt tab) {
  as above
}
main() {
  enum colour {red, yellow, blue, mauve, green, orange};
  enum_txt tab1 = {"red", "yellow", "blue", 0}
  enum_txt tab2 = {"red", "yellow", "blue",
                   "mauve", "green", "orange", 0};
  colour colour1, colour2, mixing;
  while (true) {
    cout << "Indicate two of the colours red, yellow, blue."
         << endl;
    if ((colour1=colour(get_enum(tab1)))<0 ||
        (colour2=colour(get_enum(tab1)))<0)
      break;
    if (colour1==red    && colour2==yellow ||
        colour1==yellow && colour2==red)
      mixing = orange;
```

```
        else if (colour1==yellow  && colour2==blue ||
                 colour1==blue    && colour2==yellow)
          mixing = green;
        else if (colour1==red   && colour2==blue ||
                 colour1==blue  && colour2==red)
          mixing = mauve;
        else
          mixing = colour1; // same colour
        cout << "Colour mixing will be "
             << tab2[mixing] << endl;
    }
}
```

5.9 Tables

In the array types and vectors studied so far there has been an index that could be used to select particular components from an array. This type of data structure is excellent for describing collections with several data objects, where these could be imagined lying in a long line. Texts are an example of this. Sometimes, however, we are confronted with tables, and these do not lend themselves to being described in this way. An example is Table 5.1, which gives the daily air temperature and water temperature in the Algarve in Southern Portugal. In C++, arrays with several indexes, *multidimensional arrays* or vectors where the elements are also vectors can be used to describe this type of table.

5.9.1 Multidimensional arrays

If we wish, for example, to have a table consisting of three rows and four columns, where the elements in the table are integers, we can do this with the help of the following variable declaration:

```
int m[3][4];
```

Table 5.1 Daily air temperature and water temperature in the Algarve.

	January	February	March	April	May	June	July	August	September	October	November	December
Minimum	11.5	12.0	12.9	13.5	17.0	20.5	22.2	22.5	21.5	16.0	13.5	9.9
Maximum	19.0	20.5	21.0	23.0	27.0	29.0	33.0	35.0	31.5	27.0	22.0	20.0
Mean	15.0	15.5	17.0	19.0	20.1	24.0	27.0	27.4	26.5	22.7	17.5	14.5
Water	17.0	17.5	20.5	21.0	21.5	23.0	25.0	26.0	26.0	22.7	21.0	17.5

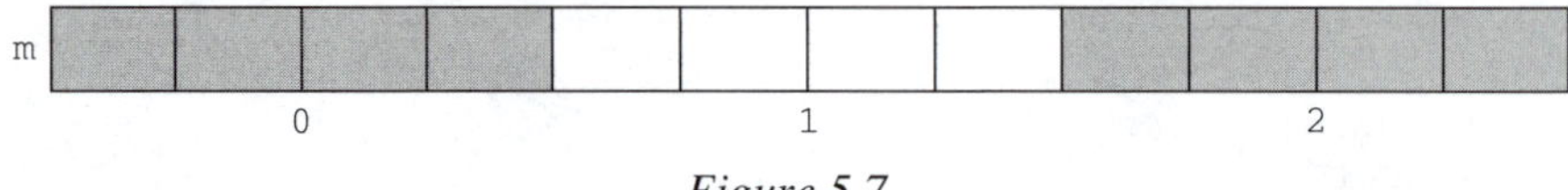

Figure 5.7

A two-dimensional arrangement with numbers is usually called a *matrix*. We can therefore say that the variable `m` is a matrix with `3` rows and `4` columns. In a declaration we are allowed to have as many indexes as we would like. In practice, however, it would be unusual to have more than two, so we shall describe this case only.

The variable `m` is actually a common one-dimensional array with `3` elements, where every element is in turn an array consisting of `4` elements of type **`int`**. We say that `m` is an *array of arrays*. An illustration of the variable `m` is shown in Figure 5.7.

Multidimensional arrays can be initialized in connection with the declaration. Table 5.1 can be described with the variable `temp`, which is declared in the following way:

```
float temp [4] [12] =
   {{11.5, 12.0, 12.9, 13.5, 17.0, 20.5,
     22.2, 22.5, 21.5, 16.0, 13.5,  9.9},
    {19.0, 20.5, 21.0, 23.0, 27.0, 29.0,
     33.0, 35.0, 31.5, 27.0, 22.0, 20.0},
    {15.0, 15.5, 17.0, 19.0, 20.1, 24.0,
     27.0, 27.4, 26.5, 22.7, 17.5, 14.5},
    {17.0, 17.5, 20.5, 21.0, 21.5, 23.0,
     25.0, 26.0, 26.0, 22.7, 21.0, 17.5}};
```

We see that in the initialization expression every line in the table is included in braces. It would have been permissible to omit the first index in the declaration, in which case the compiler itself would have computed the number of lines with the help of the initialization expression.

The easiest way of getting at a particular element in a multidimensional array is to use indexing. We can write, for example,

```
m[1][2] = 14;
cout << temp[2][4];
```

On the second line it would have been appropriate to use enumeration types to make it more readable. If we make the declarations

```
enum month { January,   February, March,    April,
             May,       June,     July,     August,
             September, October,  November, December};
enum temp_type {min, max, mean, water};
```

we can instead write

```
cout << temp[mean][May] << endl;
```

To run through multidimensional arrays we normally use repetition statements nested inside each other. For example, if we want to set all the elements in the variable `m` to zero, we write

```
for (int i=0; i < 3; i++)
  for (int j=0; j < 4; j++)
    m[i][j] = 0;
```

Where one-dimensional arrays were concerned, we saw that the array name was automatically converted to a pointer when it occurred in an expression. The pointer's type was then 'pointer to the element type'. What is the case with multidimensional arrays? Let us declare a pointer variable

```
int *p;
```

We are allowed to write

```
p = &m[0][0]; // OK
```

since the first element is of type **`int`**. By contrast, the following is not correct:

```
p = m; // Error!!
```

The reason for this is that the array name `m` is converted to the type 'pointer to an array with `4` **`int`**s', since `m` is really a one-dimensional array, the elements of which are in turn arrays. If we wish to be able to assign the variable name to a pointer, the pointer must have this type:

```
int (*q)[4]; // Pointer to an array with 4 ints
q = m;       // OK
```

We saw that, for ordinary arrays, pointers were often used instead of indexing. This can be done for multidimensional arrays, but it becomes more complicated:

```
p = &m[0][0];
cout << *(p+6);       // Writes out m[1][2]
q = m;
cout << *(*(q+1)+2); // Writes out m[1][2]
```

It is permissible to have multidimensional arrays as parameters of functions. The following function will write out the contents of a matrix in which the number of columns is `4`:

```
void write (int a[][4], int row_num)
{
  for (int i=0; i < row_num; i++)
  {
    for (int j=0; j < 4; j++)
      cout << a[i][j] << ' ';
    cout << endl;
  }
}
```

The parameter row_num indicates how many rows there are in the matrix, but it is not necessary to indicate this in the declaration of the parameter a. It can vary from call to call. Note, however, that the number of columns in each row must be indicated. This number is fixed and cannot be changed. To write out the matrix m, we can make the call

```
write (m, 3);
```

We conclude by showing a function that adds two matrices a and b, element by element, and places the result in a third matrix c:

```
void add (int a[][4], int b[][4], int c[][4], int n)
{
  for (int i=0; i < n; i++)
    for (int j=0; j < 4; j++)
      c[i][j] = a[i][j]+b[i][j];
}
```

As the number of columns must always be fixed when the parameters are two-dimensional arrays, we cannot make the functions as general as we would like them to be. One solution to this is to consider a two-dimensional array as a one-dimensional array and to give as parameters both the number of columns and the number of rows. Another solution would be to use a vector, which is demonstrated in the following section.

5.9.2 Tables with the help of vectors

You can construct a table by using a vector in which every element is a vector in its turn. To illustrate this, we construct a type that describes matrices. We write the following two declarations:

```
typedef vector<double> row;
typedef vector<row> matrix;
```

On the first line we define the type row, which describes ordinary vectors whose elements are of the type **double**. On the second line we define the type matrix. A matrix is a vector that consists of a number of elements of the type row. We can now declare a matrix variable m:

```
matrix m;
```

The matrix m does not yet have any elements – that is, no lines. To allow it to describe a matrix with 5 lines and 10 columns, we write the following program lines:

```
const int no_of_rows=5, no_of_columns=10;
m.resize(no_of_rows);
for (int j=0; j<no_of_rows; j++)
  m[j].resize(no_of_columns);
```

First we indicate the number of lines and then the length for each individual line. (It is actually possible to have matrixes in which lines are of different lengths, but this is not illustrated in the example.) Individual elements can now be indexed in the matrix `m`. For instance, we can put a multiplication table in `m` by writing

```
for (int r=0; r<no_of_rows; r++)
  for (int k=0; k<no_of_columns; k++)
    m[r][k] = (r+1)*(k+1);
```

This makes it much easier to write functions that have matrixes as parameters than when using multidimensional arrays. For instance, here is a function that prints a matrix with an arbitrary number of lines and columns:

```
void write(matrix a)
{
  for (int r=0; r<a.size(); r++)
  {
    for (int k=0; k<a[r].size(); k++)
      cout << setw(4) << a[r][k];
    cout << endl;
  }
}
```

Note that we have used the operation `size` to determine the number of lines and the length of each line. This function also enables you to print matrices in which the various lines have different lengths. You do not need extra parameters to indicate lengths. The call is thus very easy. To print the matrix `m` we worked with above, we just make the call

```
write(m);
```

We finish by giving a new version of the function `add` on page 194 that adds two matrices. The two matrices `a` and `b` will be added and the result placed in `c`.

```
void add(matrix a, matrix b, matrix& c)
{
  for (int r=0; r<a.size(); r++)
    for (int k=0; k<a[r].size(); k++)
      c[r][k]=a[r][k]+b[r][k];
}
```

Since `c` is an *outparameter* a reference must be used. The function can handle matrices of any dimension. However it is assumed that `a`, `b` and `c` all have the same number of lines, and that all lines are of the same length. (This could be checked, but we refrain from doing that in this simple example.)

5.10 Pairs

If we want a variable that contains several values of the same kind we can, as we have seen, use arrays or some of the standard classes `vector`, `deque` or `list`. However, you sometimes want to create variables that contain data of different kinds. For instance, to describe people's physical characteristics you would need a data type that contained a certain person's name, height and weight. Later in the book we see how you can use classes to construct such general data types, but here we begin by showing how you can simply build data pairs using a standard class called `pair`. In order to use this class, you must have the following line in your program:

```
#include <utility>
```

In our first example we suppose that we want to declare a variable that contains a person's name and height:

```
pair<string, int> p1;
```

The variable is called `p1`, and the expression `pair<string, int>` indicates the type that this variable will have. Inside the characters `<>` you thus write the types for the two data elements that should be included in the pair. It is possible to initialize a pair at the declaration. For instance, we can write

```
pair<string, int> p1("Maria", 170);
```

The simplest way to assign values to a pair is to use the standard function `make_pair`:

```
p1 = make_pair(string("Maria"), 170);
```

(In this case we have made an explicit type conversion from a text string to the type `string`.)

If you want to read or change part of a pair you can use the name `first` or `second` respectively, as illustrated in the following example:

```
cout << p1.first;  // writes out Maria
cout << p1.second; // writes out 170
p1.second = 171;   // changes the height to 171
```

In order to make the program a bit more readable it is often a good idea to use **`typedef`** to give the pair type a simple name:

```
typedef pair<string, int> person_type;
```

You can now use the name `person_type` instead of writing `<pair_string, int>`. We can, for instance, declare a variable:

```
person_type p2;
```

Both the variables p1 and p2 get the same type, and assignments and comparisons are allowed:

```
p2 = p1;
if (p1 == p2)
   cout << "equal" << endl;
```

Pairs can be treated like other types. It is possible to build arrays and vectors in which the elements are pairs. For instance, we can declare a vector u that can be used to store information on the heights of a number of people:

```
vector<person_type> u;
```

This can then be treated as an ordinary vector. We can, for instance, make the statements

```
u.push_back(make_pair(string("David"), 183));
cout << u[0].first; // writes out David
```

Pairs can be useful when constructing functions that need to return more than one result value. For instance, suppose we want to construct a function that has a vector with real numbers as parameters and, as a result, should give both the smallest and the largest number in the vector. Such a function might look like this:

```
#include <utility>
#include <vector>
#include <cfloat>
using namespace std;
pair<double, double> min_max(vector<double>& v)
{
   double min = DBL_MAX; // the largest number possible
   double max = DBL_MIN; // the smallest number possible
   for (int i=0; i<v.size(); i++)
   {
      if (v[i] < min)
         min = v[i];
      if (v[i] > max)
         max = v[i];

   }
   return make_pair(min, max);
}
```

We see that the function results in a pair in which the first value is the vector's minimum value and the second value the vector's maximum value. The following program lines show how you can use the function in order to determine the largest and the smallest of a number of read numbers:

```
vector<double> a;
double x;
while (cin >> x)
  a.push_back(x);
pair<double, double> result = min_max(a);
cout << "Smallest number: " << result.first << endl
     << "Largest number: " << result.second << endl;
```

An element in a pair can, in turn, be a pair. This actually makes it possible to construct functions that give more than two results. As an example of this, we give a new version of the program on page 135 that calculated the roots of a second-order equation. In this program a function called `roots` is used that needs to give three results: one value of type **bool** that indicates whether or not there are real roots, and two values that indicate the roots (if there are any). Earlier we used three reference parameters, but now we shall make use of a pair instead. We declare a type that contains the three values that should be returned as a result:

```
typedef pair<bool, pair<double, double> > root_type;
```

This type describes such pairs where the first component is of type **bool** and the second component in turn is a pair that consists of two values of type **double**. The entire program looks like this:

```
#include <cmath>
#include <iostream>
#include <utility>
using namespace std;
typedef pair<bool, pair<double, double> > root_type;
root_type roots(double p, double q)
{
  double d = p*p/4-q;
  if (d < 0)
    return make_pair(false, make_pair(0,0));
  else
    return make_pair(true, make_pair(-p/2+sqrt(d),
                                      -p/2-sqrt(d)));
}
main ()
{
  double a, b;
  cout << "p? "; cin >> a;
  cout << "q? "; cin >> b;
  root_type answer = roots(a, b);
  if (answer.first)
    cout << "The roots are " << answer.second.first
         << " and " << answer.second.second << endl;
  else
    cout << "No real roots" << endl;
}
```

Exercises

5.1 Find out how many bits are used to represent the predefined numeric types in the C++ compiler you use.

5.2 Find out (try) what happens if you write a program that tries to retrieve the value a null pointer points to.

5.3 Write a function that puts the characters in a text string in reverse order. The function should use two pointers. The only parameter of the function should be a pointer to the string.

5.4 Write a program to read in a number of integers (1000, at most) from the terminal and print them out in the same order, with any given integer being printed only once. If the integer has been printed already, it should not be printed again. For example, if the following numbers are read from the terminal:

```
45 77 -22 3 45 0 21 -1 3
```

the program should output the following:

```
45 77 -22 3 0 21 -1
```

Use pointers to deal with the array in which you have stored the numbers.

5.5 Vectors are also concepts in mathematics. The length of a vector $(v_1, v_2, \ldots v_n)$ is, however, not given by the number of elements in the vector. The length of a vector is instead defined by the formula

$$l = \sqrt{(v_1^2 + v_2^2 + \ldots + v_n^2)}$$

Write a function that calculates the mathematical length of a vector whose components are real numbers.

5.6 In mathematics we say that the two vectors $(u_1, u_2, \ldots u_n)$ and $(v_1, v_2, \ldots v_n)$ are orthogonal if the sum

$$\sum_{k=1}^{n} u_k v_k$$

is equal to zero. Write a function that determines whether or not two whole-number vectors are orthogonal.

5.7 Write a function that copies one text string to another. As well as pointers to both character arrays, the function will get a parameter that indicates the size of the array into which the text should be copied.

5.8 As we know, the function `strcat` copies a text string to the end of another text string. Using pointers, write the function `strcat`.

5.9 The value of an integral

$$I = \int_a^b f(x)\,dx$$

can be approximated, using the *trapezoid rule*, by the formula

$$I = h\left[\frac{f(a)}{2} + f(a+h) + f(a+2h) + \ldots + f(a+(n-1)h) + \frac{f(b)}{2}\right]$$

We have split the interval a to b into n subintervals of length h, that is

$$h = \frac{b-a}{n}$$

Write a function `integral` that calculates the integral of an arbitrary function whose argument and result value have the type **`double`**. As parameters, `integral` should have a pointer to the function to be integrated and the values a and b, which indicate the integration interval. Perform, in the function `integral`, repeated calculations of the integral until the difference between two calculations is sufficiently small. With every new calculation the number of intervals, n, is doubled.

Use the function `integral` to calculate the value of the integral

$$\int_1^5 x^2 dx$$

5.10 Write a program that records temperatures taken at one o'clock in the afternoon, for one week. The program should compute the highest recorded temperature and the mean of the recorded temperatures. The program variable that indicates the current day should be of the type `day_of_the_week` (see page 186).

5.11 Assume that the enumeration type `day_of_the_week` is declared as on page 186. Declare a table `tomorrow` that can be used to find out which day comes after a particular given day. The expression `tomorrow[Tuesday]` should, for example, have the value `Wednesday`, and `tomorrow[Sunday]` should have the value `Monday`.

5.12 Write a new version of the program in Exercise 3.7 on page 108. In the new version, the Roman numerals should not be read into a string variable. Instead, an enumeration type should be used to describe the Roman numerals, and they should be read one by one. The input of the Roman number is complete with the character combination for end-of-file. When you input Roman numerals you can suppose, for simplicity, that at least one blank character is written between the Roman numerals. The user can, for instance, write M C M X L I X. The program will then print 1949. *A hint*: Use the function `get_enum` on page 189.

5.13 Write a function to determine whether an $n \times n$ matrix is symmetric. In a symmetric matrix **A**, $a_{ij} = a_{ji}$ for all i and j.

5.14 A magic square is an arrangement of numbers with n rows and n columns. The sums of the values in each row, column and diagonal are the same. The following square is a magic square, for example:

```
16   9   2   7
 6   3  12  13
11  14   5   4
 1   8  15  10
```

Write a function that determines whether such an arrangement is a magic square. The number of rows and columns is arbitrary.

Another condition for an arrangement of numbers with n rows and n columns to be a true magic square is that it contains all the integers 1, 2, . . . n^2. Amend the function so that it also checks for this condition.

5.15 The simplest form of noughts and crosses is played on a board with 3×3 squares. One player plays crosses and the other noughts, and each takes it in turn to put his or her character in a square. During the game, therefore, a given square can be empty, contain a cross, or contain a nought. The first player to get three characters in a row, column or diagonal has won. Write a function that gets the board as parameter and as result indicates whether a player has won.

5.16 Tables can be constructed showing how different countries border each other. An example is shown in Table 5.2. Write a function `number_neighbours` that will result in a table like this one and a country as parameters. As a result, the function should give the number of countries the given country borders. The call `number_neighbours (tab, Sweden)` should, for example, give a value of 2. (We consider only countries with land boundaries.)

Table 5.2 Countries that border each other.

	Belgium	**France**	**Italy**	**Holland**
Belgium	–	yes	no	yes
France	yes	–	yes	no
Italy	no	yes	–	no
Holland	yes	no	no	–

5.17 The Morse code for the alphabet is shown in the following table, where dots and dashes are used to represent short and long signals, respectively.

A	.-	B	-. . .	C	-.-.	D	-. .	E	.	F	. .-.
G	--.	H	. . . .	I	. .	J	.---	K	-.-	L	.-. .
M	--	N	-.	O	---	P	.--.	Q	--.--	R	.-.
S	. . .	T	-	U	. .-	V	. . .-	W	.--	X	-. .-
Y	-.--	Z	--. .								

Write a program that reads in a message and codes it into Morse code.

Then write another program that reads in a message in Morse code, decodes it, and writes out the decoded message. In the Morse message letters are separated by one space, and words are separated by two spaces.

5.18 An efficient way of sorting the elements of an array goes under the name of *quicksort*. The method can be described by the following recursive algorithm:

1. If the array has no elements or only one element, then it is sorted. Otherwise, perform the following steps:
2. Choose an arbitrary element in the array and call it *k*.
3. Move the elements around in the array so that two groups are formed. The element *k* should be placed between the two groups. All the elements that are less than or equal to *k* should be placed in the group to the left of *k* and all the rest in the group to the right.
4. Sort the part of the array to the left of *k* using this algorithm.
5. Sort the part of the array to the right of *k* using this algorithm.

Write a function that sorts an array with elements of type `double`. Use the quicksort algorithm. The function should be able to sort arrays of different lengths.

5.19 Write a function that calculates both the mean value and the standard deviation for a set of measured values. The values are stored in a vector that is given as a parameter to the function. The mean value and the standard deviation are calculated by the following formulas (x_i denotes the values and n the number of values):

$$\bar{x} = \frac{1}{n}\sum_{i=1}^{n} x_i$$

$$\sigma = \sqrt{\frac{\sum_{i=1}^{n} x_i^2 - \frac{1}{n}\left(\sum_{i=1}^{n} x_i\right)^2}{n-1}}$$

5.20 In the program on page 97 that calculated the commission for sales representatives two vectors were used, one that contained the names of the sales representatives and one that contained the total amount for each sales representative. Rewrite the program so that it uses only one vector. The elements in this vector should be pairs containing name and amount.

6 Object-oriented program development

'Object-oriented' is an important concept in the computer world. You hear of object-oriented design, object-oriented programming, object-oriented analysis, and so on. What does 'object-oriented' mean? There is no absolute definition. One way of trying to describe object orientation is to say that it is a new approach to program development, in which a program system is built up according to the objects it involves rather than according to the functions it should perform. Another way of looking at object orientation is from a more technical perspective, in which we try to describe the idea of 'object-oriented programming'. In object-oriented programming a program is built up of a number of well-delimited units called *objects*.

In this chapter we shall give an introduction to object orientation. We shall discuss the basics of object-oriented programming and what the different words mean. In particular, we shall be discussing the concepts of *class* and *object*. When a large program is to be developed using object orientation, we say that we carry out *object-oriented program development*. Object-oriented program development is normally divided into the three different phases of object-oriented analysis, object-oriented design and object-oriented programming, and we shall be discussing these three phases.

6.1 Basic concepts

In Chapter 1 we gave the traditional picture of a data program. This was a 'box' into which input data was placed and out of which came output data. The program's function was to transform a flow of data. This way of understanding is usually called the *function-oriented* view. The *object-oriented* view is rather different. In this, a computer program is understood to be a kind of *model* of the reality alongside which the program has to work. The different variables in a program, the *objects*, are then models of real or devised things in the program's environment, and the computer program is designed to manipulate these objects. Let us begin by discussing the concept of 'object' in more detail.

Every object has a set of properties, determined by its *attributes* and its *operations*. Attributes are used to monitor the object's state, or status. Every object has a state that can be changed during execution. Every object has its own unique set of attributes. Normally you hide an object's attributes inside the object so that they are inaccessible from outside and can only be changed by the object itself. This is called *information hiding*. For instance, we can study the object `theLift`. Its state can be described with help of the two attributes `direction` and `floor`. The attribute `direction` may have some of the values `stationary`, `up` or `down`, and the attribute `floor` may contain a whole number indicating which floor the lift is on. Different object-oriented languages uses different terms for 'attributes'. The term most often used in an object-oriented context is 'instance variable'. It is used, for example, in Java. In C++ the term 'data member' is used. Because we have programs in C++ we shall use the term data member.

The second category of properties for an object is the *operations* you can perform from the object. For the object `theLift`, for instance, these may be the operations `goTo`, `stop` and `whichFloor`. You use the operation `goTo` to make the lift go to a certain floor, `stop` to stop the lift, and `whichFloor` to determine where the lift is at the moment. In object-oriented contexts, for instance in Java, such an operation is called a 'method', whereas in C++ it is called the 'member function'. We use the C++ terminology, thus *member function*.

Object

- Model of a real or imaginary object.
- A kind of variable.
- Has two kinds of properties: attributes and operations.
- Normally they are called *instance variables* and *methods* respectively, but in C++ the terms *data members* and *member functions* are used.

An object is thus a model of a real or devised thing. How then is an object described in a program? This is where the concept of *class* comes in. A class is thus a *description*. You can have different classes that describe different object sets.

Class

Description of a group of objects with the same properties.

In Figure 6.1 a graphic image of the class `Lift` is given. In this case, we are consistent throughout the book, using diagrams with the notation according to UML (Unified Modeling Language).* UML contains rules on how to present classes, objects etc.

* More information on UML may be found on the website `www.omg/uml/`. Recommended textbooks: Oestereich (1999); Stevens and Pooley (2000).

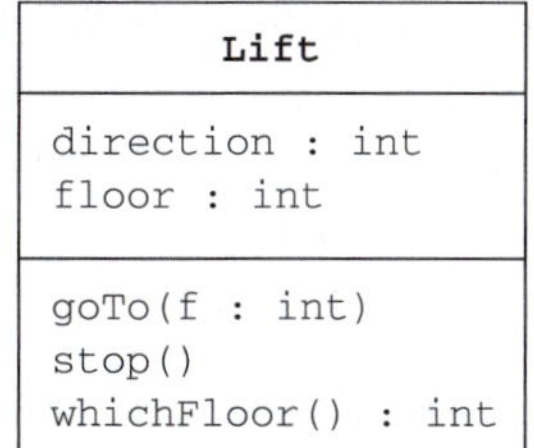

Figure 6.1 A class diagram

liftA : Lift	liftB : Lift
direction = 1 floor = 2	direction = 0 floor = 5

Figure 6.2 Object diagram

visually in conjunction with object orientation. UML has been accepted as standard by OMG (Object Management Group).

In a class diagram according to UML, the class name is placed at the top, the attributes in the middle, and operations underneath. In Figure 6.1 the types of the attributes as well as the types of the parameters for the operations and the result values have been stated. This is not always essential. UML allows you to state just the names of the attributes and the operations. (In the diagram, the direction of the lift is described with a whole number. We can let –1 denote `down`, 0 `stationary` and 1 `up`.)

An object that belongs to a certain class is said to be an *instance* of the class. Several objects can belong to a certain class. In Figure 6.2 an UML diagram is illustrated with two objects of the class `Lift`. For every object there is at the top (underlined) the name of the object, together with the class to which the object belongs and then the values of the attributes.

In the diagram there is a lift with the name `liftA` that is on the way up from the second floor and a lift with the name `liftB` that is stationary at the fifth floor. If an object's name is not relevant, UML allows you to leave it out, but the character : must be there. In this case `: Lift` must be on the first line.

6.2 Object-oriented analysis

Object-oriented program development, as discussed above, can be said to be a kind of model construction. The first question you can ask about object-oriented program development is: 'What should I construct the model from?' In order to be able to answer this question you must try to think through and establish what the new program should accomplish. This step of the program development process is usually called *object-oriented analysis*. The purpose of object-oriented analysis is to familiarize yourself with the problem in order to understand the requirements and make a first, relatively rough, model of the program to be constructed. Concretely, this means:

- finding the objects that should be included in the model;
- describing their attributes;
- establishing the relations between the different objects;
- grouping them.

These steps might need to be gone through in an iterative process, since it is important to ensure that the objects perform all the desired operations. The result of the object-oriented analysis is documented in different diagram forms that show what the model looks like. These diagrams can be supplemented with tables and other written information.

The first step, finding the objects, may appear complex. How do you find 'the right' objects? If you consider the program to be a model of the reality there is a natural way to let every real 'thing' in the reality be represented as an object. If possible, you should also try to find previously constructed objects that can be reused. These may include 'container objects', such as tables and queues, as well as objects that describe graphic pictures on the screen.

Another strategy that has been suggested is writing an informal description of what the system will do. In this description you underline all the nouns and let them be candidates for becoming objects. You let all verbs be candidates for becoming operations on the objects. This seems simple, but the problem is that you will probably end up with too many objects. Not every noun necessarily indicates a suitable object. A noun can, for instance, also indicate a property or state of an object.

You can also study how the system as a whole is intended to work, and produce a number of *use cases* or scenarios. If you think of an object as something that supplies services, you can check whether all the services are accessible. For instance, if you want to construct a program that controls a cash dispenser, you can study use cases such as 'a customer wants to withdraw money' and 'a customer wants to know her account balance'.

Of course there is not only one single set of objects that is the right one. Different sets can give equally good program designs, depending on the quality of the construction and, finally, on the programmer's knowledge, experience and intuition.

In order to use object-oriented analysis in a large program development project, you need the support of a *system development method*. This is a kind of work schedule that indicates how the model ought to be constructed – in other words, what you do to find objects, attributes and relations. The method also prescribes the different forms of diagrams that should be produced. There is usually computer support for the method – that is, programs that help to compile the different diagrams and other information needed. Some examples of common object-oriented system development methods are OMT (Rumbaugh *et al.*, 1991), Objectory (Jacobson *et al.*, 1992) and Coad and Yourdon's (1991a, 1991b) OOA-OOD.

In this case, as in the earlier section, we use the graphic notation of UML. UML is not a system development method, but different methods can prescribe that UML is to be used.

The object-oriented analysis will establish relations between the different objects. We discuss three different kinds of relation in particular:

- *knows*;
- *has*;
- *is*.

The concept *association* is used in UML to generally describe the fact that two classes are related. There is, for instance, an association between the classes `c1` and `c2` if `c1` has attributes of the type `c2`, if `c1` calls operations in `c2`, or if some of the operations of `c1` get a parameter of the type `c2`. In Figure 6.3 an association is shown between the classes `Person` and `Flight`.

An association is illustrated by a *path* between the class diagrams. The name of the association comes in the middle of the path. The small black triangle (voluntary) indicates the direction in which you should read. (It is not always essential to read from left to right.) At one end of an association path you can, if you choose, write a *role name* that indicates the role that the class plays in the association. In this example people play the role of passenger. At one end of an association path you can also indicate a *multiplicity*. This can be indicated either as a simple number or as an interval. `a..b` indicates that the number of objects of the actual type will be in the interval `a` to `b`. The character `*` means 'unlimited'. (`0..*` alternatively may be written as only `*`.) Thus Figure 6.3 should always be interpreted as meaning that a person has booked for 0 or several flights, and that a flight can have between 0 and 300 passengers.

Figure 6.3 describes a *knows* relation. A passenger must know which flights he or she will take, and a certain flight must have a passenger list. In Figure 6.3 we thus

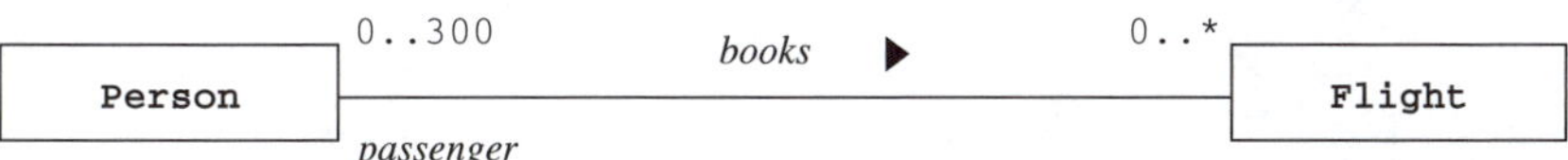

Figure 6.3 Association

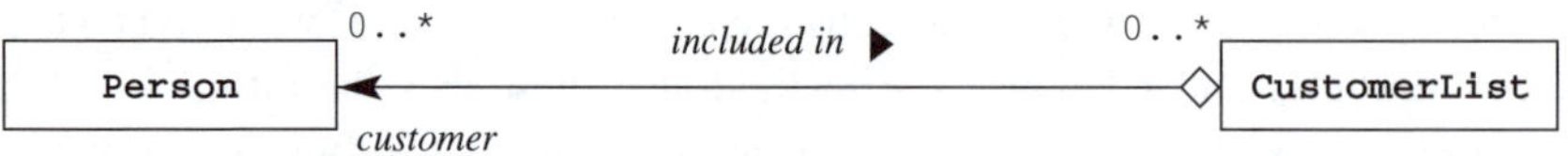

Figure 6.4 One-way association

have a reciprocal bidirectional association. But associations are not always necessarily bidirectional. Study, for instance, Figure 6.4.

A customer database must of course contain information on the people in the database, but the customers themselves do not need to know that they are included in the database. You can use arrows at the end of an association path to indicate the direction of an association – its *navigability*. In Figure 6.4 the arrow to the class `Person` shows that the association runs from right to left. UML does not define what is meant if you do not indicate the navigation arrows. The lack of arrows can mean that an association is bidirectional, but it can also indicate that you have not given information about the navigation. In order to avoid misunderstandings, you may want always to show arrows.

The 'diamond' that you find at the class `CustomerList` in Figure 6.4 indicates that the class `CustomerList` is an *aggregation*. This means that it is composed of a number of people. When the diamond is empty, as in Figure 6.4, this means that the aggregation 'knows' which parts are included in it.

There may also be associations between objects that belong to the same class. For instance, a person can be married. This is demonstrated in Figure 6.5.

Figures 6.3, 6.4 and 6.5 all describe the *knows* relation. The next relation we discuss is the *has* relation, which describes the fact that an object is constructed with the support of another object that it has it as a part. This is sometimes also called *composition*. For instance, a car has an engine and a book has a number of chapters. Figure 6.6 shows how you can graphically describe the fact that an engine has a number of cylinders. Note that the diamond should be filled in. In UML, composition is regarded as a stronger form of aggregation – a form in which the objects as parts are really *enclosed* in the aggregation. For instance, if you copy a composition its parts should also be copied.

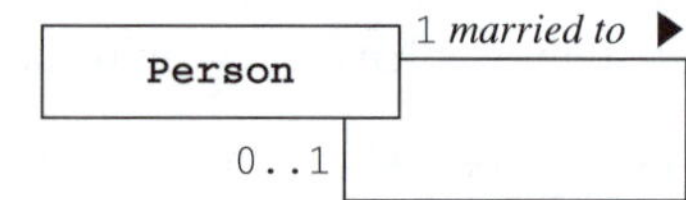

Figure 6.5 Association to the same class

Figure 6.6 Composition

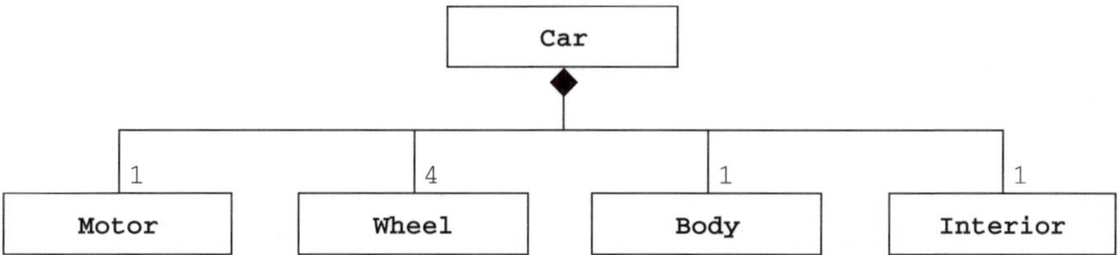

Figure 6.7 Composition with different classes

You can of course have objects consisting of many different sub-objects. Figure 6.7 illustrates how a car is composed of an engine, wheels, chassis and interior fittings.

The *knows* relation is easily confused with the *has* relation. Do not let the word 'has' fool you. That a car has an owner, for instance, does not mean that an owner is a component of the car. In a program you implement the *knows* relation by a pointer. In order to describe the fact that a car has an owner, you let the class `Car` contain an attribute that is a pointer to an object of the class `Person`.

The third important relation in object-oriented program development is the *is* relation. This is used to describe the fact that a class has certain general characteristics that may be shared with other classes: 'a squirrel is a mammal', 'a dog is a mammal'. The common characteristics are described in a separate superclass (in our example in the class `Mammal`). We can have *is* relations in several stages: 'a mammal is an animal', 'an animal is a living thing'. In Figure 6.8 *is* relations are illustrated for different kinds of vehicle. In UML the term *generalization* is used to represent relations of this kind. The superclass is a generalization of the subclasses. In the diagram this is marked with an empty arrow pointing to the superior class.

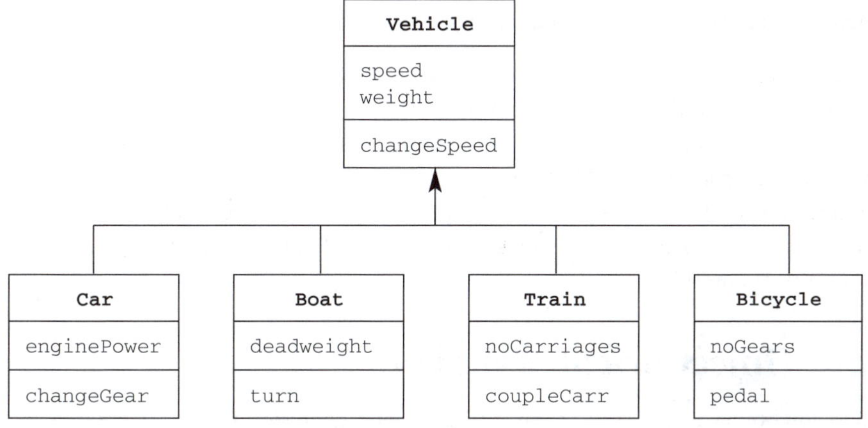

Figure 6.8 Generalization

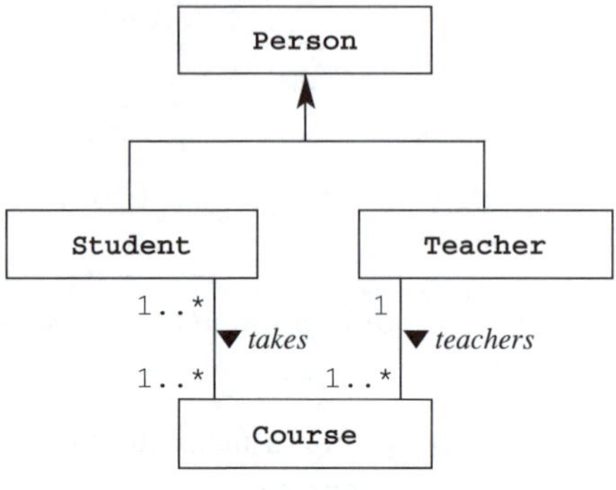

Figure 6.9

In order to describe *is* relations in object orientation you use a concept called *inheritance*. When you are going to describe a class you can start from an existing class and add new attributes or change certain attributes. You say that the new class *inherits* the properties of the old class. The new class becomes a *subclass* of the old class. The old class is said to be a *superclass* to the new class. Suppose, for instance, that we have a class `Person` that describes people. In this class there may be the attributes `name` and `address`. Suppose that we also want to describe students at the university. We can then create a new class `Student` that is a subclass of the class `Person`. The new class will then automatically have all the attributes that are in the class `Person`. We need not redefine the attributes `name` and `address`. In the subclass `Student` the only thing we need to do is declare the new attributes and relations we want. You can, for instance, imagine relations that indicate which courses a student has taken, and an operation that prints the different results a student has achieved. In Figure 6.9 both inheritance and *knows* relations are used to describe the classes `Person`, `Student`, `Teacher` and `Course`. Both students and teachers are people. A student takes a number of courses. A teacher teaches a number of courses. A course has a teacher. A course has several students.

A class that is a subclass of another class can, in turn, be a superclass with its own subclasses. A class can also have several subclasses. This makes it possible to construct class hierarchies with a tree-like structure. One of the thoughts about inheritance is that you are able to use and inherit ready-made classes kept in a *class library*. In this way the need to write new program code is reduced; also, as the ready-made classes are hopefully better tested and closer to fault-free than those that you try to construct yourself.

6.3 Object-oriented design

Up to now we have discussed mainly object-oriented analysis – the first phase in object-oriented program development. After this phase comes the *object-oriented design* phase, in which plans are drawn up and drawings are made for the object-oriented program.

The boundary between the analysis and design phases is a little vague. It could be said that in the analysis phase an idealized model is made, whereas in the design phase this model is made more concrete. Another way to express this is to say that during the analysis phase we think about *what* is to be done, while in the design phase we consider *how* these things are to be done.

The design phase can be divided into two parts: *system design* and *object design*. System design has to do with making global decisions for the system. At this point we ask questions such as how the new system is to be split into subsystems and how it will communicate with its environment. The operating system to be used is also something that needs considering. Part of the environment for our new system might well be a windows-handling system (such as Windows or the X Window system), database handlers and communications programs.

During the object design phase we start with the objects that have been selected in the analysis phase and add a number of details until each object has the form we want it to have. This may involve the application of appropriate algorithms, decisions on how the different operations are to be performed and what parameters they are to have, and so on. We also make decisions on the objects' internal construction during this phase, and decide whether we can reuse previously constructed objects.

A decision on the programming language to use to write the program must be made before the design phase is over, for the program language will affect aspects of different objects as well as the system's ability to communicate with its environment.

Object-oriented analysis and design often merge; it is not unusual for the analysis phase to encroach on the design phase. It is also an *iterative* process, in which a return to the analysis phase may be necessary if something in the design phase has to be changed. The programmer can be flexible in developing object-oriented programs, and does not have to work as rigidly as in the classical waterfall model discussed earlier.

6.4 Object-oriented programming

Our goal in the programming phase is to implement the system: that is, to realize it in the form of a computer program that can be run. Naturally, we try to write as 'good' a program as possible. A program is 'good' if it satisfies the following requirements:

- it is correct;
- it is effective;
- it is reusable;
- it is adaptable.

The first requirement is that the program should be *correct*. It should be able to perform the operations defined in earlier phases of the program development without error. Naturally, this is a very important requirement. If a program contains errors, good properties will not redeem it.

The next requirement is that a program should be *effective*: that is, it should use the resources of the computer system well. Under certain conditions this may be a deciding factor in whether the program can be used or not, but it may not always be of such importance.

Is a correct and effective program always a good program? It depends on what we mean by 'good'. To shed some light on the question, we can look at the costs of producing software. These can be divided into two parts: development costs and maintenance costs. Program development would be simplified if there were more opportunities to use ready-made program components in the same way that we have with mechanical and electronic systems. In other words, software should be required to be *reusable*. If stocks of computer software consisted of complete, reusable and well-tested components, we would soon be in a position where:

- program development costs were lower;
- program development went more quickly;
- software quality improved.

Many programmers spend a great deal of time creating variants of satisfactorily developed programs. Why is this so?

One of the reasons may be that programmers are not used to reusing programs. They may think that it must take at least as long to find a program component and find out how it works as to write it themselves. Also, it is not as easy for a programmer to find an appropriate program component as it is, say, for an electronics design engineer to find a VLSI circuit. If software components are to be reusable, they must conform to certain conditions in terms of the operating system or the ability to handle certain kinds of data. The number of variants can be endless. A reusable program component should be applicable under different conditions. In other words, it should be 'general'.

It is basically a matter of 'packaging'. How should a program component be packaged to make it 'general', so that its functions are easily understood and clearly defined?

Before continuing with our discussion of reusable programs, something needs to be said about the other side of program development costs: *maintenance costs*. A program does not deteriorate, so software maintenance costs cannot be compared with those for a car, for instance. The two main aspects of maintenance costs are correcting errors in the software that should already have been discovered during its design, and adapting software to new circumstances and requirements. That the latter should be necessary is probably caused by incorrect program specifications, or by the problem of forecasting future applications.

Maintenance costs can be low if a program has been kept free of errors from the beginning (by the use of well-tested components, for example) and if the program is intrinsically adaptable.

We can adapt a program more easily if it is constructed from several independent modules, each one being employed for a special, well-defined task. Then changes in the program will simply entail a procedure in which a component is exchanged or removed (as with, for example, the repair of a TV set). As far as possible, we want to avoid interfering with the structure of programs. If changes have to be made, they should be thought out well.

Our ability to take in a complex situation is limited. It is extremely important to minimize the number of contact situations between modules, as well as the number of each module's 'boundaries' in a system. All the information in a module that is local, which is only necessary to be known for the module itself, should be hidden. When the module is used, the user should not need to think about its internal construction. This is where the concept of *information hiding*, which was touched on earlier, comes in. Again, packaging can have a favourable effect on both development and maintenance costs.

In object-oriented programming we should try to write programs that are correct, effective, reusable and adaptable, by allowing individual modules in a program to be constructed from objects that facilitate information hiding. Such objects will be found in the design phase.

For the result to be satisfactory, an *object-oriented programming language*, a language with relevant constructs, should be used. Above all, there are two constructs that are usually required of an object-oriented programming language:

- *Information hiding*. It should be possible to put everything that defines an object's properties into one place in a program. This includes both data and information. The details of a particular object should be hidden so that other objects can neither 'see' them nor 'get to' them.
- *Inheritance*. When defining an object, we should begin with the properties of other objects, adding the new properties as required. In other words, we should try to use previously constructed objects and, making use of the inheritance mechanism, modify and adapt them to our own requirements.

There is a third programming language construct that has proven to be at least as useful as inheritance for writing reusable programs:

- *Generic program units*. A generic program unit is a kind of template that can be adapted to create new program code. Generic program units are specially useful when different kinds of *container* are created. A container is an object that can contain several other objects, an example of this being a list.

C++ and Ada are examples of programming languages that have the three important constructions – information hiding, inheritance and generic program units. C++ has a special language construct called `class`. Objects can be defined easily using this construct. It also facilitates the use of information hiding and inheritance. To construct generic program units in C++, we use something called a *template*.

Classes, inheritance and generic program units will be dealt with at some length later in the book.

References

Coad, P. and Yourdon, E. (1991a) *Object-Oriented Analysis*. Englewood Cliffs, NJ: Yourdon Press.

Coad, P. and Yourdon, E. (1991b) *Object-Oriented Design*. Englewood Cliffs, NJ: Yourdon Press/ Prentice Hall.

Jacobson, I. *et al.* (1992) *Object-Oriented Software Engineering: A Use Case Driven Approach*. Reading, MA: Addison-Wesley.

Oestereich, B. (1999) *Developing Software with UML: Object-Oriented Analysis in Design and Practice*. Harlow: Addison-Wesley.

Rumbaugh, J. *et al.* (1991) *Object-Oriented Modeling and Design*. London: Prentice Hall International.

Stevens, P. and Pooley, R. (2000) *Using UML: Software Engineering with Objects and Components*. Harlow: Addison-Wesley.

Classes

7

In the previous chapter we discussed object-oriented program development and established that the concept of *class* was central to the subject. In this chapter, therefore, we shall look at how classes are constructed in C++. We shall see how the different attributes a class can have are defined and implemented, as well as how information hiding and the two relations *has* and *knows* are realized. (The relation *is* is saved until Chapter 9.)

In C++ a class is the same thing as a type. This chapter may therefore also seem to follow on from Chapter 5, where the built-in types in C++ were discussed. Classes are more advanced types than the basic, 'ordinary' types, such as integer types and array types. For the ordinary types there is a collection of predefined operations available to the programmer. For example, integers can be added, and indexing can be carried out in arrays. In the case of ordinary types, data is also stored in a predefined way. An array, for example, consists of a series of similar elements lying one after the other in a row; indexing here always takes place from 0, and the length of the array is not stored. Where classes are concerned, it is left entirely to the programmer to decide what operations are to be used and how data is to be stored. We can declare our own array types, we can keep track of the array's length, and we can let indexing start at a value different from 0, from 1 or 100, for example. Types that contain components of different kinds can also be defined with the aid of classes. If we want to define persons, for instance, we can define a class `Person` containing both a name (of type `string`) and a length (an integer).

In computer science, a type constructed entirely by the programmer, who also defines exactly which operations to use and how to store data, is called an *abstract data type*. In C++ abstract data types can therefore be said to be constructed with classes.

7.1 Class definitions

As a first example, let us look at the following lines, which describe a clock:

```
class Clock {
public:
   void set (int hour, int min, int sec);
   int read_hour ();
   int read_min ();
   int read_sec ();
   void write(bool write_sec=true);
   void tick();
private:
   int h, m, s;
};
```

The above lines constitute a *class definition*. A definition of this kind is always introduced with the word **class**, which is a reserved word in C++. After the word **class** the name of the class is indicated, in this case `Clock`. Note that the name starts with a capital C. We shall continue to let all class names begin with a capital. It will then be easier to keep track of which identifiers denote variables and which denote classes. Since a class is the same thing as a type, `Clock` can be said to be the name of a *type*, just as **int** and **double** are the names of types. From now on, all types defined with the aid of classes will be called *class types* (when we need to differentiate them from different kinds of type, such as integer types and pointer types).

Definition of class

class *name* {
public:
   declarations of visible
   member functions and data members
private:
   declarations of hidden
   member functions and data members
};

Objects belonging to the class `Clock` have nine attributes: the six operations `set`, `read_hour`, `read_min`, `read_sec`, `write` and `tick` and the three data attributes `h`, `m` and `s`. We shall use the conventional terminology in C++ and call the operations *member functions* and the attributes *data members*. The data members `h`, `m` and `s` are used to keep track of hours, minutes and seconds. The member function `set` can be called when the clock is to be set. The member functions `read_hour`, `read_min` and `read_sec` return values of `h`, `m` and `s` respectively. The member function `write` gives a printout in the form `hh:mm:ss` or `hh:mm`, depending on whether the parameter `write_sec` is **true** or **false**. (The parameter `write_sec` has the default value **true**.) The member function `tick` is called every time a second has passed.

A declaration of a member function looks just like that of an ordinary function declaration, the only difference being that it is placed *inside* the class definition. In the same way, a declaration of a data member looks just like an ordinary variable declaration, the difference being that a member variable is declared inside the class definition. The reserved words **`public`** and **`private`** are used to obtain information hiding. The word **`public`** indicates that the attributes that are declared in the subsequent part of the class definition should be *visible* – that is, accessible everywhere – whereas the word **`private`** indicates that the subsequent attributes should be *private* – that is, accessible only inside the class. If neither of the words **`public`** or **`private`** is indicated, all the members of a class will be considered to be private.

In C++ declarations of members can be placed in any order, and this applies to the reserved words **`public`** and **`private`**. We have chosen here to put the **`public`** sections with the member functions first and the **`private`** sections with the data members last. Most authors usually put members in this order, but the **`private`** sections are sometimes put first. In this book we shall be putting the **`public`** sections first because the **`public`** section of a class definition is the most interesting for the user of the class. This section should therefore come first so that it can be seen more easily. Since the user of a class does not have access to whatever is declared in the **`private`** section, this part will be irrelevant to all the program sections except those where the class is implemented. For this reason the **`private`** sections have been put last.

Let us look at a small program that uses the class `Clock`:

```
main()
{
  Clock c;
  int hh, mm, ss;
  cout << "Set the clock!" << endl
       << "Indicate hour, min and sec" << endl;
  cin >> hh >> mm >> ss;
  c.set(hh, mm, ss);
  cout << "How many ticks? "; cin >> ss;
  for (int i=1; i<=ss; i++)
    c.tick();
  cout << "The time is now "; c.write();
}
```

A test run of the program could look like this:

```
Set the clock!
Indicate hour, min and sec
17 58 0
How many seconds should tick? 130
The time is now 18:00:10
```

To get an object that belongs to the class `Clock`, we have to create an *instance* of the class. This can be done in C++ with an ordinary variable declaration. On the third line of the program the variable `c`, which has type `Clock`, is declared:

```
Clock c;
```

The type `Clock` is handled exactly as an ordinary type. For instance, we can declare how many variables we want of this type, or declare pointers or references to variables of type `Clock`.

A member function can be called with the aid of the *dot operator*. We write the name of the object we want to perform the function for, followed by a dot, and then the function call itself with its arguments. For example, the line

```
c.set(hh, mm, ss);
```

is a call of the member function `set` for the object `c`. As usual, `hh`, `mm` and `ss` indicate the actual parameters (arguments). In more 'object-oriented' terminology it can be said that 'the message `set` is sent with the arguments `hh`, `mm` and `ss` to the object `c`'.

Note that each object of a class – that is, each variable of a type – has its own data members, which are *independent* of other objects. For instance, if we declare yet another clock:

```
Clock c2;
```

this one will have its own data members `hh`, `mm` and `ss`. The lines

```
c.set (10, 30, 45);
c2.set(15, 20, 00);
cout << c.read_hour() << ' ' << c2.read_hour();
```

give the printout

```
10 15
```

We can have pointers to other objects that belong to classes, exactly as for other types. We can write, for example

```
Clock *p;
```

The variable `p` is then a pointer to a `Clock`. To get `p` to point to a certain clock, the address operator `&` can be used as usual, or memory space can be allocated dynamically with the help of the operator **`new`**:

```
p = &c;          // p points to the variable c
p = new Clock;   // p points to a nameless new Clock
```

When a member function for an object is called via a pointer, we should use not the dot operator but the *arrow operator* `->` as in the following example:

```
p->set(21, 56, 30);
p->tick();
```

The dot operator can also be used with pointers, but then the * operator must first be employed to access the object the pointer points to. The second line above could then be written in the following way (parentheses are necessary since the dot operator has higher priority than the * operator):

```
(*p).tick();
```

So far we have seen how the class `Clock` is defined, and how it can be used in a program. In the class definition for each member function we have written only its *declaration*: that is, the line that says what the function is called, what parameters it has, and what result type it returns. For a class to be used, the *definitions* of the member functions, containing the complete implementations of the functions, must of course exist somewhere. In C++ there are two alternatives here for the definitions of member functions. They can be placed either directly in the class definition, or separately, outside the definition. To demonstrate the first alternative, we shall create another variant of the definition of the class `Clock`. We now place the definitions of the three simplest member functions `read_hour`, `read_min` and `read_sec` directly into the class definition:

```
class Clock {
public:
   void set (int hour, int min, int sec);
   int read_hour () {return h;}
   int read_min () {return m;}
   int read_sec () {return s;}
   void write(bool write_sec=true);
   void tick();
private:
   int h, m, s;
};
```

Note that the data members are directly accessible inside the member function although they were not declared in the function or given as function parameters. But this applies only to member functions. If we had had another function, not a member function in the class `Clock`, we would not have been able to access `h`, `m` and `s` in the function. When we indicate the name of a data member inside a member function, the data member that is meant is the one that belongs to the object for which the member function is called at that moment. If, for example, we make the call

```
c.read_hour()
```

then by `h` inside the definition of `read_hour` is meant the `h` belonging to the variable `c`. If we had instead made the call

```
c2.read_hour()
```

`h` in the definition of `read_hour` would have meant the `h` belonging to the variable `c2`.

The three remaining member functions, `set`, `write` and `tick`, are defined separately, outside the class definition:

```
void Clock::set(int hour, int min, int sec)
{
  h=hour; m=min; s=sec;
}
void Clock::write(bool write_sec)
{
  cout << setw(2) << setfill('0') << h
  <<':'<< setw(2) << setfill('0') << m;
  if (write_sec)
    cout << ':'<< setw(2) << setfill('0') << s;
}
void Clock::tick()
{
  s = (s+1) % 60;
  if (s==0)
  {
    m = (m+1) % 60;
    if (m==0)
      h = (h+1) % 24;
  }
}
```

Members' accessibility

- *Outside* the class only *visible* members can be accessed – those that have been declared in the `public` section of the class definition. Then the dot operator or arrow operator is used:
  object_name . member_name
  pointer_to_object –> member_name
- *Inside* a member function, all the members can be accessed without dot notation.

Member functions are no ordinary functions. They have special properties that ordinary functions do not have. A member function has, for example, direct access to the data members of a class. When a member function is defined separately, outside the class definition, it is not enough to write the name of the member function. We must also indicate which class the function is a member of. This is done by writing the class name in front of the name of the member function, with a double colon between them.

In our example, therefore, we wrote the function names `Clock::set`, `Clock::write` and `Clock::tick`.

It can be handy to define the member functions directly in the class definition, since there would be less to write, but there is good reason to be careful here. This is because the program's readability will suffer. The user of a class studies the class definition. If this is full of codes, lacking in interest, it could be difficult to distinguish what is important. The user is interested only in how the member functions should be called and not what they look like inside.

Something else should be known about the placement of the definitions of the member functions, and this has to do with how the C++ compiler translates the member functions into machine code. When a function call is made (this applies both to ordinary functions and to member functions), the compiler usually generates machine code: this means that the program *jumps* to another place in the code where there is code for the function called. When the machine code for the function has been executed, there is a *jump back* in the program to the position where the call was made. The machine code for the function itself is therefore found in only one position, and all calls will result in a jump to that position. There must be a certain number of instructions at every call to enable these jumps back and forth and to transfer the function's parameters. If a function is very simple and consists of only one or two statements, it is very likely that the machine instructions for a call will be more complicated and will demand greater primary memory space than the machine instructions for the function itself. When this is the case it would be much better not to perform a jump to the function but instead to execute the function's machine instructions directly where the call is made. Then a function is said to be *inline*, and so it is called an *inline function*. The code for an inline function is therefore duplicated at all the places in the program where the function is called.

Member functions are often very short – as, for example, the functions `read_hour`, `read_min` and `read_sec` – so it could be useful to call these *inline* sometimes. If the *definition* of a member function (that is, the member function's code) is placed in the class definition, the compiler will automatically try to convert these functions into inline functions. Since long functions are not supposed to be inline functions, it is not appropriate to define functions longer than a couple of statements in a class definition. These functions should be defined separately.

There is much to be said for keeping class definitions free of function definitions, even if it means writing a little more. They look better and are easier to read. So all functions should really be defined separately, outside the class definition, even very short ones. If we want the functions we have defined separately to be inline functions, we can always add the reserved word **`inline`** in the function definition. For instance, we can indicate that we want the member function `set` to be an inline function by letting the separate definition look like this:

```
inline void Clock::set(int hour, int min, int sec)
{
  h=hour; m=min; s=sec;
}
```

Definition of member functions

- Should be placed separately, outside the class definition:
  result_type class_name::*function_name*(*parameters*)
  { *local declarations and statements* }
- Very short member functions can be defined directly in the class definition (not recommended). They are then *inline* functions.
- Separately placed functions can also be defined as *inline*:
  inline *result_type class_name*::*function_name*(*parameters*)
  { *local declarations and statements* }

7.2 Placement of classes

We have now seen how classes are defined, and how they can be used in a program. The question now is how to divide a program into program text files and place class definitions, definitions of member functions and user programs in the best way. When writing a very small program it is possible in principle to put everything in the same file, but this is not adequate when the program is bigger. In section 4.5 we discussed how programs could be conveniently divided up. We were dealing with functions then, and we decided that we should construct program files *in pairs*. For every definition file that contained function *definitions*, or complete functions, we were to have a corresponding header file in which we placed corresponding function *declarations*: that is, declarations of the function heads. The header files were to have names that ended in '`.h`', and the definition files were to have names ending in '`.cpp`' (or a similar suffix). We should use similar principles when working with classes: we should create pairs of files, a header file and a definition file. A class definition is placed in the header file, and in the corresponding definition file are placed definitions of member functions. If we have a group of classes that are close to each other, we can put several class definitions in the same header file. In this case the corresponding definition file should contain the definitions of member functions in all the classes.

The term class *declaration* and not class *definition* would seem to be in keeping with the terminology we have used up to now, since function declarations, and not function definitions, are put into header files. But the term 'class declaration' is used for constructs of the form

```
class MyClass;   // class declaration
```

where we indicate only that the name `MyClass` denotes a class and that the complete definition will come later. We shall see that such constructs are needed when classes have to cross-refer to each other.

As an example, let us look at a new class `Flight`, which will describe regular flights. A header file is constructed with the name `flight.h`, which contains the definition of the class `Flight`. The file looks like this:

```
// The file flight.h
#ifndef FLIGHT_H
#define FLIGHT_H
#include "clock.h"
#include <string>
using namespace std;
class Flight {
public:
  void init(string flight_no,
            int dep_h, int dep_m, int arr_h, int arr_m);
  void info();
  void delay(int min);
private:
  string no;
  Clock dep, arr;
};
#endif
```

The second, third and last lines require some commentary. In C++ it is not allowed to define a class more than once in a compilation. For instance, if we wanted to have the definition of class `Flight` twice in our program, we would get a compilation error because the compiler would understand that we were trying to define two classes with the same name, which is not allowed. The risk of writing the same class definition twice in the same program text file may not be very great, but when we use header files this may very well happen. Suppose, for example, that in the file `f1.cpp` both the file `f2.h` and the file `flight.h` are included. Further suppose that we need, in file `f2.h`, the class `Flight` and have, therefore, also included file `flight.h` there. This means that when file `f1.cpp` is compiled, file `flight.h` will be read twice by the compiler.

The second, third and last lines of file `flight.h` are there to prevent file `flight.h` being included more than once in a compilation. `FLIGHT_H` is the name of a *macro*, a kind of constant that we define ourselves. On the second line there is a check as to whether a macro with this name has been defined (`#ifndef` means 'if not defined'). If it has not, the compiler will read the whole text until the line `#endif`. The first time the compiler comes upon file `flight.h`, the macro `FLIGHT_H` has not been defined. The compiler will therefore read the text. A definition of the macro `FLIGHT_H` (the macro is not given a value, but it is not needed; getting the definition is enough) occurs on the third line, which begins with #define. If the compiler should come upon file flight.h a number of times, it would jump over the text up to and including the line with #endif. The class Flight can therefore never be defined twice. We recommend this procedure for all header files containing class definitions. It is advisable to let the macro have the same name as that of the file but with capital letters.

Let us now look at the class Flight itself. It has three data members: a character array no, which contains the flight number, for example BA2078, and two clocks with the names dep and arr to indicate the departure time and arrival time respectively. Here we have an example of the *has* relation that we discussed in Chapter 6. An object of class Flight 'has' two clocks. We suppose that the definition of class Clock is in a header file with the name clock.h. To access class Clock, we must therefore include this file. This happens on the fourth line.

The class Flight has three member functions. The first one, init, is used to initialize a flight. The flight number, together with departure and arrival times, must then be indicated as parameters. The member function info writes out information about a flight, and delay is called when the flight is delayed, the length of the delay being a parameter. The function delay will then update the departure and arrival times for the flight in question.

Where functions are concerned, header files should not contain definitions with function bodies, only the function declarations. This principle also applies when we deal with classes. So we put the definitions of the member functions into a corresponding definition file with the name flight.cpp:

```
// The file flight.cpp
#include "flight.h"
#include <iostream>
#include <iomanip>
#include <string>
using namespace std;
void Flight::init(string flight_no,
                  int dep_h, int dep_m, int arr_h, int arr_m)
{
  no = flight_no;
  dep.set(dep_h, dep_m, 0);
  arr.set(arr_h, arr_m, 0);
}
void Flight::info()
{
  cout << "Flight no " << no;
  cout << ", Dep "; dep.write(false);
  cout << ", Arr "; arr.write(false);
  cout << endl;
}
```

```
void Flight::delay(int min)
{
  for (int i=1; i <= min*60; i++)
    dep.tick();
  for (int j=1; j <= min*60; j++)
    arr.tick();
}
```

Note especially that file `flight.h` must be included to make the definition of class `Flight` accessible. (File `clock.h`, on the other hand, does not need to be included, since it is already included in file `flight.h`.)

The data members `dep` and `arr` are objects of class `Clock`, and the member functions for class `Clock` are called to handle these objects. The data members in `dep` and `arr` cannot be accessed directly since they lie in the private section of class `Clock`.

A program using class `Flight` must include the file `flight.h`. As an example, we show below the following simple main program, which we shall place in a file with the name `demo.cpp`:

```
// The file demo.cpp
#include "flight.h"
main()
{
  Flight f;
  f.init("SK1853", 8, 10, 10, 55);
  f.delay(15);
  f.info();
}
```

The printout from this program will be

```
Flight no SK1853, Dep 08:25, Arr 11:10
```

For the program to be run, it must be compiled and linked. If we suppose that the definitions of the member functions for class `Clock` are in a file with the name `clock.cpp`, then three compilations will be needed. Files `demo.cpp`, `flight.cpp` and `clock.cpp` must be compiled. If a compiler that is started from the command line is used, the following commands will be necessary. (This example is from a Windows system.)

```
gxx -c demo.cpp
gxx -c flight.cpp
gxx -c clock.cpp
gxx -o demo.exe demo.o flight.o clock.o
```

The last line contains the command to link the program. Alternatively, everything can be done with one command:

```
gxx -o demo.exe demo.cpp flight.cpp clock.cpp
```

If an integrated program development system such as Visual C++ is used, the compilation commands will not be written in this way. Instead, what is called a *project* is defined, where files `demo.cpp`, `flight.cpp` and `clock.cpp` are indicated as being parts of the project. A command is then chosen from one of the menus that compiles and links all of the files in the project.

A header file should not contain separate definitions of member functions, but an important exception is the inline functions, which have to be defined in the header file. This applies to inline functions defined in the class definition as well as to those defined separately. The file `clock.h`, for example, can have the following appearance:

```
// File clock.h
class Clock {
public:
   void set (int hour, int min, int sec);
   int read_hour () {return h;}
   int read_min () {return m;}
   int read_sec () {return s;}
   void write(bool write_sec = true);
   void tick();
private:
   int h, m, s;
};
inline void Clock::set(int hour, int min, int sec)
{
   h=hour; m=min; s=sec;
}
```

Division of classes into files

- For every class, or group of associated classes, two files are created: a *header file* and a *definition file*.
- The *header file* contains the class definition and definitions of possible member functions that are inline functions.
- Use `#ifndef` and `#endif` to avoid duplicating definitions.
- The *definition file* contains definitions of all member functions that are not inline functions.

Here we have chosen to let the functions `read_hour`, `read_min`, `read_sec` and `set` be inline functions. Note that if the function `set` had not been defined inline, it would have been put instead into file `clock.cpp`.

From here on in the book we shall be assuming that class definitions and definitions of member functions have been placed in program files in the way described in this section. We shall not be discussing file division, therefore, when we give different examples of classes.

7.3 Constructors

When ordinary variables are declared, we may wish to initialize them. This is not permissible for the data members of a class:

```
class C {
  int i = 0;           // ERROR! initialization forbidden
  const int k = 0;     // ERROR! initialization forbidden
};
```

When an object of a class is declared, all the object's data members will be uninitialized unless the object is initialized in some other way. The easiest way to initialize objects automatically is to use something called a *constructor*. A constructor is a special kind of initialization function that is *automatically* called every time a variable of a certain class is declared, or when an object of the class is created in some other way – with **new**, for example.

7.3.1 Declarations of constructors

Let us return to the class `Clock` and take it as an example. We shall make a new variant of the class definition:

```
class Clock {
public:
  Clock ();
  Clock (int hour, int min, int sec);
  void set(int hour, int min, int sec);
  int read_hour(){return h;}
  int read_min(){return m;}
  int read_sec(){return s;}
  void write(bool write_sec = true);
  void tick();
private:
  int h, m, s;
};
```

What is interesting here are the two new lines

```
Clock ();
Clock (int hour, int min, int sec);
```

A constructor is a kind of member function that has the *same name* as the class it is a member of. We have therefore declared two constructors here, both with the name

`Clock`. In C++, as we know, it is possible to have overloaded functions – functions with the same name but different parameters. This also applies both to member functions and to constructors. The two constructors `Clock` have different parameters, so they are overloaded. The first constructor has no parameters, and the second one has three parameters of type `int`.

A constructor that can be called without arguments is called a *default constructor*. That a default constructor can be called without arguments means either that it has no parameters or that it has only parameters with default values. If a constructor for a class is not defined, a default constructor will automatically be defined for it. (This cannot happen, however, and the program will be faulty if the class contains data members that are constants or references or that are of a class type without default constructors. In addition, the class is not allowed to have a base class without default constructors. See Chapter 9.) An automatically defined default constructor does not do anything when it is called, and if we declare a constructor, of any kind, no default constructor will be automatically defined. In this case, therefore, if we want to have a default constructor, we have to define it ourselves.

Declaration of constructors

class_name(*list of parameters*);

- Initializes an object. Is called automatically when an object is created.
- Has same name as the class.
- Several can be overloaded with different parameters.
- A constructor that can be called without arguments is called a *default constructor*.
- A default constructor is automatically defined if no constructors have been declared by the programmer. (Compilation error if the class contains data members that are constants, references or objects lacking default constructors, or if the class has a base class without default constructors.) An automatically defined default constructor does not do anything.

Note that no return type has been indicated for the constructors. This is because constructors differ from ordinary functions in that they cannot leave a result. It is not even permissible to indicate the type `void`.

7.3.2 Definitions of constructors

Constructors are defined in the same way as other member functions, either directly in the class definition, or separately. If we want to define the first constructor directly in the class definition, we can write

```
Clock () {h=m=s=0;}
```

Here we see that this constructor simply sets the three data members `h`, `m` and `s` to `0`. If we prefer not to have the definition of the constructor in the class definition, we can instead give a separate function definition:

```
Clock::Clock ()
{h=m=s=0;}
```

Note the rather clumsy way of indicating the function name. The first word `Clock` indicates that a member function of the class `Clock` is involved, while the second `Clock` indicates that the member function is called `Clock` (which implies that it is a constructor, its name being the same as the class name).

We can define the second constructor separately in a similar way:

```
Clock::Clock(int hour, int min, int sec)
{h=hour; m=min; s=sec;}
```

Here we see that the member variables have been assigned values from the parameters.

Instead of carrying out assignment in the function body, we can have an *initialization list* in constructors, where we indicate what initialization value each data member is to have. We can then write the definition of the second constructor as

```
Clock::Clock(int hour, int min, int sec)
: h(hour), m(min), s(sec) {}
```

The initialization list is written immediately after the parameter list and is introduced by a colon. Here we see that the data member `h` should be initialized to the value `hour`, `m` to `min` and `s` to `sec`. A function definition must always have a function body, so after the end of the initialization list there must be a function body even if, as in this case, it is empty.

It is also possible to mix the initialization of data members. Some can be initialized with the initialization list and some using ordinary initialization:

```
Clock::Clock(int hour, int min, int sec)
: h(hour), m(min) {s=sec;}
```

In this constructor it does not matter if we use an initialization list or carry out ordinary assignments; but sometimes it is necessary to use an initialization list, for instance if we have to initialize data members that are constants or references, since we are not allowed to assign to these. Moreover, initialization lists can give more effective code when we initialize data members that are objects. It is therefore advisable to use initialization lists if possible, and we shall be making use of them from now on.

Definition of constructors

class_name::class_name(parameter list) initialization list
{*function body*}

- An initialization list can be omitted. Initialization lists have the form
  :*d1*(*expression*), *d2*(*expression*) . . .
  where *d1, d2* . . . are names of data members.
- References and constants must be initialized with the initialization list.

7.3.3 Calling constructors

Constructors are not called in the same way as ordinary functions. Let us, as an example, look at some program lines that create objects of the class `Clock`:

```
Clock c1;
Clock c2(8,25,30);
Clock c3 = Clock(22,15,10);
Clock *p1, *p2;
p1 = new Clock;
p2 = new Clock(14,5,40);
```

In the first line the default constructor for class `Clock` will be automatically called, which means that the data members for `c1` are set to `0`. The second and third lines show an alternative way of initializing an object when it is declared. In both of these cases the second constructor, the one with three arguments, will be called. The style of the second line is recommended, for if that of the third line is adopted, the compiler may create a temporary object of class `Clock`, which would be later copied to `c3`. On the penultimate line, an object is created dynamically using **`new`**. Since no arguments are indicated, a default constructor will be called for the object created. The last line illustrates that arguments can be given when an object is created dynamically. Here the constructor with three parameters is automatically called. The following statements can be added:

```
c1.write();  cout << endl;
c2.write();  cout << endl;
c3.write();  cout << endl;
p1->write(); cout << endl;
p2->write(); cout << endl;
```

which result in the printout

```
00:00:00
08:25:30
22:15:10
00:00:00
14:05:40
```

An expression of the form `C` (*parameter list*), where `C` is the name of a class, is an explicit call of a constructor for class `C`. What happens is that a temporary object of class `C` is created and initialized with the constructor. For example, we can write

```
c1 = Clock(19, 05, 45);
f(Clock(23, 40, 00));
```

In the first line a temporary object is created, which is then assigned to `c1`. In the second line a function `f` is called with a temporary object as argument. If we suppose that the function `f` has a formal parameter `p` of type `Clock`, the temporary object will then be copied to the parameter `p`. In certain cases the compiler is allowed to jump over a stage to form a temporary object. When the function `f` is called, it is possible, for instance, for the parameter `p` to be directly initialized with the help of the constructor without the creation of a temporary object.

We shall now see what happens when we create arrays where the elements are objects. We make the declaration

```
Clock cf[3];   // The default constructor is called
```

The variable `cf` is an array with three clocks. When this declaration is carried out, the default constructor (the one without parameters) will be automatically called for each of the three elements in the array. For this to happen there must be a default constructor for the actual class. If this is not so, we shall get a compilation error. The default constructor is also called automatically when arrays are allocated dynamically. In the following statement, for example, the default constructor will be called five times:

```
p1 = new Clock[5];   // The default constructor is called
```

An array can be initialized using a constructor other than the default constructor. If we write

```
Clock aa[] = {Clock(9,35,20), Clock(14,55,50)};
```

we get an array with two clocks, both of which are initialized with the constructor that has three parameters. (Temporary objects may be formed, and these will then be copied to the elements in the array `aa`.) We can see what some of the clocks contain:

```
aa[0].write();   // write 09:35:20
aa[1].write();   // write 14:55:50
cf[2].write();   // write 00:00:00
p1[4].write();   // write 00:00:00
```

If a class contains data members that are objects of another class, these data members can also be initialized with constructors. In order to demonstrate this we shall return to class `Flight` to add two constructors – a default constructor and one with parameters:

```
class Flight {
public:
  Flight() {};
  Flight(string flight_no,
         int dep_h, int dep_m, int arr_h, int arr_m);
  as before
private:
  string no;
  Clock dep, arr;
};
```

Observe that the default constructor has an empty function body;

We shall now define a variable of type `Flight`:

```
Flight f1;
```

No parameters are given, so the default constructor will be called. There the data members `no`, `dep` and `arr` will be initialized with the default constructors of their classes. The data member `no` is a string and it will be initialized to an empty string of length zero. The other two data members, `dep` and `arr`, are objects of class `Clock`. The default constructor for class `Clock` is automatically called, for both `dep` and `arr`. These data members will then be auto- matically initialized to the time `00:00:00`.

If we want an object of type `Flight` to get a proper flight number, and the departure and arrival times to be initialized to the correct values at declaration, we should ensure that the second constructor, the one with the parameters, is called. We therefore proceed as follows:

```
Flight::Flight(string flight_no,
               int dep_h, int dep_m,
               int arr_h, int arr_m)
: no (flight_no), dep(Clock(dep_h, dep_m, 0)),
  arr(Clock(arr_h, arr_m, 0))
{                          }
```

We use an initialization list here to initialize the data members `dep` and `arr`. Both of them are initialized with explicit calls of a constructor for the class `Clock`. If we declare a variable

```
Flight f2("TP0255", 11, 25, 13, 05);
```

the departure and arrival times for this flight will get the values `11:25:00` and `13:05:00` respectively.

7.3.4 The copy constructor

When an object is declared, it can be initialized so that it becomes a copy of another object of the same type. We can then write, for example,

```
Clock ca(7, 35, 30);
Clock cb = ca;
```

In the second line, object `ca` will be copied to object `cb`. What actually happens is that a special constructor, the *copy constructor*, for class `Clock` is called, and it is this constructor that copies the data members, one at a time, from `ca` to `cb`. We can, as we shall soon see, ourselves define a copy constructor for a class, but if we do not do this, one will be defined automatically.

An object can contain several *subobjects* that are either data members or so-called *base class subobjects* (see Chapter 9). The automatically defined copy constructor copies each subobject individually in the following way. Subobjects of a simple kind (scalars and pointers) are copied bit by bit, exactly as with ordinary assignments. If a subobject is of class type, the copy constructor for this class is called to do the copying. If, finally, a subobject is an array, each element in the array is individually copied according to the rules above. We can, for instance, declare an object, `f2`, of type `Flight` and initialize it with another object:

```
Flight f1;
Flight f2 = f1;
```

When `f2` is initialized, the automatically defined copy constructor for type `Flight` is called. This copies the data member `no` from `f1` to `f2`. Since the type `string` is a class type, the data member `no` is a subobject of class type. Therefore the copy constructor of the class `string` is called to initialize `no`. The data members `dep` and `arr` are subobjects of class type, so the copy constructor for class `Clock` is called for each one of them.

The copy constructor is not only called when variables are also initialized. It is also called when parameters are transferred to functions, or when values are returned from functions. We also count as 'initialization' the initializing of data members using an initialization list. For example, we can declare another constructor for class `Flight`:

```
Flight(string flight_no,
       Clock dep_h, Clock arr_h);
```

Apart from the flight number, this constructor has two parameters that are objects of class `Clock`. The definition of the constructor looks like this:

```
Flight::Flight(string flight_no,
               Clock dep_h, Clock arr_h)
: no (flight_no), dep(dep_h), arr(arr_h)
{                     }
```

If this constructor is called, which happens, for instance, if we make the declaration

```
Flight f3("AA7089", ca, cb);
```

the copy constructor for class `Clock` will be called twice, once at the initialization of `dep` and once at the initialization of `arr`.

Note that the copy constructor can be called only with initializations and not with ordinary assignments. If we write, for example,

```
Flight f4 = f3;    // The copy constructor is called
f4 = f3;           // The assignment operator is called
```

the copy constructor will be called in the first line but *not* in the second. Instead, the assignment operator will be called in the second line. We shall return to this later in the book.

In most cases there is no point in defining a copy constructor since the automatically defined copy constructor does exactly what we want. But when we are working with classes that allocate memory space dynamically, we often have to define our own copy constructor so that everything goes according to plan. To demonstrate this, we shall construct a class with the name `Array`. This class will describe arrays of arbitrary length with element types that are **`int`**. Unlike ordinary arrays, the class `Array` will also contain the length of an array. Another difference is that indexing will not always need to start from 0. Instead, we shall be able to choose which number the array's first element should have. Indexing will also be safe, so that it will not be possible to make the mistake of indicating an index lying outside the array.

(We construct the class `Array` for pedagogical reasons. Therefore let us for the moment forget that there is an excellent class `Vector`, which can be used instead of arrays.)

We shall use the standard function `assert` to carry out checks in the program code. An expression should be written as argument for `assert`, for example:

```
assert(n>0);
```

The function will check that the expression is true. If the expression were false, we would get an error printout of the form

```
Assertion failed: n>0, file vector.cpp, line 25
```

and the program would then be terminated. In order to use the function `assert`, the file `cassert` must be included.

```
#include <cassert>
```

The function `assert` is a good one to use during the program's development, when we are checking that everything is working as it should. When the test run is finished and we are absolutely sure that everything is correct, we can do away with checks to increase the effectiveness of the program. This is most easily done by adding the line

```
#define NDEBUG
```

just before the line that includes the file `cassert`.

Now to class `Array`. It has the definition

```
class Array {
public:
  Array(int first_index=1, int number=0);
  Array(const Array& a);
  int first() {return i1;}
  int last() {return i1+num-1;}
  int length() {return num;}
  int read(int index);
  void change(int index, int value);
private:
  int *p;
  const int i1;
  int num;
};
```

There are two different constructors. The first gets two integers as parameters, and these indicate the lowest index allowed and the number of elements. If, for instance, we want to create an `Array` object that is indexed from 101 and has 50 elements, we write

```
Array aa(101, 50);
```

Both parameters have default values. If the second parameter is omitted, we get an `Array` object that (for the time being) has no elements. The second constructor is the interesting one here, since it is our own copy constructor, which replaces the one generated automatically. We can tell that it is a copy constructor from the parameter's type because a copy constructor for a class `X` always has a parameter of type `const X&` (or only `X&`): that is, the parameter is a *reference* to another object of type `X`. This constructor is called automatically if we have declarations such as

```
Array ab(aa);
Array ac = aa;
```

There are three data members in the class `Array`. The constant integer `i1` indicates the first allowable index, and `num` indicates the number of elements. The pointer `p` is a pointer to an internal ordinary array with `num` elements. The space for the array must be allocated dynamically in the constructor every time a new `Array` object is created.

The copy constructor

class_name(**const** *class_name&*);

- Has a parameter that is a reference to another object of the same class.
- Is called automatically if there are declarations of the form

```
X x1=x2;
X x1(x2);
```

  where `X` is a class and `x2` belongs to class `X`.
- Is called only with declarations, *not* with ordinary assignment.

The three member functions `first`, `last` and `length` can be called if we want to keep track of an `Array` object's first or last index, or its length. Since these functions are trivial, they have been defined directly in the class definition. The two member functions `read` and `change` are called to read and change, respectively, a particular element in an `Array` object. (We shall later replace these two member functions by an indexing operator.) The integer parameter `index` indicates which element is concerned.

Let us look at how the different member functions have been defined. We begin with the constructors. The first constructor has the definition

```
Array::Array(int first_index, int number)
: i1(first_index), num(number)
{
  assert(num>=0);
  p = new int[num];
}
```

The data member `i1` is a constant and must therefore be initialized in the initialization list. The standard function `assert` is then used here to check that the number of elements is not negative. (But a zero number of elements is allowed.) If the number is correct, space is allocated for the array, and the pointer to the array is kept in `p`.

Our own copy constructor has the definition

```
Array::Array(const Array& a)
: i1(a.i1), num(a.num)
{
  p = new int[num];
  for (int i=0; i<num; i++)
    p[i] = a.p[i];
}
```

The new `Array` object that is initialized with this constructor should be a copy of the `Array` object `a` given as parameter. The new `Array` object should have the same index boundaries and length as the Array object a, so first the values of i1 and num are copied from the Array object a to the new Array object. The next step is to allocate an array that has as many elements as the corresponding internal array in the Array object a. Finally, we run through all the elements in Array object a and copy them to the array in the new Array object.

Why do we have to define our own copy constructor? Isn't the one that is automatically defined sufficient? Unfortunately, this one will not work here. If we used it, every data member in the Array object a would be copied independently to the new Array object, and if we copied the pointer a.p, we would get a pointer that pointed to the *same* internal array that was used by the Array object a. This would mean that the new Array object and the Array object a would *share* the internal array, and each change that was made in one of the elements in the one Array object would change the corresponding element in the other Array object, which would be absurd of course. We have to copy the *whole* internal array, not a pointer to the array. This procedure is called carrying out a *deep copy*, in contrast to using an automatically defined constructor, which results in a *shallow copy*. Generally speaking, we can state that when memory space is to be created dynamically for data members in a class, we need to have our own copy constructor.

Now all that remains is to give the definitions of the member functions that are left:

```
int Array::read(int index)
{
  assert(index >= i1 and index <= last());
  return p[index-i1];
}
void Array::change(int index, int value)
{
  assert(index >= i1 and index <= last());
  p[index-i1] = value;
}
```

These functions check both with the help of assert and see that the index indicated lies within the permitted boundaries.

To conclude this section, we shall include an example of a program that uses the class Array. The program reads a number of test values, then computes and writes out both their sum and the sum of the squares of the values. Two help functions are defined in the program: sum and square. The function sum calculates the sum of the elements in an Array object, and the function square changes the contents of the Array object so that each element is squared. Note that the two help functions are not member functions of the class Array. They are therefore called in the usual way, and they can only use whatever is declared in the **public** section of the class Array. Two Array objects are declared in the program: `a1` and `a2`. The program begins by reading how long the `Array` object `a1` is to be and then declares `a1`. `Array` object `a2` is initialized to be a copy of `a1`, and we use our own copy constructor.

```
#include "array.h"
#include <iostream>
using namespace std;
int sum(Array& a)
{
   int s = 0;
   for (int i=a.first(); i<=a.last(); i++)
      s += a.read(i);
   return s;
}
void square(Array& a)
{
   for (int i=a.first(); i<=a.last(); i++)
   {
      int x = a.read(i);
      a.change(i, x*x);
   }
}
main()
{
   int n, x;
   cout << "Number of test values? "; cin >> n;
   Array a1(1,n);
   cout << "Indicate test values" << endl;
   for (int i = 1; i<=n; i++)
   {
      cin >> x;
      a1.change(i,x);
   }
   Array a2 = a1;
   square(a2);
   cout << "The sum: " << sum(a1) << endl;
   cout << "The sum of the squares: " << sum(a2) << endl;
}
```

7.3.5 Type conversion constructors

In section 5.7.2 we discussed explicit type conversions, and we saw that an expression of the form

`typename(expression)`

was a type conversion from the expression's type to the type indicated in the type name. A constructor that can be called with only one argument has exactly this form and is therefore called a *type conversion constructor*. (That a constructor can be called with one argument means that it must have at least one parameter. If it has more than one, all of these except the first one will have default values.) Let us take a simple example. We define the following class `RatNum`, which describes the rational numbers:

```
class RatNum {
public:
   RatNum() : numer(0), denom(1) {}
   RatNum(int i) : numer(i), denom(1) {}
   declarations of several member functions
private:
   int numer, denom;
};
```

Rational numbers are numbers that can be written exactly as a quotient of integers, usually called the numerator and the denominator. (For example, the numbers 2/3, 19/5 and 23/1 are rational numbers.) We therefore let class `RatNum` have two data members, which contain only the numerator and denominator. We have defined two constructors. The first has no parameters and is therefore a default constructor. The second constructor has a parameter, so it is a type conversion constructor. If we write

```
RatNum r1, r2(5);
```

then `r1` will be initialized to `0/1` with the default constructor, and `r2` will be initialized to `5/1` with the second constructor.

The interesting thing about type conversion constructors is that the compiler tries to use them to make *automatic* type conversions. If we now write, for example,

```
r1 = 9;
```

then there are different types to the left and right of the assignment operator. On the left we have the type `RatNum`, and on the right the type **`int`**. For the assignment to be made, therefore, the value to the right must be converted to type `RatNum`. The compiler discovers that there is a type conversion operator converting from type **`int`** to type `RatNum` and so turns out code, which means that this constructor is called automatically. The result is then the same as if we had made an explicit type conversion:

```
r1 = RatNum(9);
```

Type conversion constructors can be called on all the occasions when the compiler tries to produce automatic type conversion.

A constructor can be both a default constructor and a type conversion constructor at the same time. For example, in class `RatNum`, we can manage with a single constructor:

```
RatNum(int i=0) : numer(i), denom(1) {}
```

By giving the parameter a default value, this constructor can be called either with zero or with one argument.

Let us look at yet another example. As we have seen, it is not easy to handle texts in C++ if you use character arrays. It is therefore natural to define a class that simplifies text handling. (The class `string` in the standard is an example of a class like this.) Here we shall define a class `Text` that describes objects that contain text. We can describe a text with two member variables: an integer that indicates the length of the text, and a pointer that points to a memory space allocated dynamically when an object is created.

```
class Text {
public:
   Text(int n=0);
   Text(char *s);
   declarations of several member functions
private:
   char *p;
   int length;
};
```

We have declared two constructors here. The first initializes an object so that it will contain a text consisting of `n` blank spaces. The second initializes an object so that it contains a copy of the text the parameter `s` points to. We make the definitions of the constructors separately:

```
Text::Text(int n) {
   assert(n>=0);
   length = n,
   p = new char[length+1];
   for (int i=0; i<length; i++)
     p[i] = ' ';
   p[length] = '\0';
}
Text::Text(char *s) {
   length = strlen(s);
   p = new char[length+1];
   strcpy(p, s);
}
```

We can now make the declarations

```
Text t1(5), t2("Beware of the dog");
```

The object `t1` will contain a text consisting of five blank characters, and `t2` will contain the text `"Beware of the dog"`. Since both constructors can be called with one parameter, they are type conversion operators, so that we can get automatic type conversion in expressions such as

```
t1 = "C++";
t2 = 3;
```

We sense that the first of these assignments is a natural one. We change `t1` so that it will contain the text `"C++"`. The other automatic type conversion does not occur as intuitively. If we tried to assign an integer to a text, this would generally be understood as a programming error. In fact, it is possible here. What happens is that `t2` will contain a text consisting of three blank characters. If the compiler turns out a great deal of non-intuitive automatic type conversions, it can be very difficult to understand what is happening in a program. It can therefore be desirable to prevent some of these automatic type conversions from occurring in the first place. In the standard there is a construct that makes it possible to prevent certain type conversion constructors from being used with automatic type conversion. The reserved word **`explicit`** is written in the declaration of the constructor:

```
explicit Text(int n=0);
```

And now the second of the above assignments will be incorrect. If we really want to create a text object containing a text with three blank characters, we have to make an explicit type conversion. This is still allowed:

```
t2 = Text (3);
```

7.4 Destructors

We recall from section 5.4.6 that it is a common error, when working with dynamically allocated memory space, not to release memory space that is no longer needed. In class `Array`, which we constructed earlier in this chapter, we allocate memory space, for example, every time a new object of class `Array` is created, and this happens in one of the two constructors. As we know, a constructor is called automatically every time an object is declared or created with **`new`**. There is a corresponding language construct that is automatically called every time an object ceases to exist. This is called a *destructor*. A destructor is a member function without parameters, and it is exactly like a constructor in that it is not allowed to have a result type. The name of a destructor is the same as the class name, except that it has a ~ (tilde) in front. A destructor is declared, like other member functions, in the class definition. We can add a destructor to the class `Array`:

```
class Array {
public:
  ~Array();  // Declaration of a destructor
  as earlier
};
```

The destructor `~Array` is automatically called when objects of type `Array` cease to exist. If an object has been declared in the usual way, a destructor will be automatically called when we leave the block in which the object has been declared. Again, if an object has been allocated with **new**, this will happen when we want to deallocate the object with **delete**:

```
{
   Array a1;          // A constructor for a1 is called
   Array *pa;
   pa = new Array;    // A constructor for *av is called
   ...
   delete pa;         // The destructor for *pa is called
}                     // The destructor for a1 is called
```

If a class `C1` has a data member belonging to another class `C2`, the destructors for both class `C1` and class `C2` will be called when an object of type `C1` ceases to exist. For example, if we have a class `VV`:

```
class VV {
   Array y, z;
   ...
};
```

then the destructor for `y` and `z` will be called if an object of class `VV` ceases to exist:

```
{
   VV w;   // Constructors for y, z and w are called
   ...
}          // Destructors for w, z and y are called.
```

A destructor has the task of 'cleaning' and returning any memory space we ourselves have allocated. This means that, for class `Array`, the destructor should release the array that the member variable `p` points to. Of course, the destructor can be defined directly in the class definition. Then we write

```
~Array () { delete[] p;}
```

Destructors

~class_name`();`

- Used to 'clean' an object.
- Automatically called when an object ceases to exist.
- Has the same name as the class with the character ~ in front.
- Is always without parameters. Cannot be overloaded.

But we can also define the destructor separately:

```
Array::~Array()
{ delete[] p;}
```

By constructing our own destructor for class `Array`, we can be sure that all the memory space we have allocated will be returned.

7.5 An object-oriented example

It is now time to show a longer example constructed according to object-oriented principles, which will also illustrate how some of the material we have covered in this chapter can be used. We'll write a program that allows the user to play the card game 'Twenty-one' with the computer. The game is played in the following way: the user receives one card at a time and after each card makes a decision whether or not to have another card. The user has to try to make the sum of a 'hand' as near to 21 as possible, without overstepping this number. An ace is counted as either 1 or 14. If the number 21 is overstepped, the user loses and the computer wins. But if the user stops at a number under 21, the computer has to draw one card at a time, deciding after each card whether to continue or not. If the computer has more than 21 points or a score lower than the user's, the user wins; otherwise the computer wins. The computer is therefore the winner if both have the same number of points.

We begin by defining a class `Card`, which defines the cards. We can create new cards, read a card's suit or value, or write information about a card. The parameters for the constructor have default values allowing it to function as a default constructor.

```
enum suit {clubs, diamonds, hearts, spades};
class Card {
public:
  Card(suit = clubs, int = 1);
  suit su( (){ return f;}
  int value(){ return v;}
  void write_out();
private:
  suit f;
  int v;
};
```

The definitions look like this:

```
#include "card.h"
#include <cassert>
#include <iostream>
using namespace std;
```

```
Card::Card(suit ss, int vv)
{
  assert(vv >=1 && vv <= 13);
  s=ss;
  v=vv;
}
void Card::write_out()
{
  const char *tab1[] = {"Clubs", "Diamonds",
                        "Hearts", "Spades"};
  const char *tab2[] = {"Jack", "Queen", "King"};
  cout << tab1[s] << ' ';
  if (v == 1)
    cout << "Ace";
  else if (v <= 10)
    cout << v;
  else
    cout << tab2[v-11];
}
```

To define a collection of cards, we define the class `Cardstack`. An object of class `Cardstack` can define either a card in a player's hand or the whole pack of cards.

```
#include "card.h"
#include <vector>
using namespace std;
class Cardstack {
public:
  Cardstack() {stack.reserve(52);}
  void throw_cards() {stack.clear();}
  int number_cards() { return stack.size();}
  Card look_at (int nr);
  Card deal_top();
  void lay_top(Card k);
  void new_pack();
  void shuffle();
private:
  vector<Card> stack;
};
```

A cardstack consists of ('has') a number of cards, and we put these into the vector `stack`, which is a private data member. Since it is most common to use cardstacks with 52 cards we let the constructor reserve space for 52 cards in the internal array of the vector. (This is not necessary, however.)

To lay new cards at the top of the stack we use the member function `lay_top`. If we want to change a cardstack so that it contains a new pack with all 52 cards, we can call the function `new_pack`. Cards are taken from a stack with the function `deal_top`. There is also a function `throw_cards`, which removes all the cards from a stack. The cards may be looked at without removing them from the stack, with the function `look_at`, and this will have a card number as parameter. Number 1 represents the top card in the stack, while the number of the card at the bottom can be found by calling the function `number_card`, which gives the current number of cards in the stack. Finally, the function `shuffle` will shuffle the cards in a stack. This is especially necessary if the stack contains a new pack that is to be shuffled before the game begins.

The definitions of the member functions in class `Cardstack` are given here:

```
#include "cardstack.h"
#include <iostream>
#include <cstdlib>
#include <ctime>
using namespace std;
Card Cardstack::look_at (int no)
{
  return stack.at(stack.size()-no);
}
Card Cardstack::deal_top()
{
  Card top = stack.back();
  stack.pop_back();
  return top;
}
void Cardstack::lay_top(Card k)
{
  stack.push_back(k);
}
void Cardstack::new_pack()
{
  stack.clear();
  for (suit s=clubs; s<spades; s=suit(s+1))
    for (int v=1; v<=13; v++)
      stack.push_back(Card(s, v));
}
void Cardstack::shuffle()
{
  srand(time(0));
  for (int i=1; i<1000; i++)
  {
    int n1 = rand() % stack.size();
    int n2 = rand() % stack.size();
    Card temp = stack[n1];
    stack[n1] = stack[n2];
    stack[n2] = temp;
  }
}
```

In the vector `stack`, the bottom card lies at place number `0` and the top card at the place with the number `Stack.size()-1`. In the parameter `no` of the function `look_at`, `1` means the top card, `2` the next one down, and so on. To take the right card, therefore, we must pick the card with the index `Stack.size()-no` from the stack. (We use the operation `at` in order to get index check.) Because the upper card lies last in the vector, it is easy to add and remove cards in the functions `lay_top` and `deal_top`. The operations `pop_back` and `push_back` can be used.

We run through all the combinations of suits and values in the function `new_pack`. The constructor for class `Card` is called once for each combination.

The most difficult member function is `shuffle`, which will run for 1000 rounds. At every round it randomly chooses two integers `n1` and `n2` in the interval `0` to `number-1`. It then changes the places of the cards for places `n1` and `n2` in the pack. The standard function `rand` is called to elicit random numbers. When it is called, this function returns a random integer ≥0 as result. In order to get a number in the interval `0` to `number-1` we divide this result by `number` and see what the remainder is. This remainder must, of course, lie in the required interval.

The function `rand` calculates a random number using the formula:

$$s_n = K \cdot s_{n-1} + L$$

where s_n is the new random number, s_{n-1} is the previous random number that was calculated, and K and L are two appropriately chosen constants. Repeated calls of `rand` will therefore generate a sequence of integers. We should note especially that if we generate several sequences of numbers, each time starting with the same value, s_0, then the same sequences of numbers will be generated every time. In our case this would mean that the cards would be shuffled in exactly the same way every time we ran the program, and there would not be anything particularly random about the procedure. To find a remedy for this, we have to make sure that the start value, s_0, is different each time the cards are shuffled. To indicate a start value for the function `rand` we call another standard function, `srand`. This will have an integer s_0 as parameter. To give a random value to s_0, we call a third function, `time`, which will return a large integer (equal to the number of seconds that have passed since a certain date). Every time we run our program, `time` will return different values as result. Different random sequences will be generated. We have to include the file `cstdlib` to be able to use the standard functions `rand` and `srand`, and to be able to use the standard function `time` we have to include the file `ctime`.

Note that both `Card` and `Cardstack` are completely independent of the game that will be played. They are quite general in character, and could just as easily be used to write a program for a game of patience.

Our next class is the class `Player`, which describes a participant in the game Twenty-one. This class is, of course, intended only for this game.

```
#include "cardstack.h"
class Player {
public:
   Player(Cardstack& cardpack, bool is_computer)
   : pack(cardpack), computer(is_computer) {};
   int play();
private:
   Cardstack hand;
   Cardstack& pack;
   const bool computer;
   int points();
};
```

A player has three data members: `hand` is a cardstack that describes the cards in the hand of the player, `pack` is a *reference* to the pack used in the game, and `computer` indicates whether the player is a computer or a person. The data member `computer` has been declared as a constant, since a player's properties will not change during the course of the game. The data member `pack` is an excellent example of the relation *knows*. A player must know the pack of cards used in the game to be able to draw cards from it. It is important for both players to use the same pack, so the relation *has* will not work here. If we had written

```
Cardstack pack;   // ERROR!
```

each player would then have his or her *own* pack of cards to play with, and this would be completely independent of the pack the other player played with. Clearly, it is important to have a reference to a stack of cards in order to describe the whole pack. We could also have used pointers, in which case we would have written

```
Cardstack *pack;   // Would have been all right
```

The relation *knows* can thus be described either with references or with pointers. Since a reference is a constant that cannot be changed once it has been initialized, it is appropriate to use references to describe constant *knows* relations. In this example a player will know the same pack of cards for the duration of the game. If we want to describe relations that can be changed during execution of the program, we should use pointers.

The data members in objects of class `Player` are initialized in the constructor. This has two parameters, a reference to the pack of cards used and a value of type **`bool`** that states whether the current player is a computer or not. An initialization list must be used here to initialize the data members `pack` and `computer`, since both are constants and cannot be initialized in an assignment. The third data member, `stack`, is not named explicitly but will be automatically initialized with the default constructor for class `Card`.

The member function `play` is called when it is the turn of the current player to play. This function returns as result the number of points the player scored. Coming last, in the private section of the class definition, is a declaration of a member function with the name `points`. This is a help function that is used internally at the definition of the function `play`. It is not meant to be called from outside, so it has been declared in the private section of the class definition.

Before we see how the member functions in the different classes are defined, let us look at the main program:

```
#include "player.h"
#include <iostream>
using namespace std;
main ()
{
  Cardstack pack;
  Player you (pack, false);
  Player I (pack, true);
  char answer[10];
  cout << "Welcome to twenty-one" << endl;
  while (true)
  {
    cout << "New game? "; cin >> answer;
    if (answer [0] != 'y') break;
    pack.new_pack();
    pack.shuffle();
    int p1 = you.play();
    if (p1 > 21)
      cout << "You lost!" << endl;
    else if (p1 == 21)
      cout << "You won!" << endl;
    else
    { // The computer must play
      int p2 = I.play();
      if (p2 <= 21 and p2 >= p1)
        cout << "You lost!" << endl;
      else
        cout << "You won!" << endl;
    }
  }
}
```

Now it only remains to write the definitions of the member functions in class `Player`. First comes the internal help function `points`, which calculates how many points the player's hand is worth:

```
#include "player.h"
#include <iostream>
using namespace std;
int Player::points()
```

```
{
  int p = 0, number_aces = 0;
  for (int i=1; i <= hand.number_cards(); i++)
  {
    int v = hand.look_at(i).value();
    if (v == 1) {
      p += 14;
      number_aces++;
    }
    else
      p += v;
  }
  for (int j=1; j <= number_aces and p > 21; j++)
    p -= 13;  // counts an ace as 1
  return p;
}
```

The function `play`, which is called every time it is a player's turn, looks as below. The variable `continue` indicates whether the player would like another card or not. When this applies to the computer, we use the strategy of 'sticking on' 16 points or more.

```
int Player::play()
{
  bool continue = true;
  int p;
  while (continue)
  {
    Card k = pack.deal_top();
    hand.lay_top(k);
    p = points();
    if (computer) {
      cout << "The computer got "; k.write_out();
      cout << endl;
      if (p >= 16)
      {
        cout << "The computer has " <<p<< " points" << endl;
        continue = false;
      }
    }
    else
    { // Person
      cout << "You got "; k.write_out();
      cout << " and have " << p << " points" << endl;
      if (p < 21)
      {
        char answer[10];
        cout << "One more card? "; cin >> answer;
        continue = answer[0] == 'y';
```

```
        }
        else
          continue = false;
      }
    }
    hand.throw_cards();
    return p;
}
```

Finally, here is an example of how the program can look when it is run:

```
Welcome to twenty-one
New game? y
You got Clubs 5 and have 5 points
One more card? y
You got Clubs 7 and have 12 points
One more card? y
You got Hearts 4 and have 16 points
One more card? n
The computer got Diamonds 4
The computer got Spades 4
The computer got Hearts 6
The computer got Hearts Jack
The computer has 25 points
You won!
New game? y
You got Clubs 8 and have 8 points
One more card? y
You got Diamonds 6 and have 14 points
One more card? y
You got Diamonds Jack and have 25 points
You lost!
New game? n
```

Exercises

7.1 Construct a class `Counter` that counts integers that can only take on values in a certain interval. When a counter is initialized, the start value should be indicated, as well as the least and greatest values the counter can take on. (If no boundary values are indicated, the counter should take on all the values of type **`int`**.) There should be member functions with which we can count up and down a counter with the number `1`. If a counter should then get a value that is not allowed, an error printout should result. We should also be able to read a counter's value.

Then use the class `Counter` in a program to read in a text and calculate how many blank characters occur in the text. Divide the text into appropriate files.

7.2 Complete the class `Text` on page 240 so that there are operations with which a particular character in a text can be changed and read. There should also be an operation enabling us to find out how long a text is. Construct an appropriate destructor for the class.

7.3 Construct a class `Person`. A person should have a name, an address and an age. Make use of the class `Text`. Formulate a constructor and some appropriate member functions for class `Person`.

7.4 For class `Clock` on page 216 there is a member function that advances a clock by one second. It is not practical to call this function again and again if we want to advance the clock by a larger time interval. Write a member function for class `Clock` that can advance a clock by an arbitrary number of seconds at one time.

7.5 To define a point in a two-dimensional coordinate system, it is most common to use the form (x, y), called *rectangular coordinates*. Construct a class `Point` that describes points in this way. Write appropriate constructors and a member function that calculates the distance between a given point and another. The distance, d, between two points (x_1, y_1) and (x_2, y_2) is given by the formula

$$d = \sqrt{[(x_1 - y_1)^2 + (x_2 - y_2)^2]}$$

7.6 In the previous exercise, points were described using rectangular coordinates. An alternative way of defining points is by using polar coordinates (r, θ), where r is the distance of the point from the origin. If we imagine a straight line drawn through the origin and the point, this line will form an angle with the x-axis, and this is θ. Conversion from polar coordinates to ordinary rectangular coordinates can be effected with the formulas

$$x = r \cdot \cos\theta$$
$$y = r \cdot \sin\theta$$

First define a class `Rpoint`, where the points are defined using polar coordinates, then write a type conversion constructor for class `Point` in the previous exercise, which converts from an `Rpoint` to a `Point`.

7.7 Complete the class `RatNum` on page 239 with a constructor that gets both a numerator and a denominator as parameters. When the new rational number is initialized, you should make sure that the denominator is never negative and that the nominator and denominator do not have common factors. (*Tip*: Use the function `gcd` from Exercise 4.7.)

Now write a member function `add_to` that gets another rational number `r` as parameter. The function should add `r` to the actual number. You should make sure that here, too, numerator and denominator do not have common factors.

7.8 Construct a class `Passenger` that will define a passenger on a flight. Each passenger can have a maximum of 10 departures during a flight (use class `Flight` on page 223). A passenger must therefore know (contain pointers to) this. There should be a constructor that initializes a passenger with appropriate flight departures. Here you should check that times and flights correspond, so that a person will not take a flight that leaves before the previous flight has arrived. There should also be a member function with which you can replace one flight by another. Check here, too, that times and flights correspond. If a flight is delayed, a passenger may need to change the flight that follows. Write a member function that checks whether this is necessary for a particular passenger. To solve this exercise you must add two member functions that make it possible to examine the departure and arrival times of a flight.

7.9 Complete the class `Cardstack` in section 7.5 by an operation that combines two cardstacks in one. Then use the classes `Card` and `Cardstack` to construct a program that plays the card game *Starve the Fox*. This game is played by two players. First all the cards are dealt out, with each player getting a stack of 26 cards. One of the players plays his or her top card, after which the two players take it in turns to play a card. The player who first plays a higher card of the same suit as the card first played may then take all the cards on the table and put them under his or her stack. If the card that is played first happens to be an ace, it is counted as 1; aces are worth 14 points otherwise. The player who loses all his or her cards also loses the game.

7.10 A company has a warehouse that contains several different types of article, and there may be several different examples of each article in stock. The following information will be interesting to know for each article: the *article identification* (a code of four characters), the *article description* (a text with at most 30 characters), the *number of articles* of a particular kind in stock, and the *sales price*. Write a class `Article` that defines the articles.

You need a program that keeps track of all the articles in stock. Write a program that first reads in this information about the articles and places the information into an array with elements of type `Article`. (Assume that there are no more than 1000 kinds of article in the warehouse.) Input can terminate when, for example, the article definition '`0000`' is given. The program will then repeatedly read commands from the terminal and perform the tasks required. The different commands are as follows, where `xxxx` stands for an article definition code:

`info xxxx`	Write out all current information about article `xxxx`.
`sell xxxx n`	Register that *n* items of article `xxxx` have been sold.
`buy xxxx n`	Register that *n* items of article `xxxx` have been put into the store.

More about classes

8

We have now learnt how to construct our own types with the aid of classes. In this chapter we shall be going further and learning more about what we can do with classes. The emphasis will be on how to create our own operators to work with objects in the same way as if they were built-in standard types. This we must do if the classes we construct are to be functional and maintain their 'general' character.

In order to be able to make the operators as general as we should like, we shall have to waive some of our principles regarding information hiding, for we shall be describing what are known as friends – functions or other classes – which give an insight to the private sections of classes.

In this chapter we shall also be discussing constant objects and functions as well as static data members, class variables found only in an instance that is shared by all the objects in a class.

8.1 Constant objects

We know that an object is a variable whose type is a class, and we have seen that constant variables and function parameters can be declared. This also applies to objects. For example, we can write

```
const Clock ck;
```

If we now try to call a member function that changes a constant object:

```
ck.tick();   // ERROR!
```

or call a function that has a pointer or reference to a changeable `Clock` as parameter:

```
void f1 (Clock *cp);
void f2 (Clock& cr);
f1 (&ck);   // ERROR!
f2 (ck);    // ERROR!
```

the compiler will discover this and give a compilation error.

Some member functions do not change the data members of the actual object. These are called *constant functions*. The function `read_hour` is an example of a constant function. Ordinary member functions cannot be called for constant objects, but it ought to be possible to call constant member functions. The problem is that we shall get a compilation error if the compiler does not know that the member function is constant. For instance, we would get a compilation error if we wrote

```
int hour = ck.read_hour();
```

But we can still indicate explicitly which member functions are constant in a class definition. We do this by writing the reserved word **const** after the parameter list in a function definition. We now adjust the definition of class `Clock` and indicate that the functions `read_hour`, `read_min`, `read_sec` and `write` are constant:

```
class Clock {
public:
  Clock ();
  Clock (int hour, int min, int sec);
  void set(int hour, int min, int sec);
  int read_hour() const {return h;}
  int read_min() const {return m;}
  int read_sec() const {return s;}
  void write(bool write_sec = true) const;
  void tick();
private:
  int h, m, s;
};
```

We are now allowed to call the functions for constant objects:

```
ck.write();                  // OK
int min = ck.read_min();     // OK
```

The compiler checks that we keep our word. For instance, if in the definition of the member function `write` we tried to change the actual object all the same, we would get a compilation error:

```
Clock::write() const
{
  h = 0;    // ERROR!
  tick();   // ERROR!
  ...
}
```

It is a good habit to indicate which functions are constant in the class definition, since we do not then limit the functions' usefulness unnecessarily. We shall be developing this habit from now on.

Constant member functions

- Member functions that do not make changes in the actual object.
- Are indicated by the word `const` in the function definition *result_type function_name*(*parameter list*) `const`;

8.2 The pointer this

When a member function is called, it is always for a particular object. If we make the call

```
c1.tick();
c2.tick();
```

the member function `tick` will be called for the object `c1` in the first line and for the object `c2` in the second. No object name is indicated inside the member function `tick`. For instance, there can be a line like this:

```
s++;
```

How can the member function `tick` know that in the first call it should change the data member `s` in the object `c1` and in the second it should change the `s` that is in `c2`? The answer is that all *member* functions get an extra hidden parameter that is not seen, either in the parameter list or at the call of the function. This hidden parameter is always called **this**. Its type is 'pointer to `C`', where `C` is the name of the class in question. All member functions in class `Clock`, for example, have a hidden parameter **this** of type `Clock *`.

The pointer **this** is initialized automatically so that it points to the actual object whenever it is called. Thus at the call `c1.tick()` **this** will point to `c1`, and with the call `c2.tick()` to `c2`. When the name of a member `m` is written inside a member function, the compiler will interpret this as though `(this->m)` had been written. If we write `s++` in the function `tick`, it will mean `(this->s)++`. Since **this** points to `c1` in the first call and to `c2` in the second, the correct object will be changed.

Generally speaking, we do not have to think about the pointer **this**, because the compiler automatically deals with it. But there are two occasions when we must explicitly make use of **this** in a member function. The first is when we need to call, from inside a member function, another function that will have an object of the actual class as parameter. Suppose, for example, that there is a function with the declaration

```
void plan(Flight& f);
```

which gets a reference to a flight and places this in a list of aircraft. Further suppose that we want to be able to call this function from a member function `mf` in the class `Flight`. We can then write the following:

```
void Flight::mf()
{
   ...
   plan(*this);   // give this object as argument
}
```

Another fairly common occasion when `this` must be used is when we want to return the actual object – or a reference or pointer to it – as result from a member function. This is necessary if we want to write member functions capable of being called in a single sequence. (Compare with the write-out operator `<<`.) If we want to write

```
k.set(10, 25, 30).tick().tick().write();
```

the member functions `set` and `tick` must be changed. The result from a call of these must be the actual object, so that we can directly apply the dot operator. We make the declarations

```
Clock& set(int hour, int min, int sec);
Clock& tick();
```

Here we let the member functions return a *reference* to the actual object and not to a copy of the object. The definitions of the two member functions must also be changed:

```
Clock& Clock::set(int hour, int min, int sec)
{
   h=hour; m=min; s=sec;
   return *this;
}
Clock& Clock::tick()
   { as earlier
   return *this;
}
```

Interesting here is the last line, with the expression `*this`. This expression means 'what `this` points to' – that is, the actual object. It is a reference to this object, which will be returned. There could be a question why `return this` is not used instead, since a reference really is a kind of pointer, but this would be an error, because the compiler automatically ensures that there is a reference to the object. On the other hand, if the return type from the function had been a pointer to a `Clock` – that is, `Clock *` – it would have been correct to write `return this`.

8.3 Friends

We have stated that information hiding is a very important ingredient in object-oriented programming style, and this is corroborated by the way we construct classes in C++. Whatever is declared in the private section of a class definition, is not visible outside the class. The rules of the language guarantee that only the member functions of a class have access to what has been declared there. But as we know, there cannot be rules if there are no exceptions, and so it is here. There has had to be a compromise on information hiding in C++. This is because the member functions in certain situations serve to limit the various possibilities. Now, we may indicate in a class definition that a class has certain *friends*. A friend can be either an ordinary function, which is not a member function, or another class. A friend is allowed to view a class in its entirety.

Let us take a couple of examples. On page 238 we showed a program that used the class `Array`, and in this program there is a function `square`, which squares the elements in an `Array` object. Now we can indicate in the definition of class `Array` that this function should be a friend:

```
class Array {
public:
  friend void square(Array& a);
  ...
private:
  int *p;
  const int i1;
  int num;
};
```

With this, the function `square` will have knowledge of the data members `p`, `i1` and `num` in the private section. We can now write a more effective variant of the function `square` where, instead of calling the member functions `read` and `change`, we can directly make changes in the array the data member `p` points to:

```
void square(Array& a)
{
  for (int i=0; i<=a.num; i++)
    a.p[i] *= a.p[i];
}
```

Note that `square` is not a member function. It does not belong to the class `Array`. We use a normal function call to call it, without indicating an object in front of the function name. We can write, for example,

```
Array aa;
square(aa);
```

It is controversial to use friend functions in this way, since it is contrary to our ideas on information hiding. It is important that we use friends with some discretion and common sense. If we define our friend functions with the member functions, in the same file, they could be understood to be operations that are part of the class concerned, in spite of the fact that they are not member functions. Then the function `square` might as well have been formulated as a member function, which might have been a good idea. But there are occasions when it seems natural to use friend functions, or when we simply cannot use member functions. This latter case will be discussed later in connection with operators. One instance where it is better to use friend functions is when we are dealing with *symmetrical* operations with two or more objects of the same kind as arguments. Then it does not make sense to take one of the arguments and put it in front of the function name, while the other arguments are given in the usual way. Suppose that we want to construct a function `earliest`, which gets two strikes of a clock as arguments and as result gives the earliest of the two. If the strikes of the clock, `c1` and `c2`, are to be compared and the earliest of them is to be placed in the variable `c3`, then writing

```
c3 = earliest(c1, c2);
```

will be more satisfactory than writing

```
c3 = c1.earliest(c2);
```

We can produce the first example if we formulate the function `earliest` as a friend function rather than as a member function:

```
class Clock {
public:
  friend const Clock& earliest(Clock& ca, Clock& cb);
  declarations of other member functions
private:
  int h, m, s;
};
```

We put the definition in the file `Clock.cpp`, and it looks like this

```
const Clock& earliest(Clock& ca, Clock& cb)
{
  if (ca.h<cb.h  ||  (ca.h==cb.h && (ca.m<cb.m
                 ||  (ca.m==cb.m && ca.s<cb.s))))
    return ca;
  else
    return cb;
}
```

Not only functions can be friends. Another class can be declared as a friend, in which case all of the member functions in one class can access the private members of another. This is how the class `Clock` indicates that the class `Flight` is its friend:

```
class Clock {
public:
  friend class Flight;
  ...
};
```

This makes it possible to construct a much more effective variant of the function `delay` than the one shown earlier (see page 225).

```
void Flight::delay(int min)
{
  dep.h = (dep.h + (dep.m+min)/60) % 24;
  dep.m = (dep.m+min) % 60;
  arr.h = (arr.h + (arr.m+min)/60) % 24;
  arr.m = (arr.m+min) % 60;
}
```

Here we do not have to make the clock tick forward one second at a time. We can simply add the necessary minutes.

We should exercise extreme caution before we make an entire class into the friend of another. A class `C1` should only make another class `C2` its friend when `C1` is simply a 'help class' of `C2` – that is, used to implement `C2`. We shall be showing examples of this in Chapter 13 when discussing linked data constructs.

Note, finally, that friendship is one-way in C++. A certain class itself chooses who is to be its friend and share its secrets. A class or function cannot ask to be friends with another class or function.

Friends

- In a class definition a particular function or class can be made to be a friend.

```
class C {
  friend type f(parameters);
  friend class C2;
  ...
};
```

- The function `f` and the class `C2` then have access to the private members of `C`.

8.4 Operators

In C++ there are a number of predefined operators that can be applied to the built-in standard types. For instance, we can add two variables of type **`int`** using the operator `+`, and we can compare two values of type **`double`** using the operator `<=`. These predefined operators are actually overloaded, as each one of them can be used for several standard types. For instance, one `+` operator is used for type **`int`** and another for type **`double`**. Where classes are concerned, there are almost no predefined operators. (The most important ones are the assignment operator `=`, the dot operator, the arrow operator and the address operator.) When, using classes, we declare our own types, we often wish that there were operators for these. For instance, it would seem entirely natural if for type `RatNum`, which was discussed on page 239, there were an operator `+` enabling us to write expressions of the form `r1+r2`, where `r1` and `r2` are of type `RatNum`. What we can do is define our *own* operators for our classes, and these will be superimposed on the predefined operators. For instance, if we define our own operator `+` for type `RatNum` and write the expression `r1+r2`, the compiler will automatically discover that it is a personally defined plus operator that must be called.

We shall now look at how we define our own operators for our classes – how we *overload* operators. When we declare our own operator, we write a function with the name **`operator`**`X`, where `X` is an operator symbol. If, for instance, we were to write our own addition operator, the function we declared would have the name **`operator`**`+`. The word **`operator`** is reserved in C++. We shall be giving several examples, but first some general comments are needed.

Almost all the predefined operators for the standard types can be overloaded. This applies to the following operators:

```
new      delete   new[]    delete[]
+        -        *        /        %        ^        &        |        ~
!        =        <        >        +=       -=       *=       /=       %=
^=       &=       |=       <<       >>       >>=      <<=      ==       !=
<=       >=       &&       ||       ++       --       ,        ->*      ->
()       []
```

Among these are, for instance, numeric and logical operators. Of special interest are the assignment and comparison operators, which, as we note, can be overloaded. The two operators `()` and `[]` on the last line represent a function call and indexing respectively.

When we define our own operators we must therefore use one of the operator symbols from the above table. We are not allowed to use a combination of our own, for instance `<>`, which does not appear in the table. We must also remember that there should be an equal number of operands for an operator as for the corresponding predefined operator. For instance, if we define our own comparison operator `==`, this must have two operands, and if we define our own operator `!`, it must have one operand. Some of the predefined operators exist in two variants, with one operand (unary) or with two (binary). The `-` operator is an example of this. We may write our own versions of these operators in both the unary and the binary variants.

When we write our own operator, it will have the same priority as the corresponding predefined operator. If for class `RatNum` we have defined both our own plus operator `+` and our own multiplication operator `*`, the multiplication operator will have higher priority and so will be called first in the expression `r1+r2*r3`.

In order to preserve clarity in the way a program functions, we should try to formulate our own operators so that they logically correspond to predefined operators. For example, it would be appropriate if we defined our own `+` operator

Operators

- Functions with the name `operatorX`, where `X` is the operator symbol.
- Most of the predefined operators may be overloaded for class types.
- Can have one operand (unary) or two operands (binary).
- The number of operands and the priority are the same for a corresponding predefined operator.
- Can be constructed as a member function or friend function.

for type `RatNum` so that it really added two rational numbers and did not carry out some other operation on them – subtraction, for instance.

We have two ways of constructing our own operators, by formulating them as either member functions or as friend functions. Although it is customary to use member functions, sometimes we have to use friend functions; we shall be describing both ways here. We begin by dealing with how we use member functions to construct our own operators. In the following sections we use class `Array`, defined on page 235, as an example. (The only difference is that we now declare `first`, `last` and `length` as *constant* member functions.)

8.4.1 Binary operators

In our first example, we will define our own operator `==` for class `Array`. This operator makes it possible to compare two `Array` objects `v1` and `v2` as in, for example

```
Array v1, v2;
if (v1 == v2)
```

We formulate the operator as a member function. As with other member functions, the declaration of the operator should lie in the class definition:

```
class Array {
public:
  bool operator== (const Array& v) const;
  declarations of the other member functions
private:
  int *p;
  const int i1;
  int num;
};
```

Note that the function `operator==` has only *one* parameter, and we previously stated that a comparison operator had to have *two* parameters. This is because the first parameter is understood and will automatically become the actual object. If, for example, we write the expression

```
v1 == v2
```

the compiler will understand it as if we had written

```
v1.operator==(v2)
```

That is, the function `operator==` is called for the object `v1`, and `v2` is given as argument. Thus the function's formal parameter `v` will correspond in this call to `v2`, and the pointer `this` will point to `v1`. It *is* permissible to call our own operators in this way, even if it is more normal to write an expression such as `v1==v2`. As a general rule, binary operators always have *one* parameter and unary operators have *no* parameters, where operators are declared as member functions.

Note that in the declaration we indicated that the function `operator==` should be a constant function. Of course, the actual object should not be changed when it is compared with another object. Note, too, that we did not indicate that the parameter `v` should be of type `Array` but a *reference* to a constant `Array`. By using a reference, we avoid copying a whole `Array` object in every call, and by saying that it is a reference to a constant, we guarantee that the right-hand operand is not changed when a call of the operator `==` is made.

We write the definition of the function `operator==` separately. Two `Array` objects are equal if they contain the same number of elements, each element being equal to the corresponding element in the other `Array` object. But the first index value of the `Array` object need not be the same.

```
bool Array::operator== (const Array& v) const
{
  if (num != v.num)
    return false;
  for (int i=0; i<num; i++)
    if (p[i] != v.p[i])
      return false;
  return true;
}
```

If the function here is called with the expression `v1==v2`, `num` will mean the `num` that is in `v1`, and `v.num` will mean the `num` that is in `v2`.

In the next example, we construct an operator that adds two `Array` objects, element by element. For this to be possible, the two `Array` objects must contain the same number of elements. First we must explain what we mean when we say that the operator will add two `Array` objects. By way of explanation, let us look at type **`int`**. If we have two integers `m` and `n` and write the expression `m+n`, this will mean that a new, temporary integer has been formed and that this contains the sum of the two integers. Neither `m` nor `n` will be changed because we write `m+n`. If we want to change one operand, we should instead use the operator `+=` and write, for example, `m+=n`. Then the number in `n` is added to the number in `m`, and `m` will be changed. We should like to apply the same principles to our own type `Array`, and so we construct two different addition operators, `+=` and `+`. First we deal with the operator `+=`. We can write the declaration

```
const Array& operator+= (const Array& v);
```

The definition looks like this:

```
const Array& Array::operator+= (const Array& v)
{
  assert(num==v.num);
  for (int i=0; i<num; i++)
    p[i] += v.p[i];
  return *this;
}
```

It is also understood here that the left-hand operand is the actual object. The parameter `v` refers to the right-hand operand. Since this should not be changed we will have a reference to a constant. When this function is called, it is done for the most part in statements such as

```
v1 += v2;
```

but the operator could also be a part of more complicated expressions such as

```
if (v3 == (v1 += v2))
```

Thus the operator `+=` should leave a result that we can continue to work with. This should be a copy of the left-hand operand's new value, in our example a copy of the new value of `v1`. In the declaration we have indicated that the result type should be a reference to a constant `Array`, and on the penultimate line we write that the value **`*this`** should be returned. What will be returned is quite simply a reference to the actual object, or `v1` in our example. We could also have stated that the result type should be `Array`, but the function would then have copied the actual object and left the copy as result. By using a reference, we avoid ineffective copying. It is important that the result type be indicated as a reference to a *constant*. Naturally, it would not be possible to change the actual object via the result value that has been left. For instance, the following would not be allowed:

```
(v1 += v2) = v3;   // ERROR!
```

Let us turn now to the second addition operator. The declaration is

```
Array operator+ (const Array& v) const;
```

We have declared the function as constant since the actual object should not be changed by this operator. Here is the definition:

```
Array Array::operator+ (const Array& v) const
{
   assert(num==v.num);
   Array temp(*this);   // Create a copy of this Array object
   temp += v;
   return temp;
}
```

In this function we cannot leave a reference to the actual object as result, since this object is not to be changed. Instead, we declare a local, temporary variable of type `Array` inside the function. As initializion value for this temporary vector we give the argument `*this` – that is, the actual `Array` object. The `Array` object `temp` will then be initialized with the aid of the copy constructor and will contain a copy of the actual `Array` object. If, for example, we call the function with the expression `v1+v2`, `temp` will be a copy of `v1`. We then apply the operator `+=` on `temp`, causing it to be changed. It will then contain the sum of the actual `Array` object and the right-hand operand – that is, the sum of `v1` and `v2` in our example. We give as result a copy of `temp`.

It may seem strange that we have specified neither in this function nor in the operator `+=` that the result type should be a reference. If we had, the function would have given a reference to the variable `temp` as result. This would not have been correct, as `temp` exists only inside the function `operator+`. Once the function has finished being executed, `temp` will no longer exist. As we know, a reference is a kind of pointer to a variable. If we had returned a reference as result type, therefore, we would in fact have returned a lingering pointer. (See our discussion of common errors when using pointers on page 175.)

We shall now construct two more addition operators for type `Array`, and these will also be called `+=` and `+`. The new operators both have an integer as the right-hand operand.

Binary operators

- Should have *one* parameter if it is a member function.
- Actual object `==` the left-hand operand.
- The parameter `==` the right-hand operand.
- Be careful to differentiate between operators whether or not an actual object is changed.

We should be able to write `v1+=5` to add the number `5` to each element in `v1` and `v1+10` in order to compute an `Array` object that gives a copy of `v1` but with the number `10` added to all the elements. The declarations are

```
const Array& operator+= (int d);
Array operator+ (int d) const;
```

The definitions are made in the same way as before:

```
const Array& Array::operator+= (int d)
{
for (int i=0; i<num; i++)
  p[i] += d;
return *this;
}
Array Array::operator+ (int d) const
{
  Array temp(*this);
  temp += d;
  return *this;
}
```

We shall now construct a slightly more complicated operator, a concatenation operator that we will call `&=`. With this, we shall be able to extend an `Array` object and add another `Array` object onto the end of it. If, for example, the `Array` object `v1` contains the three elements `[1, 5, 7]` and the `Array` object `v2` the two elements `[0, 3]`, we shall be able to write `v1&=v2`. After this operation, `v1` will contain the five elements `[1, 5, 7, 0, 3]`. The declaration is simple:

```
const Array& operator&= (const Array& v);
```

We also return a reference to the changed object here in order to continue working with the result. For instance, it will be possible to write `v3=(v1&=v2)`. The definition is

```
const Array& Array::operator&= (const Array& v)
{
  int *q = new int[num+v.num];  // Create new space
  for (int i=0; i<num; i++)
    q[i] = p[i];                // Copy this Array object
  for (int j=0; j<v.num; j++)
    q[j+num] = v.p[i];          // Copy v
  delete[] p;                   // Release old memory
  p=q;                          // Point to the new space
  num += v.num;                 // Increase length
  return *this;
}
```

The actual object should be changed to ensure that it contains a longer Array object than previously: in order to bring this about we have to allocate new memory space that will be big enough. It will have to accommodate num+v.num elements. We let the provisional pointer q point to this new memory space. We then copy to it the original elements of the actual Array object followed by the elements in the right-hand operand. The memory space allocated earlier for the actual Array object must then be released so that we do not consume memory that will never be released. When this has been done, we let the member variable p point to the newly allocated memory space.

We can also make a variant of the concatenation operator, one that does not change the actual object but only gives a unified Array object as result. We shall call this operator &. If v1 as before contains the three elements [1, 5, 7] and Array object v2 the two elements [0, 3], we shall be able to write v3=v1&v2. Then v3 after this operation will contain the five elements [1, 5, 7, 0, 3]. Array object v1 and v2 will be unchanged. We now write the definition

```
Array operator& (const Array& v) const;
```

The definition can be written quite simply using the operator &=:

```
Array Array::operator& (const Array& v) const
{
  Array temp(*this);  // Create a copy of this Array object
  temp &= v;
  return temp;
}
```

As with the operator +, we create here a local copy of the actual Array object. We then apply the operator &= to this copy.

Using these operators as models, we can construct several binary operators for class Array. We could, for instance, write operators for subtraction, multiplication and division.

8.4.2 Predefined comparison operators

In the previous section we defined an operator == that compares two variables of the type Array. If you have declared the operator == there should also be an operator !=, which would be easy to construct. You just have to call the operator == and negate the result. The definition of an operator != would then look like this:

```
bool Array::operator!= (const Array& v) const
{
  return !((*this)==v);
}
```

The form of this operator is actually independent of the class that it concerns. If you have defined an operator `==` for the class you can always define a `!=` operator according to this pattern. The same is true if you have defined an inequality operator such as `<`. By rewriting, you could then construct an operator `>`. In addition, if you have defined an equality operator it is also possible with the help of the operators `<` and `==` to define the operators `<=` and `>=`. In order to provide you with these circumlocutions for all classes, the standard file `util` contains a set of predefined patterns for relation operators, which can be applied to the class of your choice. You just need to define the operators `==` and `<` yourself, and you will automatically have the other comparison operators `!=`, `>`, `<=`. You thus never need to define more than two comparison operators yourself. To demonstrate this we also define the operator `<` for the class `Array`. The declaration looks like this:

```
bool operator< (const Array& v) const;
```

We compare `Array` variables according to the same principles as when texts are compared alphabetically. You start with the first elements in the two `Array` variables. If these elements are equal, the elements in the next place are compared, and so on. This is continued until two compared elements are different, or until you reach the end of one (or both) `Array` variables. If the two compared elements are different, the `Array` variable containing the smallest element is regarded as the least. If one `Array` variable is shorter than the other and all the elements in the shorter variable are equal to the corresponding elements in the longer one, the shorter `Array` variable is regarded as the least. The definition of the operator `<` then looks like this:

```
bool Array::operator< (const Array& v) const
{
  int n;   // the length of the shortest of this object and v
  if (num < v.num)
    n = num;
  else
    n = v.num;
  for (int i=0; i<n; i++)
    if (p[i] < v.p[i])
      return true;
    else if (p[i] > v.p[i])
      return false;
  return num < v.num;   // equal lengths
}
```

In order for the other comparison operators to be automatically defined it suffices to add the following lines first in the file where the class `Array` is defined – that is in the file `array.h`:

```
#include <utility>
using namespace std::rel_ops;
```

The patterns for creating relation operators are defined in a namespace called `rel_ops`, defined in the file `utility`. The second line enables this to be directly visible in all programs that include the file `array.h`. In such a program you can now, for instance, write

```
if (v1 >= v2)
  ...
```

despite the fact that we haven't defined the operator `>=`. (We assume here that `v1` and `v2` are variables of type `Array`.)

In summary, if you want comparison operators in a class that you construct yourself, you must define the operators `==` and `<` yourself. You must also add the two lines shown above at the beginning of the file where the class is defined.

8.4.3 Unary operators

As an example of a unary operator, we shall construct a unary minus operator. If we have an `Array` object `v1`, we should be able to write `-v1`. We should then get a copy of `v1` in which all the elements are replaced by corresponding negative values. The declaration of the binary operator is very simple:

```
Array operator- () const;
```

Note that, when a binary operator is formulated as a member function, the function should *not have parameters*. The operator will have only one operand where it is understood that this operand is the actual object. When we write

```
-v1
```

it is the same thing as if we had made the function call

```
v1.operator-()
```

It is permissible to write it in this way as well. The definition can now be written separately:

```
Array Array::operator- () const
{
  Array temp(*this);  // Create a copy of this Array object
  for (int i=0; i<num; i++)
    temp.p[i] = -temp.p[i];  // Negate each element
  return temp;
}
```

There are a couple of unary operators that present special problems: these are the increment and decrement operators `++` and `--`. We recall from Chapter 2 that these two operators exist in two variants: a prefix variant, where `++` or `--` is placed in front of the

Unary operator
• Should not have parameters if it is a member function • The actual object == the operand.

variable name; and a postfix variant, where ++ or -- is placed after the variable name. (See page 39.) Both variants increase or decrease their operand, but the prefix variant gives the operand's new value as result, whereas the postfix variant gives as result the operand's old value.

We look at the increment operator here, constructing our own operator ++ for type `Array`. (The decrement operator can be treated analogously.) We therefore make the declaration

```
const Array& operator++ ();   // prefix ++v
```

Since the operator ++ is a unary operator, we have declared it as a function without parameters. The problem is that both the prefix and postfix variants of the operator ++ are unary. Therefore they should both have exactly the same declaration, and it should not be possible to tell them apart. In C++ a special style of writing the declarations has made it possible to declare both the prefix and postfix variants of the increment and decrement operators. (This did not exist in earlier versions of C++, where only the prefix variant could be declared.) If we write as above, we mean the declaration of the prefix variant. If we want to declare the postfix variant, we have to declare an operator with the name ++ that has a parameter of type **int**. The declaration would then look like this:

```
Array operator++ (int);   // postfix v++
```

We can pretend that the operator ++ is binary! The integer parameter has only been added, however, to mark that we are dealing with the postfix variant. The parameter does not get a value when the function is called, and it is not used in the function definition. It has not even been given a name.

It is now time to look at the definitions of the two variants of the operator ++. We begin with the prefix variant, which increases all elements in the actual `Array` object by `1` and then returns the new value:

```
const Array& Array::operator++ ()   // prefix ++v
{
  return (*this) += 1;   // Return the new value
}
```

Here we have been able to make things very easy by making use of the operator +=, which has an integer as a right-hand operand and which we constructed in the previous

The operators ++ and --

- For class X:

```
const X& operator++();   // prefix ++x
X operator++(int);       // postfix x++
```

- The integer parameter is not used. Marks the postfix variant only.

section. As usual, we return a reference to the actual object instead of copying unnecessarily.

The postfix variant of `++` can be made almost as simple. The only difference is that instead of returning the actual `Array` object's new value, we return a copy of the `Array` object's old value. (We cannot return a reference because we would have problems with lingering pointers.)

```
Array Array::operator++ (int)  // postfix v++
{
  Array temp(*this);    // Create a copy of this Array object
  (*this) += 1;         // Increase this vector
  return temp;          // Return the old value
}
```

8.4.4 The assignment operator

In section 7.3.4 we dealt with the copy constructor, which is called when initializing an object. Then we had various problems when making initializations, and we shall experience similar problems with making assignments. When we make an assignment, as for example

```
v1 = v2;
```

the *assignment operator* is called for the class In most cases the compiler itself automatically defines an assignment operator. (But this will not happen if a class has a data member that is a constant or a reference.) The automatically defined assignment operator works well for most classes. The way in which it makes assignments corresponds to the way in which the automatically defined copy constructor makes initializations: a subobject of simple type (scalars and pointers) is copied bit by bit, just as with ordinary assignments. If a subobject is of class type, the assignment operator for this class will be called to do the copying. If, finally, a subobject is an array, each element in the array will be copied according to the foregoing rules.

In section 7.3.4 we stated that the automatically defined copy constructor did not work for classes that themselves allocate memory space. In order to carry out deep copying, we had to define our own copy constructor. On page 236 we gave a copy constructor for class `Array`. We needed to carry out deep copying when making initializations, and the same is true when we make assignments. We also need to construct our own assignment operator. A copy operator for a class `X` will have the name **`operator=`** and have a single parameter that will be of type `X`, `X&` or **`const`**`X&`. We can declare our own assignment operator for class `Array`:

```
const Array& operator= (const Array& v);
```

This will now replace the automatically defined assignment operator, and will be called every time we assign one `Array` object to another. (With initializations, however, the copy constructor will be called.) We write the definition

```
const Array& Array::operator= (const Array& v)
{
  if (this != &v)         // Copying to itself?
  {                       // No
    delete p;             // Release old memory
    num = v.num;
    p = new int[num];     // Allocate new space
    for (int i=0; i<num; i++)
      p[i] = v.p[i];      // Copy the elements
  }
  return *this;
}
```

First there is a check that an assignment has not been made to itself. If so, nothing needs to be done. But it is important to include this test, as otherwise the memory space for the `Array` object would be wrongly released.

Assignment operator

```
operator=
```

- Has a parameter that is an object of the same class or a reference to an object of the same class.
- Is automatically called with assignments

```
x1=x2;
```

- If we need to write our own copy constructor, we normally also need our own assignment operator.

If there is no assignment to the same object, the assignment operator will do the same thing as the copy constructor: that is, it will allocate memory space for an array that will contain the new value and copy the elements one by one to the new array. In addition, the memory space containing the old value must be released.

8.4.5 The indexing operator

In Chapter 7 we used the two functions `read` and `change` to read and change different elements in an object of type `Array`. This was rather clumsy. It would have been much simpler to use indexing, exactly as for ordinary arrays. This is possible if we construct our own indexing operator. It will have the name **`operator[]`** and one parameter. We can make the declaration:

```
int& operator[] (int i);
```

If we now write an indexing expression such as `v[j+n]`, for example, it will be interpreted as though we had written

```
v.operator[](j+n)
```

That is, the `Array` object we are indexing in becomes the actual `Array` object, and the index value is given as argument. An indexing expression should be able to stand both on the right and on the left in an assignment. For instance, it should be possible to write

```
v[j+1] = v[j];
```

To make this possible, the function **`operator[]`** must return a *reference* to an element so that this element can be changed via the reference. If the function had only returned an **`int`**, the result would have been a *copy* of the chosen element, and it would not have been possible to change this. Let us look at the definition. We use the function `assert` to check that the index lies within the allowed limits:

```
int& Array::operator[] (int i)
{
  assert(i >= i1 and i <= last());
  return p[i-i1];   // Return a reference
}
```

There is a little problem with this operator. Suppose that we write

```
const Array cv;
cout << cv[1];
```

Indexing operator

```
element type& operator[](int index);
element type& operator[](int index) const;
```

- The object we index in becomes the actual object.
- Index given as the only parameter.
- Appropriate to define two overloaded variants.
- Called automatically upon indexing

```
x[i]
```

When we try to compile, we can get the error printout

```
non-const function called for const object
```

Although the indexing operator does not change in the actual object, it makes it possible for the caller to change a particular element. So it should not be declared as a constant function (with the word **const**). This means that it cannot be used on occasions such as the one above, where we want to read a particular element in a constant object without changing anything. The solution is to overload the index operator. We are allowed to overload two member functions with the same parameters, where one function is constant and the other is not. We declare here a constant variant of the indexing operator:

```
int operator[] (int i) const;
```

We return a copy of element number `i`, instead of a reference. The definition looks almost exactly the same as for the non-constant variant:

```
int Array::operator[] (int i) const
{
  assert(i >= i1 and i <= last());
  return p[i-i1];   // Return a copy
}
```

8.4.6 The function call operator

The next operator we shall look at is rather special. It is the *function call operator*, indicated by parentheses `()`. We call this operator by making what looks rather like a function call. We can decide how many parameters we want the operator to have. For instance, if we decide it is to have no parameters, we can call it by writing:

```
x();
```

where `x` is an object. If we had decided that the function operator should have three parameters, a call would then have the form

```
x(p1, p2, p3);
```

An object that can be called as if it were a function in this way is called a *function object*. A function object always belongs to a class in which at least one function call operator is defined. Function objects are very useful in combination with container classes and so-called algorithms that are part of the C++ standard. This is because many standard functions are designed to accept function objects as parameters. We shall discuss this in Chapter 12.

As an example of the way we use this operator, let us construct an operator that will help us to cut *slices* out of an `Array` object. For example, if we have an `Array` object v1, consisting of five elements numbered from 1 to 5, then the elements 3, 4 and 5 constitute a slice consisting of three elements. An appropriate way of representing this slice is to write v1(3,5). We can use this style if we formulate the function call operator in the right way. For instance, we can write

```
Array v1(1,5), v2, v3;
for (int i=1; i<=5; i++)
  v1[i] = i;
v2 = v1(2,4);               // v2 == [2, 3, 4]
v3 = v1(3,5) & v2(1,2);     // v3 == [3, 4, 5, 2, 3]
```

A declaration of the function call operator should look like this:

```
Array operator() (int from, int to);
```

It evidently has two parameters that indicate the first and last index for the slice that will be cut out. As result it gives a copy of the required slice. The definition is

```
Array Array::operator() (int from, int to) const
{
  assert(from<=to && from>=i1 && to<=last());
  Array temp(from, to-from+1);  // Create a slice
  for (int i=0; i<temp.num; i++)
    temp.p[i] = p[from-i1+i];  // Copy the elements
  return temp;
}
```

Function call operator

```
return type operator()(parameters);
```

- Can have an arbitrary number of parameters.
- Automatically called with expressions of the form

```
x(p1, p2, p3 ...)
```

where x is an object of the actual class.

Note that the function call operator returns a copy of the slice. This means that the operator cannot be used in expressions such as v1(1,3)=v2 and v1(1,3)++, where the intention is to change inside a particular slice. For this to be possible, both the slice and the whole vector must refer to the *same* physical integer array (their data members p should point to the same array). But then we shall have problems with constructors and destructors. Clearly, we do not do things in this way, otherwise we shall just get into a muddle.

8.4.7 Friend functions as operators

In the introduction to this chapter we stated that operators could be formulated either as member functions or as friend functions. Why is the alternative necessary? Is it not possible simply to use member functions, as we have seen in so many examples? The problem is that there is one occasion when member functions cannot be used. All operators used as member functions require the type of the left-hand operand (or the only operand) of an operator to be of the actual class. When, for example, we use the type `Array` and write expressions such as `v1+v2`, the member functions work only if `v1` has type `Array`. Earlier we constructed an operator that had an `Array` object as left-hand operand and an integer as right-hand operand. This made it possible to write expressions such as `v1+5`. For reasons of symmetry, we would like to write `5+v1`, when the result should be the same. But we cannot do this with member functions, so we have to use a friend function. We therefore place the following declaration in the definition of class `Array`:

```
friend Array operator+ (int d, const Array& v);
```

A friend function is not a member function, and so there is no 'understood' parameter. Instead, all the parameters must be indicated in the parameter list. If a binary operator is involved here, it should have two parameters. The first parameter will indicate the left-hand operand, and the second the right-hand operand. This function can be said to belong to class `Array`, in spite of the fact that it is not a member function. We therefore put it with the definitions of member functions in the file `Array.cpp`:

```
Array operator+ (int d, const Array& v)
{
  return v+d;
}
```

This is extremely simple. By changing the order of the operands we can call the member function `+`, which is already there. (Actually, the function does not have to be a friend function, since it does not make use of anything declared in the private section of class `Array`.)

We shall give another example of a useful friend function for class `Array`. We shall write our own output operator. To obtain output at the terminal or in files, we usually use the output operator `<<` in C++. This operator is declared as a member function in the standard class `ostream`, which is defined in the file `iostream`. Class `ostream` defines what is called an *output stream*. (The variable `cout`, which we have used extensively, is, for instance, a predefined object of class `ostream`.) Since the operator `<<` is a member function of the class `ostream`, the left-hand operand of the operator should always be of this class. The right-hand operand will be the value that is output. The output operator `<<` is overloaded. There is a variant for every one of the built-in standard types. The following two member functions enable output to be made from the standard types `int` and `double`, for example:

```
ostream& operator<< (int);
ostream& operator<< (double);
```

These operators are called when we want to write, for instance,

```
cout << i;   // i has type int
cout << d;   // d has type double
```

It is important to note that the operator `<<` always gives as result a reference to the actual output stream. This makes it possible to construct chains by calling the operator. For instance, we can write

```
cout << i << d;
```

Here, the partial expression `cout<<i` gives as result a reference to `cout`, which means that the right-hand operator `<<` gets an output stream as left-hand operand.

We shall now write our own operator `<<` to function for type `Array`. Since the operator will function in the same way as the standard variants of `<<`, it must as left-hand operand have a reference to an output stream of type `ostream`, and as right-hand operand have a value of type `Array`. The result type should be a reference to the actual output stream. We must formulate our output operator as a friend function of class `Array`, so we place the following definition in the class definition:

```
friend ostream& operator<< (ostream& o, const Array& v);
```

We place the definition of our operator separately in the file `Array.cpp`:

```
ostream& operator<< (ostream& o, const Array& v)
{
  o << '[';
  if (v.num>0)
    o << v.p[0];
  for (int i=1; i<v.num; i++)
    o << "," << v.p[i];
  o << ']';
  return o;
}
```

The function writes the individual elements in an `Array` object in square brackets. The standard variant of the operator `<<` is used to write output inside the function. The actual output stream is indicated by the parameter `o`, and a reference to this is also given as result. We can now write, for instance,

```
Array v1(1,5);
for (int i=1; i<=5; i++)
  v1[i] = i;
cout << v1;
```

On the last line our new output operator is called. The parameter `o` will refer to the output stream `cout`. This output is then written as,

```
[1, 2, 3, 4, 5]
```

We can also let our output operator be part of the call chains, as in

```
cout << "v1 contains " << v1 << endl;
```

We usually construct our own output operators for our classes, and the input operators are constructed in a similar way. The left-hand operand is a reference to an object of the standard class `istream`, and the result type is a reference to `istream`. If we constructed an input operator for class `Array`, it would have the following appearance:

```
friend istream& operator>> (istream& in, Array& v);
```

Friend functions as operators

```
friend return_type operatorX (parameters);
```

- Should have the same number of parameters as operands.
- Must be used when the left-hand operand does not belong to the actual class.

8.4.8 Type conversion operators

In the last chapter we learnt that a constructor that could be called with only one parameter carried out a type conversion to the actual class. The class `RatNum` was declared, for instance:

```
class RatNum {
public:
  RatNum (int i=0) : numer(i), denom(1) {}
  declarations of several member functions
private:
  int numer, denom;
};
```

The constructor functions here as a type conversion from type **int** to type `RatNum`. It can therefore be called automatically, without this being revealed in the code. If a variable `r` has type `RatNum`, the constructor will be called automatically if we write, for instance,

```
r=5;
```

Constructors can function as type conversions only if the type that we are converting *to* is a class. If we want to define a type conversion to a type that is not a class, we have to do it in a different way. We can then define a type conversion operator. Let us take the class `RatNum` as an example. A rational number can be represented exactly as a quotient of two integers. Sometimes, however, we may want an approximate value of this quotient. It will then be a real number, which can be defined by the standard type **`double`**. Thus we construct a type conversion operator that converts from type `RatNum` to type **`double`**. The following declaration will be placed in the definition of class `RatNum`:

```
operator double() const;
```

There are some special rules for type conversion operators. Their names should be the same as the names they are converting to; they should not have parameters; and no result type can be specified. Of course, the result type should always be identical to that of the type they are converting to. We write the definition separately:

```
RatNum::operator double() const
{
  return double(numer)/denom;
}
```

Here we simply give as result the quotient of the numerator and denominator. For it to be a real number division and not an integer division, we have to make an explicit type conversion of one of the operands to type **`double`**.

Type conversion operator

```
operator type() const;
```

- Member function.
- No parameters or result type can be specified.
- Converts from the actual class to type *type*.
- Is called automatically when type conversion is needed.

This type conversion operator can now be called automatically when a type conversion from type `RatNum` to **`double`** is needed. This happens, for example, in the statement `d=r`. (Suppose that the variable `d` has type **`double`** and `r` type `RatNum`.)

8.5 Static members

Sometimes there are components common to all objects that belong to a class. In an object-oriented context these are usually called *class variables*. In C++ they are called *static members*, so we shall be using this term here. Interestingly, a static data member exists only in a single instance, but this instance is shared by all objects belonging to the actual class. A good example of a static data member is that of a variable that keeps track of how many objects of a certain type there are at a given moment. Take a bank account, for example. For every bank account there is a particular balance and a particular account holder. These items of data must of course be available in one instance for each account, and so they are ordinary data members. The interest rate, on the other hand, is a static data member. We shall use this example of a bank account to write the class definition:

```
class Account {
public:
Account() : customer_no(0), bal(0), int_earned(0) {}
  void open_account(long int customer) {customer_no=customer;}
  double balance() const {return bal;}
  void transaction(double amount);
  void daily_interest();
  void add_interest();
  static double current_interest() {return interest_rate;}
  static void change_interest(double new_interest);
private:
  long int customer_no.;
  double bal, int_earned;
  static double interest_rate;   // declaration
};
```

For every account there are three ordinary, non-static data members: a customer number; `bal`, which contains the current balance; and `int_earned`, which contains the interest earned during the year. Interest earned is calculated on a daily basis but is not added to the balance until the end of the year.

First, we shall define the member functions that have nothing to do with static data members. The constructor initializes a new account so that the three non-static data members are set to zero. The member function `open_account` is used to open a new account. A unique customer number is indicated as parameter. The function `balance` is called when the balance in a particular account is required. The function `transaction` is called each time a deposit or withdrawal is made on the account. Deposits are given by a positive amount and withdrawals by a negative amount. The function `daily_interest` will be called once every day and calculates how much interest is earned during this day. The interest earned is added to the data member `int_earned`. The function `add_interest` is called at the end of the year (or when the account is closed). This function adds the total interest earned during the year to the balance, after which the data member `int_earned` is set to zero.

There is a static data member, `interest_rate`. This is indicated by the reserved word **`static`**. There are also two member functions, `current_interest` and `change_interest`, which are used to read and change the interest rate. These functions are special in that they do not deal with individual accounts and do not use non-static variables. Member functions with this property are called *static member functions* and are marked by the word **static**.

A static data member exists only in a single instance, and there is not one for every object. We *declare* a static data member in the class definition, as was done here with `interest_rate`, but the *definition* of a static data member (the place where the variable 'is') must lie outside the class definition. We usually place it in the same file as the definitions of separate member functions. Here we put the definition of `interest_rate` into a file with the name `account.cpp`. The definition looks like this:

```
double Account::interest_rate = 0.0;   // definition
```

Note that the word **static** will *not* be put here. A static member variable can be initialized in the definition. Here it has been initialized to a value of `0`. Constructors are not used to initialize static member variables, and they cannot be destroyed by a destructor.

Static data members

```
static type_name;   // declaration
```

- The definition is placed outside the class definition:

```
type class_name::name = initialization_value;
```

- Exists only in a single instance. Shared by objects in the class.

Static data members that have been declared in the private section of a class are, like other members, accessible only inside the class, in the member functions of the class (and in the friend functions or friend classes of the class.) A static data member declared in the **public** section of a class definition is visible and accessible from outside. We then write *class name::member name*. If `interest_rate` had been declared in the **public** section, we would have been able to write, for instance,

```
Account::interest_rate = 5.0;   // Not for private members
```

Static member functions can be defined, like other member functions, either in the class definition or separately. We defined the function `current_interest` directly in the class definition but defined the second static member function separately. The word **static** cannot be put here, either.

```
void Account::change_interest(double new_interest)
{
  assert(new_interest >= 0);
  interest_rate = new_interest;
}
```

A static member function is not called for any object in particular; in fact it can be called even when there are no objects of the actual class. To change and read the interest, we can make the call

```
Account::change_interest(10.0);
cout << Account::current_interest();
```

We indicate that the functions are member functions for class `Account` by indicating their full names `Account::change_interest` and `Account:: current_interest`. Like other functions, static member functions can be called by writing the name of an object in front of the function name. For instance, we are allowed to write

```
k.change_interest(10.0);
```

Static member functions

```
class C {
  static return type name(parameters);
};
```

- Are defined like other member functions.
- Can only use static data members.
- Are not called for any special object.

```
C::name(parameters)   // call
```

if `k` is a variable of type `Account`. But this is quite meaningless since the function `change_interest` does not, in any way, read or change in `k`.

Ordinary, non-static member functions have access to static data members and can read and change these. For example, the interest rate is needed in the function `daily_interest` to calculate the interest for the day:

```
void Account::daily_interest()
{
  int_earned += bal*interest_rate/100/365;
}
```

If we change a static data member in a member function, the change will have an effect on all the objects of the actual class, since all of them share the static member variable. Now to complete our example, here are the remaining member functions for class `Account`:

```
void Account::transaction(double amount)
{
  if (amount<0 and bal+amount < 0)
    cout << "Withdrawal not possible!" << endl;
```

```
  else
    bal+=amount;
}
void Account::add_interest()
{
  bal += int_earned;
  int_earned = 0;
}
```

8.6 Pointers to members

You can have pointers to both member functions and data members, but you should then work with a special kind of pointer, discussed in this section. (Although this may not be one of the things you encounter early in the process of learning C++, we discuss it here for the sake of completeness. You may choose to skip this section, since its contents are not essential to the rest of the book.) As a starting point in our discussion we use the following class, in which, for the sake of simplicity, we have allowed all the members to be directly visible from outside:

```
class C {
public:
  double f1(int i)           // member function
  { return (x+1) * i; }
  double f2(int i)           // member function
  { return (x+2) * i; }
  static double fs(int i);   // static member function
  double x, y;               // data members
  static double z;           // static data member
};
```

We also assume that there is a common function `g` that is not put into any class and is defined like this:

```
double g(int i)  // normal function
{ return 2*i;}
```

Suppose that we find ourselves in another part of the program – for instance, in the function `main` – and have made the declarations

```
double a;     // normal variable of type double
double *dp;   // pointer to double
```

As the variable `dp` is a pointer to **`double`** it is of course possible to write

```
dp = &a;  // OK
```

but if we try to point to the static data member `z` in class `C` there will be an error message:

```
dp = &z;   // Error: z is unknown here
```

As `z` is declared in class `C` we must give the complete name for `z`:

```
dp = &C::z;   // OK
```

(On the other hand if the statement `dp = az` had been put *inside* a member function in class `C` it would have been correct.) Instead, we now try to point to one of the non-static data members by writing

```
dp = &x;   // Error: x is unknown here
```

This is wrong because `x` is declared in class `C`. (In this case, too, it would have been correct if the statement had been put inside a member function in `C`.) In the same way as for the variable `z` we try to indicate that `x` is in class `C` and write

```
dp = &C::x;   // Error: different types
```

We now get a compilation error. This is because it is not clear which `x` is being referred to. There is a data member called `x` for *every* instance when we create the class `C`. For instance, we can declare two instances, `c1` and `c2`, with class `C`:

```
C c1, c2;
```

For example, in order to indicate that the pointer `dp` should point to the `x` that is in `c1` we can write

```
dp = &c1.x;   // OK, points to the data member x in c1
```

So far the discussion concerns pointers to the data members. Let us now discuss pointers to functions. We start by declaring a variable `p` whose type is 'a pointer to a function which has an **`int`** as a parameter and which returns a **`double`**':

```
double (*p)(int);   // pointer to function
```

Because the common function `g` that was defined above has this profile, you can let `p` point to the function `g`:

```
p = &g;   // OK
```

If we try to have `p` pointing directly to a member function, for instance `f1`, it will of course be wrong because `f1` is in class `C`:

```
p = &f1;   // Error: f1 is unknown here (and of wrong type)
```

(In fact this would be wrong even if the statement was *inside* a member function in class `C`. This is attributable to the fact that the types do not correspond, which will be evident from the subsequent argument.) We can make a new attempt where we indicate that `f1` is in class `C`:

```
p = &C::f1;   // Error: different types
```

This is wrong because you do not know which `f1` it concerns: that is, to which instance of `C` the function `f1` is connected. (The result that `f1` returns is dependent on the value of the variable `x` that is a data member that can have different values for different instances of `C`.)

We shall now try to do the same as we did for data members. We indicate that we want to have the `f1` that goes together with the instance `c1`:

```
p = &c1.f1;   // Error: different types
```

But this doesn't work for member functions because a member function always has the extra concealed parameter `this`, where `this` is a pointer to an object of the actual class in question, in this example to class `C`. However, the function `f1` does not have the type 'a function that has **int** as a parameter and that returns a **double**'. Instead its type is 'member function in class `C` that has **int** as a parameter and that returns a `double`'. In C++ there is a special syntax to indicate this type. For instance, in order to declare a pointer `q` that has the type 'pointer to a member function in class `C` that has **int** as a parameter and that returns a **double**' we write

```
double (C::*q)(int);   // pointer to member functions
```

This can be compared to the declaration of the pointer `p` as seen above. The pointer `q` can now point to the member function `f1`:

```
q = &C::f1;   // OK
```

Since `f1` is a member function it cannot be called in the same way as an ordinary function. We know that if you are outside the class you must always write the name of the actual object first. For instance, we can make the calls `c1.f1(5)` and `c2.f1(3)`. The same is true when you call a member function indirectly via a pointer: you must first indicate the name of the actual object. In order to call the member function that `q` points to we write

```
(c1.*q)(5)   // for c1, call the member function q points to
```

In C++ there is a special operator `.*` for this. In this example `5` is the argument to the function that is called. (The parentheses around `c1.*q` are essential, because the left parenthesis before `5` would otherwise have had a higher priority than the operator `.*`).

Sometimes you have pointers to objects. We might, for instance, have written the lines

```
C *pc;
pc = &c2;
```

Then `pc` points to the object `c2`. If we want to call the member function that the pointer `q` points to for the object that `pc` points to we then write the expression

```
(pc->*q)(5)   // for the object pc points to,
              // call the member function q points to
```

In this case the special operator `->*` is used instead of `.*`, which was used when you did not have a pointer to the object.

To conclude we show a complete program. The class `C` is still defined as above.

```
main()
{
  C c1, c2;
  c1.x=100; c2.x=200;
  double (C::*q)(int);
  q = &C::f1;
  cout << (c1.*q)(1) << endl;    // prints out 101
  q = &C::f2;
  cout << (c1.*q)(1) << endl;    // prints out 102
  C *pc;
  pc = &c2;
  cout << (pc->*q)(1) << endl;   // prints out 201
};
```

Exercises

8.1 Complete the class `RatNum` so that it contains operators for the addition, subtraction, multiplication and division of rational numbers. You should also be able to perform these operations when one of the operands (any one) is an integer. Make sure that the denominator in a result is never negative and that the numerator and denominator do not have common factors (see Exercise 7.7).

8.2 Add operators for subtraction, multiplication and division for the class `Array`.

8.3 Overload the operators `&=` and `&` for type `Array` so that an `Array` object can be extended by one single integer. You should be able to write expressions such as `v&=5`, `v&19` and `27&v`.

8.4 Add an input operator for class `Array`.

8.5 In mathematics the scalar product of two vectors of equal length $(u_1, u_2, \ldots u_n)$ and $(v_1, v_2, \ldots v_n)$ is defined as the sum

$$\sum_{k=1}^{n} u_k v_k$$

You can use the class `Array` to store mathematical vectors. Supplement the class `Array` with an operator that calculates the scalar product of two such vectors. The operator should check that the two vectors have the same number of components, although the numbering does not need to be the same. Because C++ does not allow for overloading of functions that distinguish themselves only in the return type, you cannot use the operator symbol `*` (it has already been used in Exercise 7.2.) The symbol `^` can be used instead.

8.6 A *complex* number k can be written in the form $k = a + b \cdot \mathrm{i}$, where a and b are ordinary real numbers and i is an *imaginary* number such that $\mathrm{i} \cdot \mathrm{i} = -1$. The number a is normally called the *real* part and the number b the *imaginary* part of the number k. Construct a class `Complex` that makes it possible to work with complex numbers. Choose appropriate constructors and operators. (You need not write a division operator.)

8.7 Write a class `Dictionary` to define a very simple dictionary. A dictionary should consist of a number of entries (an array). Each entry consists of two parts: a reference word and an explanatory text. Use an extra help class `Entry` to define this. For class `Dictionary` there should be a member function with which new entries can be added. (The array does not have to be sorted.) There should be an indexing operator `[]` that gets a *text* as parameter. This text should be a reference word. The operator should look up the reference word in the dictionary and as result give a pointer to a corresponding explanatory text (or `0` if the reference word is not present).

8.8 Write a class that contains a static variable that automatically keeps track of how many objects of the class there are at any given moment. In addition, the class should contain a static member function that returns the value of the static variable.

8.9 A polynomial such as

$$f(x) = 7.4x^5 + 3.1x^2 - 10.2x + 14.9$$

can be represented by an array in which every element defines a term in the polynomial. In each element is stored the term's coefficient and degree. Construct a class `Polynomial` that defines polynomials in this way. There should be operations to add, subtract and multiply polynomials, and the results should be new polynomials. There should also be a member function that calculates the polynomial's value for any value of x. This value of x should be given as a parameter of the function. In addition, write an operator that gives the derivative of a polynomial. The derivative of a polynomial

$$P(x) = a_n x^n + a_{n-1} x^{n-1} + \ldots + a_1 x + a_0$$

can be written as

$$P'(x) = n a_n x^{n-1} + (n-1) a_{n-1} x^{n-2} + \ldots + a_1$$

Inheritance

9

The special thing about object-oriented programming is that it uses *inheritance*. Using inheritance, you can create new types on the basis of existing types, which you extend with further attributes. In the two previous chapters we saw how *has* and *knows* relations were created. The third important relation, the *is* relation, is created by the use of inheritance. For instance, we can express relations such as 'an athlete is a person' or 'a book is a document'. In C++ inheritance is introduced by creating subclasses of existing classes. In this chapter we shall be looking at how this is done.

Using inheritance, we can create objects that are only partly equal to other objects. Such objects are defined by what are called *polymorphic* classes*. When objects belong to polymorphic classes, we can have operations with the same name carrying out the same operation on the different objects, even though the operations may carry out different things, depending on the kind of object involved. Suppose, for example, that we have two different kinds of bank account: one for which the interest is calculated on a daily basis, and another for which a certain sum has to have been in the account for a certain time before it can accrue interest. The operation 'calculate interest' will carry out, logically speaking, the same thing for the two different kinds of account, but the actual calculation will proceed differently in each case. In an object-oriented language there is a mechanism called *dynamic binding*. This enables us to handle such objects uniformly. We do not actually need to see what kind of object is involved. Instead, the language mechanism ensures that the correct operation is performed automatically when the program is executed. We shall see how we can make use of dynamic binding in this chapter.

9.1 Derived classes

First, let us look at an example. (For the sake of simplicity all `#include` statements are left out in this example.) We begin with a class `Person`:

---

* of many forms

```
class Person {
public:
   const string& is_called() const;
   void change_name(const string& n);
   void write_info() const;
private:
   string name;
};
```

A person has a name. There are operations to read and change the name. We can get a printout of the name, and there is a default constructor. We shall put the definitions of the member functions separately, in the interests of clarity:

```
const string& Person::is_called() const
{ return name; }
void Person::change_name(const string& n)
{ name=n; }
void Person::write_info() const
{ cout << "Name: " << name << endl; }
```

If we want to describe persons in employment, we can define a new class:

```
class Employee : public Person {
public:
   Employee() : salary(0) {};
   long int earns() const;
   void change_salary(long int new_salary);
   void write_info() const;
private:
   long int salary;
};
```

By writing `Person` after the colon in the first line we indicate that the new class `Employee` is a *subclass* of class `Person`. (We shall not explain just now why **`public`** is in the first line.) We say that class `Employee` is *derived* from class `Person` and that class `Person` is a *direct base class* (or *superclass*) of `Employee`.

The definitions of the member functions `earns` and `change_salary` are very simple (we shall not give the definition for `write_info` yet):

```
long int Employee::earns() const
{ return salary;}
void Employee::change_salary(long int new_salary)
{ salary=new_salary; }
```

A derived class inherits all the data members from the base class. We say that it contains all of the base class as a *base class subobject*. This means that an object of class `Employee` will have the data members `name` and `salary`. This is illustrated in

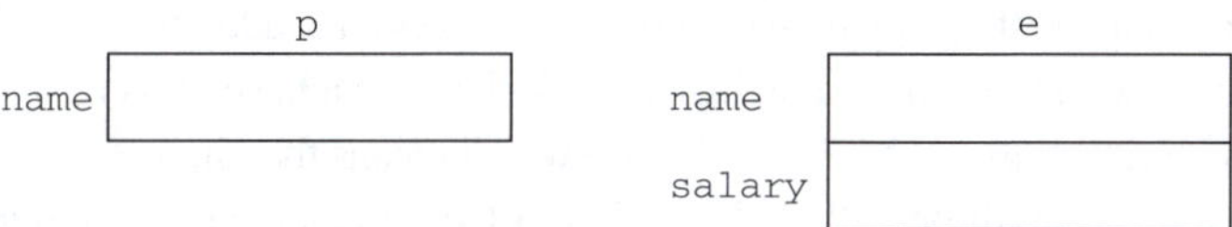

Figure 9.1

Figure 9.1, where we assume that the two variables `p` and `e`, are declared in the following way.

```
Person p;
Employee; e;
```

We see that the variable `p` has only a name, while the variable `e` has both a name and a salary.

Member functions can also be inherited. As a result, an object of class `Employee` will have the member functions `is_called`, `change_name`, `write_info`, `earns` and `change_salary`. We can also write the statements

```
p.change_name("David");
p.write_info();
e.change_name("Neil");
e.change_salary(20000);
long int s = e.earns();
e.write_info();
```

But we could not write `p.change_salary()` or `p.earns()`, since these member functions do not exist for class `Person`.

We are allowed to indicate the same name of a member in a subclass as in a base class: as a result we get a new member that *hides* the member of the base class. For instance, if we had also declared a data member called `name` in class `Employee`, an object of class `Employee` would have had two data members called `name`, but the first one would have been hidden by the second.

A new member function with the name `write_info` is declared in class `Employee`. This will hide the member function `write_info` that was declared in class `Person`. If we write `e.write_info()`, where `e` is an object of type `Employee`, the `write_info` that was declared in class `Employee` will be called. But if we write `p.write_info()`, the `write_info` that was declared in class `Person` will be called, since the variable `p` is a member of that class. The definition of `write_info` for class `Employee` looks like this:

```
void Employee::write_info() const
{
  Person::write_info();
  cout << "Salary: " << salary << endl;
}
```

The third line is interesting. It shows how we can access a hidden member. To access a hidden member with the name `m` that has been declared in a base class `B`, we write `B::m`. Here we have written `Person::write_info()`, which means that the `write_info` declared in base class `Person` will be called. The printout from the statements above will be

```
Name: David
Name: Neil
Salary: 20000
```

The first line is written out by the call `p.write_info()` and the two other lines by the call `e.write_info()`.

We must avoid function overloading between inheritance hierarchies. If a function is declared in a subclass, all the functions with the same name will be hidden in the base class, irrespective of what parameters they might have:

```
class C1 {
public:
  void f(int);    // C1::f
}
class C2 : public C1 {
public:
  void f();       // C2::f, hides C1::f
}
main()
{
  C1 a;
  C2 b;
  a.f(5);         // OK!    C1::f is called
  b.f();          // OK!    C2::f is called
  b.f(5);         // ERROR! C1::f is hidden
}
```

There are a number of functions that cannot be inherited. These are constructors, destructors, friend functions and the assignment operator `=`. Constructors and destructors will be dealt with in detail in section 9.2. The assignment operator cannot be inherited since one is always defined automatically for each class (see page 270). It hides the assignment operator of a base class.

A derived class can also have subclasses. We can, for instance, declare a class `Programmer` that is a subclass of class `Employee`:

```
class Programmer : public Employee {
public:
  const string& read_favorite() const {return fav;}
  void change_favorite(const string& f) {fav=f;}
private:
  string fav;
};
```

The data member `fav` indicates a programmer's favourite programming language.

The classes `Person` and `Employee` are *base classes* of class `Programmer`. The class `Employee` is a *direct base class*, since it is indicated in the definition of class `Programmer`. The class `Person` is an *indirect base class*. The class `Programmer` is *directly derived* from class `Employee` and *indirectly derived* from class `Person`. An object of class `Programmer` inherits attributes from all of its base classes, each of which is a subobject. This means that a programmer has three data members: `name`, `salary` and `favourite`.

Member functions can also be inherited. For instance, we can write

```
Programmer pr;
pr.change_name("Hanna");
pr.change_salary(25000);
pr.change_favourite("C++");
pr.write_info();
```

In the last line, `write_info` in class `Employee` will be called.

Derived classes

```
class D : access B {
...
};
```

(*access* = **public**, **protected** or **private**)

- Class D is *directly derived* from class B.
- Class B is a *direct base class* of D.
- D *inherits* all the members from B.
  - Exceptions: constructors, destructors, friend functions and the assignment operator `=`.
- Members with the same name are *hidden*.

```
class D2 : access D {
...
};
```

- Class D2 is *indirectly derived* from class B.
- Class B is an *indirect base class* of D2.
- D2 *inherits* all the members from B and D.

There may be several independent subclasses to a particular class. For instance, we can define a class that defines temporary employees:

```
class Temp_emp : public Employee {
public:
  Date from, to;
};
```

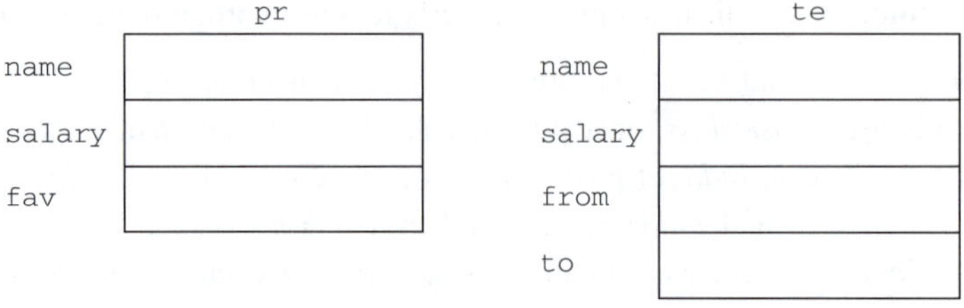

Figure 9.2

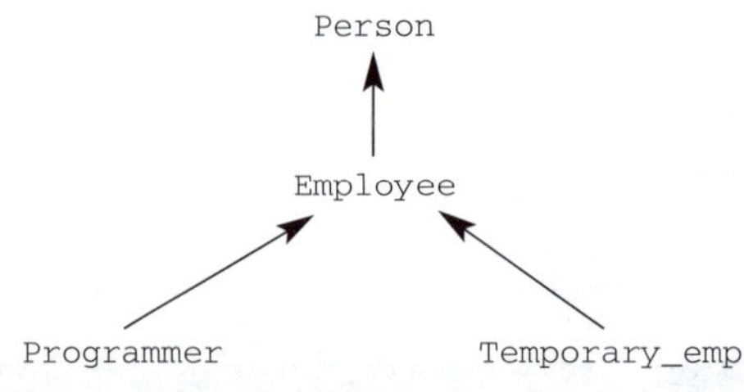

Figure 9.3

Here we use a class `Date`:

```
class Date {
public:
   int year, mon, day;
};
```

We now declare two variables – a programmer and and a temporary employee:

```
Programmer pr;
Temp_emp te;
```

The variable `pr` is composed of three parts: a `Person` part, an `Employee` part and a `Programmer` part. The variable `te` is composed of a `Person` part, an `Employee` part and a `Temp_emp` part. This is illustrated in Figure 9.2.

The relations between the classes are illustrated in Figure 9.3.

Since a derived class `D` always contains the data members of a base class `B` as a subobject, we can easily carry out a type conversion from type `D` to type `B`. The data members of the derived type are then 'peeled away' to leave the base class subobject. In this way, conversion from a derived type `D` to a base type `B` therefore occurs safely and is also one of the type conversions that can occur automatically (see section 5.7.1). This also applies to pointers. A pointer of type `D*` can be automatically converted to a pointer of type `B*`. As an example, we can look at the following function, which compares the salaries of two employees and gives the higher one as result:

```
long int higher_salary(Employee a, Employee b)
{
  if (a.earns() > b.earns())
    return a.earns();
  else
    return b.earns();
}
```

If, as before, we have the variable `pr` of type `Programmer` and the variable `te` of type `Temp_emp`, we can make the call

```
cout << higher_salary(pr, te);
```

Here the first argument is automatically converted from type `Programmer` to type `Employee`, and the second from type `Temp_emp` to type `Employee`.

Conversion in the other direction – that is, from a base type to a derived type – cannot occur automatically. It can be done explicitly, but this can be dangerous:

```
Employee *pa;
Programmer pr, *pp = &pr;
Temp_emp te;
pa = pp;                         // always safe
pp = (Programmer *)pa;           // unsafe but works
pa = &te;
pp = (Programmer *)pa;           // unsafe, may miscarry
pp->change_favourite("C++");     // and does!!
```

The first assignment `pa=pp` is safe, because we convert from a derived type to a base type. The second assignment is unsafe, because we cannot determine whether the object that `pa` points to is a `Programmer` or some other kind of employee. (But in this example it works.) The assignment in the penultimate line causes a catastrophe. The pointer `pp` should point to a `Programmer` but will, in fact, point to a `Temp_emp`. Now when we call the member function `change_favourite`, this will make a change in the object pointed to that we do not want. In section 9.6 on page 325 we shall be discussing the operator **`dynamic_cast`**, which carries out type conversion more safely.

9.2 Constructors, destructors and inheritance

Objects that belong to a derived class can be initialized, like other objects, with the aid of constructors. When a constructor is called for this purpose, the data members that have been inherited from the base class must also be initialized. This is done by calling a constructor for the base class. Then the part of the object (the subobject) that has been inherited from the base class will be initialized. The remainder of the object will be initialized by the constructor specially defined for the derived class. In this section we shall look at how this happens, and see which rules apply. In our example we use the classes `Person`, `Employee` and `Programmer`. In the class `Person` no constructor was defined: therefore the class had only the predefined default constructor. Now we add a constructor where you can indicate the name of a person. We must also define a default constructor of our own:

```
class Person {
public:
   Person() {};
   Person(const string& n) : name(n) {};
   ...
   string name;
};
```

(The two constructors could have been combined into one if we had given the parameter a default value, but in the interests of clarity we have not done this.) The new constructor is called when we make the declaration

```
Person p("David");
```

We also complete class `Employee` with another constructor:

```
class Employee : public Person {
public:
   Employee() : salary(0) {};
   Employee(const string& n, long int s) : Person(n), salary(s){}
   ...
   long int salary;
};
```

Look at the second constructor. We have used an initialization list to initialize the different parts of the object. The expression `Person(n)` is a call of the constructor for the base class `Person`. Let us now see what happens if we initialize an object of class `Employee`. We make the declaration

```
Employee e1("Lisa", 20000);
```

Because the parameter `n` in our example has the value `"Lisa"`, we get the expression `Person("Lisa")` in the initialization list. As a result, the second construçtor for class `Person` is called and the data member `name` is initialized. Then the data member `salary` is initialized to `20000`. Note that the constructor for the base class is always called *before* the data members in the derived class are initialized and *before* the statements to be executed inside the braces are executed. In the constructor above we have written `Person(n)` in front of `salary(l)` in the initialization list, but the order does not matter. The base class constructor is *always* called first.

We now initialize an object using the first constructor (the default constructor) for class `Employee`:

```
Employee e2;
```

An initialization list is also used in the first constructor, but there is no expression for the base class `Person`. Since a constructor for a base class must always be called, a call of the base class default constructor (the constructor that can be called without parameters) is generated *automatically*. Here, too, the call takes place *before* the data members in the derived class are initialized and *before* the statements inside the braces are executed. In our example, the data member `name` will be initialized to a string of length zero. Only then is the data member `salary` initialized to zero.

Of course, for a default constructor of the base class to be called, one must exist. (The class `Person` has one.) If a base class does not have a default constructor, one of the constructors of the base class in the initialization list of the constructor of the derived class *must* be called; otherwise the program will be faulty. If, for argument's sake, we suppose that a default constructor for class `Person` did not exist, we would have to rewrite the first constructor for class `Employee`:

```
Employee() : Person(""), salary(0) {};
```

If we fail to define constructors for a class, default constructors are defined automatically (as we saw on page 228). We can say categorically that base classes without their own constructors will be given a default constructor.

If we do not define our own constructors for a derived class then this, too, will have an automatically defined default constructor assigned to it. Let us take an example in which we declare a new subclass of class `Person`:

```
class Athlete : public Person {
   ...
private:
  bool elite;
};
```

Note that we have not defined any constructors. We then get an automatically generated default constructor. We might imagine that it looks something like this:

```
Athlete() : Person() {}  // automatically generated
```

The default constructor of the base class is also called, in the automatically generated default constructor, for if this did not happen we would get a compilation error.

We can now declare a variable of class `Athlete`:

```
Athlete at;
```

The default constructor for class `Person` will be called and the data member `name` will be initialized, while the data member `elite` will be uninitialized.

This is a suitable moment to recall that, when we define a class, we usually get an automatically generated *copy constructor* (see page 233) and an automatically generated *assignment operator* (see page 270). This also applies to derived classes. Both operators make an automatic assignment to the part of an object consisting of the base class, or the base class subobject. This is done when the automatically generated copy constructor calls the copy constructor of the base class and the automatically generated assignment operator calls the assignment operator of the base class.

If there are deeper inheritance relations, the call of constructors can extend to several levels. Here we give class `Programmer` from page 290 a constructor where you can indicate name, salary, and favourite language (we must also define a default constructor):

```
class Programmer : public Employee {
public:
   Programmer() {}
   Programmer(const string& n, long int s, const string& f)
      : Employee(n,s), fav(f) {}
   ...
   string fav;
};
```

A constructor – the one with two parameters – for the base class `Employee` is called here in the initialization list, and this constructor, as we explained earlier, will in turn call a constructor for its base class `Person`. This results in the initializations in class `Person` being performed first, followed by the initializations in class `Employee`, and finally the initializations in class `Programmer`. In C++, initializations must be performed in a strict order. The members of the highest base class are initialized first, and we proceed down the hierarchy until the members of the classes derived last are initialized.

Inheritance and constructors

For a derived class `D` with a direct base class `B`, the following applies:

- In the initialization list of a constructor for `D`, a constructor for the base class can be called explicitly:
  `D::D(`*parameters*`) : B(`*parameters*`), ... {`*statements*`}`
  If this has not been done, a default constructor for `B` is called *automatically*.
- If class `D` has an automatically generated default constructor, the default constructor of the base class will be called in it.
- Initialization order in a constructor:
  - a constructor for the base class is called;
  - the data members of the class in question are initialized (in the order in which they were declared in the class definition);
  - the statements inside the braces `{}` are executed.

Inheritance and destructors

- Destructors are not inherited.
- The execution order for destructors:
  - the statements inside the braces {} are executed;
  - a destructor for the base class is called.

Fortunately, destructors are much easier to deal with than constructors. Destructors are not inherited. A destructor is normally used only when a corresponding constructor has allocated memory space that must be released. Destructors are handled like constructors except that everything is done in the *reverse* order. This means that the destructor for the last derived class is executed first. Here is a simple example to demonstrate this:

```
class C1 {
public:
   C1(int n);
   ~C1();
private:
   int *pi, l;
};
C1::C1(int n): l(n)
{ cout << l << " integers are allocated" << endl;
   pi = new int[l];
}
C1::~C1()
{ cout << l << " integers are released" << endl;
   delete[] pi;
}
class C2 : public C1{
public:
   C2(int n);
   ~C2();
private:
   char *pc;
   int l;
};
C2::C2(int n): C1(n), l(n)
{ cout << l << " characters are allocated" << endl;
   pc = new char[l];
}
C2::~C2()
{ cout << l << " characters are released" << endl;
   delete[] pc;
}
main()
{
   C2 a(50), b(100);
}
```

When the program is run, we get the following printout:

```
50 integers are allocated
50 characters are allocated
100 integers are allocated
100 characters are allocated
100 characters are released
100 integers are released
50 characters are released
50 integers are released
```

9.3 Access control

We have seen how, in a class definition, we can use the reserved words `public` and `private` to indicate whether the members of a class will be accessible outside the class. There is a third possibility, a sort of compromise between `public` and `private` – the reserved word `protected`. A class definition can have the form

```
class C {
public:
   declarations of visible members
protected:
   declarations of protected members
private:
   declarations of private members
};
```

These three parts may come in any order. If nothing is written, all the members will be private. The following rules apply:

- If a member is declared in a class `C` and is *private* (declared in the `private` section), it can be used only by the member functions in `C` and by the friends of class `C`.
- If a member is declared in a class `C` and the member is *protected* (declared in the `protected` section), it can be used only by the member functions in `C`, friends of `C`, and member functions and friends of classes derived from `C`.
- If a member is *public* (declared in the `public` section) it can be used everywhere, without restrictions.

A protected member is accessible *within* the inheritance hierarchy but not outside it. We shall use class `Clock` to give an example:

```
class Clock {
public:
   Clock ();
   Clock (int hour, int min, int sec);
   void set (int hour, int min, int sec);
   int read_hour() const {return h;}
```

```
    int read_min() const {return m;}
    int read_sec() const {return s;}
    void write(bool write_sec = true) const;
    void tick();
protected:
    int h, m, s;
};
```

The only difference here is that we have written **protected** instead of **private** in the third line from the bottom. We shall now define a subclass of `Clock` – the class `Alarm_Clock`. An alarm clock has the same properties as an ordinary clock, but we have added the possibility of having an alarm at a specific time. There is a member function `set_alarm` with which we indicate when the alarm is to ring. We have also made a new variant of the function `tick`, which will hide the one declared in class `Clock`.

```
class Alarm_Clock : public Clock {
public:
    void set_alarm (int hour, int min, int sec)
                    { ah=hour; am=min; as=sec; };
    void tick();
protected:
    int ah, am, as;
};
```

The definition of the new variant of the function `tick` is most interesting here:

```
void Alarm_Clock::tick()
{
    Clock::tick();
    if (h==ah && m==am && s==as)
        cout << "\a\a\a";
}
```

First we call the function `tick`, which was declared in the base class `Clock`. This moves the clock forward one second, followed by a check to see whether it is time for the alarm to ring. But for this to happen, we must have access to the members of base class `Clock`. (We could use the functions `read_hour` and so on, but do not do so in this example.) If `h`, `m` and `s` had been private members, this would not have been possible, but by declaring them as protected we shall have access to them in the subclass `Alarm_Clock`.

As a rule, it can be said that if a class is constructed with the intention of making it the base class for various derived classes, then its data members should be declared as protected rather than as private. We then have the option of formulating the member functions in the subclasses more efficiently.

When a class D is derived from a base class B then, as we have seen, it will inherit the members of B. We then accept the inherited members as members of D and, just as for other members, the accessibility of the inherited members must be specified. We do this by writing one of the words **private**, **protected** or **public** in front of the name of the base class concerned. We can then write one of the following:

```
class D : private B {     // private inheritance
   ...
};
```

```
class D : protected B {   // protected inheritance
   ...
};
```

```
class D : public B {      // public inheritance
   ...
};
```

We call these *private*, *protected* and *public* inheritance respectively. It is more common to use *public* inheritance. We can give the following rules, where B is the base class and D the derived class:

- *Private members* of B are never visible anywhere but in B, neither in D nor anywhere outside B. Their visibility is not affected by the type of inheritance involved.
- If *private inheritance* is involved (the word **private** is used), then all the members of B that are *protected* or *public* will be *private* in D.
- If *protected inheritance* is involved (the word **protected** is used), then all the members of B that are *protected* or *public* will be *protected* in D.
- If *public inheritance* is involved (the word **public** is used), then all the members of B that are *protected* will also be *protected* in D, and all the members of B that are *public* will also be *public* in D.

We note that it is the most restrictive of any two types of access that applies. The exception is the private members of a base class that are never accessible in the derived class. Let us take some examples that illustrate the foregoing rules. We first declare a base class B with three derived classes D1, D2 and D3:

```
class Base {
public:
   int i1;
protected:
   int i2;
private:
   int i3;
};
class D1 : private Base {
   void f();
```

```
};
class D2 : protected Base {
   void g();
};
class D3 : public Base {
   void h();
};
```

None of the subclasses has access to member `i3` in the base class `B`. But all three of the base classes can access members `i1` and `i2` *internally*. In the definition of the member function `f` (the same thing applies to `g` and `h`) we shall get, for example,

```
void D1::f() {
   i1 = 0;   // OK
   i2 = 0;   // OK
   i3 = 0;   // ERROR!
};
```

Access for `i1`, `i2` and `i3` *outside* the three classes is shown in the following program:

```
main()
{
   Base b;
   b.i1 = 0;     // OK
   b.i2 = 0;     // ERROR!
   b.i3 = 0;     // ERROR!
   D1 d1;
   d1.i1 = 0;    // ERROR!
   d1.i2 = 0;    // ERROR!
   d1.i3 = 0;    // ERROR!
   D2 d2;
   d2.i1 = 0;    // ERROR!
   d2.i2 = 0;    // ERROR!
   d2.i3 = 0;    // ERROR!
   D3 d3;
   d3.i1 = 0;    // OK
   d3.i2 = 0;    // ERROR!
   d3.i3 = 0;    // ERROR!
};
```

By using private or protected inheritance we can prevent a user from accessing the members inherited from the base class from outside. An alternative method would be to use public inheritance, redeclaring all the public base class members in the derived class. Then the members of the base class would be hidden. This necessitates that *all* the public members be redeclared, otherwise they will not be hidden.

If we use private or protected inheritance there is a way of selectively making individual members of the base class more accessible in a derived class – by making what is called an *access declaration*. This is done by simply *naming* one of the members of the base class at an appropriate place in the derived class. Here are a couple of examples:

```
class D4 : protected Base {
public:
  Base::i1;  // access declaration
};
```

By naming the member variable `i1` in the **public** section of `D4` we also make `i1` *public* in `D4`. We are now allowed, for instance, to write the following in the function `main`:

```
D4 d4;
d4.i1 = 0;  // OK
```

In a similar way, we can make `i2` *protected* in `D5` by naming `i2` in the **protected** section of `D5`. This will result in `i2` being accessible in subclasses of `D5`:

```
class D5 : private Base {
protected:
  Base::i2;  // access declaration
};
```

We are not allowed to make a member more accessible than it is in the base class. For instance, if we had tried to name `i2` in the **public** section of `D5`, we would have received an error message.

In the standard, *using* declarations are recommended instead of access declarations (see section 15.1). We then write:

```
using Base::i1;
using Base::i2;
```

9.4 Reusable code: an example

We now give an example to demonstrate several of the points discussed so far. One of the fundamental ideas behind object-oriented programming is that we should be able to reuse program code by building on classes that are already available. We shall be using this technique in our example.

Sometimes it is necessary to work with really large integers, numbers that consist of so many digits that they do not have enough space in a variable of type **int** or **long int**. In this example we shall construct a class `SuperInt` that enables us to work with such large integers. Large numbers will be represented with the help of an integer array, in which a digit is placed in each element of the array. We make use of the class `Array` (from Chapter 8) and make class `SuperInt` into a subclass of this:

```
#ifndef ARRAY_H
#define ARRAY_H
#include <iostream>
#include <utility>
using namespace std::rel_ops;
class Array {
public:
   Array(int first_index=1, int number=0);
   Array(const Array& v);
   ~Array();
   int first() const {return i1;}
   int last()  const {return i1+num-1;}
   int length() const {return num;}
   const Array& operator=  (const Array& v);
   bool         operator== (const Array& v)  const;
   bool         operator<  (const Array& v)  const;
   const Array& operator+= (const Array& v);
   Array        operator+  (const Array& v)  const;
   const Array& operator+= (int d);
   Array        operator+  (int d) const;
   const Array& operator-= (const Array& v);
   Array        operator-  (const Array& v)  const;
   const Array& operator-= (int d);
   Array        operator-  (int d)           const;
   const Array& operator&= (const Array & v);
   Array        operator&  (const Array& v)  const;
   Array        operator-  () const;
   const Array& operator++ ();               // prefix ++v
   Array        operator++ (int);            // postfix v++
   const Array& operator-- ();               // prefix --v
   Array        operator-- (int);            // postfix v--
   int&         operator[] (int i);
   int          operator[] (int i) const;
   const Array  operator() (int from,int to) const;
   friend Array operator+  (int d,const Array& v);
   friend std::ostream& operator<< (std::ostream&, const Array&);
   friend std::istream& operator>> (std::istream&, Array&);
private:
   int *p;
   const int i1;
   int num;
};
#endif
```

We define the new class `SuperInt` as a subclass of class `Array`:

```
#ifndef SUPERINT_H
#define SUPERINT_H
#include "array.h"
class SuperInt : protected Array {
public:
  SuperInt(long int n = 0);
  Array::length;                    // makes length directly visible
  int operator() (int k) const;     // gives digit no. k
  SuperInt operator+ (const SuperInt& b) const;
  SuperInt operator- (const SuperInt& b) const;
  SuperInt operator- () const;
  SuperInt operator* (const SuperInt& b) const;
  SuperInt operator* (int i) const;
  SuperInt operator/ (const SuperInt& b) const;
  SuperInt operator/ (int i) const;
  bool operator== (const SuperInt& b) const;
  bool operator<  (const SuperInt& b) const;
  friend std::istream& operator>> (std::istream&, SuperInt&);
  friend std::ostream& operator<< (std::ostream&,
                                    const SuperInt&);
private:
  SuperInt(bool neg, int number)
      : Array(0, number), negative(neg) {};
  bool negative;
};
#endif
```

The class `SuperInt` contains the most important operations that allow us to work with large numbers. There is a constructor for creating new objects. There is an automatically generated copy constructor for creating copies of other objects of class `SuperInt`. There are operators for the four arithmetic operations, and the `-` operator has a further unary variant. There is a variant of the multiplication and division operators with an ordinary **`int`** as the right-hand operand. (Small integers, for instance 1, are very easy to multiply and divide by, so use is made of this.) There are a number of logical operations to compare `SuperInt` objects with each other. Finally, there are two friend functions, one to write and one to read objects of class `SuperInt`.

Protected inheritance is used in the definition of `SuperInt` (**`protected`** is on the first line). If we had used public inheritance, all the member functions inherited by class `SuperInt` from class `Array` would have been visible for the user. There are many operators for class `Array` that are not applicable to objects of type `SuperInt`. Even worse, there are operations that would give incorrect results if they were applied to objects of class `SuperInt`. For instance, the operator `++` for class `Array` increases every element in an `Array` object by `1`. If this operator were performed for class `SuperInt`, each *digit* in a number would be increased by `1`, which is not the correct way to add `1` to a number. Protected inheritance is implemented to prevent the user from making a mistake by using the wrong operator.

The only one of the inherited member functions to be made directly visible is that of `length`. This occurs in the fourth line of the definition of class `SuperInt`, where there is an access declaration. The function `length` returns the length of an `Array` object. In the case of the derived class `SuperInt`, the number of digits in a large number is returned, so this operation has some significance.

Another inherited member function that could have been made visible is the indexing operator `[]`. It would have enabled a user to directly access individual digits in a `SuperInt`. The problem here is that the user would have been able to *change* individual digits in a number – perhaps not such a good idea! (It is not possible to allow only the constant version of the `[]` operator to be visible in an access declaration.) So we have done things differently. On the fifth line we declare a function call operator `()` with one parameter. We let this operator return a single digit in a number. We can then read but not change a particular digit. Our function call operator has another advantage: if, as parameter, we give the index of a digit not in the number concerned, we shall get a value of `0`. If, for instance, we have a variable `x` of `SuperInt` and `x` has the value `123456`, the call `x(2)` will give a value of `4` (indexing takes place from the right, beginning with zero), whereas a call of `x(6)` will return a value of `0`.

Another constructor is defined in the private section of class `SuperInt`. This constructor will only be used internally when the member functions of the class are implemented. It should not be visible outside the class. We also note that, in the private section, the class has only a single data member. This is the member `negative`, which indicates whether or not a number is less than zero. All the other necessary data members are inherited from the base class `Array`. The class `Array` allows us to work with `Array` object of varying lengths. We shall make use of this fact, therefore, and let every object of class `SuperInt` consist of an array that is just as long as necessary. Every digit in a `SuperInt` is stored in an element in the array, and no leading zeros are stored. The only exception is the number zero, which is stored in an array with a single element that contains a zero. When we work with integers, we usually number the digits from the right and begin numbering with zero. Units are represented by the digit number `0`, tens by digit number `1`, and so on. We shall use this numbering sequence here. (This means that the digits in a `SuperInt` will be backwards in an array.) Objects of type `SuperInt` will be of different lengths, and the memory space for them will have to be allocated and released dynamically. We shall not have to do this explicitly in class `SuperInt`, since the constructors and the destructor in class `Array` will take care of this automatically.

Before we discuss how the different member functions will be implemented, we show a program that simulates a simple calculator. The user will enter expressions of the form *x op y*, where *op* is one of the operators `+`, `-`, `*` and `/`. The numbers that are input as data can be of arbitrary length (but the input operator can only read numbers with a maximum of 500 digits). The program replies by writing out the result, and terminates when the user writes the character combination for *end of file*.

```
#include "superint.h"
#include <iostream>
using namespace std;
main()
{
  SuperInt x, y;
  char op;
  cout << "? ";
  while (cin >> x && cin >> op && cin >> y)
  {
    if (op == '+')
      cout << (x+y) << endl;
    else if (op == '-')
      cout << (x-y) << endl;
    else if (op == '*')
      cout << (x*y) << endl;
    else if (op == '/')
      cout << (x/y) << endl;
    else
      cout << "Incorrect operator" << endl;
    cout << endl << "? ";
  }
}
```

We now show the program when it is run. (The data entered by the user has been underlined.)

```
? 1234567890123456789 * 987654321098765
1219326311370217418780678478765585
? 1219326311370217418780678478765585 /
1234567890123456789
987654321098765
? 66666644444433333377777888888999111111 +
6765765765765765
666666444444333333777785654655764876876
```

Now let us look at how the different operations in class `SuperInt` are implemented. We shall begin with the constructors. The first one, which lies in the public section, allows us to initialize a `SuperInt` with a value of type **`long int`**. This constructor also functions as a default constructor and type conversion constructor from type **`long int`** to `SuperInt`. The constructor is called automatically in the following kinds of expression:

```
SuperInt s1(6798), s2=2324, s3;
s3 = 518;
s1 = s1 + 9576;
```

In the last line the right-hand operand is converted to the type `SuperInt`. When the constructor is called it should ensure that an `Array` object is allocated exactly large enough to hold the number given as parameter. For a positive number n to be stored, $1 + \log n$ digits are needed. On the basis of this, we can write the following help function to calculate the number of digits in a number n:

```
int num_dig(long int n)
{
  if (n==0)
    return 1;
  else
    return log10((double) labs(n)) + 1;
}
```

The number 0 is treated as a special case. We called the standard functions `log10` and `labs`, which are declared in the header files `cmath` and `cstdlib` respectively (see page 41). Now we can write the definition of the constructor:

```
SuperInt::SuperInt(long int n)
: Array(0, num_dig(1))
{
  negative = (n<0);
  n = labs(n);
  for (int k=0; k<length(); k++)
  {
    (*this)[k] = n % 10;
    n /= 10;
  }
}
```

The `Array` part of the object is initialized when the constructor for the base class is called in the initialization list. The first argument indicates that indexing will begin with 0, and the second argument indicates how many elements will be allocated for the `Array` object. To compute this, the help function `num_dig` is used. The data member `negative` is initialized with the initialization of the `Array` part. The allocated `Array` object is then filled with all the digits, which are calculated one at a time by dividing the number `n` by `10` and seeing what remainder results. The expression `(*this)[k]` means that the inherited indexing operator for the actual object is called. This operator gives as result a reference to element number `k` in the array. The array cannot be accessed directly since the pointer to it lies in the private section of the base class. We must therefore use the indexing operator. (This is not a disadvantage, as the operator will check that the index lies within the allowed limits.)

The second constructor is defined directly in the private section of the class definition:

```
SuperInt(bool neg, int len)
: Array(0, len), negative(neg) {};
```

The constructor will get as parameters both a logical value stating whether or not the number is negative, and an integer indicating how many digits are to be allocated. We do not want this constructor to be accessible to outside users since it enables objects of type `SuperInt` to be created, where an array will not be correctly filled with digits. We shall use the constructor internally in class `SuperInt`.

There is a third constructor, the copy constructor. As we know, this is declared automatically and is visible from outside. It is called in expressions of the form

```
SuperInt s4(s1), s5 = s2;
```

This constructor in turn calls the copy constructor of the base class. We wrote the copy constructor for class `Array` ourselves in Chapter 7 (see page 236). It makes a deep copy. We also get an automatically generated assignment operator, which is called when we write, for example,

```
s4 = s5;
```

This assignment operator calls the assignment operator of the base class, which we also wrote ourselves (see page 271). This also makes a deep copy; when we initialize a `SuperInt` with another `SuperInt` or assign a `SuperInt` to another, we shall automatically get a deep copy. All this happens because class `SuperInt` is derived from class `Array`. It can be seen that we do not need to think of allocations of memory space and releasing memory space when we write the member functions in class `SuperInt`.

The next member function that we shall look at is the function call operator `()`, which is used to read a particular digit in a `SuperInt`. The parameter `k` indicates which digit is involved:

```
int SuperInt::operator()(int k) const
{
  if(k < length())
    return (*this)[k];
  else
    return 0;
}
```

If a number has n digits, the most significant digit of the number will lie in element number n–1, since numbering always takes place from 0. We can find out the number of digits in a number by calling the inherited member function `length`. If the function **`operator`**`()` were called with a parameter value `k` greater than the number for the most significant digit, we would realize that a zero was in this position: in fact, the function would return a value of 0. If `k`, on the other hand, contains the number of a 'regular' digit, this will be read with the help of the indexing operator.

The next operator we shall define is simple. It is the unary minus operator, which returns an object of reversed sign:

```
SuperInt SuperInt::operator- () const
{
  if (*this == 0)
    return 0;
  else
  {
    SuperInt s(*this);              // Create a copy
    s.negative = not s.negative;    // Change sign
    return s;
  }
}
```

If the number is not equal to 0, a copy of the actual object is created. (The copy constructor will be called.) We then change the sign in the copy and give it as result from the function. Note that we cannot make this change in the actual object since the function **`operator-`** is a constant function.

In class `SuperInt` we declared the operators `==` and `<`. (The other comparison operators, `>` and `!=` for instance, are defined automatically since the class `Array`, which is the superclass of `SuperInt`, includes the file `utility` and makes the name space `rel_ops` visible.)

```
bool SuperInt::operator== (const SuperInt& b) const
{
  return negative==b.negative && Array(*this)==Array(b);
}
```

The operator `==` first checks whether the numbers have the same sign. If so, the comparison operator for the base class is called to check whether the digits are equal. Note that the expressions `Array(*this)` and `Array(b)` are explicit type conversions to the base class `Array`.

Of the other comparison operators it is only the operator `<` that is slightly difficult, so we shall take it first:

```
bool SuperInt::operator< (const SuperInt& b) const
{
  if (negative && b.negative)
    return -b < -*this;
  if (negative && ! b.negative)
    return true;
```

```
    if (not negative && b.negative)
      return false;
    int n;
    if (length() > b.length())
      n = length();
    else
      n = b.length();
    for (int k=n-1; k >= 0; k--)   // Compare the digits
      if ((*this)(k) != b(k))
        return (*this)(k) < b(k);
    return false;
  }
```

First, the operands are checked in case one is negative. If both are negative, their signs can be changed along with the inequality sign. (The unary minus operator that was defined above is called.) If only one operand is negative, we can dispense with the decision whether the first is less than the second.

If both operands are positive, the digits in them are compared one by one. We begin with the most significant digit, and terminate the comparisons as soon as we have found two digits that are different. The expression `(*this)(k) != b(k)` tests whether digit number `k` in the two operands is different. Note that the operator `()` is used here, so it will make no difference if the two operands have different lengths.

Now let us tackle the operator `+`, which adds two `SuperInt`s:

```
SuperInt SuperInt::operator+ (const SuperInt& b) const
{
  if (b.negative)
    return *this - (-b);
  if (negative)
    return b - (- *this);
  // Calculate the number of digits in the sum
  int dig, i, m;  // m is the memory digit
  for (i=m=0; i<length() || i<b.length(); i++)
  {
    dig = (*this)(i)+b(i)+m;
    m = dig / 10;
  }
  SuperInt s(false,i+m);  // The sum gets the length i+m
  // Calculate the digits in the sum
  for (i=m=0; i<s.length(); i++)
  {
    dig = (*this)(i)+b(i)+m;
    s[i]= dig % 10;
    m = dig / 10;
  }
  return s;
}
```

We first test whether an operand is negative. If so, we change the sign of this operand and call the operator `-` to perform a subtraction instead of an addition. If both operands are positive, an addition should be performed. The sum will be calculated in a new temporary `SuperInt`, which we shall call `s`. Before we declare the variable `s`, we must know how many digits it is to contain. The number of digits will be equal to the length of the longest of the two operands, with 1 added if there should be a memory digit when the two most significant digits are added. To calculate how long `s` should be, we perform the additions of the two operands but we do not keep the result. The only things we keep track of are the variable `i`, which computes how many digits are added, and the variable `m`, which contains the memory digits that arise. After the last round `m` will contain a value of either `0` or `1`. The variable `s` should therefore consist of `i+m` digits. When `s` has been declared, we perform the addition once more, but this time we save all the digits that arise in the variable `s`.

We shall now turn our attention to the definition of the subtraction operator `-`:

```
SuperInt SuperInt::operator- (const SuperInt& b) const
{
  if (b.negative)
    return *this + (-b);
  if (negative)
    return - (-*this + b);
  if (*this < b)
    return -(b - *this);
  // Both numbers are positive and *this >= b
  SuperInt d(*this);     // Will contain the result
  int i, j;
  for (i=0; i<length(); i++)
  {
    d[i] = d[i]-b(i);    // Calculate digit no. i
    if (d[i] < 0)        // Borrow
    {
      for (j=i+1; d[j] == 0; j++)
        d[j] = 9;
      d[j]--;            // The first digit that is not zero
      d[i] += 10;
    }
  }
  // Compute the number of initial zeros in the result
  for (i=length()-1, j=0; i>0 && d[i]==0; i--, j++)
    ;
  if ( j == 0)
    return d;            // No initial zeros
  else
  { // j zeros. Create a new shorter result
    SuperInt d2(false, length()-j);
```

```
        for (i=0; i<d2.length(); i++)
          d2[i] = d[i];
        return d2;
    }
}
```

A test is carried out to see whether one of the operands is negative. If so, this operand is negated and an addition is performed instead. If both operands are positive, another test checks whether the first operand is not less than the second. If this is so, we let the operands change place and return the negated value of the subtraction.

If both operands are positive and the first is greater than or equal to the second, subtraction is performed digit by digit. The result is placed in a local variable `d`. In subtraction, we may need to 'borrow' exactly as if we were counting by hand. When subtraction is finished, we test whether there are zeros at the beginning of the result. There should not be any in a `SuperInt`. If there are, we declare a new temporary variable `d2`, which is shorter than `d`. We then copy the digits in `d` to `d2`, leaving out the zeros at the beginning.

The multiplication operator exists in two variants. We shall first look at the simpler of the two, the one that multiplies a `SuperInt` by an ordinary **`int`**. Our main reason for constructing this variant is that we shall need it later when we shall be multiplying a `SuperInt` by individual digits in another `SuperInt`. We give the definition below. If the right-hand operand lies in the interval from 0 to 10 the calculation is carried out directly; otherwise, the right-hand operand is also converted to a `SuperInt`, and the second variant of the multiplication operator is called to perform the multiplication.

```
SuperInt SuperInt::operator* (int i) const
{
  if (i == 0 || *this == 0)
    return 0;
  else if (i==1)
    return *this;
  else if (i>=2 && i<=9)
  { // Perform repeated addition
    SuperInt r;
    for (int j=1; j<=i; j++)
      r = r + (*this);
    return r;
  }
  else if (i==10)
  { // Move the digits one step to the left
    SuperInt r(negative, length()+1);
    r[0]=0;
    for (int j=1; j<r.length(); j++)
      r[j] = (*this)(j-1);
```

```
      return r;
   }
   else
      return (*this) * SuperInt(i);
}
```

If one of the operands is equal to 0, or if the right-hand operator is equal to 1, then calculating the result is a trivial operation. If the right-hand operand has a value between 2 and 9, multiplication is performed as repeated addition. (The value of the left-hand operand is added as many times as the right-hand operand indicates.) If the right-hand operand is equal to 10, we get the result by creating a `SuperInt` where all the digits are moved a step to the left.

With the aid of this operator we can write the variant of the multiplication operator that multiplies two operands of type `SuperInt`:

```
SuperInt SuperInt::operator* (const SuperInt& b) const
{
   if (*this == 0 || b == 0)
      return 0;
   else
   {
      SuperInt a(*this), r;
      a.negative = false;
      for (int i=0; i<b.length(); i++)
      {
         r = r + a * b(i);
         a = a * 10;
      }
      r.negative = (negative && ! b.negative) ||
                   (! negative && b.negative);
      return r;
   }
}
```

A special case arises when one of the operands is equal to zero. (This is done to ensure that the sign will be right in the result, irrespective of the sign of the other operand.) Generally, multiplication is performed exactly as we do it by hand with pen and paper. The left-hand operand (the actual object) is copied to a temporary variable `a`. The result of the multiplication will be calculated in another temporary variable `r`, which has a value of `0` from the outset. We then multiply the variable `a` with the digits in `b` a digit at a time: first the units, then the tens and so on. The result is added to the variable `r`. Between every addition `a` is multiplied by 10. To perform the multiplications we call the second variant of the operator `*`, the variant that has an **`int`** as its right-hand operand.

The last operator is the division operator `/`. This also exists in two variants, one that has an ordinary `int` as right-hand operand and one that has a `SuperInt`. We begin with the one with `int` as right-hand operand. This takes care of the special cases when the right-hand operand is equal to 1 or 10. In all other cases the right-hand operand is converted to a `SuperInt`, and the second variant of the division operator calculates the result. If the right-hand operand is equal to 1, calculating the result is a trivial operation. If it is equal to 10, we get the result by creating a copy of the actual object, one in which all the digits are moved one step to the right.

```
SuperInt SuperInt::operator/ (int i) const
{
  if (i==1)
    return *this;
  else if (i==10)
  { // Move the digits one step to the right
    SuperInt r(negative, length()-1);
    for (int j=0; j<r.length(); j++)
      r[j] = (*this)(j+1);
    return r;
  }
  else
    return *this / SuperInt(i);
}
```

The second variant of the division operator can now be defined:

```
SuperInt SuperInt::operator/ (const SuperInt& b) const
{
  assert(b != 0);
  SuperInt num(*this), den(b), r;
  int num_steps = 0;
  num.negative = den.negative = false;
  // Move den to the left as far as possible
  while (num >= den)
  {
    den = den * 10;
    num_steps++;
  }
  for (int i=1; i<=num_steps; i++)
  {
    den = den / 10;  // Move den a step to the right
    r = r * 10;
    // Subtract den from num as many times as posssible
    while (num >= den)
    {
      r = r + 1;  // Note how many times it is possible
      num = num - den;
```

```
      }
    }
    r.negative =(negative && ! b.negative) ||
                (! negative && b.negative);
    return r;
  }
```

Three local variables are used here. The numerator in the division is placed in the variable `num`, the denominator in the variable `den`, and the result in the variable `r`. The calculation proceeds in the same way as in manual calculation. First the denominator is moved as far to the left as it will go, and then we see how many times the denominator will 'go into' the numerator. This is noted, then the numerator is moved back one step to the right. We see how many times the denominator 'goes into' what is left of the numerator, and continue in this way until the numerator has been moved back to its original value.

To complete class `SuperInt` we have only to define the friend functions `>>` and `<<`, which perform the reading of input and writing of output, respectively, of objects of type `SuperInt`. The input operator `>>` is defined as follows:

```
istream& operator>> (istream& is, SuperInt& b)
{
  cin >> ws;  // Skip blank characters
  char s[500], *q=s, sign = '+';
  if (cin.peek() == '+' || cin.peek() == '-')
    cin >> sign;
  while (cin.peek() >= '0' && cin.peek() <= '9')
    cin >> *q++;
  *q = '\0';
  q = s;
  if (strlen(q) == 0)   // No digits
  {
    cout << "Incorrect integer" << endl;
    abort();
  };
  while (*q == '0')     // Skip leading zeros
    q++;
  if (strlen(q) == 0)  // The number 0 is a special case
    b == 0;
  else
  {
    SuperInt temp(sign == '-', strlen(q));
    for (int i=temp.length()-1; i>=0; i--)
      temp[i] = *q++ - '0';
    b = temp;
  }
  return is;
}
```

The manipulator ws is first used to skip leading blank characters (spacings, tab stops and end-of-line characters). Then we check whether the next character waiting to be read is a plus or a minus sign. If it is, the character is read in; if not, we assume it is '+'. Here we use the standard function peek, which tests the next character in the input stream without using it up.

A number of characters from the input stream are then read and placed in the character array s. The pointer q is used to point to the next free place in s. The input data is read as long as the character waiting to be read is a digit. When the last digit has been read, a zero character is placed last in the text string. If no digits could be read in, the user has written an incorrect integer. Then an error message is returned and the program terminated, in which case the standard function abort, declared in the header file stdlib.h, is used. If the number input is a correct integer, the function will continue by skipping all leading zeros. This is done by moving the pointer q forward until it points to the first character that does not contain the value '0'. If there are no more digits, the number 0 has been entered and this can be treated separately. If the number 0 has not been entered, a temporary variable temp of type SuperInt is declared, and the digits are placed in this variable, one by one. Note that the digits are placed backwards in temp compared with those in the text string. Finally, temp is assigned to the outparameter b.

The last function is the output operator <<. This is rather more straightforward, and no commentary is necessary.

```
ostream& operator<< (ostream& os, const SuperInt& b)
{
  if (b.negative)
    os << '-';
  for (int i=b.length()-1; i>=0; i--)
    os << b[i];
  return os;
}
```

This section has been crammed with detail and perhaps has been difficult to digest. We have tried to demonstrate the benefit of using an already completed class and building onto it, instead of doing everything from the beginning. Note especially that in class SuperInt we never had to worry about memory allocation and deallocation. The base class Array took care of all that.

9.5 Polymorphism and dynamic binding

In the so-called *typed programming languages*, such as C++ and Ada, types are used to monitor which operations can be carried out on the different data. If, for example, the variable x has type **double** and the function f(x) is called, the compiler will check whether there is a function `f` that has a parameter of type **`double`**, or whether there is a function `f` that has a parameter of type `t` and there is an automatic type conversion that can be made from type **`double`** to type `t`. If such is found to be the case, the compiler generates machine code that will cause the function `f` to be called when the program is run. Thus, which function is called is determined when the program is compiled. The call is said to be *bound* to the function `f`. In section 4.3 we saw that in C++ there can be *overloaded* functions, which means that several functions can have the same name but take different types of parameters. For example, if the call `g(x)` is made, the compiler can decide which function should be called by comparing the type of `x` with the different types of parameter that different `g` functions take.

In Chapter 14 we shall see that it is possible to construct what are known as *generic* program units for different types. We can construct a class `Array`, for example, in which the elements do not need to be of type **`int`** but can be of arbitrary type.

Overloading and generic program units are two forms of what is called *polymorphism* (having many forms) in the context of programming. This means that a program construct that has a certain appearance can mean different things (for example, calls to different functions) depending on the types of the operands involved. Binding means deciding exactly which form is appropriate. For both overloading and generic units binding occurs during compilation, and this is known as *static* or *early* binding. Alternatively, *dynamic* or *late* binding can occur, and this takes place during program execution. In languages without typing, such as Smalltalk, only dynamic binding is used, while in other object-oriented languages, such as Ada and C++, both static and dynamic bindings are allowed. The polymorphism associated with static binding is usually called *ad hoc polymorphism*; if the term 'polymorphism' is used alone it usually means polymorphism related to dynamic binding.

In the typed object-oriented languages, dynamic binding occurs in connection with inheritance. In C++ we use what are called *virtual functions* when we want to have dynamic binding. A member function is declared as virtual by writing the word **`virtual`** first in the declaration. A class that contains at least one virtual function, or which inherits a virtual function, is called a *polymorphic class*. To demonstrate polymorphism, dynamic binding and virtual functions we shall define a group of classes that describe different kinds of vehicle:

```
class Vehicle {
public:
  virtual void give_info();
};
class Motor_vehicle : public Vehicle {
public:
  Motor_vehicle(const string& no) : reg_num(no) {}
  const string& number() { return reg_num; }
```

```
    void give_info();
protected:
    string reg_num;
};
class Private_car : public Motor_vehicle {
public:
    Private_car(const string& no, int n)
      : Motor_vehicle(no), num_seats(n) {}
    void give_info();
protected:
    int num_seats;
};
class Bus : public Motor_vehicle {
public:
    Bus(const string& no, int n, bool a)
      : Motor_vehicle(no), num_pass(n), aircond(a) {}
    void give_info();
protected:
    int num_pass;
    bool aircond;
};
class Minibus : public Bus {
public:
    Minibus(const string& no, int n, bool a)
      : Bus(no, n, a) {}
};
class Truck : public Motor_vehicle {
public:
    Truck(const string& no, int l)
      : Motor_vehicle(no), max_load(l) {}
    void give_info();
protected:
    int max_load;
};
```

The root class is `Vehicle` since all the other classes are either directly or indirectly derived from this class. The function `give_info` is declared in the class `Vehicle`. Note that the word **`virtual`** stands in the declaration. This means that `give_info` is a *virtual function.* All the classes, except the class `Minibus`, each have their own variant of the member function `give_info`, and all these variants will be virtual functions. The word **`virtual`** does not have to be repeated in all the subclasses. The class `Minibus` will inherit the variant of `give_info` from class `Bus`. It is extremely important to note that the function `give_info` must have *exactly* the same number of parameters and types in the parameters. The return type must also be the same in all the variants. If the parameters are different in a variant, this variant will not be virtual. Instead, the virtual function declared in the base class will be hidden. If the parameters are the same but

New ideas

- *Polymorphism*
  A particular construct can be executed in different ways.
- *Static binding*
  The function to be called is decided during compilation.
- *Dynamic binding*
  The function to be called is decided during compilation.
- *Virtual function*
  A function that can be called with dynamic binding.
- *Polymorphic class*
  A class that declares or inherits at least one virtual function.

the return type is different, the program will be faulty (except in a special case, which will be discussed later). For our example to work in a more realistic situation, there must be more member functions than simply `give_info`. It should be possible, for example, to read the data members. These functions have been left out here, for the sake of simplicity. The definitions of the different variants of `give_info` have the following appearance:

```
void Vehicle::give_info()
{
  cout << "A vehicle" << endl;
}
void Motor_vehicle::give_info()
{
  cout << "A motor vehicle" << endl;
  cout << "Reg no: " << reg_num << endl;
}
void Private_car::give_info()
{
  Motor_vehicle::give_info();
  cout << "A private car" << endl;
  cout << num_seats << " seats" << endl;
}
void Bus::give_info()
{
  Motor_vehicle::give_info();
  cout << "A bus" << endl;
  cout << num_pass << " passengers" << endl;
  if (aircond)
    cout << "Has air-conditioning" << endl;
}
void Truck::give_info()
```

```
{
  Motor_vehicle::give_info();
  cout << "A truck" << endl;
  cout << max_load << " kg maximum load" << endl;
}
```

Suppose that we now declare three variables:

```
Private_car pc("XYZ 555", 5);
Truck       tr("ZZZ 222", 10000);
Minibus     mb("CPP 999", 10, true);
```

If we make the call

```
pc.give_info();   // static binding
```

we get written out

```
A motor vehicle
Reg no: XYZ 555
A private car
5 seats
```

Here there is a call to the variant of `give_info` that was declared in class `Private_car`. Note that this function in turn calls the variant of `give_info` belonging to `Motor_vehicle`. These are examples of *static binding*. Since the type of the variable `pc` is known at compilation, the compiler can decide which variant of `give_info` is to be called.

To demonstrate dynamic binding, we declare a pointer `fp`:

```
Vehicle *fp;
```

The pointer's type is 'pointer to `Vehicle`', which means that `fp` can point to objects of this type. Earlier in this chapter (see page 292) we saw that type conversion from a derived class to a base class was always possible and could also occur automatically. This also applies to pointers. A pointer to a derived class can be automatically converted to a pointer to the base class. Pointer `fp` can therefore be made to point to objects that belong to any of the classes derived from class `Vehicle`. For example, we can let the pointer `fp` point to a truck by making the assignment:

```
fp = &tr;
```

If a call is made (the arrow operator should be used since `fp` is a pointer):

```
fp->give_info();   // dynamic binding
```

then it will not be possible to decide at compilation what kind of object `fp` points to. We know only that it must be of class `Vehicle` or of one of the classes that have been derived (directly or indirectly) from this class. Thus at compilation it is not possible to decide which variant of the function should be called. We shall therefore get *dynamic binding*. When the program is executed, there is a check to see what kind of object `fp` points to at that moment, followed by a call to the function for it. If, for instance, this statement has been executed before the call:

```
fp = &tr;
```

then the call, above, would be output as

```
A motor vehicle
Reg no: ZZZ 222
A truck
10000 kg maximum load
```

If, instead, we had executed the statements

```
fp = new Private_car("AAA 333", 4);
fp->give_info();   // dynamic binding
cout << endl;
fp = &mb;
fp->give_info();   // dynamic binding
```

we should have had this output:

```
A motor vehicle
Reg no: AAA 333
A private car
4 seats
A motor vehicle
Reg no: CPP 999
A bus
10 passengers
Has air-conditioning
```

Note that the function `give_info` for class `Bus` is called in the last line in spite of the fact that `fp` points to a minibus. This is because class `Minibus` does not have its own variant of the function `give_info` but instead inherits the variant of class `Bus`.

In this example it is also possible to get dynamic binding with the aid of a pointer whose type is 'pointer to `Motor_vehicle`'. For instance, we can write

```
Motor_vehicle *mp;
mp = &tr;
mp->give_info();  // dynamic binding
```

In C++ we differentiate between the *static* and *dynamic type* of an expression. The static type will depend entirely on how the type of the expression has been declared in the program. The static type is determined at compilation, and is not changed while the program is executed. For instance, the static type for the expression `*fp` is `Vehicle`, since it was stated in the declaration of `fp` that it should have this type. The dynamic type for an expression is decided by the actual value of the expression, and can be changed during execution. The expression can contain a pointer or a reference. If, for instance, the pointer `fp` happens to point to a `Bus`, the dynamic type for the expression `*fp` will be `Bus`.

When a virtual function is called, the dynamic type of the actual object will determine which function is to be called, and when an ordinary, non-virtual function is called, the static type of the actual object determines which function will be called. Generally, this means that if we are to have dynamic binding, we must have *expressly* declared the function involved as virtual. If we had left out the word **`virtual`** in the declaration of `give_info` in class `Vehicle`, there would not have been dynamic binding in any of the above calls. In the call `fp->give_info()`, the static type of `fp` would have been decisive, and this would have meant that the variant of `give_info` declared for class `Vehicle` would have been called irrespective of what kind of object `fp` had happened to point to. Then

```
A vehicle
```

would have been written out in every case. One occasion when it is fruitful to use pointers to objects is when we want to monitor many objects belonging to the same group of classes – that is, classes that have a common base class. An array of pointers can be used, for instance, to define that a car hire firm owns certain vehicles:

```
Vehicle *ftab[50];
```

Now it is possible to add to the company's stock of vehicles:

```
ftab[i] = new Private_car("QWE 123", 4);
ftab[j] = new Minibus("ASD 003", 8, false);
```

Then we can write out information for all the cars of the company:

```
for (int i=0; i < 50; i++)
  ftab[i]->give_info();  // dynamic binding
```

Using dynamic binding in this type of problem can often lead to elegant solutions because we do not have to explicitly test what kind of object we are dealing with, and because we do not have to make different calls for different objects. All this is built into the mechanism of dynamic binding. And there is another advantage: it is easy to add new objects afterwards. Suppose, for example, that the car hire firm also hires out bicycles. A new class `Bike` can then be constructed:

```
class Bike : public Vehicle {
public:
  Bike(int n) : num_gears(n) {}
  void give_info();
protected:
  int num_gears;
};
```

No changes are necessary to the parts of the program already completed. If we had not used dynamic binding, on the other hand, we would have had to add a new check in all the places of the program where we checked the kind of objects involved.

We saw that we could produce dynamic binding by having pointers to objects. References can also be used. This is demonstrated in the following function, which outputs information about a `Vehicle`. This function is not a member function. Instead, it has a parameter that is a *reference* to a `Vehicle`.

```
void put(Vehicle& f)
{
  cout << "Information for a vehicle:" << endl;
  f.give_info();  // dynamic binding
}
```

For instance, we can make the call

```
put(tr);
put(*fp);
```

The static type for the parameter `f` is always 'reference to `Vehicle`', whereas the dynamic type in the first call is 'reference to `Truck`'. The dynamic type of what `fp` happens to point to is determined in the second of these calls.

We saw earlier that, when a virtual function is inherited, exactly the same parameters and return type should be declared in the derived class as in the base class. There is an exception to this rule in the case of the return type. Suppose that a virtual function `f` is declared in a base class `B1`, and that we create a subclass to `B1`, which we call `D1`. We shall create in class `D1` our own variant of the virtual function `f`. If `f` in class `B1` returns

Dynamic binding

- The actual function *must* be declared as virtual in the base class:

  `virtual` *`return_type`* `f(`*`parameters`*`);`

- It is redeclared in the subclasses with *exactly* the same parameters and return type (there is a special exception for a return type).
- The word **`virtual`** does not have to be repeated.
- *Static type* – The type an expression has according to the declarations.
- *Dynamic type* – The type an expression has at execution.
- Call of a virtual function:

```
p-> f(...);   // p is a pointer to the base type
r.f(...);     // r is a reference to the base type
```

- Which function is to be called, is determined by the dynamic type of `p` and `r`.

a value that is a pointer or reference to a class B2, we may in class D1 indicate that f should return a pointer or reference to another class D2 provided that D2 is a subclass of B2. This is especially interesting if class B1 is equal to B2 and class D1 is equal to D2.

We shall give an example of this, beginning once more with various kinds of vehicle. We shall make it possible to make copies of different kinds of vehicle. Suppose, for instance, that we have two pointers of type 'pointer to Vehicle':

```
Vehicle *fp, *fp2;
```

and that we let fp point to some kind of vehicle – a Truck, for instance:

```
fp = new Truck("BBB 777", 15000);
```

We shall now create a copy of the vehicle that fp points to. If fp points to a Motor_vehicle, we want to create a new Motor_vehicle; if fp points to a Truck, we should create a new Truck; if fp points to a Private_car, we should create a new Private_car; if fp points to a Bus, we should create a new Bus; and if fp points to a Minibus, we should create a new Minibus. We therefore construct a new virtual function that we can call in the following way:

```
fp2 = fp->create_copy();
```

Clearly, the call here must occur with dynamic binding. We put the following declaration into the definition of class Vehicle:

```
class Vehicle {
public:
  virtual Vehicle *create_copy()
  { return new Vehicle (*this);}
  as earlier
};
```

We must now define our own variants of create_copy in the subclasses of Vehicle. In classes Motor_vehicle and Truck we write the following, for example (and similarly in the other classes derived from class Vehicle):

```
class Motor_vehicle : public Vehicle {
public:
  Motor_vehicle *create_copy()
  { return new Motor_vehicle(*this);}
  as earlier
};
class Truck : public Motor_vehicle {
public:
  Truck *create_copy()
  { return new Truck(*this);}
  as earlier
};
```

Here the return types for the function `create_copy` are not identical to the return type in the declaration in class `Vehicle`, but because of the special rule just described it is allowed in any case.

9.6 The operators `typeid` and `dynamic_cast`

In using virtual functions we seldom have cause to check an object's dynamic type, but there are occasions when this may be necessary. There are two operators that we can make use of in C++: **typeid** and **dynamic_cast**. To be able to use these, we should include the file `typeinfo` in our program.

With the operator **typeid** we can directly compare an object's dynamic type with a particular type. If the variable has type `Vehicle *` as before, we can write, for instance,

```
if (typeid(*fp) == typeid(Private_car))
  cout << "This is a private car" << endl;
else if (typeid(*fp) == typeid(Bus))
  cout << "This is a bus" << endl;
else if (typeid(*fp) == typeid(Minibus))
  cout << "This is a minibus" << endl;
else if (typeid(*fp) == typeid(Truck))
  cout << "This is a truck" << endl;
```

If we had executed this statement earlier:

```
fp = new Minibus ("ASD 003", 8, false);
```

`fp` would point to a `Minibus`, and we should get the output

```
This is a minibus
```

The operator **typeid** returns a value of the predefined standard class `type_info`. Apart from the comparison operators `==` and `!=`, there is for this class a member function `name`, which can be used to find out the name of the type for an expression. The function `name` returns a text string. We can write, for instance,

```
cout << typeid(*fp).name() << endl;
cout << typeid(123+94).name() << endl;
```

We then get the message

```
Minibus
int
```

The second line shows that the operator **typeid** can also be used for types that are not classes.

Note that `*fp` must be the argument for **typeid** if the correct result is to be obtained. If we had tried to write

```
if (typeid(fp) == typeid(Minibus *))   // ERROR!!
  cout << "This is a Minibus" << endl;
```

which logically seems to be the same thing, the expression after `if` would have been false. The reason is that the expression `typeid(fp)` gives the static type 'pointer to `Vehicle`' of `fp`. This can be seen if the following statement is executed:

```
cout << typeid(fp).name() << endl;
```

We then get the output

```
Vehicle *
```

The operator `typeid` can also be used when we have references. For example, we can construct the following function, which checks whether a `Vehicle` is a kind of bus:

```
bool a_bus(Vehicle& f)
{
  return (typeid(f) == typeid(Bus) ||
          typeid(f) == typeid(Minibus));
}
```

The other useful operator is `dynamic_cast`. It can be used for two purposes: to check whether an object is of a particular type, and to make type conversion safe from a base type to a derived type. Let us take an example. Suppose that the pointer `fp`, as before, points to any kind of `Vehicle`. Now we want to know whether `fp` might possibly point to a `Motor_vehicle` and, if so, we want to write out the registration number for this `Motor_vehicle`. We can then write

```
Motor_vehicle *mp;
if (mp = dynamic_cast<Motor_vehicle *>(fp))
  cout << mp->number() << endl;
```

First we declare a pointer `mp`, which can point to `Motor_vehicle` but not to other kinds of `Vehicle` – bicycles, for example. The expression

```
dynamic_cast<Motor_vehicle *>(fp)
```

checks whether the parameter `fp` points to a `Motor_vehicle` or to an object belonging to a subclass of `Motor_vehicle`. In these cases, the value of `fp` is converted to the type 'pointer to `Motor_vehicle`', and the pointer we then get will be the result of the operator `dynamic_cast`. If `fp` does not point to a `Motor_vehicle`, the operator `dynamic_cast` will give a null pointer (value `0`) as result. In the `if` statement above, the result from the operator `dynamic_cast` is assigned to the variable `mp`. Since a value of `0` is understood as false and all other values as true, the printout statement will be performed only if `fp` points to a `Motor_vehicle`, in which case `mp` will point to this `Motor_vehicle`.

The operators typeid and dynamic_cast

The file typeinfo must be included.

```
typeid(*p) == typeid(C)
```

or

```
typeid(r) == typeid(C)
```

where p is a pointer, r a reference and C the name of a class, checks whether the object pointed to (referred to) belongs to class C.

```
typeid(*p).name()
```

or

```
typeid(r).name()
```

gives a text string with the name of the type to which the object pointed to (referred to) belongs.

```
dynamic_cast<C *>(p)
```

if p is a pointer to an object of class C or a subclass of C, then p converted to the type 'pointer to C' is given as result, otherwise 0.

```
dynamic_cast<C&>(r)
```

if r is a reference to an object of class C or a subclass of C, then r converted to the type 'reference to C' is given as result, otherwise the exception bad_cast is generated.

The operator **dynamic_cast** can also be used when there is a reference to an object. Then this reference can be safely converted into a reference to a subclass. Since references can never have the value 0, another technique is used to mark an incorrect type conversion. The operator then generates what is known as an *exception*. We have not discussed this term yet, but in order to complete our discussion we shall give an example here of how a reference to a Vehicle can be converted into a reference to a Motor_vehicle.

```
void put_no(Vehicle& f)
{
  try {
    Motor_vehicle& m = dynamic_cast<Motor_vehicle&>(f);
    cout << m.number() << endl;
  }
  catch(bad_cast) {
    cout << "Not a motor vehicle" << endl;
  }
}
```

The function is called with a reference to `Vehicle`. If the reference refers to a `Motor_vehicle`, the registration number is written out, otherwise an error message is given. (Exceptions are described in detail in Chapter 10.)

Note that the operator **`typeid`** can be used to check whether an object is of a given class `C`, while the operator **`dynamic_cast`** can be used to check whether an object is of a particular class `C` or some other class derived from `C`.

9.7 Virtual destructors

Constructors and destructors are not inherited. But they do call, as we saw earlier, a constructor and a destructor, respectively, for a base class: thus they can be said to inherit behaviour from the base class. A constructor cannot be virtual. When we create a new object, we have to indicate exactly what kind of object we want. Destructors, however, can be virtual, and this can be very useful.

To demonstrate a situation where we need to use virtual destructors, we return to the classes `Person` and `Athlete` from pages 288 and 295, respectively. Earlier, class `Athlete` had a single data member, `elite`, but now we extend the class with another data member:

```
class Athlete : public Person {
public:
   Athlete(char *n, char *k);
   ~Athlete();
private:
   bool elite;
   char *club;
};
```

We let the data member `club` be a pointer to a text string that contains the name of the athlete's club. (Of course it would have been easier to let the data member `club` be of type `string`, but in that case it would have been more difficult to demonstrate the problem.) This means that space for the text string must be allocated dynamically each time a new `Athlete` is created. This is done in the constructor, which has two parameters – the name of the athlete and the club. In the following definition of the constructor, we have included the last line merely for demonstration purposes:

```
Athlete::Athlete(char *n, char *k): Person(n)
{
   club = new char[strlen(k)+1];
   strcpy(club, k);
   cout << (strlen(k)+1)<<" bytes allocated"<<endl;
}
```

The class `Athlete` is a subclass of class `Person`. Therefore the constructor for class `Person` is first called in the initialization list to initialize the `Person` part of the object. Memory space exactly large enough to hold the club's name is then allocated dynamically. Finally, the club's name is copied into the new memory space.

Since dynamic memory space is allocated in the constructor, we must also have a destructor that deallocates this memory space when it is no longer needed:

```
Athlete::~Athlete()
{
  cout << (strlen(club)+1)
       << " bytes deallocated" << endl;
  delete[] club;
}
```

A test program that uses the classes `Person` and `Athlete` is given below for demonstration purposes:

```
main ()
{
  Athlete i1("Maria", "City Judo Club");
  Person *p1, *p2;
  p1 = new Person("Lisa");
  p2 = new Athlete("John", "Westtown AC");
  delete p1;
  delete p2;
}
```

When we run the program, we obtain the following output:

```
15 bytes allocated
12 bytes allocated
15 bytes deallocated
```

The 15 bytes allocated for the variable `i1` are deallocated, exactly as they should be when execution reaches the last right-hand brace. The variable `p1` points to an object of class `Person`. No memory space is allocated for this object, so none will be deallocated either. The problem is the object pointed to by the variable `p2`. This object is of the class `Athlete`, and memory space (15 bytes) is allocated when the object is created. When the statement **`delete`** `p2` is executed, however, memory space is not deallocated as it should be. This is because the pointer `p2` has the type 'pointer to `Person`' and not the type 'pointer to `Athlete`'. The static type is thus 'pointer to `Person`'. When a non-virtual member function is called, it is, as we have seen, the actual object's static type that determines which variant of the member function is to be called. It is the destructor for the base class `Person` that is called in this case. We did not declare a destructor in our example for the class `Person`, although there is one that is generated automatically but does nothing.

Virtual destructors

```
virtual ~class name();
```

Make sure that *all* base classes have a *virtual* constructor.

The solution to our problem is to make the destructor of the base class *virtual*, for then the dynamic type of the actual object will determine which destructor is to be called. Thus we declare a virtual destructor in class `Person`:

```
class Person {
public:
   virtual ~Person() {};
   as earlier
}
```

The new constructor does nothing: there are no statements inside the braces. Since no dynamic memory space was allocated for class `Person`, there will be nothing to be deallocated. (If class `Person` had allocated memory space dynamically, the destructor would naturally have deallocated this memory space here.) When we now test our program, we shall get dynamic binding with execution of the statement `delete p2`. Then the destructor for class `Athlete` will be called. The text written out will now be correct:

```
15 bytes allocated
12 bytes allocated
12 bytes deallocated
15 bytes deallocated
```

From this example we learn that we should *always* declare a virtual destructor in a class if this class is intended to be the base class for other classes. If this is not done, programs can be created that consume memory without releasing it, and this can lead to serious execution errors. The question arises whether C++ is poorly constructed where destructors are concerned. Surely all destructors should be automatically virtual? Then this problem would not arise.

9.8 Abstract classes

The member function `give_info` for class `Vehicle` (see page 319) is really quite meaningless, because the only thing that happens when it is used is that it writes out the text '`A vehicle`'. But we defined it because we wanted to be sure that there would be a function `give_info` for every object of a class derived from class `Vehicle`. Suppose, for instance, that we declare a new subclass `Tram` of class `Vehicle`. Further, suppose that we forget to define a new member function `give_info` for class `Tram`. Objects belonging to class `Tram` will then inherit the member function `give_info` from class `Vehicle`. The operation `give_info` should exist for all objects of a class derived from class `Vehicle` if we are to make use of the technique of dynamic binding. If, as previously, we have a pointer `fp`:

```
Vehicle fp;
```

and make the call

```
fp->give_info();
```

then the member function `give_info` must exist for all objects that `fp` could point to.

But we do not have to invent a 'meaningless' member function for a base class in order to be assured that all the objects will have this function. What can be done instead is to declare what is known as a *pure virtual function*. This member function need not be implemented (defined), in which case we shall not be able to call it. A pure virtual function is only a kind of marker for a true function. We shall show how it looks by remaking the member function `give_info` in class `Vehicle` into a pure virtual function. The definition of class `Vehicle` will then look like this:

```
class Vehicle {
public:
  virtual void give_info() = 0;   // pure virtual function
};
```

It is the initialization to `0` that indicates that `give_info` is a pure virtual function. Since `give_info` should not be implemented, we cannot write a definition for it.

A class that contains at least one virtual function is called an *abstract class* (not to be confused with an *abstract data type*, which was discussed in the introduction to Chapter 7). Since a pure virtual function cannot be called, it is not allowed to create objects of an abstract class. Thus we cannot declare variables of type `Vehicle` now. Objects can be created only for those classes in which all the pure virtual functions have been replaced by 'true' functions. For example, it is permissible to declare an object of class `Bike` if this class, as previously, has its own version of the member function `give_info`:

```
class Bike : public Vehicle {
public:
  void give_info();
  etc.
};
```

If we define a new class that is derived from an abstract class, we are not forced to declare our own versions of the base type's pure virtual functions. If these functions are not redeclared, the new class will also be abstract, and we are not allowed to create objects of the new class. If, for instance, we take away the declaration of the function `give_info` in class `Motor_vehicle`, this class will be abstract, and it will not be permissible to create objects of this class. On the other hand, we are allowed to create objects of the classes derived from class `Motor_vehicle` since these will have declared their own versions of `give_info`.

By making use of pure virtual functions, therefore, we can obtain an abstract base class. It is not our aim to create objects from an abstract class like this. It will serve merely as a pattern for the various subclasses. An abstract base class indicates which primitive operations must be present for all objects belonging to one of the classes derived from the base class. Good examples of this are applications that allow us to work with different graphic figures drawn on the screen. An abstract base class `Figure` can then be obtained. Starting from this, we can derive various subclasses for different figures such as circles, rectangles and lines. The class `Figure` can contain the pure virtual functions `draw`, `change_colour` and `move`.

To give a more concrete example of the use of abstract base classes, we shall return to the program in section 7.5, page 243. Here a player played the card game Twenty-one against the computer. A class `Player`, which defined the actions of a player, was implemented in the program. The problem with this class was that it had to define the actions of both the user and the computer. We were therefore obliged to have a member variable that indicated whether the player was a human or a computer. Let us redefine class `Player` so that it becomes an abstract base class instead:

```
class Player {
public:
   Player(Cardstack& cardpack) : pack(cardpack) {};
   virtual int play() = 0;
protected:
   Cardstack& pack;
   Cardstack hand;
   int points();
};
```

We have made two changes to the earlier version. The function `play` has been declared as a pure virtual function, and the member variable `computer`, which indicated whether or not the current player was a computer, has been removed. We now define two new subclasses of `Player`, `Human` and `Computer`:

```
class Human : public Player {
public:
   Human(Cardstack& cardpack) : Player(cardpack) {}
   int play();
};
class Computer : public Player {
```

```
public:
  Computer(Cardstack& cardpack) : Player(cardpack) {}
  int play();
};
```

These new classes each have their own variant of the virtual function `play`. If we compare these with the function `play` we had previously, we can see that they have been simplified, because each variant can be specially formulated for every subclass:

```
int Human::play()
{
  int p = 0;
  while (p < 21)
  {
    Card k = pack.deal_top();
    hand.lay_top(k);
    p = points();
    cout << "You got "; k.write_out();
    cout << " and has " << p << " points" << endl;
    if (p < 21)
    {
      char answer[10];
      cout << "One more card? " ;
      cin >> answer;
      if (answer[0] != 'y')
        break;
    }
  }
  hand.throw_cards();
  return p;
}
```

```
int Computer::play()
{
  int p = 0;
  while (p<16)
  {
    Card k = pack.deal_top();
    hand.lay_top(k);
    p = points();
    cout << "The computer got "; k.write_out();
    cout << endl;
  }
  cout << "The computer has " << p << " points" << endl;
  hand.throw_cards();
  return p;
}
```

Abstract classes

- A member function can be declared as a *pure virtual function*

```
virtual result type f(parameters) = 0;
```

- Pure virtual functions have no implementation (definition).
- A class with at least one pure virtual function is an *abstract* class.
- No objects can be created from an abstract class.
- Subclasses that do not have their own versions of all the pure virtual functions are also abstract.

Now we need only change the declarations of the two players `you` and `I` in the main program. Both of these variables previously had type `Player`. Instead we write

```
Human    you (pack);
Computer I   (pack);
```

(The parameter `pack` is a reference to the cardpack the two players have in common.) When later in the program the calls `you.play()` and `I.play()` are made, different versions of the function `play` will be called.

9.9 Virtual operators

As we saw, the concept of dynamic binding meant that it was the actual object's dynamic type that determined which function was to be called. If, for instance, we make the call `p->f(x)`, where `p` is a pointer, `x` a parameter and `f` a virtual function, it is the type of the object that `p` points to that determines which variant of function `f` is to be called. Operators are also member functions. If we write an expression

```
a XX b
```

where *XX* is an operator symbol, this would be the same thing as if we had written

```
a.operatorXX(b)
```

If the function **operator***XX* is declared as virtual and we make a call in the following form (`p` and `q` are pointers):

```
(*p) XX (*q)
```

it is then the type of the object that the pointer `p` points to that determines which variant of operator *XX* is to be called. It does not matter what the pointer `q` happens to be pointing to. *C++ allows dynamic binding in the first operator only*. This could cause confusion if we want to write symmetrical operators with two parameters of the same type. Suppose, for example, that we want to construct an operator `>` that compares two motor vehicles of the same kind. (We use the same classes as we did earlier in this chapter.) If we have two pointers `mp1` and `mp2`:

```
Motor_vehicle *mp1, *mp2;
```

we should like to be able to write, for instance,

```
if (*mp1 > *mp2)
```

That is, we should like to have dynamic binding so that different > operators would be called depending on what mp1 and mp2 happened to point to. If they point to trucks, for instance, then the maximum loads of the trucks should be compared; if they point to private cars or buses, the number of passengers should be compared. But what would happen if the pointers pointed to different kinds of vehicle, one for instance pointing to a bus and the other to a truck? The old saying that it does not do to compare apples and oranges is a good principle, and we should like it to apply here, too. Therefore we regard it as an error when the two pointers point to different kinds of vehicle, and we allow the program to abort.

We begin now by declaring the operator > for class Motor_vehicle. We let the operator be a pure virtual function, which means that class Motor_vehicle will be abstract. We do not want a situation where objects that are 'only' Motor_vehicle can be declared.

```
class Motor_vehicle : public Vehicle {
public:
  virtual bool operator> (Motor_vehicle& m) = 0;
  as previously
};
```

The next step is to declare our own variants of the operator > for the classes that are derived from class Motor_vehicle. The parameter for the operator has type 'reference to Motor_vehicle'. We begin with class Private_car. Our first attempt looks like this:

```
class Private_car : public Vehicle {
public:
  bool operator> (Private_car& m);   // ERROR!!
  as previously
};
```

Since this operator should be able to compare two private cars, we have indicated that the type of the parameters should be 'reference to Private_car'. Unfortunately, this is a mistake. The class definition can be compiled. Even the definition of the operator > can be compiled. But if we write a program and try to declare a variable of type Private_car, we shall get a compilation error because the compiler understands Private_car to be an abstract class. There cannot be objects of an abstract class. Private_car is an abstract class because the parameter type in the declaration of the > operator, of course, in class Private_car does not tally with the parameter type in the corresponding declaration in the base class Motor_vehicle. Therefore the new declaration is understood as a declaration of a *new* > operator that *hides* the one declared in the base class. The hidden operator is inherited and will still be a pure virtual function since it has not been redefined in class `Private_car`. The parameter type must therefore be the same as in the base class. Let us make another attempt:

```
class Private_car : public Motor_vehicle {
public:
  bool operator> (Motor_vehicle& m);   // Correct!
  as previously
};
```

Now the definition of class `Private_car` will be correct. Next, the definition for the > operator has to be written. Our first attempt is

```
bool Private_car::operator> (Motor_vehicle& m)
{
  return num_seats > m.num_seats;   // ERROR!!
}
```

We shall get a compilation error here! The compiler will complain about the expression `m.num_seats` and state that there is no member of class `Motor_vehicle` of that name. The parameter `m` does not have the correct type to enable us to access the data member `num_seats`. This parameter should have had type 'reference to `Private_car`' but it did not work, as we saw above. The solution to this problem is to make a type conversion. We now write the following correct definition of the > operator:

```
bool Private_car::operator> (Motor_vehicle& m)
{
  Private_car& r = dynamic_cast<Private_car&>(m);
  return num_seats > r.num_seats;
}
```

The operator **`dynamic_cast`** has been used to make a conversion from type 'reference to `Motor_vehicle`' to type 'reference to `Private_car`'. This conversion will work if parameter `m` happens to refer to a `Private_car`. If it does not, we shall understand the program to be faulty and get an execution error because the operator **`dynamic_cast`** will generate an exception. (If we want to take care of this and write an error message, the same technique can be used as on page 327.)

The > operator is defined for the other classes in a similar way. In class `Truck` we write, for example,

```
bool Truck::operator> (Motor_vehicle& m)
{
  Truck& r = dynamic_cast<Truck&>(m);
  return max_load > r.max_load;
}
```

9.10 Multiple inheritance

In all our examples of inheritance up to now we have seen how derived classes have had a single direct base class. However, a class may have several direct base classes. This is called *multiple inheritance*. We can, for example, declare a class `D` that has three different, direct base classes, `B1`, `B2` and `B3`:

```
class D : public B1, protected B2, private B3 {
  declarations of members
};
```

A class can have as many direct base classes as we like. They are simply listed after the colon, the only restriction being that a particular base class can occur only once in the list. We indicate for each one whether the inheritance should be *public*, *protected* or *private* by writing one of the words **public**, **protected** or **private**. If none of these is indicated it will be assumed that inheritance is private. It is not important in which order the base classes come in the list.

With multiple inheritance the same rules apply regarding visibility, initializations and so on as for simple inheritance. When, for example, an object with several direct base classes is created, all the base class subobjects must be initialized, either by the derived class calling the constructors of the base classes, or by their default constructors being called automatically.

We use multiple inheritance when we want to combine different properties from two or more base classes. We shall demonstrate this by adding to classes with different kinds of vehicle. Our goal is to construct a class that defines amphibious cars, a combination of cars and boats. We begin by defining the fundamental base class `Vehicle`:

```
class Vehicle {
public:
  Vehicle() { weight = length = width = 0;}
  virtual void give_info() = 0;
protected:
  int weight, length, width;
};
```

The only difference compared with the previous version is that we have added, for demonstration purposes, the three data members `weight`, `length` and `width`, and we have defined our own default constructor that sets them to zero.

We then declare two new classes: `Boat`, which defines boats in general; and `Motor_boat`, which defines motor boats. Since boats are a kind of vehicle, they have been defined as a subclass of `Vehicle`. The class `Motor_boat` is, of course, a subclass of class `Boat`.

```
class Boat : public Vehicle {
public:
  Boat(const string& material) : m(material) {}
  const string& made_of() { return m;}
  void give_info()
  {cout << "This is a boat of " << m << endl; }
protected:
  string m;
};
class Motor_boat : public Boat {
public:
  Motor_boat(const string& material, int prop)
    : Boat(material),num_prop(prop){}
protected:
  int num_prop;
};
```

Now we can define the class `Amphibious_car`, which is derived from the classes `Private_car` and `Motor_boat`:

```
class Amphibious_car : public Private_car, public Motor_boat {
public:
  Amphibious_car(const string& no, int seats,
                 const string& m,  int prop)
    : Private_car(no, seats), Motor_boat(m, prop) {}
};
```

An `Amphibious_car` has a subobject that is a `Private_car` and a subobject that is a `Motor_boat`. Both subobjects must be initialized, and this occurs when their constructors are called in the initialization list in the constructor for `Amphibious_car`. The relations of the different classes are illustrated in Figure 9.4.

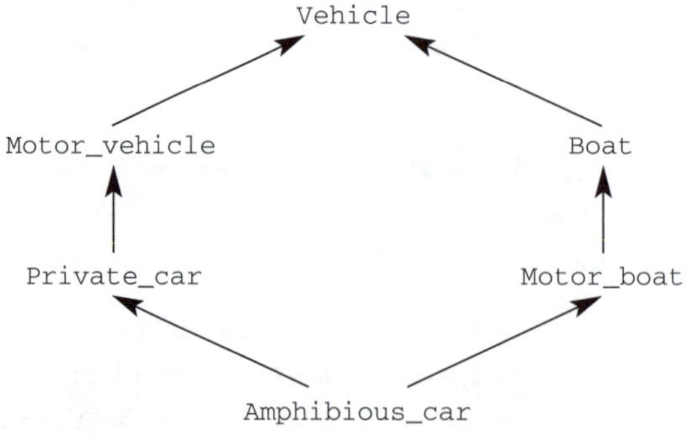

Figure 9.4

We can now declare an `Amphibious_car`:

```
Amphibious_car a("AMF 012", 4, "steel", 2);
```

An `Amphibious_car` inherits all the properties from both of its base classes. For example, we can make the calls

```
cout << a.made_of() << endl;
cout << a.number() << endl;
```

In the first line the function `made_of` is called. This was inherited by `Amphibious_car` from class `Boat`. In the second line the function `number`, inherited from class `Motor_vehicle`, is called. We shall now try to call the function `give_info`:

```
a.give_info();
```

This does not work very well. When we attempt a compilation, we get an error message giving something like

member is ambiguous

The class `Amphibious_car` has inherited the function `give_info` from two sources. The compiler does not know whether it is the function `give_info` in class `Private_car` or the `give_info` in class `Boat` that is to be called. Therefore we must explicitly indicate in the call which one is intended. For instance, we can write

```
a.Private_car::give_info();
```

A better variant would be to redeclare `give_info` in class `Amphibious_car`:

```
class Amphibious_car : public Private_car, public Motor_boat {
public:
  void give_info();
  as before
};
```

Both of the inherited versions of `give_info` can be called in the definition:

```
void Amphibious_car::give_info()
{
  Private_car::give_info();
  Motor_boat::give_info();
}
```

Now we can call `a.give_info()`, and we obtain

```
A motor vehicle
Reg no: AMF 012
A private car
4 seats
This is a boat of steel
```

Suppose that we now want to know how much an amphibious car weighs. We try to add the following line to the function `Amphibious_car::give_info`:

```
cout << "Weight: " << weight << endl;
```

This does not work. Again we get the error message

```
Member is ambiguous
```

This is because `Amphibious_car` has *two* data members with the name `weight`. The two base classes `Private_car` and `Motor_boat` are both indirectly derived from class `Vehicle`, which means that both subobjects each contain a data member with the name `weight`.

Of course, an `Amphibious_car` cannot reasonably have two collections of data members in the base class `Vehicle`. A particular `Amphibious_car` has only one `weight`, one `length` and one `width`. We must therefore make sure that only one set of data members is inherited. The solution is to use a *virtual base class*. We must then adjust our definitions of the classes directly derived from class `Vehicle` – that is, classes `Motor_vehicle` and `Boat`. We shall indicate that both of these classes are to inherit class `Vehicle` *virtually*. We do this by adding the word **`virtual`** when the base class is given. The new definitions of `Motor_vehicle` and `Boat` will then look like this:

```
class Motor_vehicle : public virtual Vehicle {
  as before
};
class Boat : public virtual Vehicle {
  as before
};
```

Multiple inheritance

- A class can have several direct base classes:

```
class D : access B1, access B2, ... {
  declarations of own members
};
```

- Each base class is included in its entirety as a subobject.
- All members from all base classes are inherited.
- Confusion with names may arise. Solved by the operator `::`
- A *virtual base class* `V` is included as a subobject exactly *once* in an object.

```
class C : access virtual V {
  declarations of own members
};
```

If in a class C it is indicated that a base class V should be virtual, then objects of all classes derived from C will contain exactly one subobject of class V.

Note that we must indicate that the base class is to be virtual as early as with the definitions of `Motor_vehicle` and `Boat`. It would be too late when we define class `Amphibious_car`. If we intend to use multiple inheritance, we must plan at an early stage, as early as with the construction of the basic base classes.

The question might arise with a virtual base class of how to initialize this single base class subobject. In this example it is quite simple because the constructor for the virtual base class `Vehicle` is not called explicitly in either of its subclasses, `Motor_vehicle` or `Boat`. The default constructor that sets the members `weight`, `length` and `width` to zero will be called here. But we could think of cases where the virtual base class is initialized differently at the different 'steps' up to the base class. What happens then? For virtual base classes there is in C++ a complicated, special rule that states that the base class subobject corresponding to the virtual base class can be initialized only once. This should be done from the constructor in the most derived class – that is, from the class at the bottom in the class hierarchy. If no explicit call of the constructor for the virtual base class is made, the default constructor of the virtual base class is called automatically. If a constructor for the virtual base class is called from an intermediate class that call is ignored.

Exercises

9.1 Beginning with class `Person`, construct a new derived class `Student` with suitable members. In addition construct a new class `Course`, relating it appropriately to class `Student`.

9.2 Complete Exercise 9.1 with class `Teacher` according to Figure 6.9, page 210.

9.3 Beginning with classes `Person` and `Motor_vehicle`, define a class `Car_owner` to define a person who can be the owner of one `Motor_vehicle` or more.

9.4 In the previous exercise it was assumed that the owner of a vehicle is always a natural person 'of flesh and bone'. Write new class definitions that allow an owner to be a person in the legal sense – that is, a corporation of some sort. A corporation has, in turn, one or more owners. Beginning with two new base classes, `Owner` and `Thing`, and making use of multiple inheritance, show whether it is possible to define the situation where certain classes, for example persons, can be the owners of one or several things and where certain other classes, for example persons in the legal sense of corporations, can be both owned and owner at the same time.

9.5 Different kinds of animal can be defined using classes and inheritance. Define some animals by beginning with a class `Animal` and deriving the different animals from this. Feel free to use such intermediate classes as `Mammal`, `Insect`, `Bird` and so on. Declare a virtual function `Sound` to define the sound made by the animal.

9.6 Descriptions of geometric figures are often used as examples in the context of object-oriented programming. First define a class `Point` that defines a point (x, y) in a two-dimensional coordinate system. Then declare a class `Figure` that contains a starting point. Let class `Figure` have a pure virtual function, `Area`.

In addition, define a number of subclasses of the class `Figure`, for example `Circle`, `Triangle` and `Rectangle`. Give them suitable members. Let each subclass have its own version of the function `Area`.

Finally, declare an array with pointers to arbitrary figures and write the statements necessary to calculate and output the area for all the figures in the array.

9.7 Complete class `SuperInt` with friend functions enabling you to perform the operations `+`, `-`, `*` and `/` when the left-hand operand has type **`long int`** and the right-hand operand has type `SuperInt`. The result of such an operation should be a `SuperInt`.

9.8 Write a virtual function `max` that as result gives the larger of two `Vehicle`s of the same make. If `fp1`, `fp2` and `fp3` have type 'pointer to `Vehicle`', it should be possible to perform a statement such as `fp3=fp1-max(*fp2)`. After this statement, `fp3` should point to the larger of the two vehicles that `fp1` and `fp2` point to.

9.9 Start from class `Array` and construct a new derived class `Matrix`, in which the elements of the matrix are integers. A matrix consists of a certain number of rows and columns. Individual elements are indicated by the row and column number. For simplicity, the numbering of rows and columns should always start from 1. The indexing operator does not allow more than one operand, so the function call operator can be used instead. Let the new class `Matrix` get an appropriate collection of member functions, and ensure that all operations visible for class `Matrix` are significant and correct for matrices.

9.10 Complete class `Matrix` in the previous exercise with the two member functions `row` and `col` with the help of which a particular row or column can be read. As result the functions should give a value of type `Array`.

Exceptions

10

When a program is executed, unexpected situations may occur. Such a situation is called an *exception*. This may be the result of an error of some kind, for example indexing outside the limits in an array, or giving faulty input data to a function. An exception is not necessarily the result of a logic error in the program. It can also arise from faulty input data.

When a function is being written, the algorithm should be as clear and easy to understand as possible. But if checks were inserted at each stage of the algorithm to handle every imaginable error and abnormal event, it would become very clumsy and hard to follow. In the latest versions of C++ a mechanism has been added to handle exceptions. This mechanism is technically similar to the one in the programming language Ada. The part of the program where the error arises generates an exception that, according to predetermined rules, is passed on to other parts of the program where the exception can be 'trapped' and appropriate action taken.

One thing that C++ has inherited from its predecessor C is its way of handling execution errors, although it might be more correct to say its way of *not* handling execution errors. As we have seen, there is no way of controlling, for example, an index so that it lies inside the allowed limits, and there are normally no controls to see that overflow does not arise in connection with numerical calculations. If controls are wanted in a program, they normally have to be put there by the programmer. This is where C++ differs from other high-level languages in which a number of execution controls are normally carried out automatically. (If, in the interests of efficiency, these are not wanted, they can usually be turned off by giving a special instruction to the compiler.) If we want to use the technique of dealing with exceptions in C++, we *ourselves* usually have to make sure that exceptions are generated when errors arise, because the compiler will not normally do so. For instance, it will not generate an exception if indexing is not correct.

Earlier, we used the standard function `assert` in programs to insert execution controls. The problem with `assert` is that, if the given condition is not true, the program will be terminated. The error cannot be taken care of, and so the program cannot be allowed to continue. But assert is not constructed for this purpose. It is meant to be used during program testing and discarded when the program has been tested. In this chapter we shall learn how to use the new technique for handling exceptions. We shall be using it from now on instead of the function assert.

10.1 Generating exceptions

Two separate stages can be distinguished when working with exceptions. In the first stage an exception is generated, and in the second stage the exception is trapped. We shall begin by describing what happens in the easier of these two stages, how exceptions are generated. How they are trapped, we shall deal with later.

An exception is generated by the execution of a **throw** statement. When this statement is executed, the block being executed will be terminated immediately. Program control will then be transferred to the part of the program trapping the exception. If no part of the program does this, the program will be terminated prematurely. (This will occur when the standard function terminate is automatically called. This function in turn calls the function abort.)

A **throw** statement has the general form

```
throw expression;
```

where *expression* can be of any type. We could write, for example,

```
throw 28;
```

Even though the expression can be of arbitrary type, we ought to use the special classes given in the standard to signal exceptions.

All the standard classes for exceptions have in common the fundamental base class exception. This has two subclasses, logic_error and runtime_error. The class logic_error is a base class for whatever classes are there to signal errors resulting from logic errors in the program, such errors as could have been avoided (at least in theory) if the program had been constructed differently. The other subclass, runtime_error, is a base class for classes used to signal execution errors that cannot be avoided by constructing a program differently. Figure 10.1 illustrates the different predefined classes.

The class exception is defined in the header file exception, and the other classes are defined in the header file stdexcept. In order to use these classes you must have the following lines first in your program. (The file exception is included in the file stdexcept: therefore you do not have to include it explicitly.)

```
#include <stdexcept>
using namespace std;
```

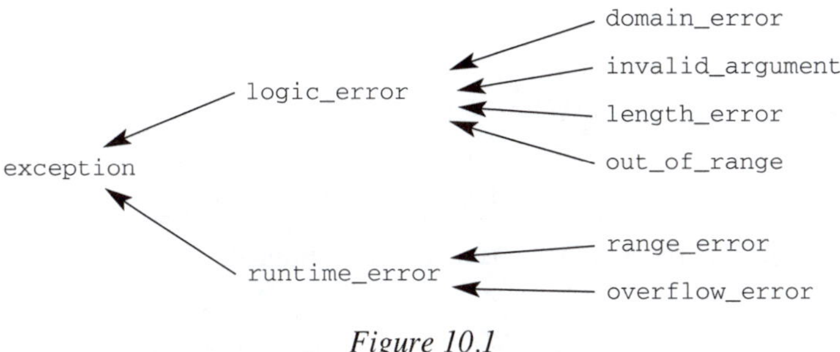

Figure 10.1

One of the most derived classes, on the right in Figure 10.1, should be used. To generate an exception, we write

```
throw exception_name("extra information");
```

To generate an exception of class `invalid_argument` we write, for example,

```
throw invalid_argument ("to my_funct");
```

When we write in this way, we create an object and 'throw away' this object so that it can be trapped later in another part of the program. All the classes in Figure 10.1, except the base class `exception`, have definitions of the form

```
class class_name : public base_class {
public:
   class_name(const string& what_arg);
};
```

We see that there is only one constructor, and that it will have an argument of the standard type `string`. Since ordinary text strings can be automatically converted to the class `string`, we can create objects of these classes by writing expressions of the form `class_name("text")`. The text given as argument can be read later when the exception is trapped. We can therefore use it to add extra information that could be useful, such as information about exactly where the error arose.

We worked with the class `Array` in Chapter 8. There we used the function `assert` to check that the parameters of member functions had values that were allowed. A better way is to generate exceptions: then a program will not have to be terminated merely because a function has been called with incorrect parameters. As an example we give a new version of one of the indexing operators. (Compare with page 273.) If the index does not lie in the allowed interval, an event of the class `out_of_range` is generated:

```
int& Array::operator [] (int i)
{
  if (i < i1 or i > last())
    throw out_of_range("Array::operator[]");
  return p[i-i1];
}
```

We have added the function's name here as additional information in the `throw` statement.

Another example is the operator `+=` on page 263, which adds elements in an `Array` to elements in another `Array`. We recall that a requirement in this function is that both the vectors involved be of equal length. The new version will be this:

```
const Array& Array::operator+= (const Array& v)
{
  if (num != v.num)
    throw length_error("Array::operator+=");
  for (int i=0; i<num; i++)
    p[i] += v.p[i];
  return *this;
}
```

The other member functions in class `Array` should also be similarly changed so that they generate exceptions.

We can also declare our own subclasses of the classes in Figure 10.1. For example, we can make the definition

```
class communication_error : public runtime_error {
public:
  communication_error(const char *what_arg = "")
  : runtime_error(what_arg) {}
};
```

We have given the parameter of the constructor a default value here. This means that we can write the expression both with and without an argument:

```
throw communication_error("Timeout in reader");
throw communication_error();
```

In certain cases the system itself will generate exceptions. If we use the operator `new` and try to allocate more memory space than is available, an exception of class `bad_alloc` is generated. (See section 5.4.5.) If we try to use incorrect type conversions with the operator `dynamic_cast` (see page 326) an exception of class `bad_cast` is generated, and if we give the operator `typeid` a null pointer as argument an exception of class `bad_typeid` will be generated. These three classes are all subclasses of class exception. The class bad_alloc is defined in the header file **new**, and the classes bad_cast and bad_typeid are defined in the header file typeinfo.

Classes derived from class exception are also used in several of the standard libraries to signal errors. This applies, for instance, to the classes string, vector and deque, and to the library that contains classes for handling streams and files. In the latter library there is a class failure, which is used to signal certain types of error with the reading and writing of data.

throw statement

throw *expression*;

where *expression* can be of arbitrary type.

- Normal execution is terminated when a **throw** statement is executed.
- It is best to use a standard class *S* derived from the standard class exception

  throw *S*("*text*");

  or a personally created class *E* derived from class exception

  throw *E*();

- The following line must be found in the program

  #include <stdexcept>

10.2 Handling exceptions

So far we have discussed only how exceptions are generated. If an exception is not trapped, the program will stop. If we have a program that controls an industrial process of some sort, it is not acceptable for the program to cease abruptly if an exception occurs. The program must deal with what has happened by writing a warning message to the operator or by closing down a critical process, for example. It is also unacceptable for a program to cease because an operator happens to have written input data in the wrong format.

There are three levels of ambition in dealing with exceptions:

1. Take control of the exception and try to take suitable action to enable the program to continue.
2. Identify the exception and pass it on to another part of the program.
3. Identify the exception but ignore it: the program will stop when the exception occurs.

The basic principle should be that the exception is controlled in the part of the program where its effect can be handled most sensibly. The third level is the one we have seen so far. We have used the function assert and allowed the program to stop. This is fine when dealing with logic errors that have occurred while the program was being tested before it was properly run.

We shall begin with an example from the following function:

```
int f(int x)
{
  int a = fa(x);
  int b = fb(x);
  return a / b;
}
```

Both of the functions that are called, `fa` and `fb`, can be two arbitrary functions. If function `fb` should return a value of `0`, we shall have a problem. If we do nothing, division by 0 will be performed, and this will give an undefined result. (Most C++ implementations ignore so-called arithmetic overflow.) If the variable `b` gets a value of `0`, this will be apparent, but what should we do? If we are operating on ambition level 1 (to take control of the exception), we have to find a suitable value to return from the function `f`. We try this:

```
int f(int x)
{
  int a = fa(x);
  int b = fb(x);
  if (b == 0)
    return INT_MAX;
  return a / b;
}
```

The constant `INT_MAX` is defined in the standard file `climits`, and indicates the largest number that can be stored in a variable of type **`int`**. If, for example, type **`int`** is represented with 16 bits, `INT_MAX` will be equal to 32 767. This is the nearest that we can get to the infinitely great number that should have been returned in the case when `b` equals `0`. Naturally, this is mathematically absurd, and we must accept that ambition level 1 is too high for this example. It is simply not possible to return a reasonable value from the function `f` when `b` gets a value of `0`. If we go to ambition level 3, the problem becomes easy. We simply add the following line after the value of `b` has been calculated:

```
assert(b != 0);
```

or we can write

```
if (b == 0)
{
  cout << "Overflow in the function f";
  abort();
}
```

But then the program will stop, and this may not be necessary. The result from function `f` may not be so important, after all. If the function that called `f` had found that an error had arisen, it might have been able to proceed anyway, even if it had not got a result from `f`. This is possible if we try to apply ambition level 2. Begin by writing a new version of function `f` to generate an exception when `b` becomes `0`:

```
int f(int x)
{
   int a = fa(x);
   int b = fb(x);
   if (b == 0)
      throw overflow_error("Error in f");
   return a / b;
}
```

Let us look at the function that calls function `f`. When we call a function that can generate exceptions, we have to indicate specially that we are prepared to trap exceptions. This we do by making use of what is called a **`try`** block, which has the general form

```
try {
   statements
}
catch (parameter) {
   statements
}
catch (parameter) {
   statements
}
etc.
```

After the word **`try`** we write a block that contains the statements to be performed, one that can possibly generate an exception. After this block there should be one or more *handlers*. Each handler is introduced with the reserved word **`catch`**, and has a single parameter. The following things happen when the statements in the block after **`try`** are executed. If no exception occurs, the statements are performed as usual, and none of the handlers will be involved. If an exception of type $type_e$ is generated by one of the statements after **`try`**, execution of this statement will be interrupted, and the program will instead jump to the *first* of the handlers that has a parameter of a type that matches $type_e$. We shall give the rules later for what is meant by 'match', but we now show an example instead:

```
void g()
{
   int i;
   while (1)
      try {
```

```
      cout << "? ";
      if (! (cin >> i))
        break;
      int r = f(i);
      cout << "The result was " << r << endl;
    }
    catch(overflow_error) {
      cout << "No result can be given" << endl;
    }
}
```

The function g keeps reading in integers from the keyboard. Input is terminated when the character combination for end-of-file is given (Ctrl-Z or Ctrl-D). For every number read the function f is called, and the result from f is written at the terminal. If a number happens to be read in such that b in the function f becomes equal to zero, the following statement is executed:

```
throw overflow_error("Error in f");
```

Since the exception that now arises does not lie in a **try** block, it will not be dealt with in the function f. Instead f will be interrupted and the exception sent further to the function g, which called f. In g there is then an exception at the point where f was called – that is, in the declaration

```
int r = f(i);
```

This line is then aborted, and since it lies in a **try** block, the program will jump to the first of the **try** block's handlers that matches the type overflow_error. In the **try** block in g there is only one handler, and since it has a parameter precisely of type overflow_error, the program will jump there. Then we obtain:

```
No result can be given
```

As soon as a handler is reached that traps the exception, the exception is eliminated. Execution then proceeds normally with the statement that comes *after* the **try** block: that is, with a statement that comes after the last of the handlers. It is important to note that there is no jump back to the statement that was aborted in the **try** block. (If in our example there had been several other statements after f(i) was called, these would not have been performed.) If we wanted to perform the statements in the **try** block again, we would have to put the whole **try** block into a repetition statement, as we did in our example, and execute the statements in it from the beginning.

The rules state that when an exception of $type_e$ arises, control will be transformed to the nearest 'suitable' handler. By 'suitable' we mean that it will have a parameter whose type matches $type_e$. And when we say 'nearest', we mean that the handler will be in the **try** block that was begun last of all the unfinished **try** blocks. This means that an exception is 'passed on' from the point where it arises – the interruption point – until there is a handler that can deal with the exception. The path the exception takes here is the reverse of the stages leading up to the interruption. If no suitable handler can be found on the way back, the program will be terminated.

We must also give the rules (in simplified form) for what is meant by types 'matching'. Suppose that there has been an exception of $type_e$. If a handler has a parameter of type `T` or type 'reference to `T`', then this parameter matches $type_e$ if:

- `T` and $type_e$ are the same type;
- `T` is a base class of $type_e$;
- `T` has type 'pointer to `B`' and $type_e$ type 'pointer to `D`', where `B` is a base class of `D`.

The most important point is, of course, the first one, which states that if the types are the same, then they match. This is the rule that was applied in our function `g` above.

We shall now extend our example to demonstrate how we can have several handlers. We did not worry before about the two functions `fa` and `fb` that were called in function `f`. Suppose that `fa` looks as follows:

```
int fa(int x)
{
  int tab[100];
  ...  // initialization of tab
  if (x < 0 || x >= 100)
    throw out_of_range("in fa");
  return tab[x];
}
```

The function `fa` generates an exception of the standard class `out_of_range` if incorrect indexing is performed.

We now extend the function `g` with yet another handler:

```
void g()
{
  int i;
  while (1)
    try {
      cout << "? ";
      if (! (cin >> i))
        break;
      int r = f(i);
      cout << "The result was " << r << endl;
    }
    catch (overflow_error) {
      cout << "No result can be given" << endl;
    }
```

```
    catch (exception& e) {
      cout << typeid(e).name() << ": "
           << e.what() << endl;
    }
}
```

We let the parameter in the new handler have type 'reference to `exception`'. This means that, according to the rules above, this parameter will match all classes directly or indirectly derived from class `exception`. This in turn means that the new handler will be a suitable handler for all the kinds of exception where the standard classes in Figure 10.1 are used. We have given the parameter in the new handler a name, `e`. It functions in roughly the same way as a parameter in a function call. When control is transferred to the handler, the handler gets the actual exception as argument. This means that we can use the parameter `e` to examine the exception in more detail. We first use the standard operator **typeid** to write out the name of the class the exception belongs to. Note that it is extremely important to let the parameter `e` be of type 'reference to `exception`' and not simply of type `exception`, because when we call **typeid** we find out which subclass of `exception` `e` refers to. If `e` is merely of type `exception`, the argument is copied to `e`, and all the parts except for the `exception` part are peeled away. The expression `typeid(e).name()` would then always return the text '`exception`'.

The standard class `exception` contains a very useful virtual member function with the name `what`:

```
virtual const char* what() const;
```

This function is inherited by all the subclasses of `exception`. When we call it, we get as result the text that was given as extra information when the exception was generated.

Let us suppose that we have a main program that makes the call `g()`. Here is an example from the program when it is run:

```
? 0
No result can be given
? -1
out_of_range: in fa
```

When we give a value of `0` as input data, function `f` generates an exception of type `overflow_error`, and we land in function `g`. When we give a value of `-1`, an exception of type `out_of_range` is generated in function `fa`. Since there is no **try** block with a suitable handler in either function `fa` or function `f`, the exception is sent on to the **try** block in function `g`. Here we land in the second of the handlers, since class `out_of_range` is derived from class `exception`. Note that we get the message '`out_of_range`' and not '`exception`'. This is because we use a reference parameter in the handler. We get the text '`in fa`' from the call of function `what`. The same text was given in the **throw** statement.

Only one exception handler can be executed in a **try** block. The first handler with a matching parameter is chosen. In our example this means that, when we get an exception of type `overflow_error`, we land in the first handler in spite of the fact that the second handler also has a matching parameter. As a general rule, it can be said that if there are several handlers, the handlers for the most derived classes should be placed first. Otherwise they will be hidden by the handlers of the base classes.

As soon as function `g` has a handler with a parameter of type 'reference to `exception`' it can trap all the exceptions that are generated in `f`, `fa`, `fb` or any other function that belongs to a class derived from the standard class `exception`. But what would happen if some other kind of `exception` arose? Suppose that function `fb` should have the following appearance:

```
int fb(int x)
{
  if (x == 1)
    throw "Now there is an error";
  if (x == 2)
    throw x;
  return x;
}
```

The function `fb` can generate two different kinds of exception. None of the standard classes for exceptions are used here (if they had been, it would have been better). An exception of type **char** * is generated in the statement

```
throw "Now there is an error";
```

And in the statement

```
throw x;
```

an exception of type **int** is generated (since `x` has this type). Exceptions of this kind are not trapped by the **try** block in function `g`. They will therefore slip through the net to go on to the function that called `g`. Let us suppose that `g` is called directly from `main`. If the call does not lie in a **try** block with a handler that can handle this kind of exception, the program will be terminated. But we might also expect to find a **try** block in `main`:

```
main()
{
  try {
    statements
    g();
    statements
  }
```

```
  catch(char *s) {
    cout << s << endl;
  }
  catch(...) {
    cout << "Unknown error occurred" << endl;
  }
}
```

A call of `g` occurs inside the **`try`** block. There are two handlers. The first one deals with exceptions of type **`char *`**. What happens is simply that the text is written out. The second handler has a parameter list consisting of three dots. This is a special way of indicating that the handler will trap any kind of exception. If we are dealing with this kind of handler, it must come last as it hides all handlers coming after it. Here is an example of how the program looks when it is run:

```
? 0
No result can be given
? -1
out_of_range: in fa
? 1
Now there is an error
The program stops here
```

`try` blocks

```
try {
  statements
}
catch (parameter) {
  statements
}
catch (parameter) {
  statements
}
etc.
```

- When an exception occurs in statements after **`try`** there is a jump to the first handler (the **`catch`** part) whose parameter matches the exception type.
- When the statements in the handler have been executed, the **`try`** block is finished, and execution proceeds with the next statement. There is never a jump back to the place where the interruption occurred.
- If there are no handlers to deal with an exception, the **`try`** block is aborted and the exception is sent on.

When we give a value of `0` as input data the function `f` generates an exception of type `overflow_error`, and when we give a value of `-1` an exception of type `out_of_range` is generated in function `fa`. Both of these exceptions are trapped, as before, by the handlers in the **try** block in function `g`. When the exceptions have been trapped, they are eliminated. Since the **try** block in function `g` lies inside a **while** statement, the whole of it is repeated again and again, and this ensures that the program continues normally when the errors have been dealt with. But after we have given an input value of `1`, the program will stop. This is because an exception of type **char** `*` is generated in `fb`. This exception is not trapped by any of the handlers in function `g`, so it is sent on to function `main`, and an exception arises at the point where `g` is called. There is then a jump to the first of the handlers that has a matching parameter. When the text string `s` has been written out, the handler is terminated, and with it the **try** block. There is no jump back to the point where `g` was called. The **try** block will not be repeated as it does not lie in a repetition statement. The function `main` has now come to its last statement and is completed in the normal way. The same thing happens when the program is run with a value of `2` given as input data:

```
? 2
Unknown error occurred
The program stops here
```

Parameters of exception handlers

Different forms:

```
catch (T)
catch (T e)
```

traps exceptions of type `T`

```
catch (T&)
catch (T& e)
```

traps exceptions of type `T` or (if `T` is a class type) of classes derived from `T`.

```
catch (...)
```

Traps exceptions of all kinds. Must come last.

Here, an exception of type **int** is generated, so we shall end up in the last of the handlers in `main`, the one that can trap exceptions of all kinds.

Thus by putting all the statements in `main` into a **try** block and letting this **try** block have a handler with the parameter `...` we can trap all the exceptions that arise in the program. Of course, there can also be handlers with the parameter `...` in other functions. To demonstrate this we write a new version of the function `f`:

```
int f(int x)
{
  try {
    int a = fa(x);
    int b = fb(x);
    if (b == 0)
      throw overflow_error("Error in f");
    return a / b;
  }
  catch (overflow_error) {
    throw;
  }
  catch (...) {
    cout << "Error in f" << endl;
    throw;
  }
}
```

All the statements in the function have been enclosed in a **try** block with two handlers. The first handler traps exceptions of type `overflow_error`, which we generate ourselves, and the second handler traps all other kinds of exceptions. We have an extra handler for type `overflow_error` because we do not want '`Error in f`' written out for exceptions of this kind. This information can be obtained, of course, by using the member function `what`. When an exception is trapped in a handler, it is normally eliminated, and execution of the program proceeds normally with the next statement after the **try** block. Meanwhile, it is possible from inside a handler to indicate that the exception trapped is not to be eliminated but should be passed on, exactly as if it had not been trapped in the first place. This is done by writing a **throw** statement without expression. The statement

```
throw;
```

in the handlers in function `f` passes on an exception to the function that called `f`. The program can be given the following test run:

```
? 0
No result can be given
? 2
Error in f
Unknown error occurred
The program stops here
```

Through the extra output text in `f`, it is now easier to discover where the error arose.

Something should be said about constructors and destructors in connection with exceptions. An exception involves a more complicated mechanism than a simple jump to an exception handler. When an exception occurs, the program 'cleans up' after itself exactly as if the functions and blocks remaining had been concluded in the normal way. This means that if variables of a class type have been declared and then cease to exist, the destructors for these variables are called automatically. But there is an important exception. Destructors are called only for objects whose constructors have been completed. Basically, this means that if an exception occurs in a constructor, the destructor is not called for this object. We should therefore take care that exceptions do not occur in constructors where memory is allocated dynamically. Care should also be taken that exceptions do not occur in destructors, since these can be called automatically while another exception is being dealt with.

10.3 Defining our own `exception` classes: an example

The standard library for reading and writing from streams is comprehensive, and contains many useful resources. The input and output operators `>>` and `<<`, for example, are often elegant and easy to use. There are shortcomings, however, and one of these is illustrated in the following lines from a program:

```
int i;
cout << "Indicate a number: "
cin >> i;
cout << "The number " << i << " was read" << endl;
```

We make a test run. In a typical C++ system, we can get the message

```
Indicate a number: 50000
The number -15536 was read
```

Another test run can give the following output:

```
Indicate a number: 80000
The number 14464 was read
```

In this example we have used a system where type `int` is represented with 16 bits. The input operator `>>` makes no check whatsoever that overflow does not arise when the digits are read in, and for this reason the result is absurd. To make the reading of integers safer, we shall construct our own function `get` for the reading of input data. The function will generate exceptions if something goes wrong.

We shall use the standard class `overflow_error` in function `get` to signal that we are attempting to read in large numbers. Two types of error can arise now. One is that an attempt can be made to read a number although end-of-file has occurred, and the other is that the user can write incorrect data, for instance letters instead of digits. We shall define our own classes to point out these errors. We begin with the declaration of our own class `io_error`:

```
class io_error : public runtime_error {
public:
   io_error(const string& what_arg)
   : runtime_error(what_arg) {}
};
```

Clearly, we have let our new class `io_error` be a subclass of the standard class `runtime_error`. This means, among other things, that class `io_error` will inherit the virtual function `what`. We now declare two subclasses of the class `io_error`. These classes will each signal a particular kind of input error.

```
class end_error : public io_error {
public:
   end_error(const string& what_arg =
             "Reading when end of file")
   : io_error(what_arg) {}
};
class data_error : public io_error {
public:
   data_error(const string& what_arg =
              "Incorrect input data")
   : io_error(what_arg) {}
};
```

We shall be using the class `end_error` to signal that we are attempting to read although end-of-file has occurred and class `data_error` to signal that the user has entered incorrect input data. For both these classes we have given a default value for the parameter of the constructor.

The input function `get` will now look like this:

```
void get(int& i)
{
   char c;
   char sign = '+';
   bool ok = false;
   i = 0;
   cin >> ws;  // Skip white characters
   if (cin.peek() == EOF)
     throw end_error("In the function get(int&)");
   if (cin.peek() == '+' || cin.peek() == '-')
     cin >> sign;
   while (cin.peek() >= '0' && cin.peek() <= '9')
   {
     ok = true;
     cin >> c;
     c -= '0';
```

```
    if (i <= INT_MAX/10 && i*10 <= INT_MAX-c)
      i = i*10 + c;
    else
      throw overflow_error("Input error");
  }
  if (not ok)
  {
    skip_line();  // See page 120
    throw data_error();
  }
  if (sign == '-')
    i = -i;
}
```

The function first skips all the blank characters. Then the standard function cin.peek is used to see whether end-of-file has occurred. If so, it is an error to try to read more, and we generate an exception of type end_error. If the user has written a plus or minus sign, this will be read and stored in the variable **sign**.

We use cin.peek in the **while** statement to see whether the next character waiting to be read is a digit. If it is, the digit is read into the variable c and converted from ASCII code to an integer in the interval from 0 to 9 by subtracting the character code for the digit '0'. Before the new digit is added to the result, a check is made to ensure that it can be added to the end without overflow resulting. Overflow will not occur if the old value in variable i can be multiplied by 10 without the result being greater than INT_MAX, the largest number that can be stored in a variable of type **int**. The condition is thus i*10<=INT_MAX, but we cannot write this since overflow would occur when i*10 is calculated. We therefore rewrite this condition and check instead whether i<=INT_MAX/10. When the old value in i has been multiplied by 10, we should be able to add it to the new number in variable c, in which case the condition i*10+c<=INT_MAX should be true. But we also have to rewrite this in order to avoid the occurrence of overflow in the test itself. Thus we check that i*10<=INT_MAX-c. If our checks show that the latest digit can be added to the result, we can perform the expression i=i*10+c without the risk of overflow, otherwise we generate an exception of type overflow_error.

After the end of the **while** statement, we check to see that at least one digit has been read. To do this, we use the variable ok. This is initialized to the value **false** but is set to **true** as soon as a digit has been read in the **while** statement. If no digit has been read, the user will have written faulty input data, and an exception of type data_error is generated. But before this is done, the actual input line is 'cleaned' with the help of function skip_line; see section 4.2.

Here is the main program that calls the function get and traps the various kinds of exception:

```
main()
{
  int k = 0;
  while (cin.peek() != EOF)
    try {
      get(k);
      cout << k << endl;
    }
    catch(data_error) {
      cout << "Faulty number. Try again!" << endl;
    }
    catch(exception& e) {
      cout << typeid(e).name() << ": "
      << e.what() << endl;
    }
}
```

A test run of the program can have the following appearance. The underlined parts have been written by the user.

```
30000
30000
50000
overflow_error: input error
-qw
Incorrect number. Try again!
-12
-12
Here the user writes ctrl-z or ctrl-d
end_error: In the function get(int&)
```

What is perhaps astonishing is that we have got the error `end_error` in spite of the fact that we made the test `cin.peek()!=EOF` in function `main` before trying to read the next number. The reason is this: when the last number, –12, was read, the last character to be consumed was '`2`'. The end-of-line character after this was not read, therefore, and this means that the end of the file was *not* reached and the test `cin.peek()!=EOF` gave the value **`true`**. When function `get` is called, it begins by skipping all the blank characters and so skips the end-of-line character. End-of-file occurs *now*, and `get` generates the exception `end_error`. A way of getting around this problem is by letting the main program itself make sure that the end-of-line character is read after every input data. The simplest thing to do is to insert a call of function `skip_line` after every call of `get`:

```
try {
  get(k);
  skip_line();
  cout << k << endl;
}
```

The only disadvantage with this is that we cannot input more than one number per line, but this may not matter in an interactive program.

10.4 Specification of exceptions

The technique of handling exceptions is based, as we have seen, on trapping the exceptions that have occurred in the functions that have been called. Various means can be applied to deal with different kinds of exception. Meanwhile, the question might be asked: how do we know what type of exception a called function can generate? One way of knowing this is of course to read the program code for the actual function, but this is not possible in practice when applied to functions that are a part of large programs and which themselves call other functions. Another way is to read the documentation available about the actual function and hope that it contains information about the different kinds of exception that can be generated. Unfortunately, such information cannot always be found.

C++ offers a third possibility. A function declaration can contain a *specification* of the exceptions that the function can generate. Suppose, for example, that we construct a function `f`, and we know that only exceptions of type `T1` and `T2` can occur in this function. We can then define the function in the following way:

```
void f(parameters) throw(T1, T2)
{ ... }
```

Last in the function head we write the reserved word **throw** followed by an enumeration of types for the exceptions that can be generated. The suffix '`throw(T1,T2,T3...)`' on the first line is called an *exception specification*. When a function `f` is now used, we can be aware of the kinds of exception that will need to be trapped. If there are functions declared in one place and defined in another, the exception specification must be in both the declaration and the definition. Earlier in this chapter we gave a new version of the indexing operator for class `Array`. We can now add an exception specification. The declaration will then be

```
int& operator[] (int i) throw(out_of_range);
```

and a separate definition can be written:

```
int& Array::operator[] (int i) throw(out_of_range)
{
  if(i < i1 || i > last())
    throw out_of_range("Array::operator[]");
  return p[i-i1];
}
```

An empty exception specification, as for example

```
void g(parameters) throw()
{ ... }
```

means that the function cannot generate any exceptions at all. If there is no exception specification such as, for example,

```
void h(parameters)
{ ... }
```

this will mean, as before, that the function can generate exceptions of any type.

If the compiler discovers that a function can generate an exception of a kind not given in the specification, this will not mean that the program is faulty. (Suppose, for example, that the function `g` were to call the function `f`, above.) This will not be regarded as a compilation error because it is, in general, impossible for the compiler to know all the kinds of exception that a function can generate. For it to be able to do this, it would have to analyse the program text in all the functions that the actual function could possibly call as well as all the functions that these functions could possibly call, and so on.

If exceptions of incorrect type are generated, these are dealt with instead when the program is executed. If, in a function `f`, an exception arises of a type not given in the exception specification, a standard function called `unexpected` will be called. If nothing else has been indicated, function `unexpected` will in its turn call another standard function `terminate`, and this will terminate the program.

For the examples that follow we shall use once again function `f` from page 348. We write a new version in which we use an exception specification to indicate the different kinds of exception that can be generated in the function:

```
int f(int x)throw(overflow_error, out_of_range)
{
   int a = fa(x);
   int b = fb(x);
   if (b == 0)
      throw overflow_error("Error in f");
   return a / b;
}
```

In the exception specification for `f` we indicated the type `overflow_error` since function `f` can itself generate exceptions of this type. To determine what other types should be listed in the exception specification for `f` we have to know what exceptions can be generated in functions `fa` and `fb`. Let us suppose that these are functions written by someone else and that we do not have access to the program codes. What we can know, however, is the declarations of the functions that will exist in an appropriate header file. Suppose that they have the following appearance:

```
int fa(int x) throw(out_of_range);
int fb(int x);
```

From these declarations we can see that `fa` can generate exceptions of type `out_of_range`, so we can include this type in the exception specification for `f`. On the other hand, the exceptions that can be generated by `fb` are unknown since we do not have an exception specification for this function.

We can now write a **try** block in which we call the function `f`:

```
while (1)
  try {
    cout << "? ";
    if (!(cin >> i))
      break;
    int r = f(i);
    cout << "The result was " << r << endl;
  }
  catch(exception& e) {
    cout << typeid(e).name() << ": " << e.what() << endl;
  }
```

Since the classes `overflow_error` and `out_of_range` are both derived from class `exception`, we have to content ourselves with having a single handler that can trap both these kinds of exception. If as input data we give a value of `0`, we could get the output text

```
? 0
overflow_error: Error in f
```

From the definition of function `fb` on page 00 we see that, if we feed in a value of 2, `fb` will generate an exception of type **int**. We then get the output

```
? 2
Program aborted
```

When the exception is passed on from function `fb` to `f`, the system discovers that `f` has an exception specification and that type **int** is not included in it. Function `unexpected` is therefore called. This in turn calls `terminate`, and the program is terminated.

We shall now illustrate how to avoid having a program terminated by redefining the function `unexpected`. We shall show the whole program:

```
#include <stdexcept>
#include <exception>
#include <typeinfo>
#include <iostream.h>
using namespace std;
void my_unexpected()
```

```
{
   throw bad_exception();
}
int fa(int x) throw(out_of_range);    // see page 351
int fb(int x);                        // see page 353
int f(int x)
throw(overflow_error, out_of_range, bad_exception)
{
   int a = fa(x);
   int b = fb(x);
   if (b == 0)
      throw overflow_error("Error in f");
   return a / b;
}
main()
{
   set_unexpected(my_unexpected);
   int i;
   while (1)
      try {
         cout << "? ";
         if (! (cin >> i))
            break;
         int r = f(i);
         cout << "The result was " << r << endl;
      }
      catch(exception& e) {
         cout << typeid(e).name() << ": "
            << e.what() << endl;
      }
}
```

To replace the standard function unexpected with our own function, we first call in main the standard function set_unexpected. As parameter we give the name of (that is, a pointer to) our own function. We have termed this function my_unexpected, and the definition is given first in the program. Now if there should be an exception in function f of a type not given in the exception specification for f, function my_unexpected will be called automatically. This function merely generates an exception of the standard class bad_exception, a subclass of the standard class exception. Since bad_exception is in the exception specification for f, the program will not be terminated. Instead, the exception will be trapped in the handler in main.

Function set_unexpected is declared in the header file exception. The definition of class bad_exception is also in this file. The classes out_of_range, overflow_error and exception have been defined in the header file stdexcept.

Specification of exceptions

- An exception specification can be added last in a function declaration:

  return_type `f` (*parameters*) **`throw`**`(T1, T2, T3 ...);`

  Then the function should generate only exceptions of the types given in the specification.
- An empty exception specification means that no exceptions should be generated by the function:

  return_type `f` (*parameters*) **`throw`**`();`

- If there is no exception specification, all types of exception can be generated:

  return_type `f` (*parameters*)`;`

- If an exception of a type not given in the exception specification is generated, function `unexpected` is called, and this terminates the program. Function `unexpected` can be replaced by the non-standard function:

  `set_unexpected(`*name_of_nonstandard_function*`);`

  This can generate an exception of type `bad_exception`.

A test run may now look as follows. Note that the program will not stop if a value of `2` is given as input data.

```
? 0
overflow_error: Error in f
? 2
bad_exception:
? -1
out_of_range: in fa
```

Exercises

10.1 Change all the member functions in class `Array` so that they generate exceptions, instead of using `assert`. Also use exception specifications to specify which exceptions the different functions can generate.

10.2 Write a version of the function `nfac` on page 140. The new function should give a floating-point number as its result and, if the result is so great that it cannot be represented by the system in use, an exception should be generated.

10.3 The function `roots` on page 135 computes the roots of a quadratic equation. Rewrite this function so that it no longer has the output parameter `ok`. Instead, the function should generate an exception of class `numeric_error`. Define this class as a subclass of the standard class `runtime_error`.

10.4 Solve Exercise 5.7 on page 199 using an exception to indicate that copying has miscarried.

10.5 Write a function `try_to_get` that can be called to read an integer from the keyboard safely. The function should have two output parameters, the first of which should be a reference to the variable to which input data will be read. The second parameter should be of type `bool`, and it should be used to signal whether or not the reading of input data has gone according to plan. *Tip*: Call the function `get` on page 358.

10.6 The function `get_enum` on page 189 reads input data from enumeration types. Make changes in this function so that it generates an exception of class `data_error` when the user writes incorrect input data, and an exception of class `end_error` when an attempt is made to read although end-of-file has occurred. Then make the necessary changes to the program on page 190 so that the new version of `get_enum` can be used.

11 Streams and files

In this book we have used the C++ standard library to read and write data from the terminal. This library is text-oriented. It relies on data being read and written in textual form. In other words, it uses the keyboard and terminal like a kind of typewriter. The mouse is not used at all. But isn't this rather old-fashioned? Surely modern programs are windows oriented: that is, they make use of a graphic screen and use windows, menus, icons and so on to communicate with the user? Shouldn't we be describing these things in a book like this? There is justification for this argument, but there are two reasons why, in spite of everything, we have used the C++ standard library. The first is that it is rather complicated to write windows-oriented programs. There are a great many help functions to be mastered, and these are, unfortunately, in no way standardized. There are many kinds of windows systems, and they are all different. Before writing windows-oriented programs, therefore, we have to decide on one particular system and learn it. The description of windows-oriented programs lies entirely outside the scope of this book, but the reader is advised to learn the basics of C++ before studying the windows system that will be important to him or her.

The other reason why we use the C++ standard library is because it is actually useful, even in windows-oriented programs. A program does not only communicate with the user. It also has to be able to read and write data stored permanently in the form of files in secondary storage, for instance on discs or CD-ROM. Sometimes we need to convert and edit data that has been read, or that will be written, using the help functions of a windows system. In both of these cases we can use the C++ standard library. It is heartening to know that we program in exactly the same way as we do when reading from and writing to the terminal. The same help functions are used – the output and input operators `<<` and `>>`, for example. What we have learnt so far is extremely useful, even for windows-oriented programs.

In this chapter we shall be looking at the general notion of a stream, and shall use this opportunity to give a summary of all the different functions for reading and writing that we have used up to now (plus a few more). The book will then be easier to use as a reference work.

We then look at how files are read and written. In this connection we shall illustrate how parameters can be given to the main program when a program is started. In particular, we shall demonstrate how objects of different classes can be stored in files with information about the class that an object belongs to. This will later facilitate reading files and re-creating objects.

Data is most often stored in files in the form of text, usually called *text files*. We may sometimes want to store data in exactly the same form as that in which it is stored in the primary memory, in what are called binary files, and this will be demonstrated.

Finally, there is a section on how to use the C++ standard library to convert and edit data internally in the primary memory.

11.1 The class `ios`

The idea of using *streams* for reading and writing data is a fundamental concept in the C++ library. A stream is simply a sequence of bytes. There are a number of operations in the library for reading from streams and writing to streams. A program can communicate with external media – for instance, disc memory – via streams. A stream can be connected to a particular file. Streams can even be connected to memory space in the primary memory or to the terminal. The interesting thing here, is that streams can always be handled in the same way, regardless of what they happen to be connected to.

In the standard library streams are implemented with the help of a number of classes. The most basic classes are the class `ios_base` and its subclass `ios`, which contains data and operations common for all kinds of stream. The class `ios` constitutes a base class for the two classes `istream` and `ostream`. These classes contain facilities to handle streams that will be read and written respectively. The class `iostream` is a subclass of both the classes `istream` and `ostream`, and contains facilities for streams to be both read and written. In order to read and write from files you use the classes `ifstream`, `ofstream` and `fstream`, which are subclasses of `istream`, `ostream` and `iostream` respectively. You can also connect streams to the primary memory. They can then be used to edit and convert data internally in the program. There are two sets of classes that can be used. The classes `istringstream`, `ostringstream` and `stringstream` are used when you want to connect streams with objects of the standard class `string`. The second set is the classes `istream`, `ostrstream` and `strstream`, used when you want to handle character arrays as streams. (These last three classes are actually not in standard C++ but are there for compatibility with older versions of C++.) Figure 11.1 shows how the different classes are related to each other. (All the classes in the diagram, except the class `ios_base`, are implemented in the standard with the help of class templates that have the same name as the class but beginning with the word `basic_`.

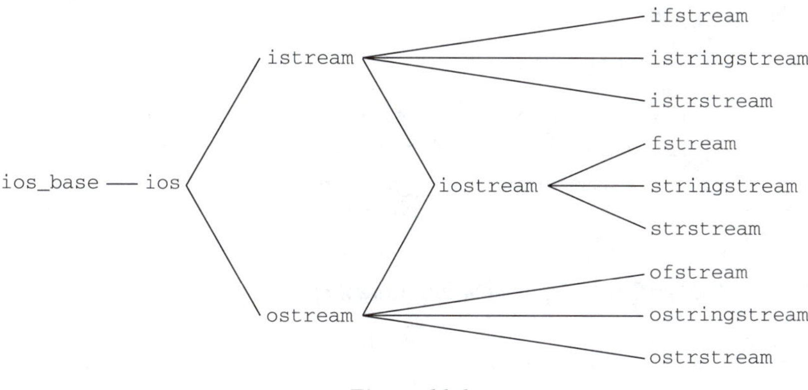

Figure 11.1

For instance, the class `ios` is implemented with the help of the class template `basic_ios` and the class `istream` with the template `basic_istream`.)

In the standard there are a number of predefined stream objects: `cin`, `cout`, `cerr` and `clog`. These are always automatically declared, so we should never try to declare them ourselves. The object `cin` is of class `istream`. It is automatically connected to 'standard input', which is normally the keyboard, but in some operating systems it can be redirected (see page 83). The other three standard objects are all of class `ostream`. The object `cout` is automatically connected to 'standard output', normally a text window at the terminal. 'Standard output' can also be redirected. The objects `cerr` and `clog` are used for output of error texts and program logs. These streams are normally connected so that output text reaches the terminal. It is a good idea to write all error messages in stream `cerr` instead of in `cout`: then error messages will be visible at the terminal even if `cout` has been redirected.

If we want to work with a stream that has not been predeclared, we have to declare our own stream objects. Then objects of one of the classes furthest to the right in Figure 11.1 are normally declared.

The classes `ios_base` and `ios` are defined in the header file `<ios>`. The predefined streams `cin`, `cout`, `cerr` and `clog` are declared in the file `<iostream>`. The classes `istream` and `iostream` are defined in the file `<istream>` and the class `ostream` in the file `<ostream>`. The classes `ifstream`, `ofstream` and `fstream` are defined in the header file `<fstream>`. The header file `<sstream>` contains definitions of the classes `istringstream`, `ostringstream` and `stringstream`. The classes `istream`, `ostream` and `strsstream` are declared in a header file called `<strstream>`.

In class `ios` there are three so-called *flags*, which indicate the condition of a stream (see Table 11.1). If none of the flags is set, the stream is all right.

Table 11.1 State flags in class `ios`.

Flag	Indication
`failbit`	That the latest input or output operation miscarried for some reason.
`eofbit`	That end-of-file occurred at an earlier attempt at reading.
`badbit`	A serious error that usually concerns the stream's internal buffer.

Table 11.2 Member functions for handling state flags.

Function	Effect
`void clear();`	Clears all the flags.
`bool good();`	Gives `true` if none of the flags is set.
`bool fail();`	Gives `true` if `failbit` or `badbit` is set.
`bool eof();`	Gives `true` if `eofbit` is set.
`bool bad();`	Gives `true` if `badbit` is set.
`bool operator!();`	Gives the result `fail()`.
`operator bool();`	Gives the result `not fail()`.

There is also a set of member functions in class `ios` that can be used to read and change the conditions in these flags. We can write, for instance,

```
if (clog.good())
  cerr << "The stream clog is all right";
if (cin.fail())
{
  cerr << "Reading miscarried";
  cin.clear();
}
```

The member function in the penultimate line in Table 11.2 is the operator `! (not)`. This can be used as an alternative to calling the function `fail`. For instance, the condition in the last of the `if` statements above can be written

```
if (!cin)
```

The function `eof` needs some explanation. When the end of a stream has been reached there is no more input to be read. If we try to read when this has happened we say that end-of-file occurs. The flag `eofbit` is then set. For this flag to be set, we must actually have tried to read when there is no more input to be read. It is not sufficient merely to have reached the end of a file. (A programmer experienced in Pascal or Ada should especially note this, since the corresponding function in these languages gives the value 'true' when the end-of-file has been reached, regardless of whether or not an attempt to read has been made.) Suppose, for instance, that we wish to compute the number of characters written in by the user. We try the following program lines:

```
char c;
int n = 0;
while (! cin.eof())   // NB! ERROR!
{
  cin.get(c);
  n++;
}
cout << "You wrote in " << n << " characters" << endl;
```

Suppose now that the user writes in the text 'abc' and then presses the enter key. Then the end of the file is marked by writing Ctrl-Z (or Ctrl-D):

```
abc
The user marks the end of the file here
```

Something rather astonishing will be returned:

```
You wrote 5 characters
```

The `while` statement is therefore executed for five rounds. In the first three rounds the characters 'a', 'b' and 'c' are read. In the fourth round the end-of-line character generated by the enter key is read. After the fourth round, there is no more input data to get, but the flag `eofbit` is not set yet. It is not set before an attempt is made to read when there is no more input. This means that the `while` statement is executed for a fifth round. When `get` is called the fifth time end-of-file occurs and the flag `eofbit` is set. (The variable `c` will then get the value `EOF`.)

To correctly compute the number of characters that have been read, we must adjust the `while` statement. We can then write, for instance,

```
while(true)   // Correct
{
  cin.get(c);
  if (cin.eof())
    break;
  n++;
}
```

After every attempt at reading we check whether the flag `eofbit` has been set. If so, the `while` statements are terminated. With the same input data as above, we now get the correct printout:

```
You wrote 4 characters
```

But a correct `while` statement can be written more simply:

```
while(cin.get(c))   // Correct and simplest
   n++;
```

This may seem rather strange. The function `get` gives as result a reference to the stream that is read. The result is therefore of type 'reference to `istream`'. The condition in parentheses after **`while`** should be of type **`bool`** (or **`int`**, if it is one of the older compilers). The compiler then tests whether there is a type conversion that can be done automatically from type `istream` to type **`bool`**. In the last line of Table 11.2 we note that for class `ios` there is a type conversion operator precisely for type `istream` to type **`bool`**. This operator will be called automatically. It gives as result the value **`true`** if the latest reading has been successful, and a value of **`false`** otherwise. In our example this means that the **`while`** statement is executed for four rounds. When the condition inside the parentheses is computed for the fifth time, reading will miscarry and the result will be **`false`**. Earlier in the book we have used the input operator `>>` in several places and written expressions of the form

```
while(cin >> i)
```

The result of the input operator is also of type 'reference to `istream`'. This means that the type conversion operator in Table 11.2 will also be automatically called in these cases.

The standard library for reading and writing in C++ was constructed before the language for handling exceptions was introduced, and this is why the procedure with flags, which has to be monitored by the programmer, is now in use. If the library were constructed today, exceptions would most probably be used instead of flags to signal errors. However, there is a mechanism that enables the programmer to indicate whether he or she wants exceptions to be generated when the flags are set.

The member function `exceptions` is used to indicate when we want exceptions to be generated. The call should have the form

```
str.exceptions(ios::flag|ios::flag|ios::flag);
```

where *`str`* is the name of the stream object in question and *`flag`* the name of one of the flags in Table 11.1. (The vertical line is the symbol for the bit operator 'or' – see section 15.2.) One, two or three flags can be indicated. If, for instance, we want an exception to be generated when the flag `eofbit` is set for stream `cin`, the following call should be inserted first in the program:

```
cin.exceptions(ios::eofbit);
```

and if we want exceptions to be generated if one of the flags `badbit` or `failbit` is set for stream `clog`, we make the call

```
clog.exceptions(ios::badbit|ios::failbit);
```

If we make use of exceptions, the exceptions generated will be of class `ios::failure`, a subclass of the standard class `exception`. Thus we can use the standard function `what`, demonstrated in Chapter 10, to get information on the cause of the error.

Finally, it should be said that in class `ios` there are also flags that indicate how data should be read and edited. These flags can be used in different ways, both with the help of special member functions in class `ios` and by using manipulators. It can all be rather complicated. In this book we use manipulators throughout since they are easiest to read and understand. We shall be looking at read and edit flags in our discussion on the reading and writing of streams.

11.2 Reading streams

Streams that we can read from all belong to class `istream`, or a class derived from it. This was illustrated by Figure 11.1. Class `istream` contains a great number of resources for reading streams. Many of the functions in class `ios` can also be used when reading. We have already demonstrated most of these in connection with stream `cin` but we shall give a brief summary here so they are all found in one place in the book.

When we read input data, we differentiate between *formatted* and *unformatted* reading. With unformatted reading, data is read from the instream just as it is stored, byte by byte. With formatted input, on the other hand, input data can be interpreted and converted. Formatted reading is carried out making use of the operator `>>`, whereas unformatted reading is done with the help of special member functions. We shall begin by describing formatted input.

11.2.1 Formatted input

The input operator `>>` can be used to read data of all the standard types. If we suppose that `is` is an object of class `istream` or of a class derived from it, we could write, for instance,

```
unsigned short int usi;
long double ld;
is >> usi >> ld;
```

The result of a reading expression is a reference to the actual stream, so several readings can be done in a chain, as demonstrated above. Normally, a reading begins with all the white characters being skipped. Note that this also applies when data is read to variables of type **`char`** and to character arrays. The user is thus free to write several items of input data on the same line, or to insert a line break between various input data items. When white characters have been skipped the characters are consumed one by one from the instream as long as the characters read can be included in a value of the actual type. If, for example, input data is read to an integer variable, the characters in the instream will be consumed as long as there are digits. Reading will stop at the first character not included in the read value.

If reading occurs to a variable of numeric type, conversion will occur from a stream of **`char`** containing character codes, to a value of the actual type. Suppose, for example, that the statements above are executed and the user enters the following input data:

```
76   -12.677
```

then the character sequence `"76"` is converted to a value of type **`unsigned short int`** and the character sequence `"-12.677"` to a value of type **`long double`**.

If, for some reason, reading miscarries (perhaps the user writes incorrect input data), the flag `ios::failbit` is set, and if end-of-file occurs when an attempt is made to read, the flag `ios::eofbit` will be set. This can generate exceptions if we have indicated that we want this to occur. As we saw earlier, we cannot be sure that an error will be indicated if there is overflow when data is converted.

Reading always stops at the next white character. This also applies when we read to a text string. For instance, if we have the lines from a program:

```
char a[11];
is >> a;
```

and give the following input data:

```
C++ From the Beginning
```

the array `a` will contain only the text string `"C++"`. The rest of the line will remain in the instream. The next character to be read is the space character in front of `F`. Note that the input operator always adds a null character at the end in the variable that is read to. Thus in array `a` a null character will be placed in position number 3. (Numbering occurs as usual from 0.)

There are a number of manipulators that can be used when input data is read. They are summarized in Table 11.3. (Some of them have been declared in file `iomanip`.)

When we read to a character array, there is no check to see that the array can hold the characters that have been read. If, in the example above, we were to feed in a connected text longer than 10 characters, the characters read would end up outside array `a` and ruin the other data. To stop this happening, we can use the manipulator `setw` and indicate the maximum number of characters that can fit into the array:

```
is >> setw(11) >> a;
```

If `setw(n)` has been written, the input operator `>>` will read at most `n-1` characters from the stream. (A null character is always added at the end.) The manipulator `setw` is good for *one* reading only.

Table 11.3 Manipulators for input.

Manipulator	Effect
`setw(n)`	Indicates the maximum number of characters that can be held in the array that will be read to.
`ws`	Jumps to the next non-white character in the stream.
`skipws`	Always skip leading white characters when the operator `>>` is used (standard setting).
`noskipws`	Do not skip leading white characters when the operator `>>` is used.
`dec`	Input data of integer type will be interpreted as decimal numbers.
`oct`	Input data of integer type will be interpreted as octal numbers.
`hex`	Input data of integer type will be interpreted as hexadecimal numbers.
`boolalpha`	Input data of type **`bool`** should be indicated as **`false`** or **`true`**.
`noboolalpha`	Input data of type **`bool`** should be indicated as `0` or `1`.

The manipulator `ws` is used to indicate that white characters should be skipped. We write, for instance,

```
is >> ws;
```

As we have seen, all white characters will be automatically skipped when the input operator `>>` is used. If we do not want this to happen we can use the manipulator `noskipws`:

```
is >> noskipws;
```

Then no white characters will be skipped from then on. Note that if input data contains a numeric value with a white character in front, there will be an input error when an attempt is made to read to a variable of numeric type. If we want to return to the standard setting, the manipulator `skipws` can be used.

The manipulators `dec`, `hex` and `oct` specify whether numeric integers that are read should be interpreted as decimal, hexadecimal or octal numbers respectively. Look at the following lines:

```
int i, j, k;
is >> oct >> i >> hex >> j >> dec >> k;
cout << i << " "<< j << " "<< k;
```

It is specified here that `i` should be interpreted as being written in octal form, `j` in hexadecimal form and `k` in decimal form. If the stream `is` contains the following input data, for example:

```
45 a7 29
```

then the output will be (written in decimal form)

```
37 167 29
```

When values are read to variables of type `bool`, input data can be written either in the form of words as `false` or `true`, or as the integers `0` and `1`. We choose the desired form with the help of the manipulators `boolalpha` and `noboolalpha`.

11.2.2 Unformatted input

Unformatted input is carried out with special member functions in the class `istream`. A summary of the functions available is given in Table 11.4.

Table 11.4 Member functions for unformatted input.

Function	Description
`gcount()`	Returns the number of characters read by the latest function for unformatted input.
`get()`	Reads and returns the next character in the stream; gives `EOF` if end-of-file occurs.
`get(c)`	Reads the next character in the stream to the variable `c`.
`getline(s, n, t)`	Parameter `t` has default value '`\n`'. Reads in a number of characters to text string `s` until the next character to be read is the same as the stop character `t`. This character is read but is *not* put into text string `s`. Input is terminated early if end-of-file occurs or if `n-1` characters have been read. A null character is always placed last in `s`.
`get(s, n, t)`	As `getline` but the stop character `t` is not read; instead remains as the next character in the stream.
`read(s, n)`	Reads `n` characters to the character array that `s` points to. If end-of-file occurs before `n` characters have been read, flags `eofbit` and `failbit` are set.
`readsome(s, n)`	As `read` but the number of read characters is given as return. If this number is less than `n`, `failbit` is *not* set.
`ignore(n, t)`	The parameter `n` has default value `1`, and `t` the default value `EOF`. Skips `n` characters in the stream. Stops earlier if the character waiting to be read is the same as `t` or if end-of-file occurs.
`peek()`	Returns the character waiting to be read, but the character remains as the next character in the stream.
`putback(c)`	Puts back the character `c` into the stream.
`unget()`	Puts back the character last read into the stream.

A common element of all of these functions is that they *never* skip white characters. All the characters are read strictly in turn. The functions can set the flag `ios::failbit` if input miscarries. The flag `ios::eofbit` can also be set if end-of-file occurs when the functions try to read. Exceptions can be generated if an indication has been made that this should occur. If nothing else is stated, the functions in the table will give as return value a reference to the actual stream.

We have seen examples of how most of the functions can be used, and we shall encounter a few more when we look at files. The functions `read` and `readsome` are used primarily when we work with *binary files*, files that do not contain text. We shall come back to this later.

We shall simply give an example containing a few statements that counts the number of lines in the instream `is`. We assume that no line has more than 500 characters.

```
const int max_length = 500;
char row[max_length+1];
int i = 0;
while (is.getline(row, max_length))
  i++;
cout << "The stream contains " << i << " rows";
```

When end-of-file occurs, both the flags `eofbit` and `failbit` are turned on. Since the member function `getline` returns a reference to the stream `is`, the type conversion operator in Table 11.2 will be automatically called, and this will return the value **`false`** when flag `failbit` is on.

11.3 Output to streams

We can write to streams that are members of the class `ostream` or a class derived from it. (See Figure 11.1.) Class `ostream` contains resources for writing to streams. With output data, we distinguish between *formatted* and *unformatted* output. With formatted output, output data is converted to a sequence of **`char`**, and it can also be edited in many different ways. With unformatted output, data is written to the outstream just as it is, without being converted.

11.3.1 Formatted output

Formatted output is carried out with the help of the operator `<<`. We have already seen many examples of formatted output to the stream `cout`, but we shall give a summary of its uses here for the sake of completeness. The operator `<<` is declared in class `ostream` for all the standard types.

With formatted output, output data can be edited in a great many ways. Editing is controlled by a collection of format flags that are defined in the base class `ios`. The

Table 11.5 Flags for formatted output in `ios`.

Format flag	Effect
`left`	Indicates that the written value should be left-adjusted: that is, any filler characters should be added after writing.
`right`	Indicates that the written value should be right-adjusted: that is, any filler characters should be added before writing.
`internal`	Indicates that any filler characters should be added between the number's sign and the first digit.
`dec`	Indicates that writing of integers should occur in decimal form.
`oct`	Indicates that writing of integers should occur in octal form.
`hex`	Indicates that writing of integers should occur in hexadecimal form.
`fixed`	Indicates that writing of floating-point numbers should occur in a fixed format with a decimal point. The number of decimal places is given by `precision`.
`scientific`	Indicates that writing of real numbers should occur in the floating-point format 999.999e99. The number of decimal places is given by `precision`.
`uppercase`	Indicates that upper-case letters should be used with floating-point writing of real numbers and with hexadecimal writing of integers.
`boolalpha`	Indicates that values of type **`bool`** should be written out in the form **`false`**, **`true`** instead of `0`, `1`.
`showbase`	Indicates that octal numbers should be written with an initial zero and hexadecimal numbers with the characters `0x` first.
`showpoint`	Indicates that the decimal point and terminating decimals with the value `0` should always be written for floating-point numbers.
`showpos`	Indicates that positive numbers should be written with the sign `+` first.
`unitbuf`	Indicates that all characters should be written directly and not buffered.

format flags that have an effect on output are shown in Table 11.5. The standard setting for all the flags, apart from `right` and `dec`, is off.

Class `ios` also monitors the three values shown in Table 11.6.

In class `ios` there are member functions (`setf` and `unsetf`) with whose help we can read and set the flags in Table 11.5 and the values in Table 11.6. We shall not describe

Table 11.6 Values for formatted output in `ios`.

Value	Meaning
`width`	Indicates the least number of output positions in the next output. Standard value = `0`.
`fill`	The character used as a filler if writing requires fewer than `width` positions. Standard value = the blank character.
`precision`	Used for writing floating point numbers. If the format is `fixed` or `scientific`, `precision` gives the number of decimal places, otherwise indicates the total number of significant figures. Standard value = `6`.

Table 11.7 Manipulators for handling formatting flags.

Manipulator	Effect
`uppercase` `nouppercase`	Turns on and shuts off, respectively, flag `ios::uppercase`.
`boolalpha` `noboolalpha`	Turns on and shuts off, respectively, flag `ios::boolalpha`.
`showbase` `noshowbase`	Turns on and shuts off, respectively, flag `ios::showbase`.
`showpoint` `noshowpoint`	Turns on and shuts off, respectively, flag `ios::showpoint`.
`showpos` `noshowpos`	Turns on and shuts off, respectively, flag `ios::showpos`.
`left`	Sets flag `ios::left`; shuts off flags `ios::right` and `ios::internal`.
`right`	Sets flag `ios::right`; shuts off flags `ios::left` and `ios::internal`.
`internal`	Sets flag `ios::internal`; shuts off flags `ios::left` and `ios::right`.
`dec`	Sets flag `ios::dec`; shuts off flags `ios::oct` and `ios::hex`.
`oct`	Sets flag `ios::oct`; shuts off flags `ios::dec` and `ios::hex`.
`hex`	Sets flag `ios::hex`; shuts off flags `ios::dec` and `ios::oct`.
`fixed`	Sets flag `ios::fixed`; shuts off flag `ios::scientific`.
`scientific`	Sets flag `ios::scientific`; shuts off flag `ios::fixed`.

these functions here, however. Instead, we shall use manipulators, which are both simpler and safer to use. Manipulators are used together with the output operator `<<`. They are defined either in the header file `iostream` or in the file `iomanip`. Table 11.7 shows the manipulators that we can use to manipulate the formatting flags.

Certain formatting flags must be handled together since they cannot all be set at the same time. This applies for instance to the flags `dec`, `oct` and `hex`. The manipulators in Table 11.7 do this automatically.

If we suppose that `os` is a stream of class `ostream` or a class derived from it, we can write, for example,

```
os << uppercase << scientific;
```

Output of real numbers then occurs in the format

```
1.234567E+12
```

If neither `fixed` nor `scientific` has been indicated, output, as we saw earlier, will be written in the format that is easiest to read, but this will depend on the actual value.

The manipulators `setiosflags` and `resetiosflags` can be used to turn on and shut off, respectively, an arbitrary flag. If, for example, the compiler being used has not implemented the manipulator `uppercase`, we can instead write

```
os << setiosflags(ios::uppercase);
```

Manipulators can also be used to change the values in Table 11.6. These manipulators are shown in Table 11.8, where a number of output manipulators of a more general kind have also been included.

Note that after every output of the form `os<<x` the value `ios::width` is automatically set to zero. (The only exception occurs when `x` has type **`char`**. Then `ios::width` is not set to zero.) This means that if we want to have a certain number of output positions, the manipulator `width(n)` must be repeated for every set of output data.

Table 11.8 Manipulators for formatted output.

Manipulator	**Effect**
`setw(n)`	Sets value `ios::width` to `n`.
`setfill(c)`	Sets value `ios::fill` to the character `c`.
`setprecision(n)`	Sets value `ios::precision` to `n`.
`setbase(n)`	`setbase(10)` same as manipulator `dec`. `setbase(8)` same as manipulator `oct`. `setbase(16)` same as manipulator `hex`.
`flush`	Empties the output buffer: that is, unwritten characters in the output buffer are written out.
`endl`	Inserts an end-of-line character in the stream, then calls `flush`.
`ends`	Inserts a zero character in the stream.

The manipulator `flush` may need some commentary. When we feed out characters to a stream, they land in a buffer. If the stream is for instance connected to a file or standard output, we cannot be certain that the actual output will take place at the same time as the program feeds out characters into the stream. In the interests of efficiency the output characters are collected into a buffer, and then written out later, all together. Normally we would not pay much attention to this, but sometimes it can be difficult to find the error when a program is prematurely terminated, for we cannot be sure that the buffer is empty. There may be unwritten characters still in it. If test output has been inserted in different parts of the program and one of these is not seen at the terminal, it need not necessarily mean that the program has not executed the statement that generates the output.

Earlier we saw several examples of the use of manipulators for editing output, so we shall not go further into detail here. Instead, it will be left to the reader as an exercise to experiment with the various manipulators.

11.3.2 Unformatted output

We carry out unformatted output with special member functions in class `ostream`. These functions are shown in Table 11.9. All the functions in the table give as return value a reference to the actual stream.

The call `os.put(c)` has the same effect as if we write `os<<c`. We discussed the effect of function `flush` above in connection with the manipulator `flush`. We shall be showing examples of how function `write` works later when we look at binary files.

Table 11.9 Member functions for unformatted output.

Function	Description
`put(c)`	Writes the character `c` to the stream.
`write(s, n)`	Writes `n` characters to the stream from the character array that `s` points to.
`flush()`	Empties the output buffer: that is, unwritten characters in the output buffer are written out.

11.4 Connecting files to streams

The variables used in a program are to be found in the primary memory of the computer, and exist only as long as the program is being executed. We have to be able to store data permanently for many programs, however. To do this we must use a secondary memory (most often a disc). Data in a secondary memory is stored in the form of *files*. A file is an arbitrarily long sequence of bytes that normally contain characters coded according to the ASCII code, or some other code. A file that contains such characters is called a *text file*. But files can exist that do not contain ASCII characters, for instance those that contain executable programs. Such files are usually called *binary files*.

A text file has a *line structure*. We can suppose that it consists of a number of lines, where each line can have an arbitrary number of characters and is terminated with a *line terminator*. The physical make-up of a line terminator can be one or more ASCII characters, but operating systems differ here. For instance, Unix normally uses a single character, LF (or 'line feed', ASCII code 10), whereas MS-DOS uses two characters, CR ('carriage return', ASCII code 13) and LF. When a C++ program reads a text file, the line terminator is automatically converted to a single end-of-line character, which is normally indicated by '`\n`' in the program. The converse also applies. When an end-of-line character is written out to a text file it is automatically converted to the character, or set of characters, that constitutes the line terminator in the text file. In MS-DOS, for instance, the end-of-line character is converted to the two characters CR and LF when output to a text file occurs.

There is no line structure in a binary file. The file consists only of a sequence of bytes that can contain any data. When binary files are read and written, therefore, there is no data conversion at all. Every byte is read or written exactly as it is.

How does the program know whether a file is a text file or a binary file? The answer is that the program must be told when the file is opened. We shall see examples of this later. If nothing in particular is indicated, it is assumed that the file is a text file.

All the programs we have studied up to now have been read from the stream `cin` and written in the stream `cout`. This means that in most cases input has come from the keyboard and output has been to a text window at the terminal. Now we shall look at how streams can be connected to files. This is essentially a very simple matter. We use the two classes `ifstream` and `ofstream`. If we want to read from a file we declare an object of class `ifstream`, and if we want to write to a file we declare an object of class `ofstream`. If we want to both read and write a file we use an object of class `fstream`. This is discussed in section 11.6. We begin by showing a program that reads a text file with the name `my_file.txt` and writes out the contents of the file at the terminal. Finally, the program writes out the number of lines in the file.

```
#include <iostream>
#include <fstream>
using namespace std;
main()
{
   int n=0;
   char c;
   ifstream f1("my_file.txt");
```

```
    while (f1.get(c))
    {
      cout.put(c);
      if (c == '\n')
        n++;
    }
    cout << endl << "The file consists of " << n
         << " lines" << endl;
}
```

In the line

```
ifstream f1("my_file.txt");
```

the variable `f1` is declared as a stream of class `ifstream`. We can indicate a text string as parameter of the constructor, as we have done here. The constructor will understand this as being the name of a file, and so when the object `f1` is initialized, the constructor will automatically link the corresponding file to stream `f1`. When a file is connected to a stream we say that the file has been *opened*. We can also declare a stream without connecting it to a file, in which case a default constructor is used for the stream. The member function `open` can later be used to open a file and link it to the stream. We also could have written, therefore,

```
ifstream f1;
...
f1.open("my_file.txt");
```

When the name of a file is indicated, either a short file name can be given, as here, or the file's complete name can be given to the file system. For example, the name `c:\own\diverse\my_file.txt`, or something similar, could be given. If a short name is given, the file must exist in the actual file folder where the program is run.

When a stream has been declared and connected to a file, we can handle it exactly as we have handled streams before. Since class `ifstream` is a subclass of class `istream`, it inherits all the members from class `istream`, and these can be used directly for its own objects. In our program, for instance, we use the member function `get` (see Table 11.4).

When the connection between a file and a stream is cancelled, the file is said to be *closed*. To close a file, the member function `close` can be used. We could have inserted the following call at the end of the program above:

```
f1.close();
```

But we do not generally need to close our files explicitly, since classes `ifstream` and `ofstream` have destructors that automatically call function `close`. This means that, as soon as a stream of one of these classes ceases to exist in the program, the file connected to the stream is closed. In our program, for instance, the destructor for `f1` is called when the program is coming to an end, and the file `my_file.txt` will be closed then.

In the next example we demonstrate that it is just as easy to write to files as it is to read from them. We shall look at a program that copies file `my_file.txt` to a new file with the name `new_file.txt`. In the program the new file is connected to an object `f2` of class `ofstream`. When the copying is finished, the program writes a text at the terminal giving the number of lines that have been copied:

```
#include <iostream>
#include <fstream>
using namespace std;
main()
{
  int n=0;
  char c;
  ifstream f1("my_file.txt");
  ofstream f2("new_file.txt");
  while (f1.get(c))
  {
    f2.put(c);
    if (c == '\n')
      n++;
  }
  cout << endl << n << " lines copied" << endl;
}
```

This program is not really very useful since it can only copy `my_file.txt` and create the copy `new_file.txt`. For the program to be more useful, it must be able to copy any one file to any other file. This is not difficult to do. We simply let the program read the file's name at execution. Let us then make a new version (the output containing the number of lines that have been copied has been removed):

```
#include <iostream>
#include <fstream>
#include <iomanip>
#include <cstdlib>
using namespace std;
main()
{
  char c;
  char name[100];
  cout << "Which file should be copied? ";
  cin >> setw(100) >> name;
  ifstream f1(name);
  if (! f1)
```

```
  {
    cout << "The file cannot be opened";
    exit(EXIT_FAILURE);
  }
  cout << "Name of the copy? ";
  cin >> setw(100) >> name;
  ofstream f2(name);
  if (! f2)
  {
    cout << "The file cannot be created";
    exit(EXIT_FAILURE);
  }
  while (f1.get(c))
    f2.put(c);
}
```

The problem is that when the user is allowed to indicate the file name, an incorrect file name can be given. If it is a file that must be read, it should exist first, among other things. Therefore, when we have tried to open a file, we should always check to see whether this has been successful or not. If the procedure has miscarried, either in the constructor or in the function `open`, the flag `failbit` will be set for the stream. We can check to see whether it has not been set. A simple way to do this is to use the operator `!` in the actual stream (see Table 11.2.). In our program the expression `!f1`, for example, will give the value **`true`** if opening the file to be copied has miscarried. If any of the files in the program cannot be opened an appropriate error message is given and, as a result, the program is terminated. To terminate a program ourselves, we can use the standard function `exit`. The function `exit` should have an integer as parameter. The value `0` means that the program has been successful, and it is then terminated in the usual way. Other values will mean that the program has miscarried. We can use one of the two predefined constants `EXIT_SUCCESS` and `EXIT_FAILURE` as parameter for `exit` to indicate whether or not the program has been successful. These constants, and the function `exit`, are declared in the header file `cstdlib`.

An alternative to using the operator `!` to check whether a file was opened is to call the member function `is_open`. This returns a value of type **`bool`**. For example, the expression `f1.is_open()` returns the value **`true`** if `f1` is open.

Every stream has an internal *buffer* where the data belonging to the stream is placed. There should be a *file buffer* for every object, and this applies especially to classes `ifstream` and `ofstream`. Characters that are read from a file or to a file will land in the file buffer. In the standard classes for input and output there are several functions that make it possible to handle data directly in a buffer but, as luck would have it, we normally do not need to use these. We can manage very well with the functions for formatted and unformatted in- and output that we demonstrated earlier. We shall only mention here a very useful and efficient operation that involves using a file buffer. This is when we want to copy a whole stream (file) to another one. In order to have access to a file buffer, we use the member function `rdbuf`, which returns a pointer to the buffer. The call `f1.rdbuf()` gives as result, for example, a pointer to the file buffer belonging to stream `f1`. The output operator `<<` is defined, as we saw, for all the standard types. But there is also a version where the right operand is a pointer to a file buffer. When we call this version, the whole buffer will be written out. This means, for instance, that we can make the statement

```
cout << f1.rdbuf();
```

We then get the output of the whole file `f1` written at the terminal. If instead we want to copy to another file, we can write, for example,

```
f2 << f1.rdbuf();
```

The *entire* file that `f1` is connected to is copied to the file that `f2` is connected to. This has exactly the same effect as writing

```
while (f1.get(c))
  f2.put(c);
```

but it is simpler and more efficient; besides, there is less risk of faulty programming.

When we open a file, we can indicate what properties the file should have. There are a number of flags defined in the base class `ios`, and these are shown in Table 11.10.

File flags can be indicated as an extra parameter when a constructor or the member function `open` is called. For instance, we could have written in the program above

```
ostream f2(name, ios::app);
```

Table 11.10 File flags in class `ios`.

Flag	Property
`in`	It should be possible to read from the file. The file should exist.
`out`	It should be possible to write in the file. If the file does not exist, a new file should be created. If the file exists earlier, it should be overwritten.[a]
`app`	It should be possible to write in the file. If the file does not exist, a new file should be created. If the file exists earlier, output data should be added at the end.
`trunc`	If the file exists earlier, it should be overwritten.
`ate`	Move to the end of the file directly when the file has been opened.
`binary`	The file will be handled as a binary file.

[a] This is not quite clear in the standard but in practice it works like this.

Table 11.11 Combination of file flags.

Combination	Property
`in|out`	It should be possible to update the file (both reading and writing). The file should exist.
`in|out|trunc`	It should be possible to both read and write the file. If the file does not exist, a new file should be created. If the file exists earlier, it should be overwritten.
`in|out|app`	It should be possible to both read and write the file. If the file does not exist, a new file should be created. If the file exists, all updating should be done at the end of it.
`out|trunc`	It should be possible to write in the file. If the file does not exist, a new file should be created. If the file exists earlier, it should be overwritten.

If the file had then existed before, it would not have been overwritten. Instead, new output data would have been added at the end.

If an extra parameter for a constructor or the function `open` is not indicated, the default value `ios::in` will apply for streams of class `istream`, and the default value `ios::out` for streams of class `ostream`. Several of the flags listed in Table 11.10 can be combined. A vertical line is then typed between the flags. If, for instance, we want to open a binary file that can be both read and written, we can write

```
f.open(name, ios::in|ios::out|ios::binary);
```

In Table 11.11 we show some combinations together with the properties that are involved. The flag `binary` can be added here, if a procedure involves a binary file. Clearly, files can be both read and written, but for this to be useful we generally have to work with files that allow direct access.

We shall now demonstrate how text files can be used to build data registers of different kinds. As an example, we shall be working with a file that contains names and telephone numbers according to the following model:

```
Anderson Lisa 0181-712-3456
Browning Neil 01362-123456
Conway Ben 0116-889-9889
```

For each person there are three pieces of information: last name, first name, and telephone number. It is an easy matter to construct a file of this sort with an ordinary text editor, but for practice we shall look at a program that generates such a file. The program should let the user write information for an arbitrary number of persons,

Opening and closing files

Declare a stream object for each file. Use class `ifstream` for files that will be read and class `ofstream` for files that will be written.

```
ifstream f(file_name, mode);
```

where *`file_name`* is a text string and *`mode`* an expression of the form

```
ios::file flag|ios::file flag|etc.
```

Alternatively, use a default constructor and call `open` later:

```
ifstream f;
...
f.open(file_name, mode);
```

A file is closed automatically when the destructor of the stream object is called. Can also be closed by an explicit call of `close`:

```
f.close();
```

and this information should be kept in the file. We shall assume that the file with the telephone number is called `telephone.txt`. If the file already exists, the new information will be written at the end of it. So as not to destroy an existing file, we indicate the file flag `ios::app` when the file is opened. The program will finish by writing out the file `telephone.txt` at the terminal. Here we make use of the technique of writing out the file buffer directly. Before the file `telephone.txt` can be read and written out at the terminal, it must be closed:

```
#include <iostream>
#include <fstream>
#include <string>
using namespace std;
main()
{
  ofstream fout("telephone.txt", ios::app);
  string ln, fn, tel;
  cout << "Give last name, first name and tel. no. "
       << "Terminate with Ctrl-Z" << endl;
  while (cin >> ln && cin >> fn && cin >> tel)
    fout << ln << ' ' << fn << ' ' << tel << endl;
  fout.close();
  // Write out contents of the file
  ifstream fin("telephone.txt", ios::in);
  cout << "Telephone list:" << endl;
  cout << fin.rdbuf();
}
```

Our next step is now to look at how we change data inside a file, and as an example we use one containing telephone numbers. We shall write a program that makes it possible to change a telephone number for one of the persons in the file. If we want to change the contents of a file, there are two ways of doing it. One is to use direct access, which enables us to change certain characters. (We shall be looking at how this is done later.) The problem with this method is that it is complicated to insert new characters or remove them, and we are usually able to simply *exchange* characters. This will not work in our example. When a telephone number is changed, there is of course no guarantee that the new number will have as many digits as the old one. We shall therefore use the second method, which involves copying to a temporary file. The program has two stages. In the first, file `telephone.txt` is read and a copy is written to file `tempfile`. If during the copying process the given person is found, the new telephone number is placed in file `tempfile`. In the second stage of the program, file `tempfile` is copied back to file `telephone.txt`. The program has the following appearance:

```
#include <iostream>
#include <fstream>
#include <string>
#include <cstdio>
using namespace std;
main()
{
  string ln1, fn1, tel1;
  string ln2, fn2, tel2;
  bool found = false;
  cout << "Give last name, first name and new te. no. "
       << "for the person who will be changed" <<endl;
  cin >> ln1 >> fn1 >> tel1;
  {
    ifstream fin("telephone.txt");
    ofstream fout("tempfile");
    while (fin >> ln2 && fin >> fn2 && fin >> tel2)
    {
      fout << ln2 << ' ' << fn2 << ' ';
      if (ln1 == ln2 && fn1 == fn2)
      {
        found = true;
        fout << tel1 << endl;  // write new tel. no.
      }
      else
        fout << tel2 << endl;
    }
  } // fin and fout are closed automatically
  if (found)
  { // Copy tempfile to telephone.txt
    ifstream f1("tempfile");
```

```
        ofstream f2("telephone.txt");
        f2 << f1.rdbuf();
    }
    else
        cout << "The person is not there" << endl;
    remove("tempfile");
}
```

Note that after the first stage files `telephone.txt` and `tempfile` will be closed, since the declarations of `fin` and `fout` lie in an internal block in `main`. The file `tempfile` created in the program will be a temporary file. This means that the program should 'clean up' after itself, removing this file from the file system. To do this, we use the standard function `remove`, which is declared in the header file `cstdio`. File `cstdio` contains declarations of the functions that are included in the C standard library for reading and writing. These functions should not normally be used at the same time as the C++ standard library functions, but it is all right to use function `remove`. Another useful function in `cstdio` is the function `rename`, which changes the name of a file. This function has the declaration

```
rename(const char *oldname, const char *newname);
```

In our program we have given the temporary file the name `tempfile`, but there is a certain risk involved. Suppose that we run the program in a file folder where there is already a file with the name `tempfile` and that this file, in spite of its name, contains important information. Our program will destroy this file. To avoid the risk of destroying an existing file, we can use the function `tmpnam`. This is declared in `cstdio` and returns a pointer to a text string containing a file name guaranteed to be unique. Thus we could insert the following declaration into the program:

```
char *tname = tmpnam(0);
```

We must then change the program so that `tname` will replace `tempfile` everywhere in it:

```
ofstream fout(tname);
...
ifstream f1(tname);
...
remove(tname);
```

11.5 File names as arguments to `main`

In traditional command-oriented operating systems such as Unix and MS-DOS a program is started by writing a command line. (This can also be done in a windows-oriented system such as Windows. You simply open an MS-DOS window that simulates a simple terminal.) In a command line, we first give the name of the program, and then what usually follow are the names of the arguments for the program. The arguments are normally names of files, but we can also have other kinds of argument such as flags of different kinds. The program and the different arguments are usually separated by blank characters. For instance, if we write the following command line:

```
> demo -x /r fill
```

it means that the program called `demo` will be run and that it will have the three arguments `-x`, `/r` and `fill`.

How do these arguments get into function `main` then? Up to now we have said that function `main` does not have parameters, but this is not really true. In fact `main` has two parameters, usually called `argc` and `argv`. (Certain C++ compilers, the Borland compiler for instance, can have additional parameters, but these are not standardized.) The first line in function `main` can therefore be written

```
main(int argc, char *argv[])
...
```

The first parameter, `argc`, is an integer that gives the number of arguments written in the command line. The program name is also counted as an argument. When the program `demo` is started by the command line above, for example, the parameter `argc` will have a value of `4`. The other parameter, `argv`, is an array where each element in the array is a pointer to a text string. The array `argv` contains `argc+1` elements. When `main` starts, `argv[0]` contains a pointer to a text string with the program name, `argv[1]` contains a pointer to a text string with the first parameter in the command line, `argv[2]` contains a pointer to a text string with the second parameter and so on. The last element, `argv[argc]`, contains a value of `0` – that is, a null pointer. An illustration of the program `demo` when it has been called by the command line is given in Figure 11.2.

We assume now that the following program has been compiled and that the executable program has been stored in the file `demo`:

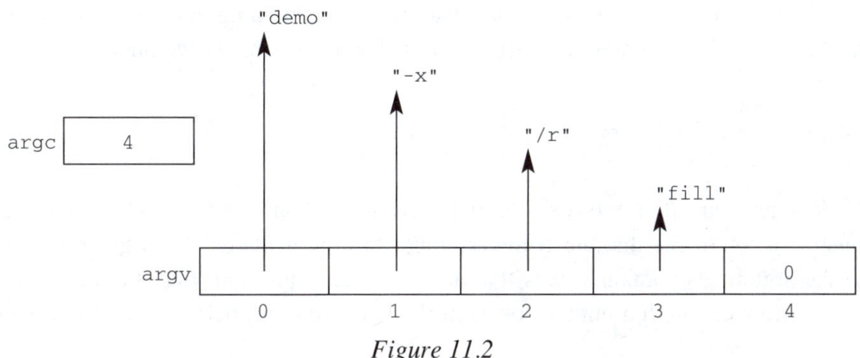

Figure 11.2

```
// The program demo
#include <iostream>
using namespace std;
main(int argc, char *argv[])
{
   cout << "program name: " << argv[0] << endl;
   for (int i=1; i<argc; i++)
      cout << "Argument " << i << ": "
            << argv[i] << endl;
}
```

First the program writes its own name and then all the parameters given in the command line when the program was started. If the program is called with the command line above it will write out

```
Program name: demo
Argument 1: -x
Argument 2: /r
Argument 3: fill
```

(Note that some compilers give the complete file name, for example `c:\own\demo.exe`.) It is common to indicate the file name as argument in the command line. Most of the standard commands in MS-DOS and Unix have file names as arguments, for example. We shall demonstrate such a program below.

We often prefer to write a tabulator character instead of several blank characters when using a text editor, but this often causes problems when we want to edit the file in another program. The program we are going to write will read a text file that contains tab characters. The text file will be copied to a new file, and all the tab characters will be replaced by a number of blank characters. The name of the file to be read and the name of the new file will be given as arguments in the command line. If we want to, we can also include in the command line, by way of a final argument, the number of blank characters that will replace each tab character in the new file. If this final argument is not given, the program will assume that every tab stop is to be replaced by three blank characters. Let us suppose that the executable program has been stored in the file `tab`. The program can then be started with one of the command lines, for instance:

```
> tab my_file.txt new_file.txt
> tab report report2 4
```

When a program that gets its arguments from the command line is written, care must be taken to see that the correct number of arguments has been given and that all the arguments contain values that are allowed. A program like this is therefore often introduced with a number of controls. Our program, below, is an example of this:

```
// The program tab
#include <iostream>
#include <fstream>
#include <cstdlib>
#include <cstring>
using namespace std;
main(int argc, char *argv[])
{
  if (argc<3 || argc>4)
  {
    cerr <<"Incorrect number of arguments" << endl;
    exit(EXIT_FAILURE);
  }
  ifstream fin(argv[1]);   // Try to open the in file
  if (!fin)
  {
    cerr << "Cannot open the file " << argv[1] << endl;
    exit(EXIT_FAILURE);
  }
  ofstream fout(argv[2]);   // Try to open the out file
  if (!fout)
  {
    cerr << "Cannot create file " << argv[2] << endl;
    exit(EXIT_FAILURE);
  }
  int n = 3;
  if (argc == 4)
    if (strlen(argv[3])==1 &&
        argv[3][0]>='0' && argv[3][0]<='9')
      n = argv[3][0]-'0';
    else
    {
      cerr << "Incorrect last argument" << endl;
      exit(EXIT_FAILURE);
    }
  char blank[] = "  ";
  blank[n] = '\0';
  char c;
  while (fin.get(c))
    if (c == '\t')
      fout << blank;
    else
      fout << c;
}
```

First the program checks that the correct number of arguments has been given. Since the program name is also counted, the counter `argc` must have a value of `3` or `4`. The program then tries to declare, each one in turn, the streams that are connected to the in file and the out file. The file names are taken from `argv[1]` and `argv[2]`.

The variable n indicates how many blank characters are to replace each tab character, and it is initialized to 3. The program then checks to see whether a final argument, argv[3], has been indicated. If so, the argument must be a text consisting of a single character (element number 0 in the text string argv[3]), and this character must be a digit. (Only values in the interval 0-9 are allowed.) If the last argument has been indicated and is correct, the variable n is changed. The character array blank is initialized with a text string consisting of nine blank characters, and the program inserts a null character in element number n. From now on, therefore, blank will be taken to be a text string consisting of n blank characters.

The final part of the program is simple. Here the in file is read character by character, and every time a tab character is encountered the text string blank is written to the out file instead.

11.6 Direct access

Up to now we have read and written all our files in a sequence, from beginning to end. Classes istream and ostream, however, contain resources that make it possible to move back and forth in a file, almost in the same way as can be done when indexing in an array is carried out. We usually say that we have *direct access* to a file. When we read or write a file, the system automatically monitors an *actual position* in the file. (This really applies to all streams, not only to those connected to files. But it is most useful for files.) The actual position marks the place in the file from which the next character will be read, or to which the next character will be written. The actual position is an integer of type streampos. (This type is automatically declared when we include the file iostream. Type streampos is the same as one of the standard types, **long int** for instance.) Numbering always takes place from 0, so that position number 0 means the file's first byte. When a file is opened, the actual position is automatically set to 0. When we read or write from a file, the actual position is automatically moved forward so that it points to the next position waiting to be read or written.

There are two operations that can be performed when we work with direct access: *tell* and *seek*. We use *tell* to read the actual position and *seek* to change the actual position. There are six different functions that can be used. These are summarized in Table 11.12. There are, as we can see, two sets of functions, one for instreams and one for outstreams (g stands for 'get' and p for 'put'). When we want to move the actual position in a file, either we can do it absolutely by calling the operation *seek* with an integer of type streampos as parameter, or we can perform a relative shift (forwards or backwards) with respect to the file's beginning, its end, or the actual position.

We now show a program that demonstrates how the functions in Table 11.12 can be used:

Table 11.12 Member functions for direct access in files.

Function	Effect
`is.tellg()` `os.tellp()`	Gives actual position in instream `is` and outstream `os`. Result is of type `streampos`.
`is.seekg(pos)` `os.seekp(pos)`	Sets actual position in instream `is` and outstream `os` to `pos` (`pos` should be a non-negative integer of type `streampos`).
`is.seekg(off, dir)` `os.seekp(off, dir)`	Moves actual position in instream `is` and outstream `os` to the point that `dir` indicates, plus `off` positions. `off` should be an integer (possibly negative). `dir` should be one of: – `ios::beg` (beginning of file), – `ios::end` (end of file), – `ios::cur` (actual position in file).

```
#include <iostream>
#include <fstream>
using namespace std;
main()
{
  ofstream fout("testfile.txt");
  fout << "First line" << endl;
  fout << "Line 2" << endl;
  fout.seekp(0, ios::beg);
  fout << "XY";
  fout.seekp(4, ios::cur);
  fout << 'Z';
  streampos pos = fout.tellp();
  fout.seekp(0, ios::end);
  fout << "The last line" << endl;
  fout.seekp(pos);
  fout << 'W';
  fout.close();
  // Print out the file
  ifstream fin("testfile.txt");
  char c;
  while (fin.get(c))
    cout << c;
  // Print out the end of the file again
  fin.clear();  // NB! Is necessary
  fin.seekg(-8, ios::end);
  while (fin.get(c))
    cout << c;
}
```

First the program writes out the two lines

```
First line
Line 2
```

to a new file with the name `testfile.txt`, then it goes back to the beginning of the file and writes out the two characters `XY`, which will overwrite the characters `Fi`. The current position after this is the third character in the first line. The program then moves four characters forward. The new current position is the one containing the character `L`, and the program overwrites this with the character `Z`. The current position is then read (this points at the character `i`) and saved in the variable `pos`. The program then moves to the end of the file and finally prints out a third line, after which it returns to the position saved in the variable `pos` and writes the character `W` there. (Thus the character `i` will be overwritten.)

The file `testfile.txt` is closed and then reopened for reading. First the whole file is printed on the screen. After that the program goes back eight characters from the end and prints these characters once more. The output is

```
XYrst ZWne
Line 2
The last line
t line
```

Note that it is important to call the function `clear` after reading the whole file for the first time. When we come to the end of the file, the flag `eofbit` is set. We shall not be able to read from the file again until this flag has been cleared. In the last line of the printout above we can see only six characters although the program went back eight positions. This is because this program has been test run on a PC where the line terminator consists of two characters `CR` plus `LF`. These two characters come last in the file.

Up to now we have shown files that we either read from or write to. (To be able to read a file that we wrote earlier, we had to close it first and then open it again.) When we use direct access, it is often necessary to have files that can be both read from and written to, and for this to be possible two conditions must be satisfied. First, the file must be opened with file flags that allow us to both read and write (see Table 11.11) and, second, there must be member functions for both reading and writing, for the stream connected to the file. The stream in question cannot be of class `ifstream`, because this only has resources for reading, nor can it be of class `ofstream`, as this only has member functions for writing. Instead we can use the class `fstream`, which is a combination of the two streams. Class `fstream` thus contains member functions for both reading and writing.

Here is a simple example that demonstrates how the class `fstream` can be used:

```
#include <iostream>
#include <fstream>
#include <cstring>
using namespace std;
main()
{
  fstream f("testfile.txt",
    ios::in|ios::out|ios::trunc);
  // Write two lines to the file
  f << "This is line no 1" << endl;
  int pos2=f.tellp(); // Line 2 begins here
  f << "Line number 2" << endl;
  // Write out the file
  f.seekp(0);
  char s[100];
  while (f.getline(s, 100))
    cout << s << endl;
  f.clear(); // NB! Necessary after end-of-file
  // Change the first word to stars
  f.seekp(0);
  f >> s;
  f.seekp(0);
  for (int i=1; i<=strlen(s); i++)
    f.put('*');
  // Write an X in the middle of the second line
  f.seekp(pos2);
  f.getline(s, 100);
  f.seekp(pos2+strlen(s)/2);
  f << 'X';
  // Write out the file
  f.seekp(0);
  cout << f.rdbuf();
}
```

The program creates a new file with the name `testfile.txt`. In the first stage, two lines are written to the file, and the file's contents are written out at the terminal. In connection with this, we use the variable `pos2` to mark the position where line 2 begins. In the second stage, two changes are made in the file. The file's first word is replaced by stars, and the character in the middle of the second line is changed to an `X`. After this the file's contents are written out again. The program's output will be

```
This is line no 1
Line number 2
**** is line no 1
Line nXmber 2
```

In the program two different ways of writing out the file are shown: by reading and writing a line at a time and by writing out the file buffer directly. Note that when a line is read at a time, the flag `eofbit` is set when end-of-file occurs. We have to call `clear` before we can carry on working with the file.

When we work with streams of class `fstream`, where reading may alternate with writing, we cannot always assume that shifts relative to the actual position will work. It is therefore best to do as in this example, by indicating absolute file positions.

We shall now look at an example that is perhaps a little more useful. It is very common to use binary files to store databases of various kinds. An example of such a program is a booking program that monitors the number of reserved places at hotels and concerts, for instance. Another example is a stores management program that monitors how many articles of a particular sort there are in stock. This type of program is characterized by the storage of *entries* in a binary file. The file will contain a number of entries of the same kind. An entry is a collection of data that belongs together. An entry can, for instance, relate to a particular room in a hotel, or a certain article in a stock program. The entries are stored in binary form in the file, which means that *no* conversion to ASCII characters will occur. The entries in the file will have exactly the same appearance as entries in the primary memory. This means in particular that numeric data is stored in the same way as integer types or floating-point number types. When entries are read and written from and to a file, a *whole entry* is transferred at a time. Thus the individual components of an entry are not read and written one at a time.

Naturally, we define entries in C++ with the help of classes. Classes that define entries must, however, be very simple. They can contain only pure data. They cannot contain pointers or references since it is pointless to store primary memory addresses in a file. (If the file was read at a later stage by the program that wrote it, or some other program, the program would no doubt be loaded into a different place in the primary memory.) In addition, classes that define entries cannot contain extra, hidden information. This means that they cannot have virtual functions or base classes. The following simple classes are used to define a bank account:

```
class Person {
public:
   char name[20];
   char address[30];
};
class Account_Entry {
public:
   long int account_no;
   double balance;
   Person account_holder;
};
```

An `Account_Entry` has three data members, all of them public. An entry contains an account number, a balance and an account holder.

Class Account_Entry contains only pure data. There are no pointers or references or hidden information. Note that it would have been an error to use type **char** * in class Person. If we had written, for instance,

```
char *name;   // ERROR!
```

The component name would have been a pointer to a text string found somewhere else. By declaring the components name and address as character arrays with given lengths, the text strings themselves will be in the entry.

We shall now look at a program that monitors bank accounts. We suppose that there is a binary file with the name accounts that contains entries of class Account_Entry. The file is sorted so that the entries are in account number order. We can imagine the program being run by an employee at a bank. Every time there is a new customer, the program will ask for an account number. It then searches for the entry in the file that contains the given account number. After this, the program will ask for an amount. A positive amount means a deposit and a negative one means a withdrawal. The program then performs the given transaction and updates the account entry in the file.

The entries in the file are numbered from 0 upwards. Since all the entries have the same length, we can calculate the starting position in the file for a given entry by multiplying the entry number by the size of the entry. A binary search is used to search for a particular entry in the file (see the discussion on page 116). We can calculate the number of entries in the file by moving to the end of the file, reading the position, then dividing this by the size of the file.

A variable with the name entry of type Account_Entry is declared in the program, and this is used when we want to read and write entries to the file. A whole entry is read or written at a time, using the member functions read and write. These will have, as a first argument, a pointer to a character array that will be read to, or written from. A pointer to the variable entry will be this argument in the program. This pointer must be converted to type **char** * to get the right type. We give the program below. The file banktype.h in the program contains the definition of classes Account_Entry and Person.

```
#include <iostream>
#include <fstream>
#include <iomanip>
#include "banktype.h"
using namespace std;
main()
{
  fstream f("account",
            ios::in|ios::out|ios::binary);
  while(true)
  {
```

```
      cout << "Account_num? ";
      long int searched;
      if (! (cin>>searched))
        break;
      Account_Entry entry;
      const int entry_size = sizeof (Account_Entry);
      // Binary search
      bool found = false;
      f.seekp(0, ios::end);
      long int entry_no, first=0,
               last=f.tellp()/entry_size-1;
      while (! found && first <= last)
      {
        entry_no = (first+last)/2;;
        f.seekp(entry_no*entry_size);
        f.read((char *) &entry, entry_size);
        if (searched < entry.account_no)
          last = entry_no-1;
        else if(searched > entry.account_no)
          first = entry_no+1;
        else // equal
          found = true;
      }
      if (! found)
        cout << "Incorrect account_num" << endl;
      else
      {
        cout << entry.account_holder.name << endl
             << entry.account_holder.address << endl
             << "balance: " << fixed
             << setprecision(2) << entry.balance << endl
             << "Amount? ";
        double amount;
        if (! (cin>>amount))
          break;
        if (amount<0 && entry.balance+amount<0)
          cout << "Withdrawal cannot be done" << endl;
        else
        {
          entry.balance += amount;
          f.seekp(entry_no*entry_size);
          f.write((char *)&entry, entry_size);
          cout << "New balance: " << setprecision(2)
               << entry.balance << endl;
        }
      }
    }
  }
```

11.7 Storing heterogeneous objects in files

We have now seen how binary files and direct access can be used to store entries in files efficiently. We pointed out that, for it to be possible to use this technique, the classes defining the entries had to be very simple. When we discussed inheritance we saw that there could be collections of objects from different classes but that the classes had to have a common, fundamental base class. We saw, for instance, how different kinds of vehicle could be defined by the creation of different subclasses of class `Vehicle`. Such a collection of objects is usually called a *heterogeneous* object collection as opposed to a *homogeneous* object collection, in which all the objects have the same type. This technique for storing objects in binary files, demonstrated in the previous section, presupposes that we are dealing with homogeneous object collections.

In this section we shall demonstrate a technique for the storage of heterogeneous object collections in files. It will be possible to write out objects of different types in a file and to read in the objects on a later occasion. A particular problem is that, for every object in the file, information about the class the object belongs to must be stored in the file so that it will be possible to re-create a similar object when the file comes to be read.

Suppose we should like to define a class with the name `Storable`. There will be two member functions in the class, `read` and `write`, which read and write objects in files. We can then define subclasses of class `Storable` that will inherit functions `read` and `write`. Before discussing the mechanism involved, we shall demonstrate the procedure seen from the user program's point of view. Suppose that we have defined a class `Animal` with three subclasses: `Dog`, `Horse` and `Cow`. We have defined class `Animal` as a subclass of class `Storable`. Let us look at the following program:

```
#include "storable.h"
#include "animal.h"
#include <fstream>
main()
{
  Storable *tab[100];
  tab[0] = new Dog("dachshund", "Nick");
  tab[1] = new Horse(5, "black");
  tab[2] = new Cow(5000);
  tab[3] = new Horse(7, "brown");
  tab[4] = new Cow(4000);
  tab[5] = new Dog("labrador", "Napoleon");
  ofstream f("animal_file");
  for (int i=0; i<6; i++)
    tab[i]->write(f);
};
```

The program creates six different kinds of animal object and keeps pointers to the objects in the array tab. Since all the objects are derived from class Storable, array tab has elements that are of type 'pointer to Storable'. When all the objects have been created, the program opens a new file with the name animal_file and writes out all six objects to this file. Function write, inherited from class Storable, is called to write the output.

When the program has been executed, the file animal_file will remain. Suppose now that on a later occasion we want to run another program that reads in the file and recreates the six objects. This program will look like this:

```
#include "storable.h"
#include "animal.h"
#include <fstream>
main()
{
  Storable *tab[100];
  Dog a_dog;
  Horse a_horse;
  Cow a_cow;
  a_dog.example();
  a_horse.example();
  a_cow.example();
  ifstream f("animal_file");
  int n = 0;
  while (tab[n]=read(f))
    n++;
  for (int k=0; k<n; k++)
    ((Animal *) tab[k])->info();
}
```

First, a similar table to the one in the previous program is declared. For the program to re-create the objects to be found in file animal_file, it must know what kind of object the file can contain. Therefore the program begins by giving examples of the three different objects that can occur in the file. With these examples serving as models, the program can then construct similar objects. Examples are given by calling the member function example that has been inherited from Storable.

In the next step, the file animal_file is opened for reading. The objects are read one at a time with the aid of the inherited function read. This gives as result a pointer to a newly created object of the right class. When end-of-file occurs, function read returns a null pointer. The pointers we get as a result from function read are stored in array tab.

In the last step, we run through array tab from the beginning, performing as many rounds as the number of objects read. At every round, the virtual function info is called, and this writes out information about the objects. Every animal class has its own version of function info. Function info is declared as virtual in class Animal. We must therefore do a type conversion from class 'pointer to `Storable`' to class 'pointer to `Animal`' for the compiler to find the function and produce dynamic binding. The program will write out

```
A dachshund called Nick
A black horse that is 5 years old
A cow that gives 5000 litres/year
A brown horse that is 7 years old
A cow that gives 4000 litres/year
A labrador called Napoleon
```

Thus we can store heterogeneous object collections in files in a relatively simple way by using class `Storable`. We shall now look at the mechanism behind all of this, and begin by looking at the base class `Storable`:

```
#ifndef STORABLE_H
#define STORABLE_H
#include <iostream>
#include <string>
using namespace std;
  class Storable {
  public:
  void example() const;
  void write(ostream& fout) const;
  friend Storable *read(istream& fin);
  enum {max=100};
private:
  virtual Storable *create_copy() const = 0;
  virtual void write_mem(ostream& fout) const = 0;
  virtual void read_mem (istream& fin) = 0;
  static  Storable *ex[max];
  static  int number_ex;
  static  Storable *search(const string& class_name);
};
#endif
```

The three functions that were called in the two programs above are declared in the public section. We use the member function `example` to say that the actual object will be an example of a class that can be found stored in a file. The member function `write` is called when we want to write out the actual object in a file. Function read reads data from a file, checks which class the read object is to have, and then creates, with the help of the given examples, an object of the right class. Function `read` cannot be a member function, since there is no actual object that the function can be called for. It is of course a function's job to create such an object.

In the private section of the function there are declarations of everything necessary to administrate reading and writing. First, the three pure virtual functions `create_copy`, `write_mem` and `read_mem` are declared. Because these are pure virtual functions, class

Storable will be an abstract class. It is not our intention to create objects that are 'only' of class Storable, but we do want the objects we create to belong to some subclass of Storable. All such subclasses that will not be abstract must have their own versions of the virtual functions. The function create_copy will create a new object of the same kind as the actual object. For instance, if we call this function for an object of type Dog, the function should give as result a pointer to a new object, also of class Dog. We shall not describe the other two virtual functions just yet.

Two static data members, ex and number_ex, are declared in the private section of the class. These are used to monitor the example objects that have been given, using the member function example. The fact that the two data members are static means, as we know, that they exist only in a single edition common for all objects belonging to class Storable or a subclass of it. The member number_ex is an integer that contains the number of given example objects, and the member ex is an array whose individual members are pointers to objects of class Storable. This array is used to point out the different example objects. The size of the array has been indicated with the aid of the enumeration value max, which has been given a value of 100 (see page 187). We usually use anonymous enumeration types in this way to indicate constants in classes. If we had declared a constant data member:

```
const int max;
```

every object of class Storable or one of its subclasses would have contained a copy of this constant. In addition, it would have had to have been initialized in a constructor for class Storable.

We place the definition of class Storable in a file with the name store.h, so the static data members should be defined in file store.cpp:

```
Storable *Storable::ex[Storable::max];
int Storable::number_ex = 0;
```

The third static member in class Storable is a function search that is used for finding a suitable example object among the examples in array ex. As parameter, this function gets a text string that contains the name of a class. The function checks the array ex and tries to find an object that belongs to a class with the given name. If it finds such an object, it gives as result a pointer to it; otherwise a null pointer is returned. An ordinary linear search is used, and the definition is quite simple:

```
Storable *Storable::search(const string& class_name)
{
  for (int i=0; i<number_ex; i++)
    if (typeid (*ex[i]).name() == class_name)
      return ex[i];
  return 0;
}
```

The function runs through the array `ex`. For every example object in the array, the operator **`typeid`** in combination with the function `name` is used to find out the name of the class that the example object belongs to (see section 9.6, page 325). This name is compared to the name that was given as parameter.

We can now give the definition of the member function `example`. The job of this function is to insert new example objects into array `ex`. There need not be more than one example for each class. Before the new example object is inserted into the array, it is checked to make sure that no example object of this class already exists in the array. Function `example` has the following appearance:

```
void Storable::example() const
{
  if (! search(typeid (*this).name()))
  {
  if (number_ex < max)
    ex[number_ex++] = create_copy();
  else
    cerr << "Too many examples" << endl;
  }
}
```

We could have kept a pointer to the actual object in array `ex`, in which case we would have written

```
ex[number_ex++] = this;   // Dangerous
```

This is rather dangerous, as we cannot be sure that the actual object exists throughout the time of execution. To avoid this problem with lingering pointers, we create another object of the same class as the actual object and insert a pointer to this object instead. This is done by using the virtual member function `create_copy`.

For class `Storable` it now remains to show the definitions of the member function `write` and the friend function `read`. We begin with function `write`:

```
void Storable::write(ostream& fout) const
{
  fout << typeid (*this).name() << ' ';
  write_mem(fout);
  fout << endl;
}
```

As parameter the function gets a reference to the stream that the data will be written in. Binary files are not used. Instead, the information is written in the file in text form. For every object written we begin by writing the name of the class that the object belongs to. We also use the operator **`typeid`** and function `name` here.

We now write out all the data members there are for the actual object. But there is a problem here. Class `Storable` will naturally have no knowledge of how all of its subclasses look and which data members they contain. Therefore the individual data members cannot be written in function `write`. This problem is solved, however, by requiring every class that will be storable to have its own implementation of the virtual member function `write_mem`. This member function will simply write out the individual members for the actual class. Function `write` can therefore call `write_mem` to produce output from all the data members. Finally, an end-of-line character is written. Thus every object will begin on a new line in the file. So that the file can be read later, there must be at least one white character – for example, a blank character – between the output of each data member. The implementations of the function `write_mem` must take care of this.

As an example, let us suppose that we shall write out an object of class `Horse`. A horse has (as we shall soon see) two data members: an integer that gives its age, and a string that gives the horse's colour. When function `write` is called for an object of class `Horse`, the following line can, for instance, be written to the file:

```
Horse 5 black
```

Class `Cow` has only one data member (an integer that indicates how many litres of milk the cow gives per year). If, instead, we want to write out an object of class `Cow`, the following line can therefore be written to the file:

```
Cow 5000
```

The job of function `read`, a friend function of class `Storable`, is to read a file that has been produced with function `write`. As result the function gives a pointer to a newly created object, or a null pointer if reading has miscarried. Function `read` has the following appearance:

```
Storable *read(istream& fin)
{
  char class_name[100];
  if (! (fin >> setw(100) >> class_name))
    return 0;
  Storable *lp = Storable::search(class_name);
  if (lp)
  { lp = lp->create_similar();
    lp->read_mem(fin);
  }
  return lp;
}
```

The function begins by trying to read in the class name to a text string. If this reading miscarries (end-of-file might have occurred), a null pointer is returned. Otherwise the function continues by calling the static member function `search`, to see whether there is an example object of the actual class. If such an object is found, `search` returns a pointer to it. We then call the virtual function `create_copy` and get as result a pointer to a new object of the same kind as the example object – that is, of the class given by the class name that was read from the file. The user must him or herself implement the virtual function `read_mem` for every non-abstract subclass of class `Storable`. This function reads in data to the individual members in an object of the actual class. Thus it functions like `write_mem` but the other way round. If, for example, the next line in the file has the appearance

```
Horse 5 black
```

and function `read` is called, it will create a new object of type `Horse` and fill in this object so that the horse becomes 5 years old and black.

The definition of class `Storable` is now finished. To complete our example, we now give the definitions of classes `Animal`, `Dog`, `Horse` and `Cow`. Class `Animal` is an abstract class and is intended to serve as base class for the other three classes. Since this class will be abstract, we do not need to implement the virtual functions inherited from class `Storable`.

```
#include "storable.h"
#include <string>
class Animal : public Storable {
public:
  virtual void info() = 0;
};
```

```
class Dog : public Animal {
public:
  Dog(const string& b = "", const string& n = "")
  : breed(b), name(n) {}
  void info()
  {cout << "A " << breed <<" called " << name << endl;}
private:
  string breed, name;
  virtual Storable *create_copy() const
  { return new Dog; }
  virtual void write_mem(ostream& fout) const
  { fout << breed << ' ' << name; }
  virtual void read_mem(istream& fin)
  { fin >> breed >> name; }
};
```

```
class Horse : public Animal {
public:
  Horse(int a=0, const string& c = "") : age(a), colour(c) {}
  void info()
```

```
   {cout << "A " << colour << " horse that is "
         << age << " years old" << endl;}
private:
   int age;
   string colour;
   virtual Storable *create_copy() const
   { return new Horse; }
   virtual void write_mem(ostream& fout) const
   { fout << age << ' ' << colour; }
   virtual void read_mem(istream& fin)
   { fin >> age >> colour; }
};
```

```
class Cow : public Animal {
public:
   Cow(int l=0) : milk(l) {}
   void info()
   {cout << "A cow that gives " << milk <<
            " litres/year" << endl;}
private:
   int milk;
   virtual Storable *create_copy() const
   { return new Cow; }
   virtual void write_mem(ostream& fout) const
   { fout << milk; }
   virtual void read_mem(istream& fin)
   { fin >> milk; }
};
```

11.8 Connecting `string` objects to streams

So far we have used streams to communicate with units outside the program (files, screen, keyboard). But it is actually possible to use streams internally in a program. With help of the standard classes `istringstream`, `ostringstream` and `stringstream` you can create streams that can read data from a `string` object or write data to a `string` object. Printing out and reading in are done in exactly the same way as when you use `cin` to read input from the keyboard and `cout` to print output on the screen. Using streams in this way is useful when you want to make type transformations to or from texts in a program, for instance if you have a real number given in the form of text and you want to convert it to the type **`double`**, or if you have an integer in the form of **`int`** and you want to convert it to text and edit it in some way.

The standard class `istringstream` is used when you want to read data from a `string` object, `ostringstream` is used when you want to write data and, `stringstream` when you want to be able to both read and write data to the same `string` object. These three classes all have definitions that look more or less as follows (very much simplified):

```
class stringstream : public iostream
{
  // constructors
  explicit stringstream();
  explicit stringstream(const string& s);
  // member functions
  string str() const;          // get the contents of the buffer
  void str(const string& s);   //change the contents of the buffer
}
```

In this case the class `stringstream` is shown, but the classes `istringstream` and `ostringstream` look the same, although they are subclasses of `istream` and `ostream` respectively.

In these three stream classes an internal buffer that you read from or write to is used. If you use the first constructor – that is, without parameters – when you create a stream object, then the buffer will initially be empty. This is natural when you use the stream for printing. If you use the second constructor, with a parameter `s` of the type `string`, then the buffer will be initialized to contain a *copy* of the text in `s`. It is of course natural to use this constructor when you want to read from a text. You use the two member functions called `str` in order to read or change the content of the buffer. Note that you always get a copy of the buffer when you read, and if you change the buffer then it will contain a copy of the parameter.

Here is a little program that demonstrates how you can read from a `string` object using the class `istringstream`:

```
#include <iostream>
#include <sstream>
using namespace std;
main()
{
  int i;
  double x;
  string s1("12 34.5"), s2("25 degrees Celsius"), s3, s4;
  istringstream sin(s1);  // init the buffer with a copy of s1
  sin >> i >> x;          // read 12 and 34.5
  cout << i << '_' << x << endl;
  sin.clear();  // needed because sin has reached 'end of file'
  sin.str(s2);  // change the buffer to a copy of s2
  sin >> i >> s3 >> s4;   // read the text in s2
  cout << i << '_' << s3 << '_' << s4 << endl;
}
```

The printout from the program will be

```
12_34.5
25_degrees_Celsius
```

In this case we use only a stream `sin` that first reads from a copy of the text `s1` and then from a copy of the text `s2`. The call `clear` is essential because the stream comes to 'end-of-file' after having read the whole text in the buffer.

The next example demonstrates what the printout to a `string` object looks like. In the program we use a stream `sout` of the class `ostringstream`.

```
#include <iostream>
#include <sstream>
#include <iomanip>
#include <cmath>
using namespace std;
main()
{
   ostringstream sout;                  // the buffer is empty
   sout << "C++ from the Beginning";    // write to the buffer
   string s1 = sout.str();              // copy the buffer to s1
   cout << s1 << endl;
   double x = 5, y = sin(x);
   sout.str("");                        // clear the buffer
   sout << "Result:" << endl            // write to the buffer
        << "sin(" << x << ")="
        << fixed << setprecision(3) << y;
   string s2 = sout.str();              // copy the buffer to s2
   cout << s2 << endl;
}
```

The printout from the program becomes

```
C++ from the Beginning
Result:
sin(5)=-0.959
```

As mentioned, streams can easily be used to perform type transformations to and from texts. As an example the following function `add_date` is shown, which adds a number of years to a certain date. The function has three parameters. The first is a reference to a `string` object that contains a date in the form `"yyyy-mm-dd"`, the second is a reference to a `string` object in which the result will be put, and the third is an integer that indicates how many years should be added. For instance, if you make the call `add_date ("2000-03-26", a 15)`, the function will fill in `a` so that it contains the text `"2015-03-26"`.

```
void add_date(const string& d1, string& d2, int n)
{
   stringstream s(d1);  // the buffer contains a copy of d1
   int year;
   s >> year;           // read year from the buffer
```

```
  s.seekp(0);           // reverse to the beginning of the buffer
  s << (year+n);        // write a new year
  d2 = s.str();         // copy the buffer to d2
}
```

In the function we use a stream `s` of the class `stringstream`. It is possible to both read to and write from this stream. We initialize the stream so that the buffer contains a copy of the first parameter `d1` from the start. Then we read the year from the buffer to a variable of type **int**. Because the class `stringstream` is a subclass of the class `iostream` it has inherited all the member functions that concern direct access. You can thus use the operations *tell* and *seek* that were described in section 11.6 on page 394 to examine what the actual position in the buffer is and to move the actual position. (The classes `istringstream` and `ostringstream` can also use direct access.) In the function `add_date` we have used the function `seekp` to move the actual print position back to the start of the buffer. We can then write the new year to replace the old one in the buffer.

11.9 Connecting text strings to streams

The classes `istrstream`, `ostrstream` and `strstream` can be used when you want to read or write directly to a character array. These classes are not actually included in the standard because the classes `istringstream`, `ostringstream` and `stringstream` that we discussed in the previous section can replace them. However, they are provisional and are implemented in several compilers. We therefore give a short description of them. We begin by describing input from text strings. To do this you use a stream of the class `istrstream`. There are three different constructors for this:

```
explicit istrstream(const char* s);
explicit istrstream(char* s);
istrstream(const char* s, streamsize n);
```

This presupposes that we have a character array that the parameter `s` points to. This character array will contain the data to be read to the stream. The first two constructors require that the text string that `s` points to should end with a null character. The third constructor can be used if there is a character array that does not terminate with a null character. So we shall indicate, instead, the length of the character array as second parameter of the constructor. (Type `streamsize` is an integer type, for example **long int**.) Here is a short program that demonstrates the use of class `istrstream`. Three different streams, `st1`, `st2` and `st3`, are created with the help of the three constructors. (This program is a new version of the program on page 409.)

```
#include <iostream>
#include <strstream>
#include <cstring>
using namespace std;
```

```
main()
{
   int i;
   double x;
   char txt1[10], txt2[10];
   istrstream st1("12 34.5");
   st1 >> i >> x;
   cout << i << '_' << x << endl;
   char s2[100];
   strcpy(s2, "25 degrees Celsius");
   istrstream st2(s2);
   st2 >> i >> txt1 >> txt2;
   cout << i << '_' << txt1 << '_' << txt2 << endl;
   char s3[3];
   s3[0] = '9'; s3[1] = '7'; s3[2]='5';
   istrstream st3(s3, sizeof s3);
   st3 >> i;
   cout << i << endl;
}
```

The printout from the program will be

```
12_34.5
25_degrees_Celsius
975
```

Output to text strings takes place analogously. Output to the stream will land in a character array instead of being written at the terminal or in a file. We make use of class `ostrstream`. To create a stream `ost` and connect it to a character array `s`, we write

```
ostrstream ost(s, n);
```

Here `s` will be a pointer to a character array, and `n` will be an integer that gives the length of the array. When we write to a character array, we ourselves have to place a null character at the end of the output so that the array will contain a text string. The simplest way of doing this is to use the manipulator `ends`, which functions analogously to the manipulator `endl`. The following program uses two streams `os1` and `os2`, which write to the two character arrays `s1` and `s2`, respectively:

```
#include <iostream>
#include <strstream>
#include <iomanip>
#include <cmath>
using namespace std;
main()
{
   char s1[100];
   ostrstream os1(s1, sizeof s1);
```

```
    os1 << "C++" << ends;
    cout << s1 << endl;
    char s2[100];
    ostrstream os2(s2, sizeof s2);
    double x = 5, y = sin(x);
    os2 << "The result:" << endl
        << "sin(" << x << ")="
        << fixed << setprecision(3)
        << y << endl << ends;
    cout<< s2;
    cout<< os1.pcount() << ' ' << os2.pcount() << endl;
}
```

Output from the program will then be

```
C++
The result:
sin(5)=-0.959
4 27
```

Note that output to both `s1` and `s2` terminates with `ends`. The text string `s1` does not contain an end-of-line character, and this is why `endl` has been added when `s1` is written out in `cout`. The text string `s2`, on the other hand, contains end-of-line characters after every line. Therefore there is no extra `endl` when `s2` is written to `cout`. On the last line, the member function `pcount` is called. This gives as result the number of characters that have been written in an outstream. Thus we can see how many characters have been written to `s1` and `s2`.

It should be said that for class `ostrstream` there is also a constructor without parameters. For instance, we could write

```
ostrstream os;
```

We do not have to indicate to which text string output data will be written. The stream itself will allocate sufficient memory space to hold the text that will be written. When the output data has been written, we can use the member function `str` to get a pointer to the text string that has been allocated:

```
os << 15*32 << ends;
cout << os.str() << endl;
```

This seems simple enough, but of course there is a snag. From the moment function `str` has been called the outstream becomes *frozen*, which means that nothing further can (or should) be written in it. In addition, we ourselves have to deallocate the memory space that was allocated for the output data. When we no longer need the text string, therefore, we have to give the statement

```
delete[] os.str();
```

When windows-oriented programs are written, the streams `cin` and `cout` are not used to read and write. Instead, there are special help functions for the windows system that is used. If we want to write output data, we can call, for example, a help function that produces a display window containing a text. There is usually a little button with 'OK' or some other qualifying text in it that we can click when we have read the message. This help function must know which text is to be written out, and it is usually indicated as a text string given as parameter to the help function. Reading input data works in a similar way. A help function is called, and this produces a window in which the user is expected to write input data. When the user has finished, the help function gives as result a text string that contains what has been written.

In this type of program, streams can be used to convert data that is to be written out or that has been read. We shall illustrate this with an example. Suppose that there are two help functions, `win_input` and `win_output`. (These functions have been invented for this example. In a real windows system they will have other names and parameters.) Both generate a window at the terminal. Function `win_output` gets a string as parameter and writes it out in the window. The function `win_input` has two parameters, both pointers to text strings. The first text string contains the question to be written out in the window, and the other text string is an outparameter that is filled in with the answer the user has given. In Chapter 2 we wrote a simple program that calculated how much it cost to rent a car. We can now write some program lines that do the same thing:

```
const int length = 100;
char text[length];
int day_number, daily_rate;
{
  win_input("Number of days? ", text);
  istrstream is(text, length);
  if (! (is>>day_number))
    throw data_error();
}
{
  win_input("Rate per day? ", text);
  istrstream is(text, length);
  if (! (is>>daily_rate))
    throw data_error();
}
{
  ostrstream os(text, length);
  os<< "Total cost: "
    << day_number * daily_rate << ends;
  win_output(text);
}
```

Note that we check whether reading has been successful. If it has not, an exception is generated. (We have used the class `data_error`, which was defined on page 358.) In this type of program we cannot write error messages in the streams `cout` or `cerr` since we are not dealing with text windows.

Exercises

11.1 Write a program that reads in text from the terminal and stores the text in a new text file with the name `myfile.txt`. The new file should have the same line structure as the text file written from the terminal. In addition, all the lower-case letters should be translated into upper-case letters.

11.2 A secret message is kept in the text file `secret.txt`. This has been stored not as straightforward text but in the form of a coded message so that it cannot be easily read without authorization. Each letter in the original message has been coded to another using this table:

```
code letters: guwyrmqpsaeicbnozlfhdkjxtv
original text: abcdefghijklmnopqrstuvwxyz
```

If, for example, the file contains the text '`lnybrt jgshsbq jrybrfygt rsqph oc`', the uncoded message is '`rodney waiting wednesday eight pm`'. Write a program to read the file with the secret message and write it out in plain language. The program should begin by reading in the code (the first line in the table above) from the terminal.

11.3 Write a program to read an existing text file and write out its contents at the terminal. No empty lines (containing only a line terminator) or lines containing only blanks should be written out. Otherwise the output should have the same structure as the text file. The program should be applicable to any text file; the text file's name should be read from the terminal.

11.4 A command that is often used in the Unix operating system is one called `cat`. The task here is to write your own version of this program. The program `cat` can be used to combine files, but it can also serve to write out the contents of one or more files at the terminal. The command has the form

```
cat f1 f2 f3 ...
```

Thus the program name is written followed by an arbitrary number of file names. The program writes out the files one at a time in standard output. If you wish to use the program to combine files, the standard output could be redirected. The following call, for instance, provides that `fc` will contain a copy of `fa` combined with `fb`:

```
cat fa fb > fc
```

Note that a redirection is not an argument that is sent to `main`. In this line, therefore, the program will get only `fa` and `fb` as arguments.

11.5 Suppose that the file `telephone.txt` with names and telephone numbers on page 387 is sorted in alphabetical order. Write a program that adds a new person. The program should read in a name and telephone number for the new person from the terminal and then insert this information in the correct place in the file so that it will remain sorted. Use a temporary file.

11.6 Information about a number of people has been collected in a binary file for statistical purposes. The information stored is the name, height, weight, shoe size, age and civil status for each person. In order to process the data the sex of every person has to be known, although this information is not included in the file.

Write a program that reads the file and creates two new files, one containing only women and one with only men. For every person in the file the program should ask the operator whether that person is a man or a woman.

11.7 A company has a register of its customers in the form of a binary file. There is an entry in the file for each customer, containing the customer's name and two lines of address including the postal code. Each of these three items is at most 20 characters in length. To send out information to customers, a program is required that can print self-adhesive address labels with the customers' names and addresses. A printing terminal is used loaded with special paper on which the labels are stuck contiguously, three in a row. The total width of the paper is 72 characters, so each label will be 24 characters wide. The height of each label is five lines.

Write a program that reads the file of customers and produces a text file that can later be sent to the customers. Use only the three centre lines of each label. The program should work even if the number of customers is not an exact multiple of three.

11.8 When we handle files, they are usually sorted. Some particular component among the entries, for instance a car registration number, is normally chosen to institute the sort procedure. This component is called the *sorting key*. A problem that often occurs is one where there are two sorted files with the same kind of entries and a new, sorted file has to be made containing the entries of both files. We say that the two original files have been *merged*. Write a program that merges two binary files containing entries that define cars. The sorting key is the car registration number. You may decide yourself what the other entries are to be.

11.9 A company has prepared a list of its employees' room and telephone numbers in a binary file. There is an entry for every employee, and each entry contains a name, a room number and a telephone number. The file is sorted in alphabetical order. Write a program that can insert entries for new employees, change already existing entries, or remove entries from the file. The program should repeatedly ask for the name, the room number and the telephone number of an employee. If a name not in the file is given, a new entry should be inserted in the correct place. If a name already existing in the file is given, the corresponding entry should be either changed or removed. The operator indicates that an entry is to be removed by writing a room number of 0 in the entry. The entries existing in the file but otherwise not indicated by the operator should not be changed. The program may require names to be read in alphabetical order.

11.10 Information about the status of football teams taking part in a league has been stored in a binary file so that for each team there is an entry in the file. An entry contains the team's name, the points it has, and the number of goals scored for and against. Entries in the file are in arbitrary order.

Write a program that sorts the file so that the team with most points comes first and the one with least points comes last. If several teams have the same number of points, the team with the best goal aggregate comes first. Teams with the same number of points and goal aggregate should be placed in alphabetical order. *Tip*: Read all the teams into an array, sort it, then write it out in the file.

11.11 A company has a sorted binary file `stockfile` with which all the articles in its stock are monitored. There is an entry for every kind of article, each entry containing the article designation (a code consisting of 10 characters), a definition of the article (a text of 30 characters), the number in stock and the price. Write a program that can deal with the following commands from the terminal:

`info` *`artno`*	The program writes out information stored for articles of *`artno`* type at the terminal.
`buy` *`artno n`*	The program should update the stock file with the information that *`n`* articles of *`artno`* type have been purchased and added to the stock.
`sell` *`artno n`*	The program should update the stock file with the information that *`n`* articles of *`artno`* type have been sold from the stock.

11.12 A sports club has stored a register with all its members in a file. The club handles several sports, for instance football, athletics and wrestling. So it has different kinds of information to be stored for its members, depending on which sport they take an interest in. Certain information is common to all its members (name, address, etc.). The different kinds of members can therefore be defined with the help of classes and inheritance. The register file is produced by a program that has used `Storable` in section 11.7 to be able to store heterogeneous objects. Define a class hierarchy that describes some different categories of member in the sports club. Then write a program that can be used for finding information about individual members. The program should first read the register file to an array. Then it should repeatedly ask for a member's name. If the member is in the register, appropriate information should be written out at the terminal. (Use dynamic binding.)

11.13 Develop the program in the previous exercise so that it will add new members or allow information to be changed for a given member of the club. The new data must, of course, be kept in the register file before the program is terminated.

11.14 Assume that the time of day is defined by a text string in the format '`hh.mm.ss`'. Write a function that updates a time of day by adding a certain number of seconds (which can be greater than 60). The function should have two parameters: a pointer to the text string to be updated, and an integer that indicates how many seconds should be added. *Tip*: Use the technique of connecting text strings to streams.

11.15 Write a program that reads a text from a text file and writes it out in edited form in standard output. The name of the file should be given as argument to `main`. As a second argument to `main`, the desired line size should be indicated in the output. (Use a connection to a stream to convert this argument to an integer.) Assume that the input file contains a number of words (sequences of non-white characters) with an arbitrary number of white characters between every word. In the output there should be one blank character between words. The line structure in the output should not be the same as that of the input file. Each line of the output should contain as many words as possible in the given line length, so that the lines are roughly the same length.

12 Container classes and algorithms

The latest trend in programming is the increasing use of ready-made program components. This development is also supported by the object-oriented approach. The standard for C++ includes several program libraries with ready-made classes and functions that programmers can use instead of having to construct all the software themselves. One important library contains program components to handle collections of data. Prior to the standardization of C++ this program library was not included in the distribution of the C++ compiler but was regarded as a supplement referred to as STL (*Standard Template Library*). An independent supplier of programs often supplied STL. Now STL is included in the C++ standard. The term STL is not used in the standard. However, one can still see it being used.

As we discussed in section 2.8, classes that handle containers are usually referred to as *container classes*. We have previously in the book become acquainted with a couple of container classes, the classes `vector` and `deque`. In this chapter we shall discuss the other container classes included in the standard. We shall also discuss so-called *algorithms*, which are a collection of ready-made functions that can be used to handle container classes. There are, for example, algorithms to sort containers and to search in them. Both the container classes and the algorithms use what are known as *iterators*, a kind of pointer-like object. We therefore, by way of introduction in this chapter, describe what iterators are and how they are used.

Container classes and algorithms are really quite sophisticated *generic* program components, a kind of *template* that can be used for arbitrary data types. For example, using the `vector` class, different containers can be established, containing different kinds of data. Fortunately, however, it is easy to use container classes and algorithms. To do so, you do not have to know how templates are constructed. Later in the book we go through the technique used in container classes and show examples of how they can be constructed. For the time being, however, we regard them as ready-made program components that we can use without being concerned about their internal appearance.

The container classes included in the standard can be divided into two main groups: *sequences* and *associative containers*:

- *Sequences*. Containers in which the elements contained logically are in a row. The following standard classes describe sequences:
  - `vector`;
  - `deque`;
  - `list`.

  The following *container adapters*, implemented using one of the above-mentioned sequence classes, are also regarded as sequences:
  - `queue`;
  - `priority queue`;
  - `stack`.
- *Associative containers*. Collections of data in which *search keys* are used to access the information in the collection. There are the following standard classes:
  - `set`;
  - `multiset`;
  - `map`;
  - `multimap`.

Of these classes we have already (in section 2.8 on page 65) gone through `vector` and `deque`. The remaining classes will be described in this chapter. Before doing this, however, we discuss iterators and algorithms.

12.1 Iterators

The standard classes `vector` and `deque` that we discussed in section 2.8 can to some extent be treated as regular arrays. It is, for example, possible to index in vectors. In section 5.4.3 we learned that pointers can be used to handle regular arrays, for example to run through them in an efficient way. The question is: can pointers also be used to handle vectors? The answer to this question is no. Pointers cannot be used, but *iterators* can be used instead. An iterator is an independent pointer-like variable that you connect to a certain container, for example to a vector or a list. Iterators can be used together with all the container classes in the C++ standard (with the exception of what are known as container adaptors). Iterators can also be used when you are working with the `string` class or with streams for reading and writing. To be able to use the standard libraries, it is important to be acquainted with iterators. There are three reasons for this:

- Iterators are used to run through containers.
- Many operations for containers have iterators as parameters.

- The independent utility functions, known as algorithms, that handle containers, all have iterators as parameters.

12.1.1 Running through containers with iterators

An iterator can point out an individual element in a container. You can compare this to the way a regular pointer points to a certain element in an array. When you run through the container you do this by using the iterator, in the same way as if the container was an ordinary array and the iterator was a pointer to the array. For iterators there are, for example, the operations `++` and `--`, which move forward and backward stepwise in the container, and the operator `*`, which gives the data element to which the iterator refers. If you have containers with iterators, these can then be handled in a uniform way. For example, you run through a set in the same way as a vector.

Let us take an example. In section 5.4.3 we had an array `f` with the declaration

```
float f[4];
```

If we want to assign the values `10`, `11`, `12` and `13` to the elements of the array, we can declare a pointer

```
float *p;
```

and then use it to run through the array (see Figure 5.4 on page 164):

```
int k=10;
for (float *p=f; p < f+4; p++)
  *p = k++;
```

Suppose now that, instead of an array, we use a vector `v` with the following declaration:

```
vector<double> v(4);
```

We can then declare an iterator with the name `it`:

```
vector<double>::iterator it;
```

The variable `it` has the type `vector<double>::iterator`. This type is declared inside the class `vector<double>`. This means that `it` is a kind of pointer variable with the capacity of pointing out individual elements inside a vector where the element type is **`double`**.

We have learned that to make the pointer `p` point to the first element in the array `f`, you can write `p=& f[0]` or even more simply `p=f`. You cannot do this when working with iterators. Instead, in every container, there is a function called `begin`. This returns an iterator that points to the first element in the container. Thus we can get the variable `it` to point to the first element in the vector `v` by writing

```
it=v.begin();
```

To be able to run through a container, we must also have an iterator that marks the end of the container. For this purpose we use the function `end`, which also gives an iterator as the result. This does not point, as we might expect, to the last element of the container, but to a fictitious element that lies just *outside* the container. (It is comparable to an array. Suppose, for example, that we have declared an array `f[4]`. Then the expression `f` is a pointer to the array's first element and the expression `f+4` a pointer to the first element outside the array.) We can now write a **for** statement that runs through the vector `v` and assigns the values `10`, `11`, `12` and `13` to its element (in the declaration of `v` we specified that `v` would have the length `4`):

```
int k=10;
for (it=v.begin(); it != v.end(); it++)
   *it = k++;
}
```

In the **for** statement, the variable `it` is initialized to `v.begin()`. The condition for continuing an additional round is that the iterator `it` has not become equal to `v.end()`. To step the iterator `it` forward so that it refers to the next element in the set the operator `++` is used. Inside the **for** statement, the operator `*` is used to access the data element that the iterator `it` refers to. We now see that, with the help of the iterator, we can handle a vector just as though it were an ordinary array.

We saw above that pointers can serve as constants. When, for example, we made the declaration

```
const int *pc;
```

it was possible only to *get the value of* the variable that `pc` points to. Trying to change it was prohibited. Thus, for instance, the following statement was not allowed:

```
*pc = 0;   // not allowed
```

Likewise, it is possible to declare iterators that point to constants. In this case, you use the type `const_iterator` instead of `iterator`. If, for example, we want only to print out the elements in the vector `v` without changing them, we can use such an iterator. In that case we can declare an iterator `cit` in the following way:

```
vector<double>::const_iterator cit;
```

and run it through the array with the **for** statement

```
for (cit=v.begin(); cit != v.end(); cit++)
   cout << *cit << ' ';
```

The printout will then be

```
10 11 12 13
```

The iterators that are defined in the container classes in the C++ standard all possess properties such that the operator `--` can be used to step backwards as well. For instance, we can write `it--`. If you wish to run through a container backwards it is, however, easier to use what is known as a *reverse iterator*. In all of the container classes a type is defined with the name `reverse_iterator`. We can make the declaration

```
vector<double>::reverse_iterator rit;
```

When you want to run through a container backwards, you should start with the last element in the container. To get an iterator that points to the last element you cannot, however, use the function `end` since it points to a fictitious element *outside* the container. Instead, you can use a function with the name `rbegin`. This results in a reverse iterator that points to the last element in the container. To know where to stop, we correspondingly use a function with the name `rend`, which results in a reverse iterator that points to a fictitious element outside the container, *before* the first element. To run through the vector `v` backwards and print out its element, we can give the statements

```
for (rit=v.rbegin(); rit != v.rend(); rit++)
  cout << *rit << ' ';
```

Note a small peculiarity: when you perform the operator `++` on a *reverse iterator*, it will step *backwards*. (The operator `--` will thus step forwards on a reverse iterator.)

The printout will now be

```
13 12 11 10
```

On page 161 we learned that you should use the operator `->` if you had a pointer to a variable of a class type and wished to call an operation for this variable. The same applies to iterators. If the iterator is pointing to a variable of class type and you wish to call an operation for this variable, you use the operator `->`. Study the following example, in which we have a container of type `deque` and the individual elements are of type `string` – that is, a class type. Initially, we put the names of some known programming languages into the container:

```
deque<string> d;
d.push_front("Pascal"); d.push_front("c");
d.push_front("c++");    d.push_front("Java");
```

Subsequently, we run through the whole container and examine whether any of the texts begin with a small c. For these we exchange the first letter for a capital C. We use an iterator of the type `deque<string>::iterator`. (In this example we also demonstrate how the iterator can be declared directly in the **`for`** statement.)

```
for (deque<string>::iterator j=d.begin(); j!=d.end(); j++)
{
  if (j->at(0)=='c')
    j->at(0)='C';
  cout << *j << ' ';
  }
}
```

Here the iterator `j` points out the individual `string` variables in the container. To access individual characters in the `string` variables we call the function `at`. In doing this we must use the arrow operator. Observe the difference when we print out the texts. Then we use the operator `*`, since we are not calling a function for type `string`, but wish to print out the whole `string` variable to which the iterator is pointing. The printout from these program lines is

```
Java C++ C Pascal
```

In the information window below, the operations that have to do with iterators and that are supported by all of the container types in the C++ standard as well as the standard class `string` are summarized.

Iterators

The following types are defined in all the container classes.
(*con* denotes a container type, such as vector or list, and *typ* the type of the elements.)
For the classes `vector` and `deque` the iterators are of the category *random-access iterator*, and for the other container classes of the category *bidirectional iterator*.

con::iterator<*typ*>	++ runs forwards
con::const_iterator<*typ*>	++ runs forwards, only for reading
con::reverse_iterator<*typ*>	++ runs backwards
con::const_reverse_iterator<*typ*>	++ runs backwards, only for reading

The following operations exist in all container classes as well as in the class `string`.

`begin ()`	gives an iterator that points to the first element
`end ()`	gives an iterator that points to a fictitious element *after* the last element
`rbegin ()`	gives a reverse iterator that points to the last element
`rend ()`	gives a reverse iterator that points to the element *before* the last element

The following operations exist for iterators of the category *forward iterator*.
(`i` and `j` denote iterators and `m` an arbitrary member of an object of class type)

`*i`	gives the element to which iterator `i` points (for *input iterators* only input, and for *output iterators* only output)
`i->m`	the same as `(*i).m`
`++i`	steps one step forwards (prefix, gives the new value)
`i++`	steps one step forwards (postfix, gives the old value)
`i = j`	assignment of iterator `j` to iterator `i`
`i == j`	comparison, equality (does not exist for *output iterators*)
`i != j`	comparison, inequality (does not exist for *output iterators*)
For iterators of the category *bidirectional iterators*, all the above-mentioned operations exist, as well as the following:	
`--i`	steps one step backwards (prefix, gives the new value)
`i--`	steps one step backwards (postfix, gives the old value)
For iterators of the category *random access* all the above-mentioned operations exist, as well as the following (compare with pointer arithmetics):	
`i += n`	steps the iterator forwards in `n` steps
`i -= n`	steps the iterator backwards in `n` steps
`i + n`	gives an iterator that corresponds to iterator `i` stepped forward `n` steps
`i - n`	gives an iterator that corresponds to iterator `i` stepped backward `n` steps
`i - j`	gives the distance (number of steps) between iterators `i` and `j`
`i[n]`	indexing, same as `*(i + n)`
`i < j`	checks whether iterator `i` is smaller than iterator `j` (if `j-i > 0`)
`i > j`	checks whether iterator `i` is larger than iterator `j` (if `j < i`)
`i <= j`	checks whether iterator `i` is smaller than or equal to iterator `j`
`i >= j`	checks whether iterator `i` is larger than or equal to iterator `j`

Different kinds of iterator have varying degrees of power. The most powerful are what are known as *random access* iterators. For this type of iterator you can, in addition to the operations demonstrated above, also perform pointer arithmetics, exactly as for regular pointers. You can, for example, add an integer (a number of steps) to an iterator, or index directly on an iterator. The classes `vector`, `deque` and `string` support random access iterators. The other container classes in the C++ standard (`list`, `set`, `multiset`, `map` and `multimap`) have somewhat simpler *bidirectional* iterators, with which you can step up and down, but not perform pointer arithmetic. There is also an even simpler category of iterators, known as *forward* iterators, which only permit you to step forwards. You can also work with *input* iterators, which are forward iterators that only permit reading, and *output* iterators, which are forward iterators that only permit writing. It is possible to connect input iterators and output iterators to streams, for example to `cin` and `cout`, as we shall soon demonstrate.

12.1.2 Operations with iterators as parameters

All container classes also have operations with iterators as parameters. Note that these operations are designed so as to alternatively allow arguments to be regular pointers instead of iterators.

We now give some examples. We begin by declaring an array

```
int a[] = {5, 6, 7, 8, 9, 10};
```

Now it is possible to declare a container, for example a `vector`, that is initialized through the elements in the array `a`:

```
vector<int> v(a, a+4);  // v contains {5, 6, 7, 8}
```

This version of the constructor demands two iterators (or pointers) as arguments. These arguments define the interval to be copied. Note that the second iterator points to the first element *after* what is to be included. You can also use real iterators in a constructor. We can, for example, give the declaration

```
list<int> l(v.begin(), v.end());  // l contains {5, 6, 7, 8}
```

Here we have used the standard class `list`. We have not yet examined this standard class very closely (it is dealt with in the next section). However, it operates in approximately the same way as the classes `vector` and `deque`. We have chosen to use the class `list` in these examples as it is more appropriate than `vector` and `deque` when you wish to insert or remove elements inside a sequence.

The operation `assign` exists in a form in which you give iterators (or pointers) as arguments:

```
l.assign(a, a+2);  // l contains {5, 6}
```

Below follow three different variants of the operation `insert`. All three have as their first parameter an iterator that points out the position in the container where the new element or elements are to be inserted. The first variant inserts an element in the position indicated:

```
l.insert(l.begin(), 0);  // l contains {0, 5, 6}
```

The second variant of `insert` makes it possible to insert an arbitrary number of equal elements at a certain position. If, for example, we wish to insert three ones in the second position we write

```
list<int>::iterator it = l.begin();
l.insert(++it, 3, 1);  // l contains {0, 1, 1, 1, 5, 6}
```

The third variant of `insert` has as its argument two iterators that point out the elements that are to be inserted:

```
l.insert(l.begin(), v.begin(), v.end());
// l contains {5, 6, 7, 8, 0, 1, 1, 1, 5, 6}
```

Note in the examples above that, if you copy elements from another container, this container does not have to be of the same kind as you are working with. (In the last example, for instance, we copied elements from a `vector` to a `list`.)

To remove one or more elements from a container, you can use the following forms of `erase`. The first form removes individual elements:

```
it = l.begin();
++it; ++it; ++it;
l.erase(it);   // l contains {5, 6, 7, 0, 1, 1, 1, 5, 6}
```

The second form of `erase` removes several elements. For example, to remove all the elements in list `l` except the last one, we write

```
it = l.end();
l.erase(l.begin(), --it);   // l contains {6}
```

The information window below contains a table of the operations with iterators as parameters, and which exist for sequences (that is, for the classes `list`, `vector` and `deque`).

Sequences: operations with iterators as parameters

`p` and `p2` denote iterators that point out positions in the sequence in question. `i` and `j` are two iterators that point out an interval in a container of the same element type as the sequence in question. `i` points out the first element in the interval, while the last element in the interval is pointed out by the iterator *prior* to `j`. The interval is called `[i,j)`. Alternatively, `i` and `j` can be regular pointers that point out an interval in an array.

sekv<*typ*> `s(i,j);`	Creates a sequence that is initialized by the interval `[i,j)`.
`s.assign(i,j);`	Assigns the elements in the interval `[i,j)` to `s`.
`s.insert(p,e);`	Inserts the value `e` in the position pointed out by `p`.
`s.insert(p,n,e);`	Inserts `n` copies of `e` in the position pointed out by `p`.
`s.insert(p,i,j);`	Inserts the elements in the interval `[i,j)` in the position `p`.
`s.erase(p);`	Removes the element in the position `p` from `s`.
`s.erase(p,p2);`	Removes the elements in the interval `[p,p2)` from `s`.

12.1.3 Iterators and streams

You can actually also have iterators that read and write streams. To make this possibility available, you include the file `iterator`

```
#include <iterator>
```

To read a stream you declare an iterator of the type `istream_iterator`. As usual, you state what type the elements have between the signs `<>`. In the following example we shall read a number of integers from the stream. Therefore we write `<int>`:

```
istream_iterator<int> iit(cin);
```

The iterator is given the name `iit`. To declare the iterator, you state as parameter the stream that you wish to read from. Here we read from the stream `cin`. The iterator `iit` will now point to the first integer that is inserted into the stream. To read all the integers in the stream we now step the iterator `iit` forward. For this we need an iterator that points to the end of the stream, so that we know where to stop. Such a stop iterator is obtained by making a declaration in which no stream is stated. We can, for example, write

```
istream_iterator<int> iit_end;  // marks the end of the stream
```

To put in a number of integer numbers from the stream and place them in a vector with the name `u`, we can now write the following statements:

```
vector<int> u;
while (iit != iit_end)
  u.push_back(*iit++);
```

The input is ended in the usual way when the user writes Ctrl-Z (or Ctrl-D). Now, a printout can be made in an even simpler way. First, you must declare an iterator that writes in the outstream:

```
ostream_iterator<int> oit(cout, " ");
```

We name the iterator `oit`. As parameters in the declaration you state what stream you wish to write on as well as a text that is to be printed out between every element. The printout from the vector `u` to the stream is now made through a simple call of the function `copy`, which we discussed earlier:

```
copy(u.begin(),u.end(), oit);
```

12.2 Algorithms: general characteristics

In the standard library there is a set of ready-made functions that you can use to handle containers. In the C++ standard these functions are called *algorithms*. We therefore also use this terminology, although the word algorithm really has a broader meaning (see section 1.5). In this section some examples are given, and characteristics common to the algorithms are discussed. In Appendix C on page 585 there is a complete list of all the algorithms in the C++ standard. The algorithms have been divided into different categories so as to make it easier to form a clear conception of what algorithms there are and what they do.

To gain access to the standard algorithms, you must include the file `<algorithm>`:

```
#include <algorithm>
```

In addition, library `<numeric>` contains some special algorithms of a numerical nature. We shall begin by demonstrating `copy`, which is one of the simplest algorithms. Assume that `v` is defined as before:

```
int a[] = {5, 6, 7, 8, 9, 10};
vector<int> v(a, a+4);  // v contains {5, 6, 7, 8}
```

We can now write

```
deque<int> d(6, 1);  // d contains {1, 1, 1, 1, 1, 1}
copy(v.begin(), v.end(), d.begin());
// d contains {5, 6, 7, 8, 1, 1}
```

The two first arguments to `copy` state the interval you are to copy from, and the last parameter points out the starting point in the container you are to copy to.

One characteristic common to all the algorithms is that they have two iterators, let us call them `i1` and `i2`, as first parameters. These iterators point out an interval in the container you wish to access. Just as before, `i1` points to the first element in the interval, and `i2` points to an element that lies just *outside* the interval. In the continued discussion we call such an interval `[i1,12)`. Thus the interval `[v.begin(), v.end())` denotes all the elements in the vector `v`, since the iterator `v.end()`, as we know, points just outside `v`.

The algorithm `copy`, as well as several other standard algorithms, has an iterator that indicates where the result is to be put. The elements that are in the indicated places will then be changed. For instance, in the example given above, the first four elements in the container `d` were changed. A prerequisite for `copy` to be able to be used in this way is thus that the container to which you are copying already has a sufficient number of elements that can be changed. Most common, however, is that you wish to add elements to a container that was previously empty, or that you wish to add new elements to a container without changing the elements already in it. In this case you can use a special kind of iterator called an *insert iterator*. There are three such iterators: `back_inserter`, `front_inserter` and `inserter`.

We shall now show some examples. We begin by declaring an empty container, `e`:

```
deque<int> e;  // e is empty
```

Now we can copy from vector `v` to `e` with the statement

```
copy(v.begin(), v.end(), back_inserter(e));
// e contains {5, 6, 7, 8}
```

Instead of giving, as the last parameter, a single iterator, we have used back_inserter. Each time copy copies something to back_inserter, back_inserter will automatically call the operation push_back for the container that has been given as parameter (e in this example). The result is that one element at a time is read from v and put last in e.

In the next example we use front_inserter instead. It works in the same way as back_inserter, except that it automatically calls push_front.

```
copy(a+4, a+6, front_inserter(e));
// e contains {10, 9, 5, 6, 7, 8}
```

Here elements 4 and 5 are read from array a and are put first in e. Note that the elements end up backwards, since a[4] is copied before a[5].

The last insert iterator is inserter. With inserter you can insert new elements at an optional position in a container, since it automatically calls the operation insert for the container in question. Assume, for example, that we have written the lines

```
list<int> l;
copy(v.begin(), v.end(), back_inserter(l));
// l contains {5, 6, 7, 8}
```

Now we can declare an iterator that points into list l:

```
list<int>::iterator it = l.begin();
it++; it++;  // it points to the third element in l
```

The following call of copy copies elements 4 and 5 from array a and inserts them before the third element in list l:

```
copy(a+4, a+6, inserter(l,it));
// l contains {5, 6, 9, 10, 7, 8}
```

Observe that inserter must have two parameters. The first states the container, and the second is an iterator that points to a position in the container.

The next algorithm to be demonstrated is equal, which examines whether the elements in two intervals are equal. To examine, for instance, whether v contains the same elements as the first part of d we write

```
if (equal(v.begin(), v.end(), d.begin()))
  cout << "equal" << endl;
```

To search for elements in a container you can call the algorithm find. If the element searched for exists, the algorithm will return an iterator that points to the element. If the element does not exist, an iterator is returned that points to the first element outside the search interval. Here follows an example. We are searching for the number 8 in d:

```
if (find(d.begin(), d.end(), 8) != d.end())
  cout << "found" << endl;
```

Another useful algorithm is `sort`, which sorts a sequence. This algorithm can be used only for containers that have iterators of category random access – that is, for containers of the type `vector` or `deque`. We now demonstrate an example:

```
char *str[6] = {"one", "two", "three", "four", "five", "six"};
vector<string> s(str, str+6);
sort(s.begin(), s.end());
// s contains {"five", "four", "one", "six", "three", "two"}
```

Note that the iterators that are given as parameters can also in most cases be regular pointers, as in the following example, where `a` is a integer array that has been declared in the same way as previously:

```
if (equal(a, a+6, d.begin()))
  cout << "equal" << endl;
if (find(a, a+6, 9) != a+6)
  cout << "found" << endl;
```

None of the algorithms that we have demonstrated up till now has made changes in the container pointed out by the first parameters. An algorithm that does this, however, is `replace`. In the following examples zeros replace all the ones in the container `d`:

```
replace(d.begin(), d.end(), 1, 0);
// d contains {5, 6, 7, 8, 0, 0}
```

Several of the algorithms that make changes in the container in question are to be found in an alternative version, referred to as the *copying version*, which does not make changes in the original container but puts the result in another container. Common features of these copying algorithms are that they all have names that end in `_copy` and that they, as an extra parameter, have an iterator that points to the starting point in the container you wish to copy to. We can, for example, do the following:

```
replace_copy(d.begin(), d.end(), a, 0, 5);
// a contains {5, 6, 7, 8, 5, 5}
vector <int> w;
replace_copy(d.begin(), d.end(), back_inserter(w), 0, 4);
// w contains {5, 6, 7, 8, 4, 4}
```

The container `d` will remain unchanged. Note that in the last example we must use `back_inserter`, since vector `w` was empty from the beginning.

12.3 Function objects

Many of the standard algorithms have, as an extra parameter, an object known as a *function object*, which describes an operation to be performed on the elements in the container. The various algorithms can have function objects of different kinds as parameters. You can divide such function objects into four categories:

- *Unary predicates.* A unary predicate, often referred to simply as a *predicate*, is used when you wish to run through a container and choose certain elements. A predicate is a function object that has one parameter of the same type as the elements in the container and that returns a value of type `bool`. Predicates are the most common form of function object. All algorithms with predicates as parameters have a name that ends in `if`, for example `replace_if`, `count_if` and `find_if`.
- *Binary predicates.* A binary predicate is used when you are working with two containers that are to be compared in some way. A binary predicate is a function object with (in the most common case) two parameters of the same kind as the elements in the containers. The function object gives a result of type `bool`.
- *Comparison operations.* A comparison operation can be used when you are working with containers that are, or are to be, sorted. A comparison operation has two parameters of the same type as the elements in the container in question. If the first parameter is smaller than the second – that is, if the first parameter is to come before the second in the sorting – the result of a comparison operation is the value `true`.
- *Other operations.* Function objects of this category have one parameter of the same type as the elements in the container. The result type can vary, depending on the algorithm.

Examples of function objects in all the above categories follow below.

12.3.1 Using pointers to functions

As we recall from section 8.4.6, a function object is an object of a class that has a function call operator. When you call an algorithm with a function object as parameter, you can alternatively give a pointer to a regular function as argument. As this is somewhat simpler, we begin by demonstrating it.

In the first example we show a *(unary) predicate*. In the last section, we saw how you can use the algorithm `replace` to change certain elements in a container. In the container `d`, for example, we changed all the elements of value `1` to the value `0`. Now assume that we wish to change all the odd elements to the value `0`. We begin by defining a function that we call `odd`. This function examines whether or not a certain number is odd. If the number is odd, the value `true` will be returned, otherwise the value `false`. The function looks like this:

```
bool odd(int i)
{
  return i % 2 != 0;
}
```

The function `odd` is an example of a *predicate*. We can now use the algorithm `replace_if` to make all the changes in `d`:

```
// d contains {5, 6, 7, 8, 0, 0}
replace_if(d.begin(), d.end(), odd, 0);
// d contains {0, 6, 0, 8, 0, 0}
```

Here the point of interest is the third parameter, a pointer to the function `odd`. What happens is that the algorithm `replace_if` runs through the container `d`. For every element the function `odd` is called with the element as parameter, and if the result of the call is **`true`**, the element in question is replaced by the value `0`.

As an example of a binary predicate, we show how you can examine whether two vectors `vx` and `vy`, which both contain elements of type **`double`**, are equal. When you compare two real numbers in a computer you must, as mentioned in section 5.2.1 above, be careful, since the numbers cannot be stored exactly. This means that two real numbers logically regarded as equal can still be conceived by the computer as unequal, since a few bits in the mantissas of the numbers may differ. For this reason you should not compare real numbers directly with the built-in operator `==`. Instead you can examine the difference between the numbers. If this difference is very small, you can regard the numbers as equal. The following function uses this principle to examine whether two real numbers are equal. (The numbers are regarded as equal if the difference between them is smaller than 10^{-10}.)

```
bool almost_equal(double x, double y)
{
  return fabs(x-y) =< 1e-10;
}
```

We can now examine whether the elements in the two vectors `vx` and `vy` are logically equal by using the algorithm `equal`:

```
if (equal(vx.begin(), vx.end(), vy.begin(), almost_equal))
  cout << "almost equal" << endl;
```

Here the elements are going to be compared in pairs. Every element `vx[i]` in the interval `[vx.begin(), vx.end())` is compared with the corresponding element `vy[i]` in the vector `vy`. For every pair, the function `almost_equal` is called. If all the calls give the result **`true`**, the whole call of the algorithm equal will also give the result **`true`**. However, if any couple is unequal, the result **`false`** will be given.

The third category of function objects is *comparison operations*. As an example we shall show how you can use the algorithm `sort` to sort roman numerals.

In Exercise 4.21 on page 146 a function with the name `rom_value`, which translated a roman numeral to a regular integer, was constructed. The function had a parameter of type `string` that contained the roman numeral. As return value, the function gave a regular integer of type **`int`**. We shall now, with the help of this function, write a program that reads in and sorts an arbitrary number of roman numerals. When you run the program it may look like this:

```
Enter Roman numbers
IX
III
VI
MM
MCMXLIX
I
The numbers sorted are
I
III
VI
IX
MCMXLIX
MM
```

Let us see how the program looks. (We assume that the function `rom_value` is defined in another file and is complied separately).

```
#include <vector>
#include <algorithm>
using namespace std;
int rom_value(string s);  // see Exercise 4.21 on page 146.
bool less_than(string s1, string s2)  // comparison function
{
  return rom_value(s1) < rom_value(s2);
}
main()
{
  vector<string> rom;  // will contain the Roman numbers
  string s;
  cout << "Enter Roman numbers" << endl;
  while (getline(cin, s))
    rom.push_back(s);
  cout << endl;
  // sort the Roman numbers
  sort(rom.begin(), rom.end(), less_than);
  cout << "The numbers sorted are" << endl;
  vector<string>::iterator i;
  for (i=rom.begin(); i!=rom.end(); i++)
    cout << *i << endl;
}
```

First we read in some roman numerals in the function `main`. Each number that is read in is put last in a vector with the name `rom`. The reading-in is ended by the user writing Ctrl-Z (or possibly Ctrl-D). After that, the vector with roman numerals is sorted. The interesting line is

```
sort(rom.begin(), rom.end(), less_than);
```

Here we give, as an extra argument, a pointer to the function that the algorithm `sort` is going to use to compare the elements when it sorts. In this example it is easy to construct such a comparison function. We call it `less_than`. In this function we simply call the already finished function `rom_value`, and compare the values it gives.

The last category of function objects is *other operations*. As an example we assume that we wish to print out all the elements in a container that contains real numbers. Therefore we begin by defining a function that we name `write`:

```
void write(double x) {
  cout << x << ' ';
}
```

Now, assume that we have declared a vector `vx`:

```
double z[] = {5, 6, 7, 8, 9, 10};
vector<double> vx(z,z+6);
```

The contents of `vx` can now easily be printed out by using the algorithm `for_each`:

```
for_each(vx.begin(), vx.end(), write);
```

For each element the function `write` will be called with the element as parameter. The result will be the printout

```
5 6 7 8 9 10
```

As a further example of function objects of the category *other operations*, we can study the algorithm `transform`. `transform` reads a number of elements from a container, performs an arbitrary operation on each of these elements, and stores the results in another container. Assume, for instance, that we have the vector `vx` according to the above, and that we wish to calculate the squares of the numbers in `vx` and put them in another vector `vy`. We then begin by writing a function that squares:

```
double sqr(double x)
{
  return x*x;
}
```

Now we can use the algorithm `transform`:

```
// vx contains {5, 6, 7, 8, 9, 10}
vector<double> vy;  // vy is empty
transform(vx.begin(), vx.end(), inserter(vy,vy.begin()), sqr);
// vy contains {25, 36, 49, 64, 81, 100}
```

Note that we must use the insert iterator `inserter`, since prior to the calling of `transform` the vector `vy` is empty.

12.3.2 Using real function objects

In all the examples thus far we have given the algorithms a pointer to a function as parameter. However, it is generally better to use real function objects – that is, objects of a class that has a function call operator. This makes it possible for the compiler to produce more effective code. Moreover, you can do things with function objects that are impossible with single functions.

Using a function object is almost as simple as using a single function. To demonstrate this, we make a new version of the last example. We begin by defining a class with the name `SqrClass`:

```
class SqrClass {
public:
   double operator()(double x) const
   {
      return x*x;
   }
};
```

Instead of, as previously, having a single function `sqr`, we let the function be a function call operator within a class. You can now, in the usual way, declare variables of the class `SqrClass`. We can, for example, declare a variable with the name `sq`:

```
SqrClass sq;
```

The variable `sq` can now work as a function object. You can thus call `sq` as if it were a function. For example, you could write the expression `sq(1.5)`, which would mean that the function call operator would be called with the value `1.5` as parameter. The result of the expression would therefore be `2.25`. We can use the variable `sq` as parameter to the algorithm `transform` and write

```
// vx contains {5, 6, 7, 8, 9, 10}
vector<double> vy;  // vy is empty
transform(vx.begin(), vx.end(), inserter(vy,vy.begin()), sq);
// vy contains {25, 36, 49, 64, 81, 100}
```

When you give a function object as a parameter to an algorithm it is not necessary to declare a variable explicitly. It is sufficient to write an expression that creates a temporary variable. In this example we might alternatively write

```
transform(vx.begin(), vx.end(),
          inserter(vy,vy.begin()), SqrClass());
```

The expression `SqrClass()` is a call of the default constructor for the class `SqrClass`. The expression creates a temporary object of the class `SqrClass`.

In the next example we show how you can, in a correct alphabetical way, sort a container that contains texts. On page 431 we demonstrated how you could use the algorithm `sort`. A problem concerning texts is, as we recall, that the sort order does not come out right when there are both lower-case and upper-case letters and letters with accents or other enhancements. If, for instance, we have the following words (from a reference book):

```
char *w[4] ={"Brontë", "attaché", "Brontosaurus", "attachment"};
vector<string> s(w, w+4);
sort(s.begin(), s.end());
//s contains {"Brontosaurus", "Brontë", "attachment", "attaché"}
```

the sort order will, as we can see, come out wrong. The reason for this is that the function `sort` uses the regular operator `<` to compare the elements included while sorting. To remedy this, we can use the alternative version of the algorithm `sort`, giving a function object as an extra parameter. The function object describes which comparison operation is to be used. We write

```
sort(s.begin(), s.end(), alpha("en"));
//s contains {"attaché", "attachment", "Brontë", "Brontosaurus"}
```

The expression `alpha("en")` is a call for the constructor of the class `alpha`, described in section 3.3. Thus we get a temporary object of this class. Objects of the class `alpha` can work as function objects since there is, in this class, a function call operator that looks like this:

```
// function call operator for comparison of string objects
bool operator()(const std::string& s1, const std::string& s2)
{ return lt(s1,s2); }
```

(The function `lt`, 'less than', is, as we recall from page 95, a member function in the class `alpha` that compares two texts in a correct alphabetical way.) Since the constructor in the class `alpha` has a language code as parameter, it is easy to obtain an alternative sorting. If, for instance, we wished to sort according to the Spanish alphabet, we would write `alpha("es")` instead of `alpha("en")`.

The class `alpha` also contains function call operators where the parameters are of types **`char`** and **`const char`** respectively. You can thus also use this class when you wish to sort individual single characters or texts that are represented as traditional text strings in C++.

In addition to the function call operator, a function object may contain member functions and data members. This makes function objects more powerful than simple functions. In the class `alpha` there is, for example, a constructor that makes it possible to state the language in question. We now study an example where the function object has a data member. Assume that a company has made a prognosis of the expected sales of a certain product for the next coming year. The prognoses are made month per month, and the expected sales figures are stored in a vector `v1` that contains one element per month. We can assume that the vector `v` contains the following information:

```
{100, 110, 130, 90, 50, 70, 80, 100, 110, 150, 200, 250}
```

To be able to plan production you need to know the total sales up to and including that month, on a monthly basis. For the month of February, for example, you would want to calculate the total sales for January and February, for March the total sales for January, February and March, and so on. To be able to do this, we begin by defining the following class:

```
class SumClass
{
public:
   // constructor
   SumClass (double init=0) : sum(init){}
   // function call operator
   double operator()(double x)
   { return sum += x;}
private:
   double sum;
};
```

The member variable `sum` is initialized in the constructor, normally to the value `0`. After that, it will increase by the value of the latest element at every call of the function call operator, and the updated value will be returned. Now, assume that we have declared another vector `v2`, which, like `v1`, contains 12 elements:

```
vector<double> v2(12);
```

We can then easily calculate the total sales figures with the help of the algorithm `transform`, and insert the results in vector `v2`:

```
transform(v1.begin(), v1.end(), v2.begin(), SumClass());
```

Subsequent to this call, the vector `v2` will contain

```
{100, 210, 340, 430, 480, 550, 630, 730, 840, 990, 1190, 1440}
```

Below is an additional example in which our class `SumClass` is used. Assume that we want the vector `v1` to contain the values `1`, `2`, `3`, etc. We begin by inserting the value `1` into all the elements in the vector `v1`. This is done most easily with the algorithm `fill`:

```
fill(v1.begin(), v1.end(), 1);
// v1 contains {1, 1, 1, 1, 1, 1, 1, 1, 1, 1, 1, 1}
```

The next step is to use the algorithm `transform`:

```
transform(v1.begin(), v1.end(), v1.begin(), SumClass());
// v1 contains {1, 2, 3, 4, 5, 6, 7, 8, 9, 10, 11, 12}
```

Function objects

A function object x is an object of a class type C, which has a function call operator. It can be called as if it were a function

```
x(parameter)
```

Many algorithms can have a function object or a pointer to a function as parameters. Often, a temporary function object is created immediately at the call

```
algorithm (other parameters, C())
```

Function objects can be divided into the following categories:

Unary predicate	Has one parameter, returns `bool`
Binary predicate	Has two parameters, returns `bool`
Comparison operation	Has two parameters `a` and `b`, returns `true` if `a<b`
Other operations	Have one parameter, give a result of optional type

Here we have used a function object of the class `SumClass`. Note it is permissible to make changes in the same container as that from which we are reading. The third parameter is `v1.begin()`, the same as the first.

12.3.3 Using predefined function objects

It is not always necessary to write function objects yourself. There is a set of predefined standard classes that you can use to create function objects. To gain access to these classes, you must include the following line in your program:

```
#include <functional>
```

In this file there are predefined classes to create function objects that can perform the ordinary mathematical and logical operations as well as make comparisons. You can also use functions known as *function adapters* to adapt your functions so that they fit. We begin with a couple of numerical examples. The classes that describe arithmetic operations are called `plus`, `minus`, `multiplies`, `divides`, `modulus` and `negate`. A function object of the type `plus` can be declared as

```
plus<double> p;
```

Since the class `plus` is a template, you must state the type for which the class is to be valid. In this case we wish to be able to add values of type `double`. Since the class `plus` contains a function call operator, the variable `p` can work as a function object. We can call it as though it were a function:

```
cout << p(4,5) << endl;   // 9 is printed out
```

The idea is, however, that the predefined function objects are primarily to be used as parameters to algorithms. As an easy example we assume that we wish to calculate the multiplication table of number 7 up to 12 × 7 and put it in a vector `v3`. In the last example we had put the values `1`, `2`, `3`, etc. into the vector `v1` that contained 12 elements. We now put the value 7 in the vector `v2`, which also contains 12 elements:

```
fill(v2.begin(), v2.end(), 7);
// v2 contains {7, 7, 7, 7, 7, 7, 7, 7, 7, 7, 7, 7}
```

We then use an alternative version of the algorithm `transform`:

```
// v1 contains {1, 2, 3, 4, 5, 6, 7, 8, 9, 10, 11, 12}
vector<double> v3(12); // v3 contains 12 elements
transform(v1.begin(), v1.end(), v2.begin(), v3.begin(),
          multiplies<double>());
// v3 contains {7, 14, 21, 28, 35, 42, 49, 56, 63, 70, 77, 84}
```

The first two parameters state, as usual, the container you are to read from. The third parameter states the starting point in another container you are also to read from. The fourth parameter states which container you are to put the results in, and the last parameter is a function object that states what operation is to be performed. In this example the elements in the vectors `v1` and `v2` will be multiplied in pairs, and the results will end up in `v3`. The last parameter is a call of the constructor for the class `multiplies`. Note the extra empty parentheses that must be included.

We provide an additional numerical example. Assume that we wish to negate all the values in the vector `v3`. We can achieve this easily using `transform` and the predefined function object `negate`:

```
transform(v3.begin(), v3.end(), v3.begin(), negate<double>());
```

The vector `v3` will then contain

```
{-7, -14, -21, -28, -35, -42, -49, -56, -63, -70, -77, -84}
```

There are three classes that you can use to create function objects that perform logical operations on their two parameters. These classes are called `logical_and`, `logical_or`, and `logical_not`. They operate in a corresponding way to the numerical function objects.

It may be of greater interest that there are also classes that you can use to create function objects that make comparisons. These classes are `logical_to`, `not_equal_to`, `greater`, `less`, `greater_equal` and `less_equal`. To give an example, we begin by placing the elements `12`, `11`, `10` etc. in the vector `v2`:

```
fill(v2.begin(), v2.end(), 1);
// v2 contains {1, 1, 1, 1, 1, 1, 1, 1, 1, 1, 1, 1}
transform(v2.begin(), v2.end(), v2.begin(), SumClass());
// v2 contains {1, 2, 3, 4, 5, 6, 7, 8, 9, 10, 11, 12}
reverse(v2.begin(), v2.end());
// v2 contains {12, 11, 10, 9, 8, 7, 6, 5, 4, 3, 2, 1}
```

Here we have used the class `SumClass`, as shown on page 438. As evidenced by the above, the algorithm reverse-shifts the elements in the stated interval around, so that they end up in backward order. Now we declare a vector that can contain 12 elements of type **`bool`**:

```
vector<bool> bv(12);
```

Now we can demonstrate how you can use a predefined function object to compare the two vectors `v1` and `v2`. We assume that `v1` has the same contents as previously – that is, `1`, `2`, `3` etc.:

```
// v1 contains {1, 2, 3, 4, 5, 6, 7, 8, 9, 10, 11, 12}
// v2 contains {12, 11, 10, 9, 8, 7, 6, 5, 4, 3, 2, 1}
transform(v1.begin(), v1.end(), v2.begin(), bv.begin(),
          greater<double>());
```

The elements in the two vectors are compared in pairs, and for every pair the result will be true if the element in `v1` is larger than the corresponding element in `v2`. The results of the comparisons are placed in the vector `bv`, which will contain the elements

```
{false,false,false,false,false,false,true,true,true,true,true,true}
```

Predefined function objects

Predefined function objects are defined in the file `<functional>`.
A temporary predefined function object is created with an expression of the form

```
operation<typ>()
```

where *`typ`* is the type for elements in the container in question.
`operation` can be any of the following (`a` and `b` denote parameters at a call of the function object):

`plus`	Gives function objects that return `a + b`.
`minus`	Gives function objects that return `a - b`.
`multiplies`	Gives function objects that return `a * b`.
`divides`	Gives function objects that return `a / b`.
`modulus`	Gives function objects that return `a % b`.
`negate`	Gives function objects that return `-a`.
`equal_to`	Gives function objects that return `a == b`.
`not_equal_to`	Gives function objects that return `a != b`.
`greater`	Gives function objects that return `a > b`.
`less`	Gives function objects that return `a < b`.
`greater_equal`	Gives function objects that return `a >= b`.
`less_equal`	Gives function objects that return `a <= b`.
`logical_and`	Gives function objects that return `a && b`.
`logical_or`	Gives function objects that return `a || b`.
`logical_not`	Gives function objects that return `!a`.

We conclude this section on function objects by demonstrating how you can use *function adapters* to adapt your function objects. The simplest are `not1` and `not2`, which are used to negate the result from a predicate. `not2` is used for binary predicates and `not1` for unary predicates. We can, for example, make a new comparison of vectors `v1` and `v2`:

```
transform(v1.begin(), v1.end(), v2.begin(), bv.begin(),
          not2(greater<double>()));
```

When the elements in the two vectors are compared in pairs this time, the result will be **`true`** for every element in `v1` that is *not* larger than the corresponding element in `v2`. The vector `bv` will then contain the elements

```
{true,true,true,true,true,true,false,false,false,false,false,false}
```

We also give an example of how `not1` can be used, but first we describe the function adapters `bind1st` and `bind2nd`. These are used to change a binary predicate into a unary predicate – that is, into a predicate with only one parameter. You do this by starting out from a binary predicate and 'binding' one of the parameters to a constant value. The function adapter `bind1st` binds the first parameter, and `bind2nd` binds the second. Of these two, `bind2nd` is the most natural to use. An example follows.

The expression

```
greater_equal<double>()
```

creates a function object that compares two elements of type **`double`** and returns a value of type **`bool`**. The expression is thus a binary predicate. We can give this expression as parameter to the function adapter `bind2nd` and write

```
bind2nd(greater_equal<double>(),8)
```

This call returns a unary predicate that, when it is called, gives the value **`true`** if its parameter is greater than or equal to 8. We have bound the second parameter in the call of `greater_equal` to 8. We can, for example, use this in the following statement, in which we call the algorithm `count_if` to examine how many of the elements in the vector `v1` are greater than or equal to 8:

```
// v1 contains {1, 2, 3, 4, 5, 6, 7, 8, 9, 10, 11, 12}
cout << count_if(v1.begin(), v1.end(),
                 bind2nd(greater_equal<double>(),8));
// prints out: 5
```

With this method it is easy to form unary predicates, starting from the predefined function objects. Alternatively, the function adapter `bind1st` can be used. However, this feels somewhat less natural. Study the following example:

```
cout << count_if(v1.begin(), v1.end(),
                 bind1st(greater_equal<double>(),8));
// prints out: 8
```

Here we have instead bound the first parameter to `8`. This means that we will count the number of elements `e` in `v1`, which satisfy the condition `8>=e`.

The function adapter `not1` can be applied to a function object that is a unary predicate. We can for example combine `not1` and `bind2nd`. In the following example we shall find the first element in `v1` that is not less than `8`. To do this, we use the algorithm `find_if`. If there is no element that satisfies the given condition, `find_if` returns the last iterator in the search interval (the one that points to the first element that lies exactly outside the interval). We write

```
vector<double>::iterator it;  // declare an iterator
it = find_if(v1.begin(), v1.end(),
             not1(bind2nd(less<double>(),8)));
cout << *it;  // prints out: 8
```

The function adapters can be used only on function objects that are constructed in a certain way. (Their classes must be subclasses to the standard classes `unary_function` or `binary_function`.) Of course, the predefined function objects satisfy these conditions.

Function adapters	
Have function objects as parameters. Give another function object as the result. (Here `f1` and `f2` denote function objects with respectively one and two parameters, and `x` denotes a value.)	
`bind1st(f2, x)`	Changes `f2` into a function object with one parameter. The first parameter is bound to the value `x`.
`bind2nd(f2, x)`	Changes `f2` into a function object with one parameter. The second parameter is bound to the value `x`.
`not1(f1)`	Gives a function object that returns the negated value of a call of `f1`.
`not2(f2)`	Gives a function object that returns the negated value of a call of `f2`.
`ptr_fun(f)`	Gives a function object that calls the function `f`.

So, if you have a pointer to a function instead of a function object, you cannot use the function adapters directly on this function. You can, however, use the function adapter `ptr_fun` to change a pointer into a function to a 'real' function object. On page 433, for example, we defined the function `almost_equal`.

The expression

```
ptr_fun(almost_equal)
```

returns a function object, the function call operator of which calls the function `almost_equal`. We may, as a slight simplification, say that the function `almost_equal` has been transformed into a function object. We can use this in the following example, in which we are looking for the first element in the vector `v1` that is approximately equal to `6`:

```
it = find_if(v1.begin(), v2.end(),
             bind2nd(ptr_fun(almost_equal),6));
cout << *it;  // prints out: 6
```

In summary, if you need a function object to call an algorithm, you can use the predefined function objects in many cases, possibly adapted with the help of a function adapter. In that case, it is not necessary to construct a function object of your own. The comparison objects `greater`, `less` and so on, adapted with `bind2nd`, are especially useful.

12.4 The standard class `list`

The class `list`, like the classes `vector` and `deque`, describes sequences. The class `list` is, however, implemented internally in a totally different way from the classes `vector` and `deque`. Arrays are not used. Instead, you use what is known as a *linked list*. If, for example, we write the program lines

```
list<int> l1, l2;
l1.push_back(5); l1.push_back(8); l1.push_back(2);
```

the list `l1` may look internally like Figure 12.1. The list consists of a number of list elements that are linked together.

Every list element contains, in addition to the data element itself, two pointers that point out the list elements that come before and after the list element in question. (The zeros mean empty pointers – that is, pointers that do not point to anything.) There are two special pointers in the figure, called `front` and `back`, which point out the first and last list elements. To reach individual elements in the list, you must go via one of these

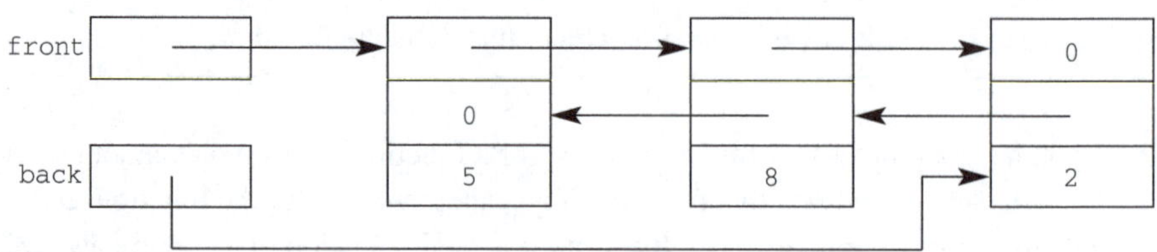

Figure 12.1 A doubly linked list

pointers and step forward to the right list element. This explains why it is impossible to do indexing. We can see from the figure that it is easy to add new elements first or last in the list. In this case, new list elements that are linked in first or last are simply created. If you use iterators, you can also get a kind of pointer to individual elements inside the list. Then it will be possible to easily remove list elements, or insert new ones in the middle of the list. No rearrangement is necessary. All you have to do is re-link the list elements. We shall discuss linked lists in greater detail in Chapter 13. Fortunately, you do not have to know how to construct linked lists to be able to use the standard class `list`. However, to understand the characteristics of the lists it is useful to understand the principle.

Lists can be handled in the same way as vectors and variables of type `deque`. All of the general operations for sequences described in section 2.8 can be used for lists. You can also use iterators as described earlier in this chapter. You can, for example, run through list `l1` and print out its contents with the statement

```
for (list<int>::iterator it=l1.begin(); it != l1.end(); it++)
  cout << *it << ' ';
```

We now study some further operations that exist only for lists. We begin by adding a few additional elements to list `l1`:

```
l1.push_front(2); l1.push_front(9); l1.push_front(8);
// l1 gets the contents {8, 9, 2, 5, 8, 2}
```

The first operation we demonstrate is `reverse`, which simply turns a list so that the elements end up the other way around:

```
l1.reverse();   // l1 gets the contents {2, 8, 5, 2, 9, 8}
```

The operation `remove` finds elements with a certain contents and removes them from the list. To remove all the twos from the list, for example, we write

```
l1.remove(2);   // l1 gets the contents {8, 5, 9, 8}
```

It is easy to sort a list, since there is a ready-made operation, `sort`, that does this:

```
l1.sort();   // l1 gets the contents {5, 8, 8, 9}
```

(Note that you cannot use the separate algorithm `sort` as described on page 431, since, as parameter, it requires iterators of the category random access.) The operation `sort` also exists in an alternative version, in which you can give a function object or a pointer to a function as an extra parameter, to state how comparisons are to be made. We could, for example, use a list instead of a vector in the program on page 434 that sorted roman numerals. If the sequence `rom` in the program had been a list, we would have sorted it with the call

```
rom.sort(less_than);
```

If you wish to perform a correct alphabetical sorting of a list that contains texts, you can use our own class `alpha`. If, for instance, the variable `s` is declared as

```
list<string> s;
```

we can sort it with the call

```
s.sort(alpha("en"));
```

The operation `unique` goes through a list and examines whether there are any groups that consist of a number of elements with the same value next to each other. For every such group, all the elements except the first are removed.

```
l1.unique();  // l1 gets the contents {5, 8, 9}
```

The next operation we show is `merge`, which merges two lists and creates a sorted list that contains all the elements in the two lists. For this to work, both the lists must be

Special operations for the standard class `list`

In addition to the operations mentioned here, there are also the operations in the information windows on pages 69 and 427.

`l.reverse( )`	Turns list `l` round so that the elements end up backwards.
`l.remove(e)`	Removes all occurrences of element `e` from list `l`.
`l.remove(func)`	Removes all the elements from the list that satisfy the condition `func(e)`. `func` is a function object.
`l.unique( )`	Removes all the occurrences, except the first, from every connected group of equal elements in list `l`.
`l.sort( )`	Sorts list `l`.
`l.sort(cf)`	Sorts list `l`. `cf` is a function object that states how the elements in the list are to be compared.
`l.merge(l2)`	Sorts list `l2` into list `l`.
`l.merge(l2, cf)`	Sorts list `l2` into list `l`. cf is a function object that states how the elements in the lists are to be compared.
`l.splice(p,l2)`	Inserts the elements in list `l2` in list `l`, before place `p`. List `l2` will become empty. `p` is an iterator that points in list `l`.
`l.splice(p,l2,i)`	Inserts the element in place `i` in list `l2` before place `p` in list `l`. The element is removed from `l2`. `p` and `i` are iterators.
`l.splice(p,l2,i,j)`	Inserts the elements in the interval `[i, j)` in list `l2` before place `p` in list `l`. The elements are removed from `l2`. `p`, `i` and `j` are iterators.

sorted prior to `merge` being called. We demonstrate this by creating one further list, `l2`, which we merge with `l1`:

```
l2.push_back(3); l2.push_back(6);
l2.push_back(7); l2.push_back(12);
// l2 contains {3, 6, 7, 12}
l1.merge(l2);   // l1 gets the contents {3, 5, 6, 7, 8, 9, 12}
```

The operation `merge` exists, just like the operation `sort`, in an alternative version in which you can give a function object as extra parameter. This function object decides how two elements are to be compared.

For the class `list` there is a special operation known as `splice`, which is used to move elements from one list to another. The operation `splice` exists in three variants. All three have a first parameter that is an iterator. This iterator points to the place in the list in question to which the new elements are to be moved. They are to be moved in *before* the element that the iterator points to. We now demonstrate with the help of some examples. First two lists `la` and `lb` are declared:

```
int z[] = {5, 6, 7};
list<int> la(z, z+3);    // la contains {5, 6, 7}
list<int> lb(2, 0);      // lb contains {0, 0}
```

The first version of the operation `splice` inserts a whole list into the list in question. We now insert list `lb` in front of the second place in list `la`. For this we use an iterator `p`, which points out the correct place in `la`:

```
list<int>::iterator p = la.begin();
la.splice(++p, lb);   // la contains {5, 0, 0, 6, 7}
                      // lb contains {}
```

Note that the list `lb` is now empty. The other version of `splice` moves an individual element to the list in question. An example follows:

```
lb.push_back(1); lb.push_back(2); lb.push_back(3);
lb.push_back(4);  // lb contains {1, 2, 3, 4}
list<int>::iterator i = lb.begin();
++i; ++i;
la.splice(la.end(), lb, i);   // la contains {5, 0, 0, 6, 7, 3}
                              // lb contains {1, 2, 4}
```

The last version of the operation `splice` moves part of another list to the list in question:

```
i = lb.begin(); ++i;
la.splice(la.begin(), lb, i, lb.end());
// la contains {2, 4, 5, 0, 0, 6, 7, 3}
// lb contains {1}
```

12.5 Maps and sets

The standard classes `map`, `multimap`, `set` and `multiset` describe what are known as *associative containers*. An associative container can be logically described as a table in which you use what is referred to as *search keys* to search for information. An example is shown in Table 12.1, in which a name is used as search key to look up a telephone number.

Table 12.1 is an example of what is known as a *map*. Each line in the table constitutes a pair, consisting of a search key and a corresponding value, a *key–value pair*. The most common situation is that a certain search key can be mapped to only one value, and that a certain search key can therefore occur only once in the left column. There are, however, situations in which it is natural to permit a certain search key to occur several times. We can, for instance, imagine that one person may have several alternative telephone numbers. This is demonstrated in Table 12.2. Such a table is called a *multimap*.

In certain situations there are no values connected to the search keys. We can, for example, have a table that contains the telephone numbers for everyone that has called us in the last 24 hours. This is illustrated in Table 12.3. A telephone number is stored only once in the table, even if that number has called us several times. The telephone numbers that are contained in the table therefore constitute a *set*.

In Table 12.3 every telephone number is stored no more than once. However, it may also be of interest to keep track of how many times a certain number has called you. In

Table 12.1 A map

Key	**Value**
Cooper Charles	0703123456
Harding Jenny	0701987654
...	...
Stevens Eric	081234567

Table 12.2 A multimap

Key	**Value**
Cooper Charles	0703123456
Harding Jenny	0701987654
Harding Jenny	031987654
...	...
Stevens Eric	081234567
Stevens Eric	0704112233

Table 12.3 A set

Key
030414141
046123499
0702123459
0704112233
0705987654
...

Table 12.4 A multiset

Key
030414141
046123499
046123499
046123499
0702123459
0704112233
0704112233
0705987654
...

that case you can let a certain number occur several times, as shown is Table 12.4. We then get what is referred to as a *multiset*.

In C++ you can use the standard classes `map`, `multimap`, `set` and `multiset` to describe tables of the kind that we have now illustrated. The search keys and the values in the tables can be of arbitrary types; they do not need to be texts. The search keys are, however, always *sorted*, as shown in our examples. If we create maps or sets by using the standard classes, the tables are not implemented with sequential tables as has been shown above. To be able to look things up faster in the tables, a more efficient storing technique is used (for example binary search trees, which will be discussed in section 13.4). This is not, however, necessary knowledge for being able to use the standard classes. Logically, it looks like the above tables.

In the following examples we shall demonstrate the special operations that exist for the standard classes `map`, `multimap`, `set` and `multiset`. However, it should be mentioned that all these classes support the technique with iterators. More precisely, you can use iterators of the category *bidirectional iterator*, which means that most of the operations that are displayed in the information window on page 424 can be used for the classes `map`, `multimap`, `set` and `multiset`. Standard algorithms may also be used.

12.5.1 The standard classes `map` and `multimap`

The standard classes `map` and `multimap` are defined in the file `<map>`. Therefore this file must be included to permit the use of these classes:

```
#include <map>   // contains map and multimap
```

The special operations for the classes `map` and `multimap` are summarized in the information window below. As an example, we demonstrate how to create a map `m1` that maps texts to integer numbers. Imagine that we wish to create a table in which the search keys are names of programming languages and the values are the numbers of programmers in the project group in question that know that language:

```
map<string, int> m1;
```

Here a variable `m1` is declared, which has the type `map<string,int>`. When stating the type, you write both the type of the search key and the type the corresponding value is to have. The elements that are to be stored in table `m1` are pairs of the type `pair<string,int>`. (Pairs were discussed in section 5.10 on page 196.) We can now use the function `insert` to put map pairs in the table:

```
m1.insert(make_pair(string("C"), 2));
m1.insert(make_pair(string("C++"), 2));
```

Operations for the standard classes `map` and `multimap`	
Below, `m` means either `map` or `multimap`. `mtyp` denotes the type of the table, `ktyp` the type of the search keys, and `vtyp` the type of the values. `x` and `y` denote maps that are either of kind `map` or of `multimap`. `c` is a comparator (a function object) and `ctyp` its type. `q` and `q2` denote iterators that point out positions in the table in question. `i` and `j` are iterators that point out an interval in a container in which the elements have the type `pair<ktyp, vtyp>`. `i` and `j` can also be pointers that point out an interval in an array.	
`m<ktyp, vtyp>`	States the type of table `(mtyp)` The type of the comparator `(ctyp)` will be `less<ktyp>`.
`m<ktyp, vtyp, ctyp>`	States the type of table `(mtyp)`. The comparator gets type `ctyp`.
`mtyp x;`	Creates an empty table. Search keys are compared by `ctyp ()`.
`mtyp x(c);`	Creates an empty table. Search keys are compared by `c`.
`mtyp x(i,j);`	Creates a table. Search keys are compared by `ctyp ()`. Is initialized with the pairs from the interval `[i,j)`.

`mtyp x(i,j,c);`	Creates a table. Search keys are compared by `c`. Is initialized with the pairs from the interval `[i,j)`.
`y = x;`	Assignment. `y` becomes a copy of table `x`.
`x.insert(p);`	Inserts the pair `p` of type `pair<ktyp, vtyp>` in `x`. If `x` is a map, the pair `<it, b>` is returned, where `it` is an iterator that points to the pair in `x` that has the search key `p.first` and `b` is a **`bool`** that is true if insertion has been performed (if the search key did not exist before). If `x` is a `multimap`, an iterator that points to the inserted pair will be returned.
`x.insert(q,p);`	As above, but begins searching for the right place in `x` where the iterator `q` points (makes it possible to increase efficiency.) Returns an iterator that points to the pair in the table that has the search key `p.first`.
`x[key]=value`	Inserts the pair `<key, value>` in `x` (if `key` did not exist before), or changes the value for `key` (if `key` existed before). Only for `map`.
`x[key]`	Returns the value for `key`. If `key` did not exist earlier in `x` the value `0` (or corresponding value) is first inserted for `key`. Exists only for `map`.
`x.find(key);`	Returns an iterator that points to a pair with the search key `key`. If `key` did not exist, the value `x.end ()` is returned.
`x.count(key);`	Returns an integer number that states the number of pairs with the search key `key`.
`x.erase(key);`	Removes all pairs with the search key `key` from table x.
`x.erase(q);`	Removes the pair that the iterator `q` points to.
`x.erase(q,q2);`	Removes the pairs in the interval `[q,q2)` from table `x`.
`x.clear()`	Remove all pairs from table `x`.
`x.size()`	Gives the number of pairs in table `x`.
`x.empty()`	Gives **`true`** if the number of pairs in `x` is `0`, otherwise **`false`**.
`x.lower_bound(key);`	Returns an iterator that points to the first pair the search key of which is not less than `key`.
`x.upper_bound(key);`	Returns an iterator that points to the first pair the search key of which is larger than `key`.
`x.equal_range(key);`	Returns `make_pair (x.lower_bound (key), x.upper_bound (key))`

The help function `make_pair` is here used to form pairs of `string` and **`int`**. The expressions `string ("C")` and `string ("C++")` are explicit type conversions from type **`char*`** to `string`.

In a table of the kind `map`, as we have here, there can only be one key–value pair with a certain search key. For this reason, nothing would happen if we tried to insert another pair with the same search key:

```
m1.insert(make_pair(string("C++"), 4));   // duplicate, no change
```

If, however, `m1` had been of the `multimap` kind, another key–value pair with the search key `"C++"` would have been inserted. For a table of the `map` kind you can use the return value from a call of `insert` to examine whether insertion has been performed – that is, whether there was no such search key previously. The function `insert` returns a pair in which the second component is a **`bool`** that is **`true`** if the insertion has been performed. We now show an example:

```
if (m1.insert(make_pair(string("C++"), 4)).second)
  cout << "inserted" << endl;
else
  cout << "already present" << endl;
```

For tables of the `map` kind you can use a special indexing operator to insert mappings. This is easier than using `insert`. We can, for example, write

```
m1["Java"] = 3;
```

Here a new pair, `<"Java", 3>`, is created, which will be put into the table. If you put in a new value for a search key that already exists, the value for this search key will *change*. Note that what occurs here differs from when you use the function `insert`. We can, for example, give the statement

```
m1["Java"] = 4;   // changed
```

Then the value for `"Java"` is changed from `3` to `4`.

The indexing operator can also be used to look up the value for a certain search key. We can, for example, have the statements

```
cout << m1["C++"] << endl;       // prints out 2
cout << m1["Pascal"] << endl;    // prints out 0
```

Here, please observe a small peculiarity about the indexing operator. If you try to look up the value for a search key that is missing from the table, the indexing operator creates a new key–value pair and puts it into the table. In the new key–value pair the value is set to `0` (or a corresponding default value, depending on what type the values have). Since, in `m1`, there is no key–value pair for `"Pascal"`, it will now be put in.

If you wish to examine the value of a certain search key without creating any new key–value pairs in the table, you must use the function `find` instead of indexing. This function returns an iterator that points to the key–value pair if it exists. If the search key in question should not exist in the table, find will return the iterator `end()`, which, as we know, points outside the table. We now demonstrate this with an example:

```
map<string, int>::iterator it;   // declaration of iterator
if ((it = m1.find("C++")) != m1.end())
  cout << it->second << endl;
else
  cout << "not found" << endl;
```

Note how the type for the iterator must be declared. It is awkward to write whole type-names in this way. To simplify it somewhat you can therefore use `typedef`. We could, for example, have given the definition

```
typedef map<string, int> tabtype;
```

In that case, the declaration of `m1` would have been simplified to

```
tabtype m1;
```

The declaration of the iterator would also have been easier:

```
tabtype::iterator it;   // declaration of iterator
```

This may also be of practical use when you need to declare iterators to run through a table. We can, for example, print out the contents of `m1`:

```
for (tabtype::iterator i=m1.begin(); i!=m1.end(); i++)
  cout << i->first << ", " << i->second << endl;
```

The output will be

```
C, 2
C++, 2
Java, 4
Pascal, 0
```

A table can be initialized directly when the declaration is made. We can, for instance, declare another table `m2` and let it be a copy of `m1`:

```
map<string, int> m2(m1.begin(), m1.end());
```

As parameters for the constructor two iterators are given, which state the interval from which you are to copy. It would also have been possible to use regular pointers. Assume, for example, that we have declared an array that contains pairs:

```
pair<string, int> ai[3] = {make_pair(string("C"), 10),
  make_pair(string("C++"), 6), make_pair(string("Java"), 3)};
```

We can then declare a new map and initialize it from this array:

```
map<string, int> m2(ai, ai+3);
```

The function `insert` also exists in a version in which you state, as parameter, the interval you wish to copy from. We can, for example, write

```
m2.insert(m1.begin(), m1.end());
```

If you wish to copy a whole table it is, however, much easier to use a regular assignment:

```
m2 = m1;
```

If you wish to find out how many key–value pairs with a certain search key there are in a table, you can call the function `count`:

```
cout << m1.count("Java") << endl;  // prints out 1
```

Note that in a table of type `map` the result from a count can be only `0` or `1`, while in a table of type `multimap` there may be several occurrences of the same search key.

To remove key–value pairs from a table you use the function `erase`. There are three versions of this function. In the first version you give a search key as parameter, and all key–value pairs with this search key are removed. In the second version you give an iterator that points to the key–value pair that is to be removed as parameter. The third version has two iterators that state an interval as parameters. We can, for example, write

```
m1.erase("Pascal");
m1.erase(it);
```

If you wish to remove all key–value pairs it is easiest to use the function `clear`:

```
m1.clear();
```

The search keys are always sorted in a map. To compare the search keys so they can be sorted, a function object is used. In a map where the search keys have the type `ktyp`, a function object of the predefined type `less<ktyp>` (see section 12.3.3 on page 439) is normally used. This means that the regular operator `<` is used to compare the search keys. This, in its turn, means that the smallest search key ends up first in the table and the largest last. Sometimes, however, you may wish to determine how the comparison of search keys is to be made yourself. You can effect this in two ways. The first is to state that a function object other than one of type `less<ktyp>` is to be used to make comparisons. Assume, for example, that we wish to create a map `m3`, in which the search keys have type `string` and the values have type **`int`**. In `m3` we want the search keys to be placed in reverse order, so the largest will come first. We can then give the declaration

```
map<string, int, greater<string> > m3;
```

Here we have stated in the type `specifier` for `m3` that the function object that makes comparisons is to have the type `greater<string>`. If, for example, we now read in the following maps:

```
m3["C++"]=2;
m3["Java"]=3;
```

"Java" would come first and "C++" last.

The function object that makes the comparisons does not have to be of a predefined type. In our examples, the search keys are of the type string. The operators < and > for the type string cannot tell the difference between lower-case and upper-case letters, which means that the order does not come out alphabetically correct. If we, for example, were to write

```
map<string, int> m4;
m4["c++"]=2;
m4["Java"]=3;
```

"Java" would come before "c++", since the operator < regards upper-case letters as smaller than lower-case letters. The solution to this problem is to use a comparison object that can make alphabetically correct comparisons. For instance, function objects of our own type alpha have that quality, and we can therefore declare m4 instead as

```
map<string, int, alpha> m4;  // gives (English) alphabetical order
```

Normally, when you declare a map a function object that is to make the comparisons is automatically created. This function object is initialized with the default constructor for the class in question. In the last example above a comparison object of the class alpha, which was initialized with the default constructor alpha(), is thus used in m4. The second way of affecting how comparisons are made does not use the above-mentioned automatically created function object. Instead, you can explicitly give a function object as parameter when you declare the map. If, for example, we had wanted correct alphabetical comparisons, but according to the Spanish alphabet, we could have declared m4 in the following way:

```
alpha comp("es");
map<string, int, alpha> m4(comp);
```

You could also have written the above like this:

```
map<string, int, alpha> m4(alpha("es"));
```

As a further example we shall show how you can create a table of the kind multimap that contains a telephone list as in Table 12.2. Since we wish to put in names that contain letters other than the 'simple' a–z, we use an object of the class alpha as a comparator. We begin by using typedef to declare the type of the table:

```
typedef multimap<string, string, alpha> teltype;
```

We want a table in which you can make mappings of names (of type string) to telephone numbers (also of type string). Therefore we have given string as the first two type parameters. The third parameter states the type of the comparator. Here we use the type alpha. We can now create a table. We want the names to be sorted according to the English alphabet:

```
teltype teltab(alpha("en"));
```

We can now put some telephone numbers in the table. Since the map in question is a `multimap` and not a `map`, we cannot use indexing. Instead, we use `insert`:

```
teltab.insert(make_pair(string("Stevens Eric"),
                        string("0704112233")));
teltab.insert(make_pair(string("Harding Jenny"),
                        string("031987654")));
teltab.insert(make_pair(string("Stevens Eric"),
                        string("081234567")));
teltab.insert(make_pair(string("Harding Jenny"),
                        string("0701987654")));
```

Now the names will end up in the correct alphabetical order, as we can confirm if we make a printout:

```
for (teltype::iterator i=teltab.begin(); i!=teltab.end(); i++)
  cout << left << setw(20) << i->first << i->second << endl;
```

The printout will be:

```
Harding Jenny    031987654
Harding Jenny    0701987654
Stevens Eric     0704112233
Stevens Eric     081234567
```

To finish off this subsection on `map` and `multimap` we show a new version of the program on page 97, which input some sales data and calculated the commission for the different sales representatives. In the version on page 97 two vectors were used, one to keep track of the names of the sales representatives and one to keep track of the amounts of their sales. In the new version, we use a table of type `map` instead:

```
#include <iostream>
#include <iomanip>
#include <map>
#include <string>
#include "alpha.h"
using namespace std;
main()
{
  const float bound=5000., pro1=0.1, pro2=0.15;
  typedef map<string, float, alpha> tabtype;
  tabtype tab(alpha("en"));  // contains name and amount
  string nn;
  float amount, commission;
  while (cin >> amount >> ws)
```

```
  {
    getline(cin ,nn);   // input next name
    tab[nn] += amount;
  }
  // write compilation
  cout << endl
       << " Amount Commission Name" << endl
       << " ====== ========== ====" << endl;
  for (tabtype::iterator j=tab.begin(); j!=tab.end(); j++)
  {
    amount = j->second;
    if (amount <= bound)
      commission = pro1*amount;
    else
      commission = pro1*bound + pro2*(amount-bound);
    cout << setiosflags(ios::fixed) << setprecision(0)
    << setw(9) << amount << setw(12) << commission
    << "  " << j->first << endl;
  }
}
```

12.5.2 The standard classes `set` and `multiset`

The standard classes `set` and `multiset` are defined in the file `<set>`. To be able to use these classes, you must include the following line in your program:

```
#include <set>   // contains set and multiset
```

The information window below shows the operations for the classes `set` and `multiset`. These are actually the same operations as for `map` and `multimap`, but there are some differences since containers of the types `set` and `multiset` do not contain any values, only search keys. We show some simple examples. Class `set` is used in the examples, but `multiset` operates in the same way. The only difference is that, in a collection of the class `multiset`, there may be several elements with the same value.

Operations for the standard classes `set` and `multiset`

Below, `s` means either `set` or `multiset`. `styp` denotes the type of the set, and `etyp` the type of the elements (that is, the same as the type of the search key).
`x` and `y` denote sets of the kind `set` or `multiset`.
`c` is a comparator (a function object) and `ctyp` is its type.
`q` and `q2` denote iterators that point out positions in the set in question.
`i` and `j` are iterators that point out an interval in a container where the elements have the type `etyp`. `i` and `j` can also be pointers that point out an interval in an array.

s<etyp>	States the type of the set (styp). The comparators type (ctyp) becomes less<etyp>.
s<etyp, ctyp>	States the type of the set (styp). The comparator gets the type ctyp.
styp x;	Creates an empty set. The elements are compared with ctyp ( ).
styp x(c);	Creates an empty set. The elements are compared with c.
styp x(i,j);	Creates a set. The elements are compared with ctyp(). Is initialized with the elements from the interval(i,j].
styp x(i,j,c);	Creates a set. The elements are compared with c. Is initialized with the elements from the interval (i,j].
y = x;	Assignment. y becomes a copy of the set x.
x.insert(v);	Puts in the value v of the type etyp in x. If x is of the kind set, the pair <it,b> is returned, where it is an iterator that points to the elements in x that have the value v, and b is a **bool** that is **true** if insertion was performed (if v did not exist before). If x is of the kind multiset, an iterator that points to the inserted element is returned.
x.insert(v,q);	As above, but starts looking after the right place in x where the iterator q points (allows greater efficiency). Returns an iterator that points to the element with the value v.
x.find(v);	Returns an iterator that points to an element with the value v. If v did not exist, the value x.end() is returned.
x.count(v);	Returns an integer number that states the number of elements with the value v.
x.erase(v);	Removes all elements with the value v from the set x.
x.erase(q);	Removes the element that the iterator q points to.
x.erase(q,q2);	Removes the elements in the interval [q,q2).
x.clear()	Removes all the elements from set x.
x.size()	Gives the number of elements in set x.
x.empty()	Gives **true** if the number of elements in x is 0, otherwise **false**.
x.lower_bound(v);	Returns an iterator that points to the first element that is not smaller than v.
x.upper_bound(v);	Returns an iterator that points to the first element that is larger than v.
x.equal_range(v);	Returns make_pair (x. lower_bound (key), x. upper_bound (key))

We start by declaring an empty set where the element type is `int`:

```
set<int> s1;   // s1 is empty
```

We can use the operations `insert` and `erase` to add and remove elements:

```
s1.insert(9); s1.insert(7); s1.insert(2);
s1.insert(0); s1.insert(1); s1.insert(7);
// s1 contains {0, 1, 2, 7, 9}
s1.erase(9); s1.erase(s1.begin());
// s1 contains {1, 2, 7}
```

Note that in a set of the kind `set` there can be only one element with a certain value. If you try to put in several elements with the same value, nothing will happen.

You can intialize a set directly when declaring by giving two iterators or pointers as parameters to the constructor. We can, for example, make the declaration

```
int a[7] = {3, 8, 2, 0, 9, 6, 3};
set<int> s2(a, a+4);
// s2 contains {0, 2, 3, 8}
```

The algorithm `copy` can be used to run through a set and copy its elements to another set. We can, for example, write

```
copy(s2.begin(), s2.end(), inserter(s1, s1.begin()));
// s1 contains {0, 1, 2, 3, 7, 8}
```

Here you must use the insert iterator `inserter`, since the operation `insert` is to be called for each element. Note that the elements that already exist in `s1` are not removed. If you wish to only make a copy of a set, you use a regular assignment:

```
s1 = s2;   // s1 contains {0, 2, 3, 8}
```

It is easy to determine whether or not a certain element exists in a set. You then use the function `count`:

```
if (s1.count(7))
  cout << "7 found" << endl;
else
  cout << "7 not found" << endl;
```

There are five algorithms that perform operations on sets. We shall demonstrate them below. To be able to do this, we declare another set and name it `s3`:

```
set<int> s3(a+4, a+7);
// s3 contains {3, 6, 9}
```

The first algorithm we show is `set_union`, which creates the set union of two sets. We can, for example, create the set union of sets `s2` and `s3` and place the result in another set `t1` by writing

```
// s2 contains {0, 2, 3, 8}
// s3 contains {3, 6, 9}
set<int> t1;
set_union(s2.begin(), s2.end(), s3.begin(), s3.end(),
          inserter(t1, t1.begin()));
// t1 contains {0, 2, 3, 6, 8, 9}
```

The first four parameters are iterators that state the two sets from which we shall create the union. The last parameter is an iterator that states where the result is to be placed. If, as is the case here, we wish to place the result in a set that was previously empty, we must use the insert iterator `inserter`.

Intersections of sets are created in the corresponding way. For example, to form a set `t2` consisting of the elements contained in both `s2` and `s1` we write

```
set<int> t2;
set_intersection(s2.begin(), s2.end(), s3.begin(), s3.end(),
                 inserter(t2, t2.begin()));
// t2 contains {3}
```

The algorithm `set_difference` chooses the elements contained in the first set but not in the second. We can, for example, write

```
set<int> t3;
set_difference(s2.begin(), s2.end(), s3.begin(), s3.end(),
               inserter(t3, t3.begin()));
// t3 contains {0, 2, 8}
```

The algorithm `set_symmetric_difference` creates a new set consisting of the elements contained in the first set but not in the second as well as the elements contained in the second set but not in the first:

```
set<int> t4;
set_symmetric_difference(s2.begin(), s2.end(),
                         s3.begin(), s3.end(),
                         inserter(t4, t4.begin()));
// t4 contains {0, 2, 6, 8, 9}
```

The last algorithm for handling of sets is `includes`. It examines whether a set is part of another set or, in other words, whether all the elements in the first set also exist in the second. For example, to determine whether `t3` is a subset of another set `t4` we can write

```
if ( includes(t4.begin(), t4.end(), t3.begin(), t3.end()) )
  cout << "t4 is a subset of t3" << endl;
```

The elements in a set are always sorted. Here, the rules are the same as for the classes `map` and `multimap`, discussed on page 454. In a set where the elements are of type `etyp`, the elements are normally sorted with a function object of type `less<etyp>`. Just as for the types `map` and `multimap`, you can affect how the sorting is done. If we, for instance, are going to work with a set of texts and want the texts to be sorted alphabetically correctly according to the English alphabet, we can use an object of the class `alpha` as sorter. We can, for example, write

```
alpha comp("en");
set<string, alpha> s(comp);
```

If, as is done here, you have stated that a comparator of your own is to be used, you must include it as an extra parameter if you call any of the following algorithms: `set_union`, `set_intersection`, `set_difference`, `set_symmetric_difference` or `includes`. If `s1` and `s2` are sets of the same type as `s`, we can, for example, calculate the set union of `s1` and `s2` and put it in `s` by making the call

```
set_union(s1.begin(), s1.end(), s2.begin(), s2.end(),
          inserter(s, s.begin()), comp);
```

To finish this section, we show a program that performs a simple comparative analysis of natural text. The program reads a number of files that contain natural text and prints out all words that occur in all the files. The names of the files are given as arguments to `main` on the `command` line. You can state an arbitrary number of files. If, for example, the program is called `analysis` and the files `essay1.txt`, `essay2.txt` and `essay3.txt` are to be analysed, you start the program with the command

```
analysis essay1.txt essay2.txt essay3.txt
```

The program looks like this:

```
#include <iostream>
#include <fstream>
#include <cstdlib>
#include <set>
#include <algorithm>
#include "alpha.h"
using namespace std;
// new_word reads a word, gives an empty string at end of file
string new_word(istream& f, alpha& a)
{
  int c;
  string s;
  // Skip all characters which are not letters
  while ((c=f.peek()) != EOF && !a.is_letter(c))
    f.get();
  // Compose a word of the letters following
  while ((c=f.peek()) != EOF && a.is_letter(c))
    s += f.get();
  return s;
}
main(int argc, char *argv[])
```

```
{
  alpha a("en");
  ifstream f;
  string word;
  set<string, alpha> s1(a), s2(a), s3(a);
  for (int i=1; i< argc; i++) {
    ifstream f(argv[i]);   // open next file
    if (!f) {
      cout << "The file " << argv[i]<< " cannot be opened"<<endl;
      exit(EXIT_FAILURE);
    }
    s1.clear();  // place the words in file no. i in the set s1
    while ((word=new_word(f, a)).size() > 0)
    {
      a.to_lower_case(word);  // translate to lower case letters
      s1.insert(word);
    }
    if (i==1)
      s2 = s1;
    else {
      // form the intersection of new words and previous words
      s3.clear();
      set_intersection(s1.begin(), s1.end(),
                       s2.begin(), s2.end(),
                       inserter(s3, s3.begin()), a);
      s2 = s3;  // s2 contains the intersection of all words
    }
  }
  ostream_iterator<string> out(cout, "\n");
  copy(s2.begin(), s2.end(), out);  // print out s2
}
```

In the program a separate function `new_word` is used to read one word at a time from a text file. For each file, all the words in the file are put in a set `s1`. The set `s2` contains the intersection of sets of all the words in the previously read files, and the set `s3` is a set that is used temporarily to create the intersection of sets `s1` and `s2`. The final printout is made with the help of an iterator that points to an `out` stream (see section 12.1.3 on page 427).

It is assumed that the read files contain text that is coded according to the standard `LATIN_1`. If the final printout is to be made in an MS-DOS window, you must add the following lines to the program:

```
#include "iodos.h"
dos_console();
```

so that letters other than a–z will be printed correctly.

12.6 Queues and stacks

Among the standard classes there are three known as *container adapters*: `stack`, `queue` and `priority_queue`. These classes are implemented using one of the standard classes `vector`, `list` or `deque`, and they offer the programmer a simplified interface with only a few operations. You cannot, for instance, use iterators.

A *stack* is a data structure in which you can place individual data elements according to the principle 'last in first out'. A stack can be compared to a pile of plates in a cafeteria. When new plates are placed on the pile, they are placed on top of the ones that are already there, and when you take a plate, you have to take the top plate on the pile. For stacks, there are the operations `push` and `pop`. The operation `push` places a data element on the top of the stack, and the operation `pop` removes the top element. If you wish to read the top element without removing it, you use the operation `top`. In addition to these operations, there are the operations `empty`, which states whether or not a stack is empty, and `size`, which states the number of elements in the stack. A stack is illustrated in Figure 12.2.

In a stack input and output take place at the same end of the data structure, whereas in a queue input and output take place at two different ends of the data structure. Thus a queue uses the principle 'first in first out'. This is illustrated in Figure 12.3. Here too

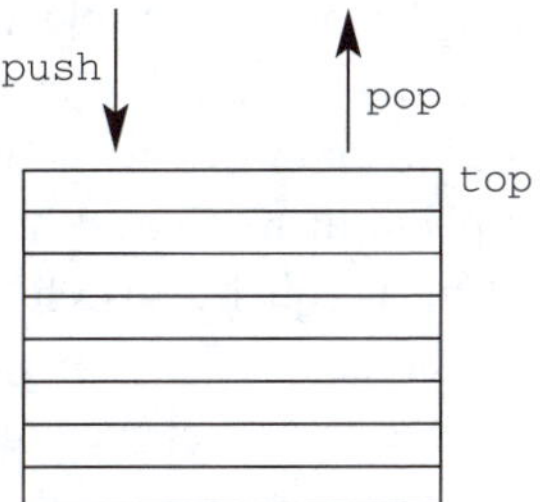

Figure 12.2 A stack

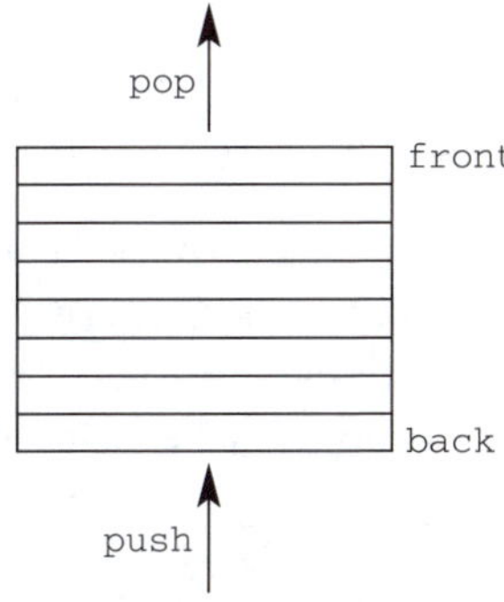

Figure 12.3 A queue

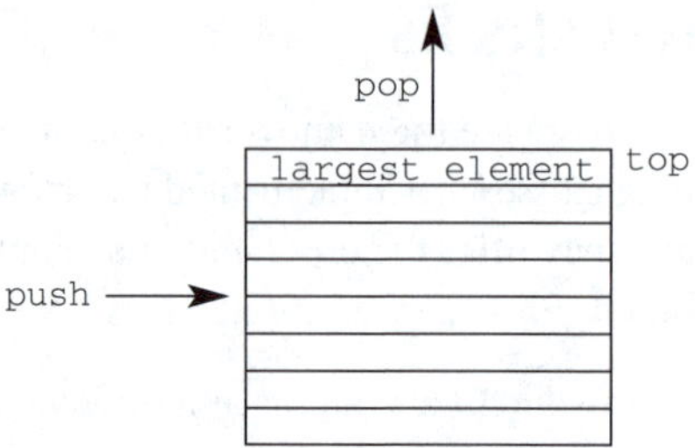

Figure 12.4 A priority queue

the operations to put in and take out elements are called `push` and `pop`. You can read either the last element or the first element using the operations `front` and `back` respectively. The operations `empty` and `size` are also available.

The third container adapter is used to create *priority queues*. A priority queue is one in which the element with the highest priority is always first in the queue. We illustrate this in Figure 12.4.

A new element is put in with the operation `push`. Where the new element ends up in the data structure depends on its value. If it is largest it is placed first, otherwise it ends up in one of the places further behind. Note that the elements do not need to be sorted. In the standard class `priority_queue` a storing principle is instead used, usually referred to as *heap*. We do not need to know exactly how this principle looks, but as a structure it is more effective to uphold than a sorted sequence. (A tree-like structure is where every node is greater than or equal to its child nodes.) The operation `pop` removes the largest element from the queue. The other elements will then automatically be rearranged, so that the next to largest element ends up first. To read the first element in a priority queue without removing it from the queue you use the operation `top`. A priority queue, like the other container adaptors, also has the operations `empty` and `size`.

In the information window below the operations available for container adaptors are summarized. Note that iterators cannot be used for container adaptors.

We now show some examples. In the first example we use a stack to input a text from the keyboard and output the text backwards. We read one symbol at a time and place it in a stack where the elements have the type `char`. The class stack is defined in the file `<stack>`, and this file must therefore first be included in the program:

```
#include <stack>
#include <iostream>
using namespace std;
```

```
main()
{
  stack<char> s;
  char c;
  cout << "Enter a text. Finish with Ctrl-Z" << endl;
  // read the text
  while (cin.get(c))
    s.push(c);
  // write out the text backwards
  while (!s.empty())
  {
    cout << s.top();
    s.pop();
  }
  cout << endl;
}
```

Operations for the container adaptors `stack`, `queue` and `priority_queue`

Below, `a` denotes `stack`, `queue` or `priority_queue`.
`atyp` denotes the type of the container and `etyp` the type of the elements.
`x` and `y` denote containers of type `stack`, `queue` or `priority_queue`.
`c` is a comparator (a function object) and `ctyp` is its type.

`a<etyp>`	States the type of container (`atyp`). For a `priority_queue` the comparator type is `less<etyp>`.
`a<etyp, vector<etyp>, ctyp>`	Only for `priority_queue`. States the type of the queue. The comparator type is `ctyp`.
`atyp x;`	Creates an empty container. For a `priority_queue` the elements are compared with an object created with `ctyp()`.
`atyp x(c);`	Only for `priority_queue`. Creates an empty queue. The elements are compared with `c`.
`y = x;`	Assignment. `y` becomes a copy of the set `x`.
`x.push(v);`	Puts in the value `v` of the type `etyp` in `x`. If `x` is a stack `v` is put on top, if `x` is a queue `v` is put last, and if `x` is a `priority_queue` `v` is put into `x` so that the largest value ends up first.
`x.pop();`	Removes the top (first) element from `x`.
`x.top()`	Reads the top (first) element in `x`. (Does not exist for `queue`.)
`x.front()`	Reads the first element in `x`. (Exists only for `queue`.)
`x.back()`	Reads the last element in `x`. (Exists only for `queue`.)
`x.size()`	Gives the number of elements in `x`.
`x.empty()`	Gives **`true`** if the number of elements in `x` is `0`, otherwise **`false`**.

In the next example some integer numbers are input from the keyboard. When all the numbers have been input, they are printed out in the same order in which they were read in. The program has the following appearance. The class `queue` is defined in the file `<queue>`.

```
#include <queue>
#include <iostream>
using namespace std;
main()
{
  queue<int> q;
  int i;
  cout << "Enter integer numbers. Finish with Ctrl-Z" << endl;
  // read the numbers
  while (cin >> i)
    q.push(i);
  // print out the numbers in the order they were read
  while (!q.empty())
  {
    cout << q.front() << " ";
    q.pop();
  }
}
```

In the third example a priority queue is used instead to store the input integer numbers. This means that the numbers that are put in will be stored according to size, with the largest number first. The class `priority_queue` is also defined in the file `<queue>`.

```
#include <queue>
#include <iostream>
#include <utility>
using namespace std;
main()
{
  priority_queue<int> p;
  int i;
  cout << "Enter integer numbers. Finish with Ctrl-Z" << endl;
  // read the numbers
  while (cin >> i)
    p.push(i);
  // print out the numbers in order, the largest number first
  while (!p.empty())
  {
    cout << p.top() << " ";
    p.pop();
  }
}
```

To be able to decide which element is the largest in a priority queue, the elements must be comparable. This comparison is made with a function object. If nothing specific is stated, a function object of the predefined type `less<etyp>` will be used. Here `etyp` denotes the type of the element. This means that the regular operator `<` is used. It is simple to specify that some other comparator should be used. If, for instance, in the last example we had declared the priority queue in the following way, the last element would instead always have been first in the queue:

```
priority_queue<int, vector<int>, greater<int> > p;
```

It is the last parameter in the type specifier that determines that `greater<int>` is to be used instead of `less<int>`.The parameter `vector<int>` must be included. It states that the priority queue is to be implemented with the help of the underlying type `vector`.

In the last example we demonstrate how you can put messages into a priority queue. Each message contains a text and an integer number that states its priority.

To describe messages, we first declare a class `Message`:

```
#include <string>
using namespace std
class Message {
public:
  // constructor
  Message(string m = "", int p = 0) : s(m), pri(p) {}
  // function call operator, compares priorities
  bool operator()(const Message& m1, const Message& m2)
  { return m1.priority < m2.priority; }
  string s;
  int priority;
};
```

We can then declare a priority queue that we call `pq`:

```
priority_queue<Message, vector<Message>, Message> pq;
```

The first parameter in the type `specifier` says that we are to put elements of type `Message` in the queue. The second element says that the queue is to be implemented with the help of the standard class `vector`. The last parameter says that comparisons are to be made with a function object of type `Message`. This is possible, since in the function object `Message` we have put in a function call operator that compares two messages and decides which one has the lowest priority.

We can now put messages into the queue with the statement

```
pq.push(Message(mess, pri));
```

Here we have assumed that the variable `mess` has the type `string` and `pri` the type **`int`**.

If you wish to read the messages in the queue in priority order, you can give the statements

```
// write out the messages in priority order
while (!pq.empty())
{
   cout << (pq.top().s) << " ";
   pq.pop();
}
```

Exercises

12.1 In Exercise 5.3 on page 199 you were asked to write a function that puts the characters in a text string in reverse order with the help of two pointers. The second parameter to the function was a pointer to the string. Create a new, simpler, version of this function. *Tip*: Use the algorithm `reserve`.

12.2 Give a new answer to Exercise 5.4 on page 199. Put the numbers in a list and use a standard algorithm to examine whether a certain number has been read in previously.

12.3 Give a new answer to Exercise 5.5 on page 199. In the new answer, use the standard algorithm `accumulate` (see page 613) to calculate the total of the squares.

12.4 Give a new answer to Exercise 5.6 on page 199. In the new answer, use the standard algorithm `inner_product` (see page 613) to calculate the sum.

12.5 In Exercise 5.17 on page 202 you were required to translate regular text to and from Morse code. Give a new answer to the second part of the exercise – that is, the part where you are required to translate from Morse code to regular text. In the new solution, use a container of the kind `map`.

12.6 Write a program that reads a file containing a C++ program and that prints out all words in the file that are not reserved words in C++. *Tip*: Use the function `new_word` on page 461.

12.7 Give a new answer to Exercise 11.10 on page 417. Read in all the items in the file to a container of the kind `priority_queue`, and thereafter print out the items on the file again. Let the class that describes the items in the file also contain a function call operator that compares two teams and decides which team is the worst. The class can then be used to create a function object that is needed to make the comparisons in the priority queue.

Dynamic data structures

13

So far we have been using the standardized container classes, `list` and `map` for instance, without worrying about how these classes are constructed internally. The use of standard classes simplifies the programming to a great degree. Sometimes, however, the standard classes are not appropriate, and you have to construct your own data structures. As a programmer you should therefore be familiar with the mechanisms used to build general data structures. This also increases understanding of the standardized container classes. Above all there are two language constructs that are of interest: *dynamic data structures* and *templates*. Dynamic data structures are discussed in this chapter, and templates are dealt with in Chapter 14.

When you want to describe many equal (or similar) objects in a program you can use arrays. Arrays are, as we have seen, very useful things, but there are situations where their value is limited. In some applications, for example, we may have collections of data without a definite idea of how many objects we need. In such cases we have to use dynamic data structures, which can grow and shrink during program execution. In this chapter we shall study how to create dynamic data structures with the help of classes and pointers. We shall be paying particular attention to the commonly used data structures *lists*, *queues*, *sets* and *trees*.

13.1 Linked lists: the basics

We shall begin by discussing *linked lists*. In this section we shall be describing the fundamental technical aspects: how linked lists are constructed, and how they are handled. There are singly linked lists and doubly linked lists. In section 13.2 we shall be using linked lists as building blocks when we construct abstract data types – stacks, queues and sets – on a higher level.

13.1.1 Singly linked lists

A linked list, with three integers, is illustrated in Figure 13.1. A linked list consists of a number of elements, and each element has two components, a pointer to the next

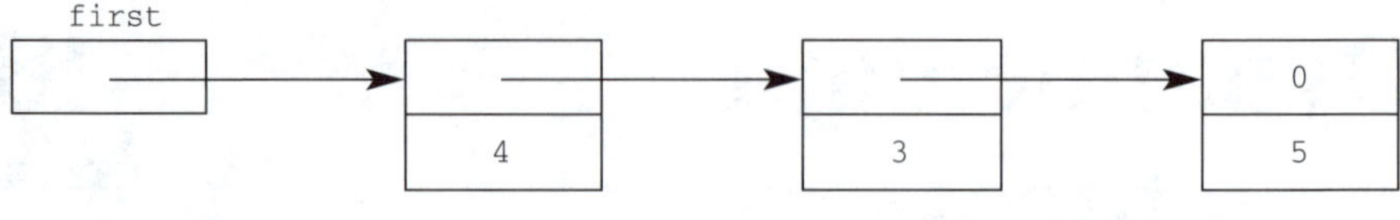

Figure 13.1

element in the list and a value, which can be of any type. In this chapter we shall assume, for the sake of simplicity, that this value is an integer. We shall see later, in Chapter 14, how this can be generalized to give components of arbitrary value. The first element of a list is usually called its *head*, and that element is pointed to by a special pointer. We have called this pointer `first`. The last element in the list contains a value of `0` – that is, a null pointer. This marks the end of the list.

Building up a list

A list element can be defined with the aid of the following class:

```
class Element {
public:
   Element *next;
   int data;
   Element(Element *n, int d) : next(n), data(d) {}
};
```

In class `Element` there are two data members: `next`, which is a pointer to the next element; and `data`, which contains the value of the list element. The type for the data member `next` is `Element *` – that is, 'pointer to `Element`'. A constructor that is called when new list elements are created has been added to class `Element`. For simplicity, we have placed all the members in the **`public`** section, where they are visible.

Now a linked list will be built up using class `Element`. We begin by declaring the pointer variable `first`, which will point to the first list element:

```
Element *first=0;
```

The pointer `first` has been initialized to a value of `0`, which says that the list is empty (has no elements). We can now create a list element and place it in the list:

```
first = new Element(first, 5);
```

The pointer `first` will point to the new element, which is initialized by the constructor in class `Element`. Since the pointer `first` earlier had a value of zero, the data member `next` in the new element will have a value of `0`. It will then look as in Figure 13.2.

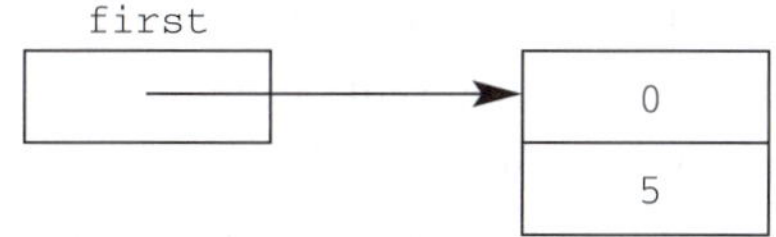

Figure 13.2

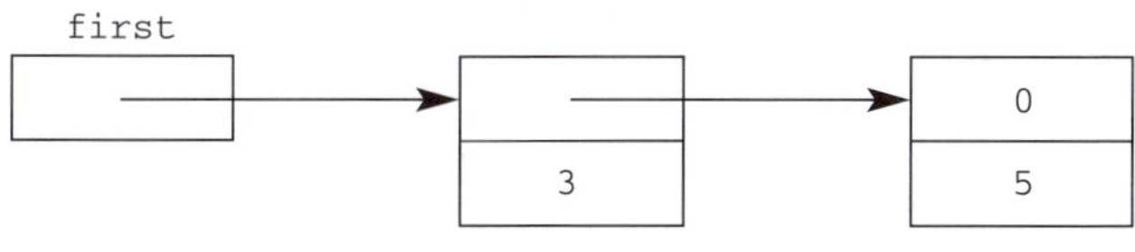

Figure 13.3

Assume now that we wish to create a new list element with a value of `3` and place it first in the list. This we do simply by writing

```
first = new Element(first, 3);
```

This is exactly the same statement that was used earlier to insert the first element! The only difference is that the value `3` has been indicated instead of `5`. Since the pointer `first` points to the element with value `5` before the statement is performed, data member `next` in the new element will point to the element with value `5`. The situation is shown in Figure 13.3.

To get the list in Figure 13.1, we can use the statement again:

```
first = new Element(first, 4);
```

Running through a list

If we want to run through all the elements in a list, we can simply start at the first element and continue until the last element is reached. The following statement can be used to write out all the elements in a list:

```
for (Element *p=first; p; p=p->next)
  cout << p->data << ' ';
```

Another pointer `p` is used here, of type 'pointer to `Element`', and this is initialized so that it points to the first element in the list. The condition for continuing is `p`, which may seem rather strange. The condition is 'true' if variable `p` contains a value not equal to `0`: that is, if `p` does not contain a null pointer. A null pointer is interpreted as the value 'false'. We could also have written `p!=0`. At every round, `p->data` is written out. Note that the arrow operator has to be used here, as `p` is a *pointer* to an object. At the end of every round the statement `p=p->next` is performed: thus pointer `p` will point to the next element in the list. In the last round, `p` will have a value of `0`.

The same technique can be used if we want to search in a list, for instance. The function below searches for a particular value in the list. As parameter, the function gets a pointer to the first element in the list and the value searched for. If this value is in the list, the function gives as result a pointer to the list element where the value is to be found. If it is not in the list, the function gives a null pointer as result.

```
Element *search(Element *first, int searched)
{
   Element *p;
   for (p=first; p && p->data!=searched; p=p->next)
      ;
   return p;
}
```

In the function, p is simply allowed to run through the list until the end (p gets the value 0) or until the value searched for has been found, in which case p will contain a pointer to this list element.

Note that the tests must be performed in the correct order in the **for** statement. We have to test whether p is different from 0 *before* the expression p->data is computed. If this is not done, there will be an execution error when p happens to be the same as 0.

Putting elements into a list and removing them

We have seen from the above that we can easily put a new element first in a list with a single statement. A function can be constructed that does this:

```
void put_first(Element *& first, int d)
{
   first = new Element(first, d);
}
```

If we want to create a list with two elements that contain the values 10 and 20, for example, we can call the function twice:

```
Element *h=0;
put_first(h, 20);
put_first(h, 10);
```

Here we use a pointer with the name h to point to the first element in the list.

The function put_first has two parameters. The second one is the value that will be put in the new list element. The type of the first parameter may look rather strange. Parameter first has the type '*reference* to a pointer to Element'. We know that we have to use a reference parameter if we want to change a parameter's value in a function, and we have to do this here, since the pointer indicated in the call must be changeable. In our example, we have to be able to change the *pointer* h *itself*. It is not sufficient to be able to change what h points to.

Thus it is not difficult to put an element first in a list. To put a new element last in a list is a little more difficult because the whole list has to be run through until the end is reached. The following function creates a new list element and puts it last in the list. We must also have a reference parameter here, since we have to be able to change the pointer itself in case the list has been empty from the beginning.

```
void put_last(Element *& first, int d)
{
  if (! first)
    // Empty list, put in new element first
    first = new Element(0, d);
  else
  {
    Element *p;
    for (p=first; p->next; p=p->next)
      ;
    // p points to the last element now
    // Put in a new element after p
    p->next = new Element(0, d);
  }
}
```

The case of the empty list must be treated separately because in that case the parameter first has to be changed. If the list is not empty, the pointer p is made to run through the whole list until the end has been reached. Note especially that the test condition in the **for** statement is p->next, not p. This means that the **for** statement is terminated when p points to the last element in the list. If the test condition had been p, we would have gone one round too many and p would have got the value 0. When the new list element has been created, the data member next in the earlier last element will contain a pointer to the new element. This is why p->next is changed in the last statement.

It is sometimes necessary to place a new element in a particular position in a linked list. Suppose, for example, we have an element in a list and a pointer p is pointing to it. Now suppose we want to put a new element with value 4 *after* this. The new element can then be created and placed in the list with a single statement:

```
p->next = new Element(p->next, 9);
```

Figure 13.4 illustrates this. The dashed line shows the situation before the statement above is executed. If we had wanted to insert a new element in front of a particular element that is pointed to, it would have been much more problematic. Then we would have had to run through the list from the beginning in order to get a pointer to the element in front of the one pointed to.

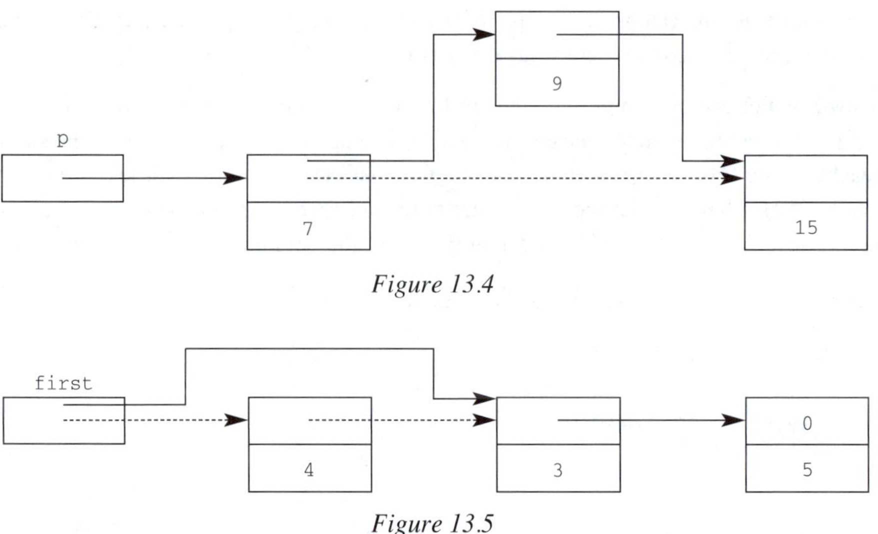

Figure 13.4

Figure 13.5

In certain cases it is simple to remove elements from a list. The first element can be removed with the statement

```
first = first->next;
```

This is demonstrated in Figure 13.5, where the dashed lines show the situation before the statement is executed. It is also easy to remove the element coming after one to which there is a pointer. For example, we can remove the element that lies after the one that `p` points to:

```
p->next = p->next->next;
```

It is a little more difficult to remove the last element in a list or a particular element in the list.

Linked lists and recursion

A list can be seen as a *recursive data type*, and it can be said that a list is either empty, or consists of two components, a *head* and a *tail*. The head is the value in the first element of the list (an integer, for instance), and the tail is a list consisting of all the elements except the first. The tail is therefore a list that is one element shorter than the original. This perspective can be extremely useful in solving certain problems involving list handling.

We saw above that it is possible to write out the contents of a list by going through the elements of the list from start to finish, using a **`for`** statement. This was easily done. It would have been much harder if we had wanted them written out in reverse order, with the last element written first, but this problem can be solved elegantly using recursion. The following function will write out a list in reverse order:

```
void write_reverse(Element *first)
{
  if (first)
  {
    write_reverse(first->next);
    cout << first->data << ' ';
  }
}
```

This says that a list can be written out in reverse order if we first write out its tail in reverse order and then write out its head. The list head is `first->data`, and `first->next` is a pointer to the list tail. An empty list has no elements, and there is nothing to write for such a list.

We have already studied the problem of placing a new element at the end of a list, but it can be solved much more simply by using recursion. The following algorithm is used: if the list is empty, then the new element is the list's only element and so is placed at the start of the list, otherwise the new element should be placed at the end of the tail.

```
void put_last_rec(Element *& first, int d)
{
  if (! first)
    first = new Element(0, d);
  else
    put_last_rec(first->next, d);
}
```

Note that there must be a reference parameter here, since we must be able to change the parameter `first`.

13.1.2 Doubly linked lists

One problem with the lists studied so far is that the whole list has to be run through – using either iteration or recursion – if an element has to be inserted or removed at the end of the list or in front of an element pointed to. If we have to work with a list and these operations are used frequently, it can be appropriate to construct a *doubly linked* list. In such a list each element contains two pointers, apart from the element's value. One pointer points to the next element in the list, and the other points to the previous element. This is illustrated in Figure 13.6. Such a list is often made circular, as in the figure, by making the forward pointer of the last element point to the first element and the first element's backward pointer point to the last element.

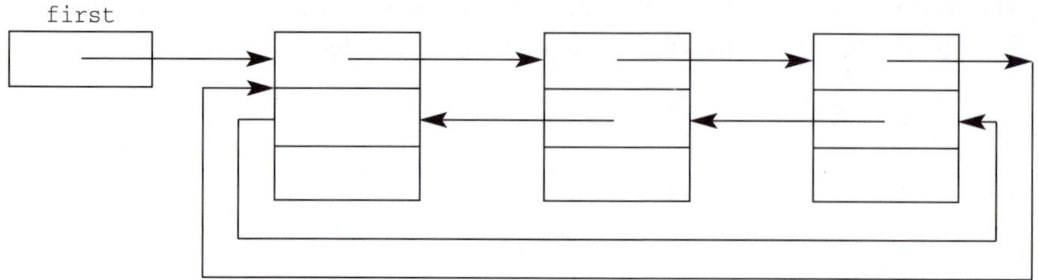

Figure 13.6

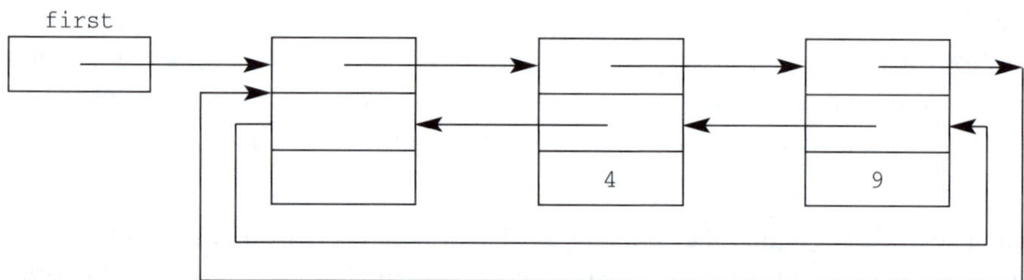

Figure 13.7

To describe an element in a doubly linked list with values of type `int`, we can use the following class. Apart from the two pointers and the value of the list element, the class contains a constructor with which new list elements can be constructed. This constructor will also function as a default constructor.

```
class Element {
public:
   Element *forward, *backward;
   int data;
   Element(Element *f=0, Element *b=0, int d=0)
      : forward(f), backward(b), data(d) {}
};
```

When working with linked lists, an empty list must be handled in a special way. This makes functions handling the lists a little longer and more complicated. To avoid this problem it is useful to let every list have a special element at the start of the list but which does not belong to the list itself. This is particularly useful when handling doubly linked lists. If, for example, we want to represent a list of integers that contains two elements, 4 and 9, we can do this with the list in Figure 13.7. Note that the first element, whose value is of no importance, does not belong to the logical list. If this technique of a special first element is used, the empty list can be described as in Figure 13.8. To build up the structure in this figure, the following statements can be executed:

```
first = new Element;
first->forward = first->backward = first;
```

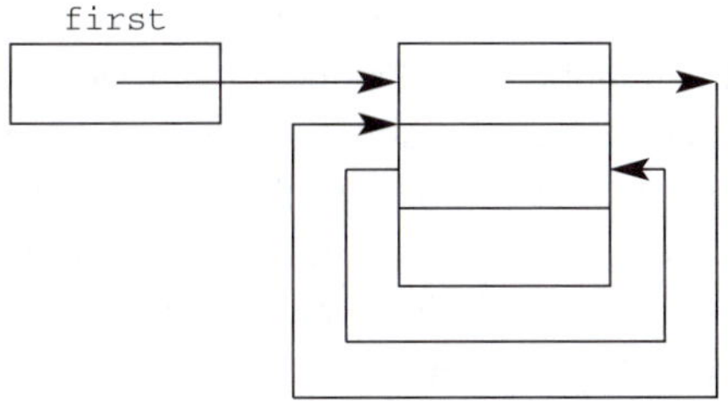

Figure 13.8

If we use a special element at the start of the list, the pointer `first` can never be equal to `0` because it will always point to this element. If we want to test whether a list is empty, therefore, there is no point in testing whether `first` is equal to `0`. But we can write instead:

```
if (first->forward == first)
```

The advantage of a doubly linked list is that it is never necessary to run through one in order to make changes. The following function, for example, removes an element from a list:

```
void remove(Element *e)
{
  e->backward->forward = e->forward;
  e->forward->backward = e->backward;
  delete e;
}
```

The parameter `e` points to the element to be removed. The first statement in the function means that the forward pointer in the element in front of the element pointed to will point to the element after the one pointed to. Correspondingly, the second statement means that the backward pointer in the element after the one pointed to will point to the element in front of the one pointed to. The result is that the element pointed to has been 'linked out' of the list. (We do not need to change the pointers in the target element, since this will be removed in the last statement.) Because there is a special element at the start of the list, it will not matter if the target element is the first, last, or some other element in the list. The code remains the same.

We shall take another example. The following function will insert a new element in front of a given element. The parameter `e` points to the element in front of which the new element will be put, and `d` is the value that the new element will have.

```
void put_before (Element *e, int d)
{
  Element *pnew = new Element(e, e->backward, d);
  e->backward->forward = pnew;
  e->backward = pnew;
}
```

Memory space is first allocated for the new element, and pointer pnew is set to point to it. The new element is initialized so that the forward pointer gets the value e (thus it will point to the element that e points to) and the backward pointer gets the value e->backward (which means that it points to the element in front of the one that e points to.) The value in the new element is initialized to d. The new list element is now initialized. It only remains to see that it is linked in the list in the right place. This is done with two statements. The statement e->backward->forward=pnew means that the forward pointer in the element in front of the one that e points to will point to the new element instead; and the statement e->backward=pnew changes the backward pointer in the element that e points to, so that it points to the new element.

Note here, too, that it is of no importance where in the list the new element is placed.

The function put_before can now be used to implement the function that puts a new element first in the list:

```
void put_first(Element *first, int d)
{
  put_before(first->forward, d);
}
```

Note that we must have first->forward and not first. The new starting point should of course be placed in front of list element 2. The special start element should always remain first in the list. However, inserting a new element after a given element pointed to is a trivial case. We can write the function

```
void put_after(Element *e, int d)
{
  put_before(e->forward, d);
}
```

Since the backward pointer in the special first list element points to the last element of the list, it will be a simple matter to insert a new element last in the list. We can also write a function here:

```
void put_last(Element *first, int d)
{
  put_after(first->backward, d);
}
```

If we want to run through a doubly linked list, we do so in the same way as with a singly linked list. When dealing with a circular list, however, the trap of a never-ending round is certainly to be avoided. The following function writes out a doubly linked list that has a special start element:

```
void write(Element *first)
{
  Element *p;
  for (p=first->forward; p!=first; p=p->forward)
    cout << p->data << ' ';
}
```

Note that `p` is initialized so that it points to the second list element in the first round. Thus we jump over the special start element. Note also the end condition `p!=first`. When `p` has reached the last node in the list, the forward pointer points to the start element, since the list is circular. If we had tested whether `p` was equal to `0`, the program would have got itself into a never-ending round.

When working with doubly linked lists, there is scarcely any need for recursion because it is as simple to scan a list forwards as in reverse order. If we want to write out a list in reverse order, we can use the following function:

```
void write_reverse(Element *first)
{
  Element *p;
  for (p=first->backward; p!=first; p=p->backward)
    cout << p->data << ' ';
}
```

13.2 Linked lists: applications

In this section we shall be constructing classes that define some common abstract data types – stacks, queues and sets. Classes will be implemented making use of linked lists. In Chapter 14 we shall demonstrate a general list class that is implemented with a doubly linked list.

13.2.1 Stacks

As we discussed in section 12.6, a *stack* is a data structure that uses the principle 'last in, first out'. The operation `push` places a data element on top of the stack, and `pop` removes the top element from the stack. To read the top element without removing it you can use the operation `top`.

A stack can easily be constructed with a singly linked list. We let the first list element contain the stack's top. A `push` operation means that a new element is put first in the list, and a `pop` operation removes the first element from the list. We can define a class `Stack` and place the definition in a file with the name `stack.h`. We shall assume that the data elements to be placed in the stack have type **`int`**.

```
// The file stack.h
#include <stdexcept>
using namespace std;
class Element;
class Stack {
public:
  Stack() : first(0) {};
  ~Stack();
  void push(int d);
  void pop() throw(length_error);
  int  top() throw(length_error);
  bool empty();
private:
  Element *first;
  Stack(const Stack&) {};
  Stack& operator= (const Stack&) {return *this;};
};
```

There are four operations: `push`, `pop` and `top`, as described above, and `empty`, which indicates whether or not a stack is empty. If we try to perform the operations `pop` or `top` on a stack that is empty, it will generate an exception of the standard class `length_error`. In the declaration of function `pop` an exception specification is used to state this.

A stack has a single data member, the pointer `first` that points to the first element in a linked list. The default constructor initializes this pointer to `0`, which means that every new stack created will be automatically empty from the beginning. There is also a destructor that releases all the allocated list elements.

The last two lines in the private section of class `Stack` are particularly noteworthy. There we define our own versions (which do nothing) of a copy constructor and assignment operator. As we know, there is an automatically defined copy constructor and assignment operator for every class, and these copy the data members one by one. If we do not define our own copy constructor and assignment operator for class `Stack`, the pointer `first` will be copied when one stack is copied to another during an initialization or assignment. This would mean that two different stack objects would point to the *same* linked list, which would, naturally, be quite wrong. By defining our own versions of the assignment operator and copy constructor and placing them in the **`private`** section, a user will not be allowed to carry out assignments and initializations of stacks. The risk of two stacks pointing to the same list is thus avoided.

Note that the file contains only a *declaration* of class `Element` and not a complete definition. Just as the user of class `Stack` does not need to know how the internal implementation of a stack looks (and should not, either), neither does the definition of class `Element` need to be in the header file. But there must be a definition that says that

`Element` is a class, otherwise it would not be possible to declare the data member `first`. We put the definition of class `Element` into the file `stack.cpp`, together with the definitions of the member functions in class `Stack`:

```
// The file stack.cpp
#include "stack.h"

class Element {
  friend class Stack;
  Element *next;
  int data;
  Element(Element *n, int d):next(n), data(d) {}
};
void Stack::push(int d)
{
  first = new Element(first, d);
}
void Stack::pop() throw(length_error)
{
  if (empty())
    throw length_error("Stack::pop");
  Element *p=first;
  int d=p->data;
  first = first->next;
  delete p;
}
int Stack::top() throw(length_error)
{
  if (empty())
    throw length_error("Stack::top");
  return first->data;
}
bool Stack::empty()
{
  return !first;
}
Stack::~Stack()
{
  while(!empty())
  {
    Element *p=first;
    first = first->next;
    delete p;
  }
}
```

Class `Element` is defined in the same way as on page 470. The only difference is that all the members have been placed in the **`private`** section (**`private`** is understood when nothing to the contrary is stated). Class `Stack` has been indicated as a friend class, and therefore has access to everything in class `Element`.

The member function `push` in class `Stack` is constructed in the same way as the function `put_first` on page 472, although the reference parameter `first` is not needed here. Instead, function `push` uses the data member `first`, which is of course directly visible since `push` is a member function.

The function `pop` is easy. If the stack is empty, an exception is generated. Otherwise, the first element is linked out of the list, and the value that was found in this element is returned. The memory space occupied by this element is deallocated.

The function `top` simply returns the value in the first element in the list. Should the list be empty, an exception is generated.

In the destructor there is a **`while`** statement that is executed until the list is empty. In every round the first element is linked out of the list and the memory space it occupied is released.

The following program demonstrates how class `Stack` can be used. The program reads a text from the terminal and writes it out in reverse order. (The individual characters that are read have type **`char`**, but they are automatically converted to type **`int`** when they are put into the stack.)

```
#include "stack.h"
#include <iostream>
using namespace std;
main()
{
   Stack s;
   char c;
   cout << "Write a text. Finish with Ctrl-Z" << endl;
   while (cin.get(c))
      s.push(c);
   while (! s.empty())
   {
      c = s.pop();
      cout << c;
   }
}
```

13.2.2 Queues

A queue is a data structure that works on the well-known principle ‘first in, first out’. If a linked list is used to implement a queue, all the new elements should be put in last in the list, and all the elements taken out of the list should be taken out from the beginning.

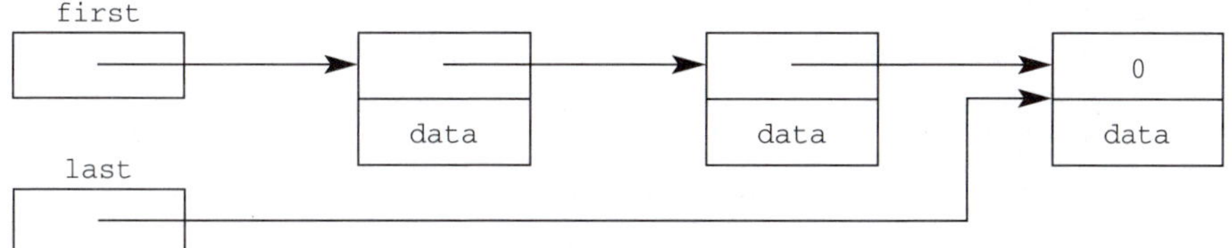

Figure 13.9

As we know, it is easy to take out the first element in a singly linked list. It is more difficult to put in a new element last. Iteration or recursion must be used to run through the whole list from the beginning. Since the operation `push` has to be performed often for a queue, this would not be very efficient. An alternative is to use a doubly linked list, when, as we know, it becomes an easy matter to put new elements last. The problem with using a doubly linked list is that it is unnecessarily complicated and uses a great deal of memory space since every list element contains two pointers instead of one.

But there is yet another alternative. We shall implement a queue with a singly linked list but, besides the usual pointer pointing to the beginning of the list, there will also be a pointer that points to the last element of the list. An illustration of this is shown in Figure 13.9.

We now define a class `Queue`, in which you can add and delete elements of type **`int`**. We let the pointers `first` and `last` be data members. We use the same names for the operations as for the standard class `queue` in section 12.6. The member function `push` is used to add an element at the end and `pop` to delete the first element. The functions `front` and `back` are used to read the first and last elements, respectively, without deleting them from the queue. Finally, the function `empty` determines whether a queue is empty. The member functions `pop`, `front` and `back` generate an exception of the standard class `length_error` if we try to delete or read an element in an empty queue. We put the definition of the class `Queue` in the file `queue.h`, which looks like this:

```
// The file queue.h
#include <stdexcept>
using namespace std;
class Element;
class Queue {
public:
  Queue() : first(0), last(0) {};
  ~Queue();
  void push(int d);
  void pop()   throw(length_error);
  int front() throw(length_error);
  int back()  throw(length_error);
  bool empty();
```

```
private:
   Element *first, *last;
   Queue(const Queue&) {};
   Queue& operator= (const Queue&) {};
};
```

In the constructor both the pointers `first` and `last` are set to null pointers, so that all new queues automatically become empty right from the beginning. The destructor goes through the entire linked list and releases all the list elements.

We have put our own versions of the copy constructor and assignment operator in the `private` section. This prevents a user from copying entire queues when initialization and assignment are carried out. (See the description of stacks on page 479.)

In the same way as when we constructed class `Stack`, we give only a *declaration* of the help class `Element` in the header file. The complete definition of class `Element` is given in the file `queue.cpp`. We shall put the definitions of all member functions there as well:

```
// The file queue.cpp
#include "queue.h"
class Element {
   friend class Queue;
   Element *next;
   int data;
   Element(Element *n, int d):next(n), data(d) {}
};
void Queue::push(int d)
{
   Element *pnew = new Element(0, d);
   if (empty())
     first = pnew;         // the queue was empty, put in first
   else
     last->next = pnew;    // put in after last
   last = pnew;
}
void Queue::pop() throw(length_error)
{
   if (empty())
     throw length_error("Queue::pop");
   Element *p=first;
   first = first->next;
   if (empty())            // the queue became empty
     last = 0;
   delete p;
}
int Queue::front() throw(length_error)
{
   if (empty())
```

```
      throw length_error("Queue::front");
   return first->data;
}
int Queue::back() throw(length_error)
{
   if (empty())
      throw length_error("Queue::front");
   return last->data;
}
bool Queue::empty()
{
   return !first;
}
Queue::~Queue()
{
   while(!empty())
   {
      Element *p=first;
      first = first->next;
      delete p;
   }
}
```

A new element is created in function `push`, and this will be 'linked in' last in the list – that is, normally after the element that the pointer `last` points to. We must also deal with the separate case when the queue was empty before insertion of the new element. In this case the new element is put first in the list. In both cases, the pointer `last` will point to the new element after it has been inserted.

We must deal separately, in function `pop`, with the case where the queue is empty once the first element has been removed. The pointer `last` then gets the value `0`.

13.2.3 Sets

The concept of a *set* is often used in theoretical mathematics. In section 12.5 we saw how the standard class `set` could be used to store a set of different objects, and how standard algorithms such as `set_union` and `set_intersection` could perform different operations on sets. Here, as an alternative, we shall demonstrate how sets can be constructed with the aid of linked lists. We can define a class `Set`:

```
// File set.h
class Element;
class Set {
public:
   Set() : first(0) {};
   Set(const Set& s);
   ~Set();
```

```
    const Set& operator+= (int d);
    const Set& operator-= (int d);
    const Set& operator= (const Set& s);
    Set operator+ (const Set& s) const;   // union
    Set operator^ (const Set& s) const;   // intersection
    bool empty() const;
    bool member(int d) const;
    bool operator== (const Set& s) const;
    bool operator<= (const Set& s) const;
  private:
    Element *first;
    Set(Element *p) : first(p) {};
  };
```

We implement a set with the aid of a singly linked list. The class `Set` contains as its only data member a pointer to the first element in the list, and the default constructor initializes this pointer to `0`. (There are also a copy constructor and a constructor in the private section, but we will be dealing with them later.)

We hide the complete definition of class `Element` in the file `set.cpp` since the user of class `Set` does not need to know what the individual list elements look like. The definition of class `Element` looks like this:

```
  class Element {
  public:
    Element *next;
    int data;
    Element(Element *n, int d) : next(n), data(d) {}
    ~Element() { delete next; }
  };
```

One difference from our previous definition is that we have let all the members be visible. Therefore it has not been necessary to indicate class `Set` as a friend class. We have done this because we shall be using help functions that are not member functions of class `Set`, and they will need to know how the list is built up. In spite of everything in class `Element` being outwardly visible, there is no risk of a user of class `Set` accessing individual list elements in a `Set` object. None of the member functions in class `Set` returns a pointer to a list element.

Another difference in the present class `Element` is that a destructor has been added. This looks quite simple but, in fact, it releases the memory space for all the elements in the linked list. Let us see how the destructor in class `Set` is defined:

```
  Set::~Set()
  {
    delete first;
  }
```

When this destructor is called, the first element in the list is released. Then the destructor for class `Element` will be called for this element. The statement **`delete`** `next` is performed, which means that the memory space for element 2 is released and the destructor for this element called. This in turn releases element 3, whose destructor is called, and so on. The destructor in class `Element` will thus be called recursively until we reach the end of the list. (If the pointer `next` is equal to `0`, nothing is performed in the **`delete`** statement.)

In this example we shall be using recursion for demonstration purposes when we implement the different member functions in class `Set`. As we saw earlier, recursive functions used in connection with linked lists have pointers to the list elements as parameters. The member functions of class `Set` do not have any such parameters. Instead, the pointer `first` to the linked list is a data member. Thus the member functions cannot be called recursively. Instead, we use a common technique in which we make the member functions call recursive help functions internally, letting them do the work. We begin by seeing how the member function for the operator `+=` is constructed. This function adds a new element to the actual set:

```
void add(Element *& p, int d)
{
  if (! p || d < p->data)
    p = new Element(p, d);
  else if (p->data != d)
    add(p->next, d);
}
const Set& Set::operator+= (int d)
{
  add(first, d);
  return *this;
}
```

A recursive help function called `add` is used here. Note that this is not a member function, but it can still know what class `Element` looks like because all the data members here have been declared in the **`public`** section.

We are working with sets that contain integers. A set is implemented with a linked list where there is one list element for each integer in the set. The different integers are placed in the list so that this is *sorted* in order of size, the smaller integers coming first. When a new integer is to be added to a set the following recursive algorithm can therefore be used in the function `add`: if the list is empty, or if the list is not empty but the new number is less than the list's first number, then the new number is placed first in the list. Otherwise, ignore the first number, and put the new number at a suitable place in the list's tail. (If the new number happens to be equal to the first number in the list, nothing at all should be done since the number will then belong to the set already.)

Note that the parameter p is a reference parameter since we must be able to change the pointer itself when a new element is put into the list.

The operator -=, which removes an element from a set, can be implemented in the following way:

```
void sub(Element *& p, int d)
{
   if (p && p->data==d)
   {
      Element *q=p;
      p=p->next;
      q->next = 0;   // NB!
      delete q;
   }
   else if (p && p->data < d)
      sub(p->next, d);
}
const Set& Set::operator-= (int d)
{
   sub(first, d);
   return *this;
}
```

If the list is not empty and the integer to be taken out from the set comes first in the list, the first list element will be linked out and its memory space released. Before this is done, we have to make sure that the pointer next has been set to 0. Otherwise, as we know, the destructor for class Element will be called recursively, and all the elements in the rest of the list will be released as well. If the integer to be removed from the set is not first in the list, we check whether the list's first number is less than the number to be removed. If it is, the number (assuming it exists) must be further along the list, in its tail, and we call the function sub recursively to remove it.

The next member function we shall look at is the assignment operator =. When data structures are implemented using pointers, we almost always have to carry out deep copying if we want to assign one object to another. If we do not define our own assignment operator for class Set, the pointer first will be copied when we make an assignment. This would mean that different set objects would be able to point to the same linked list. When one set is copied to another, all the list elements have to be copied one by one so that a new list is built up. The old list then has to be wiped out.

```
Element *copy(Element *p)
{
   if (! p)
      return 0;
   else
      return new Element(copy(p->next), p->data);
```

```
}
const Set& Set::operator= (const Set& s)
{
  if (first != s.first)   // to itself?
  {
    delete first;
    first = copy(s.first);
  }
  return *this;
}
```

A recursive help function `copy` is used here to do the copying. It can also be used when we implement the copy constructor. Deep copying must also be done here:

```
Set::Set(const Set& s)
{
  first = copy(s.first);
}
```

The member function `member` checks whether a particular integer belongs to the set. We use a help function with the name `exists`. The number searched for is in the list if it is in the first list element or the tail of the list:

```
bool exists(Element *p, int d)
{
  return (p && p->data==d) ||
         (p && exists(p->next, d));
}
bool Set::member(int d) const
{
  return exists(first, d);
}
```

To be able to define the operator `==`, which checks whether two sets are equal, we write a help function with the name `equal` that uses the following recursive idea: two lists are equal if they are both empty; if they are not both empty, then they are equal if their first elements are equal and their tails are equal.

```
bool equal(Element *p1, Element *p2)
{
  return (!p1 && !p2) ||
         (p1 && p2 && p1->data == p2->data &&
          equal(p1->next, p2->next));
}
bool Set::operator== (const Set& s) const
{
  return equal(first, s.first);
}
```

Two operations commonly performed on sets are *union* and *intersection*. The union of two sets `s1` and `s2` is a new set that contains all the elements that are in *either* `s1` or `s2`. An intersection is a new set that contains all the elements that are in *both* `s1` and `s2`. In class `Set` we have declared the two operations `+` and `^`, which compute a union and an intersection respectively. We begin by defining the operator `+`. To implement this operator we use a recursive help function, `uni`. This gets a pointer to two linked lists and gives as result a new list that contains the union of elements in the lists:

```
Element *uni(Element *p1, Element *p2)
{
  if (!p1 && !p2)
    return 0;
  else
    if (!p2 || (p1 && p1->data < p2->data))
      return new Element(uni(p1->next,p2), p1->data);
    else if (!p1 || (p2 && p2->data < p1->data))
      return new Element(uni(p1,p2->next), p2->data);
    else // same first element
      return new Element(uni(p1->next, p2->next), p1->data);
}
Set Set::operator+ (const Set& s) const
{
  return Set(uni(first, s.first));
}
```

The function `uni` uses the following algorithm: if both lists are empty, their union is empty; otherwise, we check the first element in each list and choose the list whose first data element is smallest. This element will be in the union, so a new list element is created that will contain this data element. The tail in the new list will be the same as the union of the rest of the lists. If the two lists should have the same first element, this element will only be included once in the new list. If one list is empty and not the other, we choose the first element in the list that is not empty and let this be included in the union.

In the definition of the operator `+` the function `uni` is called, and this gives as result a linked list that contains the elements to be included in the union set. The constructor that is declared in the **`private`** section of class `Set` is used to initialize the new set object to be given as result.

The next operator we shall look at is the operator `^`, which computes the intersection of two sets. The operator `^` is implemented according to the same model as the operator `+`. A recursive help function, `inter`, is used. Function `inter` gets pointers to the two linked lists as parameters. As result it gives a new list containing the elements included in both lists. A set that contains this list is given as result in the operator `^`. We give the definitions here:

```
Element *inter(Element *p1, Element *p2)
{
  if (! p1 || ! p2)
    return 0;
  else if (p1->data == p2->data)
    return new Element(inter(p1->next, p2->next),
                       p1->data);
  else if (p1->data < p2->data)
    return inter(p1->next, p2);
  else
    return inter(p1, p2->next);
}
Set Set::operator^ (const Set& s) const
{
  return Set(inter(first, s.first));
}
```

Function `inter` first checks whether one of the two lists is empty. If so, a value of `0` is returned, since no common element can be found in the lists. If neither of the lists is empty, a test is made to see whether the two first elements are equal. If they are, a list element with the value of these list elements will be included in the result. If not, we jump over the smallest of these two elements and compute the intersection of the remaining elements.

The only member function that remains to be defined is the operator `<=`, which checks whether the left operand is a subset of the right. This can be done using the member functions we have already constructed. We can check whether a set `s1` is a subset of another set `s2` by forming the intersection of `s1` and `s2`. If the intersection is the same as `s1`, then `s1` contains only such elements as can be found in `s2`: that is, `s1` is a subset of `s2`. We can now define the operator `<=`:

```
bool Set::operator<= (const Set& s) const
{
  return (*this ^ s) == *this;
}
```

13.3 Iterators: implementations

As we saw in Chapter 12, iterators play a central role in the use of standardized container classes. We have seen a large number of examples showing how iterators can be *used*. Now it is time to go deeper and study how iterators can be *constructed*.

We shall give examples of iterators that work in the same way as the iterators in standard C++. In this chapter we later construct iterators that make it possible to run through a set. In Chapter 14 we construct a generic class that describes lists. This class uses iterators and is constructed in exactly the same way as the standard class `list`.

We will now begin by completing the class `Set` with an iterator class. Our iterators should be of the category *forward iterator* (see the information window on page 424). They will have the operations `*` and `++`, and it should also be possible to compare iterators and see whether they refer to the same elements. We call the new class `Iterator`.

Since the new class will go together intimately with class `Set`, its definition is placed *inside* the definition of class `Set`. The complete name of the new class is thus `Set::Iterator`. Before we go into detail, we shall show an example of how class `Iterator` can be used. We write an output operator `<<` for class `Set` that can be used in the same way as the output operator for other types. Now suppose that we have defined a variable `s` of type `Set`, and that `s` contains the numbers `5`, `12` and `19`. We can then have the statement

```
cout << s << endl;
```

and we get written out:

```
[5, 12, 19]
```

The function **`operator<<`** has the following appearance. Note that it is not a member function:

```
ostream& operator<< (ostream& os, const Set& s)
{
  bool first=true;
  Set::Iterator it;
  os << '[';
  for(it=s.begin(); it!=s.end(); ++it)
  {
    if (! first)
      os << ", ";
    os << *it;
    first = false;
  }
  os << ']';
  return os;
};
```

The function gets as parameter the set `s` that should be written out. An iterator with the name `it` is declared in the third line, and in the **`for`** statement two new member functions – `begin` and `end` – are called. These new functions work in exactly the same way as the functions with the same names in the standard classes. Function `begin` gives as result an iterator that refers to the first element in the set. Function `end` also gives an iterator as result. This refers to an imagined first element that lies just *outside* the set.

Now it is time to look at the definition of class `Iterator`. As we explained, it lies inside the definition of class `Set`. We also add the two new member functions `begin` and `end` for class `Set`:

```
// The file set.h
#include <stdexcept>
using namespace std;
class Set {
public:
  class Iterator {
  public:
    Iterator() : point(0) {};
    bool operator== (const Iterator& i) const
                    {return point == i.point;}
    bool operator!= (const Iterator& i) const
                    {return point != i.point;}
    const int& operator* () const
                           throw(out_of_range);
    Iterator& operator++ ()    throw(out_of_range);
    Iterator operator++ (int) throw(out_of_range);
  private:
    friend class Set;
    Element *point;
    Iterator(Element *e) : point(e) {};
  };
  Iterator begin() const {return Iterator(first);}
  Iterator end()   const {return Iterator(0);}
  as before
};
```

No further changes need to be made to class `Set`. Class `Iterator` has only one data member, the pointer `point`, which points to an individual list element in the linked list that a set is built up from. The default constructor for class `Iterator` sets `point` to `0`. If we have an iterator `it` and a set `s` and write the statement

```
it = s.begin();
```

then the data member `point` in `it` will point to the first list element in the set `s`. This follows since function `begin` returns an iterator object where `point` is initialized to the value `first`. Function `end` correspondingly returns an iterator object where `point` has the value `0`.

There are both prefix and postfix versions of the operator `++`. Both versions move the pointer `point` forward so that it comes to point to the next list element for the actual set. If we reach the end of the list – that is, if `point` is equal to `0` and we try to perform one of the operators `++` – an exception will be generated. Note that the complete class name, `Set::Iterator`, must be given when the member functions are defined.

```
// prefix ++i
Set::Iterator& Set::Iterator::operator++ ()
     throw(out_of_range)
{
   if (not point)
     throw out_of_range("Iterator::operator++");
   point = point->next;
   return *this;
}
```

```
// postfix ++i
Set::Iterator Set::Iterator::operator++ (int)
                throw(out_of_range)
{
   Iterator temp = *this;   // Keep the old value
   ++ (*this);              // Move forward
   return temp;             // Return the old value
}
```

The operator `*` is used to access the data element that an iterator refers to. This operator is constructed as a member function, **`operator*`**. As result it gives a reference to the integer that is in the list element that the iterator refers to. Note that the result is a reference to a *constant* integer. This means that the operator `*` cannot be used to change an individual element in a set. Only its value can be read. (If we want to change something in a set we should use the operators `+=` and `-=` as before, to add or remove elements from the set.) If the actual iterator does not refer to a list element, an exception is generated. The definition of the operator `*` is then

```
const int& Set::Iterator::operator* () const
             throw(out_of_range)
{
   if (! point)
     throw out_of_range("Iterator::operator*");
   return point->data;
}
```

If we construct an iterator for another collection of data where we want individual elements to be changeable, a queue for example, we can let the operator `*` return a reference to a value that can be changed. The word **`const`** will then not be in the return type.

Apart from the member functions mentioned previously, class `Iterator` has a copy constructor and the two operators `==` and `!=`, which test whether two iterators are equal or unequal.

It may seem as though this is an unnecessarily complicated mechanism for writing out the contents of a set. Might it not have been easier to let the output operator `<<` be a friend function to class `Set`? Then individual elements in a set could have been accessed directly without the use of an iterator. This is true of course, but the whole point of using iterators is that they offer a general method that can be used in different contexts. Where sets are concerned, it is not necessarily the case, for instance, that we shall always want to write one out in the format `[5, 12, 19]`. As an example, we shall show a program that reads in two lines from the terminal. The program then writes out the characters that occur in one of the lines and the characters that occur in both of the lines. The program uses two sets, `s1` and `s2`. All the characters in the first line are placed in `s1`, and all those in the second line are placed in `s2`. After this the union set and the intersection of the two sets are computed.

```
#include <iostream>
#include "set.h"
using namespace std;
main()
{
  Set s1, s2;
  char line1[200], line2[200], *p;
  cout << "Write two lines" << endl;
  cin.getline(line1, 200);
  cin.getline(line2, 200);
  for (p=line1; *p; p++)
    s1 += *p;
  for (p=line2; *p; p++)
    s2 += *p;
  cout << "Characters in one of the lines:" << endl;
  Set s3 = s1 + s2;
  Set::Iterator it(s3.begin());
  while(it != s3.end())
    cout << char(*it++);
  cout << endl;
  cout << "Characters in both lines:" << endl;
  s3 = s1 ^ s2;
  it = s3.begin();
  while(it != s3.end())
    cout << char(*it++);
  cout << endl;
}
```

Here is an example of how the output might look when the program is run:

```
Write two lines
C++ From the Beginning
The Road to C
  Characters in one of the lines:
  +BCFRTadeghimnort
  Characters in both lines:
  Cehot
```

13.4 Trees

In the section on doubly linked lists we saw that each element could have two pointers. There is, naturally, no limit on the number of pointers in each element, and these pointers do not need to point in such a way as to define a linked list. Using pointers it is possible to build up data structures with elements that are connected arbitrarily. In this section we shall study *trees*. A tree is shown in Figure 13.10.

Trees
• A *root* is a node that no other node in the tree points to. • To any one node there is a *unique* path from the root. • The nodes that do not have pointers to other nodes are called *leaves*.

The elements of a tree are usually called *nodes*. The topmost node is called the tree's *root*. (It is usual to draw and think of a tree in an upside-down position compared with the real thing.) From the root there can be pointers to other nodes in the tree, but there can never be pointers to the root from any of the tree's nodes. In general there are only pointers 'downwards' from each node in the tree. To each node there is only one path from the root. (For example, in Figure 13.10 it is only possible to take path `R-S-V-Y` to get to the node `Y`.) Thus there may only be one pointer to any one node. If a node A points to a node B in a tree, the node B is said to be the *child* of A, and A is said to be the *parent* of B. The root is the only node that is without a parent. The nodes that have no children, `X`, `Y`, `W` and `U` in the figure, are usually called *leaves*, and the pointers in the tree are sometimes called *arcs*.

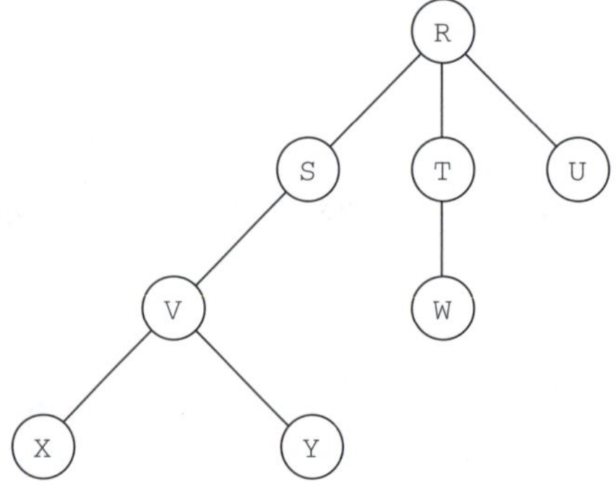

Figure 13.10

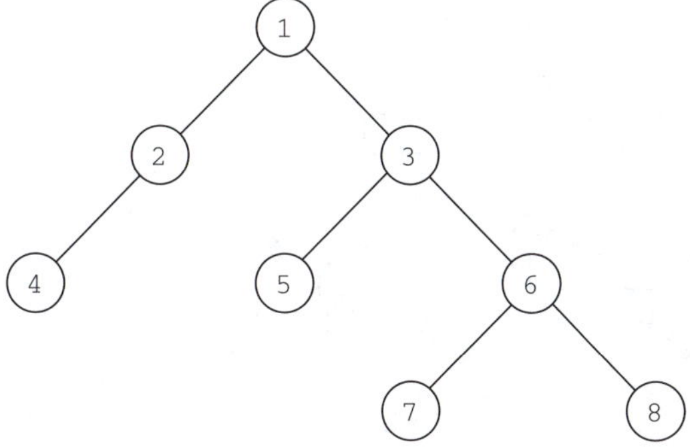

Figure 13.11

13.4.1 Binary trees

In the tree in Figure 13.10 the nodes have up to three children. We shall limit ourselves, however, to trees in which a node can have at most two children. Such trees are common in the construction of data structures, and they are generally called *binary trees*. An example of a binary tree is shown in Figure 13.11.

In C++ a node in a binary tree can be defined by a class:

```
class Node {
public:
  int data;
  Node *left, *right;
  Node(int d=0, Node *l=0, Node *r=0)
    : data(d), left(l), right(r) {}
};
```

For simplicity's sake, we let all the declarations lie in the **public** section of the class. Each node has a data member that defines the contents of the node, and two pointers that point to the node's left and right children respectively. In addition, there is a constructor that initializes all the data members. In our example the data part consists of an integer, but this can easily be generalized so that it is any information at all. If a node is lacking a child, the corresponding pointer has a value of `0`. In a leaf, both pointers are equal to `0`. The tree in Figure 13.11 can be built up as indicated in Figure 13.12. A special pointer `root` points to the root of the tree so that the whole tree can be accessed. If we have an empty tree (a tree with no nodes), then `root` has the value `0`.

Suppose that we have declared a variable `root`:

```
Node *root;
```

and want to build up a tree according to Figure 13.13. We can write the statements

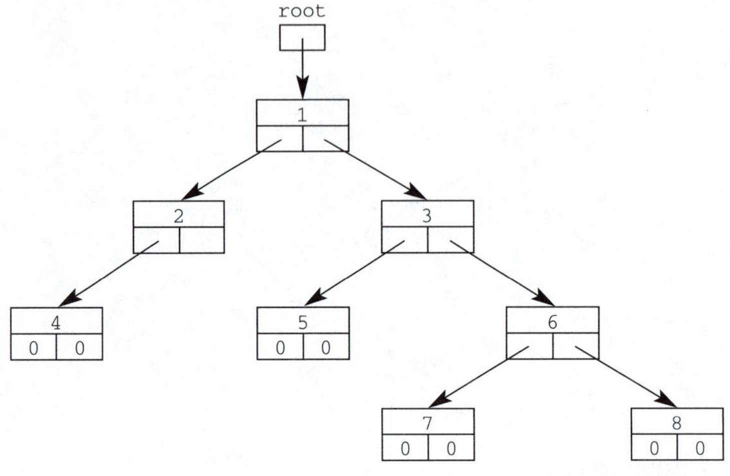

Figure 13.12

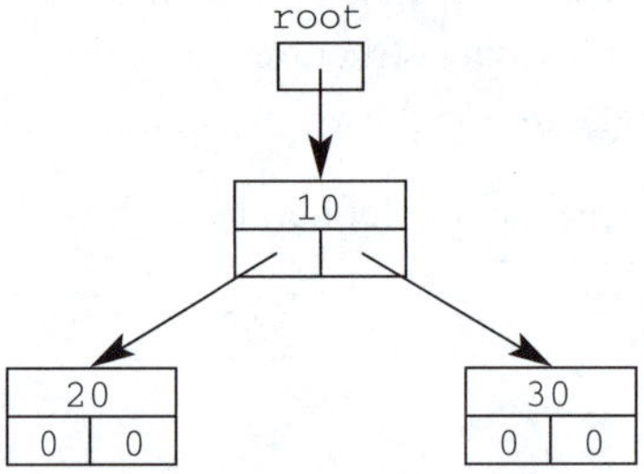

Figure 13.13

```
root = new Node;
root->data = 10;
root->left = new Node;
root->right = new Node;
root->left->data = 20;
root->right->data = 30;
```

Or, we can use a single statement:

```
root = new Node(10, new Node(20), new Node(30));
```

The nodes that lie to the left of the root can be considered as a new, smaller tree, with the left child of the root as its root. This tree is said to be the *subtree* of the original tree. In the same way, the nodes to the right of the root form a right subtree. This is illustrated in Figure 13.14. (For example, the left subtree in Figure 13.11 has node 2 as its root and comprises nodes 2 and 4. The right subtree has node 3 as its root and comprises nodes 3, 5, 6, 7 and 8.)

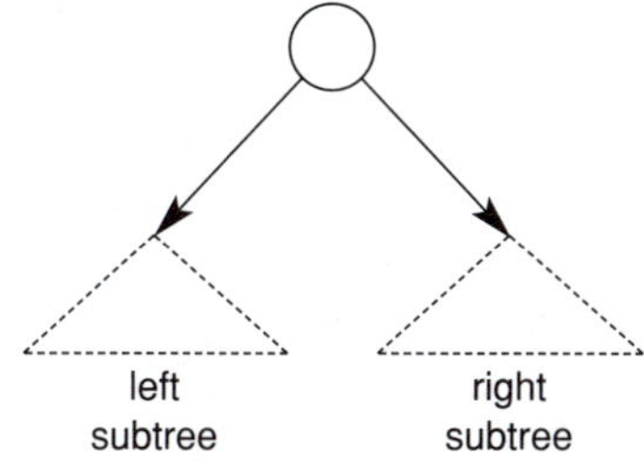

Figure 13.14

With the aid of subtrees, a tree can be regarded as a recursive data type, and the following definition can be given:

A binary tree is either
    empty (has no nodes)
or consists
    of a root, a left subtree and a right subtree.

This concept is useful in the design of programs for handling trees. We shall start by studying how to visit all the nodes of a given tree. We assume that we have a pointer `root`, which points to the root of the tree. When we considered linked lists, it was natural to visit all the elements starting at the beginning and running through to the end, but it is not that simple with a tree. It is possible to think of several alternative ways of traversing a tree. If we look at the tree in Figure 13.11, for example, we may think of visiting the nodes in the order `1-2-3-4-5-6-7-8`. However, to write a program for this (level by level) is rather difficult. It is much simpler and more common to apply the three visiting orders – *preorder*, *inorder* and *postorder* – which are defined recursively. Let us start with the most common, *inorder*:

If the tree is not empty, then:

1. Visit the tree's left subtree.
2. Visit the tree's root.
3. Visit the tree's right subtree.

We shall now try to apply this visiting order to the tree in Figure 13.11. First we note that the tree is not empty, and so the three stages of the algorithm should be carried out. The first stage, 'visit the tree's left subtree', means that the tree in Figure 13.15 should be visited. Since this is also a tree, the visiting algorithm (second instance) should be applied. The tree is not empty, and so we carry out stage 1: that is, the subtree in Figure 13.16 is visited. We now apply a third instance of the algorithm. Since the tree is not empty, we carry out the first stage, 'visit the left subtree': this means that we have to apply a fourth instance of the algorithm. This time the tree to be visited is empty because node `4` has an empty left subtree and the fourth instance of the algorithm thus

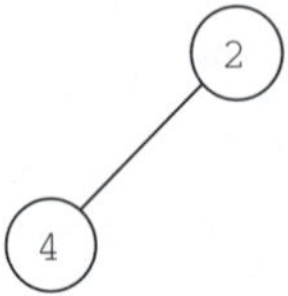

Figure 13.15

Figure 13.16

does nothing. We return to the third instance of the algorithm and carry out its second stage, 'visit the tree's root'. This means that node `4` is visited. The third stage, 'visit the tree's right subtree', starts a fifth instance of the algorithm, which does nothing because the right subtree is empty. Now all the stages of the third instance of the algorithm have been carried out, and we return to the second instance. We carry out the second stage, 'visit the tree's root', for the tree in Figure 13.15. Thus node `2` gets a visit.

Since the tree in Figure 13.15 has an empty right subtree, nothing happens when a sixth instance of the algorithm is carried out, and we return eventually to the first instance of the algorithm. We carry out the second stage, which means that the root of the original tree, node `1`, is visited. Now we have visited nodes `4`, `2` and `1`, in that order, and continue by applying the algorithm in the same way to the right subtree. We eventually find that all the nodes in the tree are visited, in the order `4-2-1-5-3-7-6-8`.

The following recursive function visits and writes out the contents of the nodes of a binary tree according to the *inorder* principle. The function gets a pointer to the root of the tree as parameter.

```
void inorder(Node *p)
{
   if (p)
   {
      inorder(p->left);
      cout << p->data << ' ';
      inorder(p->right);
   }
}
```

The functions for the other two visiting orders can be constructed in a similar way. The only difference is that the three stages in the algorithm already studied are rearranged. In the visiting order *preorder*, the value in the root is written out before the subtree is visited. We then get

```
void preorder(Node *p)
{
  if (p)
  {
    cout << p->data << ' ';
    inorder(p->left);
    inorder(p->right);
  }
}
```

In the visiting order *postorder*, the value in the root is written out after the subtree has been visited. Function `postorder` can then be written:

```
void postorder(Node *p)
{
  if (p)
  {
    inorder(p->left);
    inorder(p->right);
    cout << p->data << ' ';
  }
}
```

As we see, the algorithms for trees are naturally expressed using recursion. We shall now study a function that evaluates the *depth* of a binary tree. The function takes a pointer to the root of the tree as parameter. The depth of a tree can be defined as the number of nodes on the longest path from the tree's root to a leaf. An empty tree has depth 0, and a tree that consists of only a root has depth 1. We write the function:

```
int depth(Node *p)
{
  if (not p)
    return 0;
  else
{
  int ldepth = depth(p->left);
  int rdepth = depth(p->right);
  if (ldepth > rdepth)
    return ldepth + 1;
  else
    return rdepth + 1;
  }
}
```

The simplest case is if the tree is empty. The function then returns the value `0` as its result. If the tree is not empty, the depths of the left and right subtrees are evaluated separately and saved in the variables `ldepth` and `rdepth`. The function `depth` is called recursively

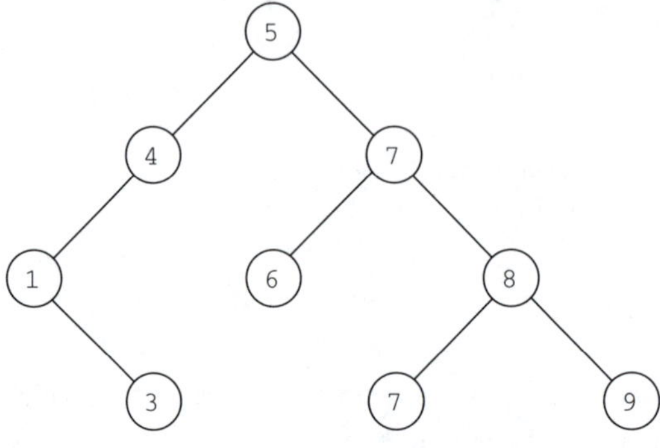

Figure 13.17

to evaluate these depths, with pointers to the respective subtrees as parameter. The function returns the depth of the deepest subtree plus `1` (the root itself) as its result.

13.4.2 Binary search trees

We shall now study a special form of binary tree, a *binary search tree*. The value of each node in such a tree is greater than the values of all the nodes in its left subtree and less than or equal to the values of the nodes in its right subtree. The tree in Figure 13.17 is an example of a binary search tree.

A binary search tree has the property that, if the principle of *inorder* is used to traverse the tree, the nodes will be visited in order of size. The nodes in the tree in Figure 13.17 will be visited in the order `1-3-4-5-6-7-7-8-9`. A binary search tree can be used when information has to be found quickly. Let us study the example of a binary search tree in which each node contains information about a person. Each node stores a person's name and membership number. We define class `Node` below. Apart from its data members, the class contains a constructor that makes it possible to initialize all the data members. This constructor can also serve as a default constructor:

```
class Node {
public:
   int memno;
   char name[20];
   Node *left, *right;
   Node(int mem=0, char *n=0, Node *l=0, Node *r=0)
   : memno(id), left(l), right(r)
   {strcpy(name, n);}
};
```

We can use the following function to find the node in the tree that contains the information about a particular person. The function has two parameters: a pointer to the tree, and a membership number for the required person. As result, the function returns a pointer to the node in which the information about the person is stored. If the person sought is not found in the tree, the function returns as result the value 0.

```
Node *search(Node *p, int searched)
{
  if (not p)
    return 0;
  else if (searched == p->memno)
    return p;
  else if (searched < p->memno)
    return search(p->left, searched);
  else
    return search(p->right, searched);
}
```

The search works as follows. First it checks to see whether the tree is empty and, if so, a result of 0 is returned because there are no entries in the tree. If the root contains the person sought then the task is easy: the result is simply a pointer to the root. In other cases it must look further into one of the subtrees. The particular subtree depends on whether the membership number required is smaller or greater than the membership number in the root. This further searching is achieved by calling the function search recursively with a pointer to the left or right subtree as parameter.

To remove nodes in such a way that the tree remains a binary search tree is somewhat complicated (see Exercise 13.16). However, to insert new nodes is simple, and we shall finish by showing a function for placing information about a new person into a binary search tree. As parameters the function gets a pointer to the root of the tree and the new person's membership number and name. The procedure will create a new node for the new person and insert it in the correct place in the tree so that it remains a binary search tree:

```
void put_in(Node *& p, int new_mem, char *new_name)
{
  if (not p)
    p = new Node(new_mem, new_name);
  else if (new_mem < p->memno)
    put_in(p->left, new_mem, new_name);
  else
    put_in(p->right, new_mem, new_name);
}
```

If the tree is empty, it is easy to insert the entry in the right place. The new node is then the root of the tree, and the pointer p is set to point to this node. Notice that the parameter p must be a reference parameter because it must be both read and updated. If the tree is not empty, a choice must be made as to whether to insert the new node in the left or right subtree, depending on whether the new person's membership number is smaller or greater than the membership number in the root of the tree.

13.4.3 A tree class

All the functions that we have used for handling trees so far have had a pointer to a node as parameter. For instance, we can make the call `inorder(root)` to write out the tree that the pointer `root` points to. This way of doing things is not in the object-oriented spirit of C++. For a C++ programmer it would have been more natural if there had been a class `Tree`. A variable `t` of type `Tree` could then have been declared and a call made of a member function for class `Tree`. We should then be able to write

```
Tree t;
...
t.inorder();
```

Is it not then possible to refashion class `Node` so that the different functions, `inorder`, for example, could be member functions instead of independent functions? Surely we could then rename class `Node` and call it `Tree` instead? Unfortunately this is not possible. The main reason is that certain operations on trees, for instance writing out trees and inserting new nodes, we must also be able to perform on empty trees. So empty tree objects must be able to exist. So far we have represented empty trees by a null pointer of type 'pointer to `Node`', but it is not possible to apply member functions to a null pointer. If we want to have a class that defines trees, we have to go about it in a different way. In this section we shall show how this can be done.

We shall define a new class with the name `Tree`. The class will have a single data member, a pointer to the root of the tree. This pointer is of type 'pointer to `Node`'. An empty tree can then be represented by a tree object where this pointer has the value `0`. We shall also change the definition of class `Node`. The type for the two pointers `left` and `right` will be changed from 'pointer to `Node`' to 'pointer to `Tree`'. This is in line with our observation that a tree is a recursive data type. A tree is either empty or it has a root and two subtrees. To demonstrate the new structure we have redrawn the tree in Figure 13.13, and Figure 13.18 shows how it now looks. We see that we need an extra pointer inserted between each node. At the bottom there are four leaves. These are empty trees and are represented by null pointers.

We begin by redefining class `Node`:

```
class Node {
   friend class Tree;
   int data;
   Tree *left, *right;
   Node(int d);
   ~Node();
};
```

Thus the type for the pointers `left` and `right` has been changed. The constructor has changed and a destructor has been added. Since **`private`** is understood here, everything

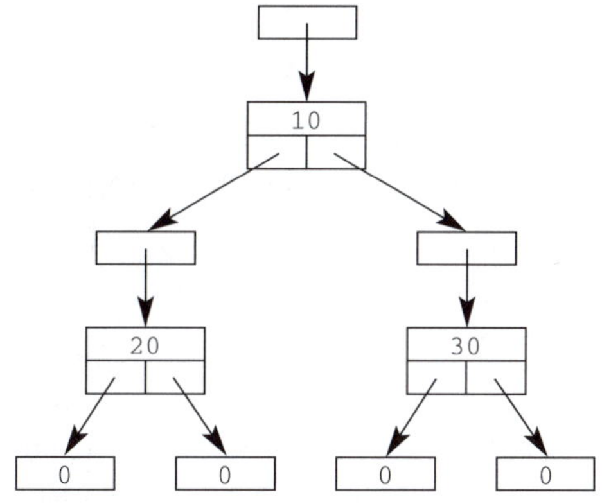

Figure 13.18

is invisible from outside except for class `Tree`, which is declared as a friend class. The definition of class `Tree` has the following appearance:

```
class Tree {
public:
  Tree() : root(0) {};
  Tree(int d) {root=new Node(d);};
  Tree(const Tree& t) {copy(t);};
  ~Tree() {delete root;};
  bool empty() const {return ! root;};
  int& value() const throw(range_error)
                  {check(); return root->data;}
  Tree& l_child() const throw(range_error)
                  {check(); return *root->left;};
  Tree& r_child() const throw(range_error)
                  {check(); return *root->right;};
  Tree& operator= (const Tree&);
  bool operator== (const Tree&) const;
  void inorder() const;
private:
  Node *root;
  void check () const
            {if (empty()) throw range_error("Tree");}
  void copy(const Tree& t);
};
```

There are three constructors. The first is a default constructor that constructs an empty tree: that is, the pointer root is set to `0`. The second is a constructor that constructs a tree consisting only of a root. This constructor calls the constructor of class `Node` and has the definition

```
Node::Node(int d)
: data(d), left(new Tree), right(new Tree) {}
```

Since the pointers `left` and `right` are initialized with the aid of the default constructor for class `Tree`, a new node will be initialized so that its two child trees are empty.

The third constructor for class `Tree` is a copy constructor that creates a tree that is a copy of another tree. The private member function `copy` is called to carry out the copying itself. We shall return to this.

There is a destructor for class `Tree`. The only thing that this does is to perform the statement **`delete`** `root`. If the pointer `root` is equal to `0`, nothing happens. Otherwise the node that `root` points to is deallocated. In addition, the destructor for class `Node` is called, and this has the simple definition

```
Node::~Node()
{delete left; delete right;}
```

Here the destructor for class `Tree` will be called for both the left and the right subtree. This means that the destructor is called recursively for all the subtrees until the leaves are reached, and here the pointer root will be equal to `0`. All subtrees and nodes will therefore be deallocated.

The member function `empty`, which checks whether a tree is empty, is easy to implement. We have only to see whether the pointer `root` is equal to `0` or not.

The three member functions `value`, `l_child` and `r_child` give as result references to a tree's root value and the left and right subtree respectively. For these functions to return a value, the actual tree must not be empty. If the tree is empty, the three functions will generate an exception. A check is made in the private member function with the name `check`.

Two operators have been defined for class `Tree`: an assignment operator that assigns a copy of a tree to another tree, and a comparison operator that tests whether two trees are equal. We begin by studying the implementation of the assignment operator:

```
void Tree::copy(const Tree& t)
{
  if (t.empty())
    root = 0;
  else
  {
    root = new Node(t.value());
    l_child().copy(t.l_child());
    r_child().copy(t.r_child());
  }
```

```
}
Tree& Tree::operator= (const Tree& t)
{
  if (root != t.root)   // to itself?
  {
    delete root;
    copy(t);
  }
  return *this;
}
```

The assignment operator first tests whether an assignment to itself is involved. If this is the case, nothing at all is done. In any other case the whole of the old tree is released. The private help function `copy` is then called to carry out copying. (This function is also called by the copy constructor.) Function `copy` is recursive. If the tree `t` to be copied is empty, then it is simple. The pointer `root` simply has to be equal to `0` in the actual tree as well. If tree `t` is not empty, the actual tree should have a root that is a copy of the root of tree `t`. A new node, initialized with the value in the root of `t`, is therefore allocated. The constructor for class `Node` sees to it that the two child trees are empty from the beginning. The two child trees in `t` must then be copied. We should not write

```
root->left=t->root->left;     // ERROR!
root->right=t->root->right;   // ERROR!
```

Then the actual tree would point to the *same* two subtrees as `t`, which would mean that the actual tree would be changed if `t` were changed and vice versa. Instead, we also have to copy the subtrees, which is done by calling the function recursively for the two subtrees.

The comparison operator is somewhat simpler. Two trees are equal if they are both empty or, if they are not, if they have the same root value, their left subtrees are equal and their right subtrees are equal. Making use of this, we can define the comparison operator. Recursion is also used here.

```
bool Tree::operator== (const Tree& t) const
  {
    return (empty() && t.empty()) ||
           (!empty() && !t.empty() && value() ==t.value() &&
            l_child()==t.l_child() && r_child()==t.r_child());
}
```

The last member function to be defined is the function `inorder`, which writes out the contents of a tree. This can be easily implemented with the help of the other member functions:

```
void Tree::inorder() const
{
   if (not empty())
   {
     l_child().inorder();
     cout << value() << ' ';
     r_child().inorder();
   }
}
```

We conclude by demonstrating how class `Tree` can be used to build up and write out the tree in Figure 13.8:

```
Tree t;
t=Tree(10);
t.l_child()=Tree(20);
t.r_child()=Tree(30);
t.inorder();
```

Exercises

13.1 A queue of cars is to be described using a linked list. Write the part of a program that creates a list describing a queue of three cars. For each car the registration number, make and year should be stored.

13.2 Write a function to evaluate the length of a linked list.

13.3 Assume you have a linked list in which the data part of each element contains an integer. Write a function to determine whether the list is sorted.

13.4 A register of club members has been built up in the form of a linked list. Each member is represented by an element in the list, in which the name, address and telephone number are stored. The list is sorted alphabetically according to the member's name. Write a procedure to insert a new member into the list, so that the list remains sorted.

13.5 Write a function that gets a pointer to a singly linked list `l` as parameter. As its result, the function should return a pointer to the new list containing copies of all the elements of `l` but in reverse order.

13.6 In Exercise 8.9 a class `Polynomial` was constructed using an array. The exercise here is to implement class `Polynomial` with the aid of a linked list, where each element in the list corresponds to a term in the polynomial.

13.7 A sparse matrix is one in which most of the elements are zero. To save storage space, such a matrix can be represented as a linked list. In the list there is one element for each non-zero matrix element containing its line and column members and its value. Write a function that gets a sparse matrix in the normal format (a two-dimensional array) as a parameter. Assume that all the elements in the matrix are integers. The function should create a list to represent the sparse matrix. The result of the function should be a pointer to the list.

13.8 Write a procedure that swaps two neighbouring elements in a doubly linked list. The procedure should take as parameter a pointer to the first of the two elements to be swapped.

13.9 Complete the class `Queue` in section 13.2.2 with an iterator class that makes it possible to read and change single elements in a queue.

13.10 Rewrite the class `Queue` in section 13.2.2 so that a doubly linked list is used to represent the queue. Complete the class so that iterators of the category *bidirectional iterator* can be used (look at information window list on page 424.) You will have to construct a new iterator class `Reverse_Iterator`.

13.11 Rewrite class `Set` in section 13.2.3 so that a doubly linked list is used to represent the set.

13.12 Write a function to count the number of leaves in a binary tree.

13.13 A binary tree can be used to represent an arithmetic expression. The expression

$$\frac{2 \times 3}{8 - 4} + 1$$

can, for example, be represented by the tree in Figure 13.19. The value of the binary tree can be defined as the value obtained when the corresponding expression is evaluated. The nodes can be defined by a class that contains the

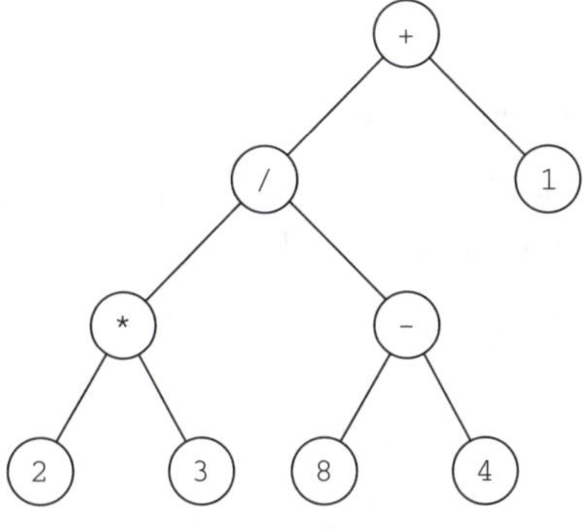

Figure 13.19

pointers to the two child trees, and we can let this have different subclasses for the different kinds of node involved. Make the class definitions necessary to describe an arithmetic expression in this way, and write a function that calculates the value of a given binary tree.

13.14 Two binary trees can be said to be reflections of one another if: (a) both are empty, or (b) both are non-empty, their roots contain the same information, and the right subtree of one is the reflection of the left subtree of the other and vice versa. Write a function that determines whether the two trees are reflections of one another.

13.15 Write a program that reads in a text from a text file and computes how many times different words appear in the text. Use a binary search tree to store the words read together with a counter. Each time a new word has been read from the text file, search to see whether it already appears in the search tree. If it does, increase the word's counter by 1. Otherwise, create a new node for the word and insert this node in the correct place in the tree. The program should finish by writing out all the words that have appeared, in alphabetical order, together with the number of times they appeared.

13.16 It is not very difficult to insert a new node into a binary search tree. To remove a node is a little harder. The following algorithm can be applied:

Call the node to be removed P.

If P is a leaf, set the pointer in P's parent that points to P to 0.

If P has a left child but no right child, let P's parent point to P's left child instead of pointing to P.

If P has a right child but no left child, let P's parent point to P's right child instead of pointing to P.

Otherwise, find the node Q in P's right subtree with the smallest value data part.

Copy the data part of Q to the node P and remove node Q.

Note that the last step is recursive, since we can apply the algorithm to remove node Q.

Write a procedure to remove a given node from a binary search tree.

13.17 Complete the tree class in section 13.4.3 with suitable member functions so that it can be used to handle binary search trees.

Templates

14

When programming, you nearly always need to use collections consisting of several objects. In order to be able to build object collections, you can use standardized container classes such as `vector`, `list`, and others. As we saw in Chapter 13, you can also construct your own container classes. For instance, we constructed the classes `Stack`, `Queue` and `Set`. The problem with the container classes we constructed ourselves is that they can only be used to build sets where the objects have the type **`int`**. For instance, if we want to construct a queue where the object is of class `Person`, then our class `Queue` cannot be used. Of course it is easy to make use of the class `Queue` as a model and to construct a new class, `Person_Queue`. All we have to do is change the type **`int`** to the type `Person` in some places in the class. However, this is awkward because it means we would have to construct a new queue class for every type of element.

Alternatively, it is possible to make use of generic classes in C++. You then write a *template* for the class, a *class template*, and the compiler automatically generates the different classes needed from this template. You do not need to write the class more than once. For instance, if you have constructed a class template called `List`, the compiler uses this to generate the classes `List<int>`, which describes an integer list, and `List<Person>`, which describes a list of people.

This is the technique that is used in standardized container classes. These classes are not really classes but class templates. This is also clear from the way in which we have declared containers of these classes. To declare a vector `v` that can contain elements of type **`int`** we have, for instance, written

```
vector<int> v;
```

You can also construct *generic functions*. For example, if you want to have a function that sorts an array, you can write a *function template*.

Templates have not always been a part of C++. Inheritance used to be used to construct object collections. If we wanted to construct a list of persons, for instance, we let class `Person` be a subclass of the predefined class `Listable`. Class `Person` then inherited the property of being able to be a part of a list. But we had a problem if class `Person` needed several properties. Perhaps we also wanted to be able to write out the class, or include it in a tree. In order to solve problems such as these, the concept of multiple inheritance was introduced into the language. Various properties could then be inherited from different sources. A difficulty with using inheritance to construct object collections, however, is that we have to decide in advance how a particular class is going to be used. As early as the definition of the class `Person` we have to know whether we want it to be listable, readable, stackable and so on. Another problem is that the programmer needs detailed knowledge of how the classes inherited from are built up in order to know what properties the new class should get. This puts a great deal of responsibility on the programmer.

It turned out that the use of generic classes was a much better method for constructing object collections than inheritance. Writing object-oriented programs does not mean that we have to use inheritance all the time. This is quite clear if, for a moment, we consider the relations discussed in Chapter 6. Inheritance defines the relation *is*. An American is a person. But is it really correct to say that a person is listable? To be able to be included in a list is hardly a natural property of any person. Persons have nothing to do with lists, so it is better to make lists independent of the things they contain. If we want to create a list containing people, we can do it with a separate class `List<Person>`.

In this chapter we shall be looking at how templates are used to construct generic classes and functions. Unfortunately, the syntax for templates is not very elegant in C++, but we shall not allow ourselves to be frightened off by that. Templates are very useful things indeed.

14.1 Class templates

14.1.1 Templates and instances

To begin our discussion of class templates, let us look at the following non-generic class that defines matrices:

```
class Matrix {
public:
   Matrix(int i=0, int j=0)
     : r(i), c(j), a(new double[r*c]) {}
   Matrix(const Matrix& m)  : a(0) {*this = m;}
   ~Matrix() {delete[] a;}
   int num_row() {return r;}
   int num_col() {return c;}
   Matrix& operator=  (const Matrix&);
   double& operator() (int i, int j);
```

```
private:
   double *a;
   int r, c;  // Number of rows and columns, respectively
};
```

As we know, a matrix is an arrangement of a number of rows and columns. The individual elements of a matrix in the above class have type `double`. To represent a matrix of `r` rows and `c` columns we use an ordinary one-dimensional array of `r*c` elements internally in the class. The data member `a` is a pointer to this array. The elements of the matrix are placed in rows in the array so that row number 1 comes first, row number 2 second, and so on. The first constructor, which can also be the default constructor, is used when we want to create a new matrix with a certain number of rows and columns. The expression `Matrix(3,5)`, for instance, indicates a matrix of `3` rows and `5` columns. The constructor initializes the data members `r` and `c` that contain the size of the matrix and allocates an array consisting of `r*c` elements. The other constructor is a copy constructor, and this uses the assignment operator to initialize a matrix to be a copy of another matrix.

The two member functions `num_row` and `num_col` are self-explanatory and are defined directly in the class definition. There are two operators: the assignment operator `=` and the function operator `()`. The assignment operator is, of course, used to assign one matrix to another. The function call operator is used to make indexing possible in a matrix. It has two parameters that indicate the row and column number respectively. If the variable `m` has type `Matrix`, then the expression `m(x,y)` gives a reference to the element that is in row number `x`, column number `y`. The operator `()` checks that the coordinates occur within the bounds allowed. The definitions of the two operators `=` and `()` are given separately:

```
Matrix& Matrix::operator= (const Matrix &m)
{
   if (this != &m)   // to itself?
   {
      r=m.r;
      c=m.c;
      delete[] a;
      a = new double[r*c];
      for (int i=0; i<r*c; i++)
         a[i] = m.a[i];
   }
   return *this;
}
double& Matrix:: operator()(int i, int j) {
   if (i<1 || i>r || j<1 || j>c)
      throw out_of_range("Matrix::operator()");
   return a[(i-1)*c + j-1];
}
```

Class Matrix makes working with matrices easy, but matrices can be constructed only where the elements have type **double**. We therefore rewrite class Matrix so that it becomes a template:

```
template<class T>
class Matrix {
public:
   Matrix(int i=0, int j=0)
   : r(i), c(j), a(new T[i*j]) {}
   Matrix(const Matrix& m) : a(0) {*this = m;}
   ~Matrix() {delete[] a;}
   int num_row() {return r;}
   int num_col() {return c;}
   Matrix& operator= (const Matrix&);
   T& operator() (int r, int c);
private:
   T *a;
   int r, c;  // Number of rows and columns, respectively
};
```

There are two changes to the earlier class Matrix. The first is that there is a new first line. The reserved word **template** indicates that class Matrix is a template and not an ordinary class. The *template parameters* (*generic parameters*) are indicated inside the characters <>. In this case there is only one template parameter, and this has been given the name T. The word **class** indicates that T is a *type parameter*. This means that T designates a type, any kind of type. (Note that T can also designate an 'ordinary' type such as **int** or **char** *, even though the word **class** is used.) As soon as T has been defined in this way it can be used *inside* class Set in the same way as a normal type name.

The second change that we have made in class Matrix is that we have changed type **double** to T everywhere. For instance, the member variable a has type T * instead of **double** *, and the function call operator () returns a value of type T& instead of **double**&.

We can now make use of the class template Matrix to create different kinds of matrix. We can write, for instance,

```
Matrix<int>    mi(5,8);
Matrix<Person> mp(3,4);   //
```

Two variables are declared here. The variable mi is a matrix whose elements are of type **int**, and mp is a matrix whose elements are of class Person. What happens here is that the compiler uses the template Matrix to generate two ordinary classes. We say that two *instances* of class Matrix are formed. (The terms *generated classes* and *specializations* are also used in the standard.) In the first instance it would seem that the type parameter `T` has been replaced by **`int`** everywhere, while in the second instance it would seem that `T` has been replaced by `Person`. The easiest way of explaining this is to say that the compiler automatically makes these changes in the text for class `Matrix` and then compiles text in the ordinary way. (In fact the mechanism works in a more complicated way than this, but it is something that the compiler does by itself.) An expression of the form `Matrix<X>`, where `X` is the name of a type (an ordinary type or class type), is the name of the class generated. This name can be used in the same way as an ordinary class name, and function parameters or variables of such a class can be declared in the usual way.

In class `Matrix` the two member functions **`operator=`** and **`operator()`** will be defined separately. Since class `Matrix` is a template, its member functions must also be templates. The definitions will have the following form:

```
template<class T>
Matrix<T>& Matrix<T>::operator= (const Matrix &m)
{
  if (this != &m)   // to itself?
  {
    r=m.r;
    c=m.c;
    delete[] a;
    a = new T[r*c];
    for (int i=0; i<r*c; i++)
      a[i] = m.a[i];
  }
  return *this;
}
template<class T>
T& Matrix<T>::operator()(int i, int j) {
  if (i<1 || i>r || j<1 || j>c)
    throw out_of_range("Matrix::operator()");
  return a[(i-1)*c + j-1];
}
```

Both definitions must be introduced by

```
template<class T>
```

that is, the same line that introduced the definition of class template `Matrix`. This says that a definition of a template follows, and that there is a type parameter called `T`. Since every instance of a class template will have its own instances of its member functions, we have to write `Matrix<T>::` in front of the function name when we indicate the full name of the member function. (If, for example, an instance should be created where `T` is equal to **`int`**, the member functions would be defined with the prefix `Matrix<int>::`.) If we want to indicate the name of a class template *inside* the class itself we do not have to write `<T>` after the class name; the class name will be sufficient. This applies, for instance, to the parameter type of the operator `=`. `Matrix` is written and not `Matrix<T>`.

Class templates

```
template<class T>  // class definition
class C {
  return_type f (parameters);
  ...
};
template<class T>  // definition of member function
return_type C<T>::f (parameters)
{ ...}
```

- `T` is a type parameter and is used as an ordinary type inside the class.
- Both the class definition and definitions of the member functions should be placed in the header file.
- *Instances* of the class are created when we write
  `C<`*type_name*`>`
  Then `T` is replaced by *type_name* everywhere in this instance.
- The expression `C<`*type_name*`>` can be used as an ordinary class name.

We spoke earlier of the placement of classes (see section 7.2), and learned that, for every class, two files should be created – a header file (which normally has a name ending in `.h`) and a definition file. We further established that the class definition should be placed in the header file and the definitions of the member functions in the definition file. For class templates we would make slightly different recommendations. Since it should be possible for the compiler to generate a class automatically from a class template, it must have access to the whole text that defines the class. The program text defining the member functions must also be accessible. This means that, for a class template, the definitions of the member functions should also be placed in the header file. As a result, there is normally no need for a definition file. (Different compilers may have solved this problem in different ways, but the recommendations given here should work for all compilers.)

On page 194 we demonstrated a function `add` that could add two matrices whose elements were integers. The problem with this function was that it only worked for matrices with four columns. We can now give a more general function that adds matrices using the class template `Matrix`. The new function gets two integer matrices `a` and `b` as parameters and as result gives a matrix that contains the sum of the two matrices. For the operation to be carried out, the two matrices given as parameters must have the same dimensions. If this is not the case, an exception will be generated. The result is calculated in a local variable `c`, initialized with the aid of the copy constructor so that from the beginning it is a copy of `a`.

```
Matrix<int> add(Matrix<int>& a, Matrix<int>& b)
{
  if (a.num_row()!=b.num_row() or
      a.num_col()!=b.num_col())
    throw range_error("add");
  Matrix<int> c(a);
  for (int i=1; i<=c.num_row(); i++)
    for (int j=1; j<=c.num_col(); j++)
      c(i,j) += b(i,j);
  return c;
}
```

Here is a program in which a matrix is read and then all its elements are updated so that their values are doubled:

```
int x, y;
cout << "Number of rows? "; cin >> x;
cout << "Number of columns? "; cin >> y;
Matrix<int> m(x,y);
for (int i=1; i<=m.num_row(); i++)
  for (int j=1; j<=m.num_col(); j++)
    cin >> m(i,j);
m = add(m,m);
```

14.1.2 Static members

Just like ordinary classes, a class template can have static data members and member functions. For example, we can complete the class template `Matrix` with a static data member `mn` that monitors the number of matrices of a certain kind and a static member function `num_matrices` that can be called to read `mn`. (Naturally, the constructors and the destructor are also changed so that they can count up and down the static data member `mn`, but we shall not show these changes here.)

```
template<class T>
class Matrix {
public:
  ...
  static int num_matrices();
private:
  ...
  static int mn;
};
```

For ordinary non-generic classes we know that a static data member is common for all objects belonging to the class. It then exists in one edition only. Where class templates are concerned, each *instance* of the class has its own edition of a static member variable. For instance, if we have the three instances `Matrix<int>`, `Matrix<Person>` and `Matrix<double>`, the variable `mn` will exist in three editions, one for each instance.

Static member functions are defined in the same way as non-static member functions. For example, the definition of the static member function `num_matrices` is

```
template<class T>
int Matrix<T>::num_matrices()
{ return mn; }
```

Static data members must always be defined outside the class definition; this applies to class templates as well. Since there will be an instance of the static data member for every instance of the class template, the definition of a static data member in a class template must also be a template and be preceded by the word **`template`**. For example, the definition of the static data member `mn` is

```
template<class T>
int Matrix<T>::mn=0;
```

Static members in class templates

- Exist in one edition for *every* instance of the class.
- Static member functions are defined in the same way as non-static member functions.
- Static data members are templates and must be defined separately. A static data member `v` in class `C` will have the definition

```
template<class T>
type C<T>::v = initialization value;
```

If there is a static member function `f` for an ordinary class `C`, then `f`, as we know, can be called in two different ways. Either we can take an object `x` from class `C` and make the call `x.f()`, or we can indicate the class name and make the call `C::f()`. The same situation applies in the case of class templates but, instead of the class name, we shall take the name of the actual instance. Let us assume, for example, that the variable `mp` has type `Matrix<Person>`. Then the following lines will write out the number of person matrices and integer matrices, respectively, that currently exist:

```
cout << mp.num_matrices() << endl;
cout << Matrix<int>::num_matrices() << endl;
```

14.1.3 Friends and help classes

If there is an ordinary non-generic class, it can be transformed into a class template in a relatively simple way. In section 13.2 we constructed a class `Stack` where the individual stack elements were of type **int**, and this was implemented with the aid of a singly linked list. We shall now remake this class into a class template. We begin with the definition (see page 480). We call the type parameter `T` and change all the **int** to `T`:

```
#include <stdexcept>
using namespace std;
template <class U>
class Element;
template <class T>
class Stack {
public:
   Stack() : first(0) {};
   ~Stack();
   void push (T d);
   void pop () throw(length_error);
   T    top () throw(length_error);
   bool empty();
private:
   Element<T> *first;
   Stack(const Stack&) {};
   Stack& operator= (const Stack&) {};
};
```

To implement a stack we use the help class `Element`, which defines individual elements in a singly linked list. Class `Element` must also be generic as the list elements will contain data elements of different types for the various instances of class `Stack`. The first line, above, is a declaration (not a definition), which indicates that `Element` is a class template with type parameter `U`. The member function `first` in class template `Stack` is declared as a pointer to an object of type `Element<T>`: that is, to a list element where the data element will be of type `T`, the same type as in the actual instance of `Stack`.

The complete definition of class template `Element` has the following appearance:

```
template<class U>
class Element {
   friend class Stack<U>;
   Element *next;
   U data;
   Element(Element *n, int d):next(n), data(d) {}
};
```

Note that class `Stack` must be able to see inside class `Element`. It has therefore been defined as a friend class. (The type parameters `T` and `U` must designate the same type. Therefore `Stack<U>` is written and not simply `Stack`.)

The definitions of the different member functions are simple to change. As an example we show the function `push` and the destructor (see page 481):

```
template<class T>
void Stack<T>::push(T d)
{
  first = new Element<T>(first, d);
}
```

```
template<class T>
Stack<T>::~Stack()
{
  while(not empty())
  {
    Element<T> *p=first;
    first = first->next;
    delete p;
  }
}
```

14.1.4 Template parameters

The class templates we have seen so far have had only one template parameter, but a class template (or function template) can have an arbitrary number of template parameters. There are two categories of template parameter: *type parameters* and *value parameters*. Type parameters are preceded by the word **`class`** or **`typename`*** and designate arbitrary types. Value parameters look like ordinary function parameters but may not be of floating-point type.

As an example we shall look at the following class template. Here we implement a stack using an array instead of a linked list. There are two data members: the array `s`, where the individual stack elements are placed, and a counter `n`, which monitors how many elements are currently in the stack. The class template has two template parameters. The first, `T`, is a type parameter used to designate the type of the individual elements in the stack, and the other, `size`, is a value parameter that indicates the maximum size a stack can have. The ordinary member functions `empty`, `push` and `pop` are defined.

* The reserved word **`typename`** is new in C++. It is not implemented in older compilers. Therefore **`class`** is most often used.

```
template<class T, int size>
class Stack {
public:
   Stack() : n(0) {};
   bool empty () {return n<=0;}
   void push  (const T& e){s[n++]=e;}
   void pop   () {n--;}
   T    top   () {return s[n-1];}
private:
   T s[size];
   int n;
};
```

When we create instances of this class template, we must give the values for both template parameters. For example, we can declare an integer stack with a maximum of 200 elements by writing

```
Stack<int,200> x;  // A stack with a maximum of 200 int
```

When the value is given to the value parameter, a constant expression must be indicated that has a value which can be evaluated at compilation.

Template parameters

- A template can have an arbitrary number of template parameters:

  `template<`*param1*`,` *param2*`,` *param3* `...>`

  where *paramN* is either a type parameter of the form

  `class T` or `typename`

  or a value parameter that looks like an ordinary variable declaration:

  type_name `v`

- A value parameter may not be of floating-point number type.
- Default values can be indicated.

Just like ordinary function parameters, template parameters can have default values. For instance, we would be able to change the first line in the class definition to

```
template<class T=double, int size=100>
```

If a template parameter has a default value then all subsequent template parameters must also have default values. When there are default values we can leave out one or more of the parameters when we create an instance of the class. We can write, for example,

```
Stack<Person> y;   // A stack with a maximum of 100 persons
Stack<> z;         // A stack with a maximum of 100 double
```

14.1.5 Property classes

When we create an instance of a class template that has a type parameter `T`, type `T` is replaced everywhere inside the class by the actual type. For example, if we create an instance of class template `Matrix` for type `Person`, `T` is replaced by `Person` everywhere. This may work perfectly well for all imaginable types in class template `Matrix` but is not the case with all class templates. To demonstrate this we shall construct a class template that describes binary search trees. We begin with class `Tree` from page 505 and rewrite the class to make it a template:

```
template<class D>
class Tree {
public:
  as before
void inorder() const;
void put_in(D d);
D* search(D d);
private:
  class Node {
    friend class Tree<D>;
    D data;
    Tree *left, *right;
    Node(D d): data(d), left(new Tree),
               right(new Tree) {}
    ~Node() {delete left; delete right;}
  };
  as before
};
```

The changes we have made to the previous definition include changing type `int` to `D` everywhere inside the class. To simplify things, class `Node` has been moved into the private section of class `Tree`. To enable binary search trees to be built up, we have also included two new member functions, `put_in` and `search`. The definitions of these have the following appearance (see the functions on page 503):

```
template<class D>
void Tree<D>::put_in(D d)
{
  if (empty())
    root = new Node(d);
  else if (d < value())
    l_child().put_in(d);
  else
```

```
    r_child().put_in(d);
}
template<class D>
D* Tree<D>::search(D d)
{
  if (empty())
    return 0;
  else if (d == value())
    return &value();
  else if (d < value())
    return l_child().search(d);
  else
    return r_child().search(d);
}
```

Now we can create an instance of the class for type `int`, for example:

```
Tree<int> t;
```

This works very well, and we can use the member functions `put_in`, `search` and `inorder` to handle the binary search tree:

```
cin >>i;
t.put_in(i);
...
cin >> i;
if (t.search(i))
  cout << "is in the tree" << endl;
t.inorder();
```

Now suppose that we have declared a class `Person` with the following appearance:

```
class Person {
public:
  char pno[10];
  char name[30];
};
```

We want to build up a binary search tree where each node contains information about a person. As search argument we shall use a national insurance number. We shall try to create an instance of class `Tree` where the type parameter `D` is set to `Person`:

```
Tree<Person> tp;   // ERROR!
```

When this line is compiled, we shall get a number of strange error messages, something along the lines of 'illegal structure operation'. There will also be an indication that the errors lie in class `Tree` and not in the program code we have written ourselves. (In the standard it is stipulated that the line where the instance is created should be indicated as incorrect, but not all compilers work like this today.)

The reason for these errors is that, in functions `put_in` and `search`, the operations `==` and `<` are carried out on objects of type `D`. In addition, function `inorder` uses the output operator `<<` to write out information in the nodes. This does not cause any problems when the type parameter `D` has been replaced by **int**, since these three operations exist for type **int**. But when we try to create an instance for type `Person` there is a compilation error, because the operations `==`, `<` and `<<` are not defined for type `Person`.

There are several things we can do to get around this. The easiest is simply to say that class template `Tree` can be used only for types where the three operations are defined. Another way of solving the problem is to make use of a *property class*. (This method is used in the C++ standard to define classes for reading and writing. The term 'traits' is used to designate property classes.) We let class template `Tree` have one more type parameter `E` that contains the necessary operations. We begin by rewriting the class definition:

```
template<class D, class E>
class Tree {
  as before
};
```

The next step is to reconstruct our definitions of `put_in`, `search` and `inorder` so that they do not use the operators `<`, `==` and `<<`. Instead we leave it to them to assume that there are three static functions with the names `less`, `equal` and `write` in class `E`:

```
template<class D, class E>
void Tree<D,E>::put_in(D d)
{
  if (empty())
    root = new Node(d);
  else if (E::less(d, value()))
    l_child().put_in(d);
  else
    r_child().put_in(d);
}
template<class D, class E>
D* Tree<D,E>::search(D d)
{
  if (empty())
    return 0;
  else if (E::equal(d, value()))
    return &value();
  else if (E::less(d, value()))
    return l_child().search(d);
  else
    return r_child().search(d);
```

```
}
template<class D, class E>
void Tree<D,E>::inorder() const
{
  if (not empty())
  {
    l_child().inorder();
    E::write(value());
    r_child().inorder();
  }
}
```

Note that the complete name of the function starts with the prefix `Tree<D,E>::`.

When we now create an instance of the class, we must give two type parameters. The first one indicates as before what type the data elements in the nodes are to have. The other is a property class that must have the three static member functions `less`, `equal` and `write`. Since the operators `<`, `==` and `<<` are defined for most of the ordinary types, it is appropriate to implement the three static member functions making use of these operators. We shall construct the following class template to be used with class `Tree` in order to avoid the need to define a property class for every ordinary type:

```
template<class D>
class TreeE {
public:
  static bool equal(const D& d1, const D& d2)
                    {return d1 == d2;}
  static bool less (const D& d1, const D& d2)
                    {return d1 < d2;}
  static void write(const D& d)
                    {cout << d << ' ';}
};
```

If we create an instance of this class for class **int**, for example, we shall get a property class that can be used when we want to create instances of class `Tree` for type **int**. As a result, we can write the following to get a binary search tree, `ti`, where the data elements have type **int**:

```
Tree<int, TreeE<int> > ti;
```

A corresponding procedure can be followed for all types where the operators `<`, `==` and `<<` are defined. For instance, if we want to have a search tree, `tu`, with data elements of type `SuperInt` (see page 304), we can write

```
Tree<SuperInt, TreeE<SuperInt> > tu;
```

According to the standard, it is allowed in class `Tree` to indicate a default value for type parameter `E` with the following as model:

```
template<class D, class E = TreeE<D> >
class Tree {
  ...
```

This is useful, since we do not then need to indicate the property class when we create instances of class `Tree`. Instead, we can write

```
Tree<char> tc;
Tree<SuperInt> tu;
```

If we have a type, for instance type `Person`, where the operators `<`, `==` and `<<` are missing, we can write a special version of the property class just for this type. This class can be called anything we please, although it could be useful to call it `TreeE`. This is because it is allowed to define a *special instance* (or 'explicitly specialized class', according to the standard) of a template for a particular class. We can then give the definition:

```
class TreeE<Person> {
public:
   static bool equal (const Person& d1, const Person& d2)
          {return strcmp(d1.pno, d2.pno)==0;}
   static bool less (const Person& d1, const Person& d2)
          {return strcmp(d1.pno, d2.pno)<=0;}
   static void write (const Person& d)
          {cout << d.pno << ' ' << d.name << endl;}
};
```

If we now declare an instance of class `TreeE` for type `Person`, this definition will be used instead of the class template above.

Finally, here is an example involving part of a program that reads a number of national insurance numbers. For each one a check is made to see whether the actual person exists in the binary search tree `tp`. If this is the case, the person's name is written out. The user is also allowed to change the person's name (but not the national insurance number). The program concludes by writing out all the persons in the tree in order of their national insurance numbers.

```
Tree<Person, TreeE<Person> > tp;
...  // Here the tree is built up
while (true)
{
   Person p;
   cout << "National insurance number? ";
   if (! (cin >> p.pno)) break;
```

```
    Person *pp = tp.search(p);
    if (pp)
    {
      char answer[5];
      cout << pp->name << endl
      << "Should the name be changed? "; cin >> answer;
      if (answer[0] == 'y')
      {
        cout << "New name? "; cin >> p.name;
        strcpy(pp->name, p.name);
      }
    }
    else
      cout << "Does not exist" << endl;
  }
  tp.inorder();
```

14.1.6 Generic standard classes

All the container classes included in the standard, for instance `vector`, `list` and `map`, are generic. They are class templates and use the technique with iterators. Earlier in the book we made use of them without knowing how they were implemented. To give the reader an understanding about how these classes are internally constructed we shall construct our own somewhat simplified variation of the standard class `list` discussed in section 12.4. We have not included all the member functions in this simplified version, and we have not defined a `reverse_iterator`.

To implement a list we use a doubly linked list with an extra start element that does not belong to the list itself (see page 476). We begin by giving a class template for the list elements. The forward pointer is called `suc` (successor) and the backward pointer `pre` (predecessor):

```
template<class T>
class Element {
public:
  Element *suc, *pre;
  T data;
  Element() {}
  Element (Element *s, Element *p, T d)
          : suc(s), pre(p), data(d) {}
};
```

We shall now show the whole definition of class template `List`. It is quite long since, in fact, it describes two classes. Class `Iterator` is declared as an internal class *inside* class template `List`.

```
template<class T>
class List {
public:
  //--------------------------------------------------------------------
  class Iterator {
  public:
    Iterator() : the_list(0), cur(0){};
    bool operator== (const Iterator& i) const
                        {return cur == i.cur;}
    bool operator!= (const Iterator& i) const
                        {return cur != i.cur;}
    T& operator* (); // Gives a ref to an actual element
    Iterator& operator++ ();     // Moves forward
    Iterator operator++ (int);   // Moves forward
    Iterator& operator-- ();     // Moves backwards
    Iterator operator-- (int);   // Moves backwards
private:
  friend class List<T>;
  List<T> *the_list;
  Element<T> *cur;
  Iterator(List<T> *l, Element<T> *c)
           : the_list(l), cur(c) {};
};
//--------------------------------------------------------------------
List() : f(new Element<T>), sz(0)
         {f->suc=f->pre=f;}
List(List& l);
List& operator= (List&);
bool empty() const {return sz==0;}
long int size() const {return sz;}
T& front();  // Gives reference to first element
T& back();   // Gives reference to last element
Iterator begin() {return Iterator(this, f->suc);}
Iterator end() {return Iterator(this, f);}
Iterator insert(Iterator pos, const T& d);
void insert(Iterator pos, int n, const T& d);
void insert(Iterator pos,Iterator i, Iterator j);
void erase(Iterator pos);
void erase(Iterator pos1,Iterator pos2);
void push_front(const T& d) {insert(begin(),d);}
void push_back (const T& d) {insert(end(),d);}
void pop_front() {erase(begin());}
void pop_back() {erase(--end());}
~List() {erase(begin(), end()); delete f;}
private:
  Element<T> *f;
  long int sz;
};
```

Class List contains two data members: f is a pointer to the first list element (the extra one), and sz is an integer that contains the number of elements in the list. The iterator class is constructed along the same lines as the iterator class that was used together with class Set in section 13.3. As we can see, an iterator has two data members. The first, the_list, is a pointer that will point to the list that the iterator is connected to. The other, cur, will point to the current list element in the list. When we make the iterator run forwards and backwards in a list, the pointer cur will be changed. But the pointer the_list will not be changed as long as the iterator is tied to a particular list. The default constructor for class Iterator initializes both pointers the_list and cur to 0. An iterator is not, therefore, connected to any special list from the beginning.

We shall first look at the member functions for class List. The default constructor creates a new empty list, and it does this by allocating the first extra list element then letting it point forwards and backwards to itself (see Figure 13.8). There is also a copy constructor and an assignment operator, both of which carry out deep copies. How this is done will be discussed later.

The member functions empty and size are very simple. Only the value of the member variable sz is used. The member functions front and back give as results a reference to the list's first and last data element respectively. If the list is empty, an exception is generated. Note that the first element in the list is the extra start element. The first data element is, therefore, in list element number 2.

```
template<class T>
T& List<T>::front()
{
   if (empty())
      throw length_error("List::front");
   return f->suc->data;
}
```

```
template<class T>
T& List<T>::back()
{
   if (empty())
      throw length_error("List::back");
   return f->pre->data;
}
```

The member functions begin and end are important. Both are defined inline and give an iterator as result. (They call the constructor for class Iterator, defined in the **private** section.) Function begin gives as result an iterator referring to the list element that contains the first data element (that is, to list element number 2). Function end does *not* give a reference to the list's last element. It gives a reference to the first element that could lie *just outside* the list. Since the list is circular, this element will be equal to the extra list element that is placed first.

There are three versions of the member function insert, which inserts new elements in a list. The first has an iterator, pos, and a new value, d, as parameter. The new value will be inserted *in front of* the element that iterator pos refers to. As result is given an iterator that refers to the newly inserted element. For the operation to be allowed, pos must be connected to the current list – the list that the member function insert is applied to. If it is not, an exception will be generated. The definition can now be written in the following way. (Function put_before from page 477 has been used as a model.) The new value d will be inserted in front of the list element that pos.cur points to.

```
template<class T>
List<T>::Iterator List<T>::insert(Iterator pos, const T& d)
{
  if (pos.the_list != this)
    throw invalid_argument("List::insert");
  Element<T> *pnew = new Element<T> (pos.cur, pos.cur->pre, d);
  pos.cur->pre->suc = pnew;
  pos.cur->pre = pnew;
  sz++;
  return List::Iterator(this, pnew);
}
```

Note that all iterator values are allowed. If, for instance, pos were equal to begin() then the new value would be placed first in the list. If pos were equal to end() the new value would be placed in front of the imagined element not belonging to the list. In other words, the new value is placed last in the list in this case.

The two other versions of insert can now be easily defined using the first version. Version number two inserts n new elements with the value d in front of the element that iterator pos refers to. It is simply a matter of calling version number one of the function n times:

```
template<class T>
void List<T>::insert(Iterator pos, int n, const T& d)
{
  if (n<0)
    throw invalid_argument("List::insert");
  for (; n>0; n--)
    insert(pos, d);
}
```

The third version of insert has three iterators, pos, i and j, as parameters. Iterator pos will be connected to the current list and i and j to another list. The function reads a number of elements from the list that i and j are connected to, and inserts them in front of the element that pos refers to. (The elements in the interval i to j are read.) The list that i and j are connected to will not be influenced by this. If we have two lists l1 and l2, we can insert a copy of l2 first in l1 by making the call

```
l1.insert(l1.begin(),l2.begin(),l2.end());
```

The definition of the third version of `insert` will have the following appearance:

```
template<class T>
void List<T>::insert(Iterator pos, Iterator i, Iterator j)
{
  if (i.the_list!=j.the_list || i.the_list==this)
    throw invalid_argument("List::insert");
  for (Iterator it(i); it!=j; ++it)
    insert(pos, *it);
}
```

The function checks that iterators `i` and `j` are connected to the same list and that they are not connected to the current list.

There are two versions of function `erase` that remove elements from a list. The first version gets an iterator `pos` as parameter and removes the element `pos.cur` that this iterator refers to. For the operation to be performed the iterator must be connected to the current list, and it must refer to an element inside the list. (The value `end()` lies outside the list and is therefore not allowed.) We then give the following definition. (Function `remove` from page 477 has been used as a model.)

```
template<class T>
void List<T>::erase(Iterator pos)
{
  if (pos.the_list != this)
    throw invalid_argument("List::erase");
  if (pos == end())
    throw out_of_range("List::erase");
  pos.cur->pre->suc = pos.cur->suc;
  pos.cur->suc->pre = pos.cur->pre;
  delete pos.cur;
  sz--;
}
```

The other version of `erase` has two iterators `pos1` and `pos2` as parameters, and looks like this:

```
template<class T>
void List<T>::erase(Iterator pos1, Iterator pos2)
{
  for (Iterator it(pos1); it!=pos2; )
    erase(it++);
}
```

The function removes a number of elements in the list from and including `pos1` up to and including the element *in front of* `pos2`.

The four member functions push_front, push_back, pop_front and pop_back insert and remove elements first and last in a list. They can be easily implemented with the aid of the member functions insert and erase. The definitions have been put inline directly into the class definition. Note that to remove the last element in a list, the call erase(--end()) should be made. If erase(end()) is written, this will mean that we are trying to remove an element outside the list.

The destructor for class template List has also been placed directly in the class definition, and it can easily be implemented using the second version of erase. All the elements are simply removed. Note that the destructor must then remove the special start element in the list.

It remains for us to define the copy constructor and the assignment operator for class List. The copy constructor will first allocate the special start element and ensure that it points forwards and backwards to itself. Then it can easily make the deep copy by calling the third version of insert:

```
template<class T>
List<T>::List(List& l) : f(new Element<T>), sz(0)
{
  f->suc = f->pre = f;  // Create start element
  insert(end(), l.begin(), l.end());
}
```

The assignment operator functions in a similar way, but it will not allocate a special start element. Instead, the old elements will be removed.

```
template<class T>
List<T>& List<T>::operator= (List& l)
{
  if (f != l.f)
  {
    erase(begin(), end());
    insert(end(), l.begin(), l.end());
  }
  return *this;
}
```

In conclusion, we shall give the definitions of the member functions in class Iterator. They are all very simple. The * operator gives as result a reference to the data part in the current list element. The operators ++ and -- are used to move forwards and backwards in the list. They exist in both prefix and postfix versions. It is permissible to move forward to the first element lying just outside the list – the element that end() refers to – but it is not permissible to move backwards in front of the first element. All the operators require the iterator to be connected to a list: that is, the member variable `the_list` may not be a null pointer.

```
template<class T>
T& List<T>::Iterator::operator* ()
{
  if (! the_list || *this == the_list->end())
    throw out_of_range("Iterator::operator*");
  return cur->data;
}
template<class T>
List<T>::Iterator& List<T>::Iterator::operator++ ()
{
  if (! the_list || *this == the_list->end())
    throw out_of_range("Iterator::operator++");
  cur = cur->suc;
  return *this;
}
template<class T>
List<T>::Iterator List<T>::Iterator::operator++ (int)
{
  Iterator temp = *this;
  ++ (*this);
  return temp;
}
template<class T>
List<T>::Iterator& List<T>::Iterator::operator-- ()
{
  if (! the_list || *this == the_list->begin())
    throw out_of_range("Iterator::operator--");
  cur = cur->pre;
  return *this;
}
template<class T>
List<T>::Iterator List<T>::Iterator::operator-- (int)
{
  Iterator temp = *this;
  --(*this);
  return temp;
}
```

This terminates our somewhat simplified version of the standard class `List`. The iterator class, as stipulated by the standard, has been defined as an internal class inside the class template `List`. This might cause problems for some older compilers, which cannot handle nested class definitions in combination with templates. If so, `Iterator` can be defined as a class template outside `List`.

14.2 Function templates

14.2.1 Definitions and instances

Classes are not the only things that can be generic. Templates, so-called *function templates*, can also be constructed for ordinary functions. In order to demonstrate how this is done we shall begin by looking at a problem that is by no means uncommon. When we write programs we often have to compare two variables with each other and see which one is the smaller. Instead of doing this in an `if` statement we can write a function to return the least value. The following function compares two integers of type `int` and gives as result the smaller of the numbers:

```
int min(int a, int b)
{
   if (a < b)
      return a;
   else
      return b;
}
```

It is not difficult to call this function. For instance, we can write `k=min(i,j)`. But if we wanted to calculate the smaller of two variables not of type `int` this function would not work. We would have to write a new version of the function. It is very inconvenient to have to write a new version of the function for every type that a parameter can have. It is better to use a function template. So we rewrite the function:

```
template<class T>
const T& min(const T& a, const T& b)
{
   if (a < b)
      return a;
   else
      return b;
}
```

The first line indicates as before that what is to come is a template and that `T` is the name of the type parameter. The following lines contain the definition of the function itself. Type `int` has been replaced everywhere by `T`. (To simplify matters we have rewritten the parameters `a` and `b` into constant reference parameters, thereby avoiding having to copy whole objects, which is an advantage if type `T` happens to designate a 'large' type.)

It is simple to create an instance of a function template. We simply make a call. We can write, for example,

```
double x, y;
long int m, n;
...
cout << min(x, y) << endl;
cout << min(m, n) << endl;
```

In the penultimate line an instance of the function `min` is automatically created where the type parameter `T` is replaced by **`double`**. On the last line an instance is created where the type parameter `T` is replaced by **`long int`**.

An instance of a function template does not have to be created explicitly. It will occur automatically when a call is made. Then the compiler will try to fit together the actual parameters with the function's formal parameters and determine which type the generic type parameters will have. If the parameters can be matched together, there is a check to see whether there already is an instance for the actual parameters. If there is not, a new instance is automatically generated.

For this to be possible, all the generic type parameters must occur in the type specification of at least one of the function's usual parameters. For example, in the function template `min`, `T` occurs in both the type specification for parameter `a` and that for parameter `b`. When instances of function templates are created, there are not the great number of automatic type conversions as there are with calls of ordinary functions. The actual parameters must correspond to the formal parameters more exactly. For instance, it is wrong to try to mix the types in a call of function `min`:

```
cout << min(m, y) << endl;   // ERROR!
```

In fact, in a function call it is permissible to indicate *explicitly* what types the generic type parameters should have, and we write this in the same way as we do when creating instances of class templates. We can write, for instance,

```
cout << min<double>(m, y) << endl;   // GOOD!
```

Normal type conversions occur here since `min<double>` is no longer a template but an ordinary function. The value of argument `m` will therefore be converted to type **`double`**.

We shall demonstrate some more useful function templates. The following function changes the value of two variables. (We have called the function `swap` since there is a standard function with that name.) We have to use reference parameters here because we want to be able to change them inside the function.

```
template<class T>
void swap (T& a, T& b)
{
  T temp=a;
  a=b;
  b=temp;
}
```

To change the values of the two **int** variables i and j we can simply write swap(i,j), and the call swap(x,y) changes the values in the two **double** variables x and y.

It is often useful to use function templates that have arrays as parameters. The following function, for instance, searches for the smallest element in an array:

```
template<class T>
T& min_element(T f[], int n)
{
   int m=0;
   for (int i=1; i<n; i++)
      if (f[i] < f[m])
         m = i;
   return f[m];
}
```

As parameters, the function gets an array (that is, a pointer to the array's first element) and an integer that indicates how many elements the array contains. As result is given a reference to the smallest element in the array. In the following call an instance is created where T designates the type **float**:

```
float a[100];
...
cout << min_element(a, 100) << endl;
```

Sorting an array is a common operation, so it is inconvenient to write a sort function for every kind of array that has to be sorted. This is an appropriate occasion to use a function template. We shall use the sort algorithm 'search for the least and swap' described on page 64. Since we already have the function min_element, which searches for the smallest number in an array, and function swap to change two values, it should be a simple matter. We write a sort function that has two parameters – an array that will be sorted, and an integer that indicates the number of elements in the array:

```
template<class T>
void sort(T f[], int n)
{
   for (int k=0; k<n; k++)
   {
      swap(f[k], min_element(f+k, n-k));
   }
}
```

When an instance of function sort is created for a particular type T, instances of functions swap and min_element will automatically be created for the same type. The call min_element(f+k,n-k) gives as result a reference to the smallest number in the subarray that begins at position number `k`. There are `n-k` elements in this subarray. We can now create instances of the sort function. For example, to sort the array `a` above we write

```
sort(a, 100);
```

Function templates

```
template<class T1, class T2, ...>
return_type f (parameters)
{ ... }
```

- `T1`, `T2` etc. are parameters and are used as ordinary types inside the function. All the type parameters must occur in a type specification in the parameter list.
- *Instances* of the function are automatically created when it is called

  ```
  f (arguments)
  ```

  The compiler then matches the arguments with the formal parameters and determines which type will replace `T`.
- We can indicate explicitly which type `T` is to have:

  ```
  f<type> (arguments)
  ```

- A *special instance* for a particular type `V` can be created. The function body is then rewritten and `T` is replaced by `V`.

  ```
  return_type f(parameters)
  { special version }
  ```

Just as if class templates were involved, we can create a *special instance* of a function template for a special type. The function template `min_element` will not work, for instance, if we have an array with text strings. A text string is of course defined by a pointer to a character array, so if we have two such pointers `s1` and `s2`, and make the comparison `s1<s2`, it is not the texts that will be compared but the values of the pointers, which is of little interest to us. We must construct a *special instance* of the template `min_element`:

```
char *& min_element(char *f[], int n)
{
  int m=0;
  for (int i=1; i<n; i++)
    if (strcmp(f[i],f[m])<0)
      m = i;
  return f[m];
}
```

Everywhere type T has been replaced by **char** *. The comparison operator < has also been replaced by a call of the standard function strcmp, which returns the value -1 if the first text string is alphabetically smaller than the other.

If we now have an array tab where the individual elements are pointers to text strings, the array can be easily sorted:

```
char *tab[100];
...
sort(tab, 100);
```

When function sort is called, an instance is created where T will designate type **char** *. When function min_element is then called from within sort, an instance will also be needed of min_element for type **char** *. But then the compiler discovers that there is a special instance and uses this one instead of generating a new instance from the template.

Of course, we can have function templates with several template parameters. Both type parameters and value parameters are allowed.

14.2.2 Generic standard functions: the algorithm library

The standardized algorithms discussed in section 12.2 are all function templates. We know that all these algorithms use the technique with iterators to handle the data sets they process. For instance, the function templates min_element and sort from the previous section exist as standard algorithms, but then use iterators. Here we show how some of the standard algorithms can be implemented. We begin by giving our own definition of the algorithm min_element:

```
template<class IT>
IT min_element(IT first, IT last)
{
  IT m=first;
  for (IT i = ++first; i!=last; i++)
    if (*i < *m)
      m = i;
  return m;
}
```

The generic type parameter IT designates an iterator or a pointer type. Suppose, for instance, that we have an integer array a:

```
double a[10];
```

Then we can call the function min_element:

```
cout << *min_element(a, a+10);
```

Since the type of a is 'pointer to **double**', an instance of function min_element is created where the type parameter IT gets type **double** *. This means that the variables first, last, i and m inside the function min_element are ordinary pointers. The operations ++ and * that are performed on these variables are the normal pointer operations. The function leaves a result of type IT – that is, a 'pointer to **double**' for this instance. This pointer points to the smallest number in the array, which means that the expression *min_element(a,a+10) is the value of the smallest number in the array, so this value will be returned.

The function templates in the algorithm library are useful not only for arrays. They can also be applied to all the container classes for which iterators exist. We can declare a list of integers, for instance:

```
List<int> l;
```

We use the class template List from page 528 here. The smallest number in the list l can now be found and written out by writing

```
cout << *min_element(l.begin(), l.end());
```

In the instance of min_element that is now created, the type parameter T will get the type List<**int**>::Iterator, since it is the type that the functions begin and end give as result. The operators ++ and *, which we ourselves defined for type List<T>::Iterator, will now be called inside the function min_element.

Here is the definition of the function template sort:

```
template<class IT>
void sort(IT first, IT last)
{
  for (IT k=first; k!=last; k++)
  {
    swap(*k, *min_element(k, last));
  }
}
```

This also has a generic type parameter IT that can designate a pointer or iterator. The parameters first and last refer to the first and last element in the data collection to be sorted. If we want to sort an ordinary array, we can make the call

```
sort(a, a+10);
```

Then an instance is created where IT gets the type **double** *. We also automatically get instances of the functions swap and min_element for this type. (Function swap, which we showed on page 535, is also a standard algorithm.) The variables first, last and k are pointers. In the call min_element the pointers k and last demarcate the subarray in which we shall search for the least value.

If we want to sort the integer list l that we defined earlier, this can be done just as easily:

```
sort(l.begin(), l.end());
```

We now get an instance where IT is equal to List<int>::Iterator and where the variables first, last and k are therefore iterators.

The operator < is used in the function template min_element. This function template, and therefore the function template sort, will work only if there is an operator < defined for the actual element type. This has not caused any problems in our examples. In one case the element type was **double**, and in the other it was **int**. In order to also make it possible to use standard algorithms for data sets where the type of element does not have an operator <, several of the algorithms exist in an alternative version in which you can give a function object as an extra parameter, as we discussed in section 12.3. We shall now demonstrate how such an alternative version can be defined. For instance, our alternative version of min_element looks like this:

```
template<class IT, class Compare>
IT min_element(IT first, IT last, Compare comp)
{
  IT m=first;
  for (IT i=++first; i!=last; i++)
    if (comp(*i, *m))
      m = i;
  return m;
}
```

Here the parameter comp is an object and the type parameter Compare is a property class that represents the type of the function object. The interesting thing is the call comp(*i, *m) that occurs on the sixth line. The object comp is called as if it was a function. In order for that to be possible we know that comp must be a function object, which means that there must be a function call operator in the class Compare.

We want to be able to compare text strings, and therefore we define the following property class:

```
class Str_Less_Than {
public:
  bool operator () (char *s1, char *s2)
  { return strcmp(s1, s2) < 0;}
};
```

Suppose now that we have declared a list in which the individual elements are pointers to text strings – that is, they have type **char** *:

```
List<char *> tl;
```

To read texts and place them in the list, statements like this can be given:

```
char s[100], *p;
cin >> s;
p = new char[strlen(s+1)];
strcpy(p, s);
tl.push_back(p);
```

Suppose now that we want to search the text in the list that comes first alphabetically. To be able to call the alternative version of function `min_element` we first have to declare an object of class `Str_Less_Than`:

```
Str_Less_Than lt;
```

This object is only a sort of dummy. It does not contain any data members, only the function call operator. We can now write out the smallest text in the list:

```
cout << *min_element(tl.begin(), tl.end(), lt);
```

As we saw above, you need not explicitly declare the function object. You can also write it in the following way. A temporary function object of the class `Str_Less_Than` is then created.

```
cout << *min_element(tl.begin(), tl.end(), Str_Less_Than());
```

We also show our own alternative version of the function `sort`:

```
template<class IT, class Compare>
void sort(IT first, IT last, Compare comp)
{
   for (IT k=first; k!=last; k++)
   {
      swap(*k, *min_element(k, last, comp));
   }
}
```

In C++ there are a number of predefined classes that you can use to create function objects. We discussed this in section 12.3.3 on page 439. On page 441 there is a list of the classes. Actually, they are not classes but templates. They all have a type parameter that indicates the type of the elements that you might compare or perform operations on. In order to demonstrate how these class templates are constructed we now construct two class templates that work in the same way as the standardized ones. We begin by defining a template `abs_val` that you can use to create function objects that calculate the absolute value of a number. For instance, suppose we have defined two vectors `v1` and `v2`,

```
vector<double> v1(5), v2(5);
```

and we have initiated `v1` to contain `{-1, 2, 3, -4, -5}`. If we now execute the following statement, `v2` will contain `{1, 2, 3, 4, 5}`

```
transform(v1.begin(), v1.end(), v2.begin(), abs_val<double>());
```

Our class template `abs_val` looks like this:

```
#include <functional>
using namespace std;
template<class T>
class abs_val : public unary_function<T, T> {
public:
   T operator ()(T x) const
   {
     if (x >= 0)
       return x;
     else
       return -x;
   }
};
```

As we see, `abs_val` is a class template that is a subclass of another class template called `unary_function`. All the predefined class templates whose function call operators have a single parameter are subclasses of the standard class template `unary_function`. The first template parameter of `unary_function` indicates the type of the parameter of the function call operator, and the second template parameter indicates the result type from the function call operator. The class template `unary_function` does not contain any data members or adaptor functions. It contains only certain type definitions that are needed when you use member functions (see page 442).

We shall also demonstrate parameter templates that can be used to create function objects with two parameters. We define a template parameter called `close` that tests whether two values are close to one another:

```
#include <functional>
using namespace std;
template<class T>
class close : public binary_function<T, T, bool> {
public:
   close(const T& eps = T()) : epsilon(eps) {}
   bool operator()(T x, T y) const
   { return abs_val<T>()(x-y) <= epsilon; }
   const T& epsilon;
};
```

As we can see, the class template `close` is a subclass of the standard class template `binary_function`. This has three type parameters. The first two indicate the types of the parameters of the function call operator, and the third indicates the result type from the function call operator. It is essential to make use of the class template `binary_function` in this way to allow the use of adapter functions.

Obviously, the function call operator returns the value **`true`** if the absolute values of the difference between its parameters are less than or equal to `epsilon`. `epsilon` is a constant that is initialized in the constructor. Using this, the programmer can decide what is meant by two values being close to each other. For instance, we can define a function object `f` that can compare values of type **`double`** and which interprets two numbers as being close to each other if the difference between them is less than or equal to 10^{-3}:

```
close<double> f(1e-3);
```

We can now, for instance, use this function object to compare the two vectors `v1` and `v2` and see whether all their corresponding elements are close to each other:

```
if (equal(v1.begin(), v1.end(), v2.begin(), f))
  cout << "close" << endl;
```

Alternatively it would have been possible to use a temporary function object:

```
if (equal(v1.begin(), v1.end(), v2.begin(),
          close<double>(1e-3)))
  cout << "close" << endl;
```

Because we have let the class template `close` be a subclass of `binary_function`, it is possible to use adapter functions. For instance, the following statement runs through the vector `v1` and replaces all the elements whose value is close to 0 with the value –1:

```
replace_if(v1.begin(), v1.end(), bind2nd(f,0), -1);
```

14.3 Heterogeneous object collections

The contents of this chapter may have given the impression that inheritance and the use of templates are two different techniques competing with each other: we must choose one or the other. However, this is not the case at all. The two methods can be used together – in fact they can complement each other to good effect. This is especially true in the case of heterogeneous object collections – those in which the objects are of different types. We shall confine ourselves here to describing collections in which the objects, though of different type, are related to each other. These different objects will all have a common fundamental base class.

We first describe how the 'classical' technique, without the use of templates, is used to construct heterogeneous object collections. Then we shall demonstrate how the use of templates and inheritance can be combined. Finally, there will be a comprehensive program involving both templates and inheritance.

14.3.1 The classical method

We now show how heterogeneous data collections can be built up simply by making use of inheritance. This technique was used before the concept of templates was introduced into C++. It is also the technique used in various object-oriented languages, such as Smalltalk, that do not have generic program units.

We begin with the following class, which defines elements that can be included in singly linked lists:

```
class ListElement {
public:
  ListElement() : next(0) {};
  ListElement *next_elem() { return next;}
private:
  friend class List;
  ListElement *next;
};
```

We see that there is only one data member, `next`, and that this is a pointer to the next element in the list. There is no data member that contains information. There is a default constructor that sets the pointer `next` to zero. The member function `next_elem` allows an outsider to read but not to change `next`. The only class that can change `next` is the friend class `List`. It has the following definition:

```
class List {
public:
  List() : first(0) {};
  void put_last(ListElement *e);
  void remove_first();
  ListElement *first_elem() {return first;}
private:
  ListElement *first;
};
```

Using class `List` we can build up linked lists in which the list elements have type `ListElement`. The only data member is a pointer `first` that points to the first element in the list. The default constructor sets this pointer to zero from the beginning. The pointer `first` can be read from outside – but not changed – using the member function `first_elem`. For the sake of simplicity, we have declared only two member functions in class `List`. These have the following definitions (compare with those on page 473):

```
void List::remove_first()
{
  if (first)
    first=first->next;
```

```
}
void List::put_last(ListElement *e)
{
  e->next=0;     // e should always be last
  if (! first)  // Empty list, insert e first
    first = e;
  else
  {
    ListElement *p;
    for (p=first; p->next; p=p->next)
      ;
    // p is now pointing to the last element
    // Insert e after p
    p->next = e;
  }
}
```

It is not particularly interesting building up linked lists with elements of class `ListElement`, because the list elements do not contain any information apart from the pointer to the next element. But now we can use class `ListElement` as a base class for objects that we may want to put in a list. On page 317 we defined a group of classes that described different kinds of vehicle. The fundamental base class in this group was the class `Vehicle`. We shall now redefine class `Vehicle` so that it, in turn, becomes a subclass of class `ListElement`. (The other classes are not changed.)

```
class Vehicle : public ListElement {
  public:
    virtual void give_info();
};
```

With this definition, class `Vehicle` and all its subclasses have inherited the property of being able to be included in lists. Every object of one of these classes will have the inherited data member `next`.

We can now declare a list and put different vehicles into it:

```
List l;
l.put_last(new Private_car("xyz111", 5));
l.put_last(new Bus("bus999", 40, true));
l.put_last(new Truck("bly555", 10000));
```

Function `put_last` expects a pointer to a `ListElement` as parameter, but pointers to private cars, buses and trucks can be automatically converted to this type since these classes are subclasses of class `ListElement`. Figure 14.1 illustrates this.

To run through the list and write out information about the different vehicles, we can do the following:

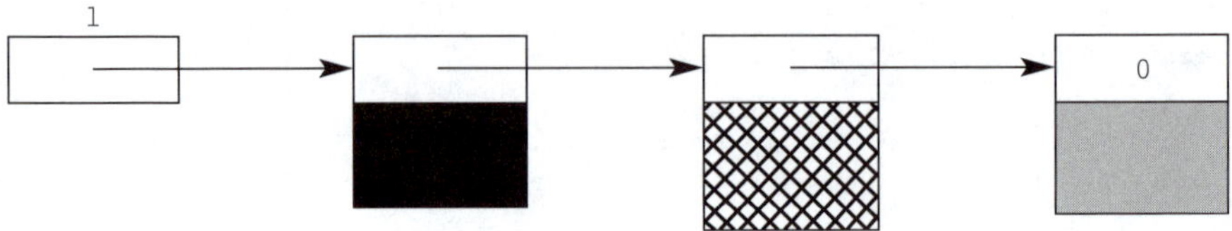

Figure 14.1

```
ListElement *p;
for (p=l.first_elem(); p; p=p->next_elem())
  ((Vehicle *)p)->give_info();
```

The expression in the last line may seem rather strange. The idea here is to call the virtual function `give_info`, which is defined in class `Vehicle`. The pointer `p` has the type 'pointer to `ListElement`'; it is also this type that the functions `first_elem` and `last_elem` give as result. So we cannot write `p->give_info()`, since there is no function with the name `give_info` in class `ListElement`. We need an explicit type conversion where the value of `p` is converted to type 'pointer to `Vehicle`'. The function `give_info` will be called with dynamic binding since it is virtual. We shall therefore get different output data for different kinds of vehicle.

The type conversion carried out here is really quite dangerous since it is performed downwards in the class hierarchy. This is one of the disadvantages of the classical method of constructing heterogeneous object collections. Apart from being obliged to make risky type conversions, there is another disadvantage. As early as the class declaration – class `Vehicle` could be an example – the decision has to be made on how the class will be used so that the inheritance of properties from the right base classes can be inherited. For instance, if we wanted to build up binary trees with vehicles instead, we would have to make `Vehicle` the subclass of a base class other than `ListElement`.

14.3.2 The combination of inheritance and templates

Templates are good tools for constructing container classes, and inheritance is an excellent method for describing objects that can be classified in different groups and subgroups. The two things can be combined. If we again take the different kinds of vehicle as an example, we can use inheritance as we did before to describe the relation between different kinds of vehicle: 'a bus is a vehicle', 'a minibus is a bus', and so on. But a vehicle is not a list element, and the relation is not natural. To construct a list, we need a class template instead. We can use the class template `List` from section 14.1.6 and declare the list `l`:

```
List<Vehicle *> l;
```

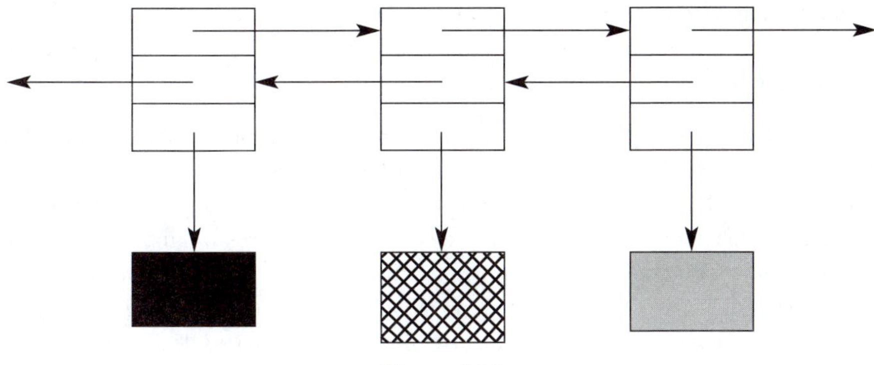

Figure 14.2

(Of course, we could as well use one of the standard classes `vector`, `list` or `deque`.)

We give the type parameter `T` the value `Vehicle *`. As a result, the type of the elements that will be stored in the list is 'pointer to `Vehicle`'. The vehicles themselves will not be stored in the list, only the pointers to them. The definition of class `Vehicle` together with all its subclasses looks exactly as it does on page 317. No other pointers or anything else need to be added. We can now create some new vehicles and insert pointers to them in the list:

```
l.push_back(new Private_car("xyz111", 5));
l.push_back(new Bus("bus999", 40, true));
l.push_back(new Truck("bly555", 10000));
```

The situation is shown in Figure 14.2. The two top pointers in each node are the pointers `pred` and `succ` used by class `List`. The third pointer is the data component `data`, which in this instance of class `List` has the type 'pointer to `Vehicle`'.

To run through the list and write out information about the different vehicles, we, of course, use an iterator:

```
List<Vehicle *>::Iterator it;
for (it=l.begin(); it!=l.end(); it++)
   (*it)->give_info();
```

The expression `*it` gives as result a reference to a list element – that is, a reference to a pointer. This pointer has type 'pointer to `Vehicle`'. The pointer therefore has the right type for us to call the virtual function `give_info`. A type conversion is not necessary.

This has none of the disadvantages that we found in the classical solution of the previous section. No risky type conversions are necessary, and we do not have to make forced decisions as to whether objects of a certain class should be capable of inclusion in lists or other kinds of object collection. If, for example, we have a matrix of cars, we can use the class template `Matrix`. Any object can even be part of several independent object collections at the same time, and there do not have to be extra data members in a particular object.

In the programming language Java, which has no generic program units, a variant of this technique is used. You let all classes, both standard classes and your own classes, become subclasses of a single common superclass called `Object`. You then create (non-generic) object collections whose elements are references (a kind of pointer) to `Object`. In this way you can develop heterogeneous data collections. This technique can also be used in C++, but the main disadvantage is, of course, that you have to make dangerous type conversions down the class hierarchy in order to deal with an object that you have collected from a data set.

14.3.3 An example: spreadsheets

Certain calculation programs work with arrangements of figures, or *spreadsheets*, consisting of a number of rows and columns. Each 'square' in a spreadsheet contains what we call a *cell*, and we access a particular cell by indicating its row and column number. (Another way of expressing this is to say that a spreadsheet is a matrix whose elements are cells.) Each cell can contain a formula. (A cell can also be undefined.) A formula is an arithmetic expression that can contain the usual arithmetic operators but it need not contain any operator at all. In its simplest form, a formula can consist of a single term. The terms in a formula can be constant values. The interesting thing about calculation programs is that a term can also be a reference to another cell in the spreadsheet. Cell number (3,4) can, for instance, contain the formula (3,1)+(3,2), which means that cell number (3,4) will contain the sum of the values in cells (3,1) and (3,2).

This type of program can be very useful when we work with budgets and accounting procedures, for example. Certain rows and columns can be defined so that they connect to other cells in the spreadsheet. The calculation program can calculate the interconnected rows and columns automatically, and all we have to do is give input data.

In this section we shall demonstrate how such a calculation program can be built up. Naturally, we are not able to show a complete program – there is not enough space – but we shall be showing the central constructions where the spreadsheet itself is built up.

We begin with the subject of *formulas*. A formula can have many forms, but all formulas have a number of common properties. One of these is that we should be able to calculate a formula and get a value as result. So we can look at formulas as a family of classes that all have an abstract base class in common, and this would have the following appearance:

```
class Formula {
public:
  virtual double calculate() = 0;
  virtual ~Formula() {};
};
```

This class has no data members. There are only two member functions: a virtual destructor, and a pure virtual function, `calculate`. Because `calculate` is a pure virtual function, class `Formula` will be an abstract class. Objects of this class cannot be created. The class exists only to be a base class.

All the subclasses of `Formula` must have their own version of the member function `calculate`. Because the destructor has been declared as virtual, the destructor of the subclass will be called when we deallocate an object with `Formula` as its base class.

The simplest kind of formula is one that contains only a constant value. Such a formula can be described with the following subclass:

```
class Constant : public Formula {
public:
  Constant(double value) : v(value) {}
  double calculate() {return v;}
private:
  double v;
};
```

The constant value is kept in the data member `v`, and function `calculate` gives as result the value of `v`. There is a constructor that makes it possible to indicate the value that `v` should have, but there is no need to have a destructor since the class does not itself allocate memory space dynamically.

We shall now study the kind of formula that has an operator with two operands: that is, expressions of the form `a` *op* `b`, where *op* is an operator and `a` and `b` are operands. As an example, let us look at a class that defines addition:

```
class Add : public Formula {
public:
  Add(Formula *left, Formula *right)
       : l(left) , r(right) {}
  double calculate(){return l->calculate()+r->calculate();}
  ~Add() {delete l; delete r;}
private:
  Formula *l, *r;
};
```

The two operands are defined with the two data members `l` and `r`, which are pointers to other formulas. So a more complicated expression can be built up in the form of a tree. The pointers `l` and `r` are given values in the constructor. The member function `calculate` is simple. It calls the virtual function `calculate` for the two operands `l` and `r` and gives as result the sum of their results. The call in the expressions `l->calculate()` and `r->calculate()` occurs with dynamic binding since `l` and `r` are pointers to the base class and `calculate` is a virtual function. Hence we do not know exactly which functions are called. It will depend on what kinds of object `l` and `r` point to.

The destructor releases memory space for the two operands so that the destructors for these formulas will, in turn, be called. So, if we deallocate an addition object, all the underlying formula objects will be deallocated.

The classes `Sub`, `Mul` and `Div`, which perform the three other modes of calculation, can easily be constructed in a similar way. The only difference, when compared with class `Add`, is that the operator `+` will be changed to `-` and `*` to `/` in the member function `calculate`. We do not have to show these classes.

To describe a formula that refers to another cell in a spreadsheet, we first have to define the class `Cell`. This class describes a particular 'square' in the spreadsheet:

```
class Cell {
public:
   Cell() : f(0), is_calculated_now(false) {}
   ~Cell() {delete f;}
   void define(Formula *form) {delete f; f=form;}
   bool defined() {return f!=0;}
   operator double();   // Calculates the cell's value
private:
   Formula *f;
   bool is_calculated_now;
};
```

There are two data members. The pointer `f` points to a formula. This pointer is initialized in the constructor to the value `0`, which means that the cell is not defined. We can check whether a cell is defined by calling the member function `defined`. To insert a formula in a cell, to define the cell, we call the member function `define`, which has a pointer to a formula as parameter. This function releases memory space for the formula that was in the cell before and puts the new formula in its place.

The other data member, `is_calculated_now`, is rather special. It has been included so that no 'circular' calculations will begin. Suppose, for example, that cell number (3,4) contains the sum of the values in cells (3,1) and (3,2). To be able to calculate these values, we must first calculate the cells. Suppose further that cell number (3,1) contains the formula (3,3)*0.5 and that cell (3,3) contains the formula 100+(3,4). There will then be a circular calculation that has to be broken. The data member is_calculated_now is normally equal to **false**, but as soon as we try to calculate the cell's value it is set to **true**. It is restored to **false** when the calculation is finished. Each calculation begins with is_calculated_now being checked. If it has the value **true**, this means that a circular calculation has occurred, and the calculation is aborted.

All of this is clarified by the definition of the member function **operator double**(). This is really a type conversion operator from type Cell to type **double**, but we use it because it is convenient for calculating the value in a cell. If, for instance, we have a variable c of type Cell and want to calculate its value and assign it to a variable x of type **double**, we can simply write x=c. Then the type conversion operator from type Cell to type **double** is called automatically. The type conversion operator has the definition:

```
Cell::operator double()
{
  if (not f)
    throw calculation_error("Undefined cell");
  if (is_calculated_now)
    throw calculation_error("Circular calculation");
  is_calculated_now = true;
  double d = f->calculate();
  is_calculated_now = false;
  return d;
}
```

We can carry out the calculation itself by calling the member function calculate for the formula in the cell. Two types of error can occur. The cell can be undefined – that is, f can have the value 0 – or a circular calculation can have occurred. If there is an error, an exception of class calculation_error is generated. This class is a non-standard subclass of the standard class logic_error:

```
class calculation_error : public logic_error {
public:
  calculation_error(const char *what_arg = "")
    : logic_error(what_arg) {}
};
```

Now class Cell has been completely defined, and we can define the last formula class, class Other, which refers to another cell:

```
class Other : public Formula {
public:
  Other(Cell *other) : o(other) {}
  double calculate() {return *o;}
private:
  Cell *o;
};
```

This is really very simple. Class `Other` has a single data member, `o`, which is a pointer to the other cell. Function `calculate` gives as result the value `*o`. This expression has type `Cell`, since `o` is a pointer to a cell. But the result from function `calculate` should be of type **double**, so the type conversion operator we defined for type `Cell` is called automatically. As a result, the value in this cell is calculated.

Now we can use the class template `Matrix` from page 514 to construct a spreadsheet, `w`, with 10 rows and 7 columns:

```
Matrix<Cell> w(10,7);
```

Since each cell contains a pointer (the data member `f`) to the base class of a family of related classes (formal classes), we have created a heterogeneous object collection with the aid of the class template `Matrix`. We are now in exactly the same situation as described in section 14.3.2. (We can ignore the fact that there is another data member in class `Cell`.)

We can now carry out indexing in matrix `w` and call the member function for individual cells. For instance, we can write

```
w(2,5).define(new Constant(15));
w(3,5).define(new Constant(20));
w(4,5).define(new Add(new Other(&w(2,5)),
                      new Other(&w(3,5))));
cout << w(4,5) << endl;   // 35 is returned
```

We can redefine one of the cells:

```
w(2,5).define(new Constant(40));
cout << w(4,5) << endl;   // 60 is returned
```

Note that the value of cell (4,5) is changed, in spite of the fact that we do not make any changes in this cell. It is simply that cell (2,5) has been redefined.

This way of defining individual cells is not very elegant. In this type of program, the situation often arises where entire rows and columns have to be handled at the same time. We may want to stipulate that column number 7 should contain the sum of columns 3 and 6 and that the values in row number 8 should be 12% of the values in row number 7. One way of making things easier for the programmer is to enclose the matrix in a class `Spreadsheet` that describes a complete spreadsheet, and to provide class `Spreadsheet` with a set of useful member functions. We make the following definitions:

```
enum op {add, sub, mul, divi};
class Spreadsheet {
public:
  Spreadsheet(int nrow, int ncol)
            : m(new Matrix<Cell>(nrow, ncol)) {}
  ~Spreadsheet() {delete m;}
```

```
    int num_row() {return m->num_row();}
    int num_col() {return m->num_col();}
    Cell& operator()(int r, int c) {return (*m)(r,c);}
    void def_row(int row, int r, op o, double d);
    void def_col(int col, int c, op o, double d);
    void sum_row(int row, int r1, int r2, op o=add);
    void sum_col(int col, int c1, int c2, op o=add);
  private:
    Matrix<Cell> *m;
  };
```

Class `Spreadsheet` has as its only data member a pointer to a matrix with cells. This matrix is allocated dynamically in the constructor, which as parameters will get the number of rows and columns, respectively, that the matrix will have. To create a spreadsheet `z` with 20 rows and 10 columns, for example, we make the declaration

```
Spreadsheet z(20,10);
```

The member functions `num_row` and `num_col`, which can be used to read the size of a spreadsheet, are easy to write. They simply call the corresponding member functions for class `Matrix`.

The function call operator `()` gives a reference to a particular cell in a spreadsheet. The expression `z(5,7)`, for instance, gives the value in the cell in row number 5 and column number 7. The function call operator is implemented using the function call operator for class `Matrix`. The expression `(*m)` is the matrix that `m` points to, and the expression `(*m)(r,c)` then means element number `r,c` in the matrix that `m` points to.

The four remaining member functions allow the programmer the possibility of indicating properties for whole rows or columns in a spreadsheet. We begin by looking at the function `def_col`, with which we can indicate that a certain column is to be calculated from another column. To indicate, for example, that column number 8 should be equal to column number 3 but with all the cells multiplied by 2.5, we write

```
def_col(8, 3, mul, 2.5);
```

Function `def_row` functions in a similar way. To indicate, for instance, that row number 10 should be equal to row number 8 but with a value of 100 added to each cell, we can write

```
def_row(10, 8, add, 100);
```

We shall soon see how function `def_col` is implemented, but first we shall show a help function, `new_formula`, which is used by all of the last four member functions:

```
Formula *new_formula(Formula *f, op o, Formula *g)
{
  if (o==add)
```

```
        return new Add(f, g);
    else if (o==sub)
        return new Sub(f, g);
    else if (o==mul)
        return new Mul(f, g);
    else
        return new Div(f, g);
}
```

This function gets as parameters the pointers `f` and `g`, which point to formulas, and a value `o`, from the enumeration type `op`. The function creates a new formula, where the functions that `f` and `g` point to become operands. The kind of formula that is created depends on the value of the parameter `o`. As result, the function gives a pointer to the new formula that has been created.

Now we can study the definition of the function `def_col`. Its purpose is to define column number `col` from column number `c`. Any changes are determined by the operator `o` and the constant `d`. The function begins by checking that the parameters `col` and `c` do not indicate the same column. (A particular column cannot be calculated, of course, from itself.)

```
void Spreadsheet::def_col(int col, int c, op o, double d)
{
    if (col==c)
        throw invalid_argument("Spreadsheet::def_col");
    for (int i=1; i<=num_row(); i++)
    {
        Formula *f = new Other(&(*m)(i,c)),
                *g = new Constant(d);
        (*m)(i, col).define(new_formula(f, o, g));
    }
}
```

The function will put new formulas in all the cells in column number `col`. (It is, of course, this column that is to be defined.) To bring this about, it runs through all the rows of the matrix. For every row, `i`, two new formulas are created, and the pointers `f` and `g` point to them. Pointer `g` will point to a formula that contains the constant `d`. Pointer `f` points to a formula that refers to a cell in the corresponding row of column number `c`. The constructor for class `Other` will have a pointer to a cell as parameter. The expression `(*m)` means what `m` points to – that is, the matrix. The expression `(*m)(i,c)` is a reference to cell number `(i,c)` in this matrix, and the expression `&(*m)(i,c)` is thus the address to cell number `(i,c)` in the matrix. The help function `new_formula`, which constructs a formula with operands `f` and `g`, is then called. The new formula will be placed in the cell in column number `col` in row number `i`, which is done by calling the member function `define` for this cell.

The member function def_row is just the same, except that the columns are exchanged for rows. New formulas are put into all the cells in row number row, and so we run through all the columns. We do not need to show this function.

The two last member functions, sum_row and sum_col, are used to indicate that a certain row or column will constitute the sum of a certain number of other rows and columns, respectively. For instance, to indicate that row number 20 will contain the sum of rows 1 to 10, we make the call

```
sum_row(20, 1, 10);
```

The last parameter has the default value add, but another operator can also be used. To indicate that row number 19 will contain the difference between row 3 and 4, for instance, we can write

```
sum_row(19, 3, 4, sub);
```

In a similar way, function sum_col will make sums of columns. For example, to indicate that column number 7 is to contain column numbers 2, 3 and 4 multiplied by each other, we write

```
sum_col(7, 2, 4, mul);
```

We shall now show the definition of sum_row. (Function sum_col is written in a similar way but with the rows exchanged for columns.)

```
void Spreadsheet::sum_row(int row, int r1, int r2, op o)
{
  if (r1>r2 || (row>=r1 && row<=r2))
    throw range_error("Spreadsheet::sum_row");
  for (int j=1; j<=num_col(); j++)
  {
    Formula *f=new Other(&(*m)(r1,j));
    for (int i=r1+1; i<=r2; i++)
      f = new_formula(f, o, new Other(&(*m)(i,j)));
    (*m)(row,j).define(f);
  }
}
```

The parameters r1 and r2 will indicate a row interval, so r1 must be less than or equal to r2. The row to be defined, row number row, must not lie in the interval between r1 and r2. It cannot be defined by starting from itself. After the preliminary checks have been made, the function runs through all the columns. For every column j it builds up a sum formula that will be put into row number row in column j. To make the sum formula, it runs through all the rows in the interval between r1 and r2. First a formula is created to refer to the cell in column j in row r1, then it is built up with references to rows r1+1 to r2. The formulas are put together by the operator o. If o has the value add, a formula will be built to indicate that the cells in column number j in rows r1 to `r2` should be added. At the end of each round the sum formula is inserted in row number `row`, and this is done by calling the member function `define`.

We finish now by showing a little main program that uses class `Spreadsheet`. The program reads a number of sales figures that are fed in exclusive of sales tax. As result it gives a printout of these initial figures, the amount of sales tax to be added to each, and the amount of each including sales tax. To conclude, the program sums up all the sales figures, the sales tax and the sales figures including sales tax. When the program is run, it can look like this:

```
Indicate amount excluding sales tax
5000
2500
1000
12500
           Amount    sales tax    incl. sales tax
            5000        1250             6250
            2500         625             3125
            1000         250             1250
           12500        3125            15625
           =====       =====            =====
           21000        5250            26250
```

The lines written by the user have been underlined. The program looks like this:

```
main()
{
   Spreadsheet s(1000, 3);
   s.def_col(2, 1, mul, 0.25);
   s.sum_col(3, 1, 2);
   cout << "Indicate the amount excluding sales tax" << endl;
   double b;
   int r=0;
   while (cin>>b)
      s(++r,1).define(new Constant(b));
   s.sum_row(s.num_row(), 1, r);
   cout<<"  Amount   sales tax  incl. sales tax"<<endl;
   for (int i=1; i<=r; i++)
   {
      for (int j=1; j<=s.num_col(); j++)
         cout<< setw(14) << s(i,j);
      cout << endl;
   }
   cout<<"   =====     =====            ====="<<endl;
   for (int j=1; j<=s.num_col(); j++)
      cout<< setw(14) << s(s.num_row(), j);
   cout << endl;
}
```

The program uses a spreadsheet, `s`, that contains three columns and a maximum of 1000 rows. Function `def_col` is used to indicate that column number 2 will be calculated as column number 1 multiplied by 0.25 (the current percentage sales tax). Then function `sum_col` is used to indicate that column number 3 will contain the sum of columns 1 and 2.

The figures fed in are then read and placed in column number 1. The variable `r` is used to calculate the number of amounts that have to be fed in. When reading has finished, function `sum_row` is called to indicate that the last row in the spreadsheet will contain the sum of rows 1 to `r`.

Now the spreadsheet is finished, and it will write out its contents. Rows 1 to `r` are written first and, finally, row 1000.

We conclude with a little warning. Class `Cell` is not complete. An assignment operator and a copy constructor that makes deep copies are missing. As the class looks now, we should not be able to assign or initialize one cell with another. For instance, we could not assign one spreadsheet to another. If we were to complete class `Cell` with an assignment operator and a copy constructor, we could also add a constructor that had a parameter of type **`double`**. This would then function as a type conversion constructor and would make it easy to add new constant values to a cell. Instead of writing `s(i,j).define(new constant(d))`, we could write `s(i,j)=d`. This is left as an exercise for the reader.

Exercises

14.1 In Chapters 7, 8 and 9 we worked with a class `Array` (the definition is on page 303). Rewrite this class so that it becomes a class template. (Not all the member functions need be rewritten; it will suffice to practise on a few.)

14.2 Rewrite class `Queue` from section 13.2.2 so that it becomes a class template.

14.3 Rewrite class `Set` from section 13.2.3 so that it becomes a class template.

14.4 Class `Set` in Exercise 14.3 requires that the operators `==`, `!=` and `<` should exist for the actual type. Write a version of class `Set` that uses a property class and which can be used for such element types where the operators are missing.

14.5 To run through a binary tree in the order *preorder*, *inorder* and *postorder* is, as we have seen, very easy. The exercise here is to write a function to visit a tree in order of level. This means that the root (at level 1) should be visited first, then the nodes at level 2, from left to right, followed by the nodes at level 3, from left to right and so on.

The following algorithm can be used. First examine how deep the tree is. Then create a separate queue for each level. Each queue should contain pointers to nodes. Then run through the tree in the order *inorder*, adding pointers to the nodes in the correct queues. Finally, run through the queues one at a time, in the correct order. Use class `List` from Section 14.1.6 to build the queues.

14.6 Write a function template that can be used to search for a particular element in an array of arbitrary type. The function should have as parameters an array and the element it is to search for. As result is given a pointer to the element searched for. If this element cannot be found, a null pointer should be returned.

14.7 The standard algorithm `reverse` changes a data collection so that the elements appear in reverse order. This algorithm has two iterators as parameters. Write your own definition of the function template `reverse`.

14.8 Complete class `Cell` from section 14.3.3 with an assignment operator and a copy constructor that makes deep copies. In addition, write a constructor that has a parameter of type **`double`**. This constructor should insert a formula like `Constant` in the actual cell.

14.9 Make your own implementation of the standard class template `priority_queue` that was discussed in section 12.6 on page 463. *Tip*: Use heap algorithms as described on page 615.

The final pieces of the puzzle

15

This last chapter will describe some constructs that we need for a complete picture of C++. These constructs have no direct connection with each other, but have been collected here for the simple reason that they did not fit in anywhere else in the book. The fact that they are being dealt with last does not mean that they are necessarily less important than earlier material. For example, name spaces, which we shall deal with first, are an important new mechanism in C++.

15.1 Name spaces

Most substantive C++ programs are composed of a number of different, separately compiled program text files. Header files are used to access declarations of program units defined in other files. Header files can be either standard files as, for example, `iostream`, or non-standard files. The total number of files included in any one compilation can be large, since header files in turn include other header files. This means that there will normally be a great number of identifiers declared when a program is compiled, with the considerable risk that two different items will be given the same name in different header files. For instance, there might be two different constants declared with the name `size`. The program cannot then be compiled since the identifier `size` will be doubly defined. It is very irritating, when something in a program has been named, to find an error message warning that there has been a double declaration when the identifier in question has been used only once.* A *name space*, a new construct in C++, can be used to solve this problem. Then we can enclose a group of declarations, for instance all the declarations in a header file, in a name space, and these declarations will not normally be visible outside this name space. The declarations will not then conflict with declarations made outside the actual name space or in other name spaces.

* The keen reader may have wondered why the identifier `divi` and not `div` was used in the enumeration type `op` on page 552. This is because in the standard file `cstdlib` there happens to be a function with the name `div`, and for some reason the file `cstdlib` was included when the program was tested.

15.1.1 Definition of name spaces

In this section we shall study how name spaces are defined. In the next section we shall see how we can access what has been declared inside a name space. A name space is a construct that has a form similar to that of a class. The construct is introduced with the reserved word `namespace` followed by the name of the name space. Then there will be a block that can contain a number of arbitrary declarations:

```
namespace name {
   declarations
}
```

Suppose now that we want to use two libraries with help functions in a program. There are two header files, one for each library. These files are called `alib.h` and `blib.h`. They have the following appearance:

```
// File alib.h
namespace Alib {
   void initialize();
   double result(double x);
   const int max_num = 20;
   void write_out(double x);
}
```

```
// File blib.h
namespace Blib {
   void initialize();
   double result(double x);
   const int max_num = 100;
   const int least_num = 2;
}
```

We see that the declarations have been enclosed in two name spaces with different names. If we had not used name spaces, and had included both the files in the same program, the compiler would have complained that the variable `max_num` was doubly defined. (The declarations of the functions `initialize` and `result` would have been compiled since it is not an error to repeat declarations of functions. But there would have been problems with linking because the linker would not have known which of the two versions was to be linked.)

The definitions – that is, the implementations – of the functions in the two help libraries are made as usual in separate definition files with names ending in `.cpp`. We can use the same syntax here as when we define member functions of classes. File `alib.cpp` can look like this:

```
// File alib.cpp
#include "alib.h"
void Alib::initialize()
{ statements }
double Alib::result(double x)
{ statements }
void Alib::write_out(double x)
{ statements }
```

The complete names of the functions can thus be explicitly indicated by beginning with the name of the name space followed by a double colon. There is a simpler way, however, because it is permissible to *extend* a name space with further declarations or definitions. For instance, file `blib.h` can have the following appearance:

```
// File blib.cpp
#include "blib.h"
namespace Blib {
   void initialize();
   { statements }
   double result(double x)
   { statements }
}
```

Here the name space `Blib`, originally defined in file `blib.h`, has been extended by the definitions of functions `initialize` and `result`. We do not then have to indicate the rather awkward `Blib::` in front of every function name. (It would be nice to be able to do this with the definitions of member functions for classes, but unfortunately this is not possible.)

We can also define *unnamed name spaces*. Then the name of the name space is simply omitted:

```
namespace {   // unnamed name space
   declarations
}
```

The definitions inside an unnamed name space are automatically accessible in the part of the program where the unnamed name space is located. But they are not accessible from a separately compiled section of the program, and we can use this fact to hide internal help functions. Suppose, for example, that functions `initialize` and `result` make use of two help functions, `internal1` and `internal2`. We can then let file `blib.cpp` have the following appearance:

```
// File blib.cpp
#include "blib.h"
namespace {
   void internal1()
```

```
   { statements }
   void internal2()
   { statements }
}
namespace Blib {
   void initialize()
   { ... internal1(); ... }
   double result(double x)
   { ... internal2(); ... }
}
```

Functions `internal1` and `internal2` are visible in file `blib.cpp`, and can be called by `initialize` and `result`, but it is not possible (by mistake) to call `internal1` and `internal2` from some other section of the program. (Alternatively, an old technique inherited from the programming language C can be used. Functions are declared with the keyword **`static`**, whereupon they become invisible to a linker. This has nothing to do with static member functions.)

Definition of name spaces

```
namespace name {
   declarations
}
```

- If *name* has not been defined before, it is a definition of a *new* name space.
- If a definition of a name space with the name *name* has been given before, it is an *extension* of this name space.
- If *name* is omitted, it is an *unnamed* name space. The definitions in an unnamed name space are directly visible in the part of the program where the definitions have been made, but they are not accessible from another, separately compiled part of the program.
- An alternative name (*name2*) can be defined instead of the original name (*name1*):

```
namespace name2=name1;
```

Name spaces can sometimes have cumbersome names. A manufacturer may be reluctant to see the company name omitted. Suppose, for instance, that a name space has the name `ChalmersSoftwareLibrary`. To avoid using this lengthy name, an alternative can be defined and used from then on:

```
namespace CSL = ChalmersSoftwareLibrary;
```

The syntax for name spaces and class definitions may look similar, but there is an important difference between a name space and a class. A class is a type: therefore instances of it can be declared. A name space, on the other hand, is not a type, so there cannot be instances of a name space. A name space is only a language construct that makes it possible to enclose a number of declarations belonging together, into a kind of package. (In fact, a similar construct in the programming language Ada is called a 'package'.)

15.1.2 Using name spaces

Whatever has been declared in a name space will be invisible from outside if no other measures have been taken. However, there are three ways of accessing the contents of a name space: with an 'explicit qualification', with a 'using declaration' and with a 'using directive'. To demonstrate these procedures, we shall assume that we have a function `f` that includes the two files `alib.h` and `blib.h`:

```
#include "alib.h"
#include "blib.h"
void f()
{
   statements
}
```

Suppose now that we put the following line in the function statements:

```
write_out(2.6);    // Error, invisible
```

We get a compilation error, because whatever is inside a name space is not directly visible. One way of accessing something that has been declared inside a name space is to use the *explicit qualification*. We can write, for example,

```
Alib::write_out(2.6);    // OK, explicit qualification
```

Every time an identifier is used, its full name is written with the name space name coming first.

The second way of making a particular declaration visible is to give a *using declaration*. This begins with the reserved word **using**, and then comes the complete name of the identifier that is to be visible. Here we make the function `least_num` in `Blib` directly visible:

```
using Blib::least_num; << endl;    // using declaration
...
cout << least_num << endl;    // OK, visible
```

A using declaration means that the identifier indicated is declared in the actual place, just as if it had been an ordinary declaration. In this way, the identifier becomes directly visible.

The third way of making declarations in a name space visible is by making a *using directive*. This makes *all* the declarations in a name space visible. The reserved word **using** is written, followed by the name of a name space. Here we make all the declarations in the name space `Alib` visible:

```
using namespace Alib;   // using directive
```

Employing a using directive means that everything that has been declared in `Alib` will be accessible, exactly as if the declarations had been made openly instead of in a name space. (There is a difference between a using declaration and a using directive. With a using declaration the identifier is declared inside the function – in this case `f`. With a using directive, however, all the declarations will certainly be visible but will lie *outside* the function.)

Now everything that has been declared in `Alib` can be used directly in function `f`. We can make the statements

```
cout << max_num << endl;   // OK, all of Alib visible
initialize();
```

Using name spaces

- *Explicit qualification*. Give the complete name every time it is used:

  space_name::*name*

- *Using declaration*. Declare *one* particular identifier at the indicated place:

  using *space_name*::*name*;

- *Using directive*. Makes the *whole* name space open:

  using namespace space_name;

Using directives can be given for several name spaces:

```
using namespace Alib;
using namespace Blib;
```

Of course, there will now be ambiguities. If we write, for instance,

```
initialize();   // Error, ambiguous
```

the compiler will not know whether the function `initialize` in `Alib` or `Blib` is to be called. So the name should be indicated explicitly:

```
Alib::initialize();
```

Using declarations or using directives can be placed anywhere in a program. To avoid unnecessarily making the contents of name spaces visible, we can ensure that our using declarations or using directives are put only in the functions or classes where the name space will be used. This is preferable to putting using directives at the outermost level in program files.

15.1.3 Name spaces and standard libraries

In the standard, a number of header files have been specified. These are both new files that are specific to C++ and new versions of all the header files that have been inherited from the programming language C. According to the standard, all standard header files should have file names that do *not* end in `.h`. The new versions of the C header files should have the same names as before but with a `c` in front. The new version of the C header file `math.h` is called `cmath`, for instance. But all the new header files will have the form

```
namespace std {
   declarations
}
```

Hence all the declarations occur in a common name space having the name `std`. Since all name spaces can be extended, the declarations in all the standard files that we include will be automatically found in the name space `std`. Declarations in header files do not automatically become visible in user programs. The three methods described in the previous section have to be used to gain access to them, so this makes it possible to include standard files without the danger of finding conflicting names when we declare something that happens to have the same name as a declaration in a standard file. If this problem does not arise, and we want everything to be directly visible (as it always used to be in C and C++), then we only have to add this line at the outermost level of our program:

```
using namespace std;
```

So that C++ will be compatible with C, the C++ standard stipulates that all the old versions of header files (those where the names end in `.h`) should remain. When a file like this is included, the using declarations are given automatically for everything declared in the file. Everything will therefore be visible without the need for any action.

Let us take an example. The header file `cmat` contains declarations of mathematical standard functions. It has the form:

```
namespace std {
   double acos(double);
   double asin(double);
   etc.
}
```

The file `math.h` then has the appearance:

```
#include <cmath>
using std::acos;
using std::asin;
etc.
```

15.2 Bit operators

From the beginning the programming language C was constructed as an alternative to assembler languages when 'machine level' programs were to be written. These were programs that worked closely with the computer's operating system and hardware. In such programs we often need to be able to handle individual bits in memory cells. In C and C++ there are a number of operators that can be used to handle integer variables as though they contained bit patterns instead of integers.

Note that the operators described here are defined only for integer types. The operator `~` is the simplest one. It has only one operand and as result gives a bit pattern in which all the zeros in the operand have been exchanged for ones, or vice versa. We shall give an example. (In the following statements we assume that all of the variables have type **`unsigned short int`** and are 16 bits long.)

```
a = 7;    // a = 0000 0000 0000 0111
b = 20;   // b = 0000 0000 0001 0100
c = ~a;   // c = 1111 1111 1111 1000
```

The operators `&`, `|` and `^` carry out the operations *and*, *or* and *exclusive or* bit by bit. The operator *exclusive or* means that a particular bit in the result will be a one if exactly one of the operands contains a one in the corresponding position. If none or both of the operands contain a one, the result bit will be zero.

```
d = a & b;   // d = 0000 0000 0000 0100
e = a | b;   // e = 0000 0000 0001 0111
f = a ^ b;   // f = 0000 0000 0001 0011
```

According to the standard, it is permissible to use the reserved words **`compl`**, **`bitand`**, **`bitor`** and **`xor`** instead of the symbols `~`, `&`, `|` and `^` respectively. The last two statements might then be written

```
e = a bitor b;
f = a xor b;
```

The operators `<<` and `>>` perform *left shift* and *right shift* respectively, moving bits to the right or the left. The left operand contains the bit pattern to be moved, and the right operator indicates how many steps the bits should be moved. (If the right operand is negative or greater than the number of bits in the left operand, the result is undefined.) When a left shift is performed, zeros are always inserted from the right; when right shift is performed on a value that is positive or **`unsigned`**, zeros are inserted from the left. (If right shift is performed on a negative value that is **signed**, it remains undefined whether ones or zeros are inserted from the left.) Here are a couple of examples:

```
g = b << 5;   // g = 0000 0010 1000 0000
h = c >> 2;   // h = 0011 1111 1111 1110
```

The operator & is often used to perform *masking*, the selection of certain bits from a bit pattern. For instance, the following statement masks the eight bits in the middle of the bit pattern contained by the variable h:

```
i = h & 0xf00f;   // i = 0011 0000 0000 1110;
```

The operator | can be used to add ones to certain bits. The following statement will put ones in the eight bits furthest to the right:

```
j = i | 0x00ff;   // i = 0011 0000 1111 1111;
```

Bit operators

- Are defined only for integer types.
- Perform all operators bit by bit.

~	compl	changes 0<->1
&	bitand	and, bit by bit
|	bitor	or, bit by bit
^	xor	exclusive or
<<		left shift
>>		right shift

Note that none of the operators we have shown here have any effect on *their* operators. If such operators are required, the corresponding assignment operators can be used. We can write, for instance,

```
a &= 0x000f;
```

which is the same thing as writing

```
a = a & 0x000f;
```

15.3 struct

In the programming language C there is a construct called **struct**. With **struct** we can construct types that are built up from several subcomponents, which can be of different type. (**struct** corresponds to the construct usually called 'record' in most other common programming languages.) When C++ was created, **struct** was used from the beginning to determine how classes were to function. The new construct **class** was similar to **struct** in C but new features were added, among them member functions and inheritance. Because C++ had to be compatible with C, it was decided that `struct` should also be present in C++, and it was allowed to have the same options as `class`. In other words, in C++, `struct` is the same thing as `class`. A `struct` can also have member functions and inherit from another `struct` or `class`. There is only one slight difference, and this has to do with access. All the members in a `struct` are automatically visible if neither of the words `private` or `public` is indicated. In a class, as we know, they would all end up in the `private` section. And the same thing applies to inheritance. When a `struct` is derived from another `struct` or from a class, public inheritance is automatically used if neither of the words `private` or `public` appears. Private inheritance is used in classes when nothing else is indicated. Here are some examples:

```
struct S1 {
   S1(int n=0) : i(n) {};
   void write() {cout << i << endl; }
   int i;
};
```

In `S1` all the members are directly visible. We can write, for instance,

```
S1 a;
a.i=7;
a.write();
```

And another `struct` can be derived from S1:

```
struct S2 : S1 {
   S2(int n, double x) : S1(n), d(x) {}
   double square() {return d*d;}
private:
   double d;
};
```

In `S2` the constructor and member function `square` are visible, whereas the data member `d` is, of course, private. Public inheritance is used here in spite of the fact that the word `public` does not stand on the first line. The following statements might be given:

```
S2 b(5, 2.5);
cout << b.square() << endl;
b.write();
```

The construct `struct` really is easier to use than `class` when we want the visible members of a class to be indicated first. It is simpler to write

```
struct D : B {
   ...
};
```

than writing everywhere

```
class D : public B {
public:
   ...
};
```

struct

The same thing as a class but data members and base classes are *visible* if nothing else is indicated.

```
struct D : B {
   ...
};
```

is exactly the same thing as

```
class D : public B {
public:
   ...
};
```

Paradoxically, the construct `class`, so central a concept in C++, is completely unnecessary. It would be just as efficient and, in fact, somewhat easier, to use `struct` in its stead. But a language that is object-oriented must, perhaps for different reasons, contain a construct that is simply called 'class'.

15.4 union

As we know, we can give a class a number of data members. We can write, for instance,

```
class C {
   int no;
   double v;
   char txt [6];
};
```

An object of class c thus contains three components: an `int`, a `double`, and a character array with six `char`. The number of bytes that are needed in the primary memory to store an object of class c is determined by the lengths of the three components. A `union` is a kind of class that can contain only *one* of its data members at a time. We can give the definition:

```
union Data {
   int no;
   double v;
   char txt[6];
};
```

If we now define an object `a` of type Data, `a` can contain either an **`int`**, a **`double`** or a character array. The three data members lie in the same place in the primary memory, thus competing for this space. An object of type `Data` will then take up as many bytes as the *longest* of its data members needs.

Unions can be used in cases where it is known that different objects can be of different kinds and that different data members will be used. In this way, memory space is saved by not reserving places for unnecessary components. Union objects can be declared and used as ordinary objects, but it must be remembered that such objects can contain only one kind of object at a time. We can write, for instance,

```
Data a;
a.no = 5;
cout << a.no << endl;
a.v=3.67;
strcpy(a.txt, "Hello");
cout << a.txt << endl;
```

The same rules apply to a **`union`** as to a **`struct`**, which means that all members will be public if nothing else has been indicated. We can then access the different data members here directly.

A **`union`** may not be used in connection with inheritance. (It cannot have base classes, be a base class itself, or have virtual member functions.) On the other hand it is permissible to have ordinary member functions, constructors and destructors. We can complete the union `Data` with some constructors:

```
Data() {}  // default constructor
Data(int i) : no(i) {}
Data(double x) : v(x) {}
Data(char *s) {strcpy(txt,s);}
```

It is now possible to write

```
Data a(5);
a = "Bye";
```

What happens if the variable `a` contains a value of a certain type and we try to interpret it as a value of another type? There will simply be an error. A **`union`** does not itself have knowledge about what type of data it currently contains. The programmer has to know this.

To avoid the risk of data being misinterpreted, we often enclose unions in a class that has an extra data member to indicate what type of data the union contains. For instance, we might want the union `Data` to describe different kinds of message.

union

- A class where the objects can contain only *one* of the data members at a time. An object is big enough to hold the largest of the data members.
- May not be used in connection with inheritance.

```
union U {
   ...
};
```

There are messages that contain a number (an integer), a value (a real number) or a text. We then construct a class `Mess` in which we enclose the union `Data`:

```
enum Kind {number, value, text, undef};
class Mess {
public:
   Kind k;   // discriminant
   Data d;   // union
};
```

The data member `d` is a union, so it can contain values of different type. Such a data member is usually called a *variant*. Data member `k` is of enumeration type and can contain one of the values `number`, `value`, `text` or `undef`. It indicates what kind of data is in `d`. The data member `k` is an example of what we call a *discriminant*. The discriminant can be tested before the value of `d` is interpreted:

```
if (m.k==text)   // m has type Mess
   cout << m.d.txt;
```

There is still room for error, but if class `Mess` were extended with a few member functions, it could be made safer. We therefore place the data members `k` and `d` in the **`private`** section so that the user cannot access them directly. All access will occur via the member functions, which will monitor that the type in `d` is correct. Here is the extended definition of class `Mess`:

```
enum Kind {number, value, text, undef};
class Mess {
public:
   Mess() : k(undef) {}
   Mess(int i) : k(number) {d.no=i;}
   Mess(double x) : k(value) {d.v=x;}
   Mess(char *k) : k(text) {strcpy(d.txt, k);}
```

```
    Kind what() {return k;}
    int the_number() {assert(k==number); return d.no;}
    double the_value() {assert(k==value); return d.v;}
    const char *the_text() {assert(k==text); return d.txt;}
private:
    Kind k;   // discriminant
    Data d;   // union
};
```

There are four constructors, a default constructor and a constructor for every possible type that `d` can contain. These constructors not only initialize `d`, they also place information on the type involved in the discriminant `k`. The member function `what` can be used to read but not change the discriminant. It can also be called to find out what is in `d`. Finally, for every one of the three types, there is a member function that makes it possible to read the value in `d`. With the aid of the discriminant, the member functions check that `d` contains the correct type. Since neither `d` nor the discriminant `k` can be changed without using one of the constructors, the data in `d` cannot be wrongly interpreted. If we were to try to use `d` incorrectly, we would get stuck in function `assert`:

```
Mess m(19);
cout << m.the_number() << endl;    // OK
m = "Hello";
cout << m.the_text() << endl;      // OK
cout << m.the_number() << endl;    // ERROR (in assert)
```

We shall very briefly mention that there is something called *anonymous union*. A union can be declared without a name, in which case a variable is declared – and not a type. We could have declared class `Mess` in the following alternative way:

```
class Mess {
    ...
private:
    Kind k;
    union {
        int no;
        double v;
        char txt[6];
    };
};
```

The union then designates a member variable in class `Mess`. The names `no`, `v` and `txt` are directly accessible in class `Mess`. (In this way, we jump over the extra level with `d` that we used earlier.) The last three member functions will, for instance, have the following appearance:

```
int the_number() {assert(k==number); return no;}
double the_value() {assert(k==value); return v;}
const char *text() {assert(k==text); return txt;}
```

15.5 Bit fields

When individual data members are declared in a class (or `struct`), we can indicate that they should be *bit fields*, which consist of a certain number of bits packed together. When we declare a bit field, we write a colon after the data member's name and then indicate the number of bits to be used for the actual data member. An example of the use of this procedure is when we have a number of objects of a certain type and want to save memory space. Suppose that we have a register of cars. For every car we wish to monitor the car's registration number (six characters), the model (a number between 0 and 99), whether the tax has been paid and the car has passed its inspection test and, finally, whether the car is no longer running (has been taken off the road). We can then give the following class definition:

```
class Car {
public:
   char reg_no[6];
   unsigned int model : 7;
   unsigned int tax_paid : 1;
   unsigned int inspected : 1;
   unsigned int not_run : 1;
};
```

The data members `model`, `tax_paid`, `inspected` and `not_run` are bit fields here. Seven bits are reserved for `model`. The other three bit fields require only one bit each. A bit field must be of integer or enumeration type. It should be indicated, as it is here, whether a bit field is `unsigned` or `signed`, since it is not clear what it will be if only `int` is written.

Bit fields can be accessed just like ordinary data members. For example, we can write the following:

```
Car c;
strncpy(c.reg_no, "abc123", 6);
c.model = 97;
c.not_run = false;
cout << c.model << endl;
if (c.tax_paid and c.inspected)
   cout << "OK";
```

(To save space, no terminating zero has been stored at the end of the registration number, so `strncpy` and not `strcpy` must be used.)

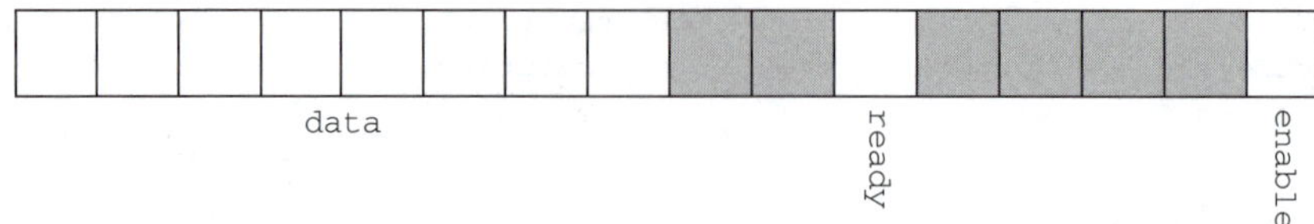

Figure 15.1

When we write machine-level programs, for example *drive routines*, which handle input and output from external units, bit fields can be very useful. We then have to access special, so-called *control registers*, which are found at given primary memory addresses. The individual bits in such a register have special functions. A register may look as it does in Figure 15.1. (We give only the general principles here. Registers may differ from system to system.)

The register consists of 16 bits numbered from right to left. (This will vary from computer to computer. Sometimes numbering occurs from left to right.) The bit on the right is set to a one if we want the external unit to be able to generate a hardware interrupt. The external unit itself puts a one in the sixth bit from the right when it is ready to accept (or has finished sending) data. The data to be sent to the external unit (or read from it) is placed in the eight bits furthest to the left. The program will fill in these bits for output while the external unit fills them in for input. The shaded bits in the register are unused in our example. We can now define a class that describes how a register will look, in keeping with Figure 15.1:

```
class Register {
public:
   unsigned int enable : 1;
                       : 4;
   unsigned int ready  : 1;
                       : 2;
   unsigned int data   : 8;
};
```

We have added *unnamed bit fields* to fill out the unused bits.

In any computer system there are several control registers, and these will be in fixed places in the primary memory. Different external units will have different control registers. As an example, let us suppose that at the (hexadecimal) primary memory address `ffa0` there is a control register that is used to write one byte at a time to a particular external unit. We can declare a pointer, `r`, to point to this register:

```
volatile Register *r = (Register *)0xffa0;
```

We have not met the reserved word **`volatile`** before. It is used to indicate that what `r` points to can be changed in some way, without it being done by the program. (Of

Bit fields

- We can indicate for individual data members the number of bits they should consist of.
- Bit fields must be of integer or enumeration type.
- Explicitly indicate **unsigned** or **signed**.
- Unnamed bit fields can act as fillers.

```
class C {
  type B1  : n1;
  type B2  : n2;
           : k1;   // unnamed bit field
  type B3  : n3;
};
```

- The address operator & cannot be used in bit fields.

course, the external unit itself changes the bit `ready`.) This is written so that the compiler will not try to make optimizations of the generated machine code for the variable `r`. This variable is initialized to the hexadecimal value `ffa0`. Since the type of this expression is **int**, an explicit type conversion must be made to 'pointer to `Register`'.

We can now access the special control register via the pointer `r`. Suppose that we want to write out a byte to the actual external unit. We have to wait until the unit is ready to accept data, then the data to be written out should be put in the register's data field:

```
while (!r->ready)   // Wait until the unit is ready
  ;
r->data = 'X';      // Write out data
```

If the word **volatile** had not been used in the declaration of `r`, the compiler might have tried to optimize the apparently meaningless **while** statement and get rid of it.

15.6 The do statement

We have used **while** and **for** statements in this book to produce repetition. But there is a third repetition statement, the **do** statement. It has the form

```
do
  statement
while (expression);
```

This statement is similar to the **while** statement. The difference is that the test expression is calculated and tested *after* instead of before each round. This means that the statement inside a `do` statement is always performed at least once. Braces can be used if several statements have to be performed at each round. We usually write `do` statements in the following way:

```
do {
   statements
} while (expression);
```

It is useful to write the right brace first in the last line so that when we read the program we are not fooled into thinking that the word `while` begins a statement.

Here is an example of a type of program where it can be expedient to use a `do` statement. In the program, repeated calculations are carried out for different input data. After each calculation, the user is asked whether further calculations should be performed.

```
main()
{
   double x;
   char answer[5];
   do {
      cout << "Give input data: " ; cin >> x;
      cout << "The result=" << res(x) << endl;
      cout << "Continue? (y, n) "; cin >> answer;
   } while (answer[0] == 'y');
}
```

15.7 The `switch` statement

A `switch` statement is one that can be used instead of an `if` statement where there is a multiple choice situation. (A `switch` statement is a primitive form of the *case* statement usually found in high-level languages such as Ada and Pascal.) We will show, by way of an example, a part of a program that simulates a very simple calculator. The program reads and calculates expressions of the form `x` *op* `y`.

```
double x, y;
char op;
while (cin >> x >> op >> y)
   switch(op) {
   case '+':
      cout << (x+y) << endl;
      break;
   case '-':
      cout << (x-y) << endl;
      break;
   case '*':
```

```
      cout << (x*y) << endl;
      break;
   case '/':
      if (y != 0)
      cout << (x/y) << endl;
      else
      cout << "Division by zero" << endl;
      break;
   default:
      cout << "Incorrect operator" << endl;
}
```

A `switch` statement is introduced with the reserved word `switch`. Then there should be a *test expression*, which must be of integer or enumeration type, in parentheses. (This can also be a value of a class type if there is a type conversion operator for the class that converts to an integer type.) Every alternative in a `switch` statement is introduced with the word `case`. The expressions that come after `case`, the `case` expressions, must be constant. There cannot be two or more `case` expressions with the same value. There may also be a `default` alternative.

When a `switch` statement is executed, the test expression after the word `switch` is first calculated, and the value of this is compared with the values of the different `case` expressions. If the test expression has the same value as a `case` expression, there is a

switch statement

```
switch(integer_expression) {
   case constant_value1:
      statement
      break;
   case constant_value2:
      statements
      break;
   ...
   default:
      statements
}
```

- Expressions after `case` must have different values.
- The `default` alternative can be omitted.
- There can be several `case` expressions in front of a given alternative.
- Upon execution there is a jump to the alternative for which the *integer_expression* is equal to a *constant_value*.
- If there is no suitable alternative, there is a jump to the `default` alternative. If there is a default alternative, nothing happens.

jump to the statement following this `case` expression. If none of the `case` expressions has the same value as the test expression, there is a jump to the statement after the word `default`. If the `default` alternative is absent and none of the `case` expressions is acceptable, nothing is carried out in the `switch` statement.

Note that a `break` statement must come last in every alternative (except in the last one). This results in the alternative being terminated. There is then a jump to the end of the `switch` statement. If there were no `break` statement in a given alternative, there would not be a jump. Instead, execution would continue with the statements in the next alternative!

It is permissible to have several `case` expressions introducing a given alternative. For example, we can write

```
switch(c) {
   case '0': case '1': case '2': case '3': case '4':
   case '5': case '6': case '7': case '8': case '9':
     number_digits++;
     break;
   case ' ': case '\t': case '\n':
     number_white++;
     break;
   default:
     number_others++;
}
```

Unfortunately this is not very elegant, as the word `case` has to be repeated.

15.8 The conditional operator

There is an operator that programmers can possibly manage without, but we should be familiar with it, in any case. This is the *conditional operator*. With this operator, *conditional expressions* can be formed. Suppose, for instance, that we want to test which of the variables `x` and `y` is the larger and then assign the greater value to the variable `z`. Naturally, this is easily done with the aid of an `if` statement:

```
if (x>y)
   z = x;
else
   z = y;
```

However, a conditional expression can also be used:

```
z = (x>y) ? x : y;
```

The conditional operator has three operands. The first is a test expression. If this is true, the second operand, the one coming after the character `?`, is calculated, and the result of the conditional expression will be equal to this operand. If the test expression is false, the third operand, the one after the character `:`, is calculated, and the result of the conditional expression will be equal to this operand.

A conditional expression is therefore a kind of `if` statement that leaves a value as result. The type of this result is determined by the last two operands. If they have the same type, the result will have this type; otherwise there will be the same kind of ordinary type conversions that occur with addition, for instance. The result type will therefore be equal to the longer of the two types.

As an example, we shall show some program lines that write out a text string `s` in such a way that all the upper-case letters (A–Z) are translated to lower-case letters. Other characters are written out unchanged. (Assume that the variable `c` has type `char`.)

```
for (int i=0; c=s[i]; i++)
  cout<< char((c>='A' && c<='Z') ? c+'a'-'A' : c);
```

The result of the conditional expression has type `int`, so an explicit type conversion must be made to type `char`.

The conditional operator

expression1 ? expression2 : expression3

- If *expression1* is `true`, the result will be equal to *expression2*, otherwise the result will be equal to *expression3*.
- If *expression2* and *expression3* have the same type, the result type will be equal to this type, otherwise an ordinary arithmetic type conversion is made so that the result type will be the longer of the two types.

Exercises

15.1 In Chapter 4 we created our own library, `simpleio`, with a few functions for reading and writing (see page 129). Adjust this library so that all the declarations in it end up in its own name space with the name `Simpleio`.

15.2 In section 13.2.3 we constructed a class `Set`. Place this class in its own name space. Several local help functions are used when the member functions are implemented. Place these in an anonymous name space so that they cannot be accessed from outside.

15.3 Assume that variable `c` of type `char` contains two small integers in the interval from 0 to 15. One of the integers is stored in the four bits on the left and the other in the four bits on the right. Write a program section that returns the sum of these two small numbers.

15.4 Suppose that we use an array, `f`, with element type **`char`** to store an array with logic values. Every logic value will be represented by only one bit, so there will be eight logic values in every **`char`**. Write a program section to show how indexing in the array can be carried out. In other words: given a variable `k`, the logic value number `k` should be taken out.

15.5 A process known as a *lexical analysis* occurs in the first stage in the workings of a compiler. The program text written by the programmer is interpreted, and divided into so-called *lexical tokens*. These lexical tokens are then sent to the second stage in the compiler. Examples of lexical tokens are identifiers, reserved words, integer constants, real constants and text strings. A lexical symbol must contain two pieces of information: there must be some indication of what kind of symbol it is, and the value of this symbol must be given. This value will depend on the kind of symbol in question. For instance, for an identifier, the value will be a text string with the identifier's name, and for an integer constant it will be an integer. Use a **`union`** to declare a type that describes lexical tokens.

15.6 Write a program that reads a date in the format yyyy-mm-dd. The program should write out the day number of the date during the year – that is, a number between 1 and 365, or 366 if it is a leap year. (Leap years are years that are divisible by 4 but years exactly divisible by 100 are not leap years unless they are also divisible by 400.) Use a **`switch`** statement with the different months as an alternative.

Appendix A Reserved words and operators

The reserved words in C++ are shown in Table A.1. The words written in brackets are alternative words for logic operators and bit operators.

Table A.1 Reserved words

(and)	continue	goto	public	try
(and_eq)	default	if	register	typedef
asm	delete	inline	reinterpret_cast	typeid
auto	do	int	return	typename
(bitand)	double	long	short	union
(bitor)	dynamic_cast	mutable	signed	unsigned
bool	else	namespace	sizeof	using
break	enum	new	static	virtual
case	explicit	(not)	static_cast	void
catch	export	(not_eq)	struct	volatile
char	extern	operator	switch	wchar_t
class	false	(or)	template	while
(compl)	float	(or_eq)	this	xor
const	for	private	throw	xor_eq
const_cast	friend	protected	true	

A compilation of the operators in C++ is given in Table A.2. Operators with only one operand, *unary* operators, have been placed in the first two boxes, and operators with two operands have been placed in the other boxes. (The exception is the conditional operator, which has three operands.) The operators have been listed in order of priority, with the operator in the first box having the highest priority. Operators in the same box have the same priority.

Table A.2 Operators

<table>
<tr><td>[] ()
. ->
.* ->*
++ --</td><td>Indexing and function call
Selection of class member
Dereferencing of pointer to member
Postfix, increment and decrement</td></tr>
<tr><td>++ --
+ -
& *
! not ~ compl
sizeof
new new[] delete delete[]</td><td>Prefix, increment and decrement
Unary + and –
Address and dereferencing
Logic NOT and bit operator NOT
Test of size
Allocation and deallocation</td></tr>
<tr><td>* / %</td><td>Multiplication, division, remainder</td></tr>
<tr><td>+ -</td><td>Addition, subtraction</td></tr>
<tr><td><< >></td><td>Shift</td></tr>
<tr><td>< > <= >=</td><td>Less than, greater than</td></tr>
<tr><td>== !=</td><td>Equal, not equal</td></tr>
<tr><td>& bitand</td><td>Bit operator AND</td></tr>
<tr><td>^ xor</td><td>Bit operator XOR</td></tr>
<tr><td>| bitor</td><td>Bit operator OR</td></tr>
<tr><td>&& and</td><td>Logic AND</td></tr>
<tr><td>|| or</td><td>Logic OR</td></tr>
<tr><td>? :</td><td>Conditional operator</td></tr>
<tr><td>= += -= *= /= %=
<<= >>=
&= ^= |=
and_eq xor_eq or_eq</td><td>Assignment operators</td></tr>
<tr><td>,</td><td>Comma operator</td></tr>
</table>

Appendix B LATIN_1 codes

Table B.1 LATIN_1 codes

\x00	*nul*	\x20	*space*	\x40	@	\x60	'
\x01	*soh*	\x21	!	\x41	A	\x61	a
\x02	*stx*	\x22	"	\x42	B	\x62	b
\x03	*etx*	\x23	#	\x43	C	\x63	c
\x04	*eot*	\x24	$	\x44	D	\x64	d
\x05	*enq*	\x25	%	\x45	E	\x65	e
\x06	*ack*	\x26	&	\x46	F	\x66	f
\x07	*bel*	\x27	'	\x47	G	\x67	g
\x08	*bs*	\x28	(	\x48	H	\x68	h
\x09	*ht*	\x29	)	\x49	I	\x69	i
\x0A	*lf*	\x2A	*	\x4A	J	\x6A	j
\x0B	*vt*	\x2B	+	\x4B	K	\x6B	k
\x0C	*ff*	\x2C	,	\x4C	L	\x6C	l
\x0D	*cr*	\x2D	-	\x4D	M	\x6D	m
\x0E	*so*	\x2E	.	\x4E	N	\x6E	n
\x0F	*si*	\x2F	/	\x4F	O	\x6F	o
\x10	*dle*	\x30	0	\x50	P	\x70	p
\x11	*dc1*	\x31	1	\x51	Q	\x71	q
\x12	*dc2*	\x32	2	\x52	R	\x72	r
\x13	*dc3*	\x33	3	\x53	S	\x73	s
\x14	*dc4*	\x34	4	\x54	T	\x74	t
\x15	*nak*	\x35	5	\x55	U	\x75	u
\x16	*syn*	\x36	6	\x56	V	\x76	v
\x17	*etb*	\x37	7	\x57	W	\x77	w
\x18	*can*	\x38	8	\x58	X	\x78	x
\x19	*em*	\x39	9	\x59	Y	\x79	y
\x1A	*sub*	\x3A	:	\x5A	Z	\x7A	z
\x1B	*esc*	\x3B	;	\x5B	[	\x7B	{
\x1C	*fs*	\x3C	<	\x5C	\	\x7C	|
\x1D	*gs*	\x3D	=	\x5D	]	\x7D	}
\x1E	*rs*	\x3E	>	\x5E	^	\x7E	~
\x1F	*us*	\x3F	?	\x5F	_	\x7F	*del*

the table continues on the next page

Table B.1 (cont'd)

\x80		\xA0	*nbsp*	\xC0	À	\xE0	à
\x81		\xA1	¡	\xC1	Á	\xE1	á
\x82		\xA2	¢	\xC2	Â	\xE2	â
\x83		\xA3	£	\xC3	Ã	\xE3	ã
\x84	*ind*	\xA4	¤	\xC4	Ä	\xE4	ä
\x85	*nel*	\xA5	¥	\xC5	Å	\xE5	å
\x86	*ssa*	\xA6	¦	\xC6	Æ	\xE6	æ
\x87	*esa*	\xA7	§	\xC7	Ç	\xE7	ç
\x88	*hts*	\xA8	¨	\xC8	È	\xE8	è
\x89	*htj*	\xA9	©	\xC9	É	\xE9	é
\x8A	*vts*	\xAA	ª	\xCA	Ê	\xEA	ê
\x8B	*pld*	\xAB	«	\xCB	Ë	\xEB	ë
\x8C	*plu*	\xAC	¬	\xCC	Ì	\xEC	ì
\x8D	*ri*	\xAD	_	\xCD	Í	\xED	í
\x8E	*ss2*	\xAE	®	\xCE	Î	\xEE	î
\x8F	*ss3*	\xAF	¯	\xCF	Ï	\xEF	ï
\x90	*dcs*	\xB0	°	\xD0	Ð	\xF0	ð
\x91	*pu1*	\xB1	±	\xD1	Ñ	\xF1	ñ
\x92	*pu2*	\xB2	²	\xD2	Ò	\xF2	ò
\x93	*sts*	\xB3	³	\xD3	Ó	\xF3	ó
\x94	*cch*	\xB4	´	\xD4	Ô	\xF4	ô
\x95	*mw*	\xB5	µ	\xD5	Õ	\xF5	õ
\x96	*spa*	\xB6	¶	\xD6	Ö	\xF6	ö
\x97	*epa*	\xB7	·	\xD7	×	\xF7	÷
\x98		\xB8	¸	\xD8	Ø	\xF8	ø
\x99		\xB9	¹	\xD9	Ù	\xF9	ù
\x9A		\xBA	º	\xDA	Ú	\xFA	ú
\x9B	*csi*	\xBB	»	\xDB	Û	\xFB	û
\x9C	*st*	\xBC	¼	\xDC	Ü	\xFC	ü
\x9D	*osc*	\xBD	½	\xDD	Ý	\xFD	ý
\x9E	*pm*	\xBE	¾	\xDE	Þ	\xFE	þ
\x9F	*apc*	\xBF	¿	\xDF	ß	\xFF	ÿ

Appendix C
Standard algorithms

C

In this appendix you will find a compilation of all the standard algorithms in C++. They have been divided into different categories to make it easier for you to understand what algorithms there are and what they can do. The following symbols are used throughout:

- `T` is the type of the elements in the container. For example, if you apply an algorithm to a list with elements of type **`double`**, then `T` represents the type **`double`**.
- `value` is a value of the same type as the elements in the actual container – that is, a value of type `T`.
- `[first, last)` indicates an interval in a container. `first` and `last` are iterators. The interval begins with the element that `first` is pointing to and ends with the elements *before* the element that `last` is pointing to. If an algorithm runs through two containers, the symbols `first1` and `last1` are the iterators in the first container and `first2` and `last2` are the iterators in the second container.
- `result` is an iterator that indicates the starting point in a container where the result of an operation is to be placed.
- `pred` is a unary predicate: that is, a function object that has a parameter of type `T` and which gives a result of type **`bool`**.
- `bin_pred` is a binary predicate: that is, a function object that has two parameters of type `T` and which gives a result of type **`bool`**.
- `comp` is a comparator: that is, a function object that has two parameters of type `T` and which gives a result of type **`bool`**.
- `op` is a function object that has a parameter of type `T` and which gives a result of type `T`.
- `bin_op` is a function object that has two parameters of type `T` and which gives a result of type `T`.

C.1 Search

find

```
find (first, last, value)
```

Searches through the interval `[first, last)` for the first element that has the value `value`. If there is such an element it returns an iterator that points to the element found, otherwise the value `last` is returned. (To look for part of a sequence: see `search` and `find_end`.)

find_if

```
find_if(first, last, pred)
```

Searches through the interval `[first, last)` for the first element `elem` for which the expression `pred(elem)` is **true**. If there is such an element it returns an iterator that points to the element found, otherwise it returns the value `last`.

Examples

See pages 443 and 444.

find_first_of

```
find_first_of(first1, last1, first2, last2)
find_first_of(first1, last1, first2, last2, bin_pred)
```

The first version searches the interval `[first1, last1)` for the first occurrence of *any* of the elements that exist in the interval `[first2, last2)`. If there is such an element in the interval `[first1, last1)` it gives as a result an iterator that points to this element, otherwise it returns the iterator `last1`.

The second version of `find_first_of` functions like the first, but with the difference that the elements in the two sequences are compared with the operator `bin_pred` instead of the operator `==`.

Example

Suppose that `l1` and `l2` are two lists of type `list<int>`:

```
// l1 contains {1, 8, 5, 42, 38, 14, 49, 63, 8, 5, 1}
// l2 contains {7, 14, 21, 28, 35, 42, 49, 56, 63}
```

The following call gives as a result an iterator that points to the fourth element in `l1`:

```
find_first_of(l1.begin(), l1.end(), l2.begin(), l2.end())
```

Suppose that we have declared a function `divisible` with the appearance

```
bool divisible (int i, int j)
{ return i % j == 0; }
```

The call

```
find_first_of(l1.begin(),l1.end(), l2.begin(),l2.end(),
              divisible)
```

then gives as a result an iterator that points to the fourth element in `l1`.

`find_end`

```
find_end(first1, last1, first2, last2)
find_end(first1, last1, first2, last2, bin_pred)
```

The first version searches backwards in the interval `[first1, last1)` for the first occurrence where the elements in the interval `[first2, last2)` appear as a part sequence. If there is such a part sequence in `[first1, last1)` it returns as a result an iterator that points to the beginning of this sequence, otherwise the iterator `last1` is returned. (To search forward: see the algorithm `search`.)

The second version of `find_end` works like the first but with the difference that the elements in the two sequences are compared with the operator `bin_pred` instead of the operator `==`.

Example

Suppose that `la` and `lb` are two lists of type `list<int>`.

```
// la contains {1, 8, 5, 42, 38, 14, 49, 63, 8, 5, 1}
// lb contains {8, 5}
```

The following call results in an iterator that points to the third element from the end in the list `la`:

```
find_end(la.begin(), la.end(), lb.begin(), lb.end())
```

The following call searches backwards in `la` for two adjacent elements that are bigger than `8` and `5` respectively:

```
find_end(la.begin(), la.end(), lb.begin(), lb.end(),
         greater<int>())
```

The result is an iterator that points to the fourth element from the end list in `la`.

`adjacent_find`

```
adjacent_find(first, last)
adjacent_find(first, last, bin_pred)
```

The first version looks for the first occurrence of two elements that appear next to each other and are equal. If there is such a pair an iterator is returned that points to the first of the two elements, otherwise the iterator `last` is returned.

The second version of `adjacent_find` functions like the first but with the difference that the two adjacent elements are compared with the operator `bin_pred` instead of the operator `==`.

Example

Assume that `l` is a list of type `list<int>`:

```
// l contains {3, 4, 4, 5, 2, 8, 8, 6, 3}
```

Then the following call returns an iterator that points to the second element in the list `l`:

```
adjacent_find(l.begin(), l.end())
```

To find the first pair of elements in the list where the first element is bigger that the second you can call

```
adjacent_find(l.begin(), l.end(), greater<int>())
```

The result returns a pointer to the fourth element in the `list l`.

max

```
max(value1, value2)
max(value1, value2, comp)
```

Returns the larger of the values `value1` and `value2`. In the first version the values are compared with the operator `<` and in the second version with the function object `comp`.

max_element

```
max_element(first, last)
max_element(first, last, comp)
```

Searches the interval `[first, last)` and returns an iterator that points to the first element that is greater than or equal to all the other elements. In the first version the values are compared with the operator `<` and in the second version with the function object `comp`.

min

```
min(value1, value2)
min(value1, value2, comp)
```

Returns the lesser of the values `value1` and `value2`. In the first version the values are compared with the operator `<` and in the second version with the function object `comp`.

min_element

```
min_element(first, last)
min_element(first, last, comp)
```

Runs through the interval `[first, last)` and returns an iterator that points to the first element that is less than or equal to all the other elements. In the first version the values are compared with the operator `<` and in the second version with the function object `comp`.

mismatch

```
mismatch(first1, last1, first2)
mismatch(first1, last1, first2, bin_pred)
```

The first version compares the elements in the interval `[first1, last1)` with the corresponding elements in the interval that begins in `first2`. As a result a pair is given that contains iterators that point to the first pair that is not the same. If all the corresponding elements in the two intervals are the same a pair of iterators are returned that point to the first element outside the intervals.

The second version of `mismatch` functions like the first but with the difference that the elements in the two intervals are compared with the operator `bin_pred` instead of the operator `==`.

Example

Suppose that we have two vectors `v1` and `v2` of type `vector<int>`:

```
// v1 contains {3, 4, 4, 5, 2, 8, 8, 6, 3}
// v2 contains {3, 4, 7, 5, 0, 8, 8, 6, 3}
```

and that we have the program lines

```
typedef vector<int>::iterator itype;
pair<itype, itype> p;
p = mismatch(v1.begin(), v1.end(), v2.begin());
cout << *p.first << ' ' << *p.second << endl;
p = mismatch(v1.begin(), v1.end(), v2.begin(),
             less_equal<int>());
cout << *p.first << ' ' << *p.second << endl;
```

We would receive the printout

```
4 7
2 0
```

search

```
search(first1, last1, first2, last2)
search(first1, last1, first2, last2, bin_pred)
```

The first version searches the first place in the interval `[first1, last1)` where the elements in the interval `[first2, last2)` appear as a part sequence. If such a part sequence appears in `[first1, last1)` it returns an iterator pointing to the beginning of this sequence, otherwise the iterator `last1` is returned. (To search backwards: see the algorithm `find_end`.)

The second version of `search` functions like the first but with the difference that the elements in the two intervals are compared with the operator `bin_pred` instead of the operator `==`.

Example

Suppose that `l1` and `l2` are lists of the type `list<int>` with the following contents:

```
// l1 contains {1, 8, 5, 42, 38, 14, 49, 63, 8, 5, 1}
// l2 contains {8, 5}
```

The call

```
search(l1.begin(), l1.end(), l2.begin(), l2.end())
```

results in an iterator referring to the second element in `l1`. The call

```
search(l1.begin(), l1.end(), l2.begin(), l2.end(),
       greater<int>())
```

results in an iterator that points to the fourth element in `l1` (since 42 > 8 and 38 > 5).

search_n

```
search_n(first, last, n, value)
search_n(first, last, n, value, bin_pred)
```

Searches in the interval `[first, last)` for a continuous succession of `n` elements with the value `value`. If there is such a succession an iterator is returned that points to the first of the equal elements, otherwise the iterator `last` is returned.

The second version of `search_n` functions like the first but with the difference that the comparison between the elements in the interval and `value` is made with the operator `bin_pred` instead of the operator `==`.

Example

Suppose that `l` is a list of type `list<int>` with the following contents:

```
// l contains {0, 0, 3, 4, 0, 0, 0, 8}
```

The following call returns an iterator pointing to the fifth element in `l`:

```
search_n(l.begin(), l.end(), 3, 0)
```

The following call looks for the first sequence with length 2 and where, for all the elements, `elem ≠ 0` is valid:

```
search_n(l.begin(), l.end(), 2, 0, not_equal_to<int>())
```

The result will be an iterator that points at the third element in `l`.

C.2 Compare, run through, count

`count`

```
count(first, last, value)
```

Returns the number of elements in the interval `[first, last)` that has the value `value`.

`count_if`

```
count(first, last, pred)
```

Returns the number of elements in the interval `[first, last)` for which `pred(elem)==true` is valid.

Examples

See pages 442 and 443.

`lexicographical_compare`

```
lexicographical_compare(first1, last1, first2, last2)
lexicographical_compare(first1, last1, first2, last2, comp)
```

Compares the elements in the two intervals `[first1, last1)` and `[first2, last2)` and returns a value of type `bool`. The result is `true` if the elements in the first interval come before the elements in the second interval. The comparison is made according to the same principles as when one arranges words alphabetically. In the first version of `lexicographical_compare` the particular elements are compared with the operator `<`, and in the second version with the function object `comp`. (Alphabetical comparison is accomplished in the following way. If two sequences are of the same length and all the corresponding elements in the sequences are equal, the sequences are regarded as equal. Otherwise the elements are compared in pairs from the beginning, and the first pair in which the elements are different decides which sequence is the least. Thus if one sequence ends before the other, the shorter sequence is regarded as the least.)

Example

Suppose that we have two vectors `v1` and `v2` of type `vector<int>`:

```
// v1 contains {3, 4, 4, 5, 2, 8, 8, 6, 3}
// v2 contains {3, 4, 7, 5, 0, 8, 8, 6, 3}
```

The statements

```
if (lexicographical_compare(v1.begin(), v1.end(),
                            v2.begin(), v2.end()))
  cout << "v1 < v2" << endl;
else
  cout << "v1 >= v2" << endl;
```

then give the print out

```
v1 < v2
```

`equal`

```
equal(first1, last1, first2)
equal(first1, last1, first2, bin_pred)
```

Compares the elements in the interval `[first1, last1)` with the elements in the interval that begins with `first2` and is composed of as many elements as the first interval. It gives a **`bool`** as a result. The first version of `equal` gives the value **`true`** if all the elements in the two intervals are equal. The second version of `equal` gives the value **`true`** if for every element `e1` in the first interval and for the corresponding element `e2` in the second interval `bin_pred(e1, e2) == true` is valid.

Examples

See pages 430 and 433.

`for_each`

```
for_each(first, last, f)
```

Runs through the interval `[first, last)` and calls `f` for every element in the interval. `f` is a function object (or a function) that has a parameter of type `T`. `f` can have an arbitrary result type. The result of `for_each` is a function object that performs the operation `f`.

Example

See page 435.

C.3 Copy and move elements

copy

```
copy(first1, last1, first2)
```

Copies the elements in the interval `[first1, last1)` to the interval whose start is pointed out by the iterator `first2`. The number of copied elements is the same as the number of elements in the interval `[first1, last1)`. It copies from front to back: that is, the first element in the interval `[first1, last1)` is copied first and the final one last.

Examples

See pages 429 and 430.

copy_backward

```
copy_backward(first1, last1, last2)
```

Copies the elements in the interval `[first1, last1)` to the interval whose end is pointed out by the iterator `last2`. The iterator `last2` thus points to a hypothetical element that lies precisely outside the interval to which you are going to copy. The number of copied elements is equal to the number of elements in the interval `[first1, last1)`. The copying occurs backwards – that is, the final element in the interval `[first1, last1)` is copied first and the first last.

This algorithm is suitable to use when one wants to move elements forwards inside a container.

Example

Suppose that `l` is a list of type `list<int>`:

```
// l contains {1, 8, 5, 42, 38, 14, 49, 63, 8, 5, 1}
```

To move all elements a step to the right and put in the value 0 first we can write the lines

```
list<int>::iterator last1=l.end();
last1--;
copy_backward(l.begin(), last1, l.end());
*l.begin() = 0;
// l contains {0, 1, 8, 5, 42, 38, 14, 49, 63, 8, 5}
```

If we had used the algorithm `copy` instead of `copy_backward`, all the elements from the second would have contained the value `1`, since copying would then have gone from front to back.

swap

```
swap(value1, value2)
```

Changes `value1` to `value2` and vice versa. (`value1` and `value2` are reference parameters.)

Example

Suppose that `l` is a list of type `list<int>`:

```
// l contains {1, 8, 5, 42}
list<int>::iterator i1=l.begin(), i2=l.begin();
i1++; i2++; i2++;
swap(*i1,*i2);
// l contains {1, 5, 8, 42}
```

iter_swap

```
swap(it1, it2)
```

Changes the values of the elements that the iterators `it1` and `it2` point to.

Example

Suppose that `l` is a list of type `list<int>`:

```
// l contains {1, 8, 5, 42}
list<int>::iterator i1=l.begin(), i2=l.begin();
i1++; i2++; i2++;
iter_swap(i1,i2);
// l contains {1, 5, 8, 42}
```

swap_ranges

```
swap_ranges(first1, last1, first2)
```

Changes all elements in the interval `[first1, last1)` to corresponding elements in the interval that begins with `first2` and vice versa.

Example

Suppose that `v` is a vector of type `vector<int>`:

```
// v contains {3, 4, 4, 5, 2, 8, 8, 6, 3}
swap_ranges(v.begin(), v.begin()+4, v.begin()+5);
// v contains {8, 8, 6, 3, 2, 3, 4, 4, 5}
```

reverse

```
reverse(first, last)
```

Places the elements in the interval `[first, last)` in reverse order.

Example

See page 440.

reverse_copy

```
reverse_copy(first, last, result)
```

Creates a sequence that is composed of the elements in the interval `[first, last)` in reverse order and places the sequence in the interval pointed out by the iterator `result`. As return value an iterator is given that points to the resulting interval, one step after the last element copied.

Example

Suppose that `l1` and `l2` are lists of type `list<int>`:

```
// l1 contains {1, 8, 5, 42, 38, 14, 49, 63, 9, 4, 0}
list<int> l2(l1.size());
reverse_copy(l1.begin(), l1.end(), l2.begin());
// l2 contains {0, 4, 9, 63, 49, 14, 38, 42, 5, 8, 1}
```

rotate

```
rotate(first, middle, last)
```

The iterator `middle` is supposed to point to an element inside the interval `[first, last)`. Rotates the element in the interval `[first, last)` as many steps to the left as necessary for the element that `middle` points to to come first.

Example

Suppose that `v` is a vector of type `vector<int>`:

```
// v contains {3, 4, 4, 5, 2, 8, 8, 6, 3}
rotate(v.begin(), v.begin()+4, v.end());
// v contains {2, 8, 8, 6, 3, 3, 4, 4, 5}
```

rotate_copy

```
rotate_copy(first, middle, last, result)
```

The iterator `middle` is supposed to point to an element inside the interval `[first, last)`. It creates a sequence that contains the elements in the interval `[first, last)` rotated so many steps to the left that the element `middle` points to comes first. The sequence is placed in the interval that is indicated by the iterator `result`. As return value an iterator is given that points to the resulting interval, a step after the last element copied.

Example

Suppose that `v1` and `v2` are vectors of type `vector<int>`:

```
// v1 contains {3, 4, 4, 5, 2, 8, 8, 6, 3}
rotate_copy(v1.begin(), v1.begin()+4, v1.end(), v2.begin());
// v2 contains {2, 8, 8, 6, 3, 3, 4, 4, 5}
```

partition

```
partition(first, last, pred)
```

Rearranges the elements in the interval `[first, last)` in such a way that all the elements that fulfil the condition `pred(elem)` are placed first and all those that do not fulfil the condition are placed last. As result an iterator is given that points to the first element that does not fulfil the condition. This does not guarantee that the relative order between the elements in the two groups is retained.

Example

Suppose that `l` is a list of type `list<int>`:

```
// l contains {1, 8, 5, 42, 38, 14, 49, 63, 9, 4, 0}
list<int>::iterator it;
it = partition(l.begin(), l.end(), bind2nd(less<int>(),10));
// l contains {1, 8, 5, 0, 4, 9, 49, 63, 14, 38, 42}
cout << "First element >= 10 is " << *it;
```

The printout is

```
First element >= 10 is 49
```

stable_partition

```
stable_partition(first, last, pred)
```

Functions in the same way as the algorithm `partition`, but guarantees that the relative order between the elements in the two groups is retained:

```
// l contains {1, 8, 5, 42, 38, 14, 49, 63, 9, 4, 0}
list<int>::iterator it;
it = stable_partition(l.begin(), l.end(),
                      bind2nd(less<int>(),10));
// l contains {1, 8, 5, 9, 4, 0, 42, 38, 14, 49, 63}
cout << "First element >= 10 is " << *it;
```

The printout is

```
First element >= 10 is 42
```

random_shuffle

```
random_shuffle(first, last)
random_shuffle(first, last, rand)
```

Rearranges the elements in the interval `[first, last)` in a random order. Note that it is a requirement that the iterators `first` and `last` are of the category *random-access iterator*. The algorithm therefore functions, for instance, on vectors and arrays but not on lists. In the second version you can give your own random number function to be used instead of the built-in one.

Example

Suppose that `v` is a vector of type `vector<int>`. The call `srand` results in different outcomes every time the program is run:

```
// v contains {3, 4, 4, 5, 2, 8, 8, 6, 3}
srand(time(0));
random_shuffle(v.begin(), v.end());
// v contains {3, 5, 8, 3, 6, 4, 2, 8, 4}
```

C.4 Change and delete elements

`replace`

```
replace(first, last, old_value, new_value)
```

Replaces, in the interval `[first, last)`, all the elements that contain the value `old_value` with the value `new_value`.

Example

See page 431.

`replace_if`

```
replace_if(first, last, pred, new_value)
```

In the interval `[first, last)` all the elements that fulfil the condition `pred(elem)==true` are replaced by the value `new_value`.

Example

See page 433.

`replace_copy`

```
replace_copy(first, last, result, old_value, new_value)
```

Creates a new sequence that is a copy of the elements in the interval `[first, last)` but with all the values `old_value` to be replaced by the value `new_value`. The sequence is placed in the interval pointed out by the iterator `result`. As return value an iterator is returned that points to the resulting interval, one step after the last element copied.

Example

See page 431.

`replace_copy_if`

```
replace_copy_if(first, last, result, pred, new_value)
```

Creates a new sequence that is a copy of the elements in the interval `[first, last)` but with all the values that fulfil the condition `pred(elem)==true` replaced by the value new_value. The sequence is placed in the interval pointed to by the iterator result. As return value it returns an iterator that points to the resulting interval, one step after the last element copied.

Example

Suppose that l1 and l2 are lists of type list<**int**>. The following lines copy to l2 a copy of l1, where all the elements less than 10 are replaced by the value 0:

```
// l1 contains {1, 8, 5, 42, 38, 14, 49, 63, 9, 4, 0,}
// l2 contains {1, 2, 3, 4, 5, 6, 7, 8, 9, 10, 11, 12}
list<int>::iterator it;
it = replace_copy_if(l1.begin(), l1.end(), l2.begin(),
                     bind2nd(less<int>(),10), 0);
// l2 contains {0, 0, 0, 42, 38, 14, 49, 63, 0, 0, 0, 11, 12}
cout << *it << endl;  // prints out: 11
```

remove

```
remove(first, last, value)
```

Deletes all the elements in the interval [first, last) that contain the value value. Returns an iterator that points one step after the last remaining value.

Example

Suppose that v is a vector of type vector<**int**>. The following lines delete all the elements from v that are equal to 3:

```
// v contains {3, 4, 4, 5, 2, 8, 8, 6, 3}
vector<int>::iterator i1, i2;
i2 = remove(v.begin(), v.end(), 3);
for (i1=v.begin(); i1 != i2; i1++)
  cout << *i1 << ' ';
```

The printout is

```
4 4 5 2 8 8 6
```

remove_if

```
remove_if(first, last, pred)
```

Deletes all the elements in the interval [first, last) that fulfil the condition pred(elem)==**true**. Returns an iterator that points one step after the last remaining value.

Example

Suppose that `v` is a vector of type `vector<int>`. The following lines delete all the elements from `v` that are greater than `5`:

```
// v contains {3, 4, 4, 5, 2, 8, 8, 6, 3}
vector<int>::iterator i1, i2;
i2 = remove_if(v.begin(), v.end(), bind2nd(greater<int>(),5));
for (i1=v.begin(); i1 != i2; i1++)
  cout << *i1 << ' ';
```

The printout is

```
3 4 4 5 2 3
```

remove_copy

```
remove_copy(first, last, result, value)
```

Creates a new sequence that is a copy of the elements in the interval `[first, last)` but with all the elements with the value `value` deleted. The sequence is placed in the interval pointed out by the iterator `result`. As return value it gives an iterator that points to the resulting interval, one step after the last element copied.

Example

Suppose that `v1` and `v2` are vectors of type `vector<int>`. The following lines copy to `v2` a copy of `v1`, where all the elements equal to `8` have been deleted:

```
// v1 contains {3, 4, 4, 5, 2, 8, 8, 6, 3}
// v2 contains {1, 2, 3, 4, 5, 6, 7, 8, 9, 10}
vector<int>::iterator it;
it = remove_copy(v1.begin(), v1.end(), v2.begin(), 8);
// v2 contains {3, 4, 4, 5, 2, 6, 3, 8, 9, 10}
cout << *it;  // prints out: 8
```

remove_copy_if

```
remove_copy_if(first, last, result, pred)
```

Creates a new sequence that is a copy of the elements in the `interval [first, last)` but with all the elements that fulfil the condition `pred(elem)==true` deleted. The sequence is placed in the interval pointed out by the iterator `result`. As return value an iterator is returned that points to the resulting interval, one step after the last element copied.

Example

Suppose that l1 and l2 are lists of the type list<**int**>. The following lines copy to l2 a copy of l1, where all the elements less than 10 have been deleted:

```
// l1 contains {1, 8, 5, 42, 38, 14, 49, 63, 9, 4, 0,}
// l2 contains {1, 2, 3, 4, 5, 6, 7, 8, 9, 10, 11, 12}
list<int>::iterator it;
it = remove_copy_if(l1.begin(), l1.end(), l2.begin(),
                    bind2nd(less<int>(),10));
// l2 contains {42 38 14 49 63 6 7 8 9 10 11 12 13}
cout << *it << endl;  // prints out: 6
```

unique

```
unique(first, last)
unique(first, last, bin_pred)
```

Deletes all occurrences, except the first, from every sequence of equal elements in the interval [first, last). Returns an iterator that points one step after the last remaining value. In the first version the element is compared with the operator == and in the second version with the function object bin_pred.

Example

Suppose that v is a vector of type vector<**int**>:

```
// v contains {3, 4, 4, 5, 2, 8, 8, 6, 3}
vector<int>::iterator i1, i2;
  i2 = unique(v.begin(), v.end());
for (i1=v.begin(); i1 != i2; i1++)
  cout << *i1 << ' ';
```

The printout is

```
3 4 5 2 8 6 3
```

unique_copy

```
unique_copy(first, last, result)
unique_copy(first, last, result, bin_pred)
```

Like the algorithm unique, but the result is placed in the interval pointed to by the iterator result. The return value is an iterator pointing to the resulting interval, one step after the last element copied.

Example

Suppose that `v1` and `v2` are vectors of type `vector<int>`:

```
// v1 contains {3, 4, 4, 5, 2, 0, 0, 6, 3}
// v2 contains {1, 2, 3, 4, 5, 6, 7, 8, 9, 10}
vector<int>::iterator it;
it = unique_copy(v1.begin(), v1.end(), v2.begin());
// v2 contains {3, 4, 5, 2, 0, 6, 3, 8, 9, 10}
cout << *it;  // prints out: 8
```

C.5 Generate new data

`fill`

```
fill(first, last, value)
```

Assigns the value `value` to all the elements in the interval `[first, last)`.

Examples

See page 438.

`fill_n`

```
fill_n(first, n, value)
```

Assigns the value `value` to the `n` first elements in the interval pointed out by `first`.

Example

Suppose that `l` is a list of type `list<int>`:

```
// l contains {1, 8, 5, 42, 38, 14, 49, 63, 9, 4, 0}
fill_n(l.begin(), 5, 9);
// l contains {9, 9, 9, 9, 9, 14, 49, 63, 9, 4, 0}
```

`generate`

```
generate(first, last, gen)
```

`gen` is supposed to be a function object that lacks parameters and which returns a value of the same type as the elements in the interval `[first, last)`. The algorithm `generate` searches through the interval `[first, last)`. For every element `gen` is called and the result of the call is assigned to the actual element.

Example

Suppose that `l` is a list of type `list<int>` that contains 11 elements, and that the class `Series` is defined in the following way:

```
class Series
{
public:
  // constructor
  Series (int start=0, int d=1) : sum(start), diff(d){}
  // function call operator
  int operator()()
  {
    int result = sum;
    sum += diff;
    return result;
  }
private:
  int sum, diff;
};
```

The following program lines places the odd numbers `1`, `3`, `5`, etc in the list `l`:

```
Series gen(1, 2);  // declaration of function object
generate(l.begin(), l.end(), gen);
// l contains {1, 3, 5, 7, 9, 11, 13, 15, 17, 19, 21}
```

generate_n

```
generate_n(first, n, gen)
```

`gen` is a function object that lacks parameters and which returns a value of the same type as the elements in the interval pointed out by `first`. The algorithm `generate_n` searches the first `n` elements in the interval pointed to by `first`. For every element, `gen` is called and the result of the call is assigned to the actual element.

Example

Suppose that `l` is a list of type `list<int>` and that the class `Series` is defined in the same way as in this example for the algorithm `generate`:

```
Series gen(0, -2);  // declaration of function object
// l contains {1, 8, 5, 42, 38, 14, 49, 63, 9, 4, 0}
generate_n(l.begin(), 5, gen);
// l contains {0, -2, -4, -6, -8, 14, 49, 63, 9, 4, 0}
```

transform

```
transform(first, last, result, op)
transform(first1, last1, first2, result, bin_op)
```

The first version searches all the elements in the interval `[first, last)`. For every element the call `op(elem)` is made and the result is assigned to the corresponding elements in the interval pointed out by `result`.

The second version searches in parallel all the elements in the interval `[first1, last2)` and the interval that is indicated by `first2`. For every pair of elements in the two intervals the call `bin_op(elem1, elem2)` is made and the result is assigned the corresponding element in the interval pointed to by `result`.

Examples

See pages 438 and 440 respectively.

C.6 Sort

The algorithms in the following paragraphs sort a container completely or partly. Common to all the algorithms is that there are two versions, one in which the elements are compared with the operator `<` and one for which one can state as parameter a function object `comp` that will make the comparisons. `comp` should return the value **`true`** if the first parameter is regarded as less than the second and the value **`false`** otherwise. For instance, if the sorting should be done in reverse order so that the greatest element is placed first, one can give a function object of the previously defined class `greater<int>` as parameter.

All the algorithms in this section (with the exception of the algorithm `partial_sort_copy`) demand that the iterators used for pointing out the container to be sorted be of the category *random-access iterator*. This means that the algorithms can be used to sort vectors and arrays, but not to sort lists and the like. (For the class `list` there is, however, a member function that does the sorting: see page 445.)

sort

```
sort(first, last)
sort(first, last, comp)
```

Sorts the elements in the interval `[first, last)`. `first` and `last` must be iterators of the category *random-access iterator*. It is not guaranteed that elements that are equal end up in their original, mutual order after sorting.

Examples

See pages 431 and 434.

`stable_sort`

```
stable_sort(first, last)
stable_sort(first, last, comp)
```

Sorts the elements in the interval `[first, last)`. `first` and `last` will be iterators of the category *random-access iterator*. It is guaranteed that the elements that are equal end up in their original, mutual order after sorting.

Example

Suppose that `v` is a vector of type `vector<int>`:

```
// v contains {1, 8, 5, 42, 38, 14, 49, 63, 9, 4, 0, 5, 3}
stable_sort(v.begin(), v.end());
// v contains {0, 1, 3, 4, 5, 5, 8, 9, 14, 38, 42, 49, 63}
stable_sort(v.begin(), v.end(), greater<int>());
// v contains {63, 49, 42, 38, 14, 9, 8, 5, 5, 4, 3, 1, 0}
```

`partial_sort`

```
partial_sort(first, middle, last)
partial_sort(first, middle, last, comp)
```

`first`, `middle` and `last` should be iterators of the category *random-access iterator*. The smallest elements from the interval `[first, last)` are placed in sorted order in the interval `[first, middle)`. The rest of the elements are placed in the interval `[middle, last)` in an unspecified order.

Example

Suppose that `v` is a vector of type `vector<int>`:

```
// v contains {1, 8, 5, 42, 38, 14, 49, 63, 9, 4, 0, 5, 3}
partial_sort(v.begin(), v.begin()+6, v.end());
// v contains {0, 1, 3, 4, 5, 5, 49, 63, 42, 38, 14, 9, 8}
partial_sort(v.begin(), v.begin()+6, v.end(), greater<int>());
// v contains {63, 49, 42, 38, 14, 9, 0, 1, 3, 4, 5, 5, 8}
```

`partial_sort_copy`

```
partial_sort_copy(first, last, result_first, result_last)
partial_sort_copy(first, last, result_first, result_last, comp)
```

Sorts the `N` elements from the interval `[first, last)` and places the result in the interval `[result_first, result_last)`. `N` is the minimum of `N1` and `N2` where `N1` and `N2` are the number elements in the two intervals. `result_first` and `result_last` should be iterators of the category *random-access iterator*, but it is sufficient for `first` and `last` to be iterators of the category *input iterator*. `partial_sort` returns an iterator that points to the end of the interval copied to, that is one step after the last element that has been copied.

Example

Suppose that `l` is a list of type `list<int>` and that `v` is a vector of type `vector<int>`:

```
// l contains {1, 8, 5, 42, 38, 14, 49, 63, 9, 4, 0, 5, 3}
partial_sort_copy(l.begin(), l.end(), v.begin(), v.end());
// v contains {0, 1, 3, 4, 5, 5, 8, 9, 14, 38, 42, 49, 63}
partial_sort_copy(l.begin(), l.end(), v.begin(), v.end(),
                  greater<int>());
// v contains {63, 49, 42, 38, 14, 9, 8, 5, 5, 4, 3, 1, 0}
```

`nth_element`

```
nth_element(first, nth, last)
nth_element(first, nth, last, comp)
```

`first`, `nth` and `last` are iterators of the category *random-access iterator*. `nth` should point to an element in the interval `[first, last)`. The algorithm `nth_element` moves the elements in the interval `[first, last)` so that the element that `nth` points to will contain the value it would have had if the container had been completely sorted. Moreover, the algorithm `nth_element` divides the elements into two groups. The group on the left consists of the interval `[first, nth)` and the one on the right of the interval `[nth, last)`. After the rearranging it is true that all the elements in the left-hand group are less than or equal to the elements in the right-hand group. (For the alternative version of `nth_element` the condition `comp(e2,e1)==false` holds for every element `e1` in the first group and every element `e2` in the second group.)

Example

Suppose that `v` is a vector of type `vector<int>`:

```
// v contains {1, 8, 5, 42, 38, 14, 49, 63, 9, 4, 0, 5, 3}
nth_element(v.begin(), v.begin()+7, v.end());
// v contains {1, 3, 0, 4, 5, 5, 8, 9, 63, 49, 14, 38, 42}
nth_element(v.begin(), v.begin()+7, v.end(), greater<int>());
// v contains {42, 38, 14, 49, 63, 9, 8, 5, 5, 4, 0, 3, 1}
```

C.7 Operations on sorted containers

The algorithms in the following paragraphs demand that all the containers they handle be sorted. Common to all the algorithms is that there are two versions, one in which the elements are compared with the operator `<` and one for which one can state as parameter a function object `comp` that will make the comparisons. `comp` should return the value **`true`** if the first parameter is regarded as less than the second and the value **`false`** otherwise. For instance, if the sorting has occurred in reverse order so that the greatest element is first, one can give a function object of the previously defined class `greater<int>` as parameter.

binary_search

```
binary_search(first, last, value)
binary_search(first, last, value, comp)
```

Examines whether in the interval `[first, last)` there is an element `e` that is equal to `value`. In this case it returns the value **`true`**, otherwise the value **`false`**. The alternative form examines whether there is an element `e` in the interval that fulfils the following conditions: `comp(e,value)==false && comp(value,e)==false`.

Example

Suppose that `v` is a vector of type `vector<int>`:

```
// v contains {0, 1, 3, 4, 5, 5, 5, 8, 9, 14, 38, 42, 49, 63}
int k;
cin>>k;
if (binary_search(v.begin(), v.end(), k))
   cout << k << " found" << endl;
else
   cout << k << " not found" << endl;
char *w[] = {"Brontosaurus", "Brontë", "attachment", "attaché"};
string s;
cin >> s;
if (binary_search(w, w+sizeof(w)/sizeof(w[0]), s, alpha("en")))
   cout << s << " found" << endl;
else
   cout << s << " not found" << endl;
```

lower_bound

```
lower_bound(first, last, value)
lower_bound(first, last, value, comp)
```

Finds the first position in the interval `[first, last)` where the value `value` can be inserted without disturbing the sorting. Returns an iterator `it` that points out the place found. For all elements `e` in the interval `[first, it)` then `e < value` is valid. (For the alternative version `comp(e,value) == true` is valid.)

Example

Suppose that `v` is a vector of `type vector<int>`:

```
// v contains {0, 1, 3, 4, 5, 5, 5, 8, 9, 14, 38, 42, 49, 63}
vector<int>::iterator it;
it = lower_bound(v.begin(), v.end(), 5);
// it points to v[4], i.e. to the first elementet with value 5
```

upper_bound

```
upper_bound(first, last, value)
upper_bound(first, last, value, comp)
```

Finds the last position in the interval `[first, last)` where the value `value` can be inserted without disturbing the sorting. Returns an iterator `it` that points out the place found. For all elements `e` in the interval `[first, it)` then `e <= value` is valid. (For the alternative version `comp(value, e) == false` is valid.)

Example

Suppose that `v` is a vector of type `vector<int>`:

```
// v contains {0, 1, 3, 4, 5, 5, 5, 8, 9, 14, 38, 42, 49, 63}
vector<int>::iterator it;
it = upper_bound(v.begin(), v.end(), 5);
// it points to v[7], i.e. after the last elementet with value 5
```

equal_range

```
equal_range(first, last, value)
equal_range(first, last, value, comp)
```

Finds the greatest interval inside which the value `value` can be inserted without disturbing the sorting. Returns a pair of iterators `<it1, it2>` that point to the interval found. `it1` is equal to the result from the call by the algorithm `lower_bound` and `it2` is equal to the result from the call by `upper_bound`.

Example

Suppose that `v` is a vector of type `vector<int>`:

```
// v contains {0, 1, 3, 4, 5, 5, 5, 8, 9, 14, 38, 42, 49, 63}
pair<vector<int>::iterator, vector<int>::iterator> p;
p = equal_range(v.begin(), v.end(), 5);
// p.first points to v[4] and p.second to v[7]
```

merge

```
merge(first1, last1, first2, last2, result)
merge(first1, last1, first2, last2, result, comp)
```

Sorts together the two sorted intervals `[first1, last1)` and `[first2, last2)` to a single sorted sequence, which is placed in the interval pointed out by `result`. The interval that `result` points to must not be overlapped by the two original intervals. Returns an iterator that points one step after the last element that is put into the result interval.

Example

Suppose that `v1` and `v2` are vectors of type `vector<int>`:

```
// v1 contains {0, 1, 3, 4, 5, 5, 5, 8, 9, 14, 38, 42, 49, 63}
// v2 contains {4, 11, 14, 20, 31, 49, 75}
vector<int> v3(v1.size()+v2.size());
merge(v1.begin(), v1.end(), v2.begin(), v2.end(), v3.begin());
// v1 contains {0, 1, 3, 4, 4, 5, 5, 5, 8, 9, 11, 14, 14, 20,
//              31, 38, 42, 49, 49, 63, 75}
```

inplace_merge

```
inplace_merge(first, middle, last)
inplace_merge(first, middle, last, comp)
```

Assumes that the two intervals `[first, middle)` and `[middle, last)` contain sorted sequences. `inplace_merge` merges these sequences and places the result in the interval `[first, last)`, which is, consequently, overwritten.

Example

Suppose that `v` is a vector of type `vector<int>`:

```
// v contains {4, 11, 14, 20, 31, 49, 75, 0, 11, 19, 40, 80}
inplace_merge(v.begin(), v.begin()+7, v.end());
// v contains {0, 4, 11, 11, 14, 19, 20, 31, 40, 49, 75, 80}
```

next_permutation

```
next_permutation(first, last)
next_permutation(first, last, comp)
```

If you start with a sorted container, you can generate all the permutations (that is, all the different ways to place the elements) in the container through repeated calls of `next_permutation`. At every call `permutation` makes a rearrangement of the elements in the interval `[first, last)`. If after such a call the container is sorted in ascending order (that is, with the least element first) the value **`false`** is returned, otherwise the value **`true`** is returned.

Example

The following program lines print out all the permutations of the words 'you', 'can', 'eat' and 'now':

```
char *word[] = {"you", "can", "eat", "now"};
sort(word, word+4, alpha("en"));   // sort the sequence first
int k=1;
do
{
  for (int i=0; i<4; i++)
    cout << ' ' << word[i];
  cout << ". ";
  if (!(k++ % 4))   // write four sentences on each line
    cout << endl;
} while(next_permutation(word, word+4, alpha("en")));
```

The printout will be

```
can eat now you. can eat you now. can now eat you. can now you eat.
can you eat now. can you now eat. eat can now you. eat can you now.
eat now can you. eat now you can. eat you can now. eat you now can.
now can eat you. now can you eat. now eat can you. now eat you can.
now you can eat. now you eat can. you can eat now. you can now eat.
you eat can now. you eat now can. you now can eat. you now eat can.
```

prev_permutation

```
prev_permutation(first, last)
prev_permutation(first, last, comp)
```

Works in a similar way as `next_permutation` but generates the different permutations in reverse order. At every call `prev_permutation` makes a rearrangement of the elements in the interval `[first, last)`. If after such a call the container is sorted in descending order (that is, with the greatest element first) the value **`false`** is returned, otherwise the value **`true`** is returned.

C.8 Operations on sets

All the algorithms under this heading require that the containers be sorted. The algorithms work well together with containers of the kind `set`.

`includes`

```
includes(first1, last1, first2, last2)
includes(first1, last1, first2, last2, comp)
```

Examines whether all the elements in the interval `[first1, last1)` also exist in the interval `[first2, last2)`: that is, whether the first container is a subset of the second. Returns the value of type **`bool`** as a result. In the first version the elements are compared with the operator `==` and in the second with the function object `comp`.

Examples

See page 460.

`set_union`

```
set_union(first1, last1, first2, last2, result)
set_union(first1, last1, first2, last2, result, comp)
```

Forms the union set of the elements in the interval `[first1, last1)` and the elements in the interval `[first2, last2)`: that is, forms a new set that contains all the elements that are included in either the first interval or the second (or both). `result` points to where the result should be located. In the first version the elements are compared with the operator `==` and in the second with the function object `comp`.

Example

See page 460.

`set_intersection`

```
set_intersection(first1, last1, first2, last2, result)
set_intersection(first1, last1, first2, last2, result, comp)
```

Forms the intersection set of the elements in the interval `[first1, last1)` and the elements in the interval `[first2, last2)`: that is, forms a new set that contains all the elements that are included in both the first interval and the second. `result` points to where the result will be located. In the first version the elements are compared with the operator `==` and in the second with the function object `comp`.

Examples

See page 460.

`set_difference`

```
set_difference(first1, last1, first2, last2, result)
set_difference(first1, last1, first2, last2, result, comp)
```

Forms a set that consists of the elements that are in the interval `[first1, last1)` but not in the interval `[first2, last2)`. `result` points to where the results will be placed. In the first version the elements are compared with the operator `==` and in the second with the function object `comp`.

Examples

See page 460.

`set_symmetric_difference`

```
set_symmetric_difference(first1, last1, first2, last2, result)
set_symmetric_difference(first1, last1, first2, last2, result, comp)
```

Forms a set that consists of the elements that are in the interval `[first1, last1)` but not in the interval `[first2, last2)` together with the elements that are in the interval `[first2, last2)` but not in the interval `[first1, last1)`. `result` points to where the results will be located. In the first version the elements are compared with the operator `==` and in the second with the function object `comp`.

Examples

See page 460.

C.9 Numerical algorithms

The algorithms in this subsection operate on all containers where the individual elements are of a numeric type. These algorithms are not defined in the file `algorithm`, but instead in another standard file named `numeric`. The following line must therefore be included in the program if one wants to use any of the algorithms that are discussed here:

```
#include <numeric>
```

accumulate

```
accumulate(first, last, init)
accumulate(first, last, init, bin_op)
```

Calculates and returns the value of `sum` of all the elements in the interval `[first, last)`. The calculation is made in the following way. `sum` is initialized to the value `init`, which is a parameter of the same type as the elements in the container. Next the statement `sum = sum + e` is executed for all elements `e` in the interval `[first, last)`. In the alternative version `sum = bin_op(sum,e)` is calculated instead.

Example

Suppose that `l` is a list of type `list<int>`:

```
// l contains {1, 2, 3, 4}
int a = accumulate(l.begin(), l.end(), 0);
int b = accumulate(l.begin(), l.end(), 1, multiplies<int>());
// a has the value 10 (=0+1+2+3+4)
// b has the value 24 (=1*2*3*4)
```

inner_product

```
inner_product(first1, last1, first2, init)
inner_product(first1, last1, first2, init, bin_op1, bin_op2)
```

Executes a parallel search of the interval `[first1, last1)` and the interval pointed to by `first2`. The first version calculates and returns a value `sum`, which is calculated as follows. First `sum` is initialized to the value `init`, which is a parameter of the same type as the elements in the container. Next the statement `sum = sum + e1*e2` is executed for all pairs of elements `e1` and `e2` in the two intervals.

In the alternative version the operator the function object `bin_op1` is used instead of `+` and `bin_op2` instead of `*`, which means that the calculations are made according to the following statement: `sum = bin_op1(sum, bin_op2(e1,e2))`.

Example

Suppose that `l1` and `l2` are lists of type `list<int>`:

```
// l1 contains {1, 2, 3, 4}
// l2 contains {0, 4, 2, 2}
int a = inner_product(l1.begin(), l1.end(), l2.begin(), 0);
int b = inner_product(l1.begin(), l1.end(), l2.begin(), 1,
                      multiplies<int>(), minus<int>());
// a has the value 22 (= 0+(1*0)+(2*4)+(3*2)+(4*2))
// b has the value -4 (= 1*(1-0)*(2-4)*(3-2)*(4-2))
```

`partial_sum`

```
partial_sum(first, last, result)
partial_sum(first, last, result, bin_op)
```

The first version searches the interval `[first, last)` and calculates, for every element, a new value that is the sum of the previous elements in the interval. The resulting sequence is placed in the interval pointed to by `result`.

In the alternative version the function object `bin_op` is used instead of `+` when the new values are calculated. An iterator is returned that points one step after the last value that was copied to the result interval.

Example

Suppose that `l1` and `l2` are lists of type `list<int>`:

```
// l1 contains {1, 2, 3, 4}
partial_sum(l1.begin(), l1.end(), l2.begin());
// l2 contains {1, 3, 6, 10}
partial_sum(l1.begin(), l1.end(), l2.begin(),
            multiplies<int>());
// l2 contains {1, 2, 6, 24}
```

`adjacent_difference`

```
adjacent_difference(first, last, result)
adjacent_difference(first, last, result, bin_op)
```

The first version searches the interval `[first, last)` and calculates a new value for every element that is the difference between the actual element and the preceding element. (For the first element the new value will be equal to the old one.) The resulting sequence of values is placed in the interval pointed to by `result`.

In the alternative version the function object `bin_op` is used instead of – when the new values are calculated. The return value is an iterator that points one step after the last value that was copied to the result interval.

Example

Suppose that `l1` and `l2` are lists of the type `list<int>`:

```
// l1 contains {3, 4, 2, 5}
adjacent_difference(l1.begin(), l1.end(), l2.begin());
// l2 contains {3, 1, -2, 3}
adjacent_difference(l1.begin(), l1.end(), l2.begin(),
                    multiplies<int>());
// l2 contains {3, 12, 8, 10}
```

C.10 Heap algorithms

A *heap* is a data structure that can logically be described as a binary tree in which every node contains a value that is greater than the value that is in the child nodes. (This is called a *maxheap*. One can also have a *minheap*, in which the value in a node is less than the values in the child nodes.) An example is shown in Figure C.1.

What is special about a heap is that it is normally stored in a sequential data structure, for example in a vector or an array. The nodes are then placed in the sequence row after row from left to right. The tree in the figure can for example be placed in an array `a` that is defined in the following way:

```
int a[] = {50, 45, 30, 27, 35, 20, 29, 18, 13};
```

In the figure the index in the array has been marked next to the nodes. For a sequential data structure to be a maxheap, the following conditions must be valid for every element `a[i]`:

```
a[i] > a[2i+1]
a[i] > a[2i+2]
```

Note that the sequence does not need to be completely sorted (even if a sorted sequence also fulfils the above conditions). A heap is an effective data structure that can be used, for instance, to construct priority queues. A heap can also be useful when you sort data. For instance, the standard class `priority_queue` that was discussed in section 12.6 on page 463 is implemented as a heap. The member functions in the class `priority_queue` call the algorithms shown in this section.

All the heap algorithms require that the iterators that describe the data sequences must be of the category *random-access iterator*. It is, for example, possible to use a vector,

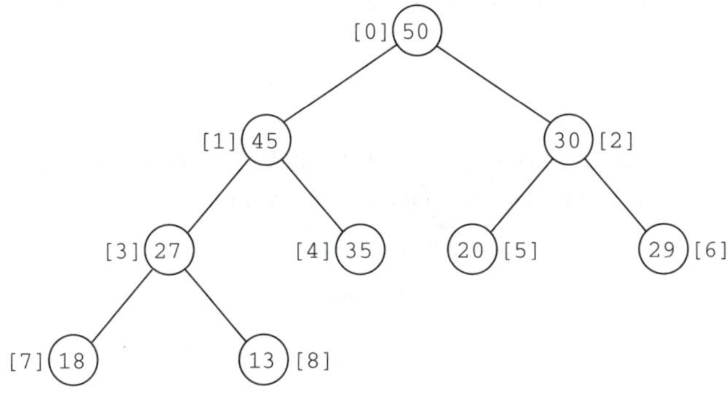

Figure C.1

which also is done in the class `priority_queue`. All the heap algorithms also exist in two versions, one in which the elements are compared with the operator < and one for which you can state a function object `comp` as a parameter. `comp` should return the value **`true`** if the first parameter is regarded as less than the second, or otherwise the value **`false`**. This means, for instance, that if you want to have a minheap instead of a maxheap you can give a function object of the previously defined class `greater<int>` as parameter.

make_heap

```
make_heap(first, last)
make_heap(first, last, comp)
```

Moves the elements in the interval so that they form a heap.

Example

Suppose that `v` is a vector of type `vector<int>`:

```
// v contains {30, 45, 35, 13, 50, 18, 27, 20, 29}
make_heap(v.begin(), v.end());
// v contains {50, 45, 35, 29, 30, 18, 27, 20, 13}
make_heap(v.begin(), v.end(), greater<int>());
// v contains {13, 20, 18, 29, 30, 35, 27, 45, 50}
```

push_heap

```
push_heap(first, last)
push_heap(first, last, comp)
```

This algorithm takes the element that is last in the interval (that is, in the position `last-1`) and places it in the interval `[first, last)` so that the elements form a heap. This presupposes that the elements in the interval `[first, last-1)` already form a heap.

Example

Suppose that `v` is a vector of type `vector<int>` and that it forms a heap. The following program lines read in a number and place it in the vector `v` so that it still forms a heap:

```
// v contains {50, 45, 30, 27, 35, 20, 29, 18, 13}
int k;
cin >> k;  // assume that the number 49 was read
v.push_back(k);
push_heap(v.begin(), v.end());
// v contains {50, 49, 30, 27, 45, 20, 29, 18, 13, 35}
```

pop_heap

```
pop_heap(first, last)
pop_heap(first, last, comp)
```

This algorithm moves the greatest element that is, the element that is in the position `first` so that it ends up last – that is, in the position `last-1`. Then the rest of the elements are moved so that they still form a heap.

Example

Suppose that `v` is a vector of type `vector<int>` and that it contains a heap. The following program lines print out the greatest value and then delete it:

```
// v contains {50, 49, 30, 27, 45, 20, 29, 18, 13, 35}
cout << v.front();  // prints out 50
pop_heap(v.begin(), v.end());
v.pop_back();
// v contains {49, 45, 30, 27, 35, 20, 29, 18, 13}
```

sort_heap

```
sort_heap(first, last)
sort_heap(first, last, comp)
```

The algorithm presupposes that the interval `[first, last)` contains a heap and moves the elements so that they are sorted in increasing order.

Example

Suppose that `v` is a vector of type `vector<int>` and that it contains a heap:

```
// v contains {49, 45, 30, 27, 35, 20, 29, 18, 13}
sort_heap(v.begin(), v.end());
// v contains {13, 18, 20, 27, 29, 30, 35, 45, 49}
```

Index

Page numbers written in bold refer to facts tables.

D

E